Studies in Erotic Art

STUDIES IN SEX AND SOCIETY
Sponsored by the Institute for Sex Research
Indiana University
Bloomington, Indiana

1. Steven Marcus / *The Other Victorians*
2. Morse Peckham / *Art and Pornography*
3. Theodore Bowie & Cornelia V. Christenson, eds. / *Studies in Erotic Art*

STUDIES IN Erotic Art

THEODORE BOWIE
OTTO J. BRENDEL
PAUL H. GEBHARD
ROBERT ROSENBLUM
LEO STEINBERG

edited by
Theodore Bowie and Cornelia V. Christenson

Basic Books, Inc., Publishers
NEW YORK LONDON

Library of Congress Catalog Card Number: 72–94288
SBN: 465-08266-1
Manufactured in the United States of America
Designed by Loretta Li

THE AUTHORS

THEODORE BOWIE is Professor of Fine Art at Indiana University. He is the author of *The Drawings of Hokusai* (1963) and *East-West in Art* (1966).

OTTO J. BRENDEL is Professor of Art History and Archaeology at Columbia University. He has done special research in Etruscan and Roman art and archaeology, and Classical survivals in Renaissance and later art.

PAUL H. GEBHARD, Director of the Institute for Sex Research, Bloomington, Indiana, since 1956, is also Professor of Anthropology at Indiana University. He is the co-author of *Sexual Behavior in the Human Female* (1953), *Pregnancy, Birth and Abortion* (1958), and *Sex Offenders* (1965). He has written numerous articles in the field of sex research.

ROBERT ROSENBLUM is Professor of Fine Arts at New York University. He is the author of *Cubism and Twentieth-Century Art* (1960), *Transformations in Late Eighteenth Century Art* (1967), and *Ingres* (1967) and has contributed articles to most of the major art periodicals.

LEO STEINBERG is Professor of Art History at Hunter College, New York, working in contemporary as well as Renaissance fields. The topics of his published essays include Michelangelo, Caravaggio, Velasquez, Borromini, Rodin, and Jasper Johns.

PREFACE

This book is the direct result of an early realization on the part of Dr. Alfred C. Kinsey of the importance of art in providing insights into man's sexual life. When royalty money from the sale of *Sexual Behavior in the Human Male* began to accumulate in the early 1950's, the Institute for Sex Research, which he founded at Indiana University, broadened its scientific and medical library to include not only standard reference books on art but also a specific collection of erotica in the form of books, works of art, and photographs. This collection, by now quite broad in its range, contains the work of children, prisoners, psychotics, and crude pornographers as well as that of famous writers and artists. A great portion of it has been contributed by the authors or artists themselves, by other donors, and by various police agencies.

The development of the collection was first entrusted to Dr. Clyde Martin. When he departed, the task was taken over by Mrs. Cornelia V. Christenson. It was thanks to her initiative that the first Conference on Erotic Art was organized at Indiana University in the fall of 1967, with the cooperation of the Department of Fine Arts and the active support of Mr. and Mrs. Lloyd Wescott, Mr. Lawrence Saunders, and Dr. Walter Alvarez, whose aid is here gratefully acknowledged.

The scholars who participated in the Conference presented more or less informal papers on the subjects which are formally discussed in this volume. The Conference was an experimental project, for which no particularly unified approach was set other than that of examining erotic art in terms of stylistic development and formal analysis—in short, the standard professional approach.

It was impressed upon the participants that, while some aspects of erotic art could be isolated and studied from the esthetic side alone, the theme tended to escape any confining limits, being by nature as "undulating and diverse" as man himself. It is probable that if a second Conference on Erotic Art were to be organized, there would be strong pressure to include psychologists, sociologists, criminologists, and historians of religion, literature, and culture generally as well as art historians. Even such a classic demonstration as Leo Steinberg's analysis of the reasons why there is a missing leg in a statue by Michelangelo is striking proof that the broader the frame of reference, the more clearly one can perceive how deeply sexual problems inform a whole civilization. The study which stands in greatest contrast with his, Paul Gebhard's commentary on Peruvian erotic pottery, is a demonstration of anthropological statistics. In favoring this method the author had to hold in check his own essential humanism simply because so few cultural data about the makers of this pottery are ascertainable. Robert Rosenblum's excursus into the symbolism of Picasso's sexual imagery might be paralleled by that of a psychiatrist. Otto Brendel's broad historical study of the artistic eroticism of classical antiquity is inevitably marked by his philosophical turn of mind, while my own approach to Japanese eroticism—which in some ways is so curiously similar to that of Greece and Rome—would be considerably more resonant than it is had I been able to contribute to it something more substantial than a bit of poor man's sociology.

In making these statements my intent is not to disarm critics: we are all keenly aware of the miscellaneous character of this volume, though no particular apology for that is needed. These are but the first few pickings in a vast quarry. Some kind of beginning had to be made.

January, 1970 THEODORE BOWIE

CONTENTS

Studies in Erotic Art

1

The Scope and Temperament of Erotic Art in the Greco-Roman World

OTTO J. BRENDEL

> . . . So did the Greeks and Romans keep all their sadnesses and gladnesses unmingled and entire. Instinctively good they did not reckon sin; nor had they any such desire to save the credit of the universe as to make them insist, as so many of *us* insist, that what immediately appears as evil must be "good in the making," or something equally ingenious. Good was good, and bad just bad, for the earlier Greeks. They neither denied the ills of nature . . . nor did they, in order to escape from those ills, invent "another and a better world" of the imagination, in which, along with the ills, the innocent goods of sense would also find no place. This integrity of the instinctive reactions, this freedom from all moral sophistry and strain, gives a pathetic dignity to ancient pagan feeling.—*William James*[1]

Representations that might be termed erotic, in one sense and another, occur frequently in Greek and Roman art. In discussing them, some principle of selection will have to be stipulated at the outset, lest the wealth of material obscure the information of more general character—historical, social, and humanistic—which the modern observer may hope to derive from studying them. Thus I do not intend to deal, for instance, with the very common phallic representations in ancient art except in these preliminary remarks, although, by comparison with the arts of many other lands and periods, the very commonness of this imagery among the classical

[1] William James, *The Varieties of Religious Experience* (New York: Collier Books, 1967), pp. 84–85.

civilizations might be judged an exceptional feature that invites discussion. By the testimony of its most frequent erotic symbol, the Greco-Roman culture ought to be declared a phallic one; by contrast, the vulva as a symbol occurs only occasionally, and known examples are rare. But it would be rash to conclude from this observation that the Greco-Roman was altogether a man's world. Other facts known about the ancient Greek and Italian societies argue against so sweeping a judgment, or at least counsel us to modify it. Even though the direction of public affairs was essentially a male domain, and the city streets, the marketplace, and the places of athletic exercise were a preserve, mostly, of men, the feminine contribution to that universal commodity called culture was considerable and, on the whole, highly regarded.

The phallic element in ancient art and religion had its own history, to be sure, though this history has yet to be written. It did not occur with equal frequency at all periods of classical art or in all areas of ancient beliefs. In the iconography of Greek art, as in Greek folklore, phallic images occupied a well-defined place. Traditionally, for instance, they formed part of the boisterous gaiety of the half-animals, mostly rather good-natured, who were the retinue of the wine god—the Sileni and Satyrs, lusty and uncouth creatures of the mythical fantasy, often depicted as comical and, sometimes, a little pathetic. Equally conventional were the stern and watchful images of the god Hermes, shaped as phallic pillars. Ancient Italy possessed a native counterpart to these inventions of the Greek myth, in the lore of the Phallus-Genius, guardian spirit of a household. Later the Romans developed from Greek precedents their proper version of a Bacchic religion, which included mystic ceremonies in which a phallic symbol was carried in a winnowing basket. Popular superstition long continued to look upon the phallic symbol both as an averter of evil and as a harbinger of
1 good luck and fortune (Fig. 1).[2]

[2] A. F. von Pauly and G. Wissowa, *Real-Encyclopädie der klassischen Altertumswissenschaft* (hereafter cited as *RE*), XIX, 2 (Stuttgart, 1938), 1701 ff., s.v. "Phallos" (Herter). Cf. O. J. Brendel, "Der grosse Fries in der Villa dei Misteri," *Jahrbuch des deutschen archäologischen Instituts* (hereafter cited as *JdI*), 81 (1966), 222 ff., 253 ff. (hereafter cited

These mythical fantasies, fears, and hopes led to images which may be said to be erotic in content. Yet to deal with their various meanings, histories, and social or anthropological implications plainly constitutes a task in itself. The catalogue of ithyphallic representations in ancient art would fill more than one volume. There are, in addition, representations of the phallus as an autonomous symbol not associated with a mythical situation or narrative. Erotic art can be, and often is, symbolic art. This aspect, like the mythical narrative, I intend mostly to bypass. It seems to me that the purpose of this investigation will be best served by turning, first of all, to the instances of art that is erotic in the most obvious sense of the term. Accordingly I propose to limit the following discussion to works of Greek and Roman art that either show sexual acts explicitly or represent situations clearly preparatory to such acts.

CATEGORIES OF EROTIC ART

The extant examples of ancient erotic art have not yet been collected systematically.[3] There is reason to believe that a great deal of pertinent material rests unused and unattended in the

---

as Brendel, "Villa"). Fig. 1: Winged Phallus, Trier, Rheinisches Landes-Museum; H. Menzel, *Die römischen Bronzen aus Deutschland,* II (Mainz, 1966), 84, no. 202 and pl. 63. The three bells probably served as an apotropaion, for added power.

[3] Only a few, rather improvised, surveys are at present available. For art, see S. Marcadé, *Eros Kalos: Essay on Erotic Elements in Greek Art* (Geneva etc., 1962), and *Roma Amor: Essai sur les représentations érotiques dans l'art étrusque et romain* (Geneva etc., 1964) (hereafter cited, respectively, as Marcadé, *Eros,* and Marcadé, *Roma*). A good collection of general—literary and historical—information, including references to art, is found in H. Licht, *Sittengeschichte Griechenlands,* 3 vols. (Dresden and Zürich, 1925–1927) (hereafter cited as Licht, Vol. I, etc.). More medically oriented studies were published by G. Vorberg: *Ars Erotica Veterum: Ein Beitrag zum Geschlechtsleben des Altertums* (Stuttgart, 1926), and *Glossarium Eroticum* (Stuttgart, 1932). Additional bibliography in Licht, *op. cit.* One also ought to consult *RE,* VIII, 1331 ff., s.v. "Hetairai" (Schneider, 1913), which offers a rich and critically assembled collection of pertinent data, not all of it in chronological order, however.

In this chapter ancient monuments shall be cited by principal publications only; bibliographical completeness cannot be attempted. References to Greek and Etruscan vases, when feasible, shall be given according to J. D. Beazley, *Attic Red-Figure Vase-*

storage rooms of many museums and art collections. Even so, and even if one applies the narrow definition here proposed, the material already available for such a study in Greek and Roman art is considerable. Since to my knowledge no serious attempt has yet been made to survey and sort this material in any scientific order, the present study must needs be an improvisation. The testimonies at hand, as well as the range of questions which these representations pose, have yet to be explored.

For instance, one may ask at this point how the rate of overtly erotic representations in classical art compares with that in the arts of other peoples and other periods. This I should call an initial question because the answer will very likely shed some light on a more fundamental matter—namely, the motivations from which such representations spring. If we search in the known history of art for the places and periods in which, for a time at least, erotic situations were depicted directly and factually as well as with a degree of frequency, originality of variation, and on a level of quality sufficient to command attention, not very many would seem to qualify. On the contrary, erotic art in the sense here stipulated appears to be the exception. Its examples are concentrated in a relatively small group of locally limited aggregations, widely separated from one another by geography and time. Five areas can be readily named in which the themes of human sexual behavior, at one time or another, have led to a yield of art that is remarkable for both its number and its quality. These areas are: the classical world, pre-Columbian Peru, medieval India, Japan during the seventeenth and eighteenth centuries, and western Europe during the eighteenth and nineteenth centuries. In this list the classical instance—Greek and Roman—appears to be the earliest.

This is not to say that pictured erotica of one kind or another are not also found in historical and geographical contexts other than those just mentioned. The use of graphic symbols of sex, often so standardized and abstracted that they resemble hieroglyphs

Painters[2] (Oxford, 1963) (hereafter cited as *AV*), or the relevant fascicles of the *Corpus Vasorum Antiquorum* (hereafter cited as *CVA*).

or reading symbols rather than bona fide representations, is more or less ubiquitous and seems to be as old as art itself. Paleolithic man possessed a fixed system of sexual signs.[4] Ever since, to judge from the most accessible evidence, it seems that erotic art by symbol has proved more common, and more persistent, than the direct representation of erotic acts. This symbolism can become highly refined. In Christian medieval art, for example, the erotic component was by no means lacking, though it is not often obvious. It can be found, especially, in the iconography of the damned in representations of the Last Judgment, where it rarely took the form of specific actions, however, but instead was realized in a rather surrealistic manner as the frantic interlacing of naked limbs and bodies. Modern art also inclines toward erotic symbolism. The impact of contemporary censorship is difficult to assess in either case, but one may doubt whether it was the only factor prompting the particular outcome. After all, symbolic art holds an intellectual attraction to which alerted minds may respond on their own volition, at any time.

Neither are the direct—not symbolic—sexual representations of art confined only to certain times and places. To proceed from prehistory to the more recent civilizations, it can be observed that summarily rendered scenes of copulation formed a part of the Mesopotamian tradition from very early times. The scenes in question occur most often on cylinder seals; they are usually explained as "sacred marriages," performed either by deities or possibly, as ritual acts, by humans.[5] If the interpretation is correct,

[4] The distinction between direct representation and representation by signs is essential for the comprehension of Paleolithic art. As for the former, "there is not a single scene of human copulation in all Paleolithic art": A. Leroi-Gourhan, *Treasures of Prehistoric Art* (New York, n.d. [1967]), p. 121. However, sexual signs and pictographs, both male and female, are plentiful; *ibid.*, pp. 144 ff. and Charts XXXII, XXXIII.

[5] Oriental "sacred marriages": H. Zimmer, "Die vorarisch-altindische Himmelsfrau," *Corolla L. Curtius* (Stuttgart, 1937), I, 183 ff., and II, pls. 62–64. E. Porada, "Iconography and Style of a Cylinder Seal from Kantara in Cyprus," *Vorderasiatische Archäologie: Studien und Aufsätze* (Festschrift A. Moortgat) (Berlin, 1964), pp. 234–239, especially p. 234, n. 2. A stone plaque that portrays an embracing couple, from the neolithic town of Çatal Hüyük (sixth millennium B.C.), testifies to the great age of this theme in the arts of Western Asia: J. Mellart, *Earliest Civilizations of the Near East* (New

these early Oriental monuments belong to the realm of religion or cult. The presumable share of early Egypt in these developments must be bypassed here, for lack of published material. But our argument does not at this point turn on the presence per se of erotic illustrations in ancient Egypt or in any other locality; at issue are the criteria of frequency, variety, and quality of such representations, wherever found. It is easy to see that the Oriental cylinder seals present erotic art. Yet by our criteria the examples from western Asia differ radically from those later found in Greece. Their theme is the same, but the artistic result is of a different order from the Greek material, which deals so freely with the variety of the human sexual experience. The latter has its parallels in those arts, already mentioned, of other times, peoples, and continents—ancient Peru, medieval India, or, nearer to modern times, Japan and western Europe. Therefore it appears that in these five local traditions—the Greco-Roman included—we are confronted with a special elaboration of the common theme, erotic art. Their testimonies differ in several important ways from the typical attitudes of other categories of erotic art. It is true that the simpler sexual symbols are not missing from the Greek material. Their presence bears witness to the unbroken link with prehistoric roots, from which all ancient civilizations grew. But the most conspicuous erotic representations of Greek art were conceived in a different vein, with a different intent—explicit and narrative or, at least, episodic. This special quality connects them, categorically, with the four other principal groups of erotic art, all having a similar intent. At present it seems a moot question whether any other, comparable body of art ought to be added to this list of five. At any event, for the time being we are faced with the likelihood that in the category here singled out for discussion—factual and freely variable portrayals of sexual situations as a theme of art—the Greco-Roman examples mark the beginning.

York, 1965), p. 95, ill. 76. Cf. also B. Goff, *Symbols of Prehistoric Mesopotamia* (New Haven and London, 1963), p. 71 and n. 61; p. 77.

MOTIVATIONS OF EROTIC ART

I should call the outcome of the preceding, admittedly preliminary survey a matter of reflection on several counts. In the first place, it leads to the conclusion that erotic situations, in the sense here assumed, occur less often among the themes of art than might have been expected at the outset. Secondly, one may wonder why they have become an acknowledged and special theme of art, each time with a tradition of its own, in only so few, widely separated instances. Thirdly, there is cause for surprise that the history of this theme began, as apparently was the case, so late in the universal history of the world's art. Other themes, such as the hunt, or battle, or the tending of herds, precede it by far.

Apparently, man, as a common being, has no intrinsic need to represent his erotic acts in art. Yet these acts form an inseparable part of the existence of humans as a species, and of man as a natural animal. Obviously a distinction must be made here, as with so many other propositions of art, between an underlying human reality and the wish for its externalization. Sexual activities are natural and universal, insofar as they are common to the race in its entirety. Their outward representations, such as in a picture, evidently are optional. Hence, when their portrayal occurs it must be considered an expression of choice. Why, then, and under what circumstances did erotic themes come to be represented at all? Their absence from the repertory of art at any particular time may be due to one of two extremes. Either the matter has not been deemed sufficiently important to invite representation; for example, it ranges below other topics, such as the hunt or war, in urgency. Or, on the contrary, its importance has been deemed uncommonly high; in this case it may be protected by taboos that prevent its representation in art, or at least reserve such representations for rare and special occasions. Either condition can arise under various circumstances, both primitive and civilized. Neither requires discussion here. But, since experience shows that erotic art is on the whole the exception rather than the rule, the question of what prompts these exceptional occurrences, if and when we find them, ought not to be bypassed. In this chapter the question receives added interest from the fact that classical art provides us with the earliest, highly developed instances of the theme that are still extant.

Primitive religion as a possible source of erotic representations has already been mentioned. The early Oriental "sacred marriages" certainly fall into this category. It seems that similar representations, variously explained, were also found in early Greek sanctuaries. None is preserved, however, and the scarce literary references to monuments of this sort tend to show the rarity, rather than the commonness, of their occurrence. For instance, paintings allegedly illustrating the "sacred union" of Zeus and Hera are mentioned as having been known in the large temple of Hera at Samos and in her equally famous shrine at Argos. The descriptions leave little doubt about the erotic character of both paintings.[6] Unfortunately they give us no hint as to the age of both works; hypothetically, I am inclined to ascribe them to the archaic rather than to any later period of Greek art. They are probably best understood as Greek variations on the older Oriental theme. It seems to be characteristic that, according to the ancient testimonies, both paintings belonged to sanctuaries dedicated only to the female partner of the divine pair. This circumstance, also, relates the goddess to the more ancient, probably eastern, forebears. The great mothers of the Asian religions, be they mistresses of the heavens like Istar or of the good earth like Cybele, show in all their numerous hypostases a tendency to emphasize, if not the supremacy, at least the autonomy of the female. This of course is primarily a sociological consideration, but one which reflects on their erotic habits also. Their male companions often appear to be incidental, or relegated to a role of attendants, of secondary status.

[6] Representation of a "sacred marriage" of Zeus and Hera, in Samos: Varro, quoted in Lactantius, *Inst.*, I, 17; Origenes, *Cels.*, IV, 48, 54. A similar painting at Argos: Clemens Alexandrinus, *Hom.*, V, 18.

So Tammuz was attached to Istar, Adonis to Aphrodite; so, in a transparent poetic transposition, Paris became an appendage to Helen of Troy. Since time immemorial the religions of ancient Asia, and the mythical fables ensuing from them, liked to equip the the archetypical goddesses of their beliefs and speculations with the attributes of erotic dominion and initiative. Often the men with whom they associate are in deadly danger.

One senses in these conceits the makings of a natural and elemental theology. The erotic component of the myth is subordinated to this cosmic theology. The meeting of two divine partners, if it is at all mentioned, confirms the sexual bipolarism of nature, of common experience, thereby sustaining all life on earth. It is, however, a meeting of principles rather than of persons. Obviously such a manner of thinking is better served by abstract symbols than by natural representations. This may be one of the reasons why little erotic art, other than the sparse examples here mentioned, was motivated by the speculative thoughts of ancient Asia, even when myths with namable divine protagonists were formed from them. The mute neolithic Asian symbols, the *lingam* and the *yoni,* proved a more effective way of carrying the same insights through the millennia, in the lore of the Hindu religion.[7]

It may be interesting to ask why, in ancient Greece, the phallic symbol so much prevailed over its female counterpart. Answers can only be tentative, since no single cause apparently accounts for the outcome. One contributing circumstance—perhaps a decisive one—may be sought in Greek religious thought; this differed from other early Mediterranean religions insofar as it addressed itself more to the human encounter than to cosmic reality. Hence it tended to be socially and morally oriented. Deities were powers that operated, and opposed each other, in a structured

[7] H. Zimmer, *The Art of Indian Asia* (L. Campbell, ed.) (repr., New York, 1964), I, 22–25.

society. They became prototypes, not so much of natural forces as of human attitudes and actions, defined by social status and special interests. In this process, apparently, the paradox came to pass that the polarism between the sexes was not always equitably incorporated into representative characters, such as the pair Zeus and Hera. Whenever this fictitious humanization failed to take place evenly, it was the male principle which retained its impersonal, symbolic form. The phallic pillar of Hermes, marker of tombs, guardian of the gate, does not differ significantly from the *lingam* symbol.[8] Contrariwise, the myth defined Demeter, the earth goddess, as a mother with human traits, united with her daughter by a common fate and personal history. In her cult no male partner was mentioned; phallic symbols seem to have played a part, however.[9] Precisely because the popular belief held her to be a queen of old, and autonomous in her realm of creation, which was the fecundity of the fields, the complementary biological principle did not need to be personified. In a father-oriented society such as the Greek was, perhaps male power is always apt to appear as a suprapersonal quality or an abstraction in its own right; witness the amputated male organ of Uranus which, in conjunction with the sea, created Aphrodite. Its sexual counterpole, the power of the female, remained fully vested with the attributes of human reality.

The Greek myth knew other deities of unnatural birth, without the aid of either a father or a mother, or of even a parent in any ordinary sense. Yet it seems that these fancied anomalies did not spring from a wish to negate natural conditions or the social institution of a family. Rather these strange tales, in effect if not in original intention, isolated one single aspect from the larger context of social experience which binds the members of a family to one another—mother to daughter (Demeter-Kore), daughter to

[8] *RE*, XIX, 2, 1688 ff. (Herter). R. Lullies, *Die Typen der griechischen Herme* (Königsberg/Pr., 1931), bibliography, p. 10, n. 5.

[9] Cf. Herter, preceding footnote; Brendel, "Villa," p. 222 and n. 27.

father (Zeus-Athena), twin brother to sister (Apollo-Artemis). This social involvement of the gods and goddesses in Greek mythology is worth noting here. It sets the intellectual basis of Greek mythical thinking aside from the natural religions—for example, those of early Asia. In a natural exegesis of the world at large, the polarity of sex is likely to emerge as the supreme force because it regulates and sustains the lives of the known species. It becomes a metaphor of the life force itself and a prototype for all acts of creation. By contrast, in a social interpretation of the human existence, the sexual diversity must be viewed as a condition of natural man, and fitted into the larger framework of affective situations that arise from our associations with others.

RELIGIOUS MOTIVATIONS IN GREEK EROTIC ART

Here another relevant point becomes increasingly clear: the distinction between sexual symbolism and erotic representations of art is valid, and it remains significant. Primitive beliefs and religious reflection on the natural order are alike inclined to express themselves symbolically, often by means of highly abstracted ciphers of the natural form. Erotic representations, on the other hand, seem from the outset to follow a narrative and episodic or, if we may call it so, a "reporting" bent. The impact of religious motivations on the creation of the latter kind of imagery appears slight. This verdict, however, leaves the mythical histories out of consideration. Yet myth by definition is narrative; and much Greek mythology must be classified as religious narrative that deals, in the words of Cicero, with the "nature of the gods." In the guise of myths, the religious heritage of antiquity made a considerable contribution toward a tradition of erotic imagery in classical art.

The loves of the gods and heroines may be cited first in this context. Conspicuous among these famous stories is the pairing of humans with a divine animal: an eagle rapes Ganymedes, a bull abducts Europa, Pasiphaë loves a bull. The two last-named inci-

dents probably preserve reminiscences of the bull worship carried on in the Cretan and Mycenaean palaces. In fact, the stories of this sort generally seem to relate novelistic versions of legends and cult practices that hailed from much earlier strata of Mediterranean culture. Yet in spite of their amorous content they have not as a rule led to representations that one would term erotic by modern standards. The only exception, for reasons that escape us, are the illustrations of Leda receiving the Jovian swan. Like many of Zeus' female companions, she, too, is a princess; the myth insists on a social stratigraphy then long obsolete. Wrapped in her legend, as in the myths of other heroines like her, we may once more recognize the age-old message of the essentially self-sufficient woman, for whom the meeting with the (unrecognized) male is but a fleeting moment. Only in the case of Leda, however, has art represented that moment. The iconography of her strange love can be traced back as far as the early fourth century B.C. Commonly, she is
2, 3 shown standing (Figs. 2 and 3).[10] Only at a later stage of Greek art
47 appears the type of the reclining Leda (Fig. 47), which so much captivated the fancy of Michelangelo.[11]

Mythical too, but in a different sense, is the subject of a totally different fantasy preserved in several Hellenistic and Roman
4 variations. One, a rather fine marble relief in Boston (Fig. 4), shows a rustic laborer or perhaps a shepherd—his Pans pipes are lying nearby—taking his midday nap. What he is dreaming about is clear

[10] Standing Leda (Fig. 2). Statue by Timotheos (early fourth century B.C.), Rome, Capitoline Museum, Sala delle Colombe 804; Helbig,[4] II, n. 1254 (Roman copy). A different type, Fig. 3, probably derived from a Hellenistic model. It was rendered frequently in Roman reliefs, including sarcophagi; additional examples in Marcadé, *Eros*, pp. 13, 16, 17.

[11] Leda reclining: like the foregoing reliefs, this composition probably echoes a Hellenistic prototype—possibly a painting. Examples occur chiefly in Roman minor arts, such as engraved stones and terracotta lamps. The Roman lamp, Fig. 47, gives an exceptionally fine version; J. Perlzweig, *Lamps of the Roman Period, First to Seventh Century after Christ* (The Athenian Agora, Results of Excavations conducted by the American School of Classical Studies, VII) (Princeton, 1961), p. 119, n. 781, and frontispiece. Roman, first half of the third century.

enough. A Siren-like creature, at once attractive and repulsive, has taken possession of him. This is the hour of Pan, known for odd dreams, and the demon seems to be one of his emissaries; in medieval folklore she might be described as an incubus. The mood is idyllic, though the implications may turn out eerie.[12] In the popular lore of many lands there is a strange connection between the thought of death and the erotic fantasy. Perhaps this is why two sketchily painted groups of lovers found a place among the decorations of the so-called "Tomb of the Bulls," in Etruscan Tarquinia (Fig. 5). If this is the reason, these groups, likewise, ought to 5
be counted as erotic art, prompted by a religious impulse or at least a not uncommon superstition.[13]

To this somewhat scattered evidence one large religious complex of cults and myths remains to be added, which for centuries proved an abundant source of erotic themes in classical art. I refer to that cluster of ideas, legends, and celebrations which assembled around the person of the wine god Dionysos. Apparently, in the Bacchic religion traces of an early cult of vegetative growth were combined with a deliberate emphasis on enthusiastic psychic conditions. In its wake, also, a special iconography of art came into being; during its long history it achieved a typical imagery of well-known characters shown, more often than not, in traditional situations. In these monuments, chiefly the numerous Greek vase paintings, the inclusion of erotic elements soon became standard.

Yet, as the same monuments clearly tell us, the erotic inclination habitually associated with Bacchic liberties was in fact

[12] C. Vermeule, "Greek, Etruscan, and Roman Sculptures in the Museum of Fine Arts, Boston," *American Journal of Archaeology*, LXVIII (1964), 334, and pl. 104, fig. 24.

[13] Tomb of the Bulls: H. Leisinger, *Les peintures étrusques de Tarquinia* (Lausanne, 1953), pls. 12–19; L. Banti, "Problemi della pittura arcaica etrusca; la tomba dei Tori a Tarquinia," *Studi Etruschi*, XXIV (1955–1956), 179 ff. There are indications that the erotic groups had been planned somewhat differently from the design eventually executed; J. de Wit, "Die Vorritzungen der etruskischen Grabmalerei," *JdI*, XLIV (1929), 31–84.

characteristic of only one group among the Bacchic personnel, the capering troop of Satyrs and Sileni. Not fully human, exhibiting visible signs of their animal nature such as horsetails and ears, these boorish children of the woods constitute something of a social class by themselves. They have not entirely made the grade of civilized behavior. The god Dionysos tolerates them, even enjoys their presence, for reasons of his own. But they are scarcely fit for ordinary human company. Their phallic nature has already been pointed out; it is their essential characteristic. To say that no other religious conception or mythical fancy did so much to establish phallic symbols and representations in the life and art of the ancient Greeks, is probably no unfair statement. By way of this traditional iconography, the phallus became the emblem of Dionysian activities everywhere, including the theater: witness the astonishing
6 phallus monuments excavated in Delos (Fig. 6).[14] It is important that we judge these circumstances realistically, without undue romanticism. Obviously no classical phallic representation of this kind can be described as a religious monument in any direct sense; none was an object of cult; nor did any function as the embodiment of a religiously revered symbolism.[15] We may, however, call these representations the results of a mythical tradition. In this way—not as an object of cult or a subject of speculative theology, but as the continuous action of a mythical fantasy rooted in religion—a religious motivation can indeed be said to underlie all erotic art connected with the dominion of Dionysos and his noisy crowd. Moreover, this body of material forms the largest single complex of classical erotic art for which a religious origin can at all be claimed.

[14] Fig. 6, Monument of Karystios, Delos: E. Buschor, "Ein choregisches Denkmal," *Mitteilungen des deutschen Archäologischen Instituts, Athenische Abteilung* (hereafter cited as *AthMitt*), LIII (1928), 96 ff.; Ph. Bruneau and J. Ducas, *Guide de Délos* (Paris, 1965), p. 130, No. 81.

[15] For bibliography, see n. 8, and preceding footnote.

The matter is important for another reason as well. Mythical fiction endowed the unruly folk of Satyrs and Sileni with generic traits which changed but little over the centuries. Humanness perplexes them, but animals are their friends. Most erotic scenes of ancient art that I can cite showing a male lover coupled with an animal partner represent Satyrs or their likes. The choice seems logical: the sons of the wilds congregate lightly with their fellow creatures. Thus the Silenus portrayed on an Eretrian vase, himself
moving with an animal elegance, has captured a doe (Fig. 7); the 7
Pan represented by the much later Roman statue in Naples finds
his pleasure with a goat (Fig. 8). We are to understand that a 8
natural affinity exists between these partners. Relations between Satyrs and women are not equally easy. In the majority of monuments the enthused maenads of Dionysos reject their satyresque
suitors (Fig. 9), though exceptions to the rule can be found. More- 9
over, some of the earliest erotic representations in Greek art show Sileni or Satyrs joined by women who, in these latter instances, probably ought to be described as nymphs—nature's own daughters and obliging spirits, denizens, themselves, of the lonely wilds, kin of their uncouth lovers. In the case of companionship either with animals or with nymphs, the mores of the wood people raise a question which one ought to consider in evaluating these early erotica. It opens up a critical aspect which seems to apply not only to the Greek examples at hand but also to much, if by no means all, erotic art: the illustration of sexual actions may imply an element of ridicule, satire, or caricature. What Satyrs do is funny, by Greek standards. The not-quite-humans ape the humans—or is it vice versa? In the play of Satyrs the idea of the comical is never far off, and its critique is based on an assumed social distance which is precisely the reason why the doings of others appear comical or, at least, entertaining. In the early Greek portrayals of the Satyrs and Sileni, it seems that both the erotic situations and the postures have been styled accordingly. The Sileni stalk their prey in the
woods (Fig. 10), or approach their mates from the back, both 10

11 partners standing—animal style, *more canum* (Fig. 11): it all fits the setting and the characters.[16] Apparently these early Greek and Etruscan vase paintings, dating to or near the middle of the sixth century B.C., mark the beginnings of the new erotic art. Myth formed the characters and situations; a realistic appraisal of the mythical happenings perhaps prompted their representation. The spirit which informed this expansion of the range of art, we conclude, was the curt archaic wit. Its literary concomitants were the ready obscenities of Hipponax; and the first exercises of the new genre may be described as mythical banter in a Dionysian vein, in keeping with the "phallic" songs and antics of the incipient comedy.[17]

[16] Fig. 7, Silenus and doe: Eretrian amphora, Athens, National Museum; Furtwängler and Reichhold, *Griechische Vasenmalerei* (hereafter cited as *FR*), Text II (Munich, 1932), p. 215 and fig. 104. Fig. 8, Pan and goat, Naples, National Museum; Marcadé, *Roma,* p. 114. Figs. 9, 10, Satyrs and nymphs: Chalcidian cup, Würzburg, Martin von Wagner-Museum, n. 164. E. Langlotz, *Griechische Vasen* (Munich, 1932), I, 23 ff.; II, pls. 26–27.

Maenads opposing the advances of satyrs: Brendel, "Villa," p. 223 and n. 28. Examples to the contrary exist but remain exceptional: e.g., the cup by Makron, *AV,* I, 462, n. 43.

Groupings, non-mythical, of humans with animals occur on Roman terracotta lamps; in these small reliefs the humans may be men as well as women, the animals are mules or donkeys. Perlzweig, *op. cit.,* pp. 122 f., no. 829; K. Kübler, *JdI,* LXVII (1952), 107, no. 48; H. Menzel, *Antike Lampen* (Mainz, 1954), p. 539, fig. 47, 3. The pairing of women with donkeys evidently was an ancient cliché; for Roman examples, see Perlzweig, *op. cit.,* nos. 831–833; pl. 18. The chances are that the fable of the asinine lover in Apuleius' "Metamorphosis," which recurs in Lucian's "Lucius or the Ass," rested on a broad basis of folklore. Its ostensibly secular aspect may indeed cover hidden memories of popular religion; cf. W. Krebs, "Zur kultischen Kohabitation mit Tieren im Alten Orient," *Forschungen und Fortschritte,* XXXVII (1963), 19 ff. The grotesque dancers that decorated the ceremonial mantle of the "Despoina" at Lycosoura in Arcadia, as represented by Damophon (M. Bieber, *The Sculpture of the Hellenistic Age*[2] (New York, 1961), pp. 158 f.; Brunn-Bruckmann, *Denkmäler,* pls. 478–480), also seem to belong to this order. So do Titania and Bottom, in Shakespeare's *A Midsummer Night's Dream,* "when . . . it came to pass, Titania wak'd and straightway lov'd an ass" (III, ii, 33 f.).

[17] Hipponax: author of highly realistic poetry, mostly on personal matters; second half of the sixth century B.C. Only fragments are preserved; E. Diehl, *Anthologia Lyrica,* fasc. 3[3] (Leipzig, 1952).

EROTIC ART, NON-MYTHICAL: THE "ANCIEN RÉGIME"

Religious belief, mythical fiction, and ritual custom were the three agents that evidently helped to establish the illustration of sexual themes in Greek art. But once it was set up as a thematic genus, the new erotic art soon turned to nearer matters. From here on, as the following survey will show, the importance of religious and mythical motivations dwindles fast. The vast majority of Greek erotic art deals with social situations and the actions of real, not mythical, people.

While a remarkable range of free invention must be allowed to these representations, this is not to say that they were not also subject to certain iconographic habits. Rather, I suggest that a new iconography of erotic themes emerged in Greece during the late archaic period, after about 530 B.C., defined chiefly by the attending circumstances in which such doings were shown: banquets, symposia, and other similar gatherings. We must assume that these occasions were considered a frame of social reality into which the erotic episodes have been fitted as a matter of custom and common usage. In the artistic records of the period, love is companionable.

The monuments on which these scenes occur are almost all vase paintings. This fact, also, is not without significance because the painted vases count among the comparatively few objects of contemporary Greek art that were turned out primarily for private use. They thereby confirm the predominantly secular and private destination of the art which concerns us here. Most late archaic vases with erotic representations are drinking cups. All can be ascribed to painters and ateliers of acknowledged reputation and to leading masters of their profession. They were articles made for the connoisseurs and the affluent.

Nevertheless, their most characteristic topic, the inclusion of erotic scenes with the representation of banquets, was probably not a fresh invention. It seems to have started outside Greece some time before it made its appearance on the Attic red-figured vases.

The first example, chronologically, which I can cite is a bronze bowl of Cypro-Phoenician make in the British Museum, decorated
12 with incised design (Fig. 12). Its likely date, before 550 B.C., certainly precedes the Attic examples by at least a generation. The frieze around the outer rim on the inside begins with a small band of musicians. There follows a row of dining couches; some of the banqueters are entertained by naked women. The presence of waiters who offer drinking vessels, and of the musicians, suggests that a banquet is in progress. This festivity may have been held on some special occasion, possibly of the religious calendar, but there is no certain sign of any determinable purpose, and the tenor of the whole representation strikes us as decidedly worldly. The decorations on this class of Phoenician metal bowls often repeat identical motives. Probably the scenes illustrated on the sample in London also render an established, even stereotype composition. There are reasons to assume that other, similar representations once paralleled those still preserved, and that some may have come to the attention of the Greeks. We are entitled to consider the bowl in London an immediate antecedent of the erotic banquets which about thirty years later made their appearance on the Greek painted vases.[18]

If the iconographic type of the erotic banquet was then already in existence, however, the Greek ceramists gave it status, variety, and a range of interpretation far beyond the limits and ambitions of any previous art. A review of vase paintings produced between approximately 530 B.C. and 470 B.C., dealing with this subject matter, shows the growing strength of the humanistic and secular outlook. It also demonstrates the essentially reportorial, narrative character of these representations. Most of them seem to tell us something about what people do or did, something that happened or may have happened—no more and no less. Ostensibly their attitude is one of simple realism; though in some instances a

[18] Cypriote bowl, London, British Museum, Br. 186: E. Gjerstad, "Decorated Metal Bowls from Cyprus," *Opuscula Archaeologica,* IV (1946), 8 f. and pl. V.

degree of criticism, sympathetic or perhaps faintly mocking as the case may be, does not seem to be wholly excluded. At any event, it is now up to us to decide how to read their stories or comment on them.

A fine cup by the so-called Tarquinia Painter, now in the Antiken-Museum at Basel, shall be cited first although it is a relatively late representative of this essentially archaic iconography, dating to about 470 B.C. It well exemplifies, however, the narrative method typical of these banquet scenes.[19] The representation around its outer side forms a continuous frieze which even the two handles do not noticeably interrupt. The symposiasts are lined up along this zone: a few men, of different ages, and naked girls are all comfortably settled on couches, presumably, though the furniture is not expressly shown, only the blankets and pillows. A frieze, of course, is a manner of composition that may convey multiple meanings: it may consist of isolated, disconnected images, or its images may suggest a succession of events that follow one another in time. Neither of these alternatives applies to the cup in Basel. No progress of events is indicated, nor are the groups and persons isolated from each other. Actually the painter has taken all possible pains to make it clear that the persons assembled together are partaking of the same situation and, hence, that their actions and gestures are simultaneous. The question is, how to describe the situation. No food is shown, and drinking has almost ceased, or so it seems. A bearded gentleman appears to be singing, while the girl in whose lap he rests his elbow awards him with some leafy

[19] Red-figure cup, Tarquinia Painter, Basel: *AV*, II, Addenda I, 1673. It should be understood that the symposia on Greek red-figure vase paintings have a richly documented and varied iconography. The theme was most popular with the painters, but banquets including erotic episodes also occur in reliefs: Ch. Karousos, in *AthMitt*, LXXVII (1962), 121 ff. and Beil. 35. This larger context in which the above examples find their proper places cannot be treated here; nor will it be possible to discuss all pertinent details, such as the erotic implications of the frequently illustrated "Cottabus" game, for which cf. P. Mingazzini, *Archaeologischer Anzeiger* (1950–1951), pp. 35 ff. Related Etruscan materials: S. de Martinis, *La tipologia del banchetto nell'arte etrusca arcaica* (Rome, 1961).

branch, the prize of a winner. Genteel dalliance, conversation, invitations to love; evidently the symposium is about to enter into its next stage, turn to a different kind of pleasure. Yet even in this relaxed condition the tone of converse remains remarkably polite. The wreaths of flowers in the hair of the ladies stay unruffled, or at least they have stayed so thus far.

13 Perhaps a somewhat earlier cup in Berlin (Fig. 13), by the Thalia Painter, can be taken to illustrate the same convivial joys, if in a more advanced stage and on a higher pitch. Here, the gaiety has reached its peak; cultivated politeness has given way to rather dissolute groups of men and women clearly engaged in sexual actions. Although ostensibly lined up along the frieze on the outside of the bowl, these noisy merrymakers, too, must be understood as acting within a context. Unfortunately the imperfect preservation of the painting makes it difficult to read all the details properly.[20] Ten men and seven women, all unclothed, seem to be milling around, pursuing their amorous sports. Just where in reality the revel is supposed to take place is a question. Three high lampstands—the only furniture—indicate a place inside some building, and probably also convey the idea that what we see happens at nighttime. Among the women is a dancer with rattles who might well take part in some lighthearted drinking bout, except that nobody seems to pay much attention to her. It is not unlikely that, nevertheless, one ought to describe the whole carousal as a scene of symposium; drinking vessels are carried about, if not used, and at least one of the men wears the broad ribbon knotted around his brow, worn formally by the symposiasts. In that event, however, the complete absence of comfortable equipment, such as banquet couches and pillows, must be called to attention. There is no furniture on which to sit or rest. The fact is worth noting because the same observation holds true of other late archaic representations of related themes. Perhaps, in these instances, one faces a special iconographic tradition not yet fully understood.

[20] Red-figure cup, Thalia Painter, Berlin 3251: *AV*, I, 113, no. 7. *CVA*, Berlin (2), pl. 56, 4; interior, pl. 59, 4. C. Vermeule, "Fragments of a Symposium by Euphronios," *Antike Kunst*, VIII (1965), fig. 6.

Even though the compositional scheme can be considered a conventional one, the opposite must obviously be said about the details. The persons and their behavior are all represented with a stress on their variety, mixing a pointed wit with invention and realism. Most of the participants busy themselves with railleries, preludes to love. Some chase each other, ready to catch and be caught. Some dance, or perform rather grotesque pantomimes. Much of the frieze is given to the illustration of these preparatory actions, which one may compare to the love dances known to occur among certain animals. People are apt to behave oddly in such situations. One cannot help feeling that the painter recorded their oddities with a smile—himself a cool observer. Many details are in need of further inquiry and more accurate description than can here be undertaken. But it is clear that amorous episodes of a preparatory character occupy the greater portion of the frieze. Only two couples are shown in actual sexual contact, one by cunnilingus (man to woman, which is rare in Greek art), the other pair standing upright near the first. Apparently these actively erotic scenes are to be understood as unconnected with the rest but simultaneous, all forming part of the common revel.

The circular picture on the inside of the same cup (Fig. 14) 14
likewise renders an erotic group, but in a different mood. Evidently it deals with the ultimate stage of a feast like the ones just described—a symposium or banquet of some kind. A lamp still burns on its high stand but the loud merrymakers have disbanded or, at least, are no longer in sight. Instead we see a group of four people. Two make love together, lying on a couch—a bearded man and a woman. They seem to belong to the elegant set of Athenian society, to judge from their stylishly dressed hair, their only adornment. The gaiety of midnight has passed, however, and we infer that some time has since elapsed; the small hours of the morning are imminent.

The whole group was drawn in a rather complicated manner, and the damage the cup has suffered makes the details still more difficult to read. It may prove helpful to recall the famous ending of that other "Symposium" described by Plato about a century later, which, it seems to me, tells of a similar occasion with even a comparable sense of narrative: the end of the feast, the hour of departure, the last glimpses remembered by a participant about to leave.[21] The picture in the Berlin cup, obvious differences notwithstanding, may be described in a similar vein, thus: "Before closing the door behind me I turned around one moment. Most of the guests had already left. The girl, Smikra, had fallen asleep on the floor, using a footstool for her headrest. Megakles was still there, on his couch with Callisto. But either he had lost interest or perhaps he was distracted by the sight of Smikra, sleeping so near his bed; for Callisto seemed to punish him, or else merely to make an attempt at reawakening his spirits, with a sandal held in her raised hand. Meanwhile Megakles' boy, sitting nearby in a corner, entertained himself as best he could, and also shouted intermittently, to spur his master. So I left them alone and went out into the street, with the daylight already approaching."

I am aware that several details of this improvised description are capable of different interpretations and subject to future corrections.[22] What my fictitious paraphrase may nevertheless bring out, over and above the questions of detail, concerns a certain quality of the representation in its entirety as a work of art—namely, its persuasiveness as a momentary situation, formally expressed. The methods of all early painting tended to be analytic and successive. It is true that a heightened sense of simultaneity comes to the fore in many Greek late archaic vase paintings. Yet even by their standards a degree of immediacy such as that conveyed by the painter of the Berlin cup must be considered rare. What we call a "situation" binds together many dimensions of time, circumstance, and

[21] Plato, *Symposium*, 223. All names in my paraphrase are invented, except Smikra, which seems authentic; see preceding footnote.

[22] Details are debatable. It is likely that the reclining man, second group from the left in Fig. 13, is in actual contact with the woman who stands before him; but one cannot say that the representation makes this quite certain. The girl Smikra in Fig. 14 may have been masturbating, as A. Greifenhagen recently suggested, following Vorberg; *Jahrbuch Berliner Museen*, IX (1967), 25, n. 82. It is certain only that she has fallen asleep. For the sandal as an instrument of punishment, cf. F. Wolters, *AthMitt*, XXX (1905), 405 ff.; also the group of Pan and Aphrodite from Delos, in Athens, M. Bieber, *The Sculpture of the Hellenistic Age*² (New York, 1961), p. 147 and figs. 629–630.

consciousness in one remembered moment; such as here the disorder, the irrational charms, and the impending fatigue, of a declining feast. To be sensitive to the experience, and to retain something of its wholeness and compactness in the forms of vision, goes to the credit of any artist, be he ancient or modern. In this respect, and quite aside from the merits of his theme, which may be judged variously, the painter of the Berlin cup was extraordinarily successful. His work ranged with the finest and most subtle of his time and craft.

The material at our disposal is at present hardly sufficient to chart either a general anthropology or a sociology of Greek erotic art. Nevertheless, some pertinent questions may be raised at this point with the proviso that the answers can claim no more than a temporary validity. For instance, the late archaic samples so far examined have all dealt with heterosexual acts. Yet the Greek writers have much to tell about homosexual activities in their society, chiefly among men but among women as well. The monuments do not disclaim this information. Yet the ratio of distribution between these two manners of love seems, in Greek erotic art, to favor the heterosexual more decidedly than some famous sources, such as the Platonic dialogues, would lead us to expect. At least in this special category of art, and not counting the representations which treat erotic contents in a broader sense, such as myth or allegory, the majority of known examples pair men with women.

One remarkable example to the contrary is the outer frieze around the well-known drinking bowl with paintings by Peithinos
(Fig. 15).[23] On one side four fashionable young men dally with 15
four younger boys. Everybody stands upright, two together, each pair a closed unit; there is no noticeable connection between one couple and the next, although all appear to be assembled in a

[23] Berlin 2279; *AV*, I, 115, n. 2. About male homoeroticism in ancient Greece, see D. M. Robinson, *A Study of Greek Love-Names* (Baltimore, 1937), esp. Ch. II, pp. 15 ff. Men in women's clothing: A. Rumpf, "Zu einer Vase der Sammlung Robinson," *Studies Presented to D. M. Robinson* (St. Louis, 1951–1953), II, 84 ff.; L. D. Caskey and J. D. Beazley, *Attic Vase-Painting in the Museum of Fine Arts* (Boston and Oxford, 1931–1963), II, 55 ff.

common locale which may be a palaestra, to judge from the athletic equipment hung from hooks on the rear wall, as was customary. All wear finely spun, transparent cloaks, and the young boys cover the backs of their heads with the tops of their mantles, as the society girls were wont to do at that time. We also should note that in this instance the lovers are consistently divided into pairs of profile figures that confront each other, heedless of anyone else. There is something precious and ceremonious about this formal order, and the artful flatness of the drawing adds to the impression of restraint and elegance: the attributes of a select and cultured class. No loud merrymaking here; at the most, we imagine whispered conversations. But the details belie the apparent quiet. Desires are aroused, intimate caresses are offered or solicited, kisses are exchanged. The last-named detail should be especially noted. For the kiss of lovers that is so important, for instance, to the Kama-Sutra and the illustrative art of India, occurs but rarely in the erotic representations of Greek archaic art.

16 The other side of the same cup (Fig. 16) shows young men of similar bearing in the company of equally elegantly dressed and nicely behaved young ladies, as if to restore the balance between the two kinds of love. Here, also, the visitors confront their hostesses in pairs, but the conversations are carried on at measured distances. Either we are to assume that the temperature of mutual attraction is less, in these polite meetings between the two sexes, or that the rules of the game—of offering and acceptance, proposal and rejection—are somehow different in their encounters.

Thus far, it seems, we have been dealing with the ways of the upper classes. I am not so certain whether this is the case in some other representations of similar kind, such as the cup attributed to
17 Skythes, or a follower of Skythes, in the Louvre (Fig. 17).[24] All persons in this frieze are nude. A woman, belly down, has stretched herself across a four-legged chair to practice fellatio on a man bending over her from the left, while another man behind

[24] Paris, Louvre G13; *AV*, I, 86, "Pedieus Painter (?)."

her busies himself with her back. To the right of this group of three, another woman has gone down on her knees to perform the same service, like her companion on the left, to a man standing before her. Fellatio, exercised by women on men, seems to be the dominent theme of the Skythes frieze; the only exception is the next group to the right, consisting of a man threatening with a lampstand the kneeling (?) woman at his feet. It seems to me that, all in all, the Skythes frieze recalls episodes of a brothel, in the style of Jean Genet. The haggard, avid, worn-out features of the women also suggest an explanation along these lines. We do not find their like in other Greek representations of the same category. I consider the cup of Skythes in the Louvre to be an early example of erotic art that is intended as a vehicle of social criticism. The suggestion, if accepted, would place this work of a Greek vase painter at the head of a long line of erotic representations which express either a protest against social manners or, more generally, impatience with human nature as such. In the rich texture of erotic art over the centuries, this derogative tendency forms a special strand which, it now appears, stretches from Skythes to Rembrandt, and to moderns such as George Grosz.

Apparently related by outlook, though hardly quite as barbed, are a number of other erotic representations in a lighter vein, from the same ambience of Greek archaic art, intended to be comical or perhaps satirical. Most illustrations of women who avail themselves of artificial phalli seem to belong to this category, such as the girl on a cup by Nikosthenes who handles two of these objects simultaneously (Fig. 18).[25] A similar explanation seems to apply to a 18
little narrative by the painter Onesimos in which an elderly gentleman, standing before his willing girl companion, holds an object of the same kind—rather than a sandal—in reserve behind his back (Fig. 19).[26] This is evidently a satire, but at the same time a rather 19
good-natured comment on that unending theme, the human comedy.

[25] London, British Museum E815; *AV*, I, 125, n. 15, "Nikosthenes Painter."
[26] I. Rácz, *Antikes Erbe* (*Meisterwerke aus Schweizer Sammlungen*) (Zurich, 1965), p. 54.

I finish this part of my essay in the Greek fashion, by a Satyr play. For the Satyrs had not been forgotten by the Greek public. Their antics still were, and remained for a long time to come, a favorite theme of the arts and, especially, of the vase painters. But in several respects their condition has changed. In art, they now appear as Bacchic creatures entirely. The friendly nymphs have all but disappeared, and the Maenads of Dionysos mostly shy away from them. Such also seems to be the reasoning
20 that underlies the painting shown in Fig. 20. A troop of Satyrs, left to themselves, celebrate the orgies in their own way, keeping each other's company.[27] The implications are obvious and, perhaps, a trifle sad. Notice the lonely fellow at the right who approaches the crouching Sphinx—a most unapproachable creature. She, in turn, behaves as if she were the feminine mystique incorporate, the female enigma. Sphinxes, of course, are supposed to be enigmatic, and long-inherited mythical archetypes provided the basis for this fantasy. Both they and the Satyrs behave according to their established characters. Yet, iconographically, these groups of Satyrs, who bend and swing so decoratively, do no more than repeat the same human actions which are shown in many other, more or less contemporary, representations; they have become the apes of humanness.

In this context one may also mention a relief of related content, once decorating an Etruscan ash urn. It renders a bacchanal of Satyrs styled as a banquet; this bacchanal, however, includes
21 women (Fig. 21).[28] The Etruscan relief is interesting for yet another reason—namely, as an example of erotic art created for funerary purposes. Possibly it illustrated the pleasures of the dead in their new station—that is to say, another kind of mythology, one quite different from the Greek.[29] But what matters in both the Greek

[27] Red-figure cup, Berlin 1964.4. *AV*, II, Addenda II, 1700: "Circle of Nikosthenes Painter"; M. Robertson, *Österreichisches Archaeologisches Institut, Jahreshefte* 47 (1964–1965), 114, n. 44.

[28] R. Herbig, *Die jüngeretruskischen Steinsarkophage* (Berlin, 1952), pl. 108a.

[29] See above, n. 13; also below, n. 31. Such beliefs, if indeed they had been implied with the Etruscan representations, were alien to Greek thought; Karousos, *op. cit.* (above, n. 19).

vase painting and the Etruscan relief, from the point of view of this inquiry, is the iconographical schema; this focuses on the variety of the sexual positions, recording them, as it were, as much for entertainment as for instruction. Gradually the synoptic, situational character of the archaic erotic monuments moves out of sight. A new, separative, and cataloguing tendency begins to take its place, whose impact will become fully apparent only later, in the art of the Hellenistic period.

THE "BANQUET TYPE": CONCLUDING REMARKS

After about 480 B.C. came the approximately 150 years during which Greek art underwent that extraordinary process of expansion and self-realization now generally known as its classical period. Somewhat later, perhaps, starting around 470 B.C., a new attitude toward erotic representations makes itself felt which differs markedly from the archaic. Yet in contrast to the generally expansive mood of Greek art at that time, so bent on innovation, the first obvious signs of change in this special category of subject matter must be described as negative. The most telling symptom is a sudden decline of frequency. Works of erotic content that are datable between about 470 B.C. and the end of the century are conspicuously rare. Hardly any example known today can be ascribed to the thirty years—about the length of a cultural generation—immediately after the year 470 B.C., the periodic turning point we shall assume for this sector of Greek art. Even in the later fifth century and during much of the fourth, erotic representations are appreciably scarcer than was true of archaic art.[30] Not before the Hellenistic period will their number be found to be on the rise again.

Iconography, also, reflects the change. The convivial settings which the archaic vase painters usually choose for their erotic

[30] A. Rumpf, *Malerei und Zeichnung* (*Handbuch d. Archaeologie*, IV, I) (Munich, 1953), p. 117.

themes disappear fast from the monuments of the new era. Their last vestiges can be recognized in a small number of representations dating to the years around 440 B.C. Characteristic of these monuments are curiously contrived groups of two or three men who are dealing with a single woman in various more or less plausible fashions. But the heroic style of the decades which produced the Pheidian cult images and the paintings of Polygnotus proved ill-suited for such levities. The men go about their business earnestly, in squarely staged groupings and with straightforward manners that seem to belie their sportful pastimes. The zest has gone out of these somewhat Victorian-looking extravaganzas. If we here mention them at all, it is because they testify to a belated attempt, probably on behalf of a small and epigonous group, to re-enact the companionable gaieties of their elders.[31] When eventually, at the close of the century, a classical style of erotic representations did evolve in Greece, it will be seen that the change came about, in no small part, through a new understanding of the theme itself and not through a revival of the ancient iconography.

Another symptomatic change, characteristic of the new era, ought to be mentioned here. According to archaic habits, drinking cups were the preferred carriers of erotic illustrations; this suggestive association between the convivial cups and the themes of sexual love ended with the archaic period. In classical art, erotic representations, when they occur at all, are found on sundry types of vases and on various other objects—for example, mirror cases. Around 400 B.C. the ancient sources also mention erotic paintings by famous masters; these were probably on small tablets, independent of any utility.[32] We may conclude that the erotic subject matter, now separated from its previously restricted social context,

[31] Marcadé, *Eros*, p. 137 (Athens, National Museum); p. 143 (Paris, Louvre). *AV*, II, 1029, n. 16 (Polygnotos). For a comparable triad of late archaic style, from an Etruscan tomb, see M. Moretti, M. Pallottino, W. Lerici, *Nuovi monumenti della pittura etrusca* (Milan, 1966), pl. 138.

[32] Rumpf, above, n. 30 (paintings by Parrhasios); also below, n. 64.

instead constituted a theme of art in its own right, to be rendered freely for any purpose an artist or his patrons might deem appropriate or profitable.

In retrospect it appears that the late archaic period saw the greatest flowering of erotic art in ancient Greece. Only the Hellenistic period matched the archaic in productiveness, and none equaled the archaic in variety of invention or quality of execution. Since, however, the Greek archaic example also happened to be the earliest instance in history of an erotic art fully conscious of its allotted range, any such statement about it carries rather far-reaching implications.

It is interesting, for instance, that the representation of erotic themes in Greece reached its early height at the time of the Persian wars, which was indeed a time of vigorous thought and action. The contemporaries of this art were the founders of the Athenian empire, the fighters of Marathon and Salamis—a generation of unusual force and enterprise that enjoyed spectacular successes. There is thus no reason to assume that the creators and supporters of an erotic art of note must necessarily be discouraged societies of declining fortunes, apathetic to public concerns.[33] It seems more reasonable to suppose that every case rests on diverse conditions, whether of strength or of weakness.

Clearly the sociology of erotic representations also poses questions, although here we can touch upon them only briefly. Moreover, the sociological aspect has a bearing on the wider problem, that of explaining the various appearances, in separate

[33] Thus H. Kahn and A. J. Wiener ("The Next Thirty Years: A Framework for Speculation," *Daedalus*, 1967, pp. 705 ff.) classify erotic art as "Sensate," thereby distinguishing it from pornographic art, which is listed among "Late Sensate" propensities; p. 707, with reference to P. Sorokin. Since the terms "Sensate" and "Late Sensate," though in this instance applied to the arts, describe collective symptoms that concern the whole society, a change from the first to the second condition can be construed as representing a collective, necessary, and predictable event. Similarly, the excavators of the debris that was thrown from the Acropolis after the Persian invasion of 480 B.C., were astonished at the frequency of erotic themes among the potsherds—ostensibly the remnants of a heroic age: *AthMitt*, XIV (1889), 339.

times and places, of erotic arts distinguished by specific formal and ethical characteristics. For our comprehension of their underlying causes, and for the evaluation of these manifestations of art as public symptoms, a measure of sociological understanding is indispensable. Thus the "banquet type," to call it so, of late archaic Greece has social connotations which are probably determinable. In almost every instance the men in these representations appear to belong to a rather coherent, if perhaps none too numerous, social group. We may describe them as members of an upper class having aristocratic leanings, though all of them need not have been heir to the wealth and privileges of the landholding archaic nobility. We cannot speak for the less famous and the forgotten ones, but among those long remembered we would count among their number both the adventurous noble Miltiades and the utterly resourceful upstart Themistocles. At the time of the Persian wars this class constituted the leading society in most Greek city-states, and especially in Athens; by income and prestige its members were equipped, if not always ready, to pay for their ambitions and their fun.[34]

The social condition of the women who keep company with these men in the same vase paintings is not quite so easily established. That they were prostitutes of a sort one cannot doubt. But this observation no more than describes the legal and social limitations of their status. It does not determine their place on the different scale of values which measures social attainment by the virtues of higher cultivation and by the attraction of worldly refinement. Judged on the latter scale, the range of difference among the prostitute women of the early Greek urban societies was evidently very great, probably wider than is usual with generally homogeneous professional groups. It is obvious that on the Peithinos
16 cup (Fig. 16) the ladies are quite the equals of their male visitors in elegance of manners and fashion. They act and dress as members

[34] According to his ancient biographers, Miltiades upon his death left a large legal debt unpaid, which he owed to the Athenian republic; his son, Cimon, *did* pay it, however. Demosthenes, XXIII, 205; Plutarch, *Cimon*, 4, and others.

of an upper class, not unlike Japanese geishas. Apparently they shared the tastes of their visitors for genteel entertainment that included the luxuries of polite deportment, conversation, and attire; and they were prepared to meet these standards. In turn, it seems that their social graces earned them a measure of social esteem in the eyes of their callers. One ought not to forget that in the ancient city-societies—or in any other society similarly structured—the prostitutes represented not merely a profession but also a social group of distinct risks and chances. Theirs was the only class of emancipated women which these societies were likely to tolerate. This condition leaves to the individual a considerable chance of personal success and development; it also causes the conspicuous inequality of status that is often observable among the members of this group. In the emerging city-states of archaic Greece, the three-fold division of the women according to their social usefulness, which Demosthenes much later stated rather drily, was still in the making.[35] The time had not yet come when the learned sought the company of an informed courtesan, as Socrates felt instructed by Aspasia, and when every successful courtesan had to have her philosopher, as Leontion claimed her Epicurus.[36] Nevertheless, in the archaic period, an incipient gradation between socially different

[35] Demosthenes, LIX ("Against Neaira"), 122: "Mistresses (or courtesans, *hetaíras*) we keep for the sake of pleasure, concubines (or rather female slaves, *pallakás*) for the daily care of our persons, but wives to bear us legitimate children." Trans. by A. T. Murray, Loeb Library (Cambridge, Mass., and London, 1939); alternative suggestions by myself. Compare this to the even blunter saying current among the manor houses and *latifundia* of Brazil reported by G. Freyre, *The Masters and the Slaves* (New York, 1966), p. 13 and n. 31.

[36] Epicurus and Leontion: Diogenes Laertius, X, 4 ff.; Alciphron, *Epist.*, IV, and others. Paintings which represented Epicurus and Leontion are mentioned by Pliny, *Historia Naturalis*, XXXV, 9; 144. One of them, probably the painting by Theoros, may be recognized in a Roman copy now in Naples, National Museum (wall painting from the Villa of Boscoreale); Otto J. Brendel, *American Journal of Philology*, LXXV (1954), 406 f.

Socrates and Aspasia: F. Fuhrmann, "Gespräche über Liebe und Ehe auf Bildern des Altertums," *Mitteilungen des deutschen archäologischen Instituts, Römische Abteilung* (hereafter cited as *RömMitt*), LV (1940), 78 ff.

About the status of women in Greek society generally, cf. N. E. Paoli, *La donna greca nell'antichitá* (Florence, 1966).

strata can probably be stipulated, within the class of the prostitute women, on the testimony of the contemporary art. On the strength of the same testimony, however, one would have to admit that the contemporaries of the Persian wars were apparently a tumultuous crowd altogether, on any social level. What the vase painters show us can have been no more than one facet of an effusive temperament shared, it seems, by the entire generation, and amply evinced by its leaders. I refer to that coincidence so often apparent in the conduct of the latter, of aristocratic tastes with hard action and of a rare recklessness in the pursuit of both.

After this brief summary of social circumstances, gleaned from their reflection in works of art, the time has come to assay the share of the artists in creating the pictorial records of manners here before us. If indeed the Greek late archaic was the earliest instance of an erotic art both mundane in spirit and unrestricted in its choice of themes, ecological conditions doubtlessly favored its coming into being; but it was up to the artists to realize that art. At this point, with the reservation that the following suggestions can be no better than tentative, awaiting further scrutiny, I should propose three factors, the concurrence of which probably proved essential for the formation of any erotic art on a level of quality comparable to the Greek. First, any erotic art of this description must for its encouragement and subsistence depend on a closed social group, of cultivated habits. The second factor also seems to reside chiefly, if not exclusively, in the supporting group; it may be described as a secular and pragmatic outlook, a frankly appreciative and humanized attitude toward sex, and an extrovert taste for the communication of social pleasures. In regard to this second factor, however, the participation of the artists is also an effective element. Though hardly the social equals of their lively clients, the artists must have partaken to some extent of their clients' sensibilities and tastes or at least been no strangers to them.[37] Actually

[37] About the social condition of the Attic vase painters at the end of the archaic period not much can be said with confidence. The apparent facts indicate that they were a literate group, and that their ranks included some remarkably independent characters.

in the Greek archaic instances, a paradoxical relation seems to prevail between the two groups, the artists and their patrons. If these examples can be accepted as typical, the erotic representations of the kind here discussed are apt to assign a strangely ambiguous function to the upper classes to which they address themselves: the supporters become at once the patrons and the target of that art. Certainly in archaic Greece the customers of these representations also furnished the subject matter for much of the ware which they bought.

Since this ware, sexual representations informed with free-spoken realism, was then a cultural innovation, we should further investigate the special conditions of art that are necessary to bring this event to pass. Required, evidently, was not only a favorable intellectual climate but also a certain general conception of art sufficiently flexible to undertake the illustration of themes so freely selected. A commensurate freedom of thematic choices—the competence to deal with the matters of experience at will, not merely in conformity with set norms of iconography or formal rules—thereby emerges from our query as the third prerequisite factor for the formation of an erotic art that demands a range of meaning and variety beyond the primitive.

Greek art at the end of the sixth century B.C. was predisposed for such a venture by general condition and by the direction of its progress. Among the many imaginable themes of art, erotic subjects as defined by the ancient Greeks must rank as genre scenes, generally speaking. This definition unites them within a special class of art. It also aligns them with a leading trend that is notice-

---

The first known self-portrait in the history of art was due to one of their numbers: Smikros the painter, who ascribed his name to a participant in a most elegant symposium, on the *stamnos* in Brussels A 717; *AV*, I, 20, n. 1. Still earlier, Euphronios, an older painter, perhaps portrayed the same Smikros as a young man; fragment of a *krater*, Munich 8935. A. Greifenhagen, "Smikros, Lieblingsinschrift und Malersignatur," *Jahrbuch Berliner Museen*, IX (1967), 22 ff., and bibliography, notes 72 ff. Cf. also the name of the girl Smikra, in the cup of the Thalia Painter, above, n. 20. Such incipient autobiographical tendencies among artists must be deemed a significant phenomenon. They concern alike the history of art and social history.

able in all Greek late archaic art but favored especially by the vase painters. At no other time was Greek art so inclined toward realistic portrayals of the contemporary milieu; nor was its choice of subject matters ever again so large, its range so free, its approach to the social aspects of human existence so direct. The conspicuously uninvolved, detached objectivity that informs the erotic representations of the period fits their definition as genre scenes. To make love is a part of people's social lives, and so the artists of that time registered the various ways of doing it with a keen and sensitive perception of fact, with a gusto that is most likely sympathetic, but with no trace of sentimentality. Primarily, their work turns out to present a picture of manners not essentially different from other themes of genre, such as women meeting at the well house or shopping for a pair of new shoes. The erotic representations, like other genre pictures, describe people, their actions and the situations in which they act, all truly reported. A sign of sentiment, or of affection exchanged between the lovers, is rarely if ever seen in these illustrations of love. We may recognize in some of these works a hint of thoughtfulness or perhaps a critical comment. But then it is always the artist who comments on the people and the situations, as if he were an impartial eyewitness and onlooker. The persons he represents follow their whims and sports. Their loves, described so objectively, may show shared pleasure, but the ingredient of a mutual sentiment is mostly lacking, or, at least, not mentioned. Exceptions to this rule are extremely rare; the cup by Peithinos
15, 16 described above (Figs. 15 and 16) may be one of them.

All this the coming generations were ready to change, however, as the works of art shall soon tell us. The new republic that began to rebuild Athens after the Persian invasion followed a different bent of mind. For the frivolities of the old society it seems to have had little use. The days of the archaic dandies and of their last lusty companions, the robust generation that fought and won the wars against Persia, were then already numbered. The year 471 B.C., when Themistocles was exiled, sets the symbolic date for the end of their era.

❁ TWOSOMES: CLASSICAL AND HELLENISTIC

Groups comprising no more than two participants occur among the erotic themes of Greek vase paintings at the close of the archaic period, even when they still were greatly outnumbered by the serially arranged friezes and the representations of the banquet type. They found a natural place in the roundels inside the drinking cups (Figs. 22, 23, and 24). Yet it is not difficult to see from 22, 23, 24
the start that these pairs of lovers in self-contained compositions, not participants in a crowd, represented something more than a mere variant of the banquet theme. I regard them as a different iconographic type and, in Greek art, a new thematic concept having special implications. The dyad, isolated by a frame, added to the sexual theme those connotations of privacy and intimacy for which the gay revels had left but little room. For the first time the possibility of a more psychologically oriented interpretation of sexual episodes moved within the range of the visual arts; the merely factual illustrations of the older type had neither sought nor achieved such interpretations. Now a chance opened up, to view and express with sympathy that intense and exclusive concern—the affective accompaniment of the sexual union—which emotion demands and often establishes between two persons, if only for the while of a shared pleasure. This new interest in showing the life of the soul (*animi sensus,* in the language of Pliny), not as an appendage of our outward actions, but as their very source and origin, conforms with a ruling trend of all classical art.[38] Sentiment, the capacity for feeling, is an airy element and properly beyond vision; yet from the late fifth century B.C. and far into the fourth it was a main concern of the Greek artists to give a visual account of man as a sentient being. This was the time when the winged figures of Eros and the fluttering Erotes became the common allegories of sentimental love, as ubiquitous in the Greek art of that era as angels were in later Christian art, when their

[38] *Animi sensus:* Pliny (on Myron), *Historia Naturalis,* XXXIV, 58.

number increased so notably during the Baroque period and the so-called Age of Reason. It is an interesting fact, however, that these popular visualizations by symbol were not often used in the erotic representations which here concern us. The erotic illustrations remained an art of genre even on the classical level, and aim at direct and realistic representation. Only on rare occasions did their makers avail themselves of what, to them, may have seemed unnecessary allegorical embellishments or circumlocutions.

The early monuments in this category—pairs of lovers by themselves—are vase paintings, still in the late archaic style. A cup by the Panaitios Painter, in the British Museum, offers an example
22 (Fig. 22).[39] A pretty young woman half lies, half kneels on a bed, face downward; her right hand reaches back expectantly to her partner, who kneels behind her. The man is characterized as elderly and clearly embarrassed. The joke is on the ineffective lover, as so often in comedy. All this has been very delicately drawn, not unlike a modern cartoon of a rather sophisticated sort. The satire is obvious and typical of its time. Something new comes to the fore, however, in the use of the frame as a seclusive device. The frame isolates the little comedy, styled as an episode of the boudoir, an amusing indiscretion. One ought also take notice of the comfortable furnishings within the small enclosure—bed, pillow, the lady's wool basket hanging on the wall.[40] In this type of erotic representation accessories seem important; they connote comfort

[39] Red-figure cup, London E44 (Panaitios Painter): *AV*, I, 318 f., no. 2. In contrast to this painting, other early representations of erotic pairs in the circular fields of red-figure drinking cups continue to be styled as episodes, derived from the traditional banquet situation. In a cup attributed to a painter of Beazley's "Pioneer Group," Yale 163, *AV*, I, 36 (a), two lovers embrace and kiss, drawn with the neatness of a Japanese woodcut. The woman is a flute girl: a reminiscence of the banquet. Similarly, in the splendid cup by the Triptolemos Painter at Tarquinia (Fig. 24), *AV*, I, 367, no. 93, the woman reclines on a wineskin; again, the memory of the banquet determined the choice of the furnishings.

[40] The feminine surroundings of a well-settled *hetaira* did not differ greatly from more ordinary households; G. Rodenwaldt, "Spinnende Hetären," *Archaeologischer Anzeiger*, 1932, 7 ff.

and privacy. Even when, on the inside of a somewhat later bowl at Tarquinia, a similarly engaged couple is seen standing instead of kneeling (Fig. 23), the woman still manages to lean her head on a large cushion, presumably propped against the wall of her room.[41] 23

Another item on our list of twosomes confronts us with an entirely different set of circumstances, with regard to both its formal style and its humanistic outlook. It is a small jug in Berlin, most elegantly designed by an Athenian artist who must have worked near the end of the fifth century B.C. (Figs. 25 and 26). 25, 26
Since the time of the Panaitios Painter (Fig. 22), more than half a century has elapsed.[42] In the interval the cultural and intellectual climate of Greece changed profoundly. The painter who placed an erotic scene so deftly on the shoulder of his jug, its sole decoration, in the middle of the front side just below the neck, evidently was a man of lively spirits. Like his late archaic precursors, he, too, belonged to a founding generation—the inventors and perfecters of the mature classical style, a race of innovators in their own right. 22

The subject matter of his little painting is unusual. A young man sits on one of the comfortably built chairs with a high curving back which were in fashion during the late decades of the century. A girl, stripped except for her broad hairband, makes ready to join him headfirst. The action may seem clear enough, but the circumstances in which it is set require some discussion. First of all, the participants of this happy meeting are two very young people—younger than those in most other Greek portrayals of erotic subjects. Indeed, I should call them adolescents; the young man has

[41] Red-figure cup in Tarquinia (Briseis Painter): *AV*, I, 408, no. 36. Identical with Marcadé, *Roma*, p. 38, cited as being in Naples. The oath of Lysistrata (Aristophanes, *Lysistrata*, 231), jokingly compares the bent back of a woman in this position to the handle (shaped as a crouching lioness?) of a cheese grater; cf. P. Jacobsthal, *AM*, LVII (1932), 1 ff. Popular speech, less metaphorically, may call her a "Katapýgaina." For the latter expression and related descriptive epithets, see M. Milne and D. von Bothmer, *Hesperia* XXII, (1953), 215 ff.; I thank E. Harrison for this reference.

[42] *Oinochoë*, Berlin 2414 (Shuvalov Painter): *AV*, II, 1208, no. 41 (shape 9); *CVA*, Berlin (3), pl. 145, 2. The shape appears to be unique. Relation to the regular *choës* is likely; E. Buschor, *FR*, Text II (Munich, 1932), 316 and fig. 150.

fine, uncut locks but as yet shows no trace of pubic hair, and the girl is hardly older. An explanation of these unusual circumstances may come from the related vessels by the same painter which belong to the class of the so-called *choës*—small jugs turned out in quantity for the annual Athenian spring festival, a sort of carnival, known as the Anthesteria. On that occasion, two days were dedicated to the wine god; the barrels containing the preceding summer's vintage were opened and officially declared ready for use. Much merrymaking went on and much attention was paid to the young, including the very young, whose playful pictures appear frequently on the vases of this type. The couple on the Berlin jug of course are not children; but can we not say that, as the wine has come of age, so have they? The implied parallel between the young wine and human maturing does not seem at all implausible, if one considers the specifics of the monument and the context of folklore from which it came.[43]

Be this as it may, the tenor of the picture differs palpably from archaic satire. It makes the outspoken veracity of the latter seem harsh by comparison. But the representation on the Berlin jug is not a simple exercise in erotic art, of interest only for its surface meaning. On the contrary, it seems to imply a great deal more than the data represented, and to leave much to a knowing interpretation of implicit references. To a contemporary beholder this little scene may have suggested a smiling yet clearly readable allusion to a popular feast on the local calendar. Such appreciative, or even indulgent, interest in the home environment and the native folkways certainly is an amiable trait; it also bespeaks a romantic attitude. For "classical" and "romantic" modes are not always so clearly divided as the literary critics of the nineteenth century stipulated. They do not seem in every instance to be wholly incompatible. The emotionalism which much classical Greek art expresses is a romantic element. By the same token we may here observe that the humanistic interpretation of erotic situations in

[43] Brendel, "Villa," pp. 228 f., n. 38; p. 230, n. 41; p. 244, n. 68.

Greek art on the classical level was apt to express itself in a romantic vein.

According to that interpretation, the sexual meeting of two individuals is predicated, ultimately, as a result of sentiment. This concentration on the emotional aspect was in keeping with the psychological interests of a society which, at that very time, subjected the human experience of love to the questioning thought and analytic inquiry of the dramatic poets and the discourses of the sophists. The awesome emotional dynamics that underlie and govern all human affairs, public and private alike, thus became the concern and, indeed, the discovery of the intellectually alert. Among these irrational powers, affection and disaffection were bound to reveal themselves as the prime movers. Perhaps it is advisable to distinguish here between the representations of sexual themes as one kind of erotic art and another range of erotic themes having much broader meaning. At the height of the Greek classical era a great portion of its art, especially in drama and vase painting, must be called "erotic" in the latter sense—dealing with the themes of love. This art drew its subjects chiefly from myth and legend—namely, the loves of the gods and heroes. The illustrations of sexual situations constitute a different case; they followed a different tradition and continued to deal with the loves of actual, not mythical, people. A human reality, socially conditioned, had been their proper subject matter from the start. But the established genre was not incapable of accepting the romantic and sentimental propensities inherent in the new eroticism, and this the *oinochoë* in
Berlin (Fig. 26) shows persuasively. Its small picture has no need of 26
a boundary line to isolate the lovers. Even without a frame we realize that they are alone, wholly absorbed with one another. Their foreheads touch, their glances meet.[44] Clearly the erotic iconography has taken a fresh turn. In this instance at least, it has

[44] Brendel "Villa," p. 242, n. 62; also p. 248, n. 74. The Renaissance resuscitated the ancient trope; for still later examples, see P. A. Tomory, "Profane Love in Italian Early and High Baroque Painting: The Transmission of Emotive Experience," *Essays in the History of Art Presented to R. Wittkower* (London, 1967), pp. 182 ff.

come to imply, as a concomitant of the explicit action, an element of gentle passion or of love requited.

We have already mentioned the paucity of erotic monuments during the fourth century B.C., and this survey must here proceed across considerable chronological gaps. But among the relatively few extant examples some will be found of excellent quality, such
27 as the relief on the cover of a bronze mirror in Boston (Fig. 27). The style and workmanship of this Greek relief ought to be credited to a Corinthian or Southern Italian, rather than an Attic, workshop. Its date probably lies within the decade after the middle of the century.[45] The subject—a man and a woman in sexual contact—is self-explanatory. Here I may note, as a general observation, that from the fourth century B.C. onward the erotic monuments of Greek art, and of the subsequent Roman art as well, tend to deal with their sexual themes in a more obvious, if topically more limited, manner than was usually true of the earlier examples. As a rule they require less explanation, insofar as the sense of their representations is plainly evident and their compositional schemata became in the course of time quite standardized. They invite commentaries of another sort, however. The relief on the Boston mirror, which stands at the beginning of the new trend, in many ways represents a highly individual creation. By originality of interpretation, this still is a classical monument. Nevertheless, it can be shown that its composition probably started from a small series of preconceptions, silently accepted, which was eventually to turn into a new, standard iconography. First, the erotic act involves two people of different sex. This will remain the rule, almost entirely; homosexual representations of an assuredly late classical

[45] Bronze mirror, Boston, Museum of Fine Arts: W. Züchner, *Griechische Klappspiegel* (Berlin, 1942), pp. 66, 94 (KS. 95). Said to have been found in a grave, either at Corinth or at Megara; since the provenance is not certain, a Southern Italian origin ought to be considered also. Only the relief on the outside is here at issue; the engraved drawing on the inside of the lid (Marcadé, *Eros*, p. 123) seems to me by a modern hand. The mirror appeared on the Paris art market about 1881; cf. Züchner, *op. cit.*, p. 78, to KS. 123. A group of remarkably similar design occurs on a terracotta fragment, probably
28 of a Roman lamp (Fig. 28).

or Hellenistic origin are rare.[46] Second, the couple is shown to be alone, presumably in secluded quarters. Third, the prerequisites of physical comfort—bed, mattress, pillow—are clearly described. The insistence on these three iconographic conditions amounts to a rule that is but rarely violated, and sets the limits for the latest stage of Greek erotic art. The implications appear to be chiefly sociological. A newly developing, prosperous, urban bourgeoisie has thus spelled out its demands of comfort and gracious living. By contrast with the austere bareness of locale which characterized so many erotic happenings in the archaic tradition, the erotic idyl here appears tamed, civilized, domesticated. Overtones of a new morality may also be recognized in these iconographic changes; social standards and standards of conduct often intertwine. The interiors and furnishings that are shown or indicated in the erotic scenes after the new fashion seem to reflect a wider problem of society—namely, the proprieties of making love. In their own way the illustrations of art answer to a fashionable—or popular—quest for seemly surroundings. The scene must be set indoors, privately; a bed is *de rigueur.* We must assume that the new iconography responded to a current notion of properness when it was first adopted. At any rate, the prescript was followed for centuries afterward, as a convention of art.

The cover relief of the mirror in Boston, though ostensibly

[46] A few examples, at random: Terracotta medallion with stamped relief (bottom of a cup?) in Berlin, Hellenistic, from Pergamon; second half second century B.C. O. Deubner, *Archaeologischer Anzeiger* (1939), 346, fig. 10; I thank O. Deubner for this reference. Cast bronze relief (center of a bronze bowl), Roman in a rather neo-classical manner, probably early first century A.D.; Naples, National Museum: Satyr and young boy. Marcadé, *Roma,* p. 36. About the authenticity of a presumed Roman silver cup which was made known recently, I reserve judgment, having not seen the original: C. Vermeule, "Augustan and Julio-Claudian Court Silver," *Antike Kunst,* VI (1963), 33 ff. and pl. 14, figs. 2, 4, 6 (London Art Market). But the Roman bronze *situla* from Herstal, now in Brussels, Musées Royaux d'Art et d'Histoire, which illustrates four dignified scholastics at work in the main frieze and at play in the shoulder frieze, ought to be mentioned here. The satirical intent of the representation was made sufficiently clear by F. Cumont: *Annales de la Société d'Archéologie de Bruxelles,* XIV (1900), 401 ff.; pls. XXXI, XXXII, XXXV. Late first century A.D., about the time of Domitian, a coin of whom formed part of this find.

designed only to decorate a useful utensil, is no mean work of art. On the contrary, it is a remarkably fine object in its own right, and it bears the marks of a noble ancestry. If we compare it with the materials discussed so far, we find much that appears new and special. First the facts. The lover, a young man, embraces his partner from the rear, both half reclining. One might expect that in the tradition of ancient art two persons so recumbent side by side would be illustrated in profile, but here the pair is shown almost frontally; the legs and body of the woman extend diagonally, between foreground and background. A tendency to create complicated and somewhat strained representations of reclining groups is to be noticed early in Greek erotic art and perhaps
14 follows naturally from its subject matter (see Fig. 14); but the wish ingrained in all arts of antiquity, to produce complete and unabridged images, also seems to have had a share in these pictorial adventures. Certain it is that the artist who designed the Boston mirror could avail himself of drawn models that represented similar groupings. I count the work as an echo of the painted erotica for which Parrhasios had been famous, himself a much-admired draftsman.[47] The two artists may have been near

[47] Pliny, *Historia Naturalis,* XXXV, 67; see also above, n. 30. One of Parrhasios' erotic themes can be named specifically, "Meleager and Atalante": evidently a mythological travesty. The painting, a small tablet *(tabella),* was later kept in the collection of the emperor Tiberius, where Suetonius mentions it; below, n. 64.

References to mythological parody occur also in connection with other fourth-century painters, e.g., in the circle of Apelles: Pliny, *op. cit.,* 140. The erotic themes, of course, were not new; neither was the travesty of myth. But in the fourth century B.C. we hear more of both, either because new and perhaps more capricious attitudes toward subject matter came to the fore, on the part of the artists, or because the paintings were more spoken of. Toward the close of the fifth century B.C., easel painting began to assert its supremacy over vase painting. It seems that in the wake of this turn from a principally decorative to a freer use of the painter's art, a certain painting could and quite frequently did become a matter of public concern, in a manner that was hardly true of any vase painting. Thus about the time when painted *tabellae* with erotic content first appear in the lists of ancient writers on art, the first expressions of adverse criticism of such themes are heard in the discussions of the contemporary literate public. The two events are probably not unconnected. Previously, the vase painters had not drawn this kind of attention, although they represented the same subjects most freely. Obviously, about 400 B.C. the mutual relations between art, artists, and

contemporaries, for all we know. At any rate, the representation on the mirror, though a toreutic relief, ought to be valued first of all as the tour de force of a skillful and sensitive designer. It is in every essential respect a painterly work, intended to realize a softly melting perspective in the design of the woman who leans backward. The converging perspective lines culminate in the kiss of the lovers. The passionate temperament of the scene is beyond doubt: the lovers meet under the wings of Eros, who hovers visibly in the air. All this belongs to the best style of Greek fourth-century art and thought. The two modes of emotion—active and passive, *thymos* and *pathos*, attack and abandon—unite in the pleasures of the senses consummated by the impressible mind. The kiss, never so shown before in any monument on our list, appears here as the agent and the symbol of that union. The thought is good psychology, by classical standards; the illustration is realistic, by ours; the mood, romantic.

The kiss combined with physical union recurs in a terracotta group of two young lovers which was excavated at Delos (Fig. 29). 29
A woman facing forward sits astride her partner, who appears to be seated rather than reclining. Like the relief in Fig. 27, this small group also decorated an object of use, probably a terracotta lamp.[48]

---

the public had begun to change. As the freedom of the artists grew in one direction, it became narrowed in another by the social criticism it started to evoke.

The arguments that underlie these early symptoms of social censure, directed at erotic representations, cannot be discussed here. They were hardly quite the same as the objections raised in more recent periods. Aristotle's critique of the work of the painter Pauson probably is the best-known example (*Politics,* 1340, a, 33); the same Pauson had previously attracted the scorn of Aristophanes. At stake, it seems, was a contrast about which these critics felt strongly, between the heroic themes of the older muralists such as Polygnotus and the lowly subjects of the popular genre preferred by Pauson; the latter included erotic matters (below, n. 64). We must conclude that, in general, vase painting, an applied art, was measured differently from easel painting, as to the social values expected from either art. In the fourth century B.C. one encounters a new public sensitivity to this situation: what once had been right for the vase painters was not necessarily right for the easel painters also. For a short collection of references, see P. Moreno, "Il realismo nella pittura Greca del IV secolo A.C.," *Rivista d'archeologia e storia d'arte,* XIII–XIV (1964–1965), 84, notes 10, 11.

[48] Terracotta group, late second century B.C.; Delos, Museum. Marcadé, *Eros,* p. 43.

It is a fully modeled work of sculpture, however, and of fine craftsmanship. The style is definitely Hellenistic; a date after the middle of the second century B.C. seems to fit both the stylistic characteristics and the Delian history. We must assume that an interval of about two hundred years separated the terracotta group from the mirror at Boston. Nevertheless, the two seem related by temperament. The fact that the frontal position of the two lovers has been retained gives both works a remarkable formal similarity. It necessitates the same somewhat forced turn from the foreground toward the back in both representations. Essentially this must be called a pictorial device—in the Parrhasian taste, I am now inclined to say; it was scarcely a sculptor's invention. But we have come to see that this formal arrangement, wherever it is employed, greatly enhances the emotional effect of the scene. Clearly the romantic tradition, the noble style of Greek erotic art, did not end abruptly with the fourth century B.C. It had Hellenistic followers, as the group from Delos convincingly demonstrates. Rarely has its distinguishing mark, the kiss of lovers, been shown more emphatically. At no other point of its history did Greek art move so close to the impassioned sensualism which, centuries later, animated the Tantric reliefs of India.[49]

ART FOR THE MULTITUDE: HELLENISTIC AND ROMAN

During the Hellenistic period the frequency of erotic representations was again on the rise; it reached its peak under the Roman
29 Empire. But the terracotta group from Delos (Fig. 29) can hardly be called typical of this production. The quality of its execution is superior, as are the spirit and spontaneity of its invention. The bulk of the Hellenistic and Roman material shows quite different characteristics, and lends itself to a more summary survey than was the case with the preceding phases. It lacks the individualism which so signally distinguishes the earlier examples.

[49] Tantric reliefs: H. Zimmer, *op. cit.* (above, n. 7), pp. 129 ff.

Exceptions to this rule are few. On the whole, the erotic art of the Hellenistic and Roman periods appears surprisingly homogeneous. It exhibits little change over the centuries, either of style or of principle. For this reason I shall here treat it as a typological unit; its evolvement must be regarded as a special occurrence in the universal history of art, despite the wide area of distribution and the long duration of its typical manifestations. The monuments which fall in this category come from every part of the Mediterranean area; their time of origin ranges from the third century B.C. to the end of the third century A.D.

Objects made of inexpensive materials such as clay predominate. Paintings on a modest scale are known from Roman Campania, chiefly Pompeii (below, pages 61 ff.). The workmanship is often careless, the execution cursory; this holds true, also, of the paintings. The iconography is on the whole restricted to the representations of couples on their beds or mattresses. In many instances it is obvious that one is dealing with a routine art and a proliferation of stereotypes. Nevertheless, a degree of variety is not wholly lacking, not even among the humble objects which will from here on increasingly demand our attention, such as the numerous Roman terracotta lamps; for these simple utensils, which were in everybody's hands, now become frequently the carriers of erotic representations. In the new order of monuments it is the scope of the variety that has changed. The new era reverted from the humanistic diversity of the classical examples to a simpler level of fact, without, however, aiming at that variousness of events which the archaic vase painters cultivated. The typical erotic monuments of the Hellenistic and Roman periods present themselves to us as a popular art, designed for a broad appeal to many people rather than reserved for only a few. While the "couple on the bed" remains the standard theme, diversity was realized by the positions assigned to the various couples. The sole emphasis lies on this strictly factual specification, and its blunt depiction constitutes the exclusive message of almost every erotic representation after approximately 200 B.C. We must conclude that the erotic art of the Hellenistic Greeks and the Hellenized Romans found its proper range of diversity in the variations of a single representational schema. Whatever grade of refinement it was to attain developed within the intellectual and iconographic limits of this given theme. The technicalities of the *ars amatoria* came to form the obvious matter of interest. A more humanistic interpretation of the variousness of love may still concern the literati, from Herondas to Ovid. Yet even in their work seriousness and sympathy will now often hide behind a somewhat supercilious realism which comments benevolently on the ways of commoners; or it will take cover under a polished surface of elegant frivolity. The visual arts will have none of the former and little of the latter.

The confluence of originally separate national histories which together produced the Hellenistic culture and its heir, the Roman Empire, also shaped the conditions of the new erotic art. I should mention expressly two factors. The first and perhaps most generally important consists in the rapid increase of easily exportable art, mass-produced in molds. To this category belong not only the ornate tableware and other implements of metal, often precious, for which the demand was rising steadily, but also the fine ceramics and the cheap earthenware decorated with stamped reliefs. Fine metalwork and inexpensive ceramics could be turned out in quantity, and both types of work were widely distributed. By far the greater portion of the preserved monuments are objects of small value, as to material and cost of production. The second factor was of a different nature. The traditional Roman sense of gravity was apt to frown on any manner of frivolousness, for either of two rather opposite reasons: because it was held to be an expression of aristocratic luxury, always suspect in ancient Rome, or because it was regarded as an entertainment tolerable, to an extent, among the lower classes but unbecoming to a person of rank and responsibility. Either condition tended to encourage an erotic art on a relatively low level of quality and of small intellectual ambition, and to discourage personal comment. Either trend, whether toward a rising quantity of output or a concomitant decline of artistic quality, can already be noticed during the Hellenistic period. Both trends increased with the centuries, in proportion to the growing Roman influence upon the ancient civilizations. After the first century B.C., almost all extant erotic representations belong to one or another class of this popular art. The exceptions must be discussed separately when the occasion arises.

There was a third factor, however, which probably also put its mark on these developments: the art of Alexandria almost certainly had an impact on the new erotic iconography. Unfortunately its contribution is difficult to assess. Too little is known of the aulic art and the public monuments of the Hellenistic metropolis. The court, it seems, favored an art of cultivated leisure, erudite and sophisticated. The contrast between this higher level of art and a very active, popular production was probably more sharply defined in Alexandrian Egypt than in any other Hellenistic territory; the frequent local terracotta statuettes and middle-class tombstones may be taken as representative of the popular trends. There are also indications that on both levels the share of the native Egyptian tradition reached further than has been assumed. The evidence supporting this observation can probably be augmented in the future. It does not concern the erotic imagery alone, but points to a general condition of the Hellenistic art in Alexandria. Symptoms of cultural interpenetration appear in the realm of concepts underlying the theological definition of the monarchy, which was borrowed from Pharaonic Egypt and incorporated with the courtly allegories of the Hellenistic rule; they appear also in formal developments, such as the continuation of portrait sculpture in a native vcin but Hellenized to a greater or lesser degree.

From this state of affairs arises an interesting question. While the evidence of erotic art in early Egypt appears thus far to be minimal, a rather special type of erotic representations in a late Egyptian manner comes to the fore during, or perhaps shortly before, the Hellenistic period. This type includes small groups carved from the local limestone, as well as the famous illustrated
papyrus scroll in Turin (Fig. 30). Most of these representations 30
show highly fantastic actions, resembling the oddity of dreams.

Often the male figures—including children—are given absurdly oversized phalli. Even when the sexual situations can be read as essentially "natural," they tend to be depicted with grotesque exaggerations and willful distortions, in a fashion of caricature. That an element of phallism of prehistoric origin was inherent in certain aspects of Egyptian thought and cult, as in the religion of Osiris, is a well-attested fact. Moreover, fables, often humorous, and legends involving phalli of more than ordinary extension can be found in the folklore of many peoples, including those of the African continent. Thus the late Egyptian erotica may be related to an earlier native lore, but they can hardly be fully explained by it. The resulting imagery can assume a native look, as in the statuette groups. Conversely, it may offer strange variations of much more ancient ideas or, possibly, an imported iconography, as was perhaps the case of the Turin papyrus.[50] At any rate, an Alexandrian component must be expected within the spectrum of Hellenistic erotic art. Among its constituent characteristics I count the following:

1. *Symplegmata* in an open-air setting: this representational scheme is unusual in post-archaic erotic art, but examples occur in Roman wall paintings that show it in considerable detail. The setting may include water and boats, awnings hung between trees, trellises overgrown with flowers; the people are represented as small, commensurate with the landscape in which they move about. Decidedly, the scenery was not meant to depict a wilderness, but cultured landscapes, such as a garden near a river or
31 canal (Fig. 31).[51] It is typically related to the "Nilotic" landscapes in Hellenistic style which, in turn, accommodated many elements

[50] Turin papyrus: below, n. 69. Phallism in Egypt: J. Boardman, "A Greek Vase from Egypt," *Journal of Hellenic Studies*, LXXVIII (1958), 8.

[51] Fig. 31, Roman painting, from Pompeii: a picnic in the Egyptian style. Naples, National Museum; Marcadé, *Roma*, p. 36; cf. pp. 65, 68. In Rome the open-air banquet under a canopy was regarded as an Alexandrian luxury; cf. Propertius, III, XI, 45, with implied—unsympathetic—reference to the lavish entertaining of Cleopatra during her Roman visit: "*Ausa* (sc. Cleopatra) . . . *foedaque Tarpeio conopia tendere saxo.*"

of earlier Egyptian river scenes. When erotic groups are added to this kind of setting, they appear as a by-play in the larger context.

2. Caricature: the protagonists are represented as pygmies, comically distorted. Again the "Nilotic" landscapes furnish the nearest parallels, as they are frequently populated with pygmies of similar invention.[52]

3. A conspicuous phallism, in the sense just defined. Any representation in Hellenistic or Roman art that contains one or more of these three typical elements is for this reason likely to stem from an ultimately Alexandrian source, even when such a work was found outside Egypt.

To complete this survey, mention must be made of two particular erotic themes which, though not entirely new, became fashionable during the Hellenistic and Roman periods. Both subjects seem to have been contributions to the Hellenistic *koiné* by the Asian continent. First is the demonic gardener, Priapus, probably venerated originally in the rural districts along the Asiatic borders of the Black Sea and in the city of Lampsakos. He was primarily a grower and guardian of trees, vines, and fruits, but in the course of time he came to be looked upon as an impersonation of the generative powers of all nature. The Hellenistic cultural expansion carried this rather secondary and locally limited deity south and westward, where its enormously phallic, grotesquely friendly aspect gained universal popularity. Egypt, too, received the Asian immigrant favorably, comparing him to her own Horus. As an object of religion, Priapus need hardly be taken seriously, especially in these relatively late stages of his cult, though his odd appearance gave to the Hellenistic world a popular phallic image, a visible address for every vague wish of happiness and success, and a target of many an irreverent joke. His simple, rustic

[52] Pygmies, caricature, Nilotic landscapes: Otto J. Brendel, "Der Affen-Aeneas," *RömMitt*, LX–LXI (1953–1954), 153 ff.; painting in Naples, National Museum: A. Maiuri, *Roman Painting* (Geneva, n.d. [1953]), p. 111.

sanctuaries enliven the countryside in countless Roman idyllic paintings, as they probably also did in reality.[53]

32 The second specifically Hellenistic theme that here requires at least a brief notice is the hermaphrodite (Fig. 32). Its progress from Asia to the West parallels that of Priapus. But, different from that universally popular phallic dispenser of bounty, the fantasy of the *hermaphroditus* led from the start to rather esoteric theological and anthropological speculations. In the Near East, as perhaps also in Greece, speculative fictions of a bisexual divinity or a bisexual aboriginal race of humans preceded the legend of the youth who became one with the nymph Salmacis.[54] Yet it was in the terms of a myth that the lore of the hermaphrodite established itself in Hellenistic and Roman thought, and that the ineffable appeal of the man-maiden became a favored theme of Hellenistic and Roman art.

The outcome, in art, was a generic being of mythical status whose impersonal youthful image invited admiration and curiosity because of its inscrutable dual nature—a conversation piece to adorn the houses and gardens of the literate and the rich. Therefore, within the overwhelmingly popular erotic art of the period, the representations of the hermaphrodite form an exception. The relatively high number of marble statues on our list of examples and the quality of their execution sufficiently bespeak the social status and financial ease of the clientele for which they were designed.[55] This, it seems, was a theme to suit refined minds. For the ancient argument still went on about the original oneness of being, though by now it was conducted in a more secular mode that, by modern standards, one should call psychological. The story of Tiresias, wise and old, furnished its representative parable. This cryptic tale can be traced to the Asian Greeks as far back as the

[53] *RE*, XXII, 2 (Stuttgart, 1954), 1914 ff., s.v. "Priapos" (Herter and Lullies).

[54] M. Delcourt, *Hermaphrodite: mythes et rites de la bisexualité dans l'antiquité classique* (Paris, 1955).

[55] All preserved ancient statues of hermaphrodites are Hellenistic or later. Most are Roman copies of Hellenistic prototypes; below, n. 58.

late fifth century B.C. It imparted a human nature to the mystic hermaphrodite and a personal name as well. A miraculous fate turned Tiresias into a woman, then after a time restored him to manhood. When, upon being questioned, he declared that a woman's pleasure in love surpasses the masculine ninefold, Hera blinded him and Zeus granted him the gift of prophecy.[56] The vexing problem of wholeness, severed by diversity, thus was restated in different terms. It was not even a new slant, in presenting the problem, to lay the stress on the natural division of sex. To be either man or woman is part of the human condition—the finiteness of man. Up to this point the myth merely confirms the ancient speculations about a pristine unity incorporated in a bisexual being. But a new intellectual turn appears in the prospect of a practical answer to the problem. For was Tiresias not both a man and a woman successively? This seems to be the message of his story. Whosoever is able to experience the pleasures of the other sex, and can combine them with his own, may thus in himself restore the original union of nature and transcend the barriers of the limited self. The thought of self-transcendence, in any form, is essentially mystical. For those so inclined, the legend of the *hermaphroditus,* in the form of the Tiresias myth or in any other, easily turns into a transparent fable. It becomes the mythical allegory of a daydream with philosophical overtones or of a state of being that is perhaps unattainable but not unthinkable.

We know about these rather *recherché* expositions of myth mostly from literature.[57] The monuments hardly hint at them. At best they provide a vision of the substance on which such speculations—and an expectation of the extraordinary—may well have

[56] The *locus classicus* is Ovid, *Metamorphoses,* III, 318 ff.

[57] In addition to the ancient literary testimonies, one may also note the echo which the myth of Tiresias elicited from modern writers. I quote from T. S. Eliot, *The Waste Land,* III ("The Fire Sermon"): "I Tiresias, though blind, throbbing between two lives,/Old man with wrinkled female breasts, can see/At the violet hour . . . ," and "Notes on the Waste Land," to v. 218: "The whole passage from Ovid is of great anthropological interest." The reference is to the passage above, n. 56.

turned. Of such kind probably was the allure of the once much
32 admired "sleeping hermaphrodite" (Fig. 32); the occasional standing
statues may have carried religious connotations, as of a cult image
revealing itself to its devotees. But when the bisexual wonder became involved with the more conventional, mythical tribe of the
Satyrs, the step from the sublime to the commonplace was easily
made. The hermaphrodite attacked by a disappointed Pan or Satyr
may seem a rather stale joke to us, but the theme was evidently
popular in Hellenistic art; it became quite common in Romano-
33 Campanian painting (Fig. 33).[58]

THE NUMBERS GAME

Under this heading I propose to set down some observations on the common and often rather abridged erotic representations that form the majority of the Hellenistic and Roman material. There is little need to discuss them in a strict chronological order. If anything requires explanation in these representations, it is the uniformity and stability of their chief characteristics; compared to this, the regional and chronological differences appear secondary. It should be kept in mind, however, that the monuments in this category constitute the latest and ultimate stage of erotic art in the Greco-Roman world. The tradition that determined and sustained their long-persistent iconographic types—their coherence of outlook and of their intellectual level—poses the problem here.

[58] Sleeping Hermaphrodite: Rome, National Museum, Brunn-Bruckmann, *Denkmäler,* pl. 505 and text; also Villa Borghese 1552. Additional copies and bibliography in G. Lippold, *Handbuch,* p. 366 and pl. 130, figs. 1, 2; M. Bieber, *The Sculpture of the Hellenistic Age*[2] (New York, 1961), pp. 146 f.

Standing Hermaphrodite from Pergamon: Lippold, *op. cit.,* p. 359, with n. 3 and pl. 126, fig. 1. Others: Bieber, *op. cit.,* pp. 124 f. and fig. 492.

Hermaphrodite attacked by Satyr or Pan, statuary groups: Brunn-Bruckmann, *Denkmäler,* pl. 731, with list of replicas; Bieber, *op. cit.,* pp. 146 f. Painted version of the same statuary groups: P. Herrmann, *Denkmäler d. Malerei d. Altertums* (Munich, 1904–1931), pl. 124, 2.

We turn first to a Hellenistic example, a work of modest price in its own time—the fragment of a terracotta pot from Delos, dating from near the middle of the second century B.C.[59] Reliefs representing erotic groups have been stamped on its outside. The best-preserved group shows a pair of lovers on a bed. The box-like shape of the bed results from the large cloth hanging from its side almost down to the floor. It resembles the corresponding furniture on the earlier mirror case in Boston (Fig. 27)—a reminder that the link with the classical tradition was not yet entirely broken. On the bed one sees a woman from the rear, reclining, her arms closing around the neck of her kneeling lover and her left leg bent across his back; she holds him firmly, as in a Hephaestus' net. The design is very apt and on the whole securely outlined, but details are treated sketchily; the facial features, especially, are barely recognizable. 27

The arrangement of these groups raises a problem of interpretation, however. The fact that several reliefs illustrating erotic couplings were lined up around the walls of a single vase, without dividing frames or any other visible separation, brings up once more the questions of locality and of simultaneity of action. Yet a narrative context, be it a temporal sequence or the simultaneous episodes favored in archaic vase paintings, cannot often be construed from the Hellenistic and Roman stamped reliefs. Their erotic episodes are mostly treated per se. They do not as a rule add up to unified situations. In the Delian fragment, every little composition formed a closed unit and, according to the common practice in ancient relief ceramics, each representation was produced by a separate mold. It is therefore likely that in this case, as in most similar decorations, no general context was contemplated, beyond the sharply drawn outlines of each group. Neither of the two couples still visible seems aware of the others; the order in which they follow each other holds no apparent meaning. In the molded

[59] Terracotta relief, fragment from Delos: Marcadé, *Eros*, p. 47. Cf. the similar material from Pergamon, J. Schäfer, *Hellenistische Keramik aus Pergamon* (Berlin, 1968), pp. 79 f.

decorations, frames and base lines can be dispensed with, and the sequence of the stamped units can be altered to accommodate the craftsmen's whims or needs. Regardless of whether an action was shown as a single item or in combination with other representations, it retains its own exclusive content within the confines of each relief. Nor, for a similar reason, do the faces matter much. Personal character or sentiment was not a prime consideration, if it was considered at all, in this new class of erotic art. The first lesson to be derived from the mass-produced ware is that the conditions of its manufacture may entail a loss of reality in the scenes illustrated. The sexual episodes are separated from particulars of reality such as a certain time and place. Their message has become typified, de-individualized, and to that extent absolute; such prototypical images require little reference to surroundings. Their groupings can be staged by puppetlike figures, rather nondescript as persons, and acted out without much regard to environment. A sense of reality attaches only to the actions themselves.

The above characteristics, of both concept and presentation, remained constant throughout the entire Hellenistic-Roman period, with only minor variations. If from the Delian potsherd one turns to a Roman-Alexandrian terracotta flask (*lagynos*), which now belongs to the Antiquarium of West Berlin, the continuity of the
34, 35, 36 iconographical tradition becomes very clear (Figs. 34–36). The Berlin *lagynos* dates in the third century A.D.—about four hundred years later than the fragment from Delos.[60] Four small reliefs illustrating four manners of coition decorate the sloping shoulder of the vessel. Details differ, but the ordering principle has hardly changed in the interval since the similarly decorated relief vase from Delos was fashioned. True, the groups in this late antique Alexandrian instance seem united by the scrolls of vine and grapes into which they were inserted. While this device ostensibly creates a decorative order, it may also carry connotations of meaning in keeping with the local tradition; it may evoke reminiscences of

[60] Roman-Alexandrian *lagynos*, Berlin, Antiquarium: A. Greifenhagen, *Beiträge zur antiken Reliefkeramik* (Berlin, 1963), pp. 67 ff.

the ancient connection between Bacchic and erotic scenes, or it may be read as a late remembrance, equally vague, of those open-air banquets interspersed with erotic episodes which apparently were a specialty of earlier Alexandrian art. The oversized phallus of the reclining man (Fig. 35) can, too, be counted as a stylistic 35
symptom, typical of a regional Alexandrian tradition (see above, pages 49 ff.). For all that, the individual groups remain isolated, with no meaningful connection or clear reference to one another. The basic principle of arrangement—molded reliefs lined up around the walls of a terracotta vessel—was only modified, not essentially altered, by the ornamental vines. The modeling of details is quite unequal; some of the figures appear typified to an extent that heralds the future Coptic style of art in Egypt (Fig. 36). 36

About midway between the times of the relief vase from Delos and of the Berlin *lagynos* dates the numerous class of the so-called Arretine pottery. This famous *terra sigillata* ware requires a brief consideration, because within the family of mass-produced decorated ceramics to which it belongs it must for several reasons be called exceptional. It originated in a small Roman municipality, now the town of Arezzo, whence it was widely exported. The most active period of the Arretine potteries was in the early Empire, more or less coincident with the rule of Augustus, and their output reflects the Augustan taste. Their specialty was a finely wrought tableware of red-glazed clay, often decorated with delicately modeled reliefs; this new fashion replaced the earlier black-glazed household ceramics of Hellenistic make. Clearly the designers of these rather ambitious ceramics were modernists within their own time; their work aimed at a cultivated clientele, or at least a class of buyers conversant with, and emulating, the preferences of their social betters. Among the various molded reliefs which were the stock in trade of the Arretine potteries one finds a series of erotic scenes, on a level of quality unrivaled in post-Hellenistic ceramics.[61]

The erotic reliefs are usually on the outside of deep, open

[61] Erotic series, stamped reliefs, Arretine: Greifenhagen, *op. cit.*, pp. 79 ff.

37 bowls that probably served as drinking vessels (Fig. 37). They
share with all ancient molded ceramic decorations the characteristics of a serial product, except that their design and execution are better than is true of most others. Being stamped by molds, each relief constitutes a finished composition. The molds can be
38 used singly (Fig. 38), or the impressions can be lined up in rows; the latter is the more common method. Representations can be selected and distributed at will; the types are interchangeable. In the erotic series all the reliefs represent pairs of nude lovers—a man and a woman at a time—on low beds that are often covered with furs. The postures of the couples may alternate or vary, within a rather narrowly limited range; either the female partner
39 reclines, or the male (Fig. 39). Minor differences of detail occur not rarely in the variations of an essentially identical pattern,
40 according to the matrixes employed for each impress (Figs. 40
41 and 41).

In spite of the separateness inherent in the stamped reliefs, the ensembles which result from the sequence of scenes around an individual vessel often seem to suggest a planned context. In this respect, also, I find that the Arretine material diverges from the contemporary standard; no ancient erotic art since the archaic period approaches more nearly the banquet type of the Greek red-figured vases than do some of the Arretine bowls. The resemblance can hardly be incidental. As the fastidious formalism of their design pronounces the Grecizing and neo-classic spirit of Roman art under Augustus, so, I suggest, the erotic theme in the hands of the same artists assumes a Grecizing, retrospective slant. Indeed, it is not at all improbable that a reference to Greek art was consciously implied with this amatory imagery. But if such was the case the convivial setting—the ostensible occasion of the erotic happenings—itself acquires a fictitious, not realistic, quality. In a Roman surrounding any allusion to the banquets of Greek fame must be deemed a neo-classic thought, a reconstruction of a romantically viewed past. The concepts underlying this dainty imagery, both its formal style and its styled contents, were neo-classic on either count. Conversely, this renovative attitude may also have been a self-conscious response to actual contemporary conditions. Its calculated classicism, cool and aloof, can be an attempt at restoring to the erotic theme an air of social refinement and aristocratic exclusiveness which the prevailing opinion denied to this genre. For once, a group of Roman artists tried to raise the social standing of erotic representations; and their way of accomplishing this was to recall the Greek paragons. In this somewhat esoteric undertaking the ease and naturalness of the prototypes went by the boards, to be replaced by a new and impeccable formal elegance. In Rome the erotic banquet, Greek style, would in any event have seemed a rather contrived situation. Only in contemporary poetry were concurrent voices sounded. The episodes which Propertius chose to make the leading theme of two elegies involving the poet himself, his friend Gallus, and the latter's mistress (I, XIII; cf. I, X), find their visual equivalent in the work of the Arretine designers. Thus the intellectual climate of Augustan classicism produced the last notable instances, in Greco-Roman history, of an erotic art viewed positively—not as social satire—and addressed to the happy (or unhappy) few.

Still the pretended exclusiveness of the Arretine vases was more apparent than real; it was a matter of esthetic perfection rather than of substance. Comparison with other, lesser products in the same iconographic tradition shows that the Arretine potters had no exclusive rights to their themes, nor to the patterned representational formulae which they elaborated. A pair of lovers
depicted on a Roman lamp from Crete (Fig. 42) does not look much 42
different from the similarly posed couple on the Arretine bowl (Fig.
40). The Cretan version came from a mold which produced a less de- 40
tailed image and somewhat cloudy surface modeling.[62] These minor

[62] Roman lamp, Irakleion (Crete): Marcadé, *Eros,* p. 58. Occasionally the Arretine erotic schemata were translated into marble reliefs: A. Balland and Ch. Goudineau, "Un oscillum de Bolsena," *Mélanges d'Archéologie et d'Histoire,* LXXIX (1967), 567 ff.

differences notwithstanding, both reliefs render the same erotic action and both make use of the identical profile composition representing that action. Both evidently followed a common prototype. Nor are such formal coincidences restricted to this one branch of monuments, the ceramic reliefs. In a small Roman painting
43 ing at Naples (Fig. 43) the group of a young woman straddling her reclined partner appears remarkably like the analogous group
39 known from Arretine molds (Fig. 39). We must conclude that, in both categories, stamped reliefs and popular erotic paintings, the artists often drew on a common stock of models. Their works are interrelated insofar as the painters and ceramists both seem to deal in the same prefigured types.

The continuous interrelation within these various crafts—the arts of the painters, the ceramists, and probably also the silversmiths and other metalworkers—must be recognized as a conditioning factor of the tradition which here concerns us. It accounts for the typical quality that characterizes the products of this tradition. Two kinds of monuments are especially involved in this exchange of patterns: the various classes of molded reliefs, including the numerous terracotta lamps, and the small erotic paintings which once embellished the walls of the more or less affluent bordellos in the Roman cities around the gulf of Naples.[63] Both groups must be described as popular art. A rapid survey of the Roman lamps with erotic scenes will suffice to impress on us the principle followed by all their representations. Their subject, the variety of sexual positions, is modeled, as it were, in each instance by one pair of protagonists. The figures are small, rendered quite impersonally, and often abbreviated to the point
44 of resembling marionettes (Fig. 44). Nevertheless, within these

[63] Roman lamps, various types: see Menzel, *op. cit.* (above, n. 16); photographs of the Irakleion series, Marcadé, *Eros,* p. 58. The small Roman paintings—wall paintings imitating *tabellae*—also are best illustrated in Marcadé. Those now kept in the National Museum at Naples seem well preserved on the whole, though an examination of possible repairs still is a desideratum and might revise this evaluation.

restrictions the lamps offer richer material than the comparatively narrow selection found in the Arretine ceramics (Figs. 37–41), 37, 38, 39, 40, 41
although the latter are esthetically the superior product. The anthropological value of these testimonies is considerable, however modest the artistic merit of the lamps may often appear to us. The outspokenness, freshness, and variousness of their small representations make this an entertaining and enjoyable group of popular erotic art, for all its unconcern with decorum. Regrettably, no modern comprehensive catalogue of the erotic representations on the Hellenistic and Roman lamps is thus far available. Yet their types invite cataloguing by brief factual descriptions, such as "woman on her knees, male partner kneeling
behind her" (Fig. 45), or "male partner on his back, female kneels 45
in opposite direction, double oral-genital contact" (Fig. 44). 44
Altogether, they constitute themselves a pictured catalogue of erotic actions.

I should say much the same about the painted Roman "Bordeeljes." Their number is fewer than that of the lamps, but in these representations, too, the variety of couplings is the obvious subject matter. In addition to iconography, however, other aspects of interest result from the different medium. Painting gives to the individual artist more freedom than that enjoyed by the ceramist, who assembles a selection of stamped reliefs. Even when the painter merely reproduces a common schema, much depends on his individual performance. He may introduce variations in the application of color and in the formal arrangement, and these may affect the interpretation of content. Therefore, the paintings are less stereotyped than the terracottas; they have a greater range of diversity. Like the terracotta lamps, they ought to be sorted according to subject and type. But they also deserve a study in the terms of artistic criticism. The painted erotica from Pompeii and Herculaneum, though of very unequal quality, include some rather spirited performances; some are treated as miniature
paintings (Fig. 46), others are lightly drawn, little vignettes. All 46
seem to date from a comparatively short stretch of time starting,

approximately, in the early first century A.D. and ending with the disastrous outbreak of Monte Vesuvio in 69 A.D. Their drawing often seems inept, by classical standards, but it is rarely amateurish. Sometimes the painters employ popular devices which can be read as antecedents of late antique art, such as a bed viewed from above in an oblique and slanted perspective. For the most part they work in established Hellenistic-Roman traditions of imagery and professional training. About the antecedents of this art we know nothing. It seems to me that classical reminiscences, in a "Parrhasian" vein, may still be detected among its preserved products.[64] Apparently, to borrow a term from sociology, one is confronted with sunken cultural goods which survived on a lower level of class, as folk art.

If we draw the sum of these observations, the serial character of this type of erotic art, unchanged from the Hellenistic period to the end of antiquity, shall probably be declared its most special quality. From this basic characteristic derive the features which all its products share, such as the closed and isolated groups, the frequent repetitions of typical groupings, the bluntly factual depiction of the standard coital positions. It should be noted, also, that these stylistic symptoms recur on quite different levels of quality, and that they seem independent of the artistic medium. More important, however, is the often-attested tendency to combine familiar erotic compositions into sequences numbering two or more—that is to say, into series. This manner of arrangement, likewise, was not bound to any one medium, although it evidently came most naturally to the potters who assembled their stamped reliefs in rows, as in Arretine ceramics. But the paintings, also, were put together in sequences, such as around the walls of a

[64] Menzel, *op. cit.*, p. 6 and n. 55, reached a similar conclusion concerning certain erotic groups on Roman lamps. This coincides with our previous remarks, above, p. 44 with notes 45, 47; also J. Schäfer, *op. cit.*, n. 59. Yet the paintings are even more likely to include reminiscences of famous, earlier *tabellae*. As long as no valid typology has been established, however, comprising all relevant classes of monuments, the question must rest.

room. Every evidence indicates that in this category of erotic art there must have operated an unusually close nexus, relating its components to one another and thereby implicitly suspending their individuality. For it now appears that each specimen on this list can be evaluated only as a link in a long chain of similar representations. All are interconnected and all complement each other. Even when, as on the Roman terracotta lamps, only one of the available patterns becomes singled out for representation, the character of uniqueness is denied to these compositions. Unless they happen to render a namable event, such as the myth of Leda (Fig. 47), they deal in generalities.[65] In the majority, the sexual 47
episodes do not present personal situations but typical actions; they appear to be variations of a common theme. Ideally, if not actually, each representation connects with all the other variations of the theme, or at least is apt to be so understood by the beholder. This all-pervasive context transcends the range of meaning which one may ascribe to any individual example. On the grounds of this diagnosis I consider the erotic art in this category a closed group, reflecting a rather unified tradition, and its various representations a continually interrelated—that is, cyclical—iconography.

Iconographic "in-groups" of this description often arise from the need, or wish, to illustrate standard literary or other intellectual topics that were first formulated outside the visual arts. It seems likely that the iconography of the small-scale Hellenistic and Roman erotic monuments came into being in much the same way. I submit that the broader context, of which so many of them evidently partake, was the essentially literary idea of an erotic catalogue.

That famous books of this type existed in antiquity is a documented fact. None has survived, but sufficient information about them has been preserved for us to form an idea of their

[65] Above, n. 11.

contents and make-up.[66] Their descriptive and enumerating method conformed to the post-Aristotelian systematizing and compiling literature proper to the Hellenistic period; it ought to be distinguished from the graphic portrayals and the more novelistic written biographies of celebrated courtesans (*pornai,* hence the Greek term *pornographos* and modern "pornography"), which probably preceded them.[67] By "erotic catalogues" we shall here understand the apparently not infrequent treatises, possibly versified according to Hellenistic custom, which expounded the modes ("schemata") of copulation. Their principal content consisted of lists in which the various sexual positions were enumerated and described in detail. The emphasis on a numerical count, applied to a catalogue of embraces, links these Hellenistic compilations with the later Sanskrit prose treatises on the same subject, which were based on the Kama-Sutra of the fifth century A.D. The latter probably represents the most elaborate known example of an erotic catalogue in the ancient manner. A certain mystique of numbers,

[66] F. Susemihl, *Geschichte der griechischen Literatur in der Alexanderzeit* (Leipzig, 1891–1892; repr., Hildesheim, 1965), I, 843 and n. 48; Licht, Vol. III (supplement, 1928). The "Schemata Synousias" by Philainis seem to have started this series of catalogues; J. Schäfer, *op. cit.* (above, n. 59), p. 79 and n. 94. See also below, notes 68, 69.

[67] *Pornographos* can mean a person who writes about courtesans or draws their likenesses, or does both; just as a *topographos* can be a writer on geography, a painter of localities, or even a mapmaker. Among the four classical painters mentioned for their erotic subjects—Parrhasios, Pausias, Aristeides the Younger, and Nicophanes, all of the fourth century B.C.—only Pausias receives the epithet of *pornographos* expressly. Moreover, Pliny (*Historia Naturalis,* XXXV, 125 ff.) tells a little romance about a painting by the same artist, said to have portrayed the mistress of his early years as a girl binding (or selling) flowers; her name is given as Glykera—surely a *hetaira.* Aristeides the Younger was among the painters credited with a portrait of Leontion (Pliny, *Historia Naturalis,* XXXV, 99); for this subject, see above, n. 36. The evidence points to a coherent tradition of more or less novelized data from the lives of famous *hetairai.* To the already named examples one may add the story of Apelles and Pancaspe, as well as various similar anecdotes which involve no artists but other men of fame; cf. also P. Moreno, *op. cit.* (above, n. 47), p. 84, n. 11. This entire body of material appears homogeneous in character, insofar as it represents a genre of *historia* in its own right, which may well have combined a romantic-literary with an iconographic tradition. We can accept it as a reflection of the literary *pornographiae* composed of precisely this kind of anecdotes, much like Brantôme's *Vies des dames galantes.*

or at least a rationalized principle of numerical order, was implied with this literary method. Among the Hellenistic materials, titles indicating lists of twelve are mentioned several times; *mille modi Veneris* said Ovid (*Ars Amatoria,* III, 787) in a similar counting vein, though he himself seems to enumerate only seven—possibly a meaningful number also.[68] His witty and elegant passage almost certainly mirrors in Latin a Hellenistic model. It is the most complete reflection still accessible of this peculiarly Greek literary genre, the didactic erotic poem.

How well the monuments here at issue fit into the intellectual framework of this literature is apparent. Even though they were not book illustrations, they conform to the need for such illustrations, to be inserted into the written columns of an ancient book. Their seemingly contradictory characteristics, the separateness as well as the intrinsic seriality of their compositional types, are also probably best explained if we assume that their makers followed the habits of the illuminators. Their explanatory and typical—not narrative—intent accords with the spirit of the literary catalogues.[69]

[68] Erotic catalogues, arranged by numbers: among the earliest appears to have been the *Dodekatechnon* by Paxamos; Licht, Vol. III (Supplement), p. 160, with parallels. As the title proclaims, this book dealt with its subject in twelve sections. Ovid, *Ars Amatoria,* III, 771 ff., catalogues but does not enumerate his topics; what is and what is not a separate item on his list is not always clear. Certainly 783 f. cannot be so designated; Apuleius, *Metamorphoses,* II, 17, may be compared. Whether 775 f. ought to be understood as a separate *figura Veneris* or a mere variation of the first is in doubt. Representations of art such as the Pompeian painting in Marcadé, *Roma,* p. 59, favor the latter interpretation. But opinions to the contrary can be sampled: O. Lewis, *La Vida* (New York, 1968), p. 286 ("A Day with Felícita in San Juan"). A philological matter, not to be followed up here, concerns the names that were applied to various sexual positions, from Aristophanes to the advanced Roman period. See above, n. 41. Leaving aside Aristophanes, who presents a special case, it appears that most terms were borrowed from either conventional mythology (Ovid) or the *palaestra* (Apuleius): the latter remark also holds for the similar catalogue in Lucian, "Lucius or the Ass," 8 ff.

[69] A note about the possible or even likely astronomical connotations of these numbered catalogues may be in order here. Twelve, the number of the zodiacal signs, obviously agrees with the title of the *Dodekatechnon.* The erotic papyrus in Turin (above, p. 49), though not a Hellenic monument, also ought to be remembered in this context. Since a publication of the papyrus is being prepared by Dr. J. A. Omlin, I wish here merely to refer to a drawing from the collection of the Institute for Sex Research, Indiana University (Fig. 30), which seems independent of the similar drawings 30

At any rate, our diagnosis seems in keeping with the observation that ancient custom inclined to regard illustrations in books as a means of demonstration. Instructive pictures in scientific treatises, added to an expository text in order to increase its usefulness, are among the earliest book illustrations preserved. The sense of the erotic catalogues was of this kind; it, too, was instructional.

The most renowned representative of this Hellenistic literature was the work of an authoress known as Elephantis—probably a learned courtesan from Alexandria. Illustrated editions of her books were current; about the entertainment which the emperor Tiberius derived from them, one may consult Suetonius.[70] Whether the

---

kept in the Brooklyn Museum. The drawing in Indiana gives a rather schematic, though on the whole apparently consistent, illustration of the original; it may be somewhat older than the Brooklyn drawings. On these testimonies, barring further inquiries, it appears that twelve erotic episodes of quite fantastic character were lined up in a frieze-like, centered composition. According to information kindly put at my disposal by Dr. Omlin, the original dates to the XXth Dynasty, somewhere between the reigns of Ramses II and Ramses III. Dr. Omlin also calls my attention to the fact that the left end of the papyrus is not complete. It is certain, however, that one episode was given special emphasis, and indeed a central place. This group—according to the drawings known to me—may either be counted as the seventh from the left, or the sixth from the right end. Among the remaining representations it is unique, not only because of its central place but also because in this one episode the woman, reaching down from her high bed, is shown above the man reclining on the ground below her; for the significance of this detail, cf. H. Zimmer, *op. cit.* (above, n. 5). The comments scribbled on the drawing in Indiana by a former owner seem without foundation. It is nevertheless possible that the pictures carried some allegorical implication—for instance, allusions to the annual cycle may be involved, possibly in a vein of parody. But pending the forthcoming publication of the accompanying text this matter may be left in abeyance.

That the astrological order of seven survived in medieval Islamic erotic literature, one may infer from *The Seven Stories of the Seven Princesses* by Nizami, written about 1197, The king, Bahram, visits his seven princesses of seven different lands, who live each in a palace furnished in the color and with the jewels of her proper planet; with each he spends a night of a week—starting with black Saturn, ending with white Venus, from Saturday to Friday—to hear her story and share her love. (German translation by R. Gelpke, Zurich, 1959.)

[70] Elephantis: the name (which is not unique) may refer to the Egyptian county of Elephantine. Alexandrian origin is likely: *RE,* V, s.v. "Elephantis," 2324 f. Several references to her work have survived; the most detailed is Suetonius, Tiberius XLIII. At least some editions of her poem had illustrations: *Carmina Priapea,* 4. Apparently her work, in several books *(volumina),* consisted of versified treatises of which the *figurae*

imperial copy was also illustrated, we do not know. At any rate, the report by Suetonius makes quite clear how closely words and pictures complemented each other in this genus of literature. Tiberius kept the volumes of Elephantis in a *cabinet sécrêt* of his villa on Capri, together with a collection of erotic paintings (*tabellae*) and *sigillae;* in the context, the latter term more likely refers to stamped terracotta reliefs than to statuettes. The collection, accordingly, contained art objects of exactly the sort with which the present discussion concerns itself. Apparently the eminent collector regarded this material as a topical group, held together by a common meaning and related to written texts. The account given by Suetonius leaves no doubt that the purpose of the books, as well as the illustrations, was to instruct.

It is too early to say whether a single model book or diverse picture series ought to be stipulated as the source of all, or some, of the monuments here contemplated. Certainly the methods that guided their various compositions look uniformly alike. It also becomes clear that the appearance and wide distribution of these typical series mark a decisive change in the style of ancient erotic art, from freely invented, original, and variable creations to an illustrative, standardized, instructional, and taxonomic iconography. Even when the new monuments did include classical reminiscences, they were nevertheless conceived, collected, and preserved in a cataloguing spirit. The Alexandrian share in this development seems to have been considerable. Not only do the demonstrable parallels in Alexandrian letters recommend this assumption. One may also point out that the technical outlook and the enumerative mind—in short, the serial character of the new erotic iconography—have their antecedents in much earlier Egyptian art. Thus in several tombs at Beni Hasan which date from the Middle Kingdom one finds rows of wrestlers in various positions, shown as continuous series. Each pair demonstrates a professional trick or a

---

Veneris seem to have occupied only one; others dealt with *pharmaka,* beauty recipes, and similar professional advice.

special hold, all recorded with a schooled eye for the technicalities
48 of wrestling (Fig. 48).[71] Such action series of professional character could at a later time easily have been transferred to pictured scrolls, or broken up into separate episodes and inserted into the columns of a written book. I think it likely that the many small erotic representations of Hellenistic and Roman manufacture derived from comparable illustrative series, possibly reflecting a long-established Egyptian-Alexandrian tradition.[72] As with the Pharaonic wrestlers from Beni Hasan, their purpose was a demonstration of fact, or a classification of variety such as a naturalist

[71] Wrestlers from Beni Hasan: Several such friezes exist; for an illustration of one, see G. Farina, *La pittura egiziana* (Milan, 1929), pl. 22 (tomb no. 15). The tradition was older, however, and not limited to Beni Hasan; cf. W. Wolf, *Die Kunst Aegyptens* (Stuttgart, 1957), pp. 369 f. and 695, n. 5. This analogy from Pharaonic art seems the more relevant, as in the Hellenistic-Roman literary tradition; likewise, the amorous duel was often described in terms of athletic sport or combat. See above, n. 68, for Apuleius and Lucian; also Ovid, *Ars Amatoria*, II, 728. Similarly, in the myth and iconography of Atalante, love and the wrestling context appear as analogues. The passage in Lucian (n. 68) is of special interest here, because it not only elaborates the conventional simile but also maintains the instructional character of the erotic catalogue which it imitated, or perhaps parodied: the maid, Palaestra, enacts the instructor.

[72] The sources of this iconography need not have been books in the ordinary sense —texts interspersed with illustrations. They may just as well have been pictured scrolls, with a minimum of explanatory text. In the latter genre, which aims at instruction through pictures without a current text, the illustrations can be expected to show how certain objects are recognized and labeled (e.g., plants) or how something ought to be done (e.g., how the actors are to stand with regard to each other, or to gesticulate, in a certain dramatic scene). Therefore, in series of this kind the pictures cease to be illustrations in the true sense; rather, they take the place of a verbal exposition. About such pictured scrolls before the Christian era, we know as yet very little; it is nevertheless likely that they existed. The research in medieval manuscripts shows that professional model books, designed for use in artists' workshops, kept for a considerable time the antique format of the horizontal *rotulus*, then long obsolete; see R. Branner, "The Saint-Quentin Rotulus," *Scriptorium*, XXI (1967), 256 f. and notes 14, 15, 19; also "Le Rouleau de Saint Éloi," *Information d'histoire de l'art*, XII (1967), 55 ff. For this reason alone we may assume that similar collections of models for painting were used in antiquity as well, at least since the Hellenistic and Roman periods, and that, like their Byzantine and medieval successors, they were of the *rotulus* type. Cf. H. Kenner, "Griechische Theaterlandschaften," *Jahreshefte des österreichischen archäologischen Instituts*, XLVII (1964–1965), 42 f. and 61 ff., for the evidence of workshop traditions, including model books, in ancient painting.

might undertake, in the style of Linné. It differed sharply from the humanistic concern with personal interpretation and narrative. The serial illustrations of the new type present erotic art on the level of late antique scholasticism. Gradually, like the texts they perhaps accompanied, they entered into the limbo of compendia, encyclopedias, primers, and manuals which were the bequest of the classical world to the Middle Ages, both west and east.

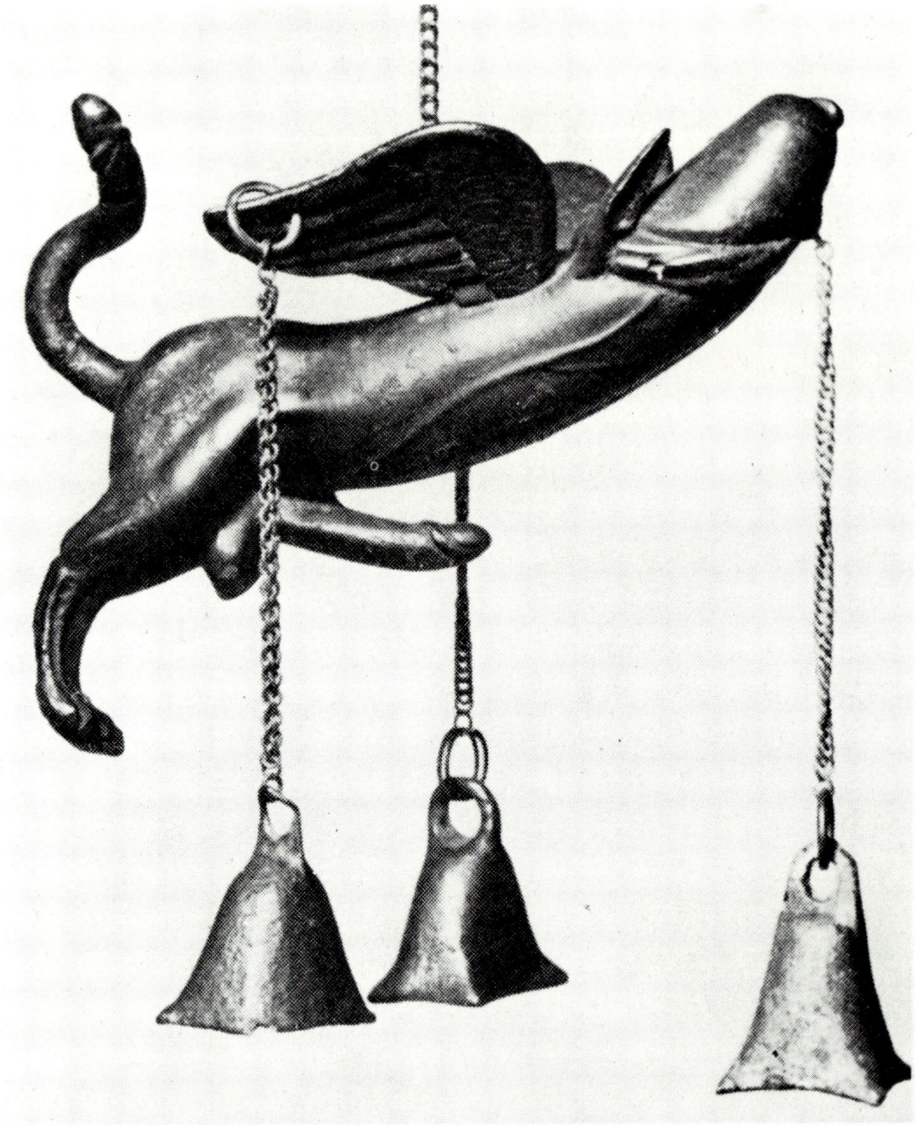

1. Winged phallus. (*Trier, Rheinisches Landes-Museum.*)

2. Standing Leda. Statue after a lost work by Timotheos, early fourth century B.C. Roman copy. (*Rome, Capitoline Museum.*)

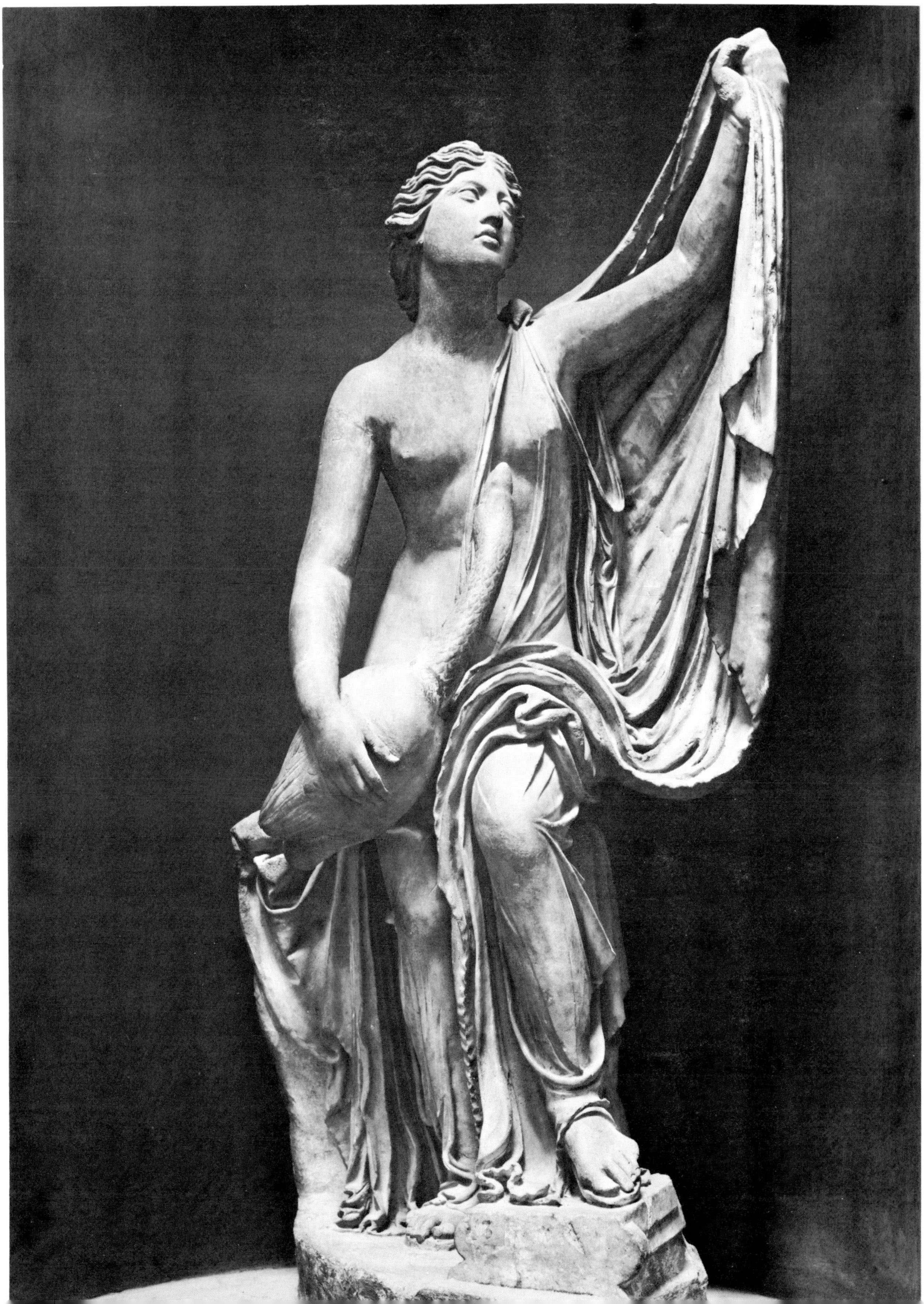

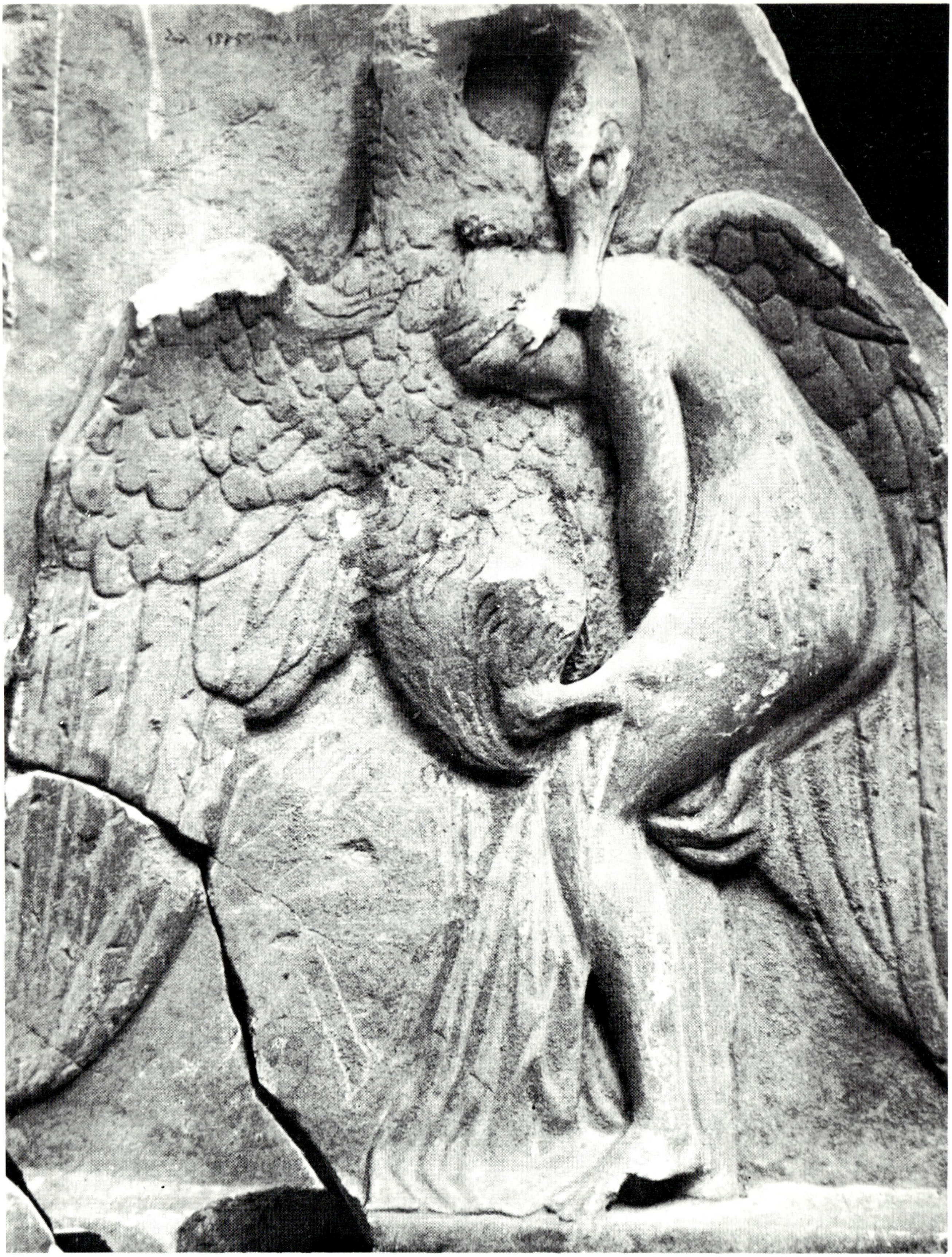

3. Standing Leda. Relief. (*Athens, National Museum.*)

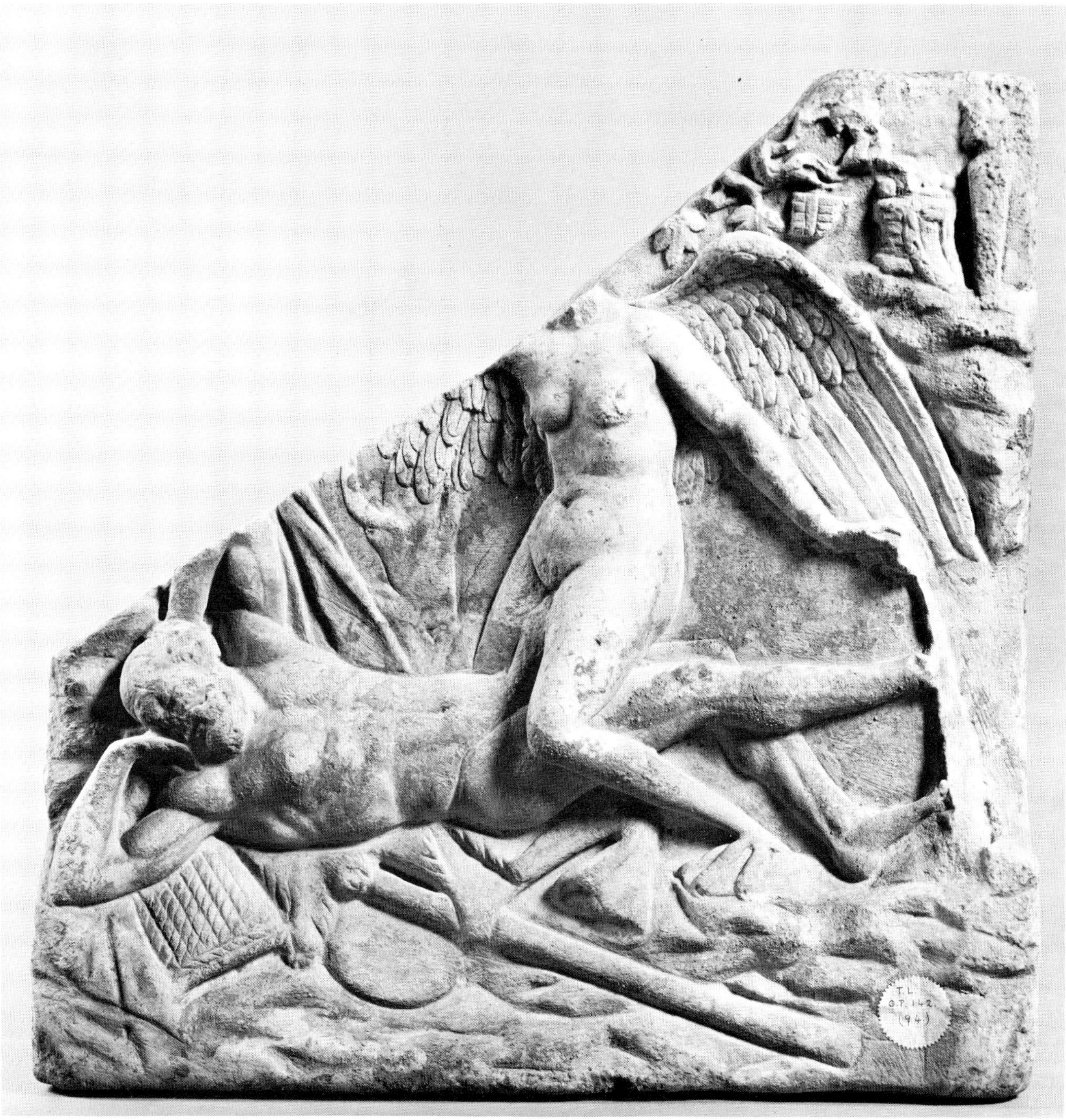

4. Erotic group, sleeper and winged demon. Relief. (*Boston, Museum of Fine Arts, Gift of E. P. Warren.*)

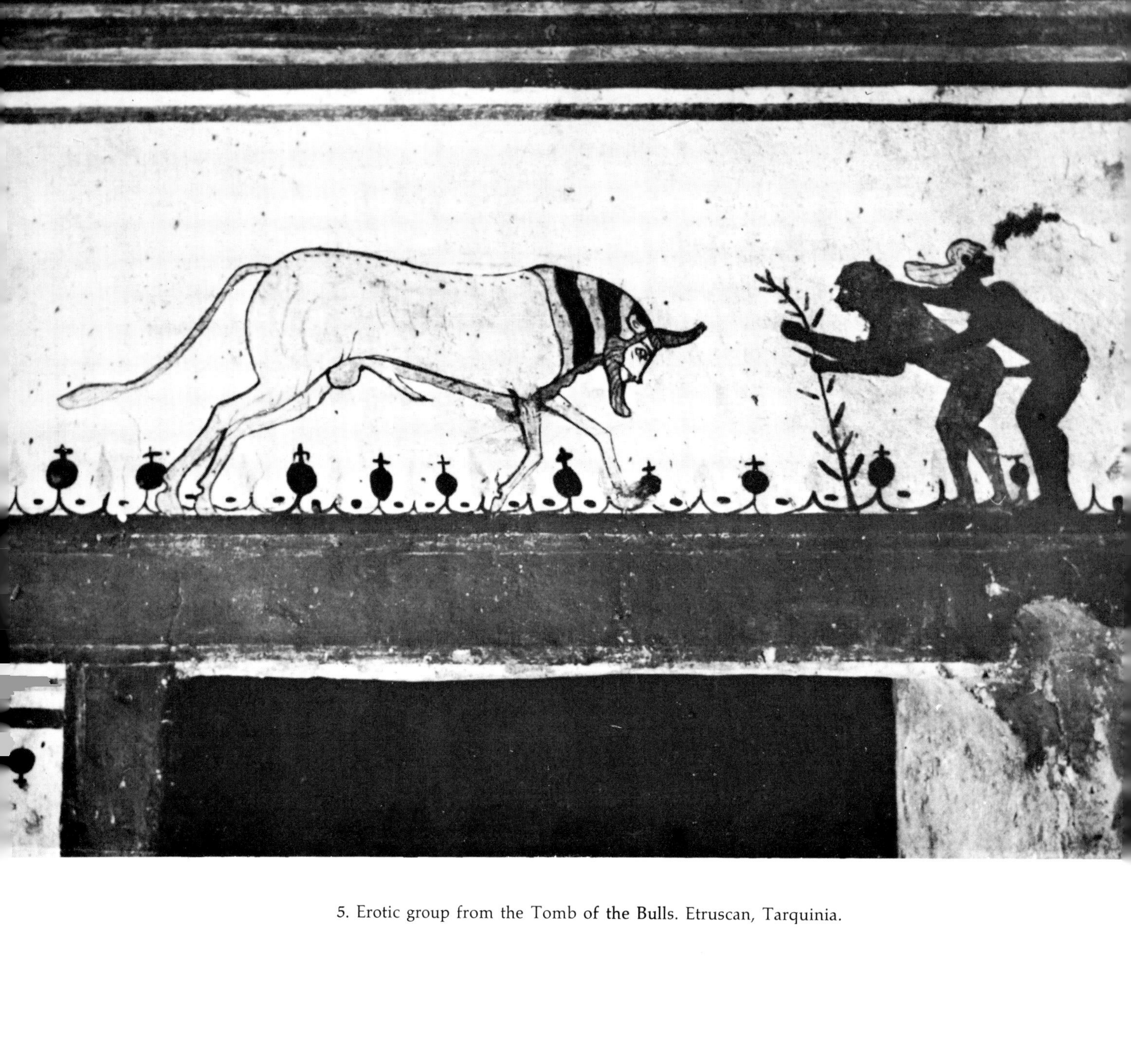

5. Erotic group from the Tomb of the Bulls. Etruscan, Tarquinia.

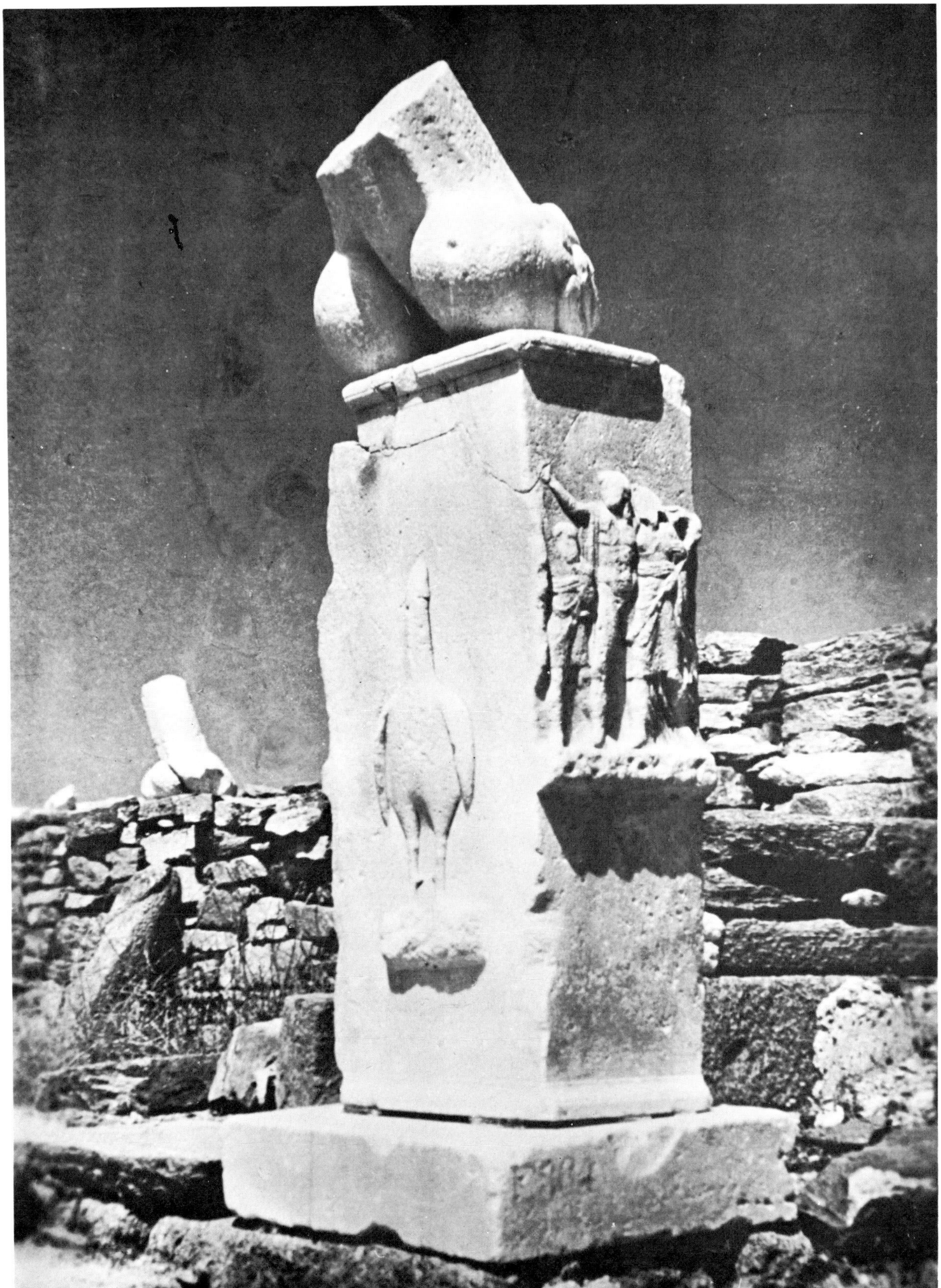

6. Choregic monument of Karystios. (*Delos.*)

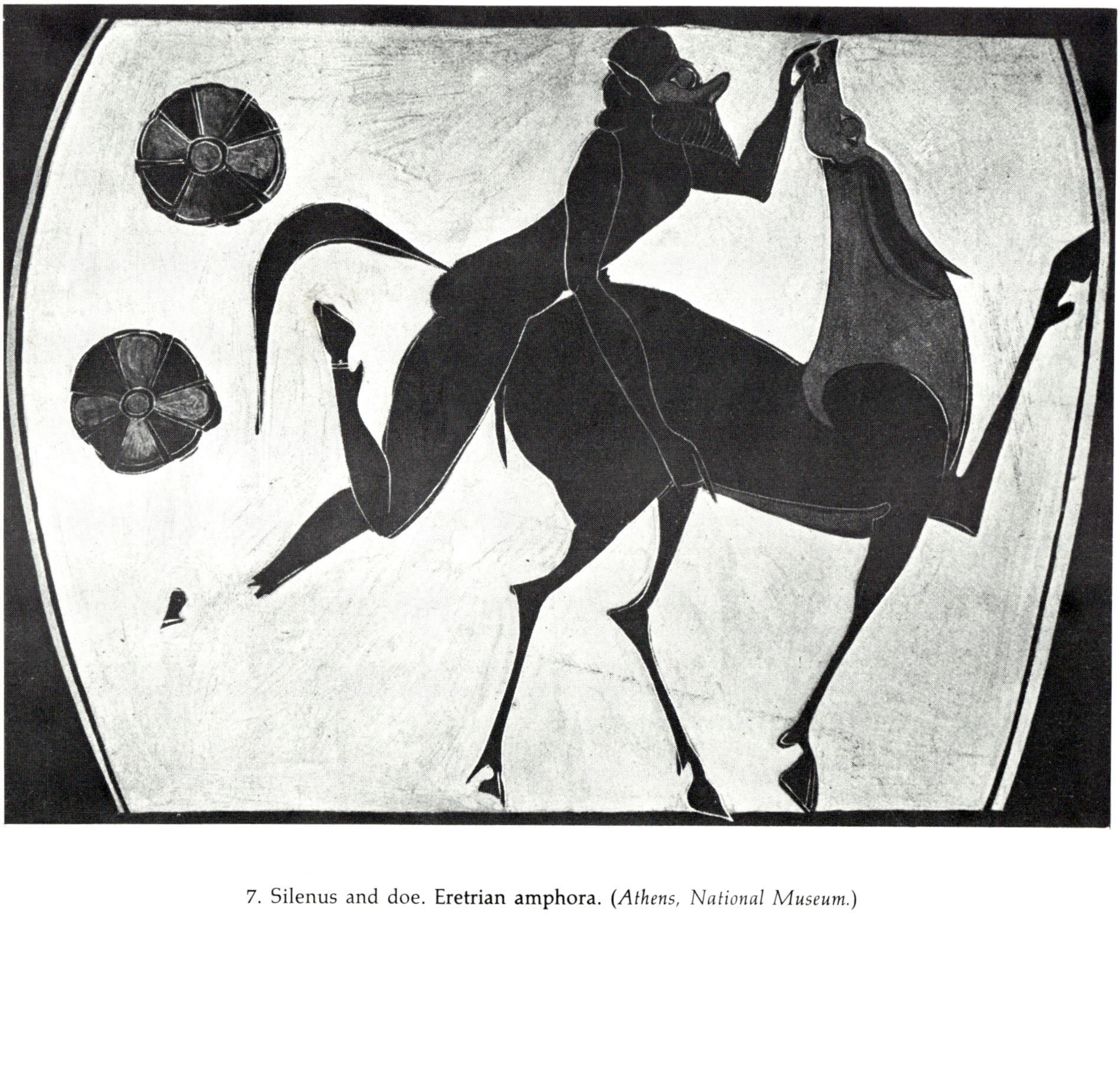

7. Silenus and doe. Eretrian amphora. (*Athens, National Museum.*)

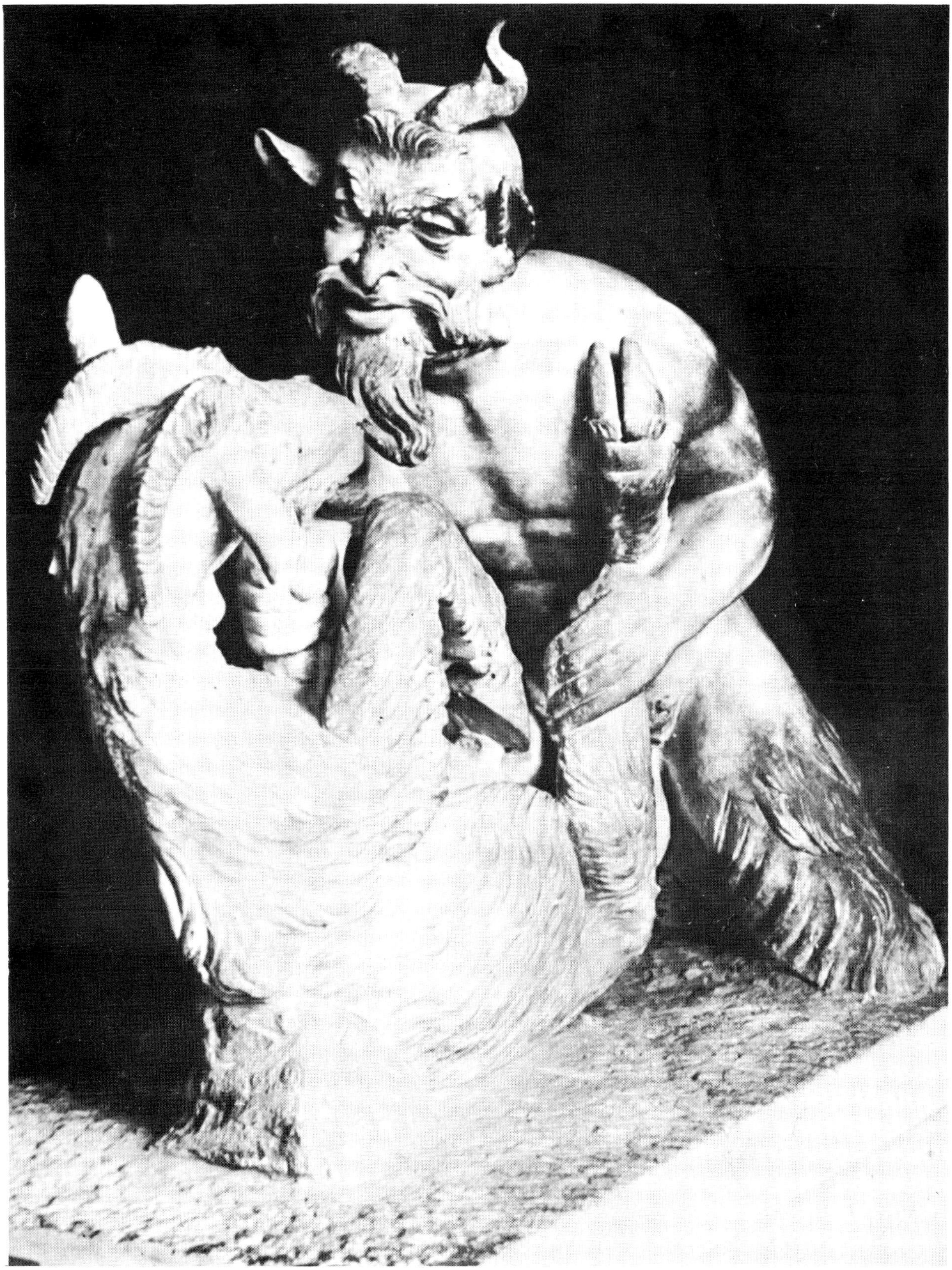

8. Pan and goat. Roman. (*Naples, National Museum.*)

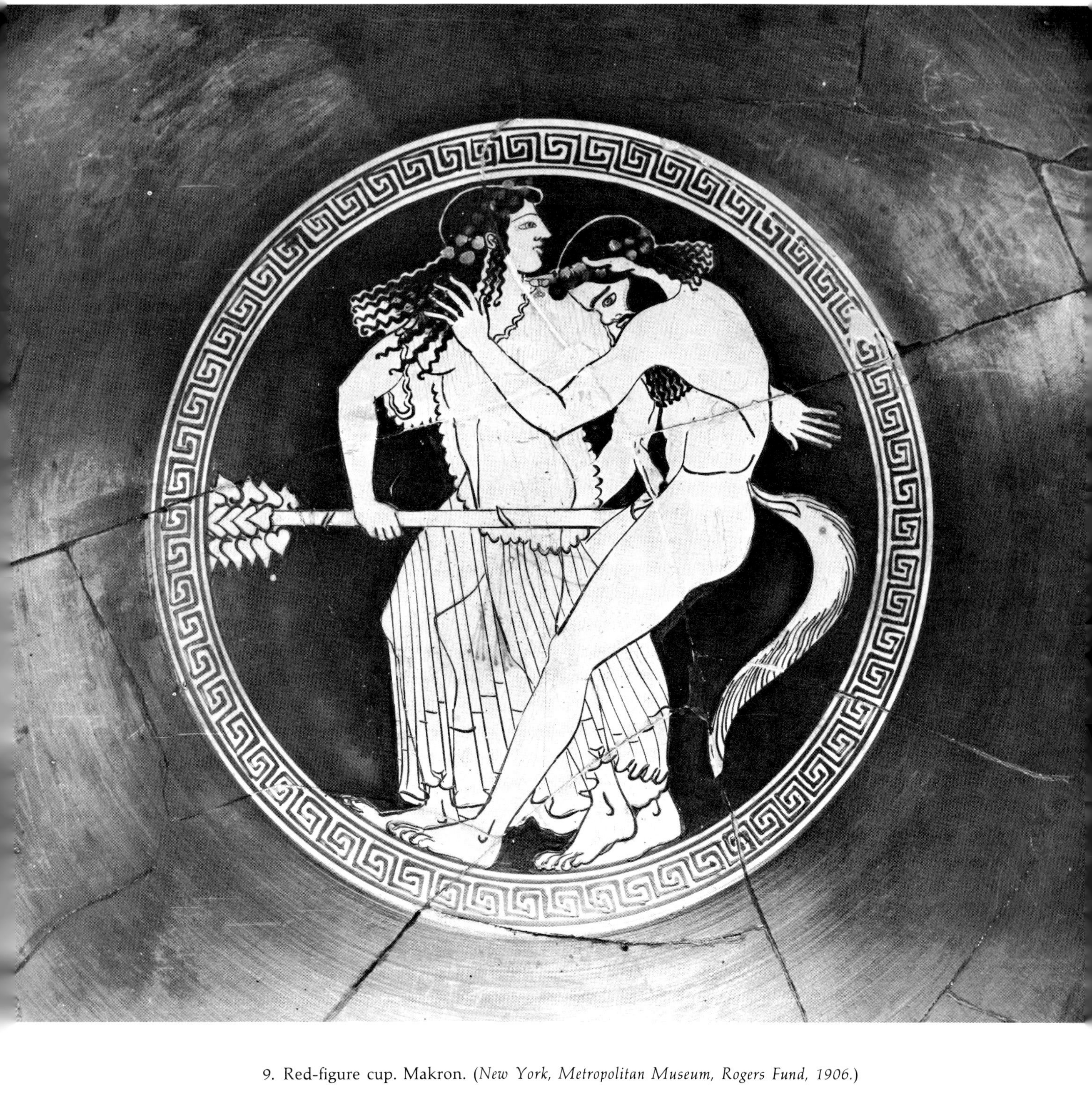

9. Red-figure cup. Makron. (*New York, Metropolitan Museum, Rogers Fund, 1906.*)

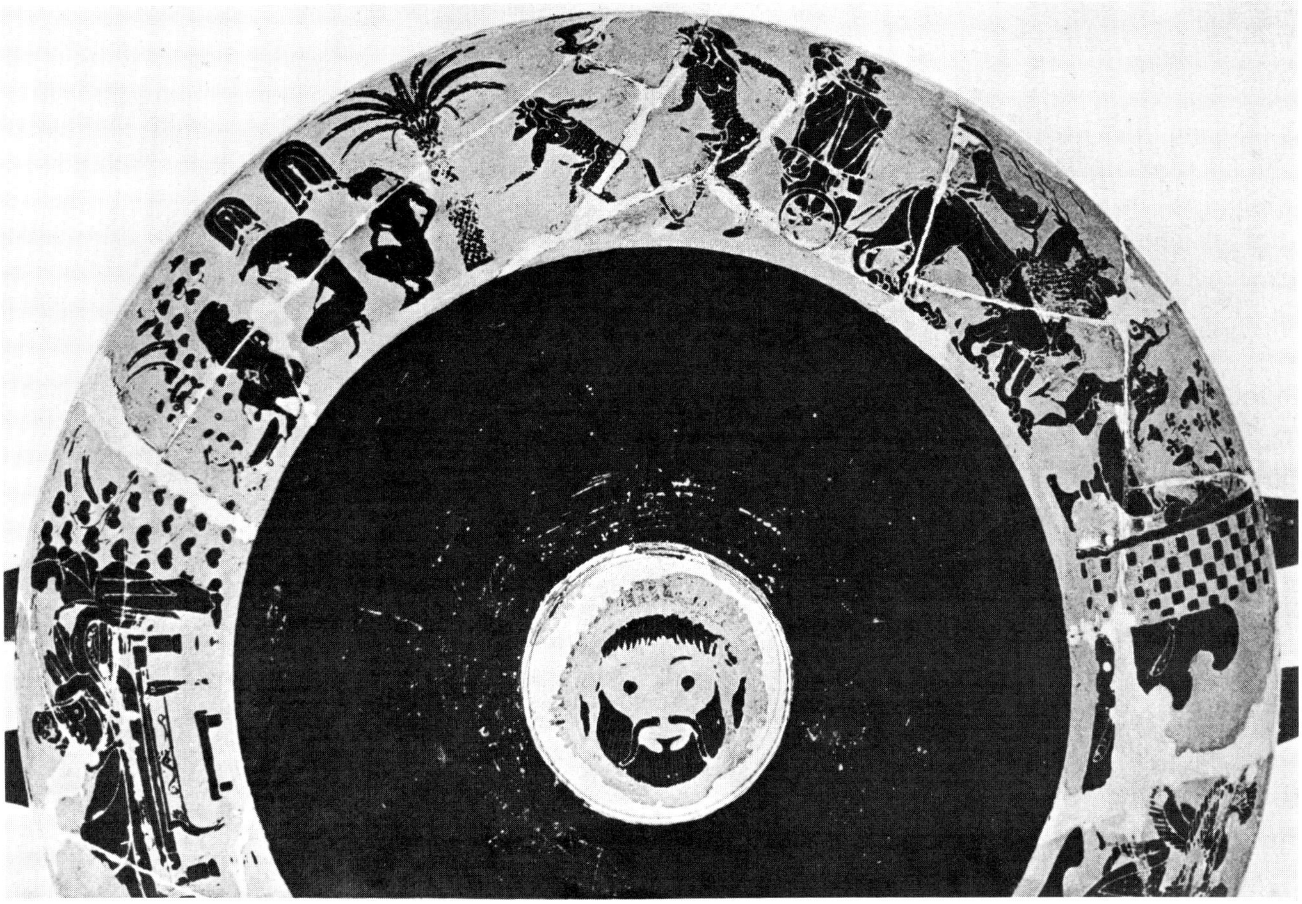

10. Satyrs and nymphs. Chalcidian cup. (*Würzburg, Martin von Wagner-Museum.*)

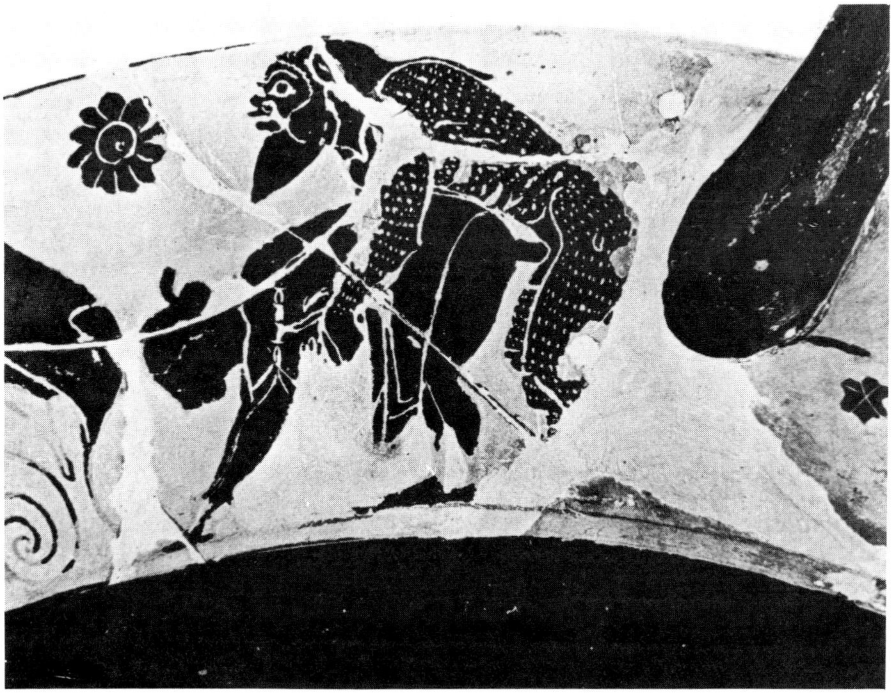

11. Detail of Chalcidian cup, Fig. 10.

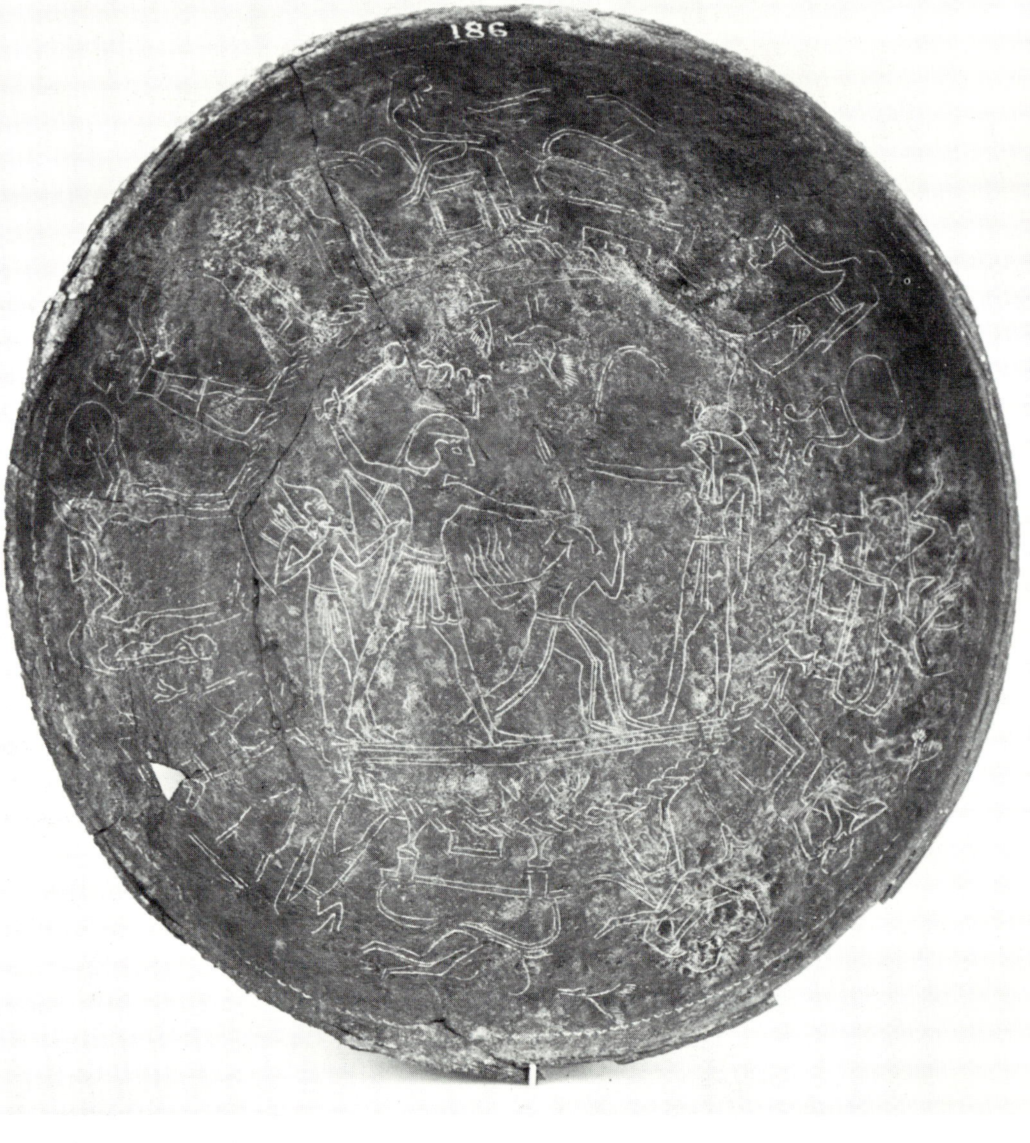

12. Bronze bowl. Cypriote. (*London, British Museum.*)

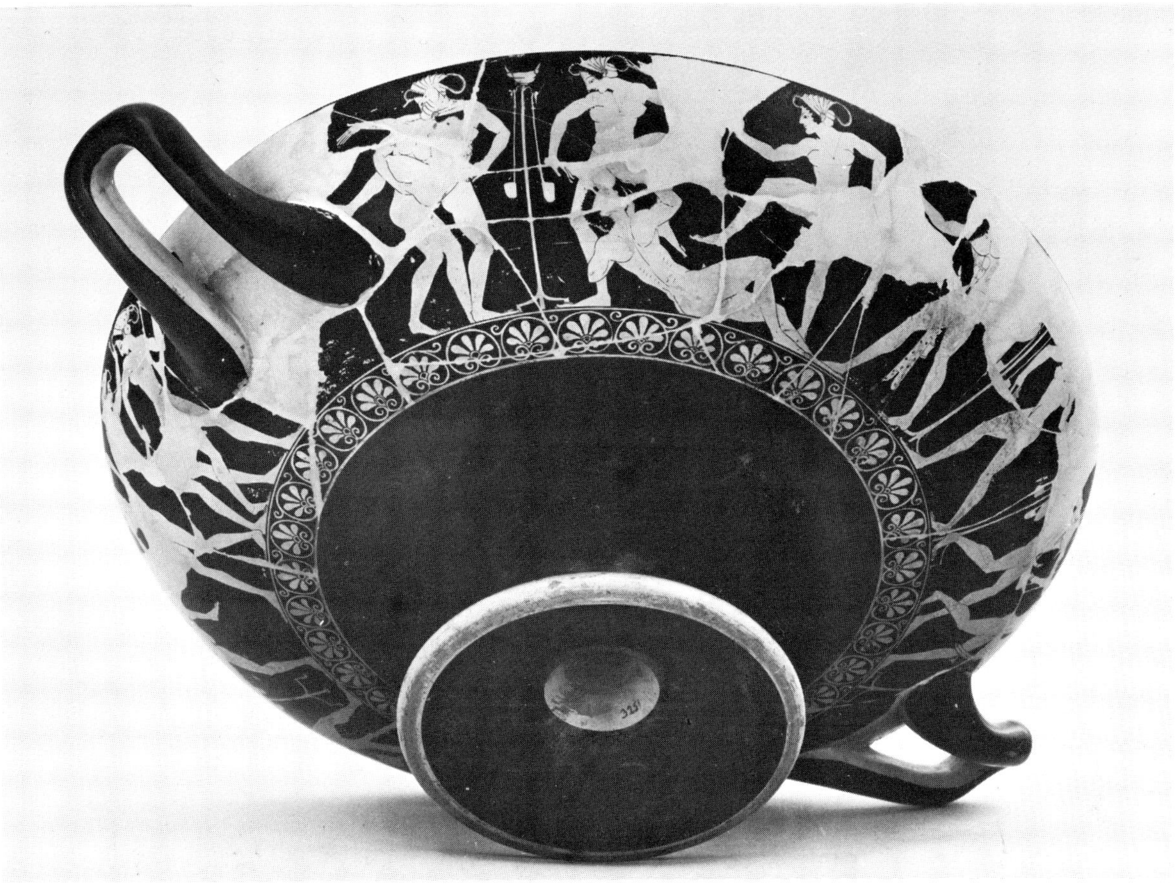

13. Red-figure cup. Thalia Painter. (*Berlin, Stiftung Staatliche Kulturbesitz.*)

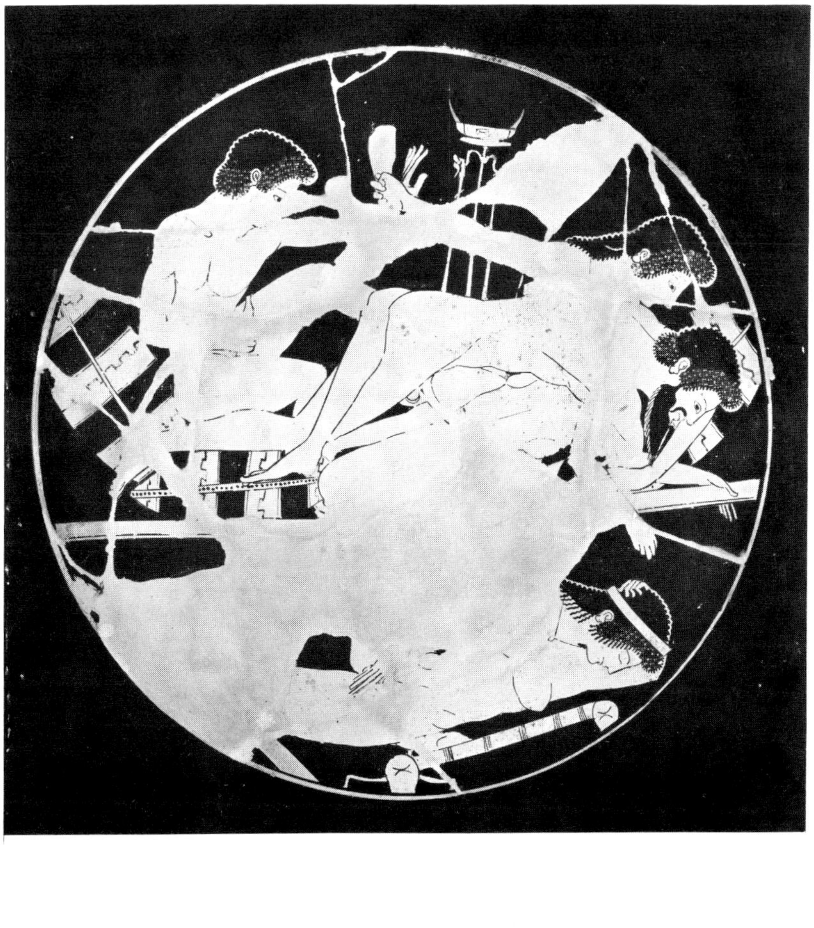

14. Interior of Fig. 13.

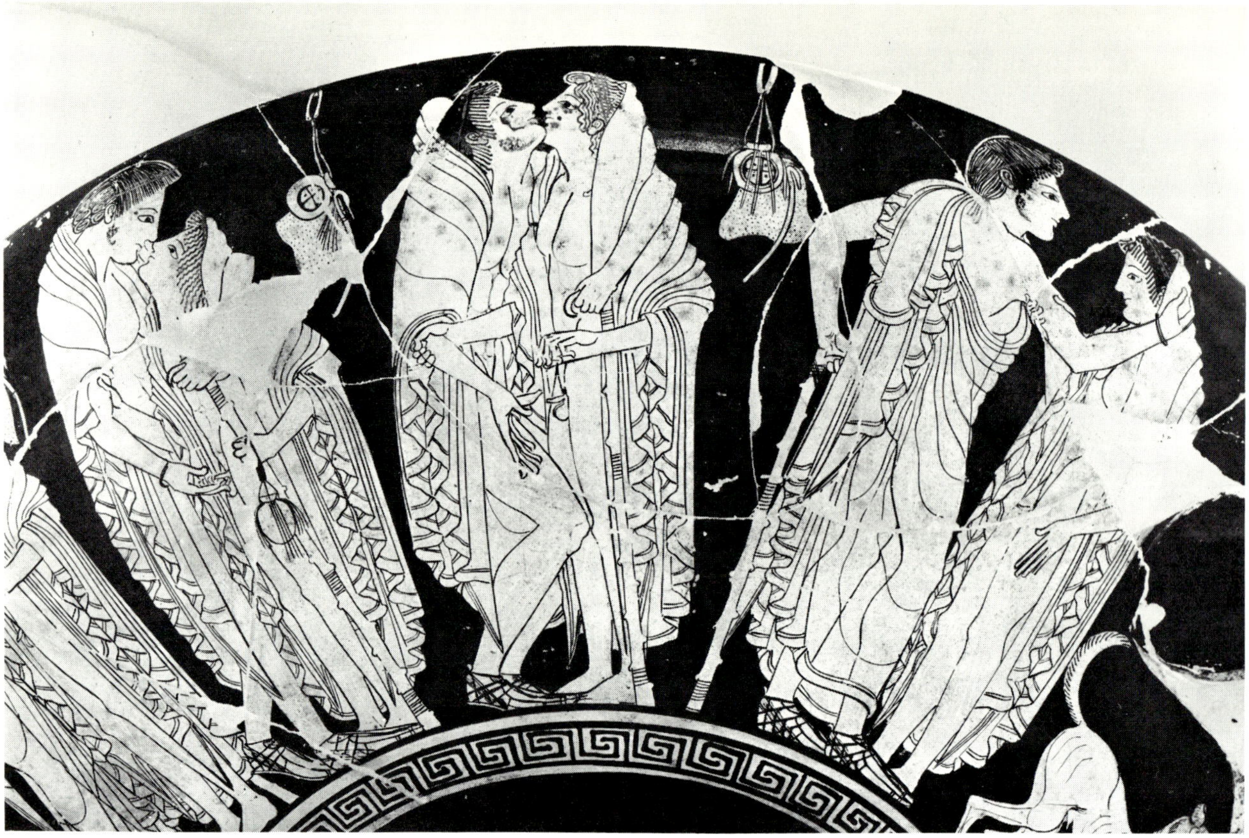

15. Red-figure cup. Peithinos. (*Berlin, Stiftung Staatliche Kulturbesitz.*)

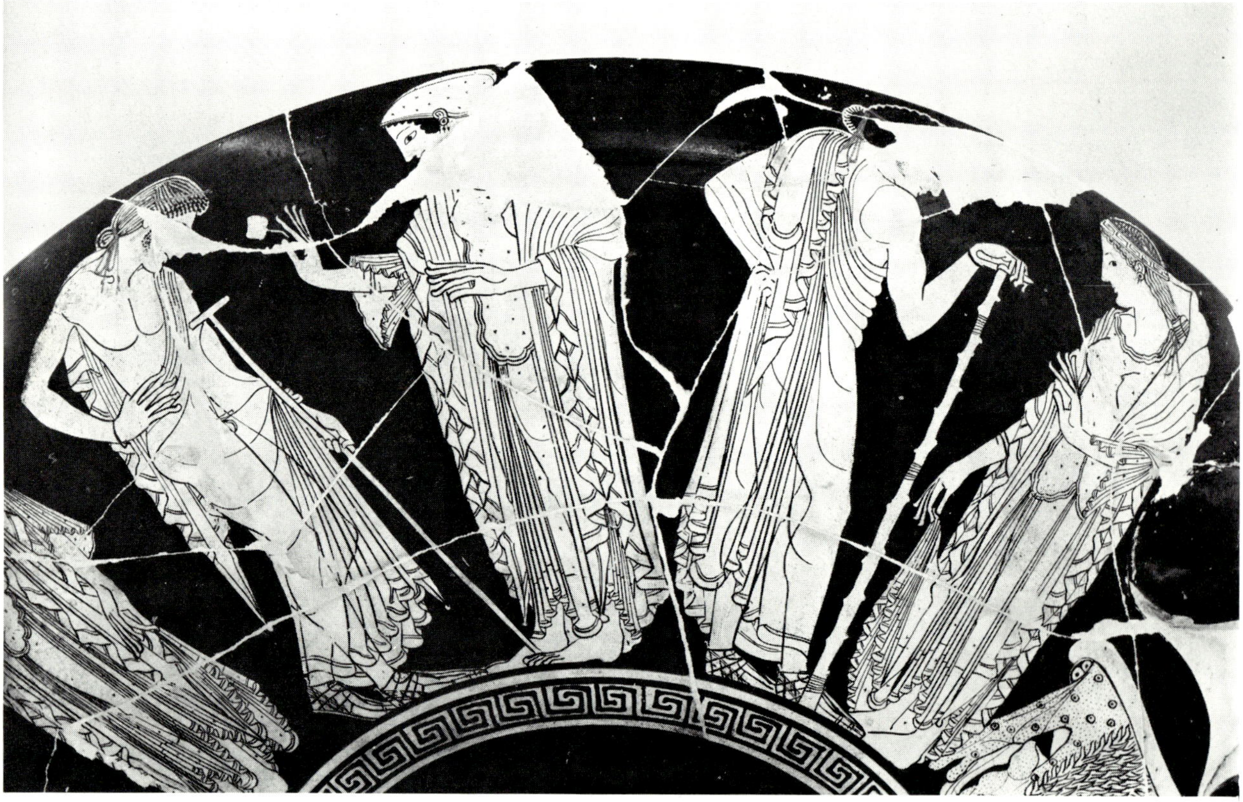

16. Reverse side of Fig. 15.

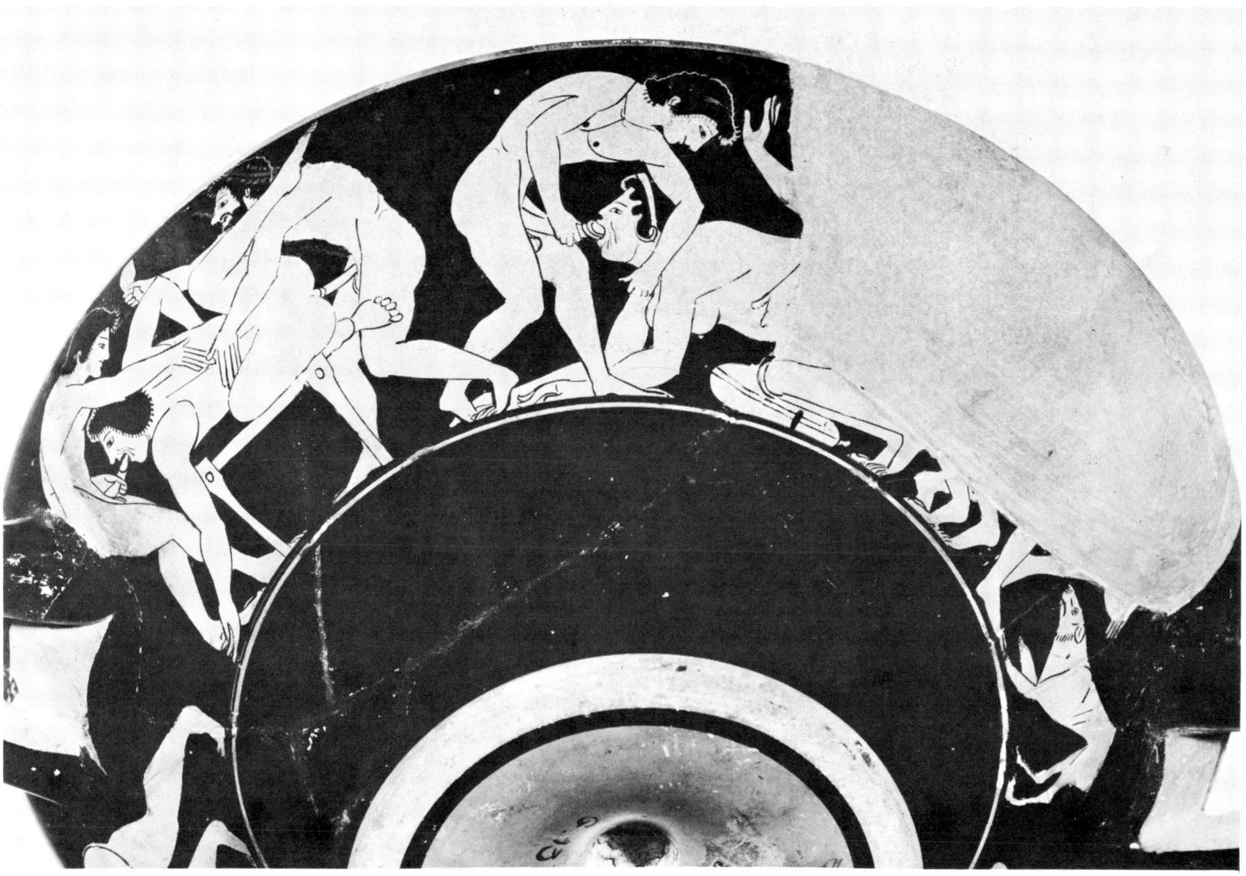

17. Red-figure cup. Pedieus Painter(?). (*Paris, Louvre.*)

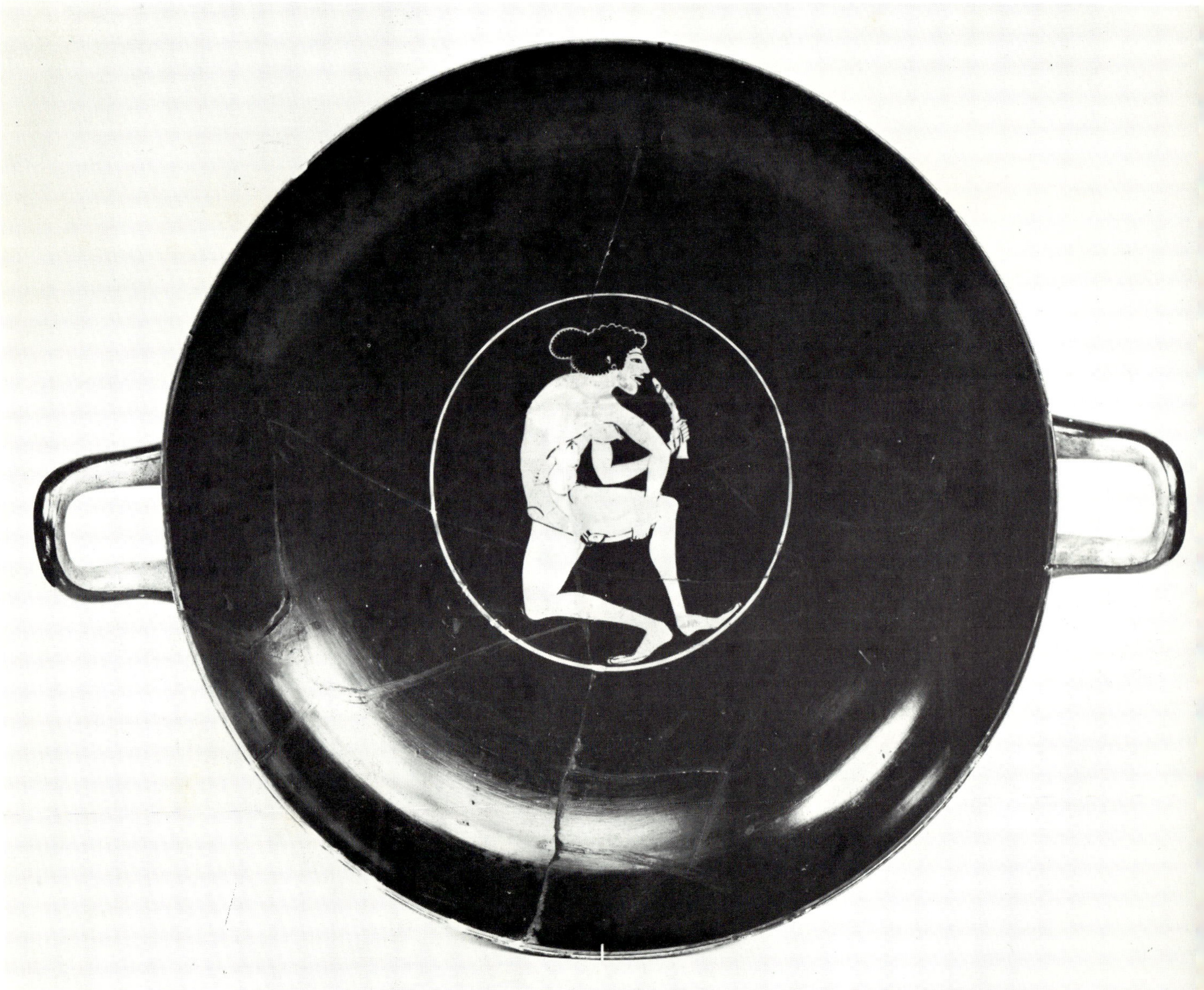

18. Red-figure cup. Nikosthenes Painter. (*London, British Museum.*)

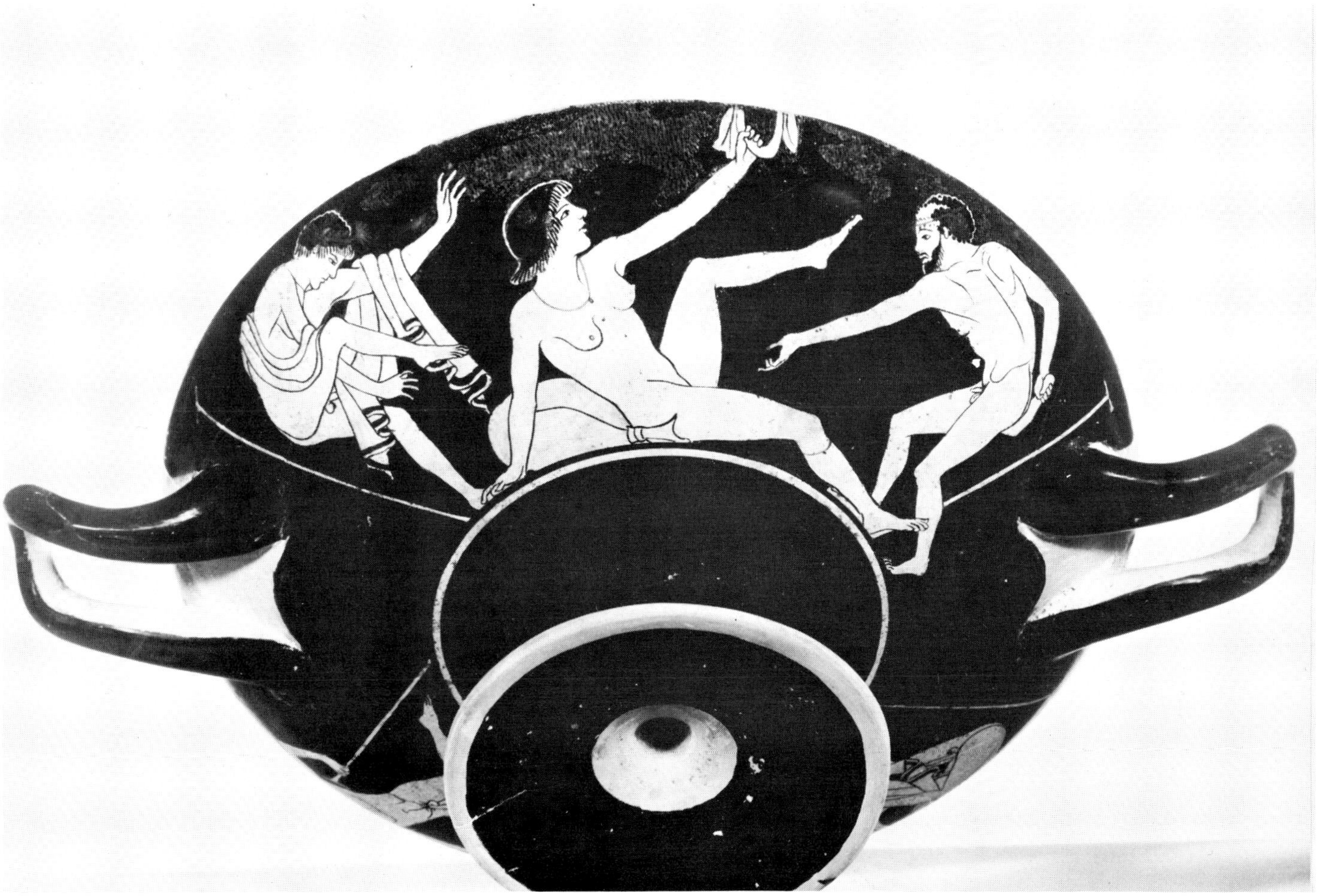

19. Red-figure cup. Onesimos Painter. (*Basel, Antiken-Museum.*)

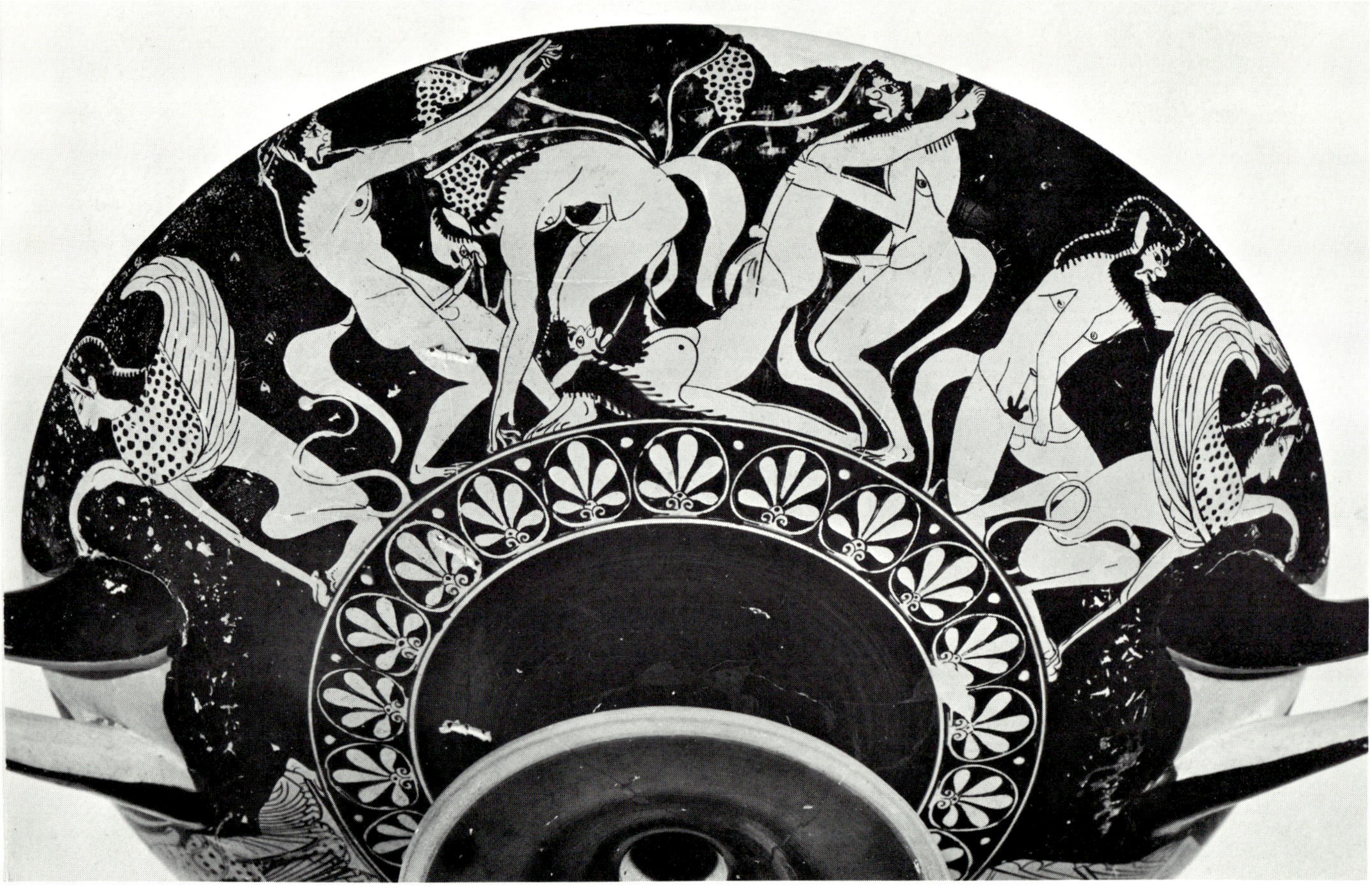

20. Red-figure cup. Circle of Nikosthenes Painter. (*Berlin, Stiftung Staatliche Kulturbesitz.*)

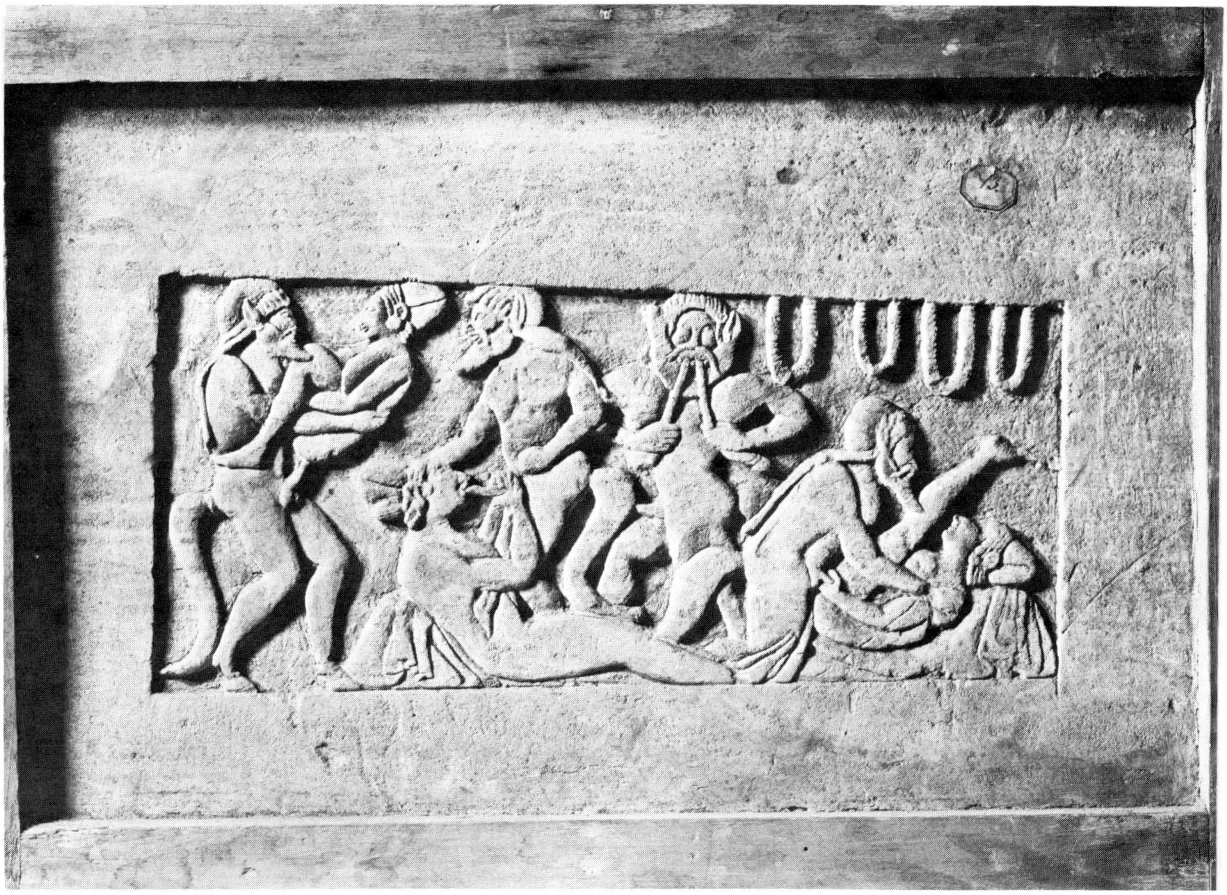

21. Ash urn. Etruscan, from Chiusi. (*Paris, Louvre.*)

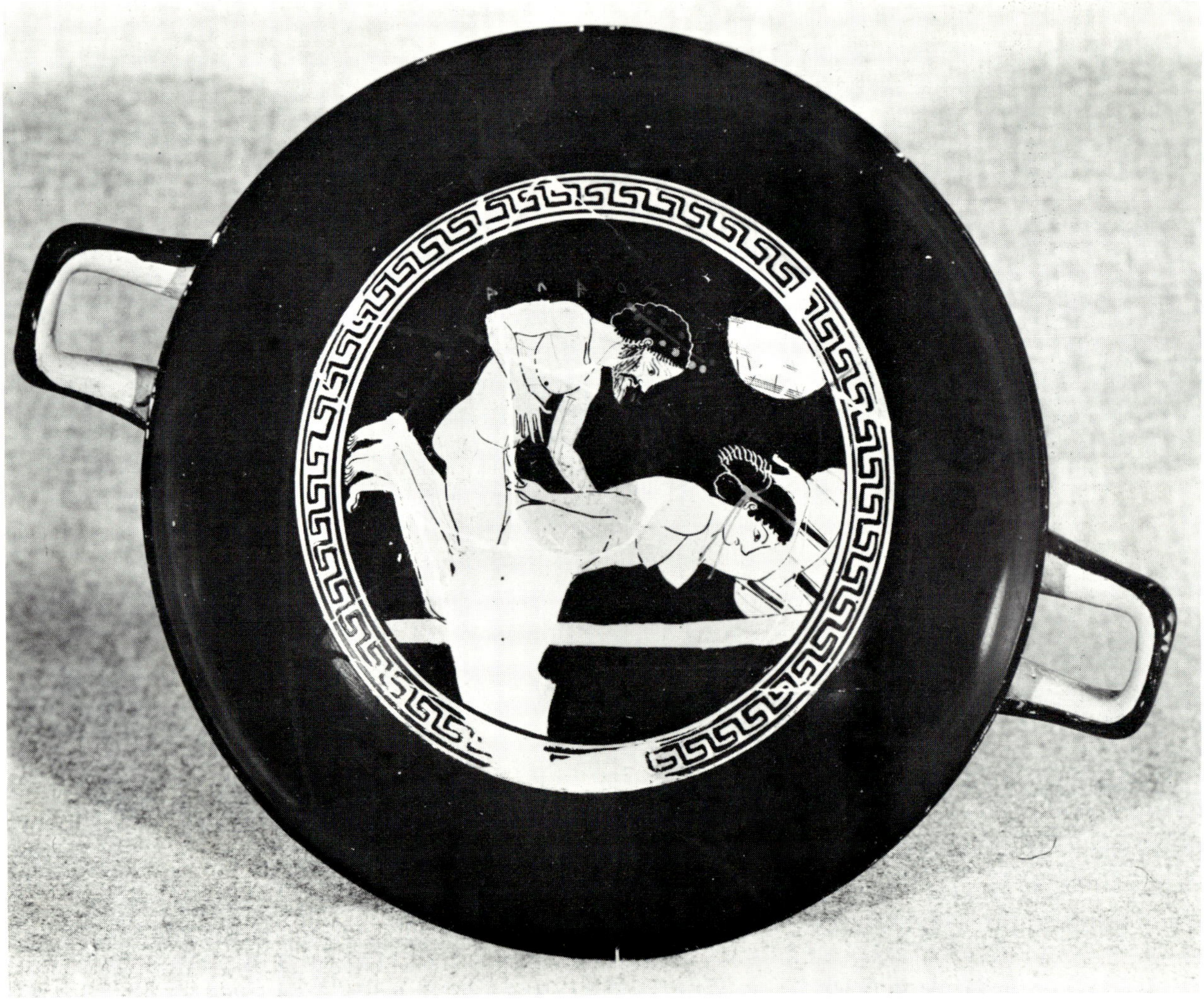

22. Red-figure cup. Panaitios Painter. (*London, British Museum.*)

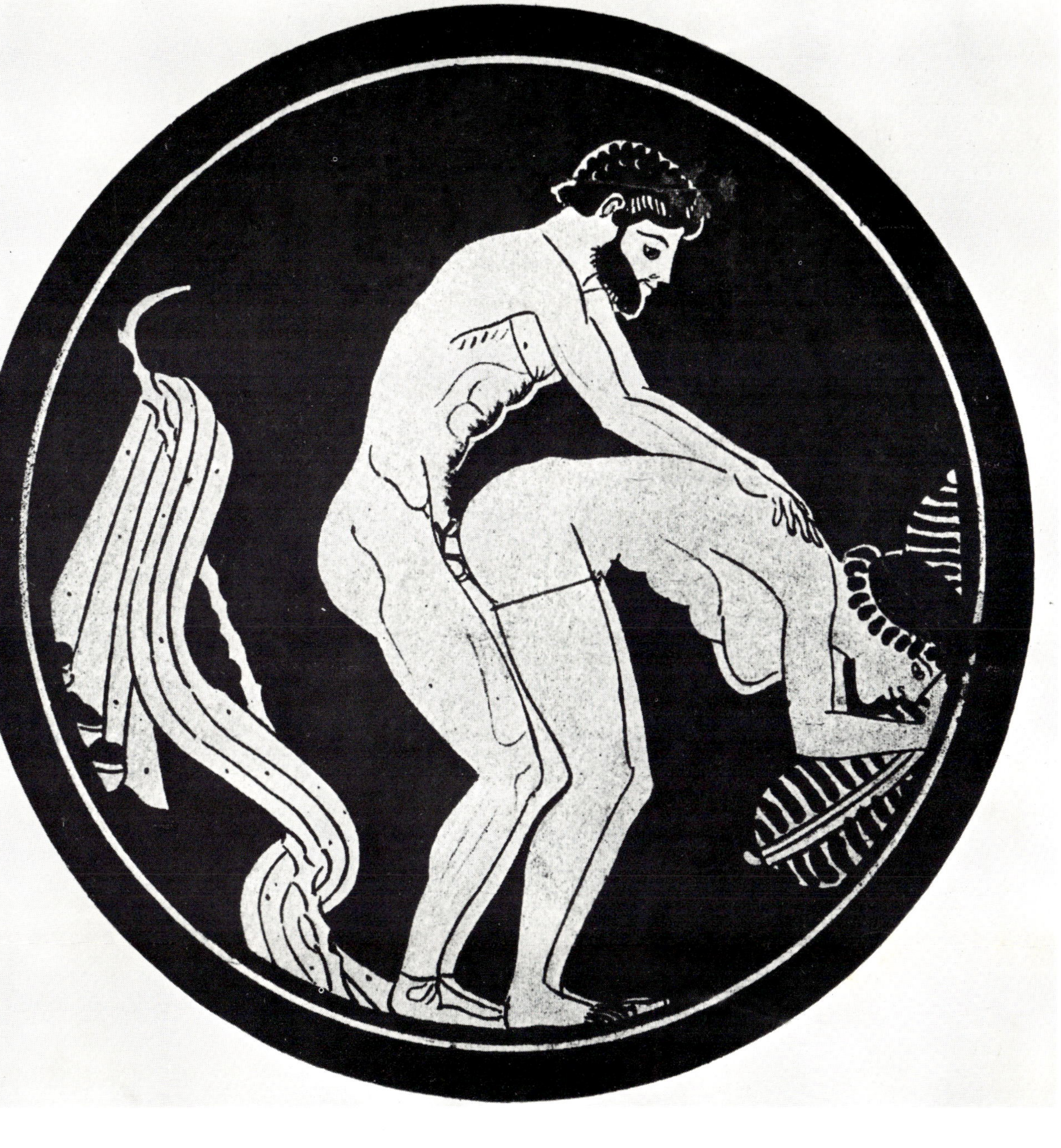

23. Red-figure cup. **Briseis Painter.** (*Tarquinia, Museum.*)

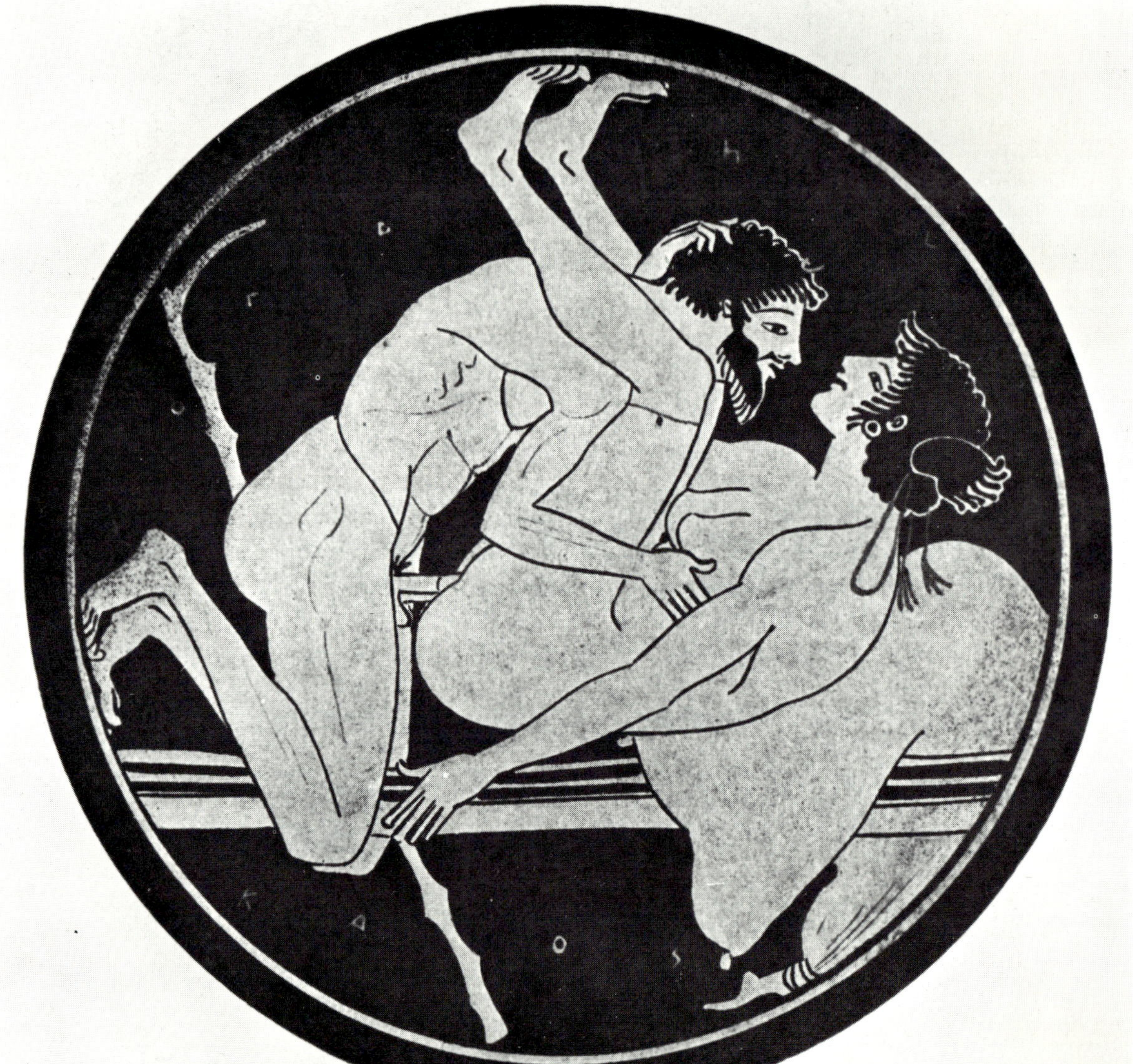

24. Red-figure cup. **Triptolemos Painter.** (*Tarquinia, Museum.*)

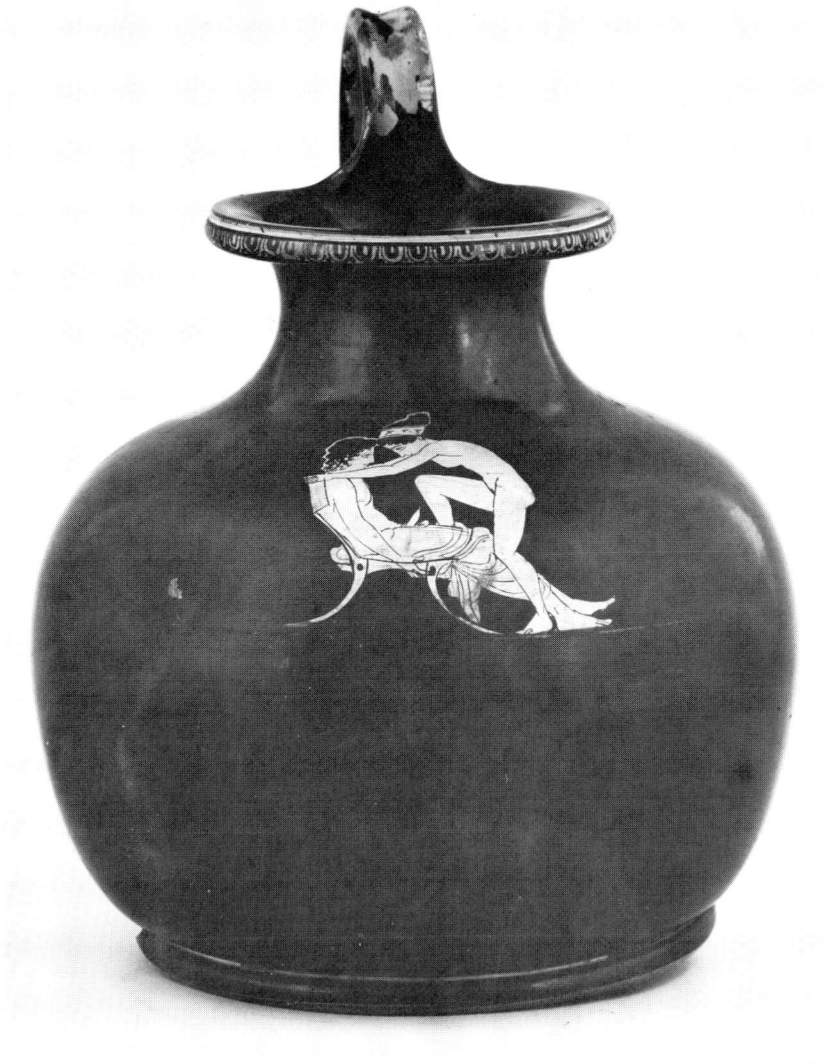

25. Red-figure *oinochoë.* Shuvalov Painter. (*Berlin, Stiftung Staatliche Kulturbesitz.*)

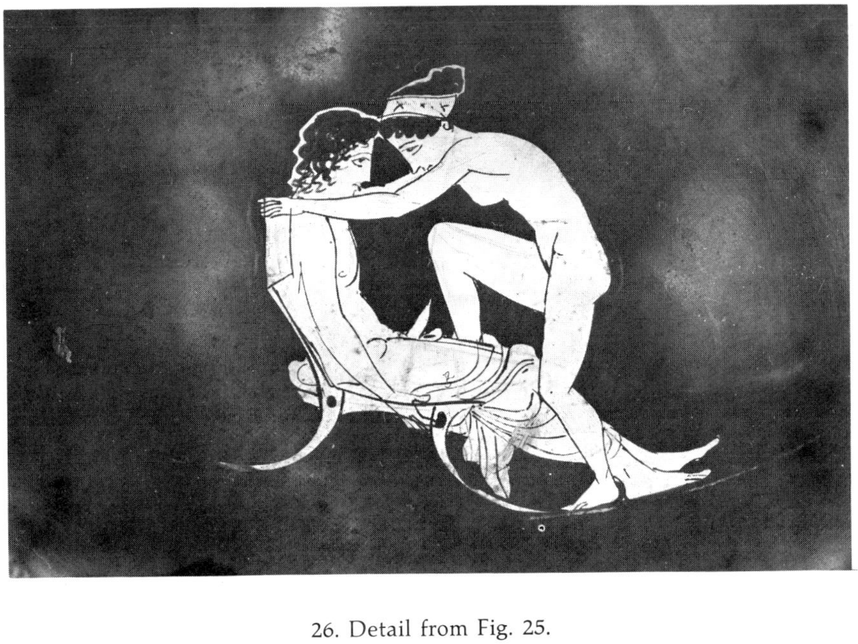

26. Detail from Fig. 25.

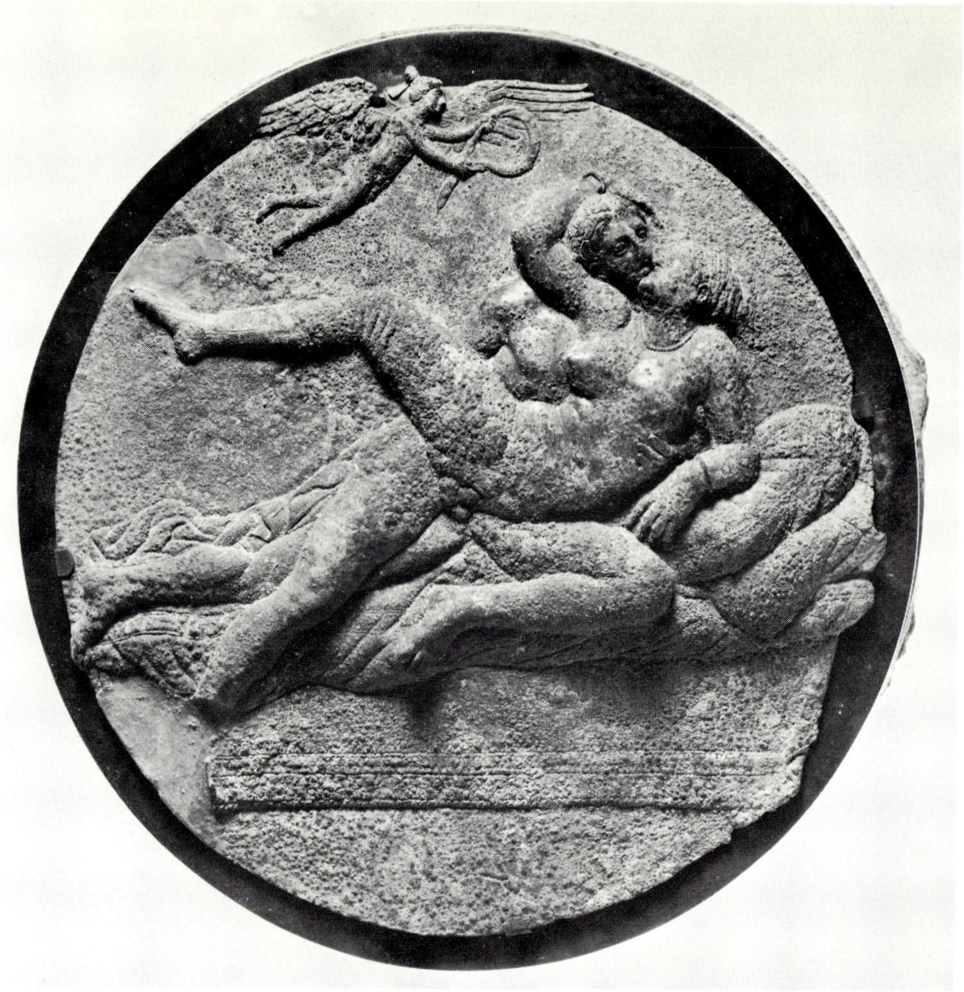

27. Bronze mirror cover. Corinthian or Southern Italian. (*Boston, Museum of Fine Arts. Gift of E. P. Warren.*)

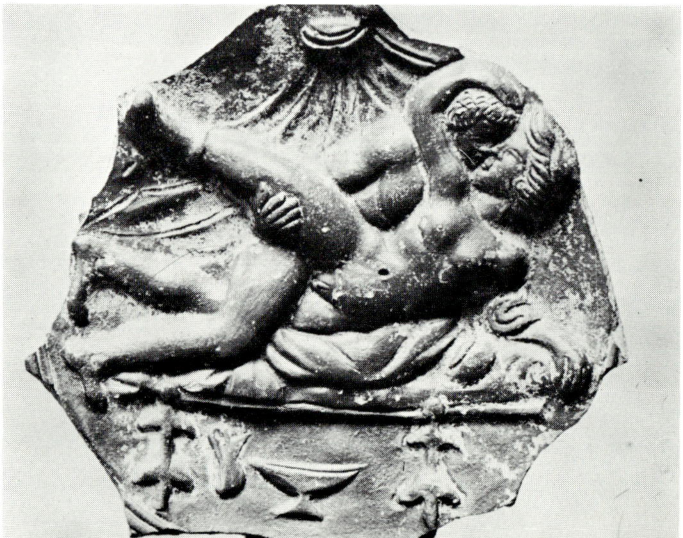

28. Terracotta fragment. (*Berlin, Stiftung Staatliche Kulturbesitz.*)

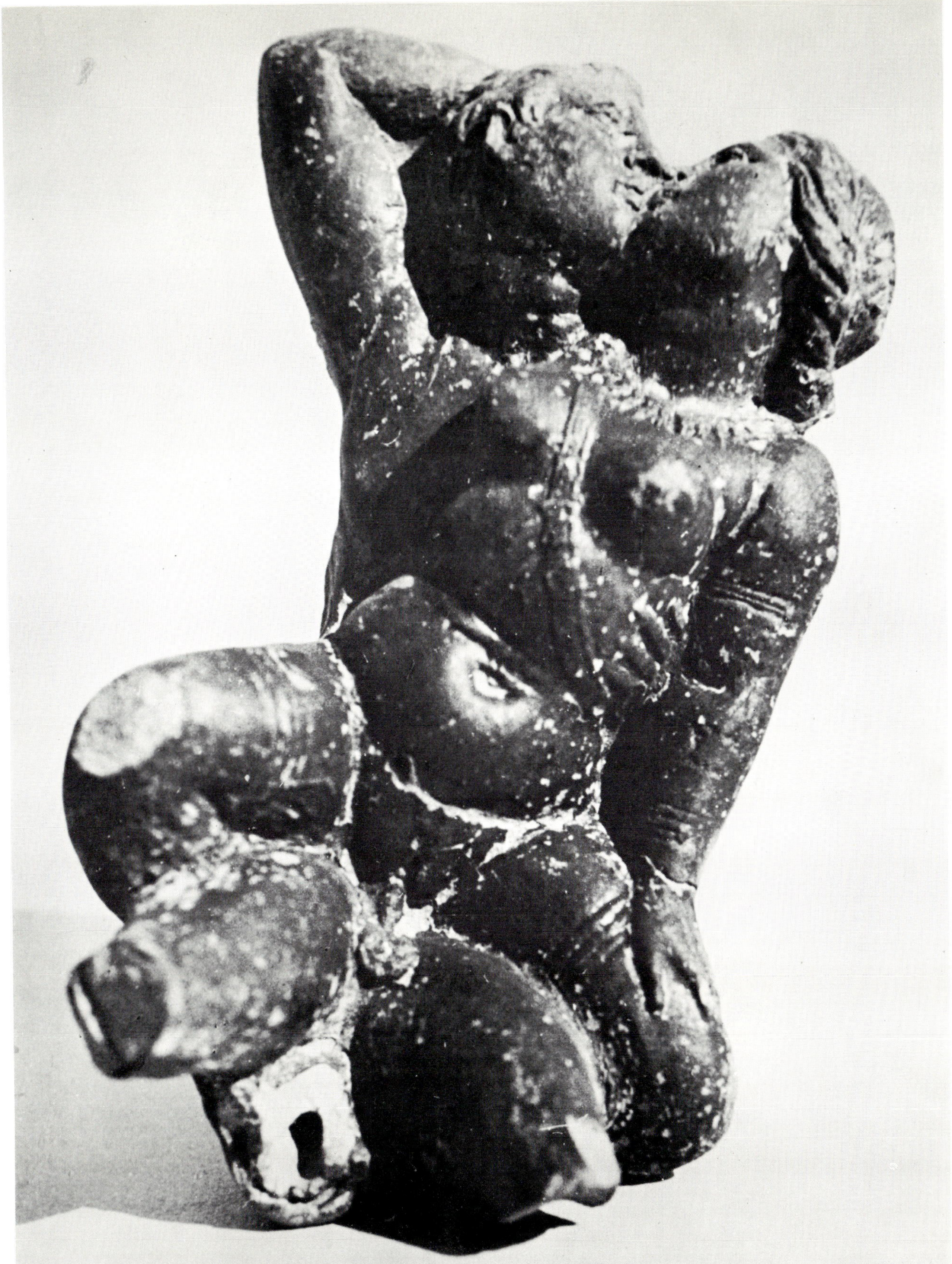

29. Terracotta group. (*Delos, Museum.*)

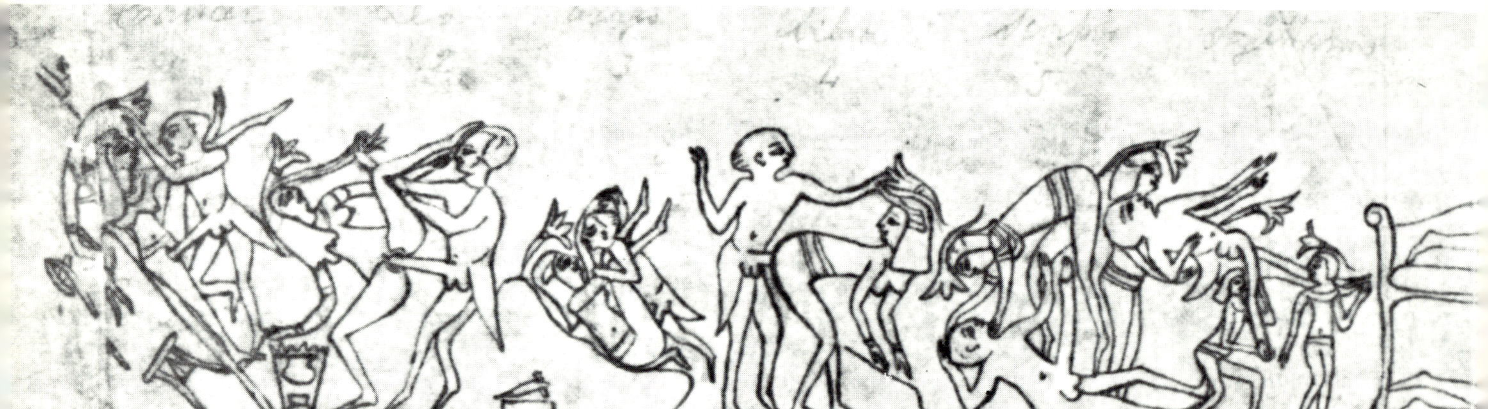

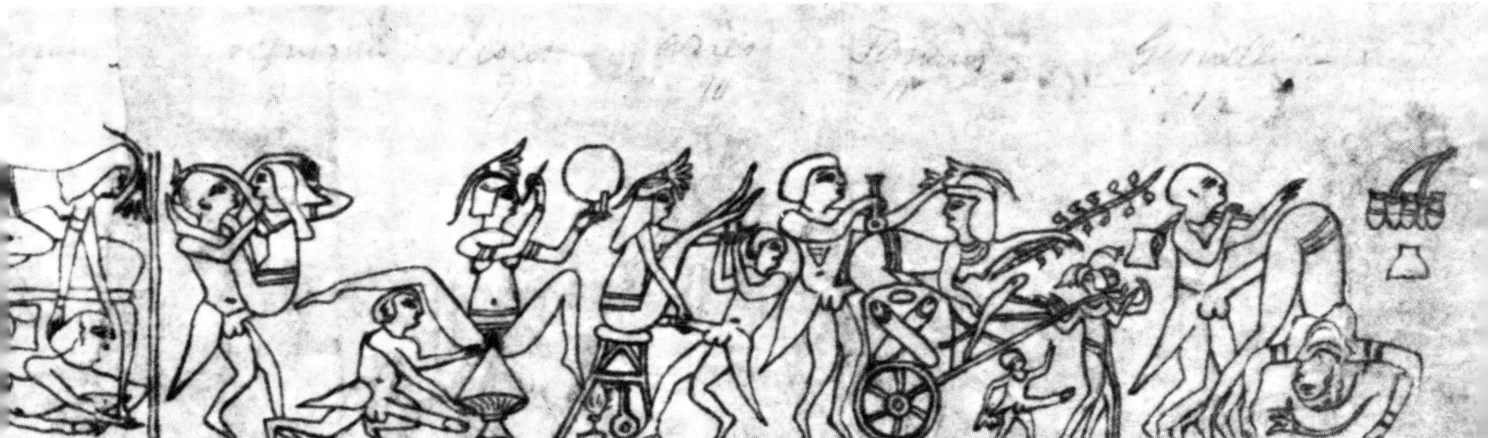

30. Egyptian papyrus, Turin. Drawing. (*Bloomington, Ind.,* ***Archives*** *of the Institute for Sex Research.*)

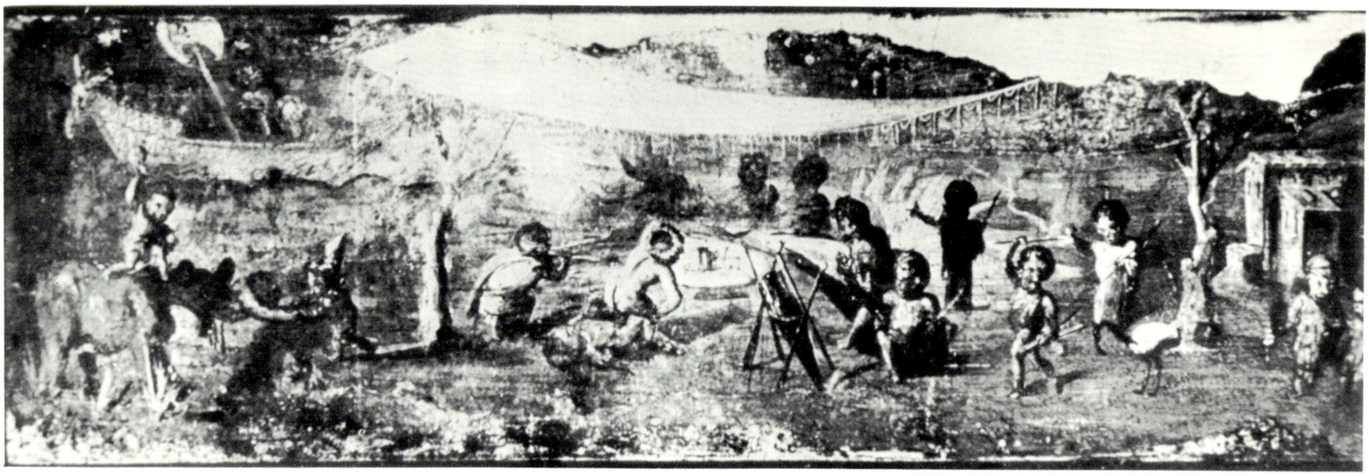

31. Roman painting from Pompeii. (*Naples, National Museum.*)

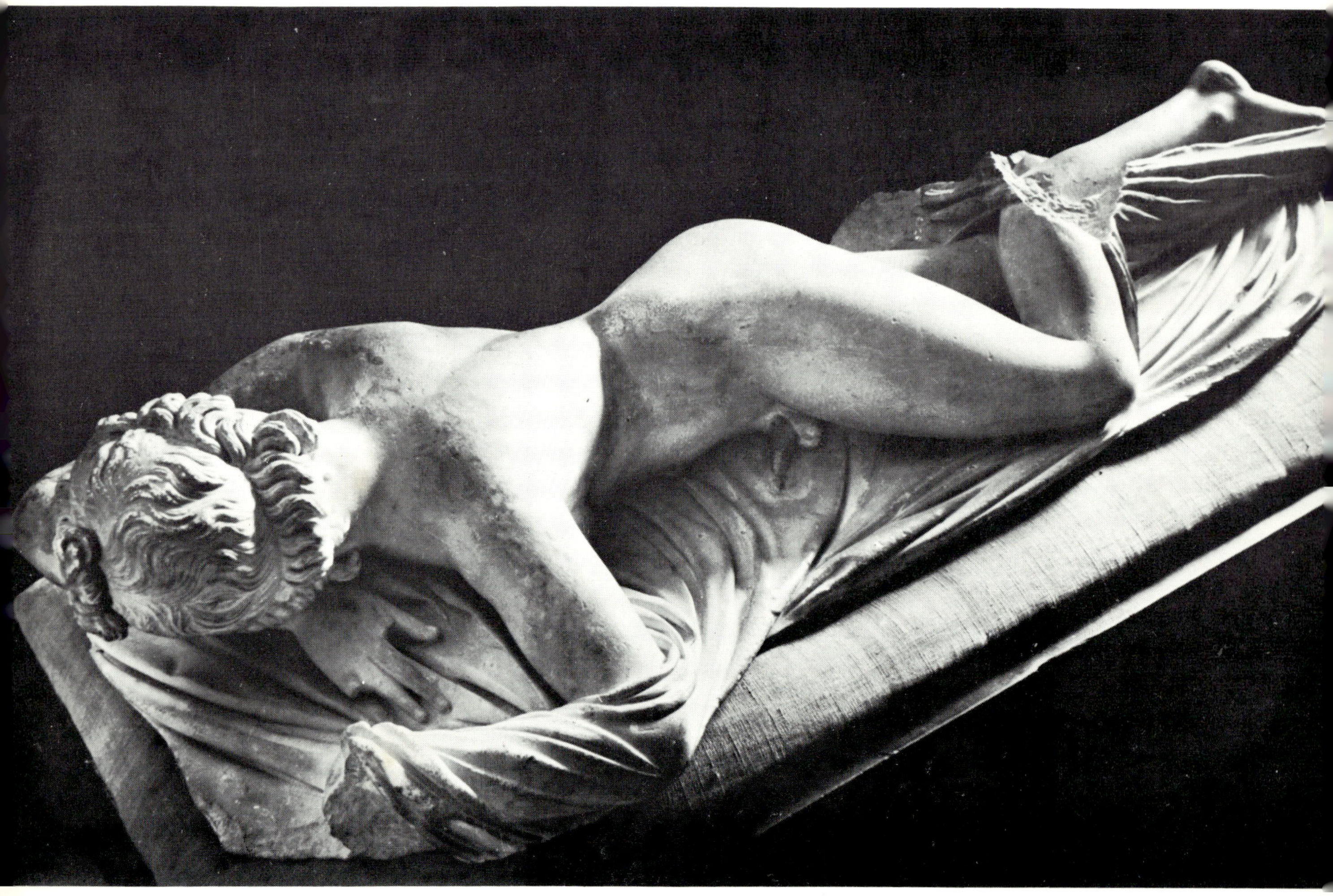

32. Sleeping hermaphrodite. (*Rome, National Museum.*)

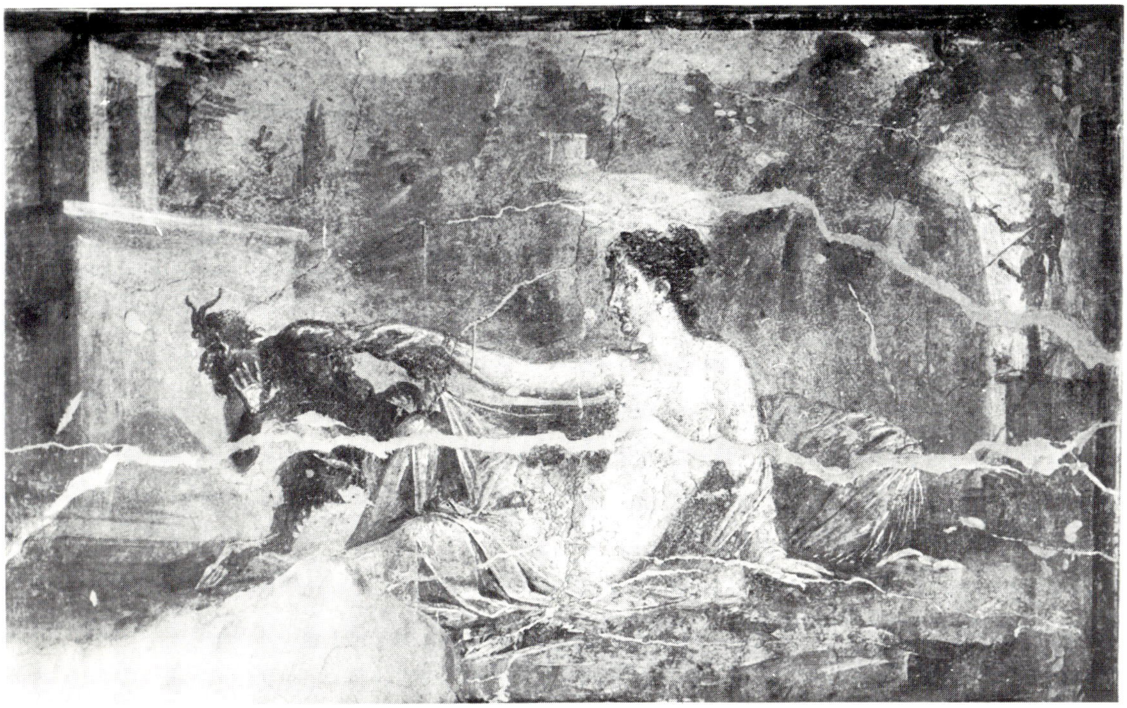

33. Hermaphrodite attacked. Painting. (*Naples, National Museum.*)

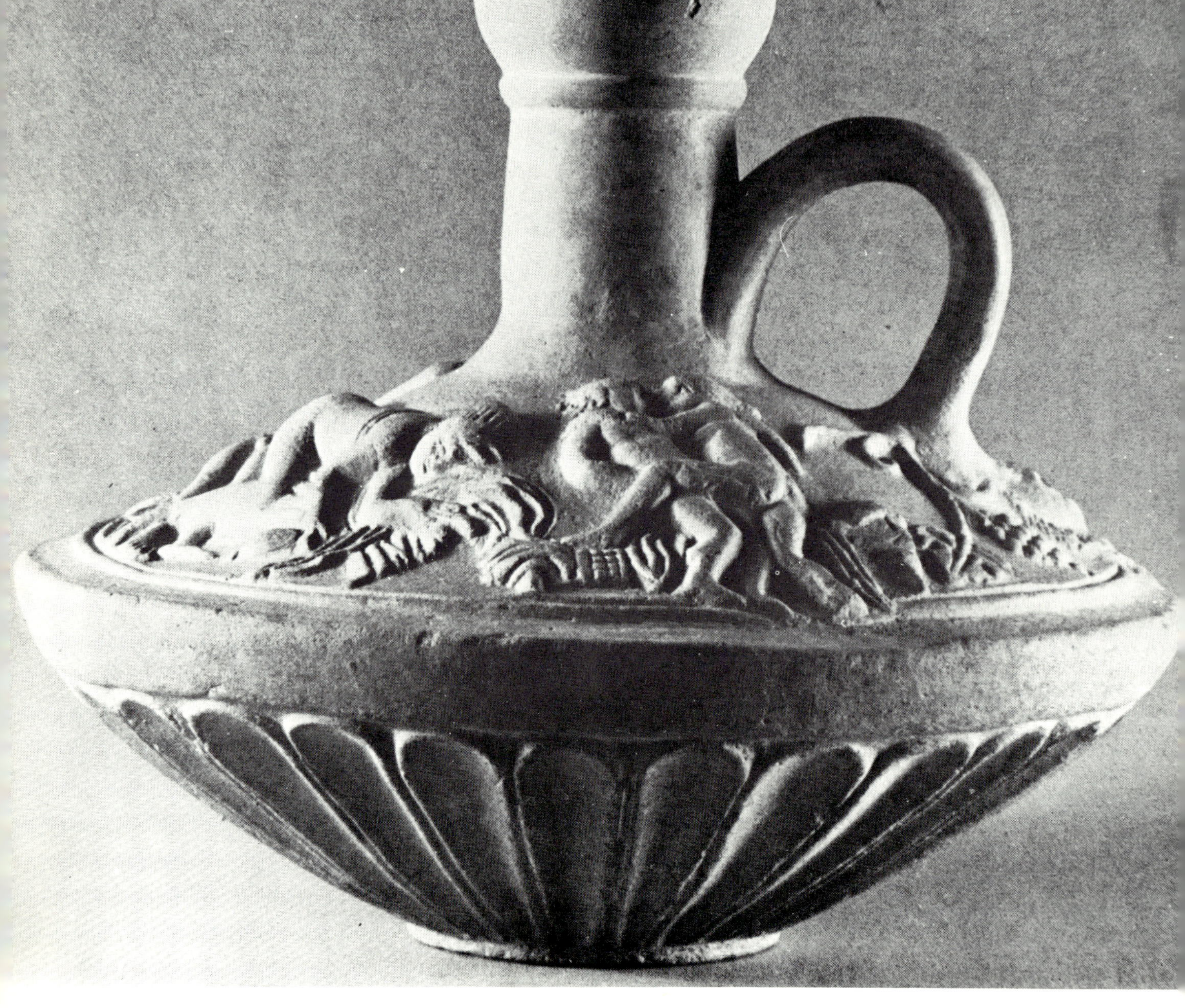

34. *Lagynos,* Roman-Alexandrian. (*Berlin, Stiftung Staatliche Kulturbesitz.*)

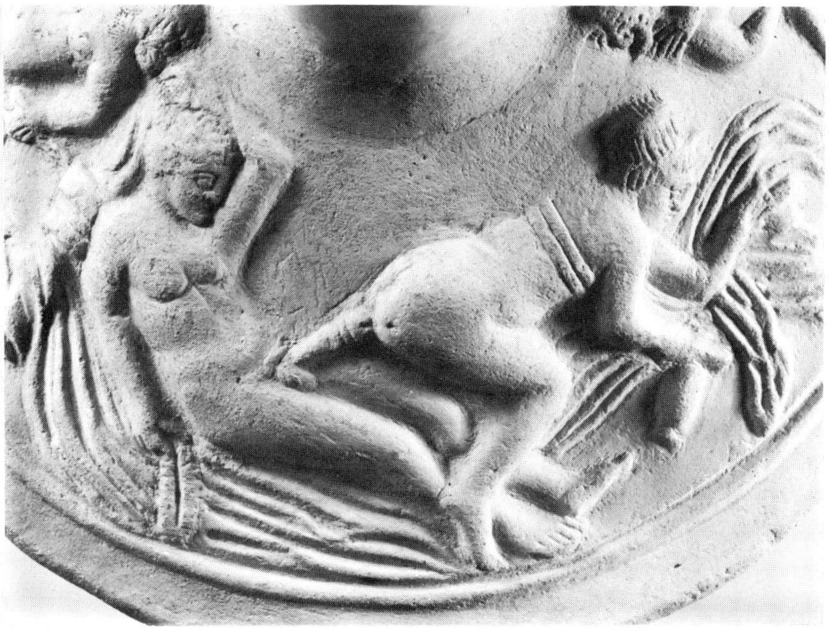

35. Detail from Fig. 34.

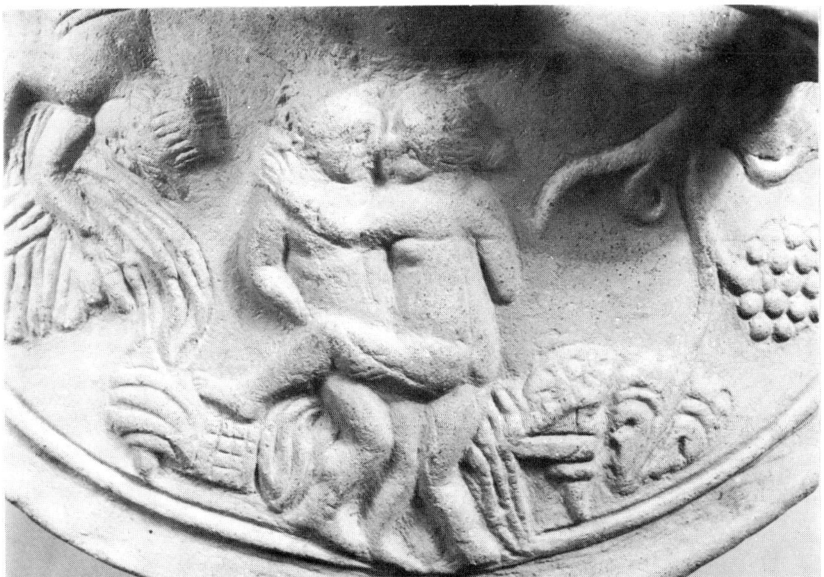

36. Detail from Fig. 34.

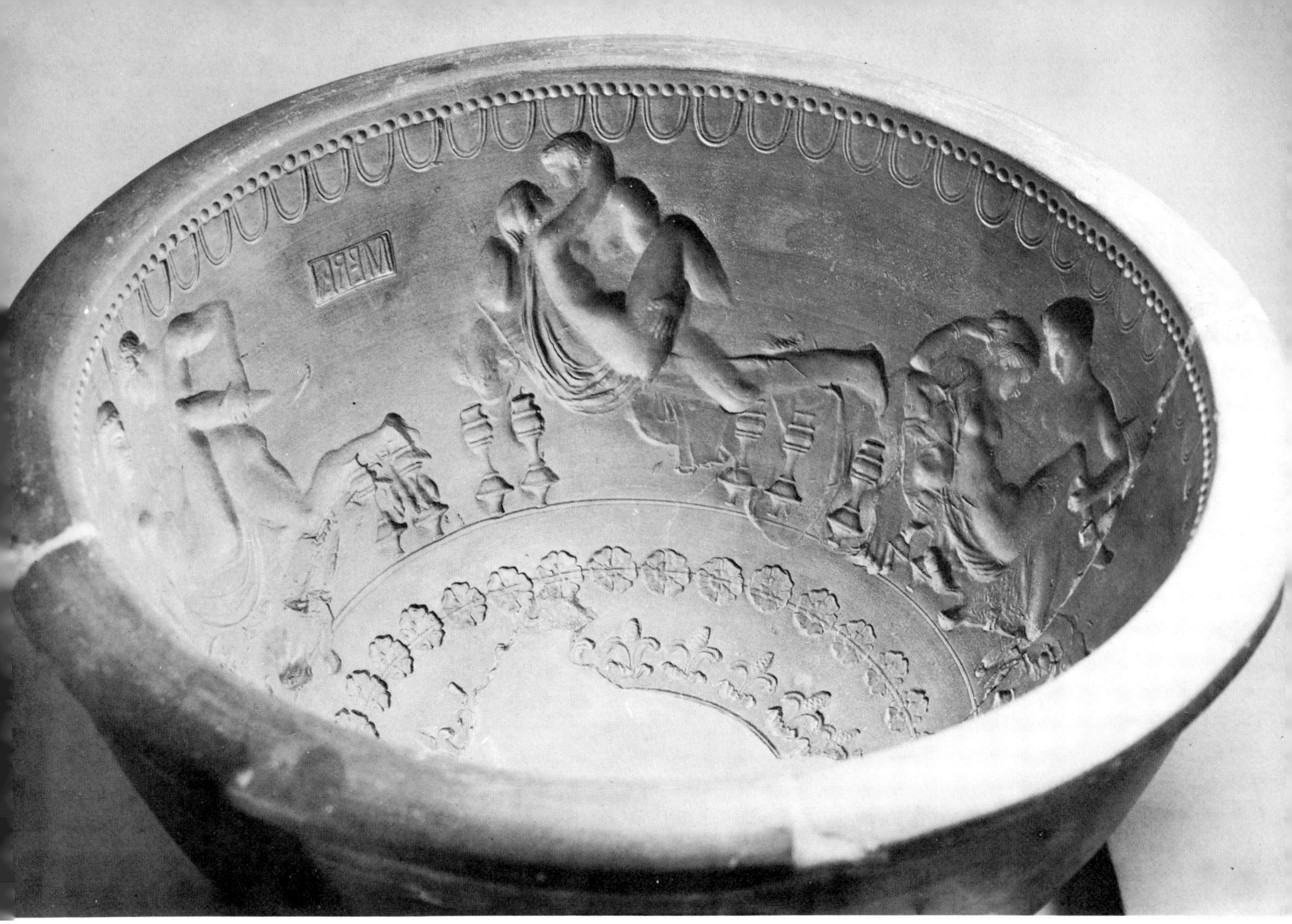

37. Erotic reliefs. Arretine mold. (*Berlin, Stiftung Staatliche Kulturbesitz.*)

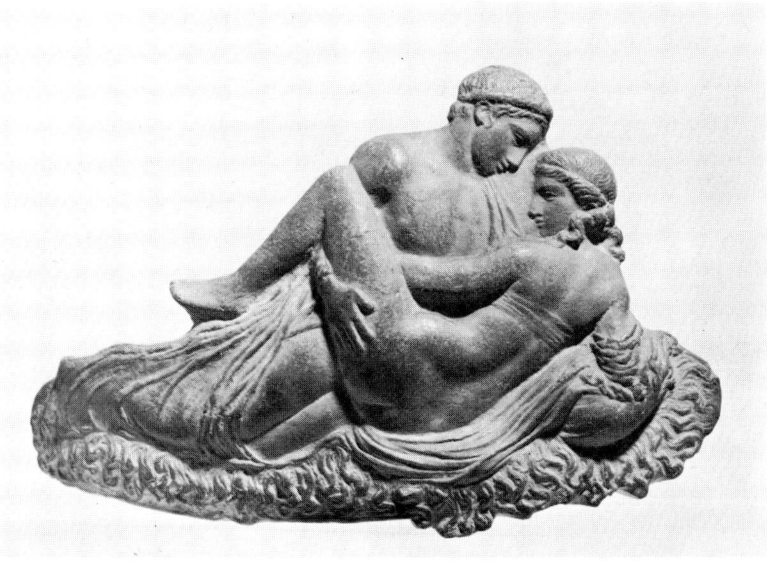

38. Stamped relief. Arretine. (*Berlin, Stiftung Staatliche Kulturbesitz.*)

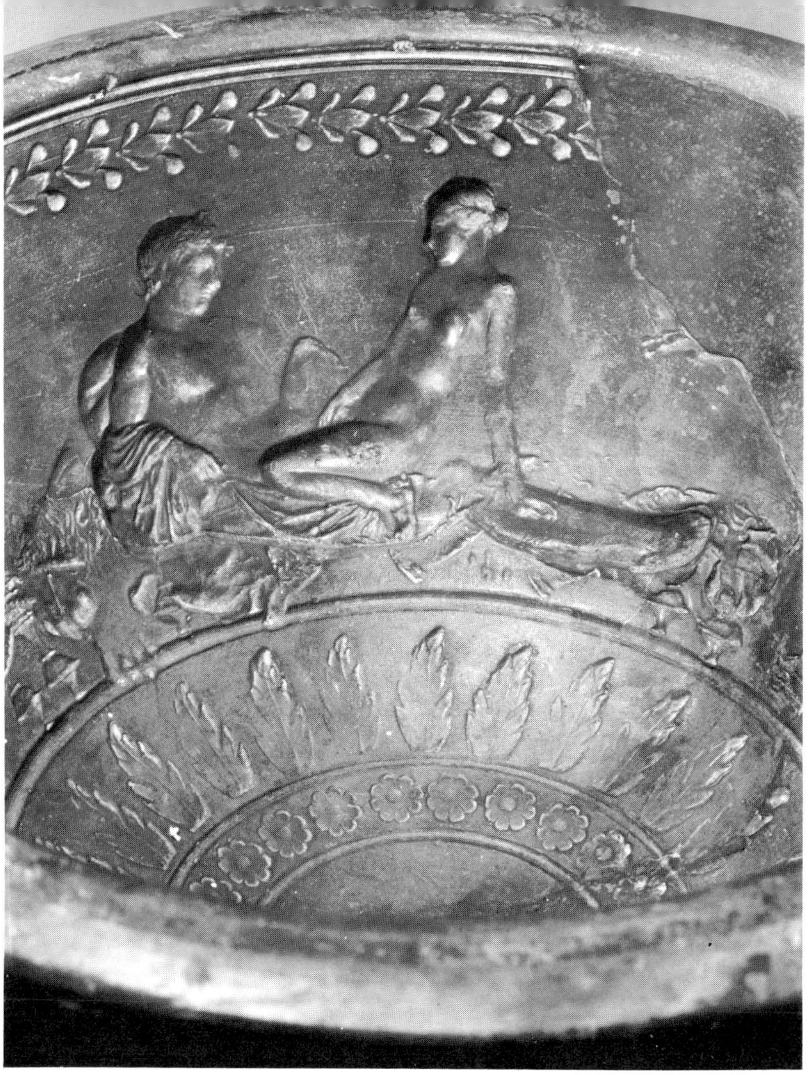

39. Erotic group. Arretine **mold.** (*New York, Metropolitan Museum, Rogers Fund, 1941.*)

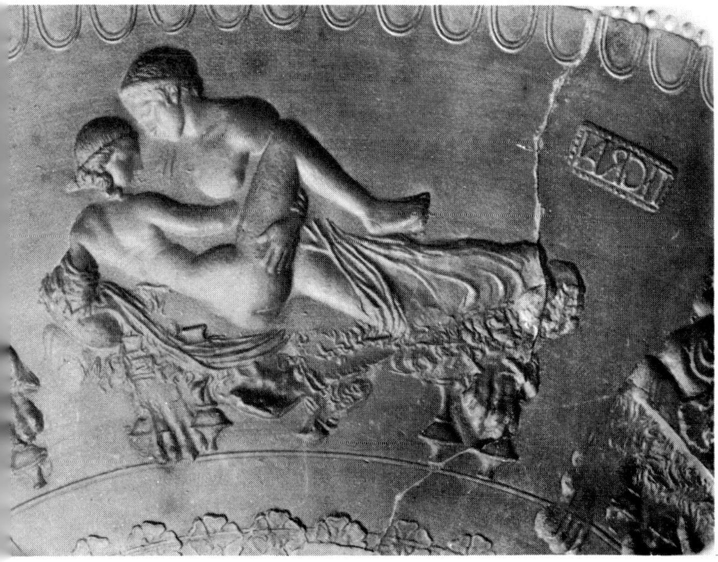

40. Detail from Fig. 37.

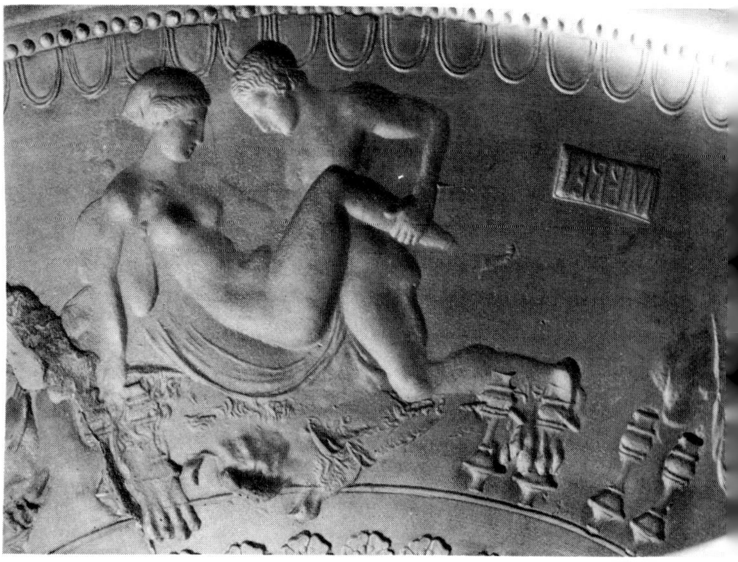

41. Detail from Fig. 37.

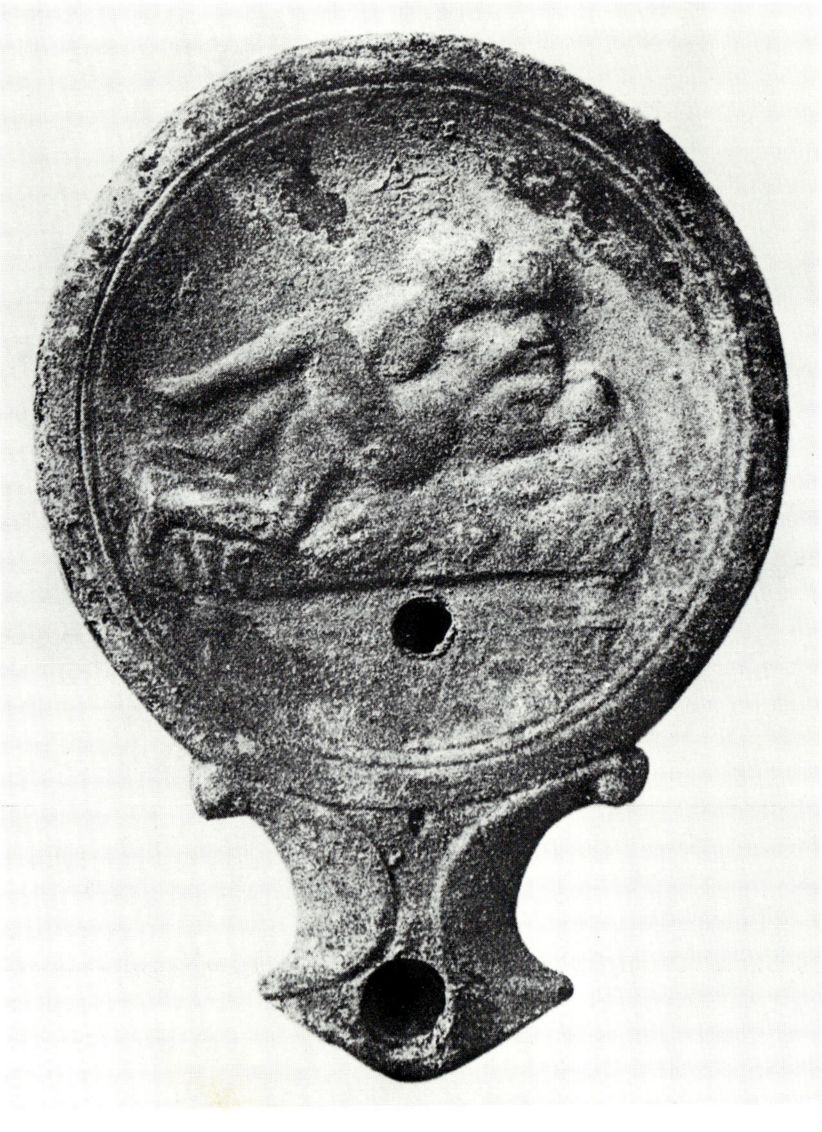

42. Roman lamp. (*Formerly Munich, private collection.*)

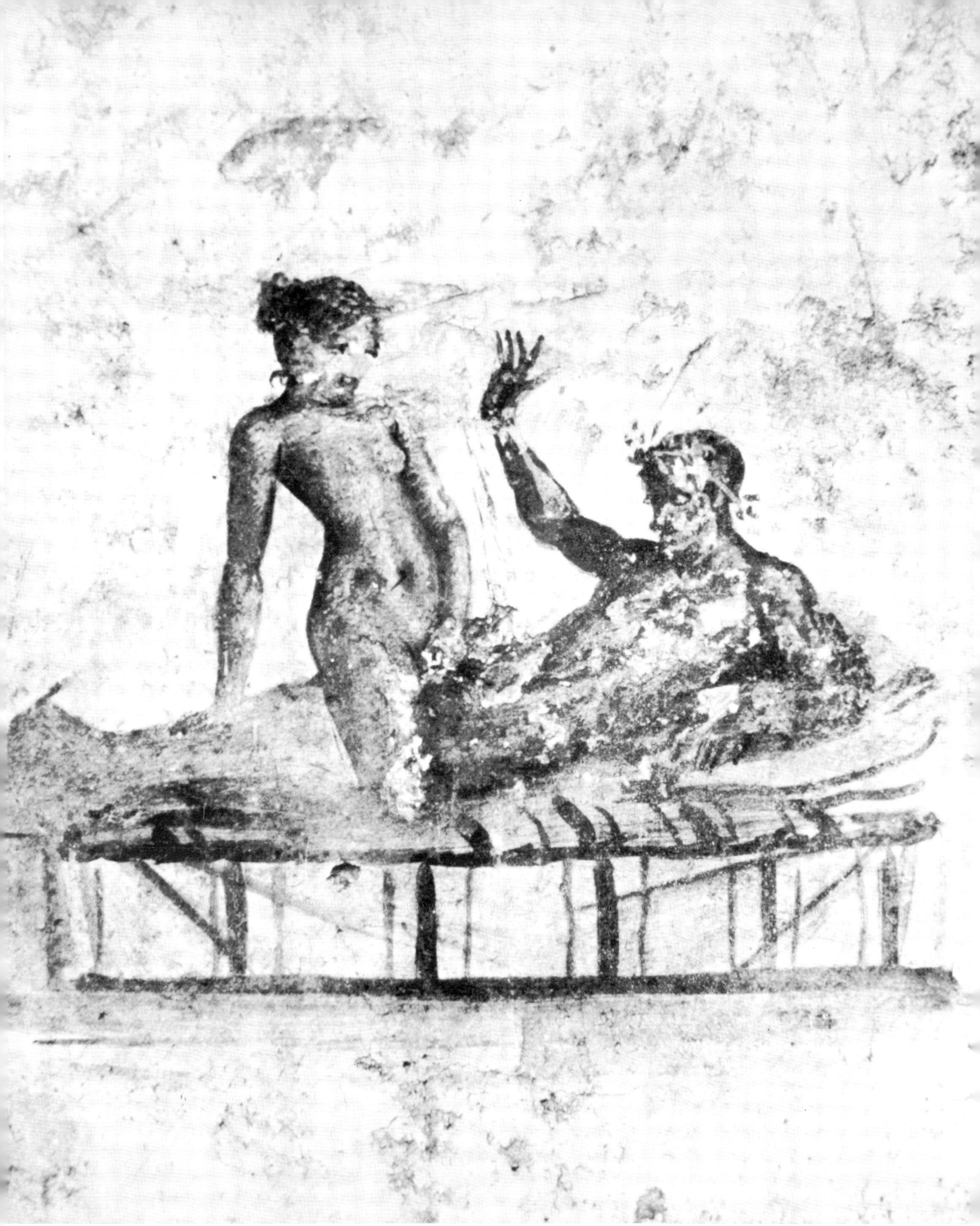

43. Roman painting. (*Naples, National Museum.*)

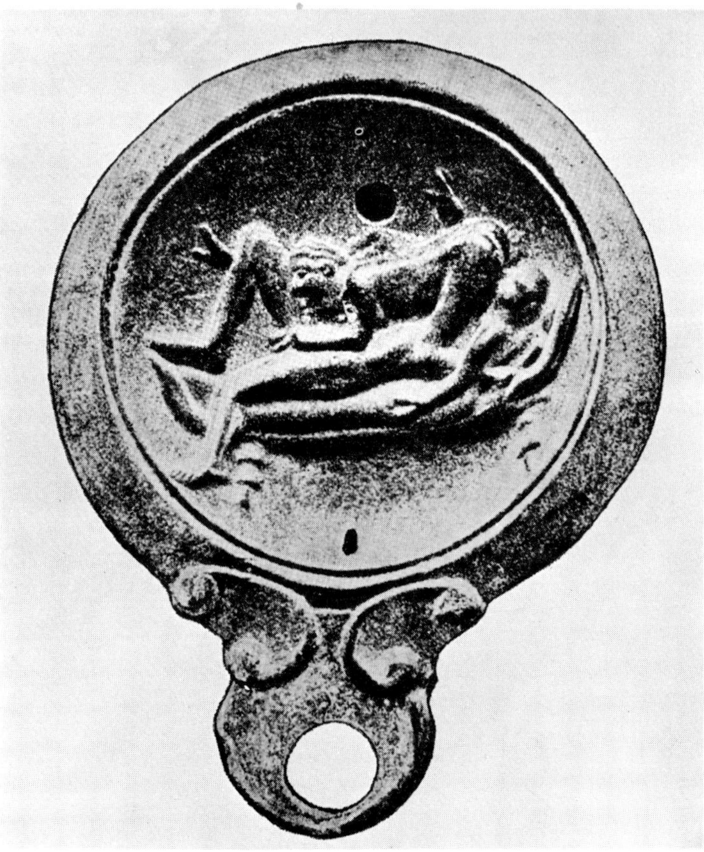

44. Roman lamp. (*Formerly Munich, Antikensammlung.*)

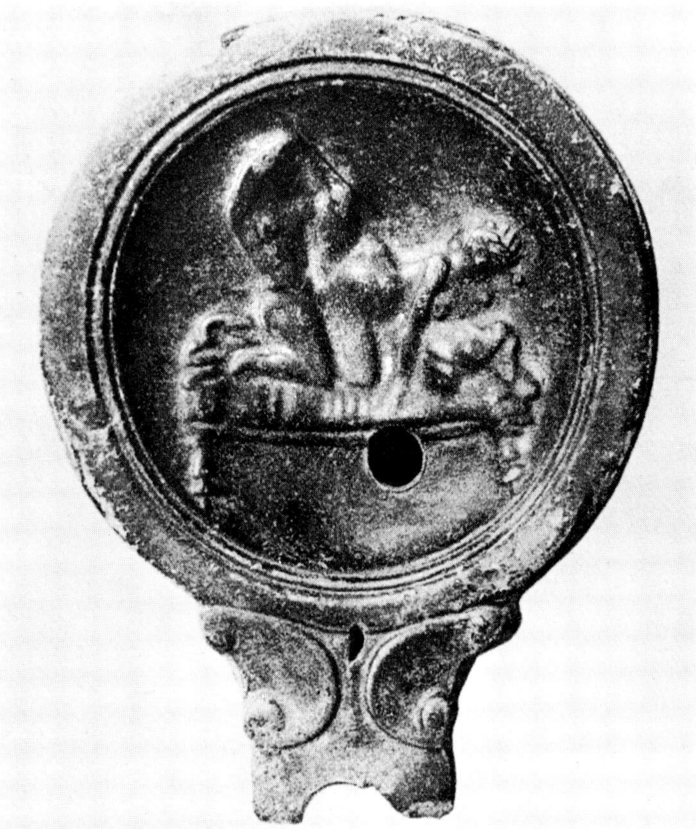

45. Roman lamp. (*Formerly Munich, private collection.*)

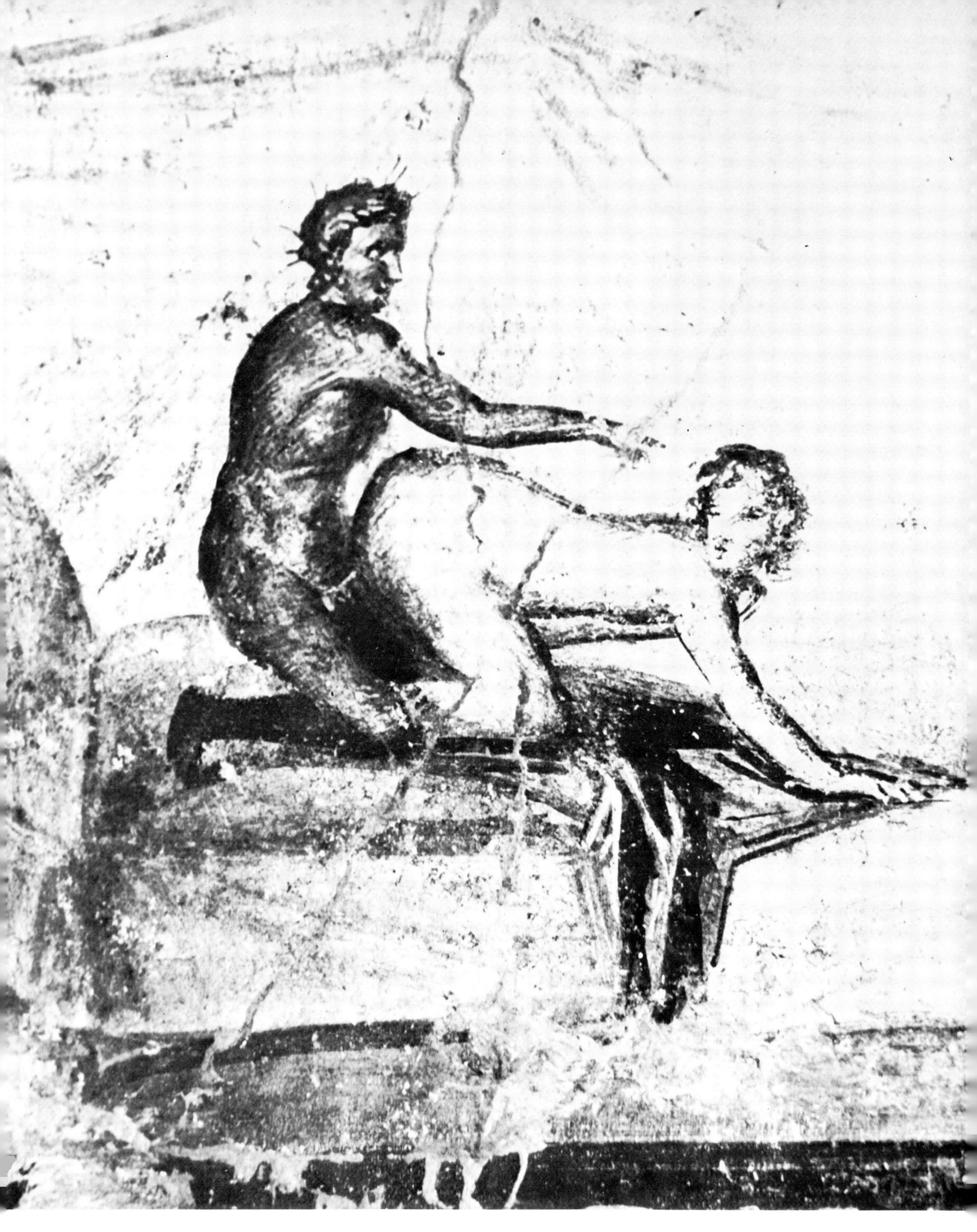

46. Roman painting. (*Naples, National Museum.*)

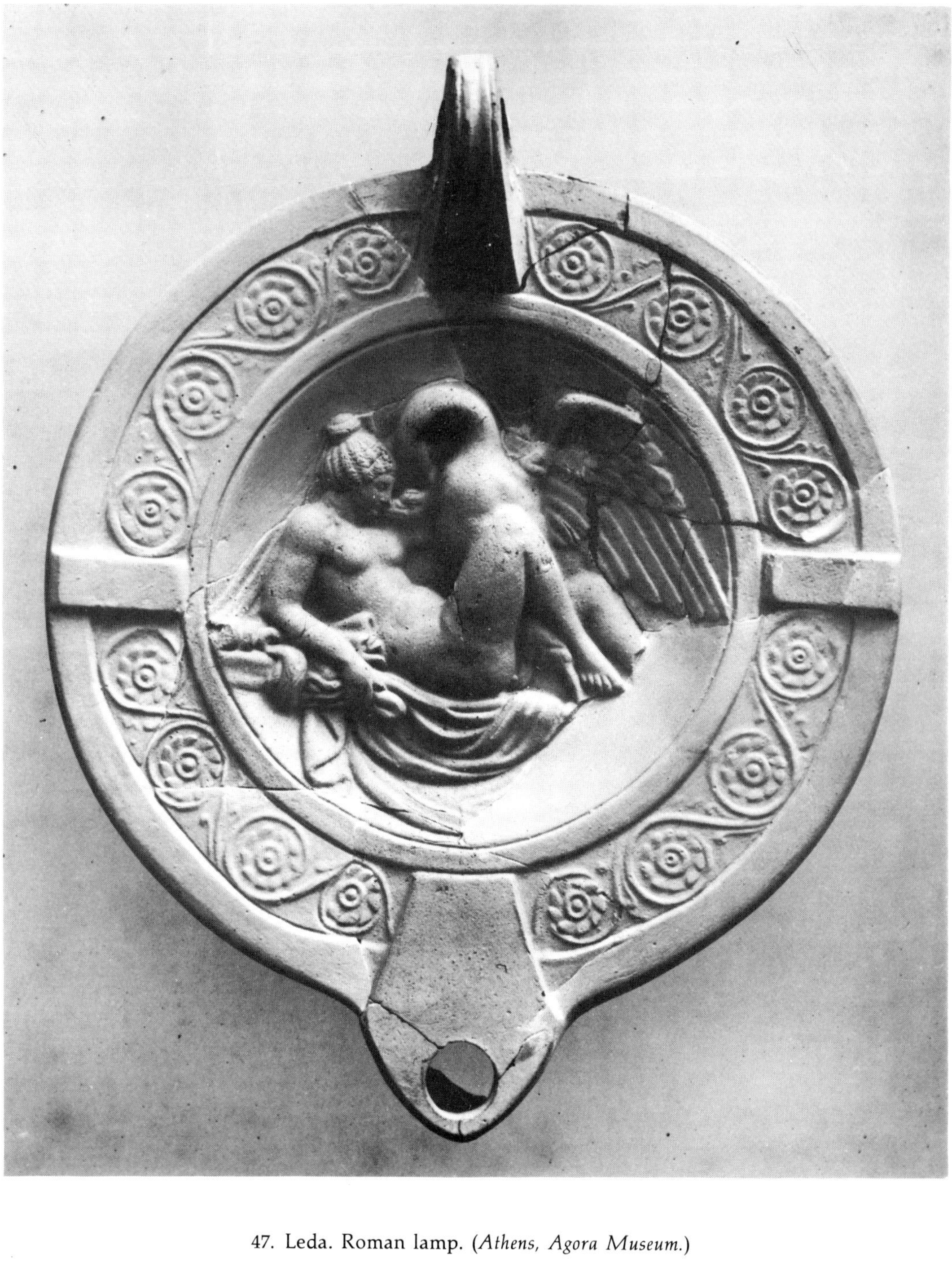

47. Leda. Roman lamp. (*Athens, Agora Museum.*)

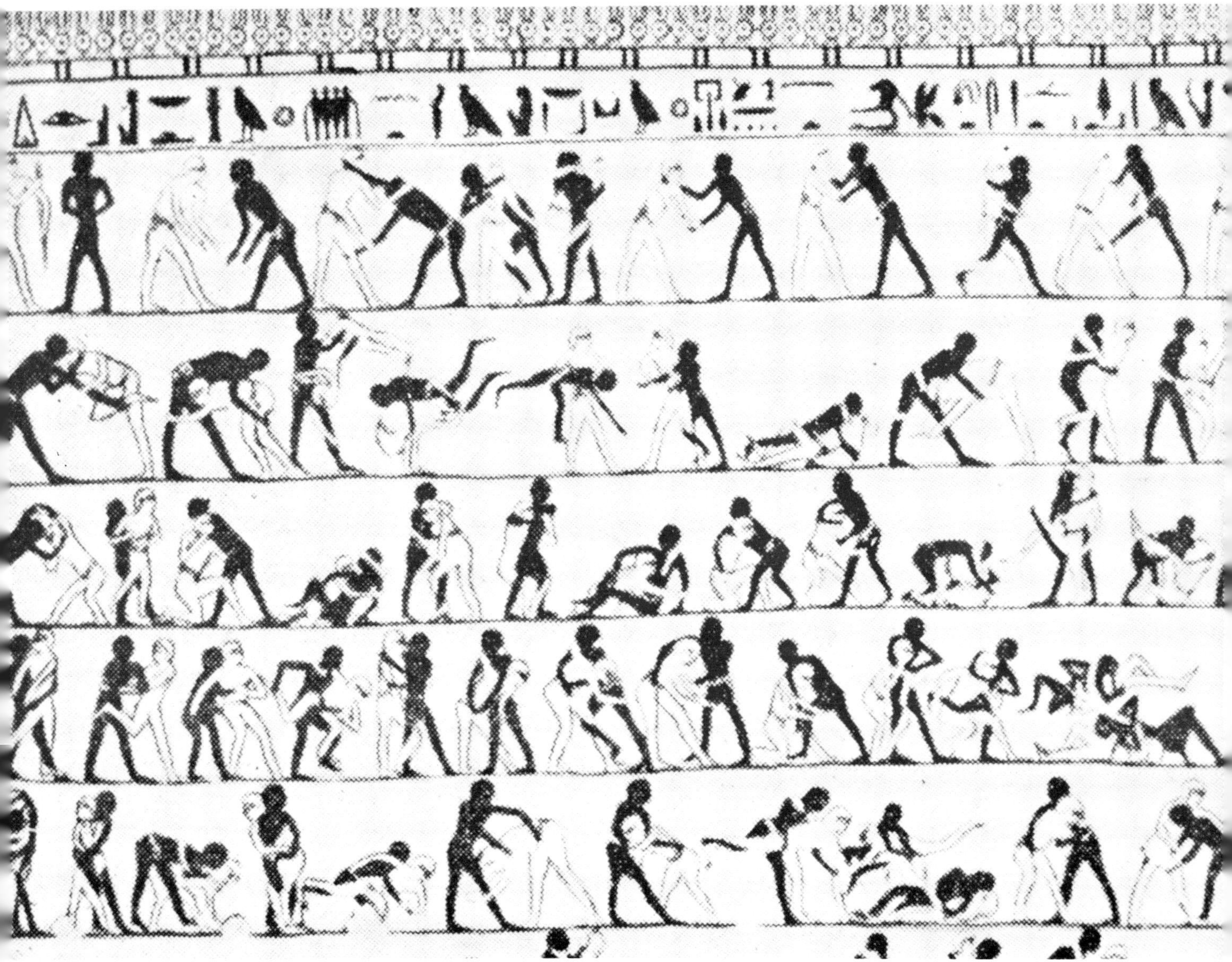

48. Westlers. Beni Hasan, Tomb No. 15.

2

Sexual Motifs in Prehistoric Peruvian Ceramics

PAUL H. GEBHARD

The ancient inhabitants of Peru learned to make ceramics around 1500 B.C. The vast majority of ceramic products were vessels for fluids and solids, but figurines, whistles, panpipes, and sundry other artifacts were also made of clay. The ceramics were often decorated with varying degrees of skill by modeling and/or painting. In certain cultures a substantial percentage of this decoration was in the form of representational art, and this good fortune gives the archaeologist a much better knowledge of past artifacts and behavior than he could otherwise have hoped for.

In addition to finding vessels bearing depictions of warfare, religious rites, and various genre scenes, the early archaeologists were astonished to find that sexual activities were also represented. Such sexual themes are not common, but in certain cultures they are not rare either. Nevertheless, a spurious rarity has been given them through their omission in museum displays (a forgivable submission to our societal demands) and the scant treatment they receive in the literature. Some books and articles simply fail to mention erotic ceramics, whereas others dismiss them with almost curt brevity. Unless one reads extensively in archaeological literature, one would receive the impression that ceramic erotica were limited to one culture, the Mochica, and that it was rare there.

The sexual vessels did not accidentally escape attention but were, rather, the victims of the prudery of our own culture. Scholars avoided what they feared might be construed as an undue interest in them, and museum officials not infrequently concealed these items from inquiring scientists or brought forth only a portion of their collections. Even one of the leading archaeologists and collectors, Rafael Larco-Hoyle, strained to convince himself and others that some of the sexual scenes were meant to be moral lessons and admonitions as to the consequences of certain acts. Prior to Larco's recent book on sexual pottery only a few journal articles were specifically devoted to the subject and these, as one might guess, were in German anthropological periodicals during the first quarter of this century.[1]

Shortly after joining Dr. Alfred Kinsey in 1946, I brought my scant knowledge of erotic Peruvian ceramics to his attention and suggested that these cast light upon the sexual interest of a long extinct culture and one which was never influenced by the religions which shaped the sexual thinking of Europe and Asia. Dr. Kinsey asked that during interviewing field trips I visit nearby museums to seek out and photograph these vessels. After William Dellenback joined the Institute for Sex Research as a photographer, he assumed this task, photographing a small private collection in 1949 and the larger Wassermann-San Blás collection[2] in 1951. Kinsey's interest was by then sufficient to negotiate with Rafael Larco-Hoyle for permission to photograph his large collection, most of which was at that time housed at the Hacienda Chiclin near Trujillo. This collection included the greatest amount of erotic Peruvian pottery known, roughly double the holdings of the Peruvian National Museum. An agreement was made in which the Institute promised not to make photographs available for research until Larco-Hoyle published his book on sexual pottery

[1] For example: Enrique Brüning, "Beiträge zum Studium des Geschlechtslebens der Indianer im alten Peru," *Anthropophyteia,* VI (1909), 101–112. Enrique Brüning, "Beiträge zum Studium des Geschlechtslebens der Indianer im alten Peru. Auszug von verschiedenen alten Geschichtwerken, das Geschlechtsleben der Indianer Perús betreffend," *Anthropophyteia,* VIII (1911), 199–202. R. Lehmann-Nitsche, "Zu den Anthropophyteia aus Alt Peru," *Anthropophyteia,* VI (1909), 99–100. Arthur Posnansky, "Die erotischen Keramiken der Mochicas und deren Beziehungen zu occipital deformierten Schädeln," *Gesellschaft für Anthropologie, Ethnologie und Urgeschichte,* Festschrift (1925), Band 2, pp. 67–74.

[2] See B. J. Wassermann-San Blás (ed.), *Céramicas del antiquo Perú, de la colección Wassermann-San Blás* (Buenos Aires: Jacobo Pueser, 1938).

(he hoped with Kinsey as co-author) or until his death. As fate would have it, both events occurred within eighteen months in 1965–1966.

Dr. Kinsey, Mr. Dellenback, and I visited Peru in 1954 for the purpose of seeing, describing, and photographing every prehistoric artifact of apparent sexual significance in the collections of Larco-Hoyle and the National Museum. We were able to accomplish this in less than two months and we also photocopied all relevant items in the Prado Museum, the Trujillo Museum, and several private collections.

This chapter is based almost wholly upon the materials we examined and, in most cases, photographed. In a few instances I have made use of photographs sent to us by interested individuals; in addition, Larco-Hoyle provided us with photographs of roughly fifty items which he no longer possessed. I have been able to include in this present study nearly all of the raw data we collected; only in a relatively few cases did the fragmentary nature of the object or of my notes prevent utilization.

This study is primarily descriptive and analytical. Formulating and testing hypotheses is premature until one has taken the necessary first step, that of becoming well acquainted with the subject material. Since the study deals not with living creatures but with art unfettered by anatomic realities, a number of curious taxonomic problems arose. Whereas gender can almost always be accurately determined by anatomy, hair style, and dress, the Mochica often depicted cadavers engaged in sexual activity. These lack gender distinguishing traits in many instances and I have been forced to attribute gender on the basis of context. For example, if a cadaver is behaving with a human female as a human male would, I have assumed that the cadaver is (or was) male. Some persons have suggested that these cadavers in actuality represent mutilated but living humans. I disagree. The Mochica did depict individuals suffering from diseases and mutilations, but they did so with a skillful realism that made clear that the individuals were still alive. The cadavers, on the other hand, usually display a tissue loss incompatible with life. The eyes are gone, there is no flesh on the face, the ramus of the jaw is visible, and the ribs show clearly. A few cadavers are less decomposed, and these might represent ill but living humans. When corporeal realism conflicts with a sexual theme, the realism is sacrificed on the altar of art, for one sees that many cadavers have miraculously retained their phalli. Another problem was the classification of coital positions. Anatomically impossible postures are not infrequent, such as the female crouching yet having coitus with a standing male. This was often achieved by making the male smaller than the female and by shortening his legs. Whether coitus was vaginal or anal was frequently ambiguous, but I have not labeled coitus as anal unless it was clearly shown to be so. Lastly, it is extremely difficult to differentiate between exhibition of erect male genitalia and masturbation. Generally if the male's hands were on the shaft of his penis, one might construe the activity as self-masturbation, but in some cases it is quite possible that he was merely supporting his enormously exaggerated phallus.

A more frequent problem was whether or not to consider the depiction of genitalia as falling within the scope of this study. I have chosen to include such instances only if the genitalia were exaggerated in size, tumescent, or ostentatiously displayed.

Although the bulk of sexual pottery is confined to the Mochica and the later Chimu cultures of the northern coast of Peru, examples have also been found in roughly a dozen other Peruvian cultures. In order to appreciate historical changes and to note how contemporaries influenced one another, it is necessary to use the various cultures as the frame of reference.

THE FORMATIVE PERIOD

Prior to the Formative Period, which extends from about 850 B.C. to 200 B.C., no examples of erotic ceramics are known. In the early part of the Formative Period, two cultures in the northern coastal area of Peru began producing pottery with sexual activity depicted —the Vicus, a recently discovered culture with which I am not familiar, and the Salinar.

Vicus

All the Vicus examples seem to be modeled anthropomorphic vessels. The crudity of the modeling makes for a certain amount of ambiguity, but insofar as I can tell from the text and illustrations in Larco-Hoyle's most recent book,[3] the Vicus potters depicted only a few sexual themes: heterosexual coitus, heterosexual petting with genital manipulation, display of genitalia, and use of the penis as a spout or tripod leg. The coitus occurs in several positions, often in dorso-ventral fashion with the female's back toward the male so that vaginal penetration is from the rear. I do not know how many sexual Vicus ceramics are known, but I have the impression that there are no more than a dozen.

Salinar

The Salinar pottery is also modeled, but somewhat more skillfully. The vessels are not painted, whereas the Vicus specimens were. The modeling is simple and rather childlike: bodies often are cylindrical, limbs are noodle-like, digits are indicated by a few incisions, and eyes are mere punctuations or coffee-bean-shaped. Nevertheless, despite the absence of detail and delineation, some of the anthropomorphic vessels convey great facial animation. Individuals' lips may be retracted to expose the teeth, a feature that is not common in most ancient Peruvian sexual art. Another unusual feature of the Salinar pottery is that, whereas female breasts are in low bas-relief or even more sketchily indicated,

[3] Rafael Larco-Hoyle, *Checan* (Geneva: Nagel, 1965).

the nipples are generally clearly shown. In a number of vessels the clitoris is carefully depicted.

There are only a few sexual Salinar vessels; we know of only twelve, all anthropomorphic. Of these, four are in the form of females with genitalia emphasized, four are males with erections or prominent phalli, two depict heterosexual petting, and two show coitus. The petting consists in one instance of the male touching the female's breasts while his erect penis is near her open vulva, and in the second instance of a female touching
49 the partly erect penis of a male seated beside her (Fig. 49). In both coital scenes the female lies supine, but in one the male lies prone atop, whereas in the other he kneels between her legs.

Gallinazo

In the latter part of the Formative Period, or roughly from 450 B.C. to 200 B.C., the Gallinazo (or Viru) culture existed in the northern coastal area. Sexual ceramics are extremely rare, consisting in our sample only of genital display plus one unique and curious vessel in the form of a hermaphrodite inserting its penis into its own vulva.[4] Two vessels show female genital display: both figures are nude and one has exaggerated genitalia. Similarly, of the two vessels showing male genital display, one clothed male has a normal-size penis and one nude male has an erect penis of
50 exaggerated size (Fig. 50). Lastly, under the heading of genital display is a phallic whistle. The Gallinazo examples, all modeled rather crudely and sometimes painted as well, nevertheless exhibit stylistic parallels with the Salinar pottery.

In summary, ceramics with sexual themes seem to have first begun during the Formative Period and to have been confined to the northern coast of Peru. The themes were generally limited to

[4] I know of only one other depiction of a hermaphrodite. This is a Mochica specimen, and the hermaphrodite appears to be amputating its penis.

heterosexual coitus (often in dorso-ventral fashion), simple manipulation of genitalia, display of genitalia, and use of the penis as a functional and probably humorous part of a vessel. The expression of sexual themes was through modeling, not painting.

THE FLORESCENT OR CLASSIC PERIOD

From approximately 200 B.C. to 600 A.D., most of the regions of Peru attained a technological and artistic zenith. During this time the erotic pottery also reached its peak both quantitatively and qualitatively, and was no longer confined exclusively to the northern coast.

Nazca

This culture, located on the southern coast of Peru, stressed painting more than modeling for ceramic decoration. Consequently, some sexuality is depicted solely by painting and in many of the modeled examples the limbs and other details are expressed by painting rather than modeling. Nevertheless, purely painted erotica were a definite minority.

Stylization is characteristic of Nazca art and, though some nonsexual vessels are decorated with intricate painting, the designs and depictions of the sexual ones tend to be simplified. The latter phases of the Nazca culture show a technological deterioration in the art.

In our sample we have twenty-four Nazca examples. The bulk of these, seventeen, depict genital display. Five are vessels in the form of a female; three of them have exaggerated genitalia. Two are bowls with female genitalia used on the exterior as designs. The clitoris is often shown and the pubic hair elaborated into geometric patterns. This use of female genitalia alone as a motif is uncommon in Peru. There are ten cases of male genital display: two are wholly painted, the others are modeled in the shape of a man. In seven instances the penis is erect and exaggerated; in two (the painted examples) the penis is flaccid but still exaggerated. In addition, there is one vessel in the shape of a nude male who may be masturbating or, possibly, displaying his partially erect normal-size penis.

There are no Naza vessels in our sample in which petting is shown.

There are six coital specimens, all the coitus being vaginal. No kissing or breast stimulation accompanies the coitus. In three cases the female is supine with the male prone on top of her
51 (Fig. 51); in one case the female is again supine, but the male kneels between her legs; and in another case the female is prone with the male prone on her back. All of these five are anthropomorphic vessels. The sixth specimen is a bowl with the figures painted in the interior bottom and with the genitalia alone in low relief. The coital position here is unusual: the figures lie supine with their heads in opposite directions while genital intromission is nevertheless maintained.

Maranga

On the central coast to the north of the Nazca area was the Maranga or Lima culture. Erotic pottery was extremely rare; our sample contains only two examples. One is a vessel in the form of a standing male holding or masturbating his erect penis, which is
52 a functional spout (Fig. 52). On the top of the second vessel is a female on her side with exposed and emphasized genitalia; the male with whom she was having coitus has been broken away, so that only his feet, hands, and a trace of penis remain. The coitus was anal rather than vaginal. The themes and general treatment lead me to suspect that these two pieces may have been inspired by the adjacent Mochica culture to the north.

Recuay

The first sexual pottery to be found in the Peruvian highlands occurs in the northern highlands in the Recuay culture, also known as the Copa or Huaylas. All examples are modeled, generally with supplementary painting. The modeling is ordinarily crude, the bodies being rather amorphous and the limbs noodle-like. We have record of eleven sexual vessels. There are two instances of male genital display which might have been excluded from the study, since the genitalia are not exaggerated even though they are prominently shown and may be partially erect. Aside from these two, all nine other examples represent vaginal coitus.

The Recuay seem to have had a near monopoly on one type of anthropomorphic vessel. The male and female, both fully clothed, appear to copulate in a seated position facing one another, with the hands on one another's shoulders or arms. There are five such vessels in our sample (Fig. 53). Of the remaining four sexual 53 scenes, only one merits particular note. The Recuay very frequently had several modeled figures on top of their vessels and sometimes these figures are under an arbor or canopy. The specimen in question shows a couple in coitus under such a canopy while surrounded by four female spectators. This is the only example in our entire collection of voyeuristic bystanders. One wonders if they represented the audience at ceremonial coitus or merely servants waiting at a discreet distance. Of the remaining coital vessels, two have the female supine with the male squatting between her legs, and one has the female supine with the male prone atop.

Mochica

This culture, once known as Early Chimu, of the northern coast of Peru has by far the greatest amount of sexual pottery. It is difficult to estimate the number, but assuming that the Larco-

Hoyle collection and the museums of Lima and Trujillo contain at least half of the known specimens, the grand total would be in the vicinity of eight hundred. The sample upon which this study is based consists of four hundred and fifty-six specimens. The general consensus of those authorities whom I questioned is that less than 1 percent of the Mochica vessels are sexual in nature and that these are found almost exclusively as funerary offerings in graves. However, one must recall that the majority of reasonably intact vessels also come from graves. Interestingly enough, the age and gender of the deceased seem to have no connection with the presence or absence of erotic ceramics in the grave. Another complicating factor is this: If one shatters a sexual vessel into one hundred pieces and enumerates them separately, one has perhaps ninety-eight nonsexual shreds while only the remaining two bear the critical sexual representations. If less than 1 percent of the vessels were sexual to begin with and if breakage thus serves to reduce the apparent number of sexual vessels, it is not surprising that fragments with sexual motifs are not reported from habitation sites.

Virtually all of the Mochica sexual pottery is modeled. While there are some bowls and plates, most vessels are rectangular or globular in shape and equipped with a spout; such vessels consequently have an upper surface area supporting modeled figures as well as the spout. In our sample most of the vessels had modeled figures on their tops, while in a substantial minority the entire vessel was in anthropomorphic form. Painting was often added as a supplement but was seldom important in delineating anatomical features. The modeling was far superior to that of any other prehistoric Peruvian culture, and some of it must be rated excellent in terms of realism and artistic skill. It proved impossible to distinguish wholly handmade vessels from those made by the usual Mochica two-piece mold and subsequently "touched up" by hand.

The Mochica sexual themes may be categorized in various ways, but I have found it most convenient and analytically profitable to formulate seven categories based on the type of sexual activity depicted.

GENITAL DISPLAY

Thirty-four examples, or 8 percent of all the Mochica vessels, are in this category. These depicted individuals not engaged in activity with anyone and not masturbating, but simply displaying their exaggerated and/or erect genitalia. A simple nude with normal-size genitalia not in a tumescent state would not be classed as a case of genital display unless some unusual posture focused attention upon the genitals.

There were ten instances of male display, including two cadavers, and the individual was alone in six of the ten cases. The penis was of exaggerated size in three specimens. It was partly erect in four, fully erect in another four, and in two cases breakage prevented judgment.

While I did not include them in this study, mention should be made at this point of the numerous depictions of nude prisoners of war. These seated men have ropes around their necks, and while their phalli are not tumescent, seven such specimens merit note here because the terminal end of the rope is in the form of a snake head biting the captive's penis. Perhaps this symbolized the anguish and emasculation of captivity.

Of the twenty-four examples of female genital display, fourteen belonged to a highly distinctive form of vessel—a bowl at the bottom of which lies a supine female with a gaping vulva. One is reminded of a woman lying in a large bathtub. The female does not constitute the bottom of the bowl; there is space beneath her. Hence any fluid poured into the bowl runs down through the vulva and into the reservoir beneath, and conversely when one pours from the vessel the fluid flows from the vulva (Fig. 54). 54
Four other vessels were in the form of females whose vulva served as the spout. In the remaining six cases the displayed genitalia were not functional apertures. Genitalia were exaggerated

in eighteen cases (the bowl and vulvar spout specimens described above). The clitoris was usually carefully depicted; this clitoral recognition is unusual in the ancient or primitive art elsewhere in the world.

MASTURBATION

There are eighteen Mochica vessels (or 4 percent of the sexual examples) showing self-masturbation by males. In all but two instances the individual is alone; in the two exceptions the male was with a female. Cadavers outnumber living males by a margin of three specimens. It is noteworthy that, although cadavers are often shown petting with women, their female partners never fellate them or have coitus with them.

In half of the cases in which it was possible to ascertain the size of the penis, it was exaggeratedly large. The phalli were fully erect in all but one case in which the erection was partial.

I labeled as masturbation any instance in which a male had one or both hands grasping his penis. Where one hand was used,
55 it was generally the right hand (Fig. 55). In those cases in which both hands were used, especially if they seemed to be supporting an exaggerated penis, there is the possibility that the Mochica artisan intended to depict genital display rather than self-masturbation. There are no cases of female masturbation in our sample, and I have heard of only one or two possible but dubious specimens. However, Larco alludes to female masturbation.[5]

HETEROSEXUAL PETTING

A relatively large number (22 percent) of Mochica vessels depict heterosexual petting. The individuals involved are generally seated side by side in close contact. One arm of each person is used for embrace and the other arm is free for manipulative

[5] Larco-Hoyle, *op. cit.*, p. 110.

activity. The embracing arms are often concealed behind the bodies. The female is shown as masturbating the male (in 49 percent of the petting specimens) far more often than the reverse (10 percent). Mutual masturbation is rare (2 percent). The male being masturbated frequently cups the female's chin in his hand (Fig. 56), an affectionate gesture still employed by Peruvian Indian 56
males. Such chin holding appears to be a Mochica and Chimu monopoly, and occurs in 21 percent of the petting specimens.

Kissing is also depicted, but this is always tongue-kissing, the insertion of the tongue into the other's mouth or the touching of tongues. Tongue-kissing occurs in 12 percent of the petting scenes. Tongue-kissing appears to be a feature only of the Mochica pottery. Stimulation by the male of the female breast, so standard a technique in our culture, is uncommon among the Mochica; only 9 percent of the vessels depicting petting show breast stimulation. One particular type of vessel showing a cadaver tongue-kissing a female consistently has the cadaver manipulating her breast (Fig. 57). All Mochica breast stimulation is manual; no 57
cases of oral stimulation are known to me.

Not infrequently more than two people are involved in petting scenes; some 76 percent of the Mochica ceramics with a petting theme represent two persons, and 25 percent three. There are no cases of four or more participants. Cadavers seem peculiarly prone to group petting; at least one cadaver is involved in every instance! There are no cases of three petters in which all participants are living humans. Curiously enough, where three individuals are represented, as a rule only two are engaged in petting while the third sits passively by doing nothing more than maintaining body contact with the person of the opposite sex. If the non-functional member of the trio is male, he may, on rare occasions, masturbate himself. In the trios, the central individual is always a female if the other two are male, or a male if the other two are female (Fig. 58). The petters are always grouped together; in our sample 58
there were no cases of one person off by himself or herself. In only one instance was an infant, sleeping, present in a petting scene.

It is most interesting that in the petting portrayals a cadaver male and a living female are the commonest participants, constituting the majority of the examples (37 percent). Second commonest is a living couple (26 percent). Third is a cadaver male with one or more cadaver females (24 percent). Fourth is a living female with two cadaver males (5 percent). Other combinations are rare.

The participants in petting are often clothed, but if only one is nude it is always the female. Cadavers are ordinarily nude or wearing a hooded cloak which covers the back but leaves the front of the body bare. In 25 percent of the cases the degree of male nudity could not be ascertained, and the same was true of females. Males were completely nude in 16 percent of the cases, whereas 32 percent of the females were nude. Some 25 percent of the males were fully clothed and somewhat more (34 percent) of the females. In 30 percent of the males, but in none of the females, the torso was nude but the pelvis clothed. Seven percent of the females wore a cloak which left the ventral surface of the body nude; no males were thus cloaked. One couple was petting under a blanket.

HETEROSEXUAL MOUTH-GENITAL CONTACT

Although a substantial number (8 percent) of the Mochica vessels portray fellation (that is, female mouth on penis) not one example of cunnilingus (male mouth on female genitalia) is known to me. Larco-Hoyle refers to cunnilingus in Mochica pottery,[6] but no examples could be found in his collection and a subsequent published statement of his suggests that he simply inferred that this technique existed among the Mochica.[7]

[6] Rafael Larco-Hoyle, "A Culture Sequence for the North Coast of Peru," in J. Steward (ed.), *Handbook of South American Indians* (Washington, D.C.: Bureau of American Ethnology, Bulletin 143), II, 174.

[7] *Checan*, p. 81. In discussing the humorous false-bottomed bowls, in which fluid pours from a vulva, he says, "These vessels show that the Mochica practiced cunnilinctus."

The male is seated in 60 percent of the cases of fellation, standing in 5 percent, and lying on his back or side in 34 percent. If he is lying, the female with him is almost always fully represented, but if he is seated or standing, only her body from the waist up may be depicted and she appears to be embedded in (or arising from) the floor (Fig. 59). I believe this to be an 59
artistic short cut, eliminating that portion of the female's body not necessary to the sexual action. This "half a woman" convention occurs in 70 percent of the depictions of fellation, being commonest in instances in which the male is seated. The female often grasps the male's legs, less often his penis, and he may hold or touch her head. There are but two instances of more than two persons in any fellation scene, and here the extra figures are infants. Evidently mouth-genital contact was more a private matter than coitus or petting.

Cadavers are virtually never involved in fellation; there are no portrayals of a male cadaver fellated by a living female, and only one shows a female cadaver fellating a living male. No fellation occurs between cadavers.

In all but 7 percent of the fellation depictions it was possible to ascertain the degree of nudity on the part of the male. In 28 percent of the ascertainable cases he was completely nude; in 20 percent he wore only a pelvic covering; in 9 percent only his upper torso was covered; and in 43 percent he was fully clothed.

It was often difficult to determine whether the females were nude or not, as their body surfaces were frequently smooth and without detail. In only about half of the cases could one be reasonably certain as to the degree of nudity. In this ascertainable group, about 70 percent of the females were wholly nude, 26 percent were fully clothed, and the remaining 4 percent wore only a cloak which was open in the front.

I should add that there are no examples of self-fellation, but the concept was not unknown, for at least one vessel depicts an animal in this activity.

COITUS

Heterosexual coitus was the most popular sexual theme of the Mochica potter, comprising some 39 percent of all the vessels with sexual content. Despite its popularity, the positions and situations depicted are surprisingly limited. No more than two individuals, aside from an occasional infant, are portrayed. Infants, sometimes suckling, lie by the female's side in 24 percent of the coital scenes
60 (Fig. 60). The coitus takes place upon either a bed or some nondescript smooth surface; one gains the impression that it was indoors. No coitus in unusual situations was illustrated, and despite the prevalence of throne-like chairs in fellation scenes, such chairs were never utilized for coitus. The coital positions are somewhat restricted; five account for virtually all of the specimens. The coital positions shown are:

1. Female supine, male prone on top of her (9 percent).
2. Female on her side, male behind her lying on his side, spoon fashion (29 percent).
3. Female on her side, male either lying partially on top of her or squatting by her buttocks; in either case vaginal or anal penetration is from the rear (9 percent).
4. Female supine, male kneeling or squatting between her legs (9 percent).
5. Female kneeling or on all fours with the male squatting or standing behind her (18 percent).
6. Female prone with the male prone on her back or squatting behind her buttocks (18 percent).
7. Male supine with the female on top of him either squatting or seated (3 percent).
8. Both seated, face to face (2 percent).
9. Other positions, chiefly unclassified variations of the above, account for only 4 percent.

There were no instances of coitus with both partners standing, or with both seated with the female's back to the male, or with both kneeling face to face, or with both lying on their sides facing each other. This paucity of positions makes one wonder whether those depicted were not in actuality the positions in general use.

Essentially all of the coitus occurs between living males and females. In only two instances in our sample is there coitus between a living female and a cadaver male. In a handful of cases the female's partner is either a supernatural being or a masked man, probably the former. Living males do not copulate with cadaver females, and cadavers never engage in coitus with one another.

Coitus generally occurs with the female nude, except perhaps for a broad necklace and sometimes a head covering. This is true in 75 percent of the cases. The male, on the contrary, is completely nude in only 12 percent of the scenes. In 38 percent of the scenes he wears a pelvic covering resembling modern jockey shorts or else some breech clout; the garment is pulled aside to let the penis protrude. In some cases (20 percent) he is fully clothed, and in fewer still (6 percent) his torso is covered by a garment while the lower part of his body is nude. Females are rarely fully clothed; only one example exists. One female had her torso nude but her pelvis covered, and two (1 percent) had the torso clothed but the pelvis nude. The degree of nudity of some couples is obscured by the fact that copulation occurs under a blanket, but the blanket is, in every case but one, so arranged that the genitalia are visible. Even in this one case, where the blanket covers the pelvic areas of both partners, the artist has carefully shown the outline of the penis and vulva under the fabric. Males are blanket-covered in 10 percent of the cases, females in 11 percent.

Two males (1 percent) were depicted wearing a cloak which left the ventral surface of the body nude; no females were thus clothed, although a few females wore cloaks in petting scenes.

Ascertaining the degree of nudity of the coital partners is not always easy, owing to the frequent absence of details, the inability to differentiate between a bracelet and a cuff, and similar ambiguities. Some 13 percent of the males and 11 percent of the females could not be categorized as to degree of nudity.

Whereas in our culture coitus is frequently accompanied by kissing, the reverse is true in Mochica pottery. Neither kissing nor breast manipulation during coitus is depicted, despite the fact that both techniques do occur in the portrayals of petting. Not only is kissing conspicuous by its absence; the heads of the coital partners are usually some distance apart, so that even cheek contact is seldom seen. This disinterest in body contact is indicated by many of the coital postures in which only the genital areas are touching. Moreover, the female frequently is not embracing the male, and he, like as not, uses his hands and arms, not to clasp
61 her, but to maintain his posture (Fig. 61). One is left with the impression that to the Mochica coitus was strictly a genital affair.

One of the most interesting aspects of the Mochica depictions of coitus is that 21 percent is anal rather than vaginal. This is a minimum figure, since I counted only those instances in which the
62 penis could be seen entering the anus (Fig. 62). In a number of other cases the body postures suggested anal coitus but the genitalia were either concealed or not clearly modeled. At one time I thought that perhaps this high incidence of anal coitus was an artistic device whereby one could show female genitalia and coitus simultaneously; the obscuring of the erotically interesting vulva and penis by the act of vaginal coitus has always posed a problem for pornographers. Now I am not so sure; anal coitus may in fact have been quite prevalent, probably as a contraceptive measure, and this, coupled with the lack of manual stimulation of the female by the male, may explain the disinterest which many females seem to display in the activity.

Speaking of disinterest, it is noteworthy that neither male nor female seems to be particularly excited. The faces are sober, placid, or solemn. There are no closed eyes, smiles, open mouths, or orgasmically contorted faces. This same sobriety is characteristic of the portrayals of fellation. Yet all these expressions were within the technological powers of the artist. Indeed, in several vessels showing male masturbation the man is grinning, and a few depictions of petting show some facial animation.

There is diversity in the degree of female participation.

Whereas some lie passively, cooperating only in assuming a coital posture, others grasp the male or clasp their legs about him. A few facilitate intromission by guiding the penis or by spreading their buttocks. Some seeming female passivity stems from the fact that if the male is behind her there is little she can do beyond maintain a suitable position. Gestures of rejection are extremely rare and not clearly identifiable as such; there may be two or three cases in which the female seems to be pushing the male away.

Although artistic license with regard to body size confuses the issue, there is no clear evidence of coitus between adults and children. This absence of pedophilia seems to be true of all other forms of sexual activity.[8] There is also no sadism, masochism, or voyeurism in Mochica coital scenes. The only theme in which a third person is witness to coitus is one which can scarcely be called voyeurism: a bird-headed man is throwing a bowl of fluid at the copulating couple.

HOMOSEXUALITY

In all of the hundreds of Mochica vessels with sexual themes only two illustrate male homosexuality. One instance consists of a male lying on his side while a male cadaver lies behind him, spoon fashion, and apparently has anal coitus or at least presses his penis against the living male's buttocks. However, this vessel has another unique feature: the male's eyes are closed and Larco-Hoyle may be correct in suggesting that the scene represents a homosexual dream.[9]

One other vessel depicts two cadavers lying prone, side by side, with an arm around each other and tongue-kissing. This kissing is remarkable since one of the pair is simultaneously play-

[8] *Checan*, p. 122, agrees that pedophilia is absent. There is occasionally a discrepancy in the size of the male and the female, but in only one instance is this marked enough to suggest child-adult contact. This is a case in which an adult female is masturbating a very small supine male—possibly a child.

[9] *Checan*, p. 112.

ing on a set of panpipes. The cadavers are dressed like males.

Female homosexuality is completely absent and there are no specimens which even hint at it.

ANIMAL CONTACT

Sexual contact between humans and animals is commonplace in the mythologies and jokes of many peoples, but such depictions are virtually nonexistent in Mochica ceramic art. A few females are shown with creatures having animal heads and human bodies, but these, one assumes, are supernaturals or masked men, not animals. I know of only one rather clear case and one probable case of human sexual contact with an animal, and in both instances the human is female.

The first represents a seated woman cuddling against, and probably embracing, a penguin-like bird as large as she. One of her hands is in the area of the bird's genitalia. The total position is the same as that found in human petting scenes.

The second is a vessel currently in the Chicago Art Museum. Larco-Hoyle illustrates it and discusses it.[10] A female is shown lying on her back with her legs spread and her genitalia visible. A huge dog stands over her with his forepaws on her shoulders and his rear paws on her thighs, as though he were holding her legs apart. His penis is broken, but the stump is oriented toward the woman's vulva, which appears to contain a fragment of the penis. Larco-Hoyle thinks this vessel may represent a woman who has been knocked down by a dog, but her spread-open legs, the detail with which her genitalia are depicted, and the evident tumescence of the dog's penis make one believe the scene is sexual.

One must be careful not to confuse sexuality and combat. One vessel, which I at first assumed represented an animal copulating with a woman, on closer inspection clearly showed that the animal was satisfying not his sexual appetite but his hunger.

[10] *Checan;* cf. footnote on p. 34 and illustration on p. 126.

ANIMAL SEXUAL BEHAVIOR

In addition to depicting humans, the Mochica potters also showed animals in sexual activity. The great majority of scenes (over 90 percent) are coital and the animals are generally mammals (Fig. 63). Most of the mammals were quadrupeds which I could not identify; they could have been deer, llamas, vicuñas, or similar ungulates. Some of the vaguer, more generalized ones could have been dogs. Concerning the coital depictions, some 27 percent of the animals were unidentifiable quadrupeds; 13 percent were llamas; 16 percent were rats or mice; 19 percent were frogs or toads; and 19 percent were mythological creatures. One pair of jaguars, one pair of crustaceans, and one mixed couple complete the census. 63

The positions are generally appropriate to the species, but in a few instances the coitus is shown with one animal supine and the other prone on top in human fashion.

No fellation occurs, aside from one instance of self-fellation; masturbation is very rare; and genital exhibition is uncommon.

NONBEHAVIORAL SEXUALITY

About 8 percent of the Mochica sexual vessels did not illustrate sexual activity but were nevertheless sexual in nature. Most of them, about a dozen, were vessels with vertical spouts in the shape of a penis. Several of the phalli had been given a human face (just below the glans of the penis) and tiny arms, and four were holding their nostrils—a crude allusion to genital odor (Fig. 64). 64 An almost equal number of specimens, which I label "phallic persons," exist. These are representations of men, and possibly a woman in one instance, generally in a kneeling position with a headdress which, if viewed from the rear, is seen to be a glans penis. Somewhat similar are two vessels showing a person, beating a drum, whose hair falls over his face with only the tip of his nose protruding—the whole arrangement suggesting female genitalia.

There are four clay whistles of phallic shape, two vessels are beautifully executed representations of male and female genitalia, and a third vessel has a penis draped over the top. A few miscellaneous specimens constitute the remainder.

HUMOR

Although not one of the basic categories used in this study, a record was made of specimens that seemingly had a humorous value for the Mochica. About 15 percent of the ceramics were humorous—most of them falling into the categories of genital display and nonbehavioral sexuality, and a few concerned with masturbation and petting.

The commonest form of humor centered on having a person drink from a penis or a vulva. There are vessels with vertical spouts in the shape of a penis, and there are male figures displaying or masturbating phalli which serve as functional spouts. In some (perhaps five to ten) instances the drinker was forced to use the penis spout because the rim of the larger aperture through
65 which the vessel was filled was perforated (Fig. 65).

The female counterpart consists of bowls (fourteen in our sample) with a recumbent nude female in the bottom forming a false bottom, the fluid flowing through the gaping vulva. A few other vessels with vulvar apertures are in our collection.

The "phallic persons" described under nonbehavioral sexuality and the phallic whistles are patently humorous.

In addition to these obvious items of humor, there are other instances of what may have been humorous to the Mochica. Some specimens consist of two vessels linked in Siamese-twin fashion, or a single vessel with two internal compartments, which when filled with fluid and tilted produce a vacuum in one vessel or chamber as the fluid flows into the other. The vacuum sucks air through a specially made aperture, producing a moaning whistling sound. When such whistling vessels, as they are called, depict coitus, the combination may have been motivated by a sense of humor. Other possibly humorous specimens are those in which the genitalia are grossly exaggerated although not functional spouts or apertures. Also possibly humorous are a few individuals engaged in self-masturbation, genital display, or petting and shown with facial expressions suggesting hilarious enjoyment or mental deficiency. All such individuals are male and none are in the act of coitus, which was evidently a more serious matter not subject to levity.

THE FUSIONAL OR TIAHUANACO PERIOD

After the Classic Period, with its well-defined and distinctive cultures, Peru entered a period of artistic and technological deterioration and there is reason to believe that the era was marked by political confusion. A unifying influence was the spread of one art style over all of Peru. This style, which originated in Bolivia and the southern highlands of Peru, is associated with the Tiahuanaco culture, and the extent and rapidity of its spread suggest that it was also associated with a religion. In many ways one is reminded of the fall of Rome and the spread of Christianity with its technically inferior art style.

During this Fusional Period, which extended from 600 A.D. to 1100 A.D., sexual art suffered a marked decline in quantity and quality. The Tiahuanaco culture produced no sexual ceramics and the spread of the Tiahuanaco art style must have discouraged erotica. Indeed, the style itself is not hospitable to erotica, since figures are treated in an extremely conventionalized and simplified manner, often being reduced to angular geometric designs.

Huara

One culture on the northern coast, the Huara, reflected the collapse of the Mochica and the dominance of Tiahuanaco art. In our sample there are only five sexual vessels. Four of then represent vaginal coitus with the female supine and the male prone on top. There is no kissing or breast manipulation. The typical

Mochica spouts are gone, and in these examples the male's hat serves as the neck of the vessel or else a large funnel-like neck or spout emerges from his back. The modeling is very crude, the
66 bodies resembling potatoes with thin limbs (Fig. 66). Three of the four vessels are painted as well as modeled. Degree of nudity can be ascertained in only two instances, in which it appears that the female is fully clothed. The one remaining Huara vessel is modeled with a skill not much inferior to the Mochica and portrays a male monkey in self-masturbation.

Huari (Wari)

In the northern highlands, the Huari culture is represented in our sample by ten vessels. Seven of these are similar and very distinctive, sharing the following traits:

1. Coitus occurs with the female supine and the male prone on top.
2. One or both wear a garment which radiates feather-like projections much like a full-length Plains Indian war bonnet. These projections often terminate in serpent heads.
3. Generally little monkey-like animals surround the couple.
4. Headdresses or coiffures are elaborate.

These curious and somehow vaguely ceremonial scenes occur only on the sides of the globular vessels in bas-relief; they were prob-
67 ably mold-made (Fig. 67). At least two are very crudely executed, so that the first impression is of copulating centipedes, but the others are clearer.

I have the feeling that these vessels derive from the earlier Mochica examples, again always in bas-relief on the sides of vessels, showing a female in coitus with a deity or masked man with a fair amount of surrounding detail suggestive of ritual. The Mochica deity also wears an elaborate headdress. One other Huari-Mochica similarity occurs in these vessels: in two of the seven, the male holds the female's chin in his hand. All seven vessels are bottles with globular bodies and central spouts.

The remaining three Huari vessels consist of one crude vessel in the form of a man grasping his exaggerated erect penis which forms a spout, one depiction of llama coitus, and one portrayal of toad coitus. All of these are, of course, continuations of Mochica themes.

Ica

One Ica, or possibly Chincha, vessel is in our sample. It is in the shape of a squatting female with tiny protuberant conical breasts and with a huge pubic area. The vulva is gaping to reveal a large clitoris and a circular vaginal aperture. To be frank, I am not persuaded that this is an Ica product, but I have accepted the museum's attribution.

Lambayeque

Toward the end of the Fusional Period on the northern coast, the Tiahuanaco influence was largely cast off or assimilated and a renewal of old Mochica motifs occurred. This revival is best seen in the Lambayeque culture, though the modeling is inferior to that of the Mochica and there is less use of painting. The stirrup spout, so popular among the Mochica, is less common in the Lambayeque, in which a long tapering spout with a bridge leading to a figure is the favorite type. An unusually large percentage of the Lambayeque sexual ceramics are whistling vessels (32 percent).

Of our total of thirty-seven Lambayeque vessels, eighteen depict human coitus. Of these, at least five seem to be instances of anal coitus. The commonest position, represented by seven examples, is with the female kneeling and the standing or squatting male having coitus from the rear. Three specimens show the female supine with the male prone on top, and another three display the female on her side with the male prone or squatting

on top of her (or slightly to one side), making penetration from the rear. Two vessels show the female prone with the male crouched behind her; two show the female supine with the male
68 squatting or kneeling between her legs (Fig. 68). Only one vessel represents both the male and the female having coitus on their sides, spoon fashion.

Fellation of the male by the female is the second commonest portrayal. We have seven examples. In four the male is prone; in three he stands. In three instances the male is much smaller than the female. The penis is always exaggeratedly large and thick, a trait not usual among the Mochica.

Male genital display and/or masturbation accounts for five examples, four of which are in the form of men, while the fifth is a vessel with a penis spout. Three of the four vessels in the form of men have the usual enormous penis serving as a spout and the perforated rim (formed by their hats) forcing the use of the spout for drinking.

Animal coitus is represented by four vessels, of which two depict a mythical creature wearing a hat or crown and copulating with a toad.

One bottle shaped like an erect phallus and one vague petting scene complete the inventory.

In summary, Lambayeque conforms to the Mochica tradition; no activity is represented that was not in the earlier culture.

CITY-BUILDER PERIOD

By 1100 A.D. the Tiahuanaco influence was gone and there was a renaissance of local Peruvian cultures accompanied by an increase in construction and, evidently, an increase in population. This period existed until roughly 1400 A.D., when Inca domination put an end to it. Although many traditions and old styles were revived, erotic art did not regain the prevalence it had during the Classic Period. For all practical purposes, it was confined to the Chimu culture of the northern coast, the traditional stronghold of Peruvian erotic art. However, a few examples also occur in the Chancay culture of the adjacent central coast.

Chancay

There are eleven Chancay items in our sample. Eight are not vessels but large hollow figurines. These are extremely simplified and remind one of gingerbread men. All are standing with outstretched arms, but the arms are so short that the hands seem to issue from the shoulders. These nude figurines would not be classed as erotic were it not for two features. First, the genitalia are carefully depicted in detail, whereas other body parts are given summary treatment or ignored. Second, the penis is partially or fully erect in three of the four male figurines. There are three female figurines, two with the clitoris depicted and the third with a somewhat emphasized genital area. The genitalia are not exaggerated in size. Aside from these crude and stereotyped figurines, we have three vessels. One is rather well modeled but fragmentary, consisting of a seated male with an erect penis of normal diameter protruding upward beyond the waist of his pelvic cover. This vessel has a stirrup spout. The second is a unique double vessel portraying, crudely, a seated male with an enormous penis. A female with her back to the male sits astride this great penis, the head of which protrudes beyond her. The third vessel has on its side, modeled in full round, a male being fellated by a much smaller female (Fig. 69). 69

Chimu

The great kingdom of the Chimu took up the old erotic tradition of the Mochica, a tradition kept alive in feeble form by the Huara and Lambayeque during the anti-erotic Fusional Period. The

Mochica technological excellence was never equaled and many of the former variations were not revived, but there was a rebirth of sexual ceramics along generally pre-established lines.

In keeping with Chimu pottery characteristics, most of these vessels are unpainted black ware, frequently made by mold rather than by hand. We have 111 examples.

The majority (50 percent) of the vessels portray coitus between a man and a woman. Cadavers, so prominent in Mochica art, vanished with that culture, and masked men or supernaturals no longer appear. Coitus, in brief, is confined to living humans. By far the commonest position is that with the female supine and the male prone on top. The second most frequent is with the female on her side with the male behind her, and about equally frequent is the position in which the female is on her side but the male is on top of her making entry from the rear. This is a coital repertoire even more limited than that of the Mochica. The presence of an infant, rather common among the Mochica, is seen on only two vessels. One variety of coital scene is unique to the Chimu: modeled atop a vessel, a single male lies on his side between two adult (or at least nubile) supine females, having coitus with one of them. There are a number of such examples, and the neglected female is not sleeping, for her eyes are open. It is possible that the neglected female represents a grown daughter, and perhaps among the Chimu adolescent daughters slept with their mothers. Adolescent sons are never depicted sharing the marital bed.

The old gesture of holding the female's chin is seen again on occasion, but the Chimu depart from Mochica tradition by frequently depicting kissing during coitus in the common position. Actually this is not kissing in the usual sense; the male is kissing or mouthing the female's chin as she bends her head back.

Anal coitus occurs, but less often than among the Mochica.

Heterosexual petting is shown on eighteen vessels (16 percent of the total), consisting of embracing and/or masturbation. The female generally masturbates the male. No breast stimulation occurs. In marked contrast to the Mochica, there is no fellation. The absence of mouth-genital contact is remarkable, since it was a major Mochican theme and one which carried over into the Lambayeque culture immediately antecedent to the Chimu. In five examples there is the theme, just described, of a male lying between two females. But here the erect penis is not in the vagina; hence these vessels were placed in the petting category (Fig. 70). 70

There is no homosexuality, and no vessels represent sexual contact between humans and animals. One vessel showing of a jaguar atop a man appeared at first glance to be sexual, but on closer inspection the jaguar was seen to be satisfying his gustatory rather than his sexual appetite.

Nine vessels (8 percent) were classed as genital exhibition, all male. The humorous exploitation of female genitalia, as in the Mochican false-bottomed bowls, has vanished.

Male masturbation is represented by eighteen vessels (16 percent); no female examples are known.

Only three vessels (2.7 percent of the total) illustrate animal coitus; this is an unexpectedly small number, since proportionately more occur in the preceding Lambayeque culture and the following Chimu-Inca culture.

One curious small vessel consists of a bottle-like vessel representing the testes from which protrudes a large phallus. At the base of the phallus is a shield-like affair through which the phallus protrudes—much like the guards on modern douche nozzles which prevent too deep insertion. This is no douche, however, since the phallus is imperforate.

Lastly, six zoomorphic vessels (5 percent of the total) consists of a mythological quadruped with a face covered with circular warts and chevron-shaped stripes which issue from the nose and run down the cheeks. This creature is variously depicted as exhibiting his erect penis or masturbating or, in one case, fellating himself. Not included as being sexual are two such creatures shown sucking their tails.

Chimu-Inca

After the Inca conquered the Chimu, some sexual pottery continued to be made for a time. We have twenty-seven examples.

By far the commonest sexual activity was human coitus, depicted in twenty vessels. Three are anthropomorphic bowls with the male prone upon the supine female. The bodies are crudely
71 formed, resembling two potatoes lying on one another (Fig. 71). The kissing-during-coitus theme occurs in two of these three. On the tops of ten vessels are modeled figures showing the female kneeling and the male squatting behind her. Only one coital act appears to be anal. Two vessels carry on the earlier Chimu theme of the male on his side copulating with one female while another lies beside him. Three other vessels have modeled figures on top showing the female supine and the male kneeling between her legs, the male and female on their sides spoon fashion, and the female kneeling with the male kneeling behind her. Lastly, there are two anthropomorphic vessels, one with the female supine and the male prone on top and the other with the female supine and the male squatting between her legs. No infants share the bed with any of these couples.

Only one vessel depicts petting: a male lies on his side between two females, with his arms and legs on one, but his penis is not inserted.

One vessel is clearly humorous, consisting of a phallus with a human face and arms.

One anthropomorphic vessel of a male may be classed as genital display, since a vague bas-relief erect penis is visible.

The remaining four vessels are of animals. One shows two birds standing belly to belly with their heads upturned; the others illustrate copulating dogs, llamas, and two unidentifiable creatures.

Inca

With the conquest of all of Peru and immediately adjacent regions by the Inca, the production of ceramics with sexual themes came to an end. The Inca did not have a tradition of pottery decorated by modeling, and their painted decoration was predominantly geometric rather than representational. When life forms were depicted, they were almost exclusively floral or of nonhuman forms of life.

Although this could explain a reduction in human sexual representations, it does not explain why in the conquered areas there was not at least some persistence of sexual themes, since local ceramic traditions were not wholly supplanted. The answer seems to be that the Inca were opposed to sexual representations in any medium. This "anti-sexuality," if one can so term it, is suggested by various Spanish accounts which speak of the Inca as having been disturbed by local sexual mores, particularly those of the northern coast of Peru—the heartland of sexual ceramics.

SUMMARY

Sexual depictions in prehistoric Peru seem to have been confined to the ceramic medium. This statement cannot be made with much certainty, since textiles and wood rarely survived the corrosive soil of the northern coastal area, which was the major area for sexual representation. However, we do know that sexuality was never, or almost never, depicted in stone or metal. We also know that the textiles in central and southern Peru were similarly deficient. It would be important to know whether or not pottery was made by one gender and textiles by the other, since elsewhere in the world the males have a monopoly on the production of graphic erotica.

Sexual ceramics seem to have originated during the Formative Period on the northern coast of Peru and remained confined to that area during that time. The themes were few and simple: petting, vaginal coitus, genital display, and some humor.

In the following Classic Period, the northern-coast Mochica culture became Peru's greatest producer of sexual ceramics. More sexual themes were added to the repertoire: anal coitus, kissing, masturbation, fellation, coitus between animals, and even a tiny amount of homosexuality and human contact with animals. Probably owing to Mochica influence, some sexual ceramics appeared during this period along the central coast (Maranga culture), the southern coast (Nazca culture), and in the northern highlands (Recuay culture). However, it must be added that the Nazca treatment of sexuality is quite unlike that of the Mochica and a case could be argued for independent invention. The other cultures of Peru, and particularly those in the central and southern highlands, seem to lack erotic pottery.

The Fusional or Tiahuanaco Period saw the majority of indigenous Peruvian art styles drowned out by, or at least strongly diluted by, the artistic traditions of the Tiahuanaco culture of Bolivia. This art style may well have been connected with a religion that frowned upon sexual representation, and the angular, highly conventionalized nature of the style made it a less suitable medium for erotic presentation. In any case, sexual ceramics seem to have become extinct except in the northern coast and northern highlands. In the former, the Lambayeque culture preserved, in modified and aesthetically deteriorated form, many of the Mochica sexual themes.

With the subsequent City-Builder Period, the Peruvian cultures were emancipated from the domination of the Tiahuanaco style and there was a renaissance of Classic traditions. On the northern coast among the Chimu, the sexual pottery shared in this rebirth and became commoner, but the excellence of the Mochica wares and the diversity of themes were never recaptured. In terms of geographic distribution, the sexual ceramics seem to have lost ground; aside from a few borderline instances on the contiguous central coast, all examples seem confined to the northern coast in the Chimu culture.

In the fifteenth century the Inca completed their conquest of all of Peru. If sexual pottery was not already dead, one can assume that the Inca gave it the *coup de grâce.* Only in the Chimu area—an area which resisted the Inca stubbornly and successfully for years—did ceramic erotica persist, but eventually it died out. The demise must have antedated the conquistadors, who in their eagerness to ferret out sin would not have left erotica to languish unreported.

Despite the varied history of Peruvian sexual ceramics, they show a remarkable consistency in many respects. The basic themes were heterosexual coitus, petting, and genital display—the latter often including elements of humor. Upon this base the Mochica made additions and elaborations which tended to persist thereafter. The unity of the Peruvian ceramics can best be emphasized by pointing out a series of singular omissions:

1. Although male self-masturbation is shown, there is no clear instance of female masturbation.
2. Although coitus is a common theme, there is no group coitus.
3. Fellation of the male by the female is depicted, but never cunnilingus by the male on the female.
4. Mouth-genital contact between animals is not shown.
5. Homosexuality is represented by only two vague male examples, and we have no case of two living humans in homosexual contact. Female homosexuality is completely absent.
6. There are a few cases of females in sexual contact with animals, but no male is seen in such activity.
7. There is little lip kissing and no kissing of the breast.
8. There seem to be no paraphilias represented, such as sadomasochism (although torture scenes are not rare), pedophilia, or voyeurism.

This uniformity suggests to my mind that the depictions reflect the activities and taboos of the ancient Peruvians.

The study of this pottery, and here let us confine our attention to the Mochica culture which accounts for most of it, leaves one with a list of unanswered questions. The Mochica operated under what seems to us to be curious constraints. If living females petted with cadavers, why did they not engage in fellation or coitus with them? Why didn't cadavers have coitus or fellation with one another? Why are cadavers found only in the Mochica culture? Why are there no animal cadavers? Why do couples kiss, including tongue-kissing, during petting, but never during coitus? Why are the faces so bland when the Mochica were capable of depicting animated expressions? Why is virtually all of the sexual representation done by modeling, despite the fact that the Mochica were quite prolific in depicting nonsexual scenes in painting? These and still other questions may go forever unanswered, but the presence of the uniformities, the diversity of themes, and the unexpected omissions combine to make this a rich field for inferences and deductions which must stem from further and more intensive research.

TABLE 1

CULTURE AND PERIOD	Number of sexual ceramics in sample	Coitus	Anal coitus	Coitus in dorso-ventral position	Petting	Kissing	Breast stimulation	Fellation	Homosexuality	Human-animal sexual contact	Genital display	Sexual humor	Masturbation	Animal coitus	Cadavers
CITY-BUILDER PERIOD															
Chimu-Inca	27	X	X	X	X	X					X	X		X	
Chimu	111	X	X	X	X	X					X		X	X	
Chancay	10				X			X			X				
FUSIONAL PERIOD															
Lambayeque	37	X	X	X	X			X			X	X	X	X	
Huara	5	X													
Huari	10	X										X	X	X	
Ica	1										X				
CLASSIC PERIOD															
Mochica	456	X	X	X	X	X	X	X	–	–	X	X	X	X	X
Recuay	11	X									X				
Maranga	2		X	X								X	X		
Nazca	24	X									X	?	X		
FORMATIVE PERIOD															
Gallinazo	6										X	X			
Salinar	12	X			X		X				X				
Vicus	12?	X		X	X						X	X			

X = Present
– = Rare

TABLE 2
COITAL POSITIONS
(Calculated for cultures with over a dozen examples)

POSITION	CULTURE			
	Mochica	Lambayeque	Chimu	Chimu-Inca
	%	%	%	%
Female supine Male prone on top (V.V.)	9	17	65	20
Female on side Male on side (D.V.)	29	6	13	15
Female on side Male prone or squatting (D.V.)	9	17	13	0
Female supine Male kneeling or squatting (V.V.)	9	11	0	10
Female prone Male prone or squatting (D.V.)	18	11	5	0
Female sitting on top Male supine (V.V.)	3	0	0	0
Female sitting Male sitting (V.V.)	2	0	0	0
Other	4	0	0	0

V.V. = ventro-ventral or the ventral surfaces of the body together or facing.
D.V. = dorso-ventral. The back of the female toward the male so that entry is made from the rear.

FIGURES

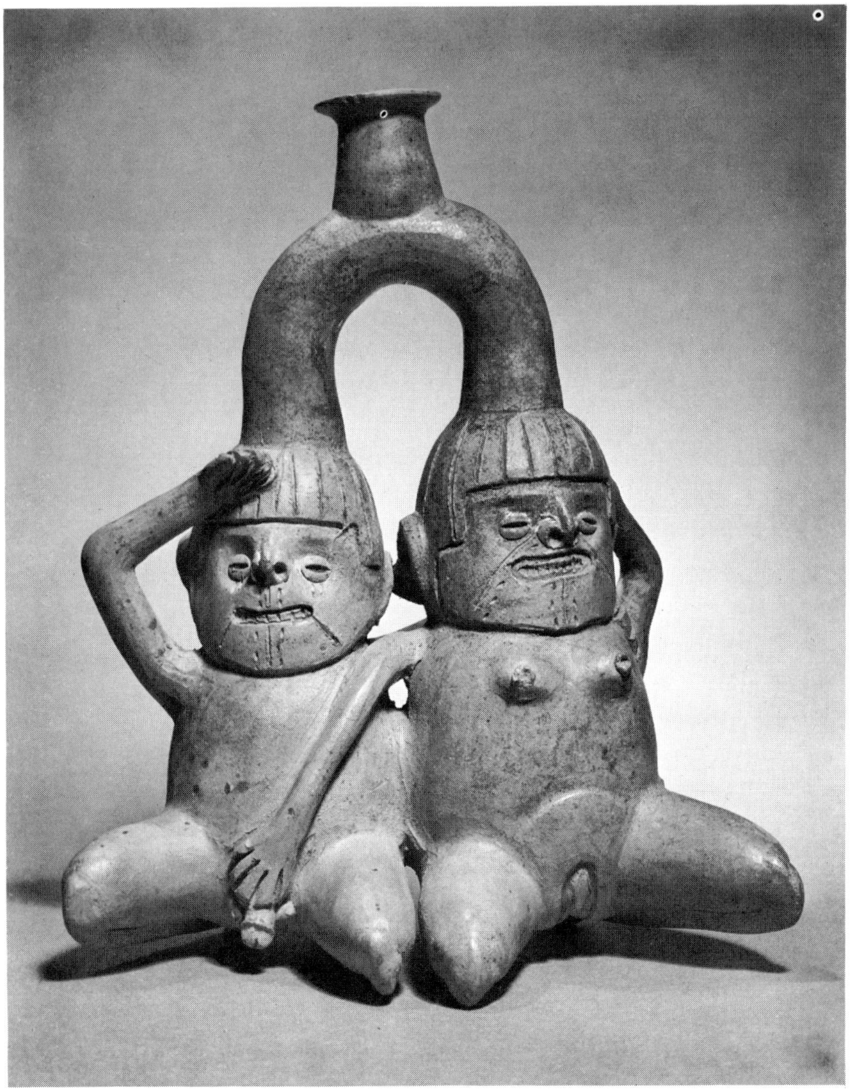

49. Petting. Salinar culture.

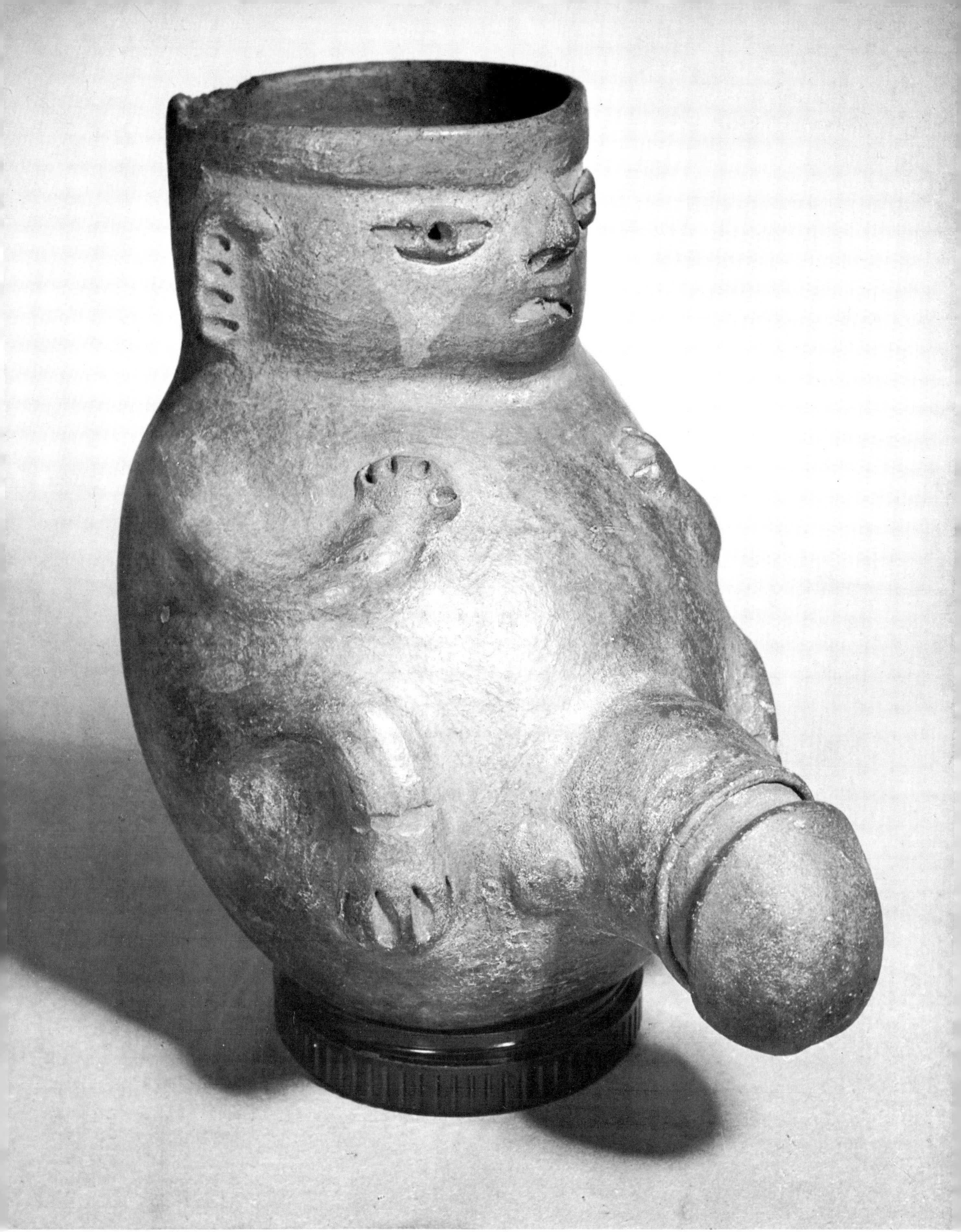

50. Genital display. Gallinazo culture.

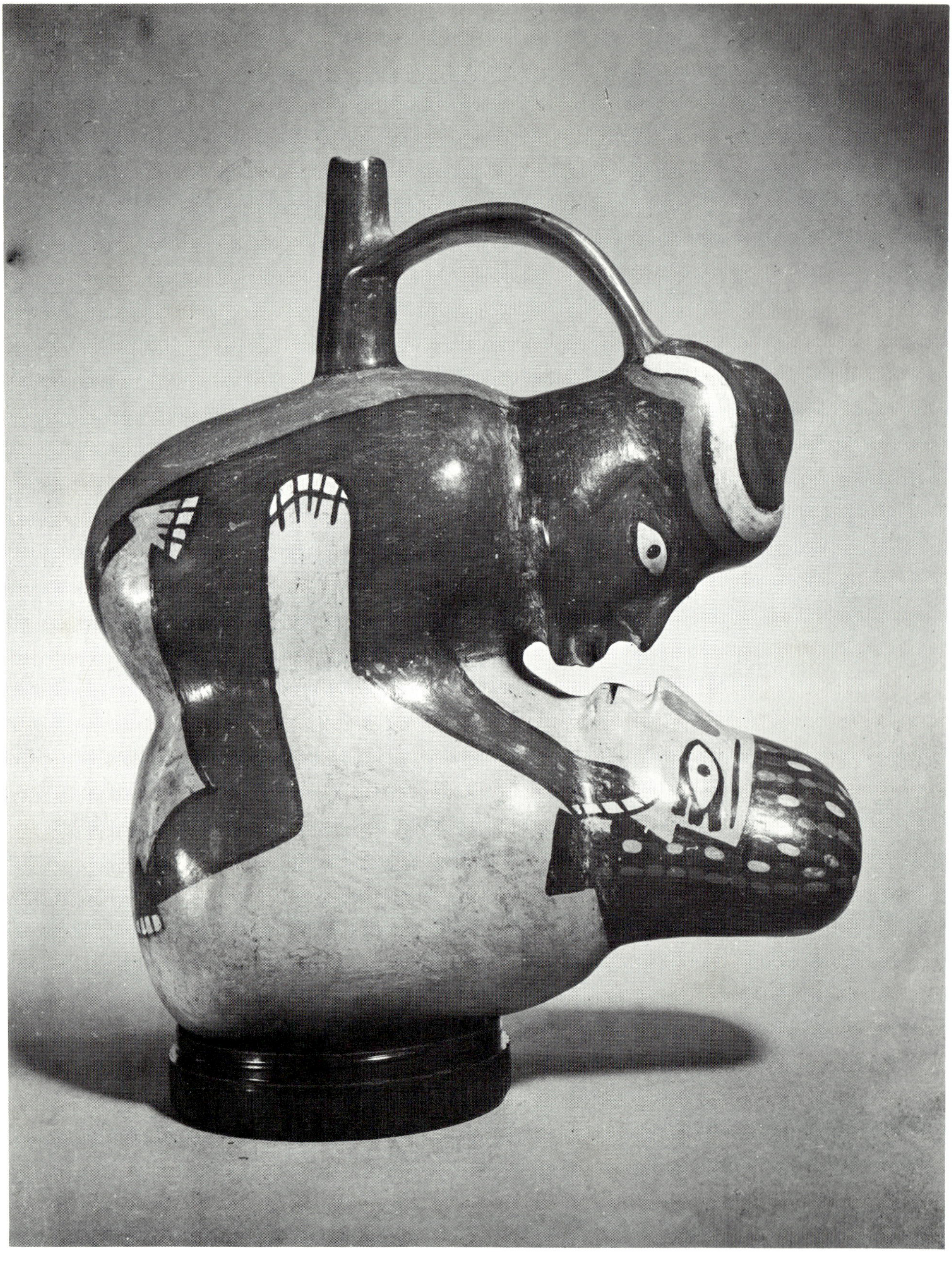

51. Coitus. Female supine, male prone. Nazca culture.

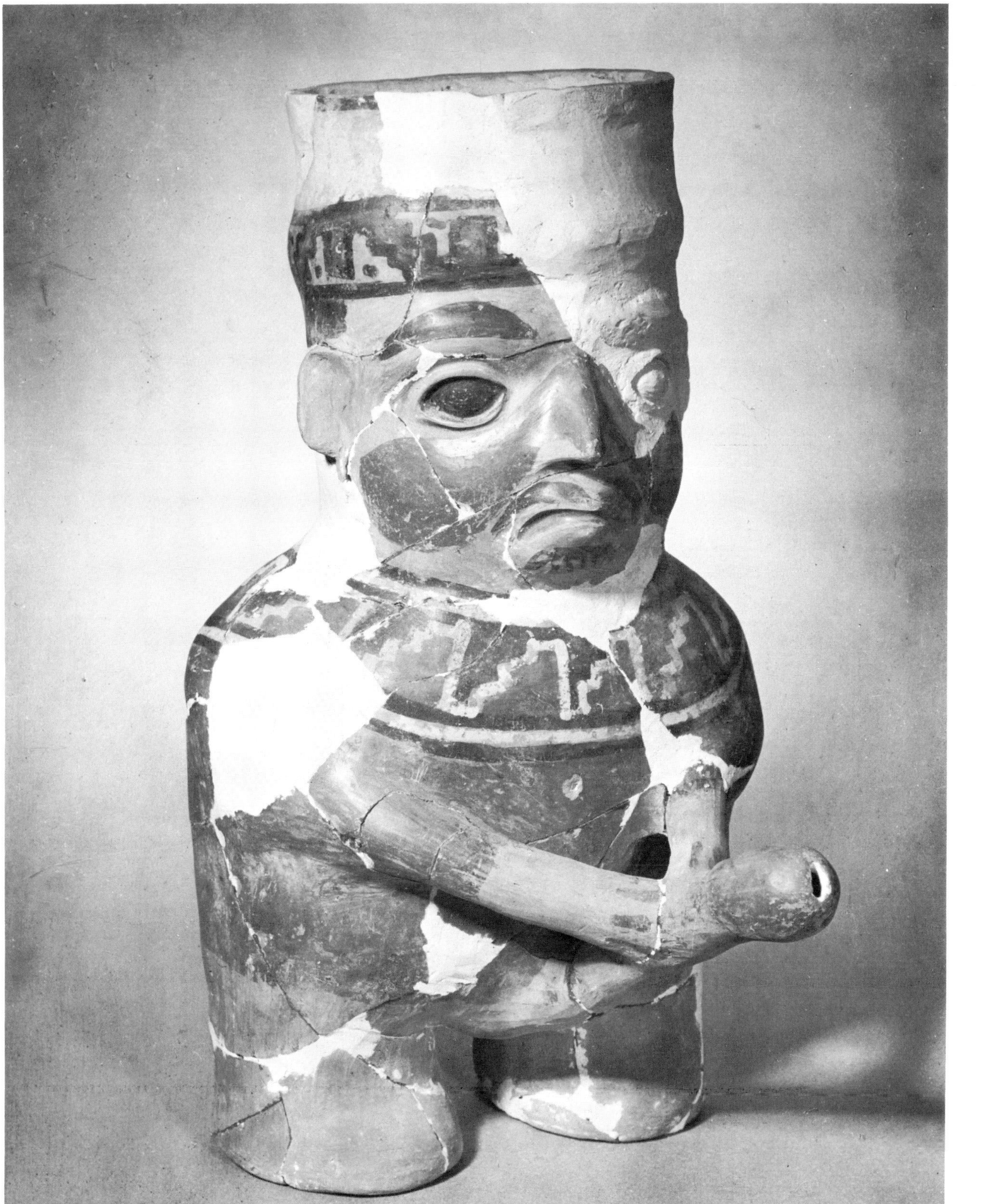

52. Masturbation. Maranga culture.

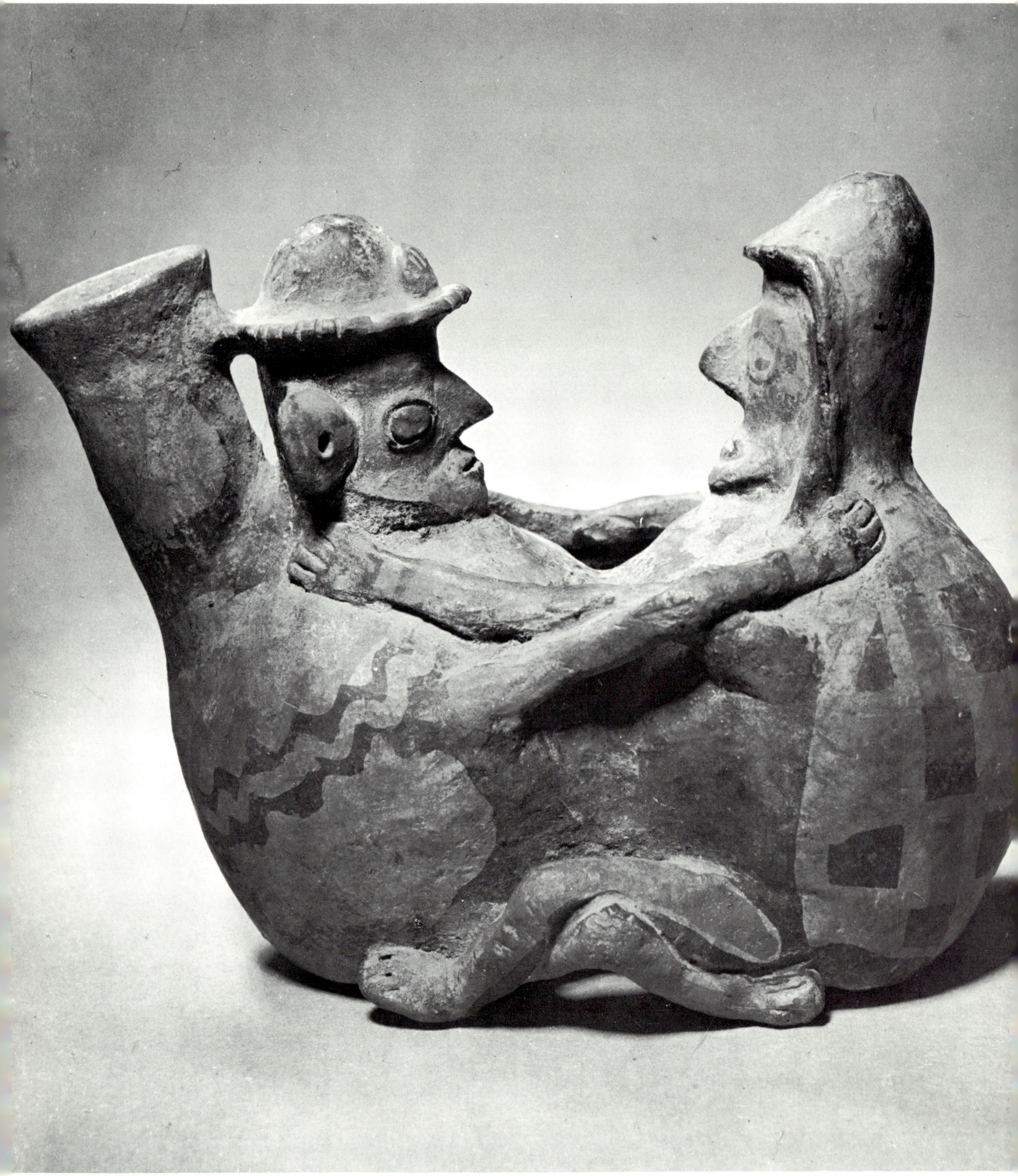

53. Coitus with couple seated face to face. Recuay culture.

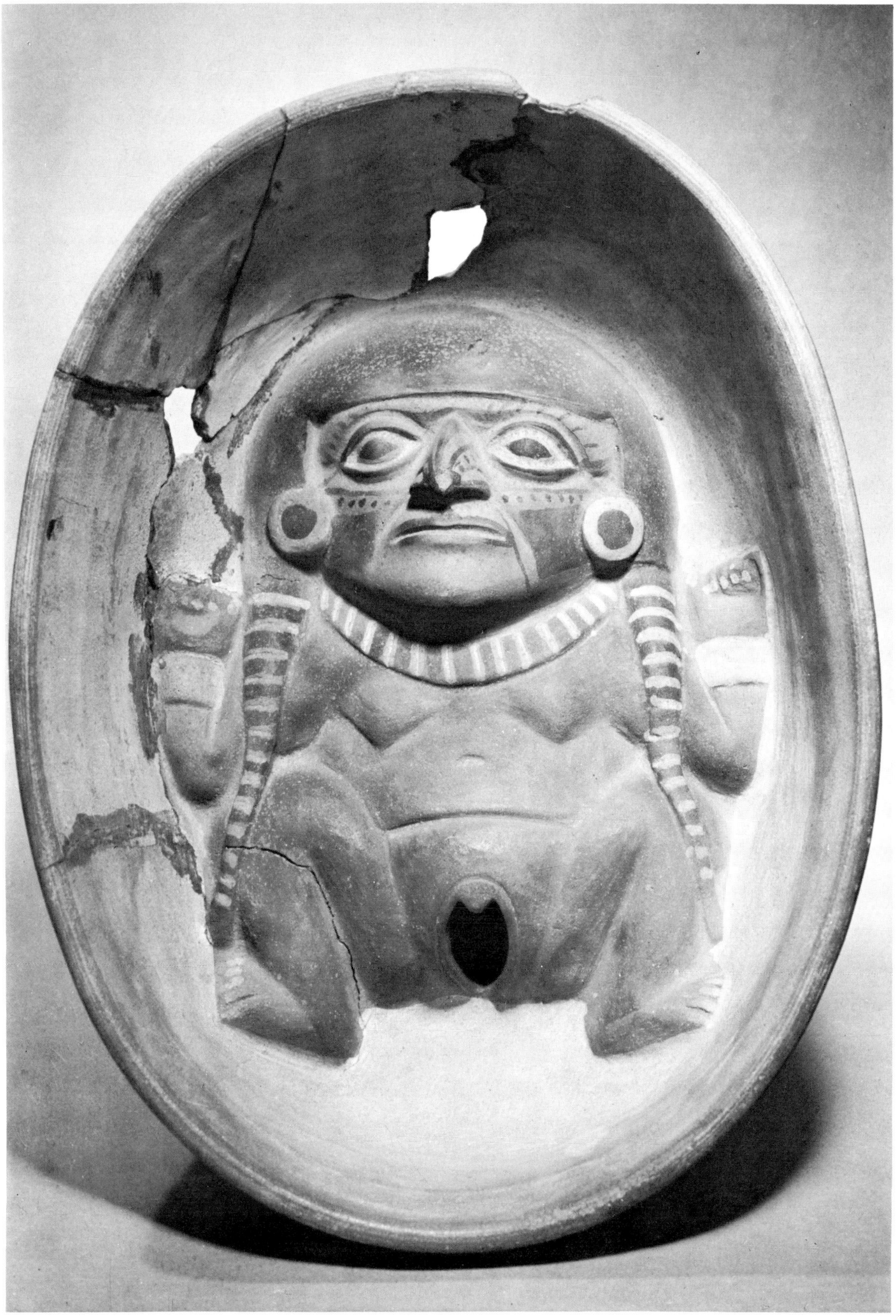

54. Humor. The nude female constitutes a false bottom of the bowl. Fluid flows in and out of the vulva. Mochica culture.

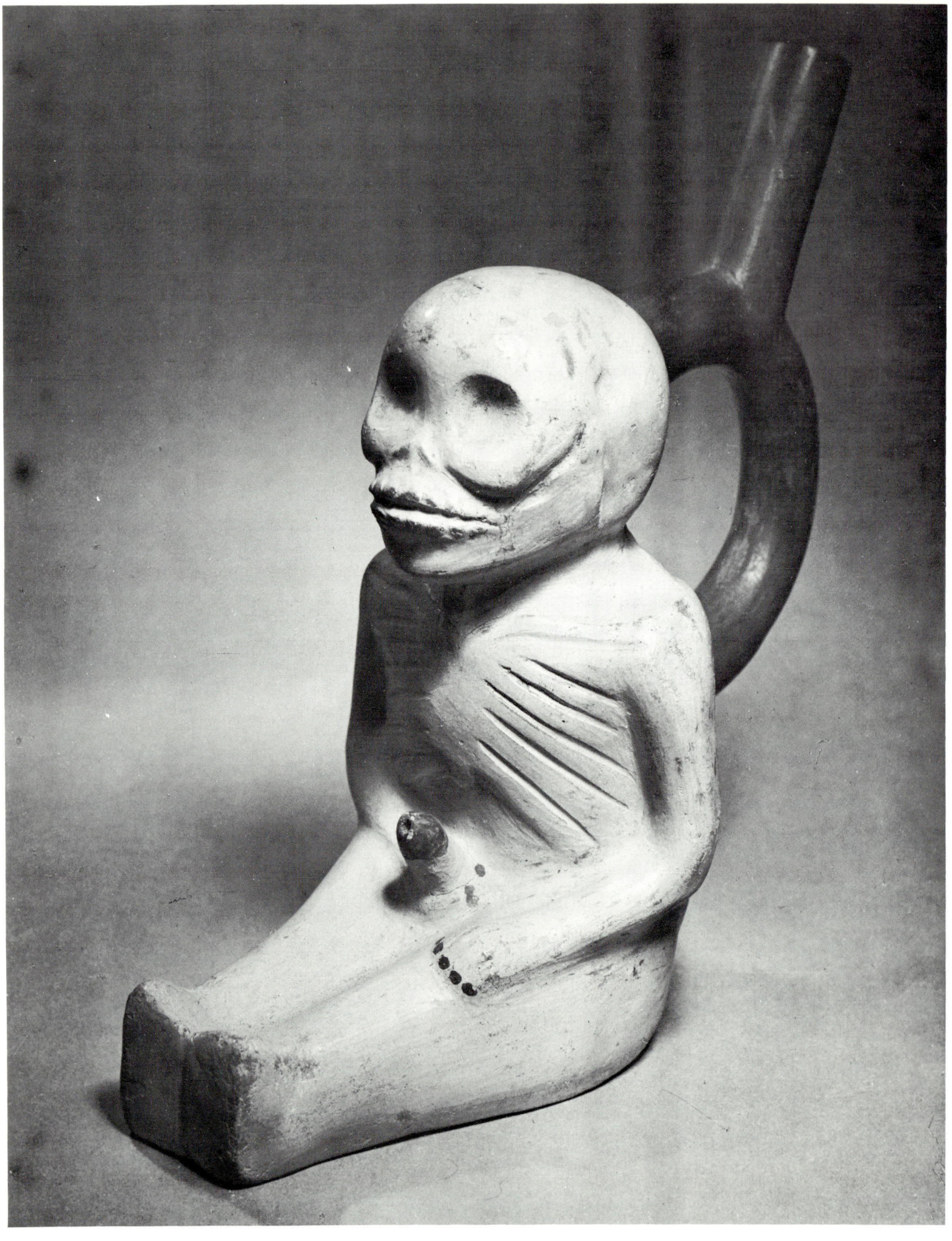

55. Masturbation by a cadaver. Mochica culture.

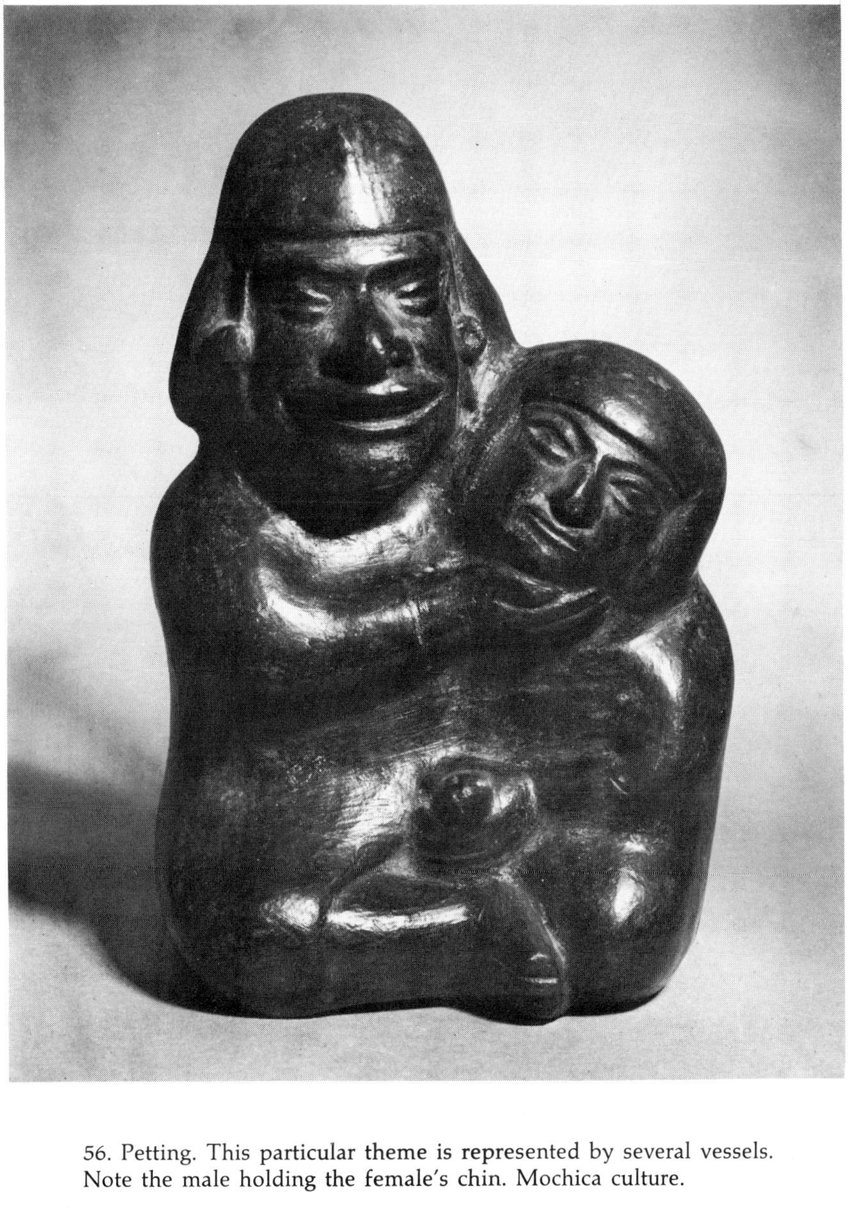

56. Petting. This particular theme is represented by several vessels. Note the male holding the female's chin. Mochica culture.

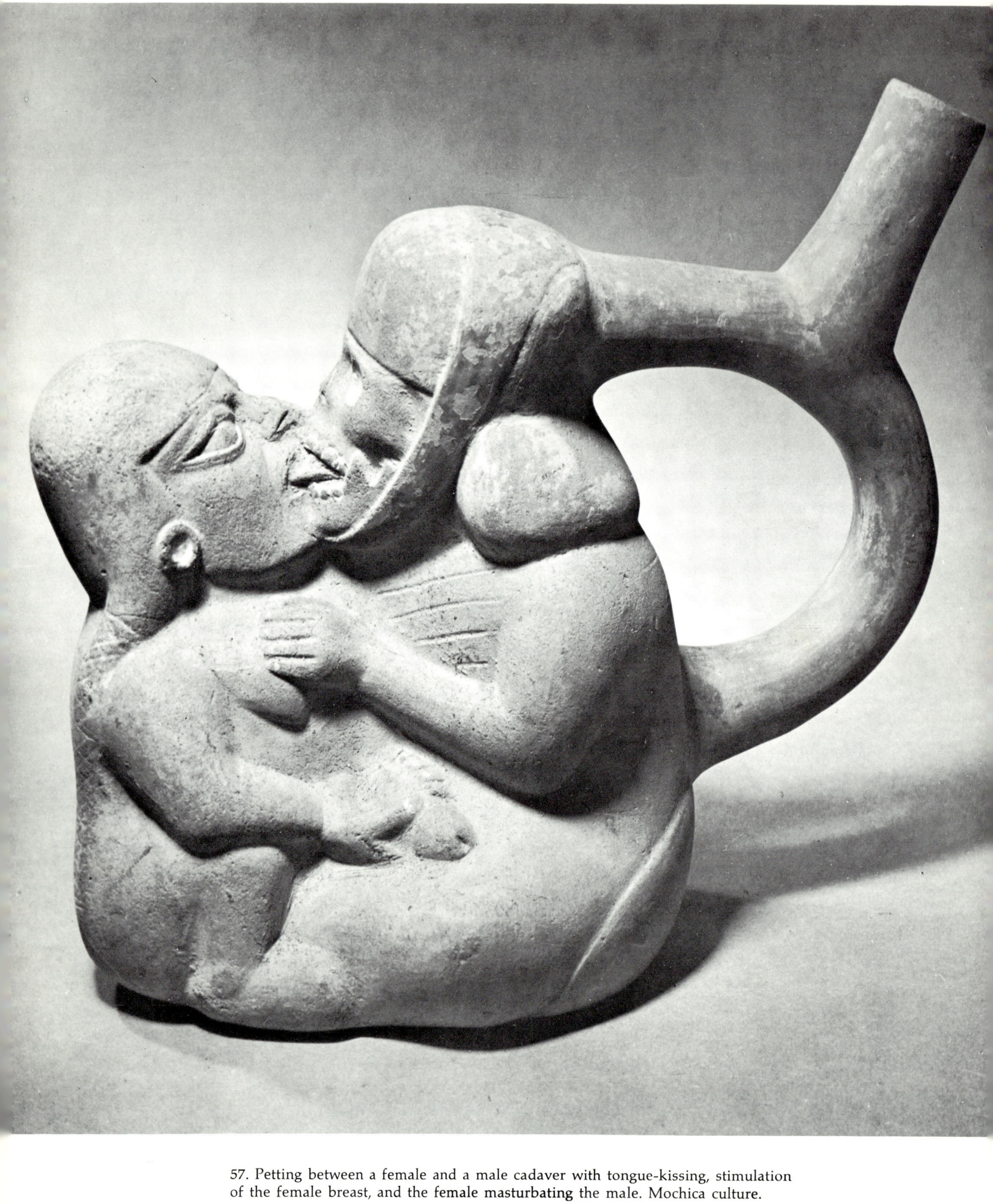

57. Petting between a female and a male cadaver with tongue-kissing, stimulation of the female breast, and the female masturbating the male. Mochica culture.

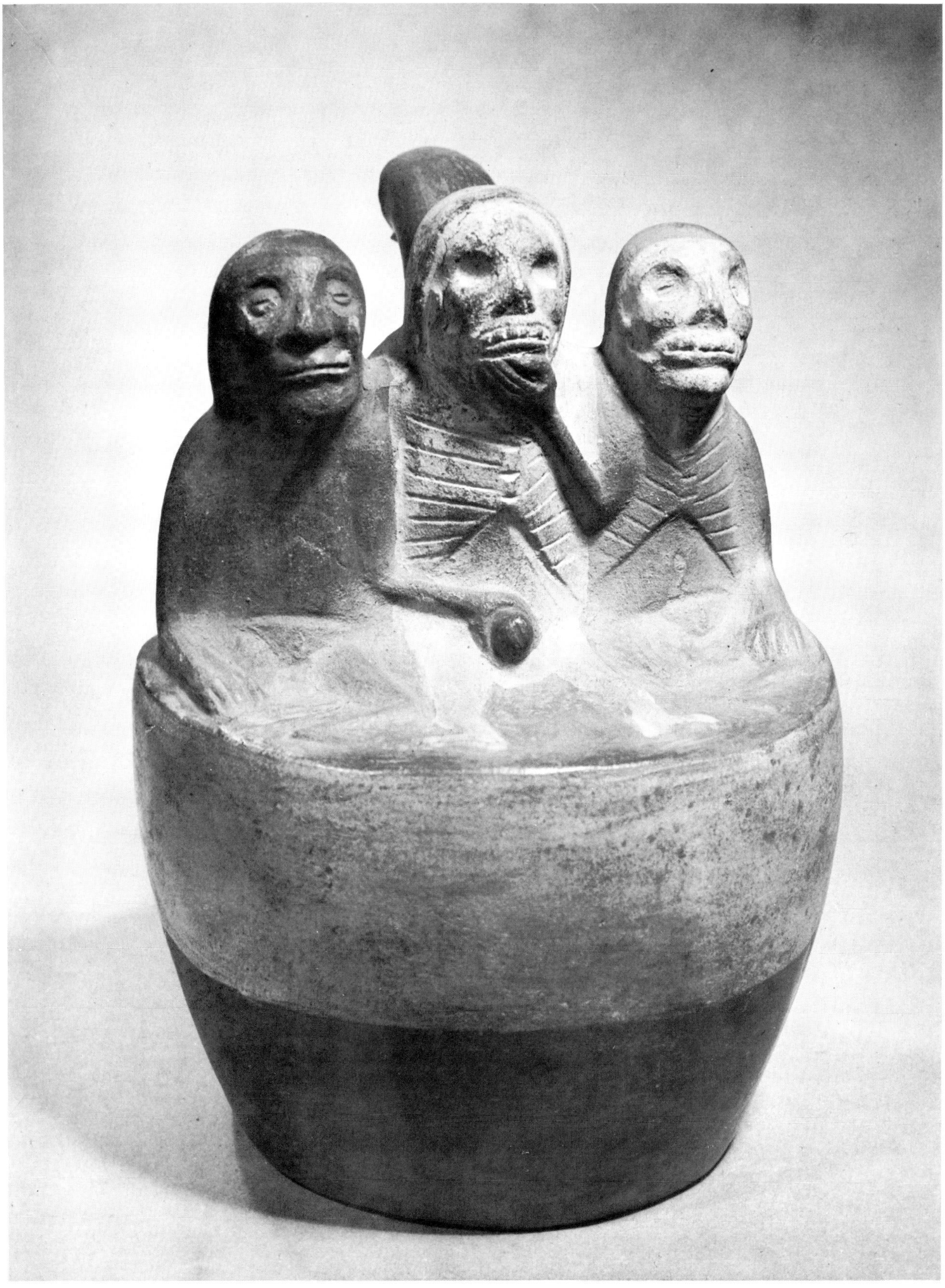

58. Petting between three cadavers. The male is seated between two females. One female masturbates him while the other holds his chin. Mochica culture.

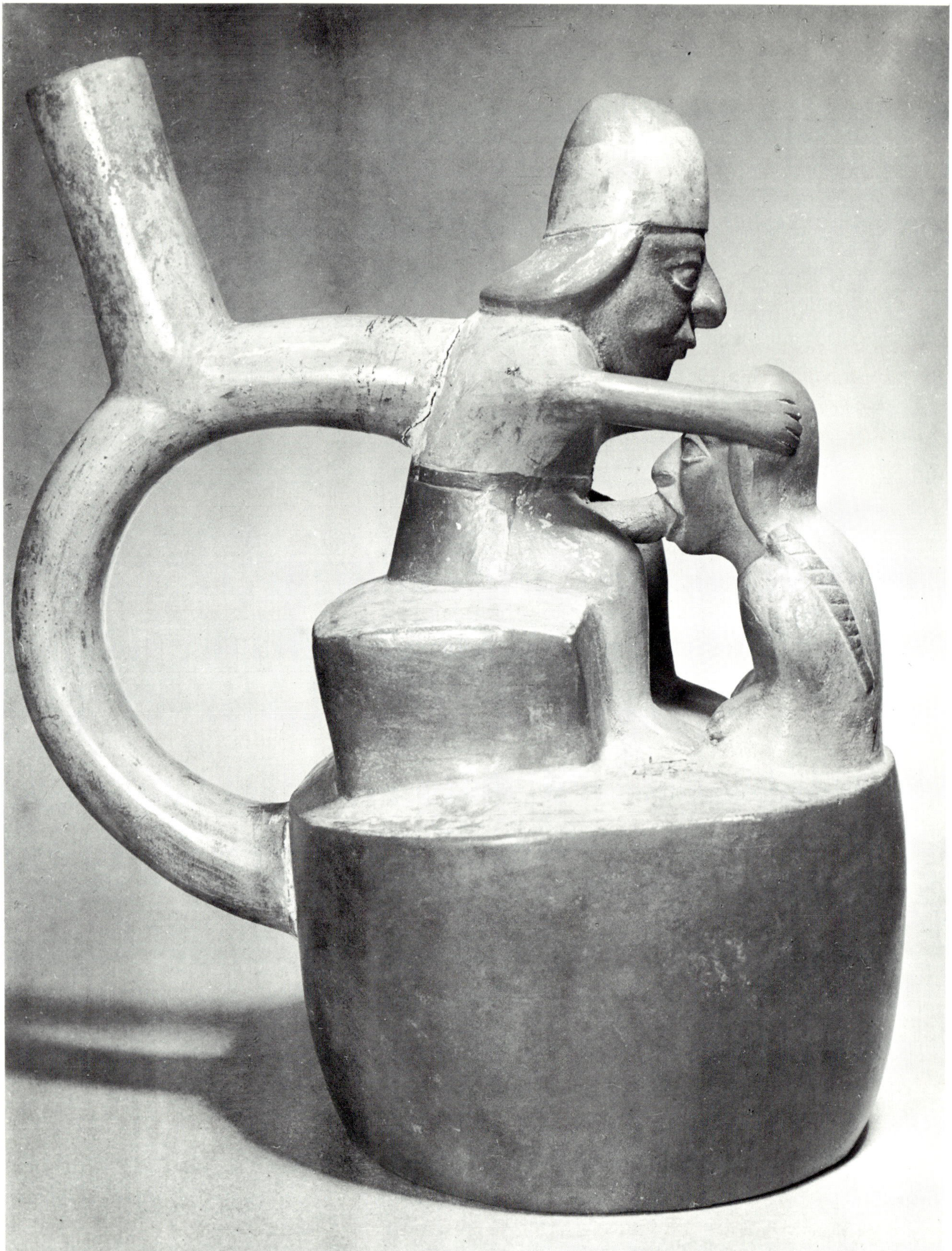

59. Fellation with the male seated and only the upper body of the female depicted. Mochica culture.

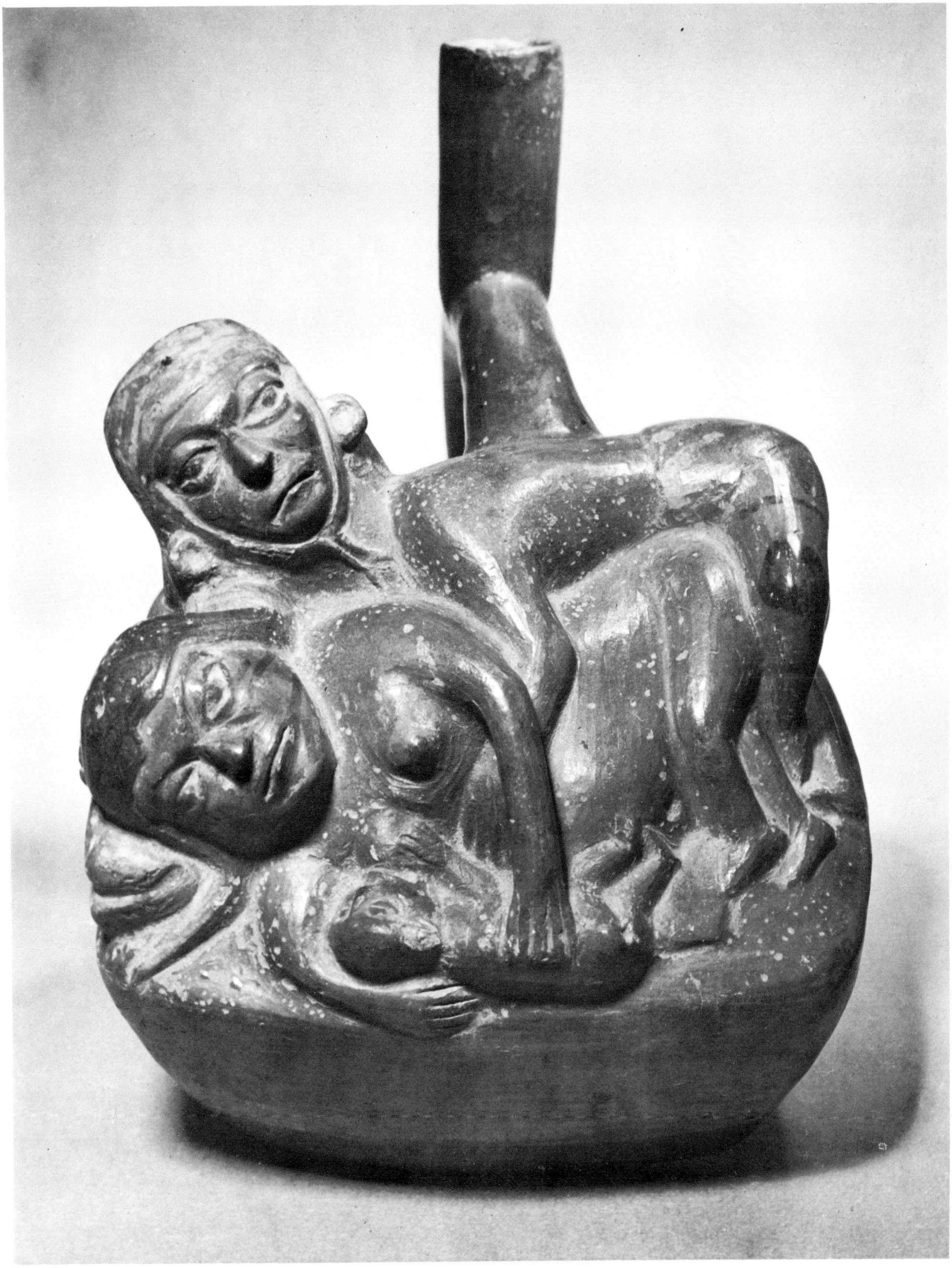

60. Coitus with the female on her side and the male on his side behind her, spoon fashion. Note the suckling infant. Mochica culture.

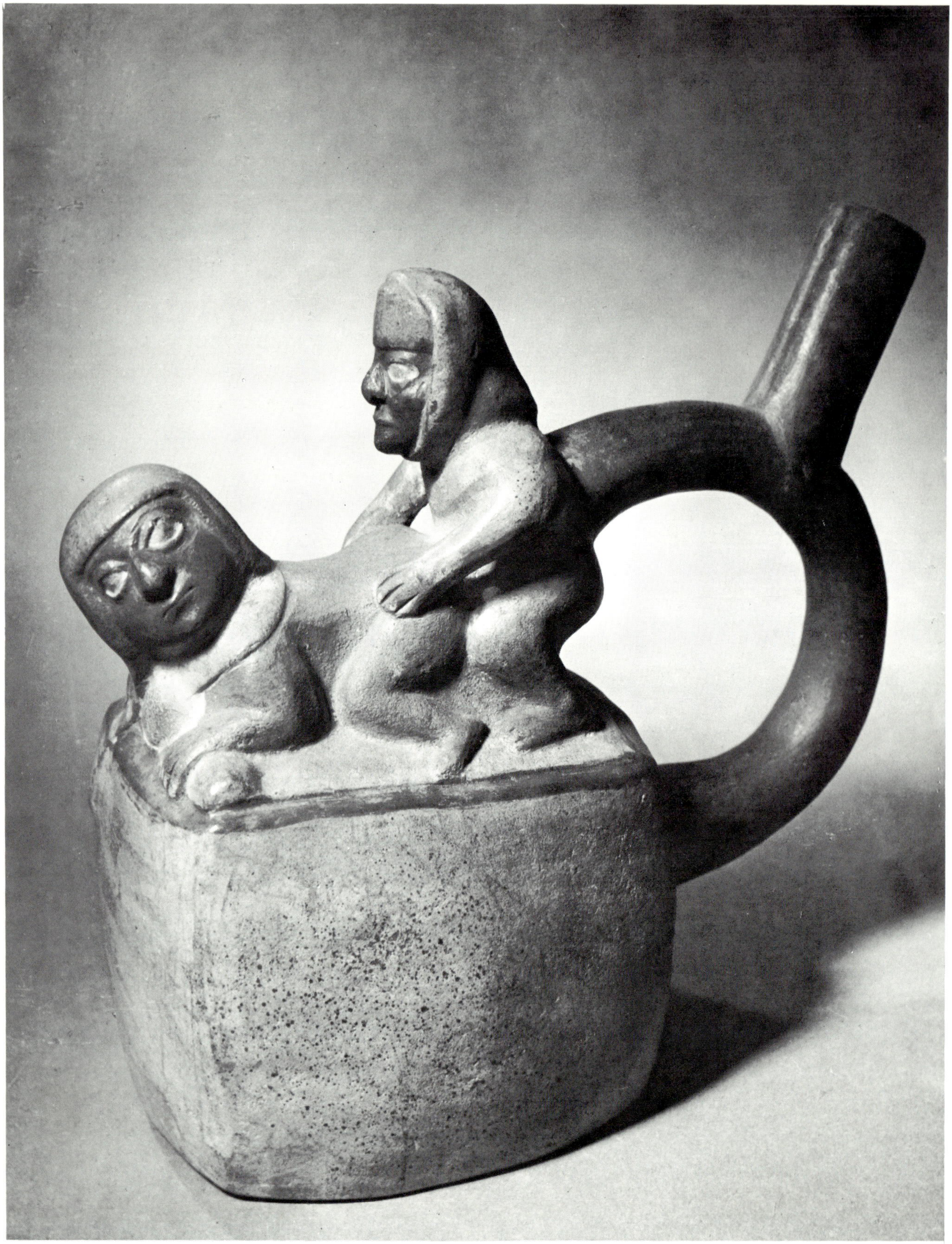

61. Coitus with the female kneeling and the male squatting behind her.
Mochica culture.

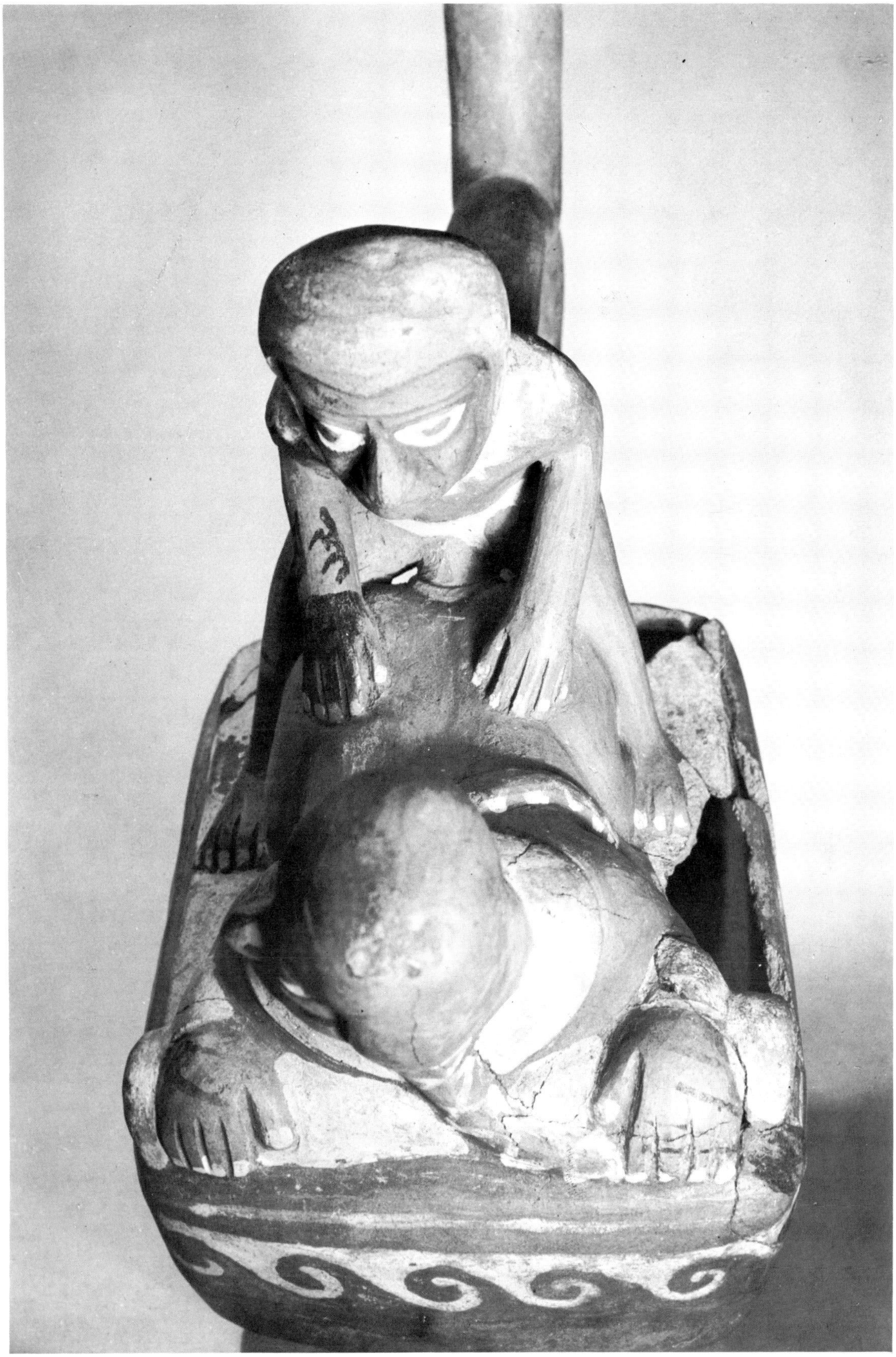

62. Anal coitus with the female kneeling and the male standing behind her. When viewed from the rear, the vulva is seen below the penetrated anus. Mochica culture.

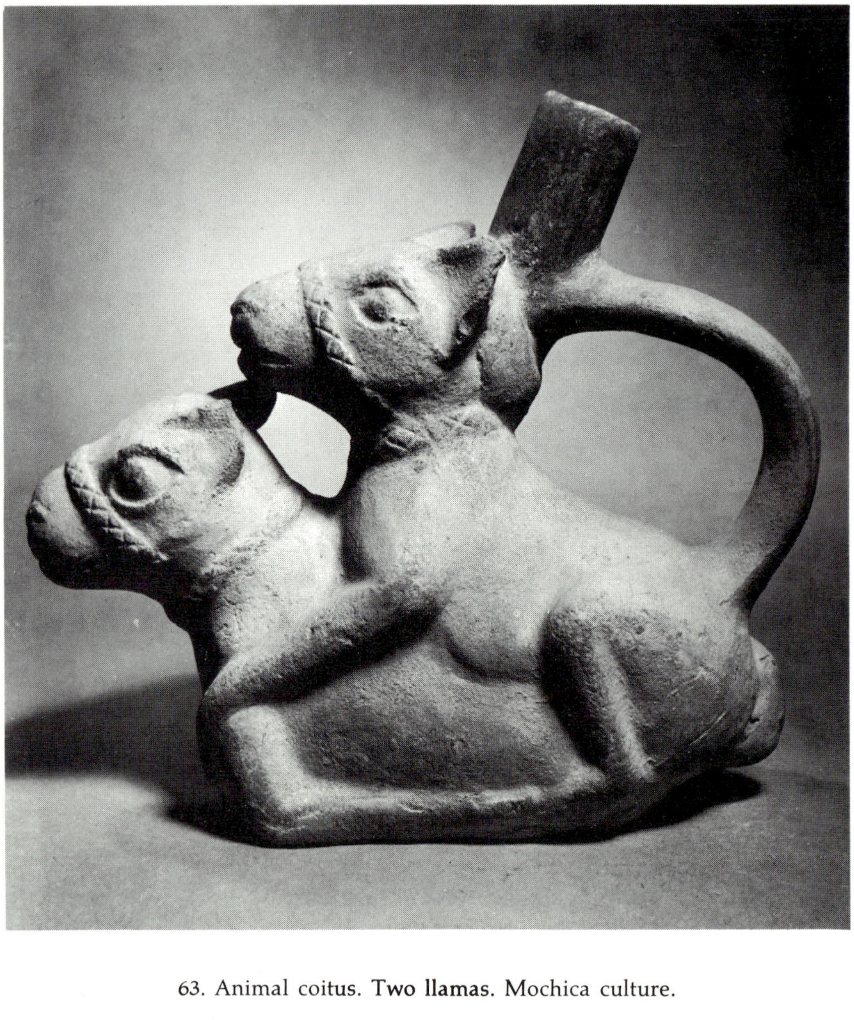

63. Animal coitus. Two llamas. Mochica culture.

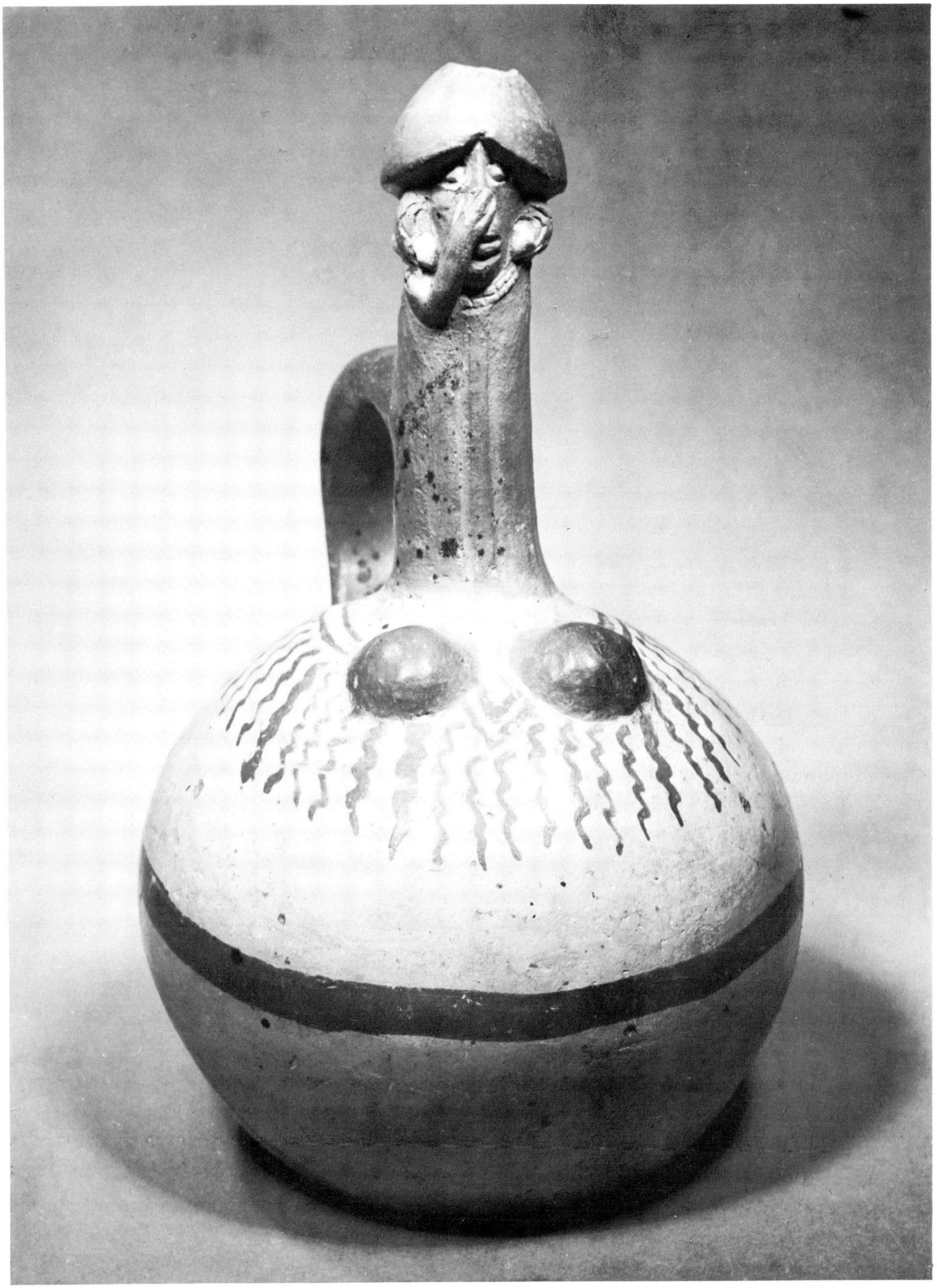

64. Anthropomorphic phallic spout holding its nose. The painting at the base is thought to represent the vulva aperture, indicating that the phallus is in the vagina. Mochica culture.

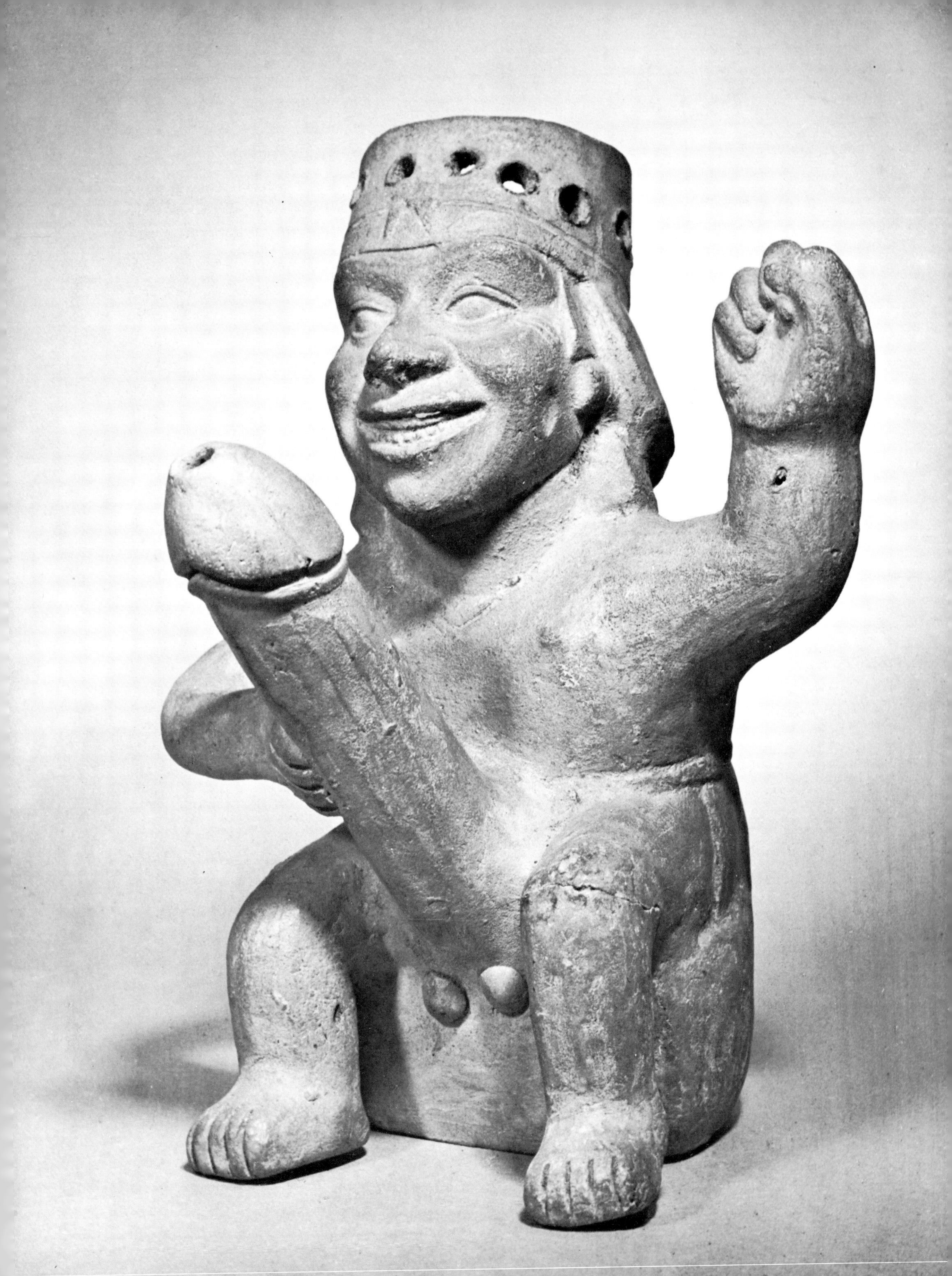

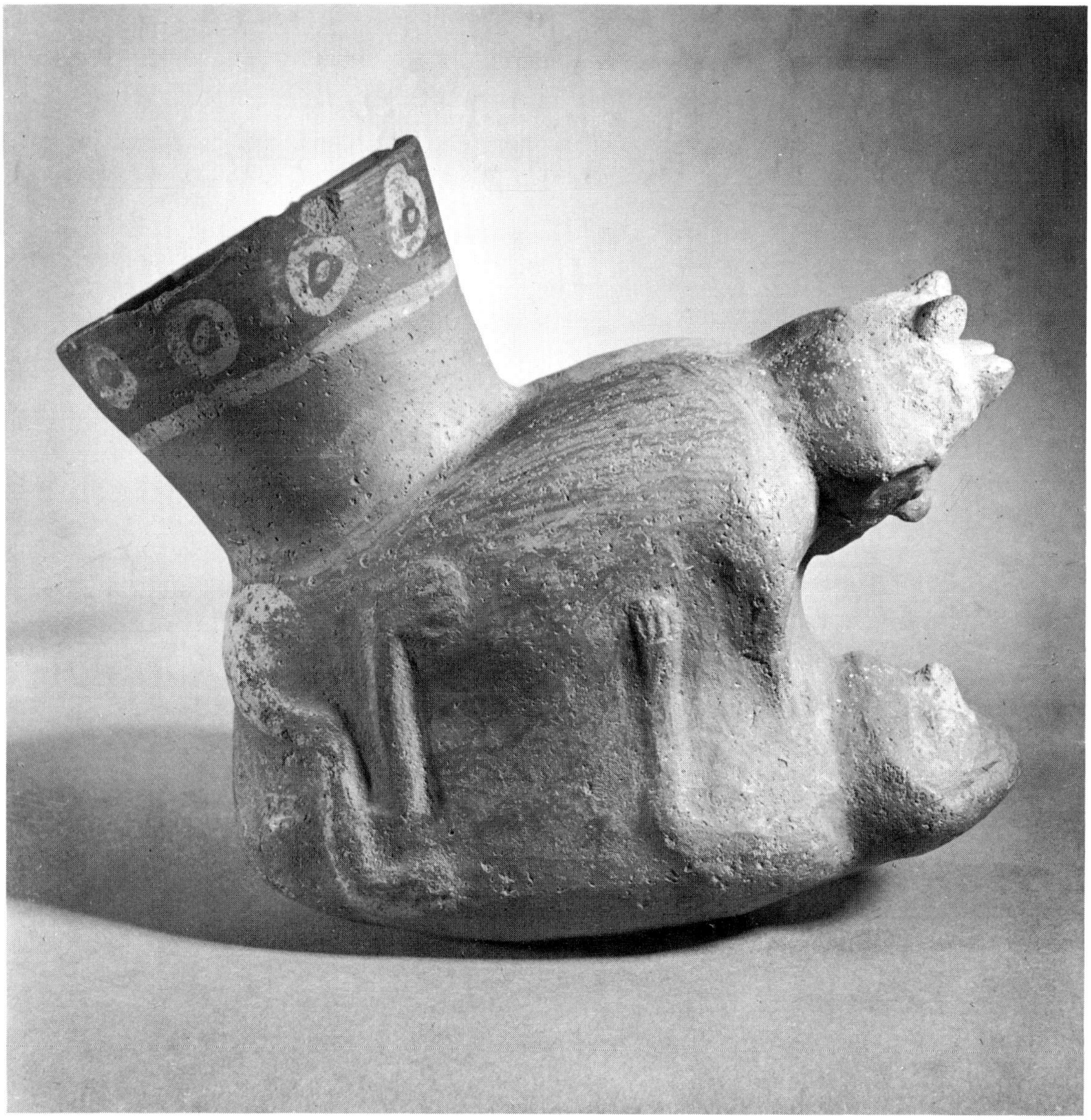

66. Coitus with female supine. Huara culture.

65. Humor. Vessel with a perforated rim which forces the drinker
or pourer to use the phallic spout. Mochica culture.

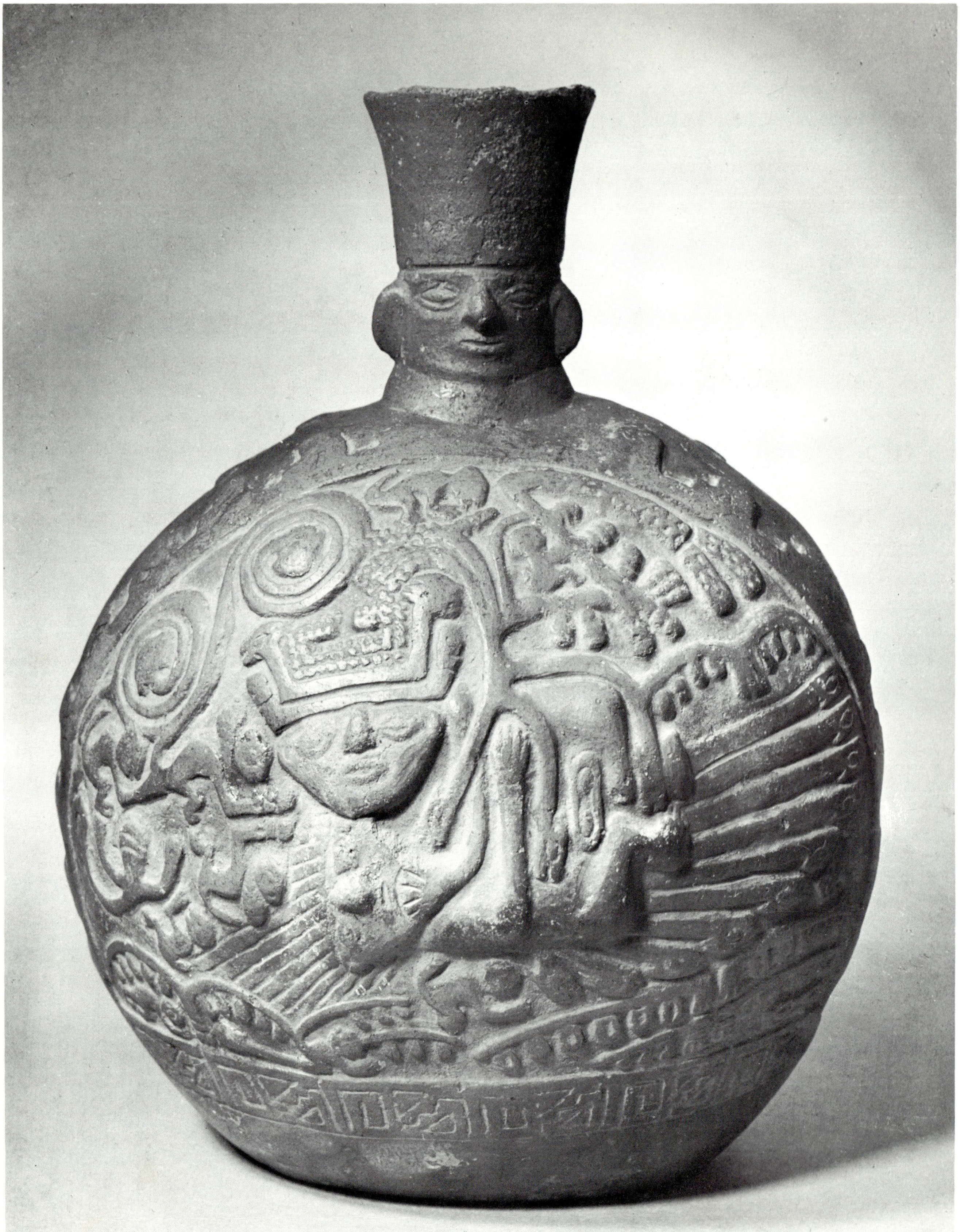

67. Coitus with female supine. Bas-relief, probably mold-made.
Note the hand on the chin. Huari (Wari) culture.

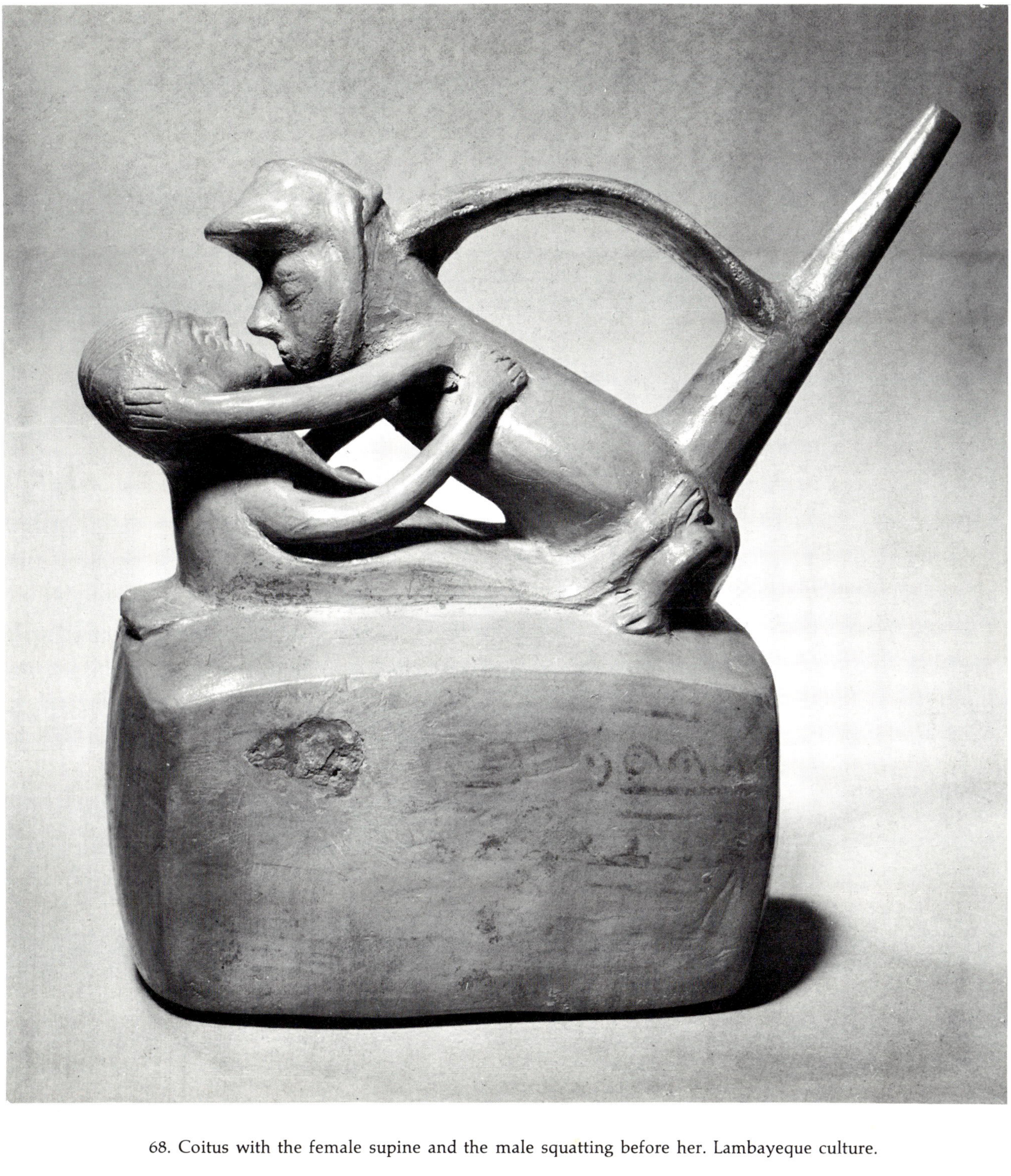

68. Coitus with the female supine and the male squatting before her. Lambayeque culture.

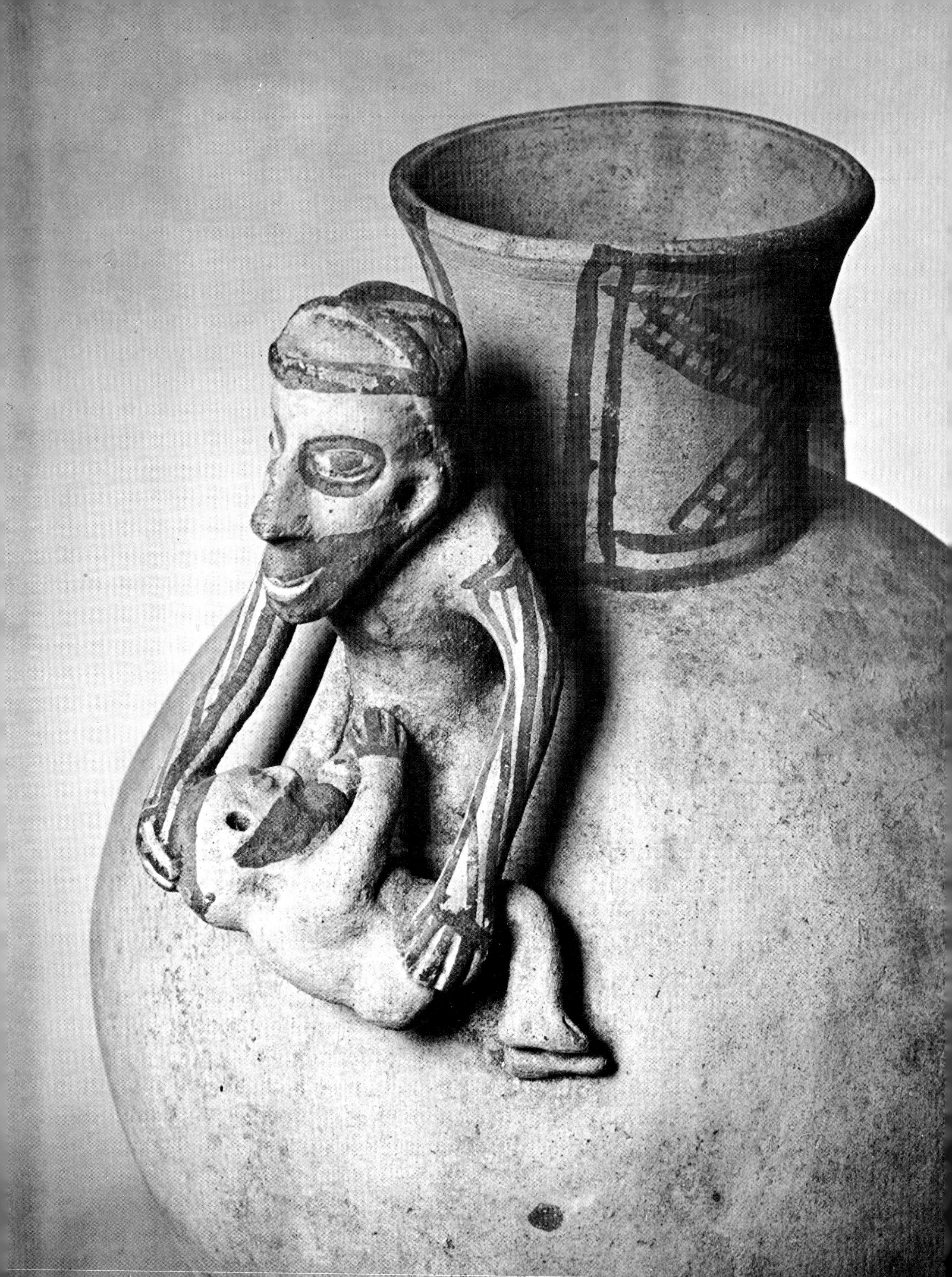

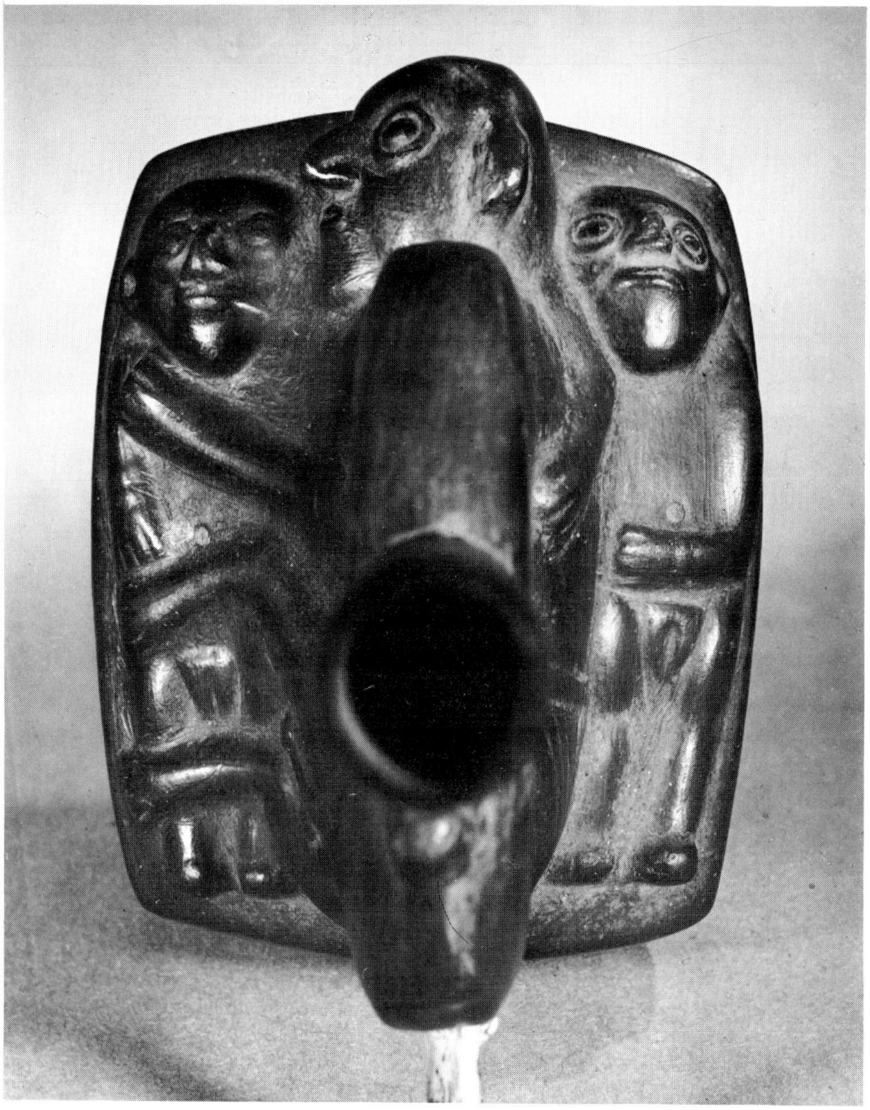

70. Petting. A male lies between two females with his legs and one arm over one of them. Almost identical vessels showing coitus have been found. Chimu culture.

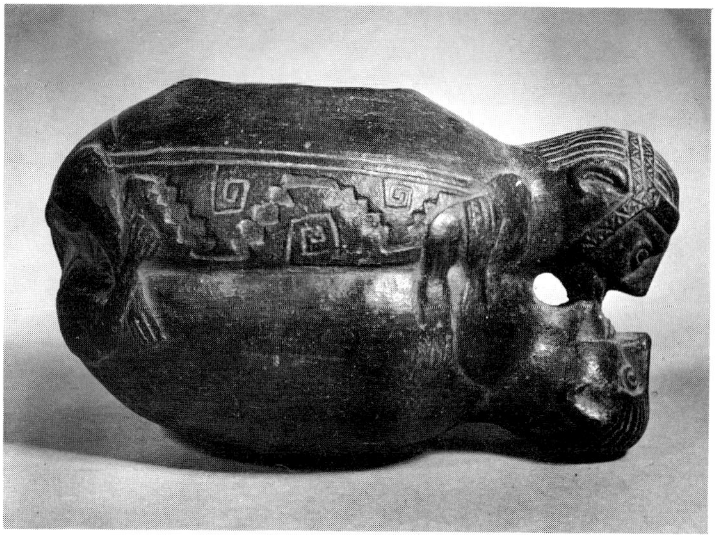

. Fellation of a male by a much
aller female. Chancay culture.

71. Coitus with the female supine and the male prone. Note the chin kissing. Chimu-Inca culture.

3

Erotic Aspects of Japanese Art

THEODORE BOWIE

Japanese erotica have long attracted the attention of Western connoisseurs and collectors. Few scholars, however, have made systematic or formal studies of the subject, and there exists no translation in any Western language of the work of such Japanese specialists as Kozo Hara, Yoshizaku Hayashi, Teruji Yoshida, and Kiyoshi Shibui—the competence of the latter being particularly buttressed by his splendid collection of representative prints. Probably the only authority in English on the artistic aspect of the Japanese erotic print is Richard Lane, who lives in Japan and whose occasional articles appear in journals which are not widely disseminated. Happily, he has contributed a substantial chapter, "The Shunga in Japanese Art," to a recently published book.[1]

My principal aim in this study, then, has been to seek answers to several fundamental questions: Are erotica a separate category or an integral aspect of Japanese art? How much of what is erotic is imaginative projection and how much of it realistic representation? Are the conventions used by this form unique or do they possess universal validity? How does the erotic element relate to other aspects of Japanese culture, such as religion, mythology, literature, and folk art?

[1] In Philip Rawson, *Erotic Art of the East* (New York, 1968), pp. 283–375. For other studies, see: Marianne Densmore, *Les Grands Erotiques Japonais* (Paris, 1962); L. E. Gichner, *Erotic Aspects of Japanese Culture* (privately printed, 1953); Genchi Kato, "A Study of Japanese Phallicism," *Transactions of the Asiatic Society of Japan,* supplement to 2nd Series, I (1923–1924), 5–70; F. S. Kraus, *Japanisches Geschlechtsleben* (2 vols.; Leipzig, 1931); Richard Lane, "Floating World Morals vs. *Ukiyo-e* Scholarship," *Ukiyo-e Art* (Tokyo), No. 12 (1966), pp. 7–24; François Poncetton, *Les Erotiques Japonais* (Paris, 1925).

Erotic expression in Japan is graphic rather than plastic, and secular rather than religious. (This is the exact contrary of the case in India.) Kenneth Yasuda, of Indiana University, is of the opinion that there is no Japanese painter of any renown who has not, at some time in his career, produced an erotic work; indeed, he goes so far as to say that the production of erotica was required of him as proof of his mastery. If one were to take this literally, one would have to postulate the existence of an enormous corpus of erotic pictures accumulating since at least the end of the twelfth century, a date which is accepted as the beginning of Japanese artistic autonomy. If there is such a corpus, very few examples dating earlier than the seventeenth century have been published. Most of what we know of this type of work belongs to the period, roughly from 1600 to 1850, in which flourished the school of artists known as *Ukiyo-e,* the Art of the Fleeting (or Floating) World. There is every reason to believe that the artists of *Yamato-e,* the school of Japanese art par excellence, which flourished in the thirteenth century, was even more realistic in its description of life than were the *Ukiyo-e* painters and draftsmen. But such early erotica are not easily come by, either directly or in facsimile or reproduction, so that we are reduced to inferences based on the works we do know, which are rarely devoted to erotic subjects.

From the second half of the fourteenth century to the end of the sixteenth, the major artistic developments in painting stressed either the adoption and expansion of certain Chinese ideas concerning the poetic or philosophic interpretation of nature, or the native interest in formal design and decorative values. We have first the flourishing of the Ashikaga Idealist School, which took its cue from Sesshu and other Zen masters; this led to the growth of the Kano School of painters. What characterizes these schools is their relative lack of interest in the human figure or in human activity. This is equally true of the so-called Decorators of the second half of the sixteenth century. While it is therefore conceivable that such artists as Sesshu, Shūbun, Sōami, Kano Masanobu,

Tōhaku, and Sōtatsu were capable of rendering any kind of realistic subject involving human beings, their interests lay elsewhere. If, as is supposed, each of these masters produced erotica (of an overt kind—if esoteric, the Westerner would surely miss it), examples of this work have not yet come to light. It is therefore difficult to generalize about eroticism in Japanese painting in the seven centuries of its most vigorous growth. Being largely limited to the productions of the *Ukiyo-e* school, we have a narrow view of the subject.

Historically, Japanese schools of art are a class phenomenon. The painters of the *Yamato-e* period, who gave the world that notable form called the *makimono* or handscroll, with its stress on continuous visual narrative, were for the most part court artists. Themselves members of the minor nobility, they worked for a small, aristocratic public with whose ways and point of view they were thoroughly familiar. Their depiction of life in the palace and in the military camp, in ceremonies and in war, affords invaluable documentary evidence about the history of Japan in the feudal epoch. In describing the life of the lower classes, the peasants, farmers, and quasi-serfs who toiled for them, their manner was condescending and mocking and realistic to the point of caricature. The productions of this school also included scrolls painted by Buddhist monks; these are historical in the sense that they portray the foundation of various orders or the life of the particular saint to whom they paid obeisance and whose memory they wished to perpetuate. Such artists were likewise members of the nobility, who could afford to satirize the lower classes. Anything with sexual connotations that can be found in these particular *makimono* would therefore be somewhat biased.

The *Ukiyo-e* school reflects the shift in economic power from the court to the city and the gradual decline of the samurai class and the corresponding rise of the merchant class. From the sixteenth century on, the cities of Edo, Nagoya, and Osaka grew at a fantastic rate and became centers of culture as well as of trade.

As the merchants acquired wealth and power, they tended to emulate the aristocracy; in decorating their homes they could afford to employ the same kind of artists. But there soon arose among the middle class of merchants a demand for art which was met by city artists, a professional group whom it is not inaccurate to describe as a kind of proletariat, since they were hard-working, usually ill-paid, and more often than not members of the artisan class. These people did not know the palace, but they knew the city, its pleasures and its varied life. Actors, wrestlers, and courtesans were among their favorite subjects; the theater, the brothel, the bathhouse, and the street, their principal scenes. While on the whole the style that prevails in the rendering of these subjects is a realistic genre, a tendency to glorify or poetize and to employ a somewhat mannered form of expression should put us on our guard against relying too heavily on *Ukiyo-e* works as objective documents.

Ukiyo-e started as a school of painting, but its productions were soon popularized through the medium of the print. Its first form is that of an illustration for a book; eventually the detached single sheet becomes the norm. This early connection with the printed word is of great importance. Sociologically, it means an ever-widening public, whose tastes are catered to; artistically, it means that, although the picture eventually liberates itself from its secondary role as illustration, it never completely sheds a verbal element which is part visual pun, part allusion to a literary or mythological tradition which is of a piece with the general culture and which is totally lost on anyone not brought up in it.

This art of the city must not be confused with folk art, which is the most ancient and most fundamental expression of Japanese culture. More than in any other country, folk art in Japan provides a solid underpinning for all of its artistic manifestations. It is the voice of a robust, hard-working, ingenious, and imaginative people, endowed with incredible gifts for fanatical devotion to causes or beliefs and dogged resolution to overcome obstacles and catastrophes, as well as the capacity to invent fantasies and myths of the most harrowing cruelty or the most tender subtlety, and to enjoy life in its most Rabelaisian aspects. Anything erotic which comes from this source is sure to be expressed with a bawdy gusto which may strike some as vulgar but which has the merit of refreshing honesty.

I have had, over the years, many opportunities to view Japanese erotic works of art, the great majority of them prints. In particular, the chance to examine a few in the vast collection belonging to Kiyoshi Shibui, in Tokyo, convinced me, as it would any unprejudiced person, that to question their artistic qualities and merits is a futile exercise. Unhappily, photographic reproduction does not convey the full artistic quality of a well-made print, so that that essence created by the harmonious blending of composition and design, color and line, has to be taken on faith. This must be kept in mind, since all the examples reproduced here are taken from slides in the archives of the Institute for Sex Research. When the slide reproduces a print or book illustration, its conversion into a photograph does not entail too great a distortion. The same may not be said of a painting, where delicacy of line and tone is an important esthetic element. Moreover, it is difficult to judge from any kind of reproduction whether a work which purports to be of an early period (such as the thirteenth century) is truly an original, a late copy, or merely a clever pastiche "in the manner of." This is one reason why the remarks I make about works which seem to belong, stylistically, to periods earlier than the seventeenth century are ventured with many reservations.

One last generalization: whatever philosophy of beauty may have been evolved by Japanese estheticians, it is certain that it is not based on the harmonious proportions of the human body. The human nude is not the revelation of perfection. There is no equivalent in Japanese mythology for Apollo, Aphrodite, Eros, or even Priapus. Phallicism seems to have prevailed since earliest times, but it did not produce the kind of deified *lingam* which becomes the god Siva, destroyer as well as creator, or the all-things-to-all-women concept for which Krishna stands. The expression of pan-sexuality occurs at the most directly immediate level which we may call realism—the only exception being the intrusion of fantasy, which is a world with its own laws, where elements borrowed from the so-called real world are recombined at will.

The method followed below has been to take some thirty-seven pictures and to examine them, first under two main headings, the realistic and the fanciful, and then, by pairing them, to analyze them in terms of the specific kind of sexual behavior portrayed. Some attention is also paid to formal points of stylistic analysis, especially composition.

OBSERVED REALITY

The Nude

72 Fig. 72 reproduces a large single-sheet print by Kiyonaga (1752–1815), who, by training or family connections, is in a straight line of descent from Moronobu, the reputed founder of the *Ukiyo-e* school.

The keynote of the tradition that he represents is one of straightforward portrayal of every-day life. The bathhouse scene that is the subject of this print shows a family group drying themselves after the bath. There are two young men and two young women, two children, two women of indeterminate age seen only in part, and an older man. Every one of the personages except the old man is stark naked. The two younger men have erections; their penises are not particularly exaggerated. The pubic regions of some of the women are fully exposed. The whole atmosphere seems relaxed, and we are left free to suppose that some sexual activity—masturbation in one case and copulation in the other—is about to take place. Whether intentionally or not, one of the effects of the situation is to provide sex education for the young. Many people today would regard the scene as indicating a healthy frame of mind. But how normal is it? If the setting were European, one could immediately say that the bathhouse was a specific kind of bagnio, an establishment providing opportunity for illicit amusement. This is clearly not the case here, as the artist has been careful not to give his figures sensuous poses or lurid expressions; they all look innocent, and are not to be thought of as indulging in any kind of exhibitionism. As a frequenter of bathhouses, the artist was so familiar with the human body that he undoubtedly depended entirely on his visual memory in creating his composition. The flow of his line is very smooth, though it is clear that his way of representing bodies reflects the conventional manner of a school that did not provide precise training in anatomy.

For the sake of contrast we may examine Fig. 73, which 73
reproduces one panel of a scroll painted by Maruyama Okyō (1733–1795). A close contemporary of Kiyonaga, Okyō did not subscribe to the tenets or the style of the *Ukiyo-e* school or indeed of any other; he was by temperament an independent investigator. Among other things, he looked into Western modes of painting; his kind of realism (or, more accurately, naturalism) included formal study of human anatomy. In the scene illustrated, we see a man and woman in the preliminaries of intercourse. With one hand the man is inserting *rin-no-tama* (pleasure balls) into the woman's vagina, while wetting the fingers of his other hand preparatory to lubricating his penis. The sexual organs of both partners are not unduly exaggerated, and the facial expressions of each are carefully studied with greater insight into the anticipation of pleasure than most artists before Okyō usually display. The bodies are carefully observed, though there is no sign that the linear pattern—the hallmark of a tradition in which only the brush is used—is different from that of any other Japanese artist. And here, as almost always elsewhere, the painter makes his line flow from limb to covering cloth with a constant attention to design.

Sex Organs

74, 75 Figs. 74 and 75 reproduce four pages from a work in which an artist named Koikawa Shozen demonstrates a quasi-scientific delineation of male and female genitalia and of varieties of sexual poses. Nothing much is known about Shozen except that he seems to have devoted a large amount of his time and energy to copying hundreds of erotic prints by artists of every period in order to produce an encyclopedia of sexual practices. From the samples shown here it is presumed that his motivation was accuracy of rendering. Since there are sixteen volumes in this encyclopedia, composed almost entirely of illustrations, with little text other than the notes and indications given in each picture, it may be presumed that we have here a kind of running history of Japanese erotic art, with particular reference to the imagery created for the books illustrated by *Ukiyo-e* artists.

Scatology

76 In Fig. 76 the artist (not identified) portrays a woman defecating and a man urinating in full view of their companions. Probably peasants, they perform their bodily functions without interrupting their eating. There is nothing specifically sexual in the situation; these children of nature are so habituated to a complete lack of privacy that acts which are usually performed more or less secretly do not arouse the slightest curiosity in them. The picture is something in the nature of a social document, and any inference that the artist is either deploring or mocking the coarseness of his
77 subjects is gratuitous. In Fig. 77, a print by Utamaro (1754–1806), we have something much more subtle, a commentary on the implications of voyeurism and the special delight it conveys when sex and scatology are combined. There is the added feature of the *voyeur vu,* involving the viewer of the erotica in identifying himself with the youth watching, behind a fence, a young woman (holding

tissue paper in her mouth) about to defecate. The youth is so posed as to indicate clearly that he is masturbating while at the same time inviting sodomy, a complication obviously not unintended by the artist.

Rape

Violent crimes, including rape, must have been frequent at times when Japan was torn by clan wars and other forms of social unrest. Rape is, accordingly, a frequent subject for illustrators, but, in the nature of things, it is not too likely to occur before witnesses. There is only a relative amount of realism, and a considerable reliance on imaginative power in a work such as is illustrated in Fig. 78. Kunisada (1786–1865) here portrays a young 78
woman bound and gagged, with her legs held wide open by being tied to a pole, in the act of being raped by a fierce, hirsute bandit. Much depends on the use of color to convey the sense of horror and gloom, and some of that atmosphere comes through even in the black-and-white reproduction. The design of the bodies indicates an incomplete solution to the problem an artist has to solve when trying to depict copulation when a man faces a woman. He has to reconcile what the eye can naturally perceive, which is not much, with the need to stress the genital organs. This is perhaps why positions other than the supposedly customary one for sexual congress are so popular with many Japanese artists.

One of the favorite attitudes shown is penetration from the rear, which in some cases implies assault or rape. Such is the case in Fig. 79. The scene is a country lane in wintertime. A young 79
farmer, wearing a straw coat and a straw hat, is assailing a young woman from behind. She, not too reluctantly, balances herself on a basket while biting a corner of her kerchief. Her left leg is raised sufficiently high for everyone to see that intercourse here is not anal. The tender colors used by the artist, the pleasant pattern formed by the contrast between the clothing of the partners and

their naked limbs, their air of intense preoccupation, all contribute to make this work a masterpiece of harmonious serenity. The brutality of the context is sublimated; it has become something idyllic, scarcely different in spirit from the poetic pictures of well-behaved and demure young ladies and their placid suitors on which the fame of Harunobu rests.

The Chinese Precedent

It has often been suggested that the Japanese borrowed the idea and the manner of illustrating erotic books from the Chinese. The Ming period in China saw the development of the erotic novel, among which the *Chin P'ing Mei* and the *Golden Lotus* are the ones the West knows best. Popular editions illustrated with woodblocks undoubtedly reached Japan in the early part of the seventeenth century; their vogue stimulated numerous imitations. No opinion is offered as to the literary merits of the Japanese texts. There is no doubt, however, about the improvement in the quality of the illustrations and the heightening of their boldness and lewdness.

80 Fig. 80 shows a characteristic example of the Chinese manner. The artist is quite clearly ill at ease in handling the human body. No one disputes the Chinese genius for inventing exquisite and complicated pleasures and tortures. But whatever skill may have been developed among painters between the fifth and twelfth centuries, when the demands of Buddhistic art required the limning of men and gods in varied activities, was of little help in the prevailing fashion of painting landscapes from which the human element is almost totally absent. Add to this the fact that the Chinese are not accustomed to seeing nude men and women or even children. The need to represent men and women devoid of the flowing robes which the brush can so gracefully portray reduces the painter to creating doll-like figures more reminiscent of earthworms than of human beings.

The theme of Fig. 81, by a Japanese artist, is virtually the same as the one used by the Chinese illustrator: a copulating trio. The latter places his group far away from us on a bed which looks like a stage, and shows us stiff little tubular forms which so verge on the abstract as to have almost no erotic significance. By comparison, the Japanese painter, who is classified as a primitive because of the characteristic awkwardness of his style, is infinitely more adept at solving the problem posed by an essentially improbable acrobatic performance. The viewer is brought up close to the actors, who look solidly fleshed and flexible; at the same time, in spite of all the exaggerations, the pattern of the composition is coherent. 81

The Yamato-e Tradition

Figs. 82 and 83 are two successive scenes in a *makimono* attributed to Nobuzane, a celebrated court painter of the first half of the thirteenth century. The style is typical of the school of which he was an outstanding member. There is a fair probability that we are looking at erotic situations involving aristocrats as seen by a man of their own class. We are therefore led to make the following inferences about the sexual habits of such people: that love play among the nobles of the Heian and later courts included cunnilingus; that, whether copulation took place indoors or outdoors, partners might be totally clothed, partly clothed, or totally nude; that attention is called to the genitalia through the devices of increasing their dimensions somewhat and heightening their color, though not to the extent (which may be described as gross exaggeration) which occurs in the seventeenth and eighteenth centuries; that sexual excitement on the part of the woman, and the approach of orgasm, are signaled by her closed eyes and the crispation of her toes. On the other hand, no matter how tumultuous the engagement, neither the man's headdress nor the woman's hairdo is likely to be disturbed. All this, with variations, 82, 83 will recur in *Ukiyo-e* works, where the subjects are clearly not of the nobility.

One might ask whether Nobuzane or other court painters had actually witnessed these scenes. He certainly had a good notion of the way portly ladies and gentlemen look when engaging in amorous sport. There is nothing improbable in the belief that high-born personages were as ready to exhibit themselves as the lesser breeds are reputed to have been, provided no scandal occurred. A court painter might well have been invited to record such activities for the benefit of his friends.

Instruction in Sexual Techniques

One of the principal rationalizations proposed for the depiction of erotic scenes is their educational function. The uninitiated, who include mostly young married couples, need to be fully instructed about the private aspects of marriage. Brides in particular are expected to accept their future lords' and masters' sexual whims and even to anticipate them. Hence the commissioning of so-called "pillow books," which are family heirlooms and presumably passed on from mother to daughter.

I have chosen from various books illustrated by Kunisada (1786–1865) four scenes which might constitute the main sequence
84 in such a manual. The first one, Fig. 84, opens in a richly decorated room in which a woman is receiving a painting lesson. In the traditional manner she is kneeling on the floor with the paper unrolled before her, and she holds the brush perpendicular to the paper. Crouching above her and pressing her closely is her teacher. A bit of flesh among the robes tells us that an exploratory arm is reaching toward her pudenda. The scene is watched by two little children, partly hidden by a curtain; we will not see them again. As in many other similar illustrations, there is a certain amount of text. The burden of the captions here is that learning how to make love needs as much thorough instruction as learning how to paint.

This first stage of love play is likely to be succeeded by one or more scenes in which the stimulation is more overt and pressing. Before long a first conjunction is reached, as is seen in Fig. 85. 85
Both partners are fully robed, but there is enough baring of the lower parts to reveal active copulation. Mutual kissing, apparently not indulged in at the preliminary stages, is a frequent accompaniment to specific sexual action. As an indication of the relatively cultivated audience toward which this kind of work is aimed, the artist is likely to make special literary and artistic allusions. The cartouche in the upper-left corner reproduces a well-known *waka,* or short poem, and the vignette to the right of it illustrates a passage from a love epic such as the *Tale of Genji,* painted in the standard style. Neither picture nor poem is inherently salacious; they are merely capable of being so interpreted.

With Fig. 86 we reach a later phase. The partners have now 86
abandoned their heavy robes in favor of cotton *yukatas* and engage in coitus from behind. This is one of Kunisada's most splendid achievements, both in his ability to convey the passionate intensity of the actors and in his skill in creating a design based on the contrast between flesh and cloth and the rhythmic flow of curving bodies against the geometrical design of the furnishings. His handling of color, which can scarcely be guessed at in the black-and-white reproduction, adds to the effectiveness of the scene.

The crumpled papers scattered on the floor, in the scene depicted in Fig. 87, suggest that the partners have already engaged 87
in a half-dozen bouts and are trying a change of pace. They are now totally nude, except for the inevitable piece of cloth around the woman's waist. The text states explicitly that both are enjoying the cunnilingus, but that the woman is having difficulty performing fellatio and would prefer a return to copulation. This raises several interesting questions. The representation of fellatio, at least until relatively modern times, seems to have been rarely essayed by Japanese artists. This cannot be because the practice was not indulged in; but why did artists eschew this particular theme? Is it because conventions required that the woman be shown with a tiny mouth and the man with an enormous penis? The present

illustration and numerous others show plainly that the Japanese do not hold with the theory, propounded by Casanova in his *Memoirs,* that a woman's mouth and her vulva have identical proportions and that a man may know what to expect of a woman simply by observing her mouth.

Professional Sex Instruction

A bride's manual of the type suggested above might also serve for the training of a prostitute or for the arousal of a client. Given the practical nature of the Japanese, there is nothing improbable in
88, 89 what Figs. 88 and 89 (which should be seen as one picture; they are a part of a polyptich with several parts omitted) seem to represent: a sexual performance for the benefit of young trainees in the Yoshiwara. The gorgeously robed ladies are obviously taking a professional interest in the scene being enacted before them, and will presumably engage in a critique of it at the right moment. Whether such events ever took place, the Western historians of Japanese night life do not say. But when an artist depicts the *mores* of his country, what he dredges up from his imagination may be just as validly revelatory as the actuality he portrays.

Public Performances

90 The same remark applies to the two scenes shown in Figs. 90
91 and 91. They represent sexual bouts of an acrobatic character between wrestlers and prostitutes, taking place before mixed audiences whose reactions are clearly enough indicated by their attitudes and expressions, though care has also been taken to provide many captions. Fig. 90 is slightly more realistic and hence more plausible than Fig. 91. In both situations, but especially in the former, there is an element of contest: in Fig. 90, a referee on the left is clearly taking his responsibilities seriously. The Japanese are very fond of games and contests of all kinds; a sex

contest would be perfectly natural, even though we cannot document the fact beyond such pictures as these.

Bawdy Humor

Much of what we have seen so far has been humorous only incidentally, though there was no intention of suggesting that the Japanese tend to be solemn about sex. On the contrary, they have a raucous sense of humor, which is given free play particularly when some kind of ambiguity is involved. In Fig. 92 we see a man 92
assailing a woman from behind, while under a net another man sleeps peacefully. We inevitably conclude that he is a husband being cuckolded literally under his own nose. This is a universally comic theme, but here the treatment is as strongly spiced a version of it as we will ever experience.

The situation in Fig. 93 is somewhat more ambiguous and 93
needs the interpretation of the text. A man, long deprived of feminine company, finds his pleasure interrupted by an intruder, who will not go away but proceeds to have anal intercourse with the woman. The latter is obviously not overly displeased. The ambiguity is heightened by the pictorial allusion on the folding screen in the upper left of the picture (actually it is on the same level as the bed mat, but the perspective is slightly distorted). What is depicted is a famous pair of rocks offshore at Futamigaura on the southern coast of Honshu, near Ise. They are known as Meoto-Iwa, the wedded creators of Japan linked by a heavy straw rope. The artist here has given both of them an unmistakable phallic look, with implications left to the viewers' imagination.

Sodomy

There is little ambiguity in Fig. 94, in which the explicit 94
drawing is further elucidated by the text. A noted courtesan has been disappointed by the flabby performance of a youth. They are

intruded upon by an older but clearly vigorous man, a monk, who proceeds to have anal intercourse with the boy while inserting his hand into the woman's vagina. A comic note is added by the monk's pretense that he is actually entering the woman. Monks are often the subjects of satire in this branch of Japanese art, but there is no particular suggestion of disapproval of their lusty proclivities.

95 The situation depicted in Fig. 95 is intended to elicit our mock sympathy for the plight of the man with an enormous erection. He is unable to insert it into the fundament of the youth without causing serious damage. A courtesan peering behind the curtain offers her services, but one suspects that they will not be accepted.

These last two book illustrations are the work of Utamaro, who was reputed to have spent so much time in the Yoshiwara that he could be considered the official painter of the night-life quarters of Tokyo. One is led to surmise that he saw at first hand enough of what was going on to give us a fair idea of the possibilities of the place, even though these scenes and others like them that he drew might be sheer inventions.

Lesbianism

Utamaro is also the author of a large single-sheet print, Fig.
96 96, in which two nude women, presumably prostitutes, are about to engage in lesbian activity with the aid of a large dildo. The text specifies that the woman on the left is expressing her impatience while her companion is pausing before inserting some pellets—lubricant or aphrodisiac or both—into her. The dildo is exaggerated to the conventional dimensions given to the penis, and the vulvas are correspondingly enlarged. Aside from this distortion, the women's bodies are delineated with Utamaro's characteristically graceful mannerism, and the composition exudes a kind of serene sensuality which brings this work close to being a masterpiece.

97 Fig. 97 represents a special kind of masculine wish fulfillment.

This is a jousting contest between two women, each of them armed with poles, with tampons on the ends, which penetrate their vulvas. The woman on the right is in the throes of an orgasm, indicated not only by her attitude but also by an emission spouting from her vagina. The belief that women ejaculate the way men do is often expressed by artists, but before we dismiss this as an example of ignorance or faulty observation, we should ask ourselves whether it is not intended as an artistic metaphor. The contest aspect is further indicated by the presence of a referee, who is evidently interrupting his score-keeping to masturbate under his robe. The cartouche on the left is framed by four phalli.

The Orgy

Scenes in which multiple partners of both sexes are locked in amorous combat are frequently represented by artists, who normally scamp the artistic problem involved by simply linking the groups along a horizontal plane. A more interesting type of composition, which describes a special type of orgy, is seen in these next two figures. The basic theme is that of one man engaged with a number of women. In Fig. 98 the male has taken on six of 98
them. He indulges in straight copulation with the first, and he kisses the second (note that such kissing in Japan has very specific erotic connotations) on the mouth. The four others he arouses and satisfies with his fingers and his toes. All the bodies are naked except for the usual cloths about their waists; and they are flung about in poses suggestive of the wildest abandon. It is an open and explosive composition, in sharp contrast with that of Fig. 99. 99
Here one man is involved with ten women. His responsibilities are correspondingly greater, so that in addition to his natural limbs and organs he uses dildoes strapped to his elbows and knees. The composition here is closed, suggesting that a self-contained rhythmic movement is being generated. Both of these artistic solutions are extraordinarily ingenious and esthetically satisfying,

with the Dionysian abandon of the first work perfectly balanced by the controlled tension evident in the second.

❀ THE WORLD OF SEXUAL FANTASY

The line between observable reality, described in the preceding group of examples, and projective fantasy, which is the theme of this section, is not hard and fast; nor is it always easy to locate. As used here, the term "fantasy" is intended to connote the kind of situation in which recognizable everyday reality is transcended, either through the process of distorting or exaggerating natural forms or by creating totally new forms and contexts through the joining or juxtaposition of elements borrowed from different realms of being: human and animal, dreams and actuality, or any combination through which a certain kind of shock is intended. It might well be argued that when an artist depicts a man as possessing an enormously exaggerated erect penis, which he wields in an environment in which all other elements are reasonably normal, he is stressing the fantastic at the expense of the real. But in this particular case we are dealing with an artistic convention that we can interpret as a metaphor. In most of the examples that follow, we are invited to enter a surreal world where we must plainly suspend our disbelief and simply accept the given premises. Under those conditions, there should be no difficulty in agreeing that Japanese imagination, when unbridled, has produced some remarkable results.

The Comic Contest

The Japanese have an engaging fondness for fun and games and contests of different sorts. Artists have often recorded this national trait in a number of works, the best known of which go back to the thirteenth century. The celebrated Toba Sojo, or Abbot Kikuyu of the Kōzan-ji in Kyoto, is famed for his "Animal Scroll"

and is also regarded as the author of three other scrolls of drawings. Two of these deal, in a humorous and even caricatural style, with humans at play. Regardless of the correctness of the attribution, the term *Toba-e,* or art in the manner of Toba Sojo, has come to be applied to a whole series of works, of varying artistic merit, in which contests are the principal theme. Among the breezier examples of this genre one might cite the "Farting Contest." Fig. 100, illustrating the measuring of penises, shows details from a 100
handscroll which is probably a nineteenth-century version of a comparable work done in the Kamakura period (thirteenth and fourteenth centuries). The setting is probably that of the imperial court of the eighth century. The reason for saying that pictures like this record fantasies is clearly the fact that they express longings and desires, secret aspirations brought to light, and vainglory paraded in the only place where they could have meaning, the world of make-believe.

That the tradition persists at the popular level is shown in
Fig. 101. Here the intent of the artist is to sing the praises of male 101
potency. The great tumescent penises shown here are put to tests which demonstrate their virtues: hardness, resistance, and durability. As in the previous work, a great deal of humor is evident. In the handscroll from which Fig. 100 derives, great lords display magically magnified endowments in the presence of court ladies, each of whom claims that her own obviously much smaller vagina is capable of accommodating the proudest man. In Fig. 101, the peasant, the farmer, and the lowly artisan boldly proclaim their own versatility, and their implied superiority over the effete upper classes.

Ghosts and Demons

Dreams of unsatisfied lust or sexual fears or morbid desires are the subject of a kind of transformationism in which the artist endows sexual organs with a separate identity, in terms of humans, animals, or monsters. A double page by Kunisada, Fig. 102, gives us 102 a set of examples of all three. These forms may be regarded as traditional, and are possibly very ancient, proceeding from a substratum of primitive folk beliefs.

103 The artist who made the print illustrated in Fig. 103 may have wanted to point a moral by ringing his particular changes on a popular theme. Once again we have an orgy, with one man a prey to twenty or more females. Each of them is a personified vagina, greedily seeking out the male in the lurid light of a flaming hell. The caption calls this scene "The Purgatory of Fiery Vulvas." There is no doubt that the governing concept here is that of a punishment to fit the crime, an odd one in fact, since no one would have supposed that excessive sexuality was ever a crime in Japan.

Witchery

Foxes are sometimes thought of as being demons sent to bewitch humans. Hence the three samurai who are consorting with three naked trollops suddenly find themselves, in a parallel
104, 105 composition (Figs. 104 and 105), making love to foxes while they themselves are demoted to the rank of farmers. The concept here too is very striking, and not a little gruesome.

Bestiality

The coupling of humans with dogs, sheep, boars, and other animals is often represented in a matter-of-fact and even humorous fashion which would seem to indicate that the Japanese do not particularly disapprove of such behavior. The examples of bestiality pictured in this group belong, however, to a special category. Fig.
106 106 shows copulation between a woman and a stallion. Photographs exist which seem to prove that such a conjunction, monstrous as it may seem to us, is not physically impossible. One thinks also of

Pasiphaë and Semiramis, those queens of classical antiquity whose unnatural lusts could scarcely be satisfied by mere mortals. The question here is whether we are looking at an actual performance or a symbolic projection. The probability that it is the latter is heightened by the knowledge that in Hindu mythology there exists the concept of the *Nāyikā,* a minor female divinity whose function is to be receptive to the male in all his manifestations. In the chapter on India in Philip Rawson's *Erotic Art of the East,* two eighteenth-century Indian miniatures are reproduced; one of them (Plate XII) shows *Nāyikās* coupling with all kinds of animals. Another (Plate 121) is specifically devoted to depiction of the intercourse of such a female with a stallion. Rawson's commentary makes the point that "the Nāyikā who couples with the stallion recalls the old Vedic rituals centered on the horse-sacrifice. This sacrifice could only be performed by a king whose power was such that his chosen stallion had wandered freely for a year without anyone daring to capture him. It was thus an emblem of the solar power of the king. At a certain point in the sacrifice his queen lay coupled with the horse. The horse in our picture is obviously a symbol for the masculine libido, and as such can function as a highly illuminating symbol even today."

In view of the amount of Vedic lore which was absorbed by Japan after the sixth century, and of the separate but probably equal symbolic significance of the horse in Shinto belief, it is more than likely that Fig. 106 is in effect a religious picture.

The situation depicted in Fig. 107 is clearly a flight of the 107
imagination. This large print, by Hokusai, is one of the most sensuous works ever made by any artist anywhere, both in what is shown and in the general implications of the composition. A woman, lying on her back, is being enveloped by the tentacles of two devilfish. The smaller and younger octopus is kissing her on the mouth while the older and larger one buries his head in her vulva. She offers no resistance whatever, and if we could not surmise it from the drawing itself, we would learn from the abundant text which surrounds it that her pleasure is more than

shared by the beasts. The woman is not a victim, but a deliberate partner, and the animals evidently are meant to be paraphrases of humans.

Memento Mori

If the artist who created "The Purgatory of Fiery Vulvas" can be said to have anticipated Freud's *vagina dentata,* and if Hokusai's fisherman's wife is close kin to Joyce's Molly Bloom, then Kunisada's
108 vision of man copulating with a female skeleton, in Fig. 108, takes us right back to the Psalmist. Vanity of vanities! This notion is fully supported by the text inscribed at the upper left of the picture. It is a poem from the Zen Buddhist monk Ikkyu (1394–1481), whose main burden is that all women are sisters under the skin. Kunisada was one of the main purveyors of erotic pictures of his time. It is fitting that he should provide a note of moral insight on which to close this particular investigation.

The foregoing group of examples is but a small sampling of what it is possible to find even in an incomplete archive of Japanese erotic art. They may, however, serve as a basis for tentative answers to the questions posed at the outset.

1. The erotic is not a special category of Japanese art; paintings and prints which contain an erotic element should be judged by the standards applied to any other works of their particular school or period.

2. As such works are predominantly realistic in treatment, they may be said to reflect the psychology of the particular public for which they were intended. Whether one can generalize from this to saying that any erotic work by a Japanese artist is a valid revelation of the national psychology depends on the thoroughness with which all available evidence has been examined. No such claim is made here.

3. A true appreciation of Japanese eroticism in art requires full familiarity with the literature, mythology, and, inescapably, the language of Japan.

4. There is very little symbolic imagery of a subtle kind which the untutored foreign eye can discern. There is much more to it than using a clam for a vulva or a mushroom for a penis.

5. About the only artistic convention used (if indeed that is what it can be called) is the portrayal of enormously enlarged penises on otherwise normal masculine bodies. Artists are by no means consistent in the use of this convention, which may find its origin in traditional phallic cults.

6. In its total lack of false shame, Japanese erotic art suggests that a very healthy as well as uninhibited response to sex was a national characteristic which prevailed until the influence of Western notions of puritanical restraint began to be felt in the latter part of the nineteenth century.

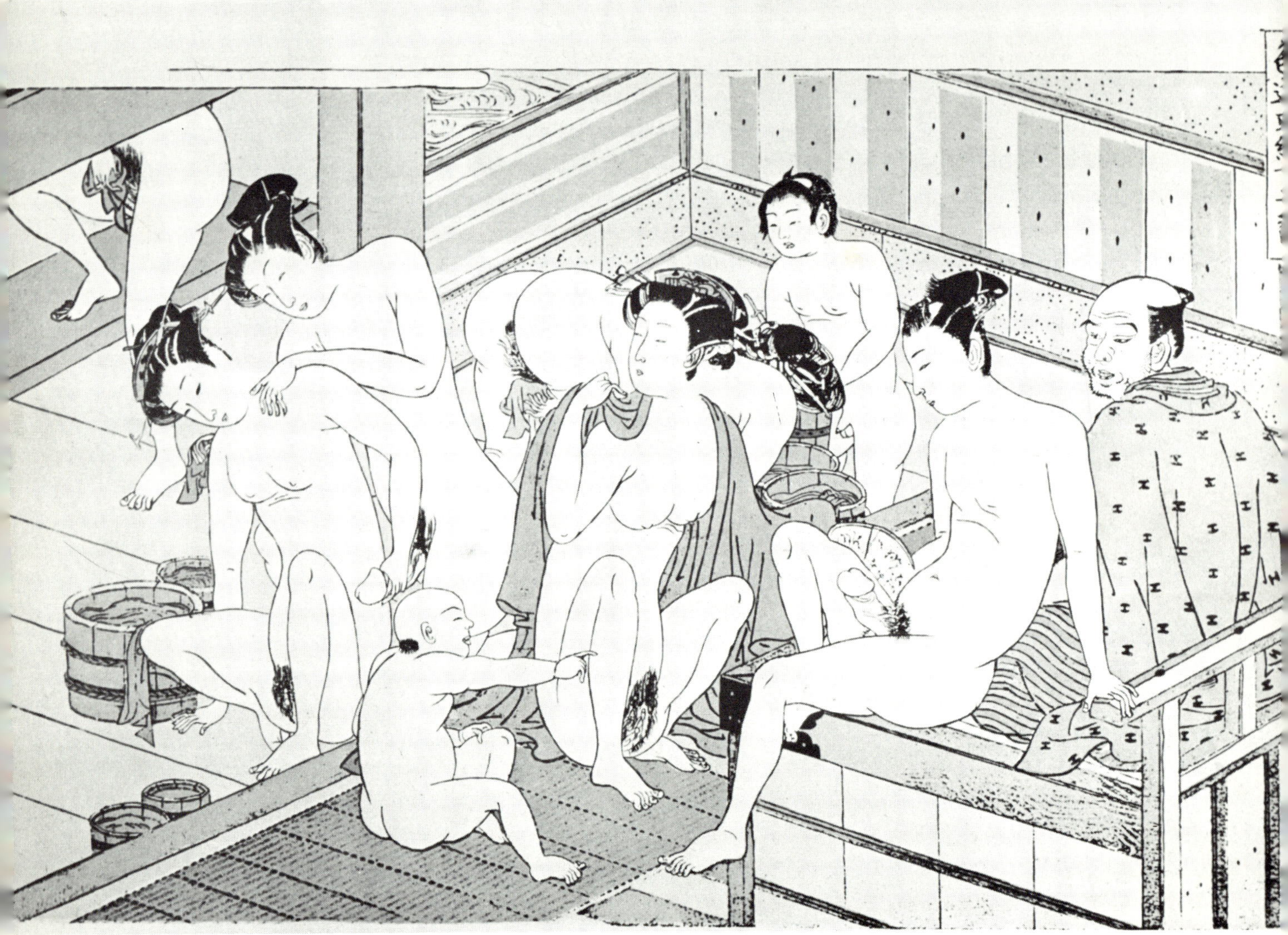

72. Bathhouse scene. Single-sheet print by Kiyonaga (1752–1815).

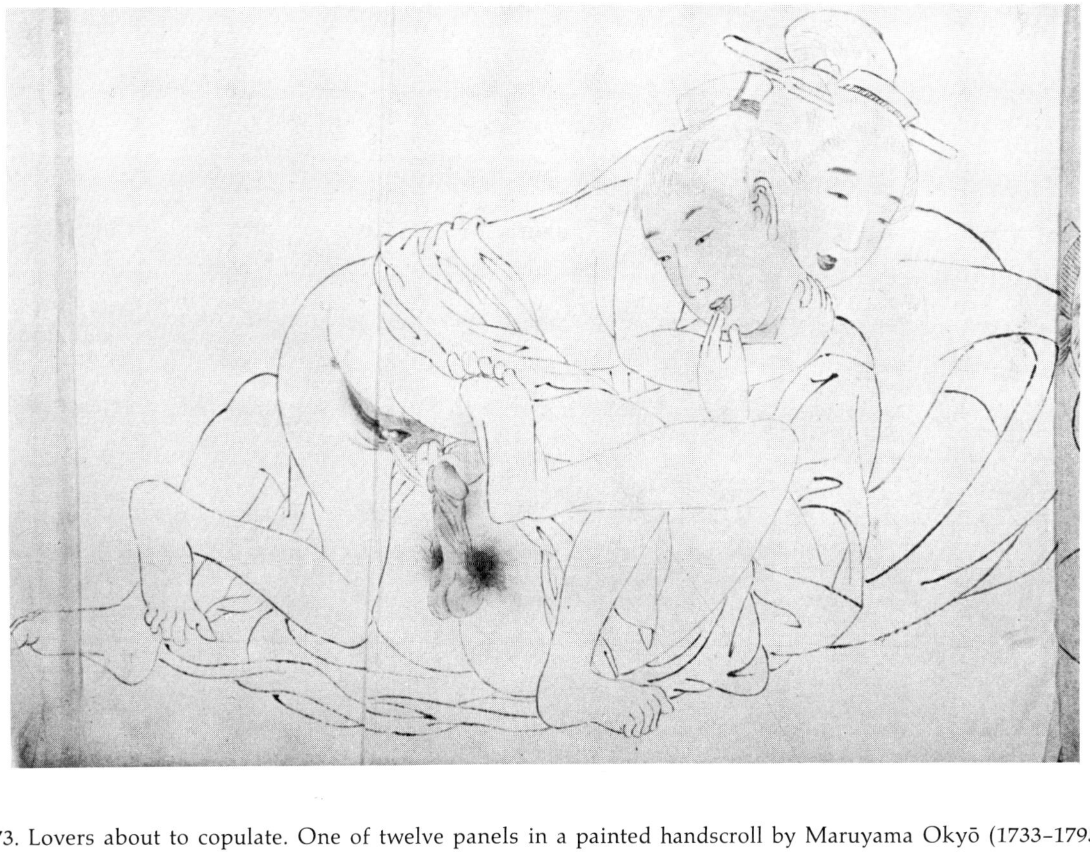

73. Lovers about to copulate. One of twelve panels in a painted handscroll by Maruyama Okyō (1733–1795).

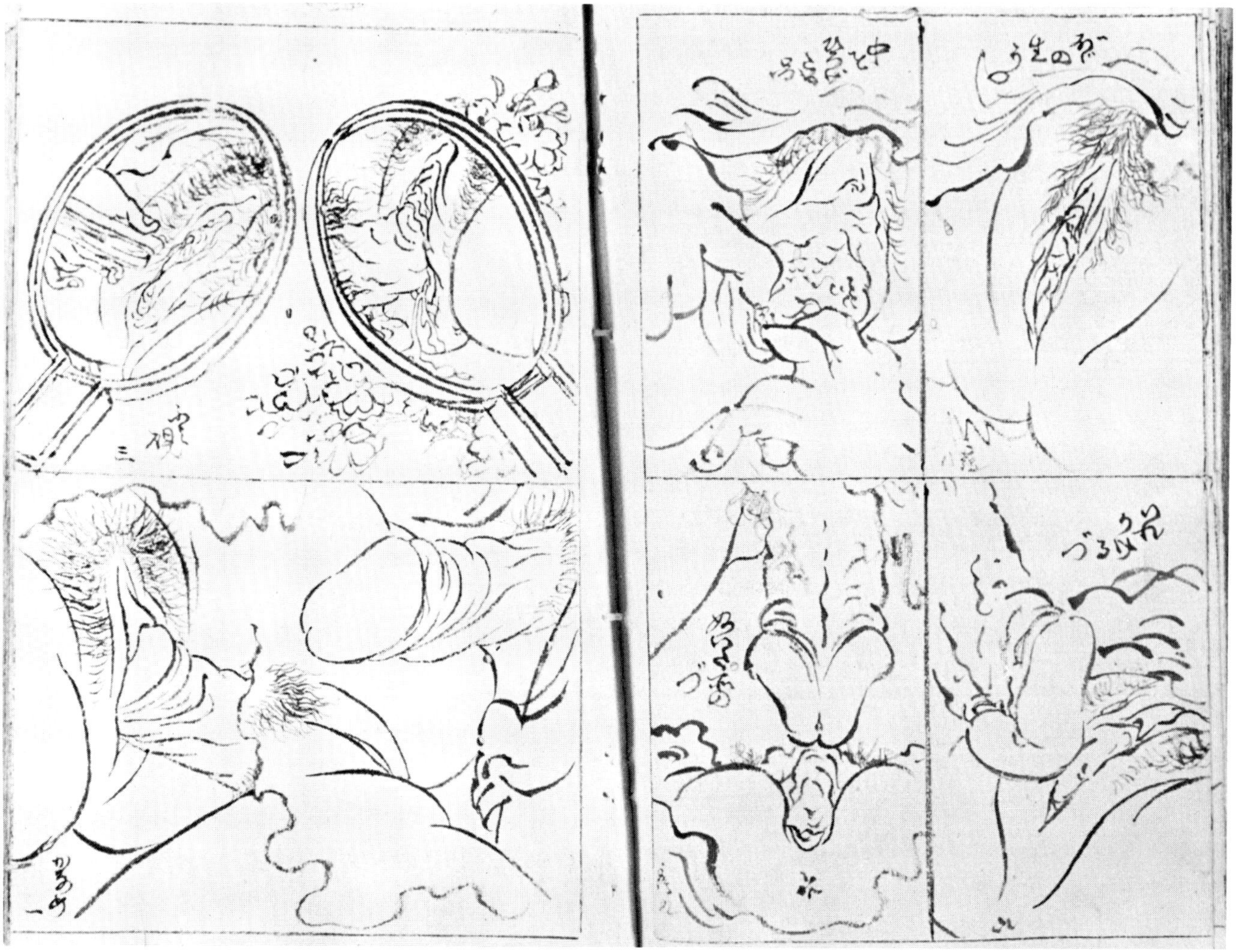

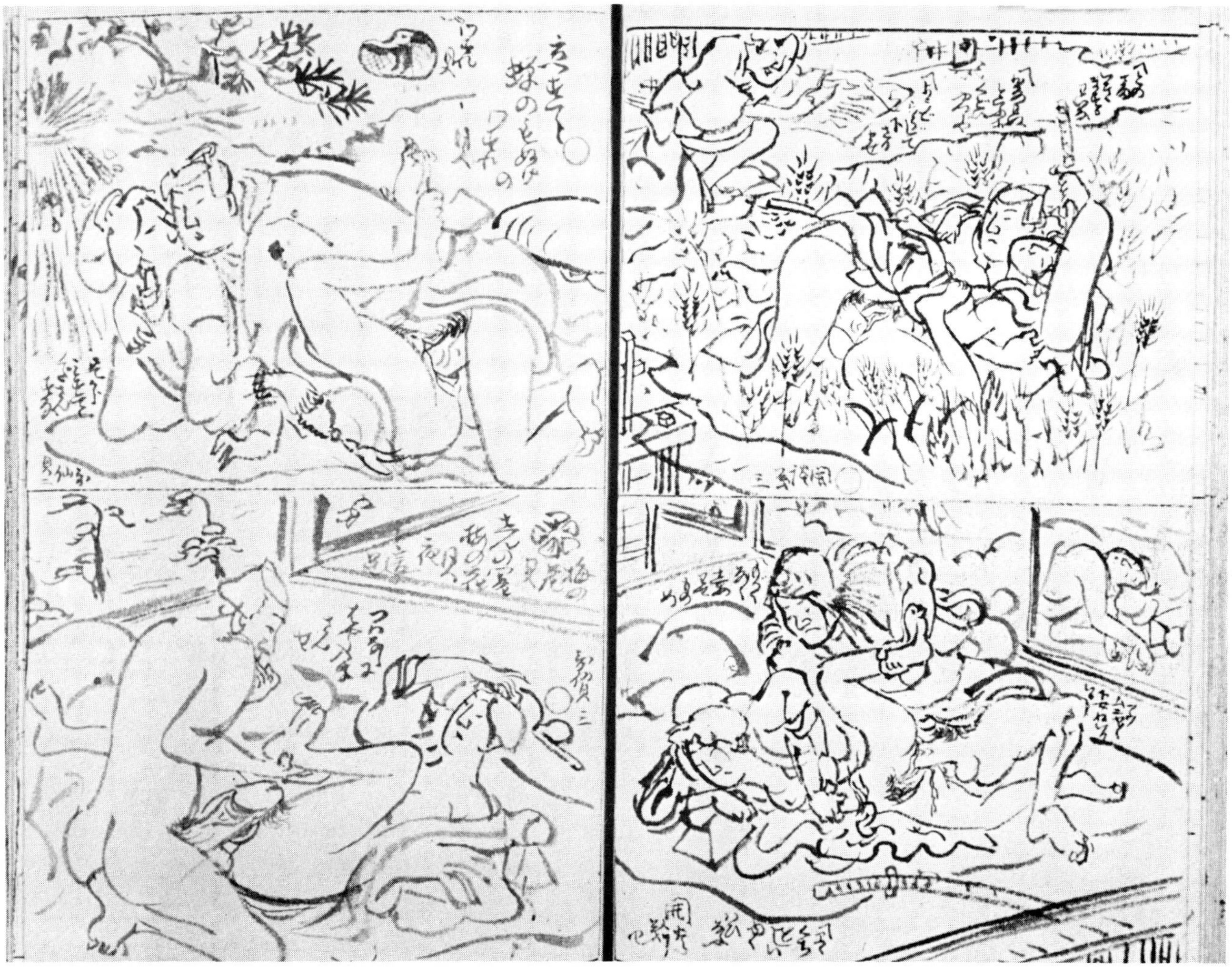

74–75. Two double pages of sketches of sexual organs and positions from Koikawa Shozan's *Kokan Makura Taizen,* a kind of encyclopedia of sexual lore derived from paintings and drawings, in sixteen volumes (middle of the nineteenth century).

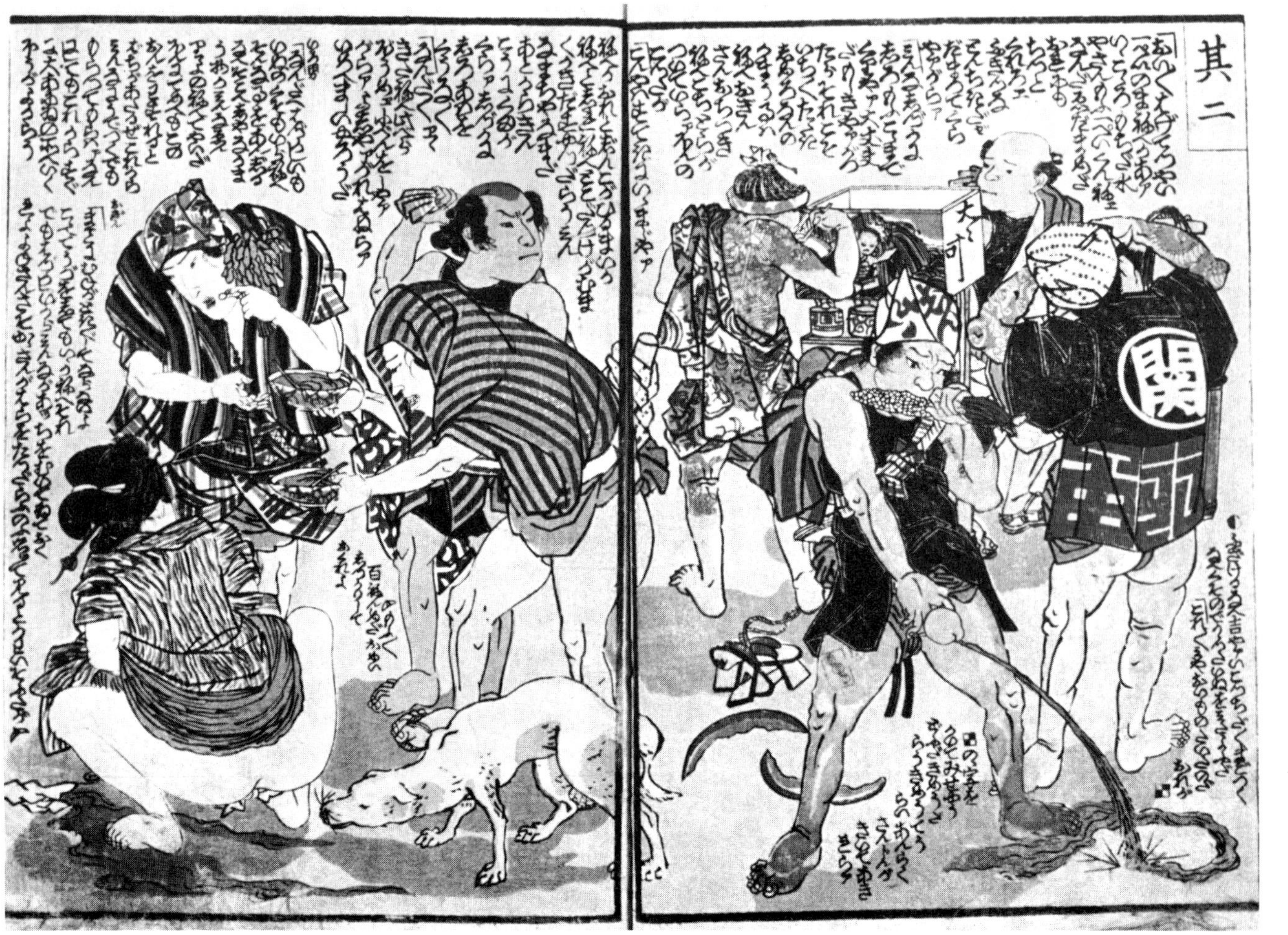

76. Country manners. By an unidentified nineteenth-century artist who contributed to a three-volume work called *Oeyama.*

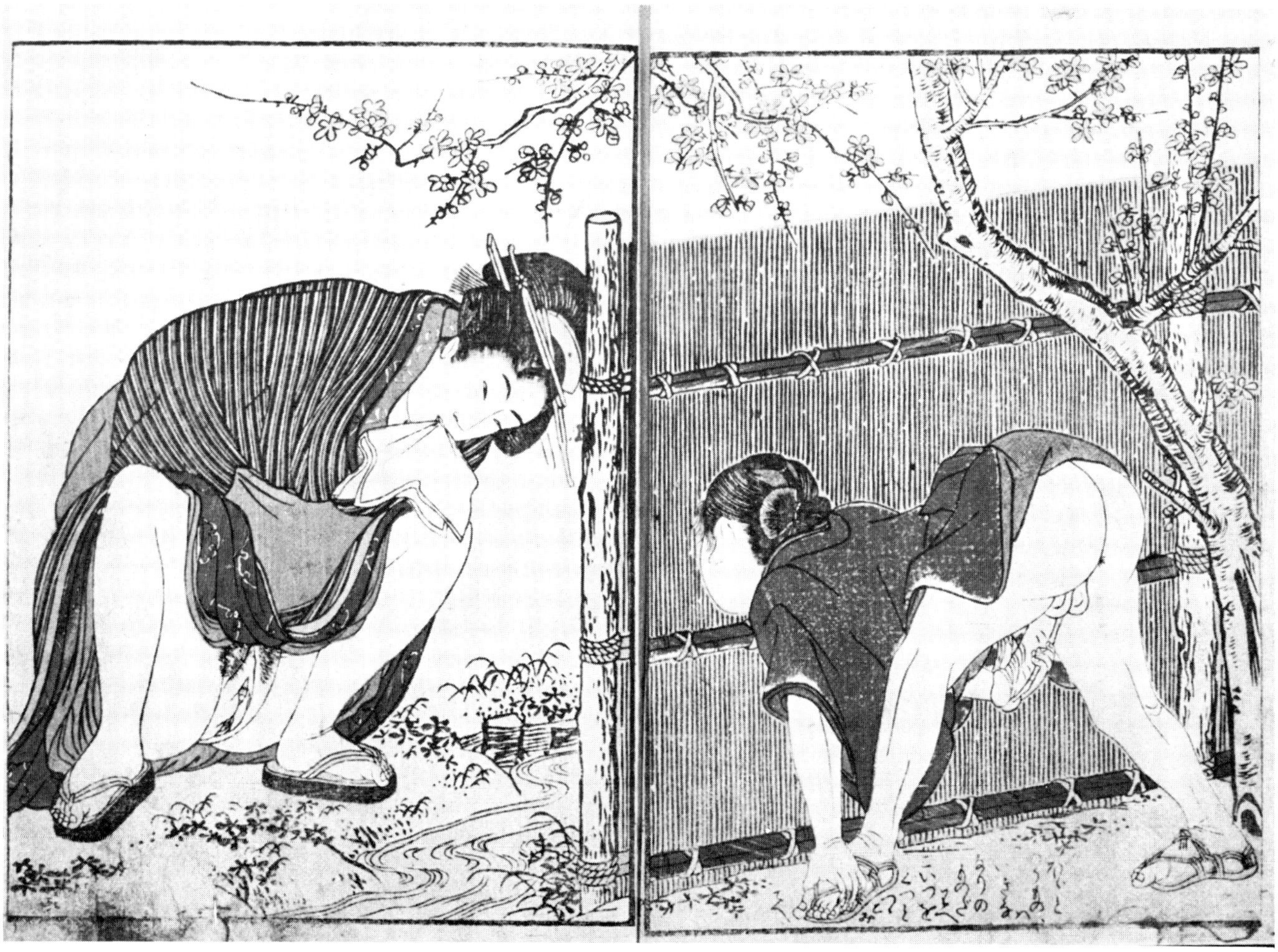

77. The voyeur. Woodblock illustration from *Kiku no Tsuyu* (*Dewdrops on Chrysanthemums*) by Utamaro (1754–1806)

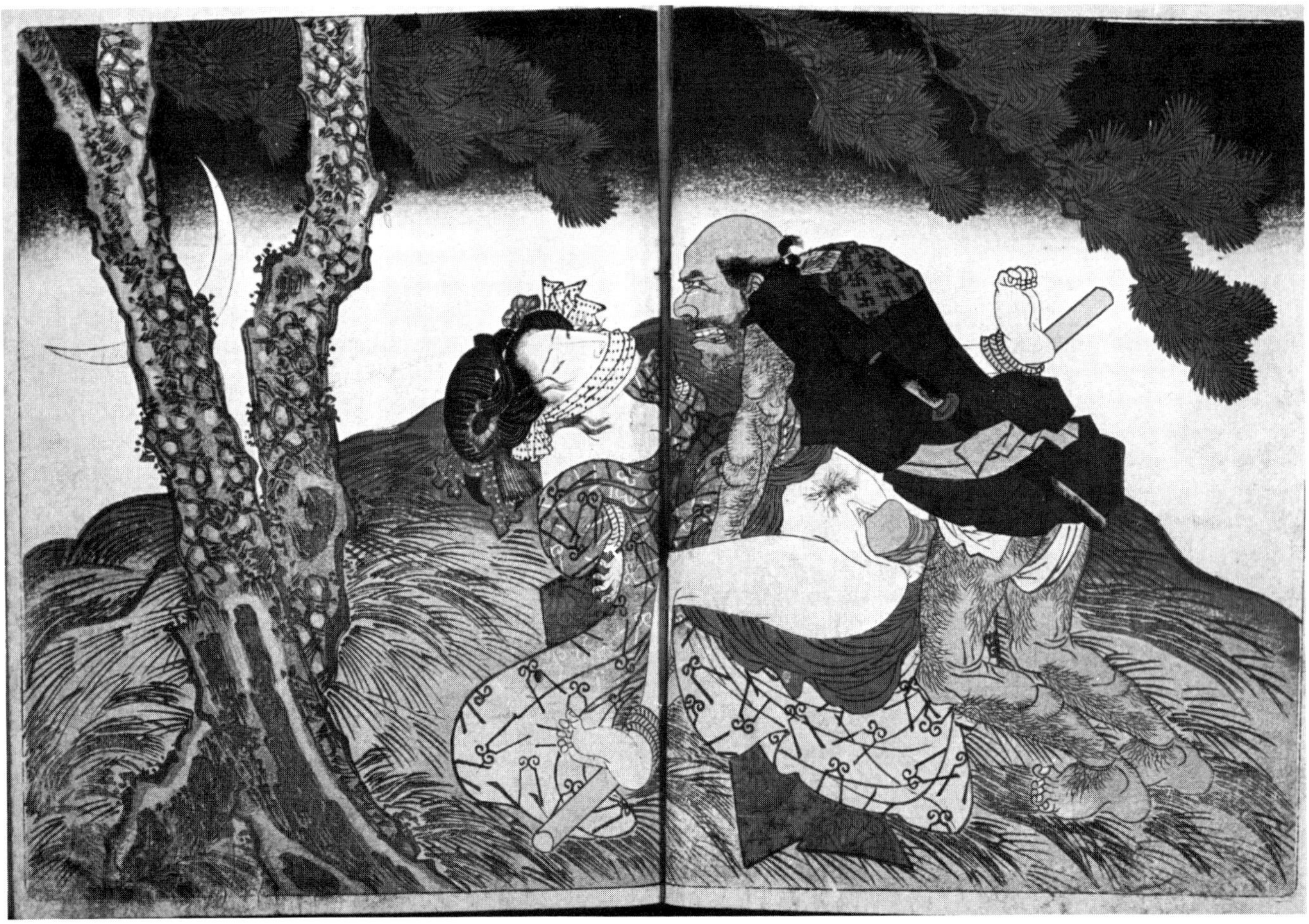

78. Rape. From *Shiki no Nagame* (*The Scenery of the Four Seasons*) (1829). Illustration by Kunisada.

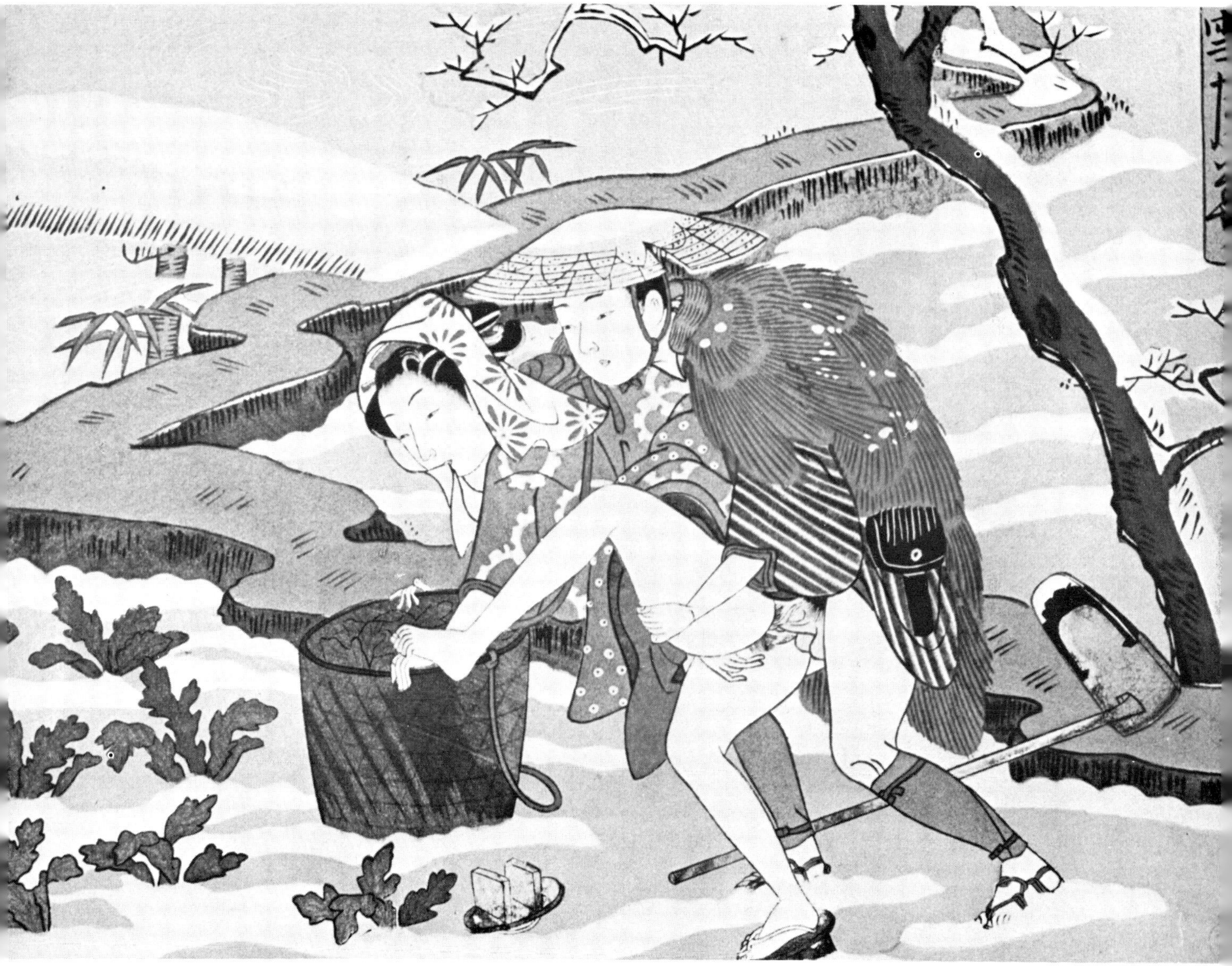

79. Attack from behind. Single-sheet print by Harunobu (1724–1770).

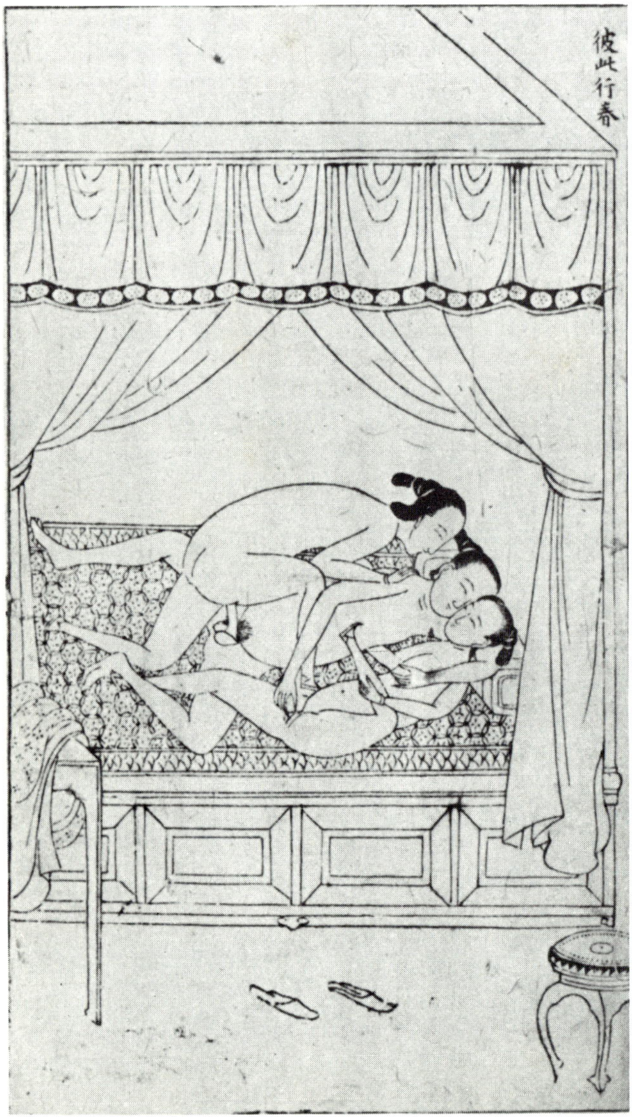

80. Copulating trio. Illustration from the Chinese novel *Chün Kung Tu,* by an unidentified artist of the Ming period.

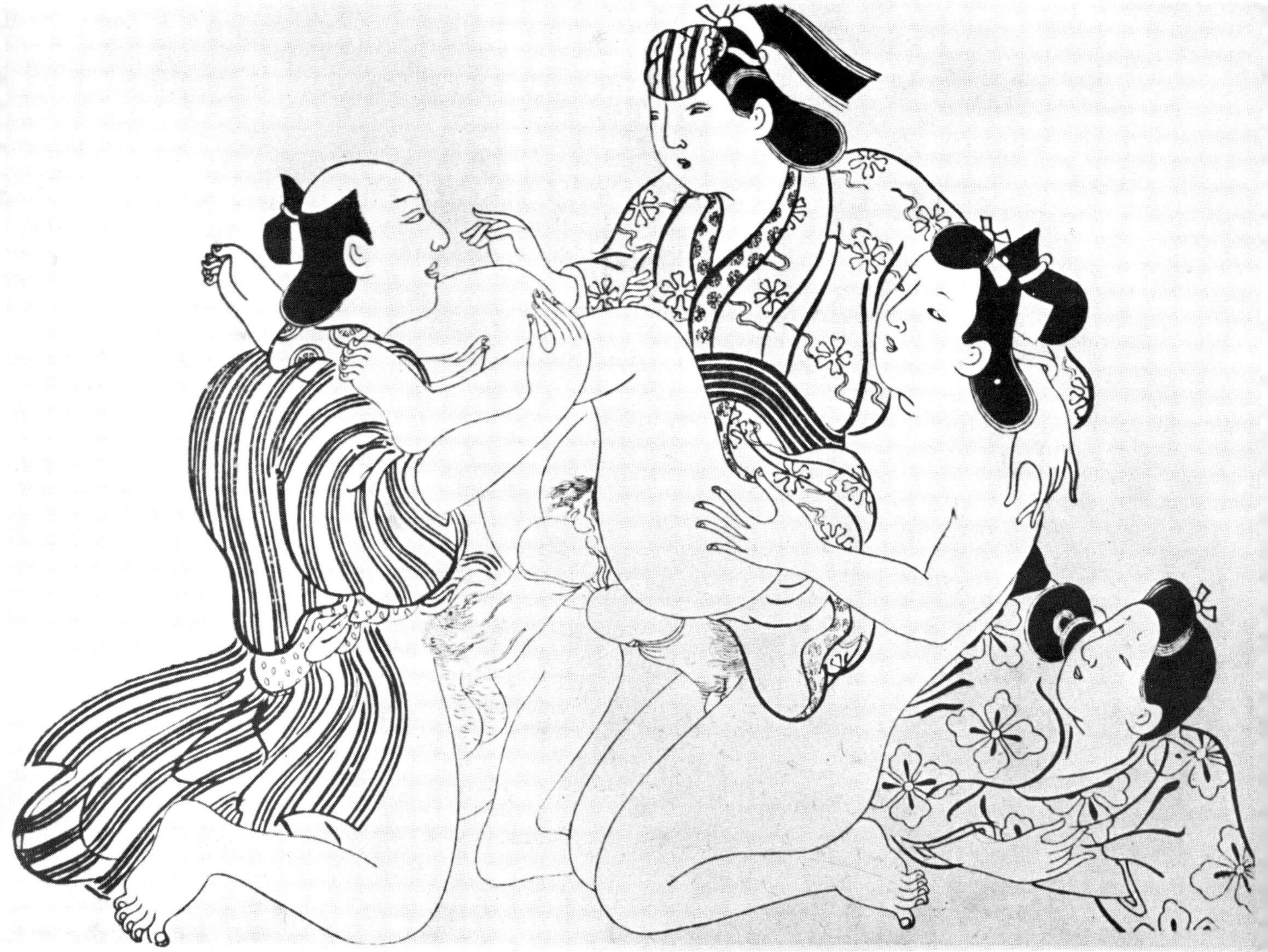

81. Copulating trio. Single-sheet print by Sugimura (late seventeenth century).

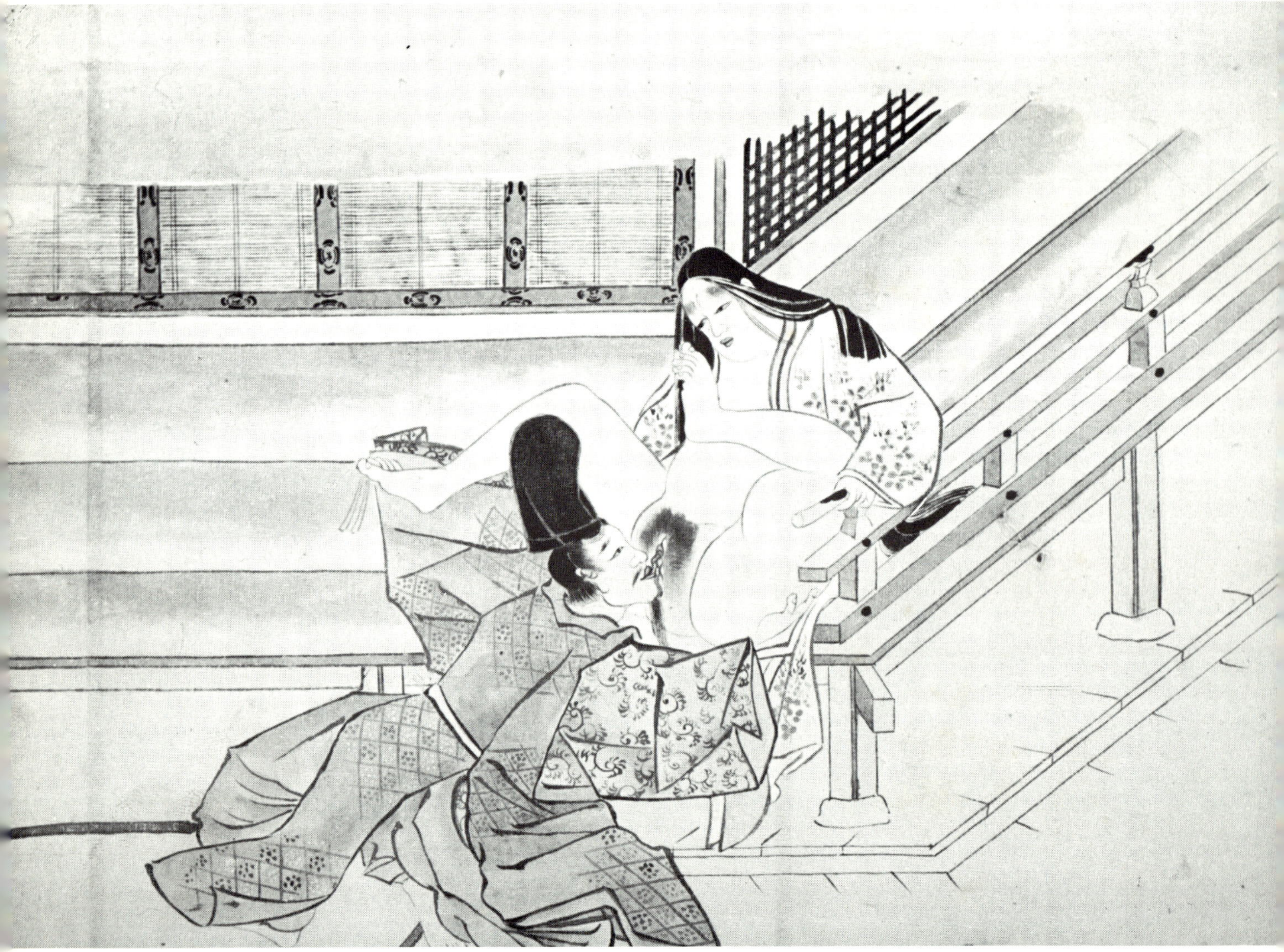

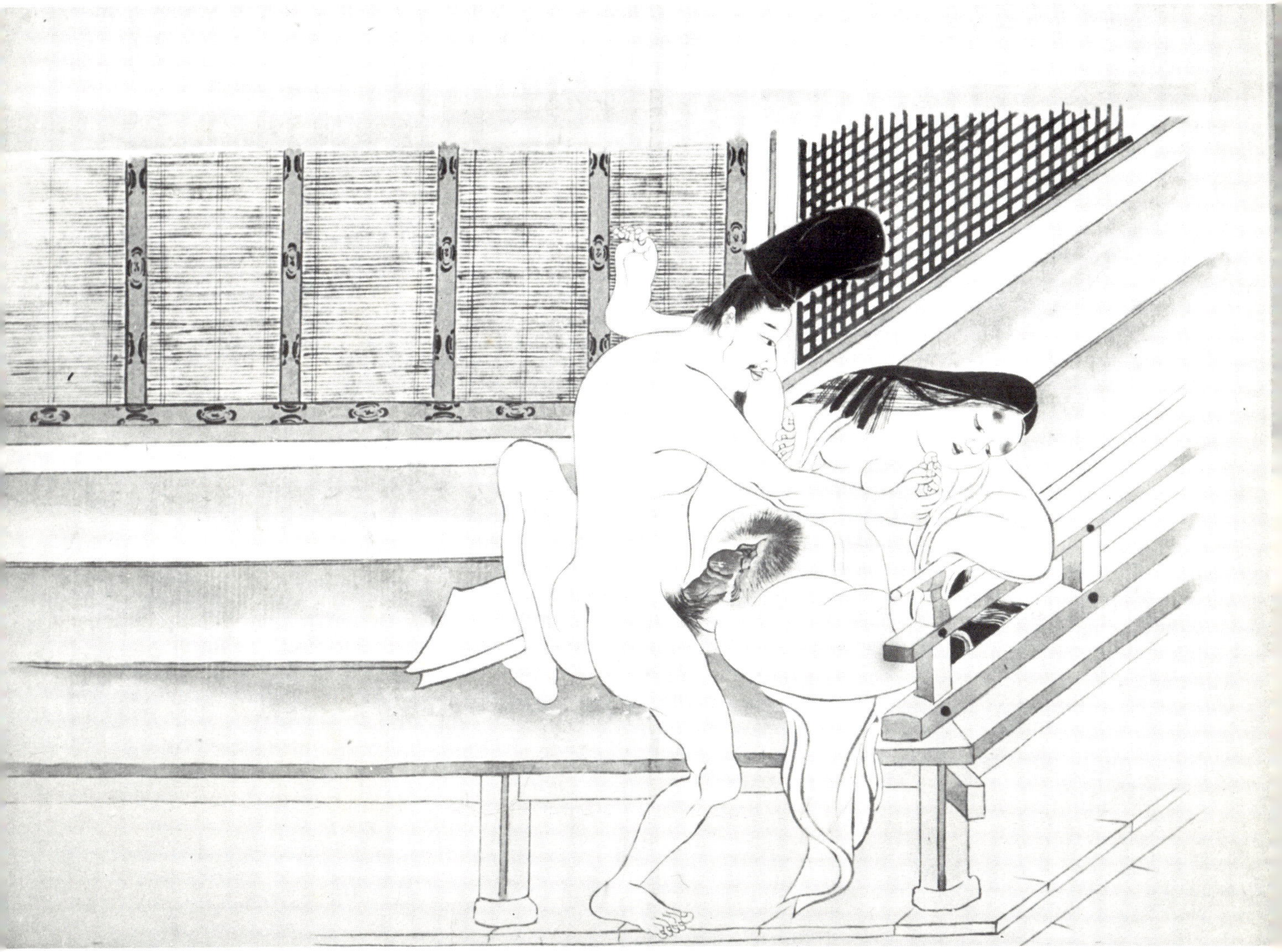

82–83. Love play and copulation. Two scenes from *Koshibagaki Sōshi,* a handscroll attributed to Fujiwara Nobuzane (1176–1268). This facsimile was probably made in the nineteenth century.

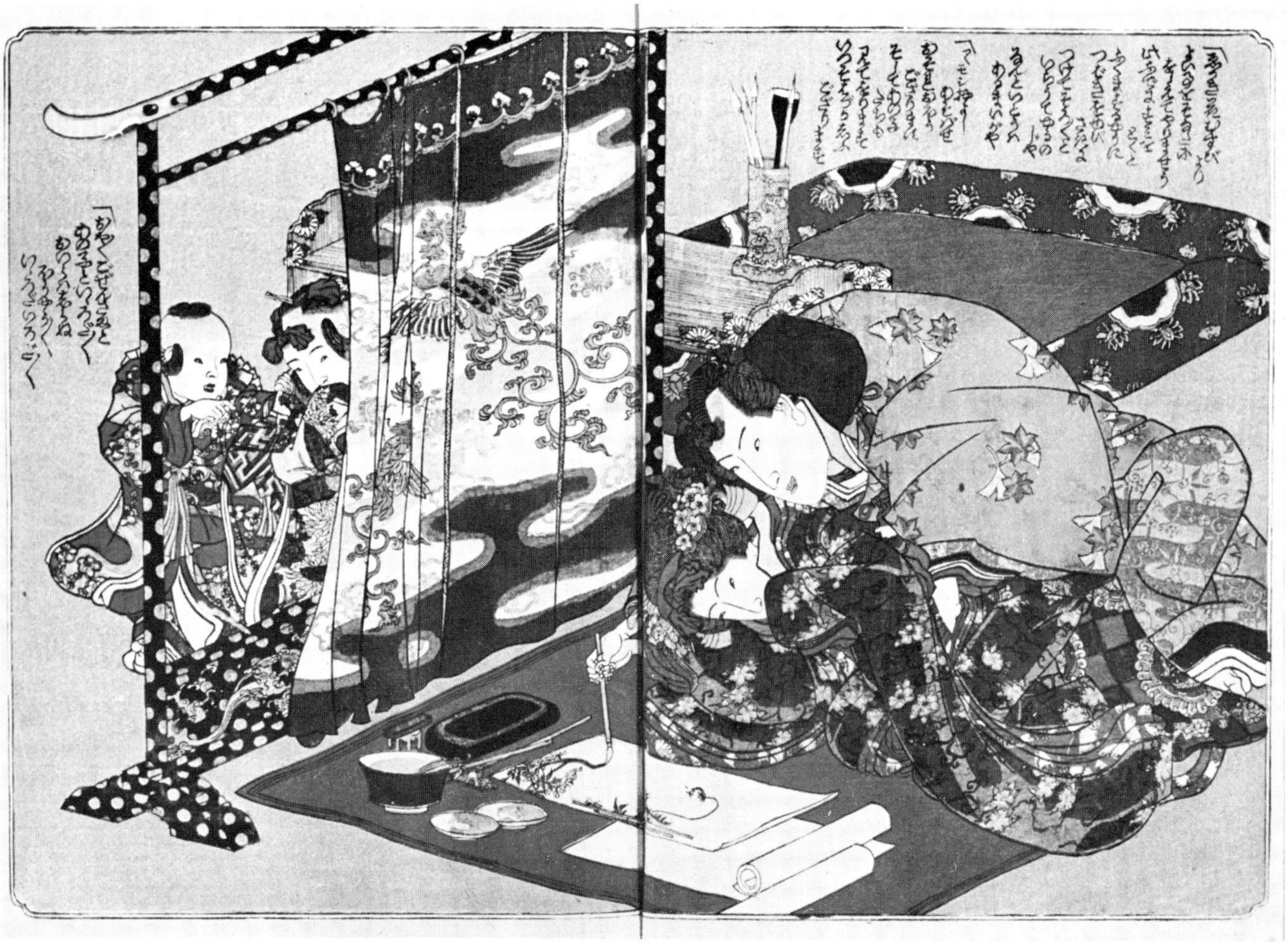

84. Love play. From Kunisada, *Enshi Gojūyojo* (*Parody of the Tales of Genji*).

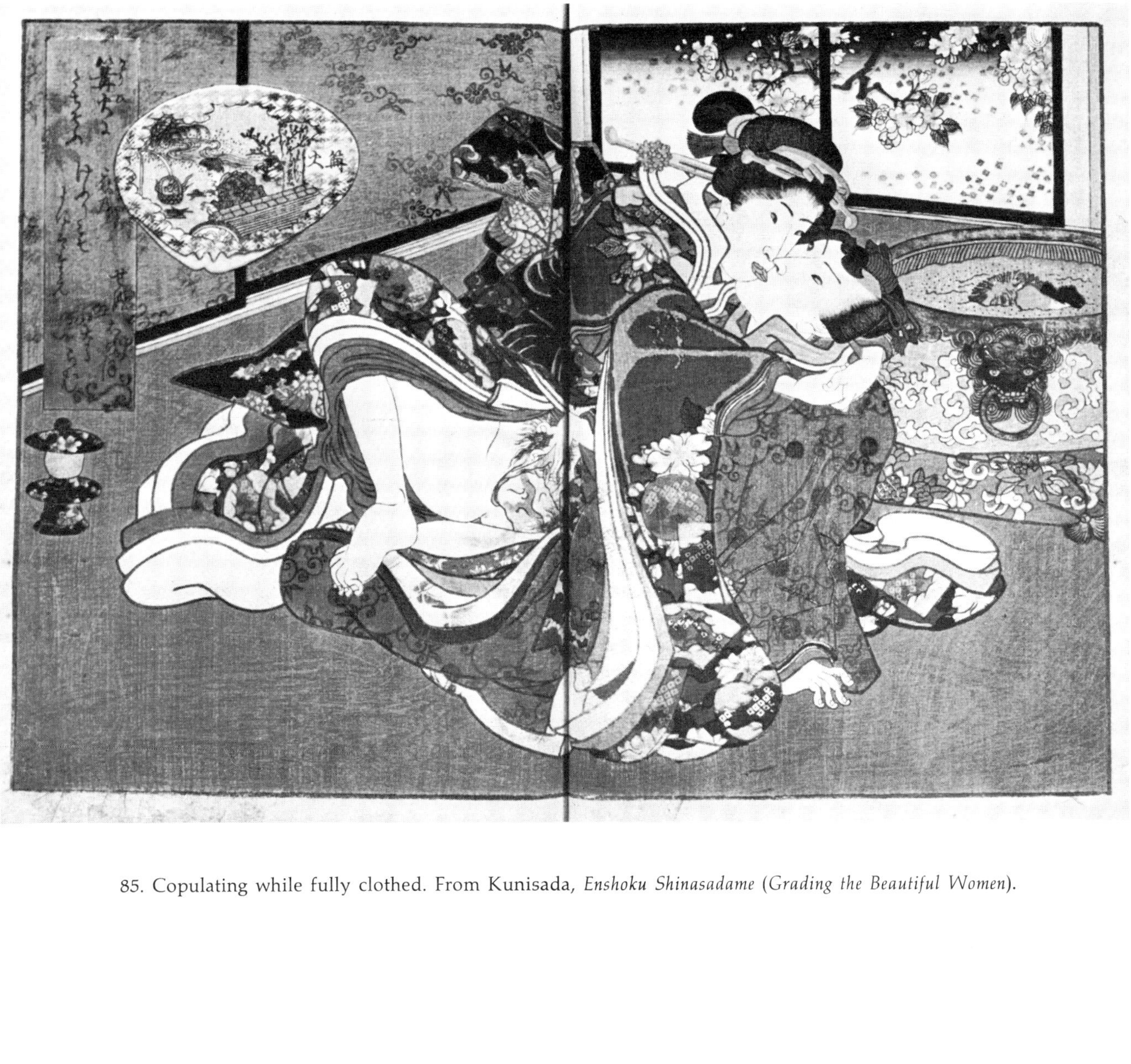

85. Copulating while fully clothed. From Kunisada, *Enshoku Shinasadame* (*Grading the Beautiful Women*).

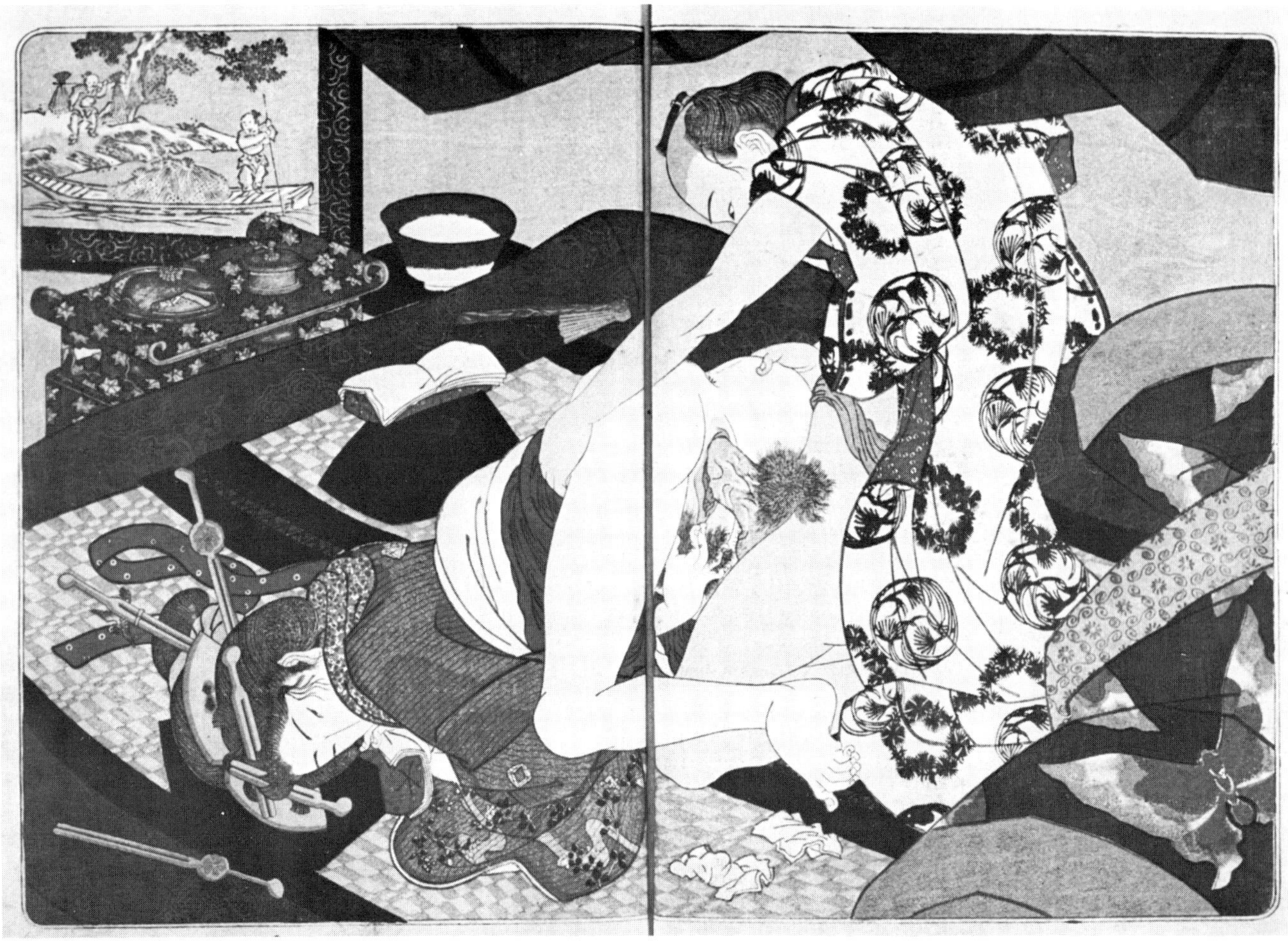

86. Penetration from behind. From Kunisada, *Kachō Yojō Azumi Genji* (*Modern Tales of Genji*).

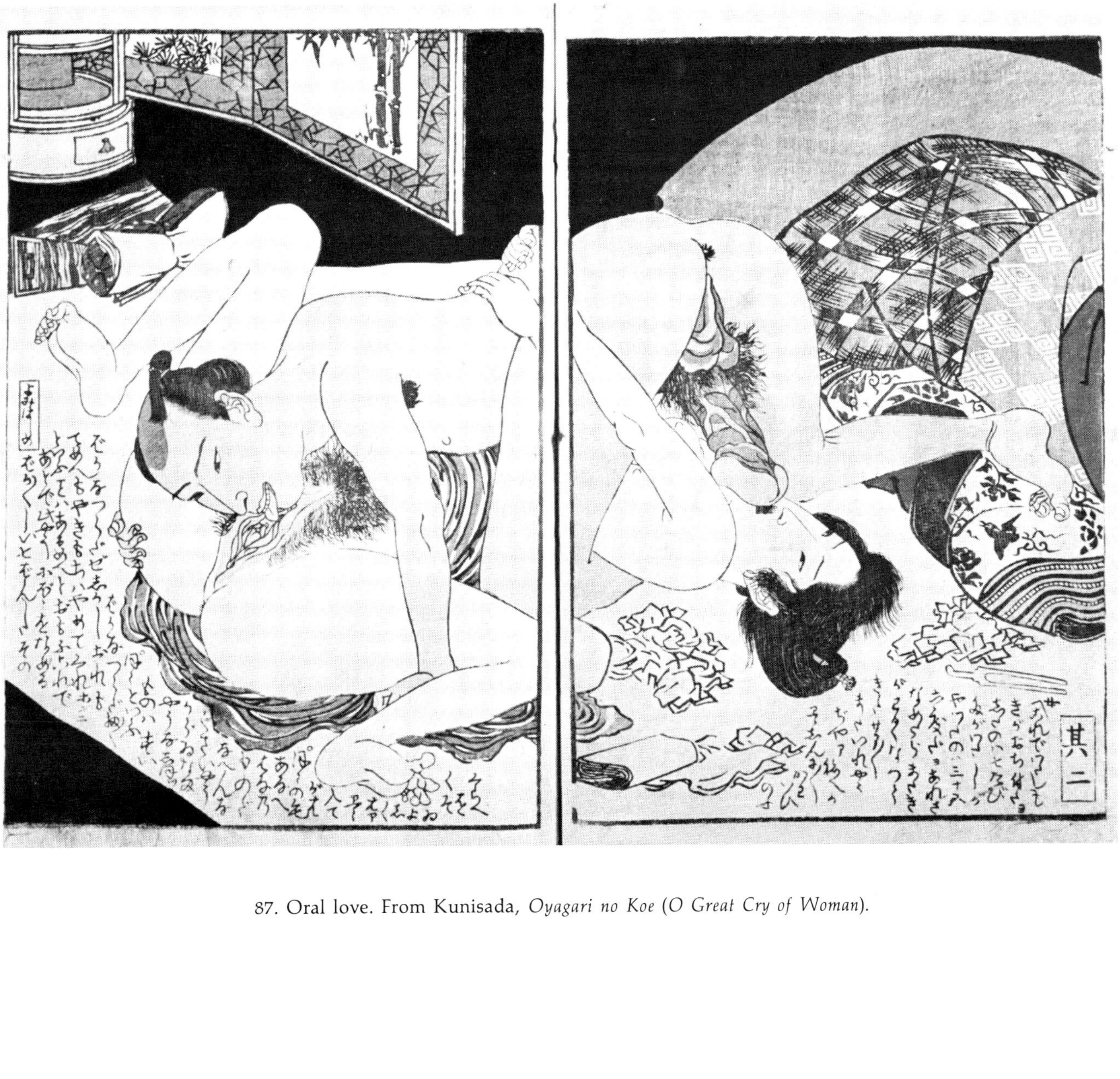

87. Oral love. From Kunisada, *Oyagari no Koe* (*O Great Cry of Woman*).

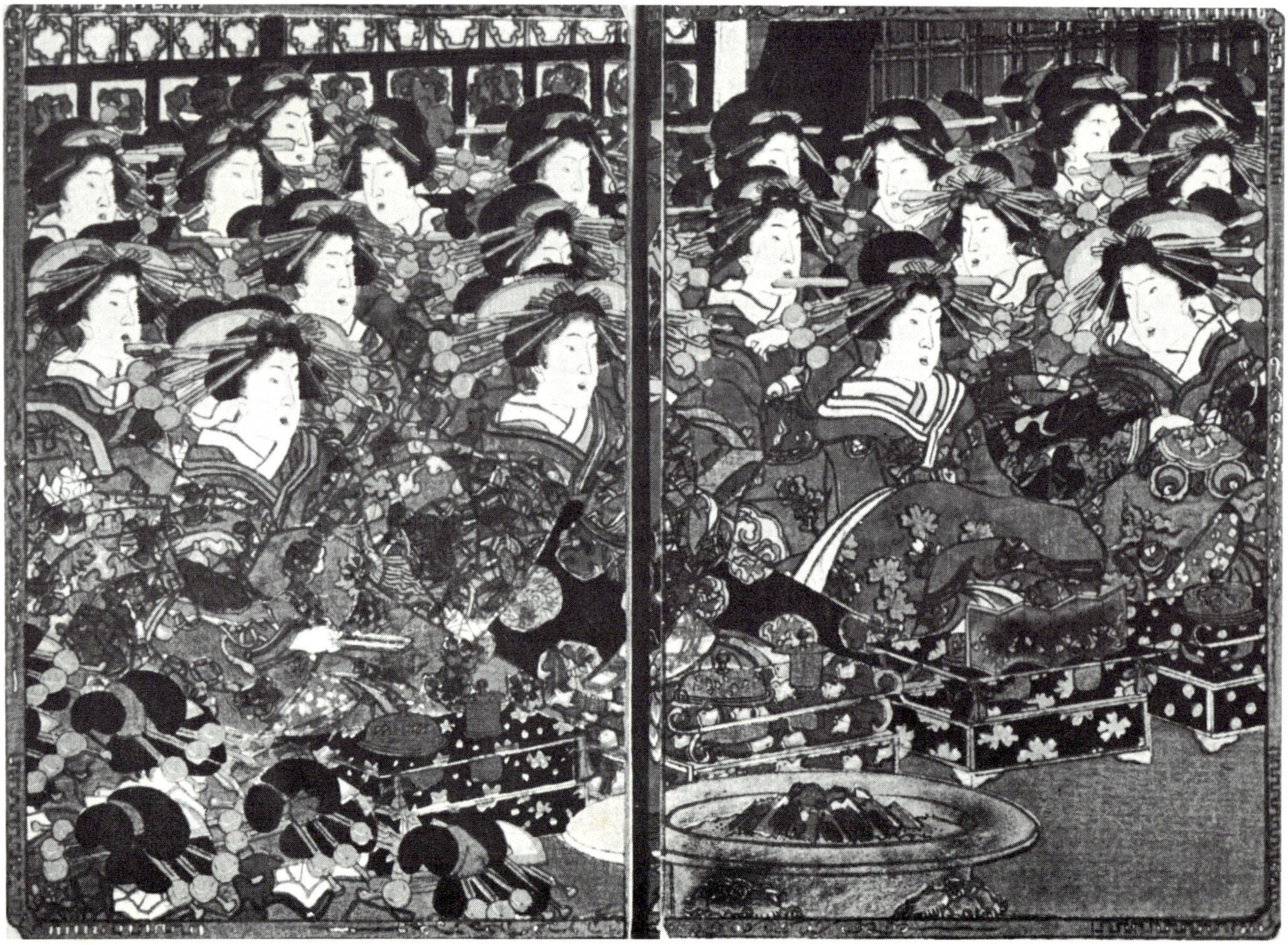

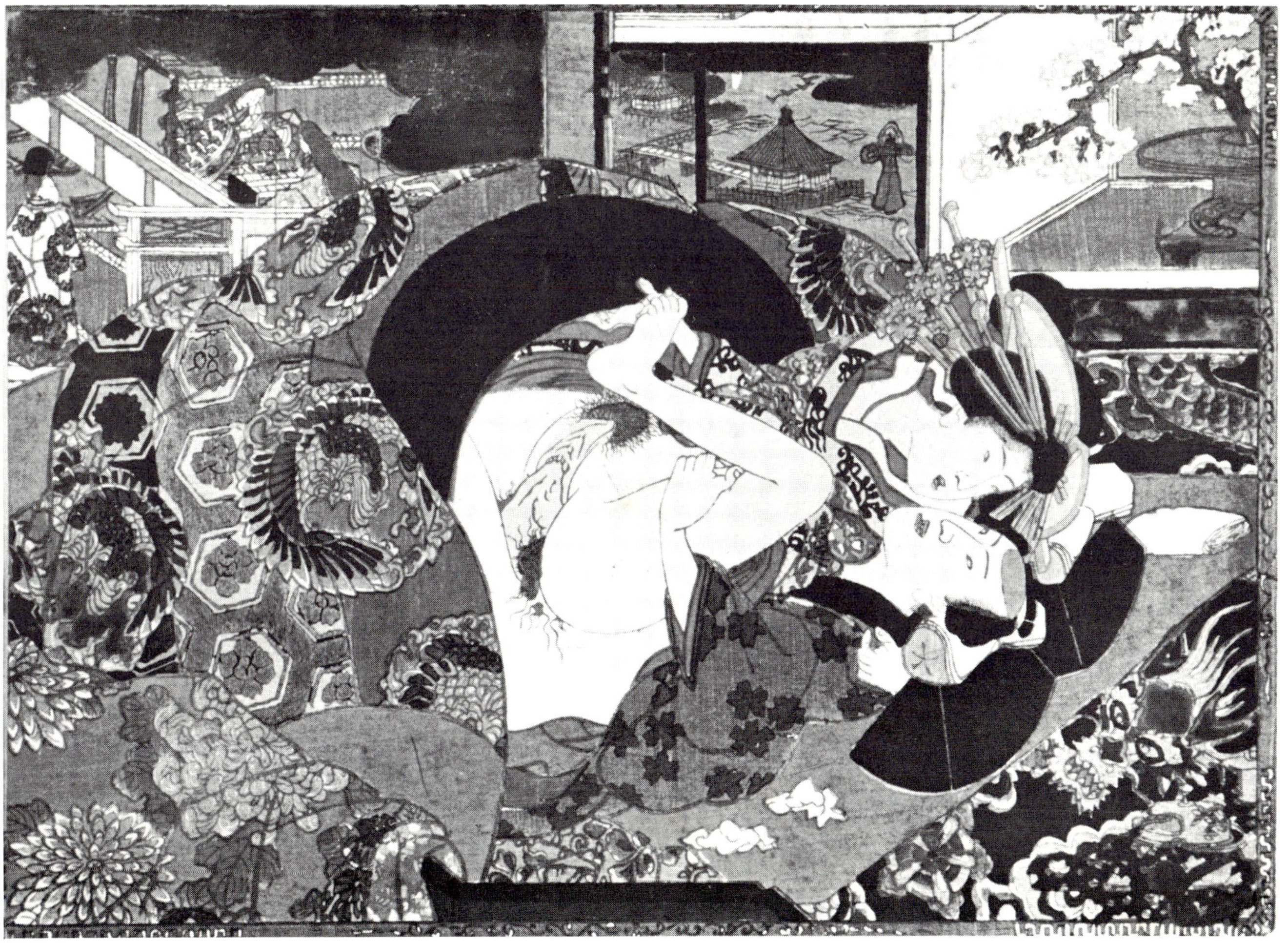

88–89. Performing before professionals. Two panels from a woodblock polyptich illustrating *Irojiman Murasaki no Hitomoto,* by an unidentified artist of the middle of the nineteenth century.

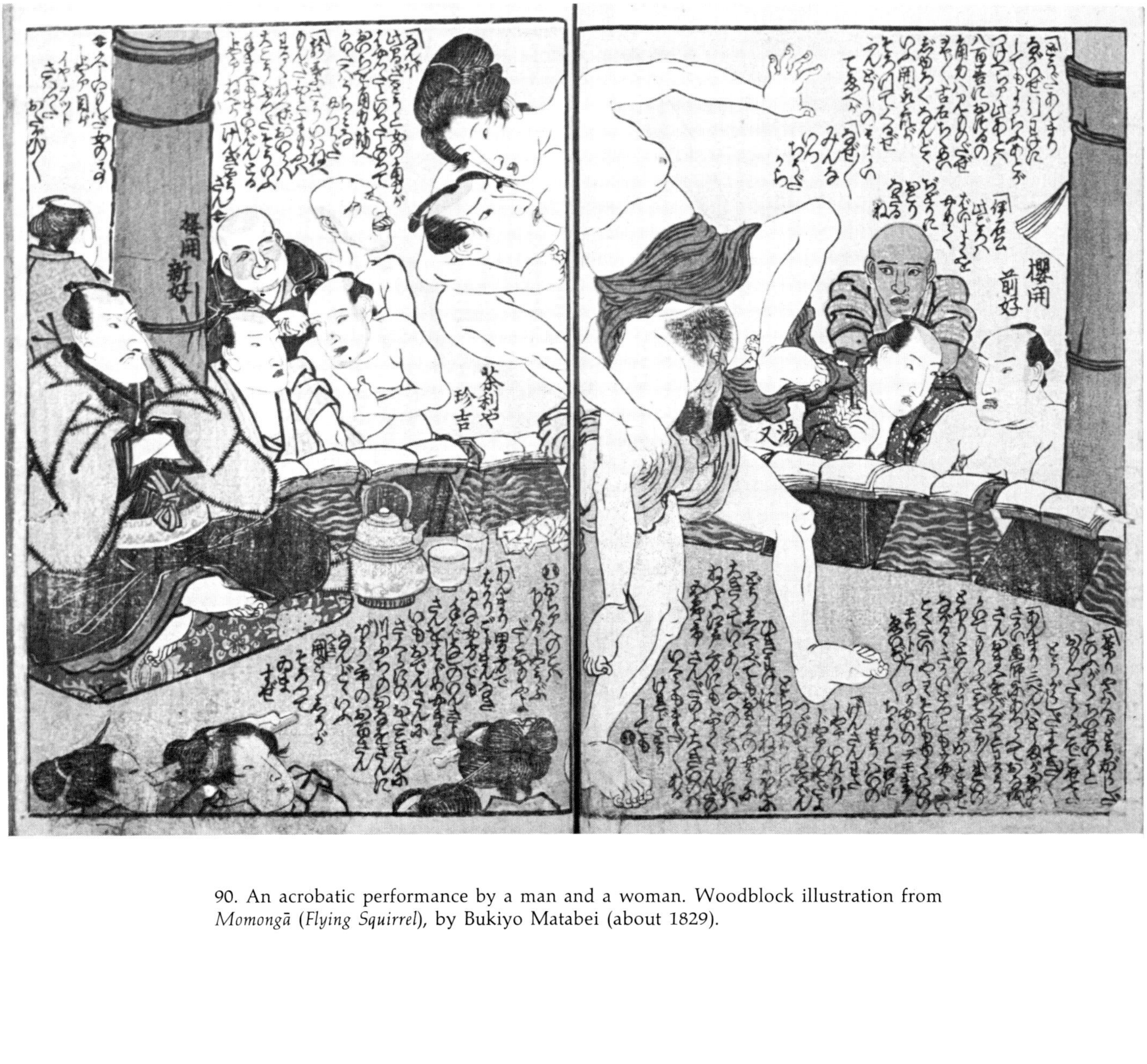

90. An acrobatic performance by a man and a woman. Woodblock illustration from *Momongā* (*Flying Squirrel*), by Bukiyo Matabei (about 1829).

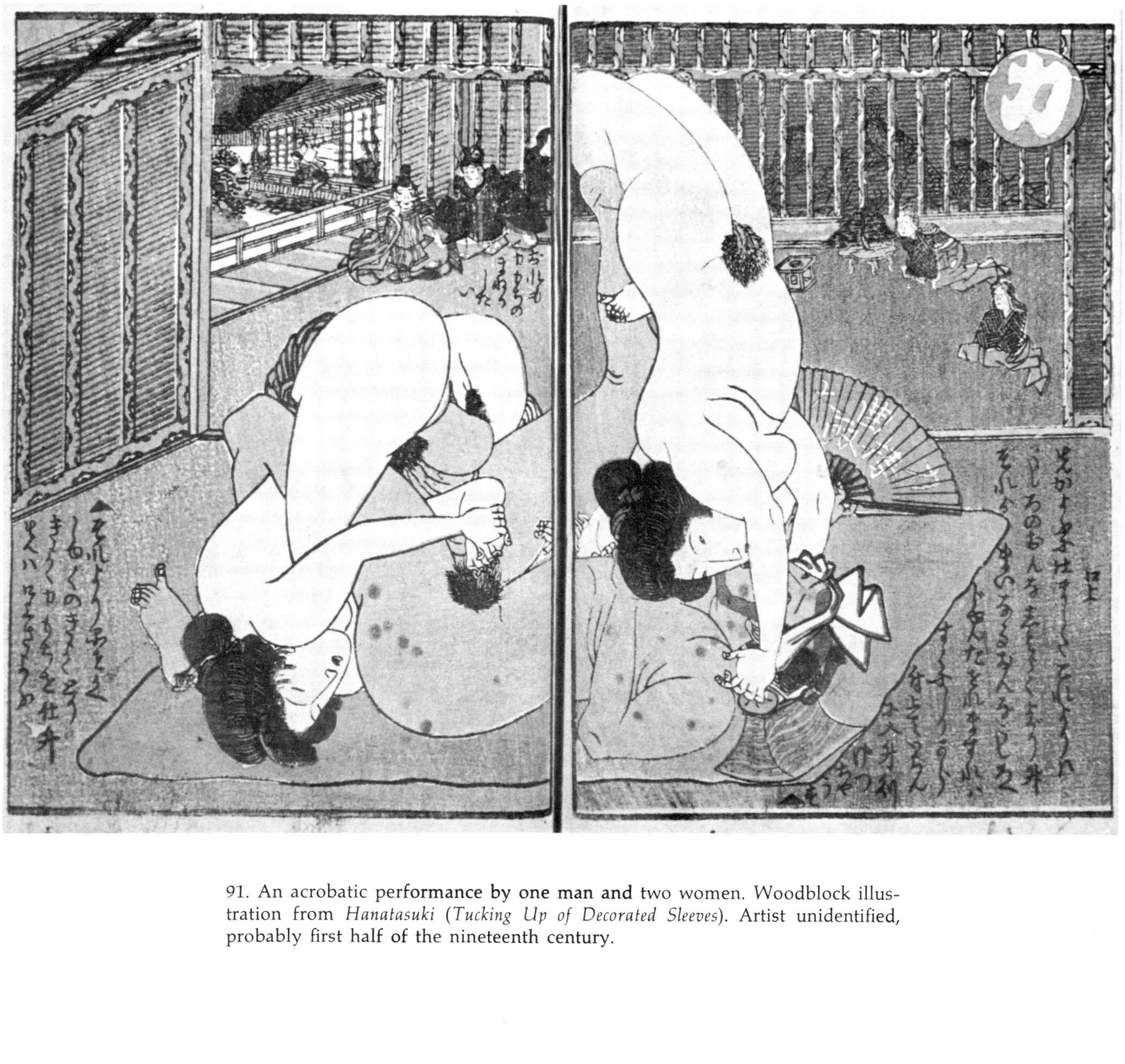

91. An acrobatic performance by one man and two women. Woodblock illustration from *Hanatasuki* (*Tucking Up of Decorated Sleeves*). Artist unidentified, probably first half of the nineteenth century.

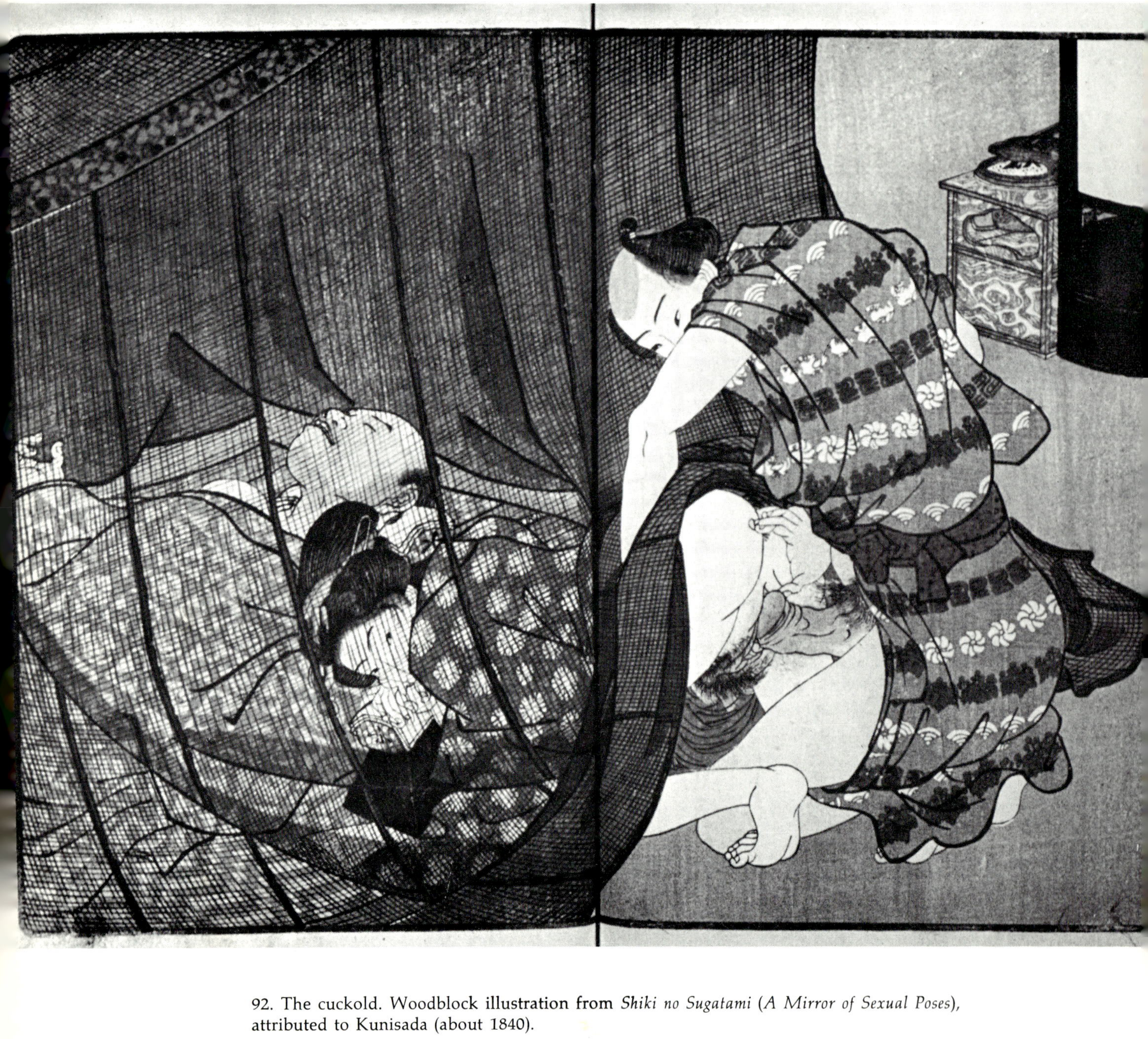

92. The cuckold. Woodblock illustration from *Shiki no Sugatami* (*A Mirror of Sexual Poses*), attributed to Kunisada (about 1840).

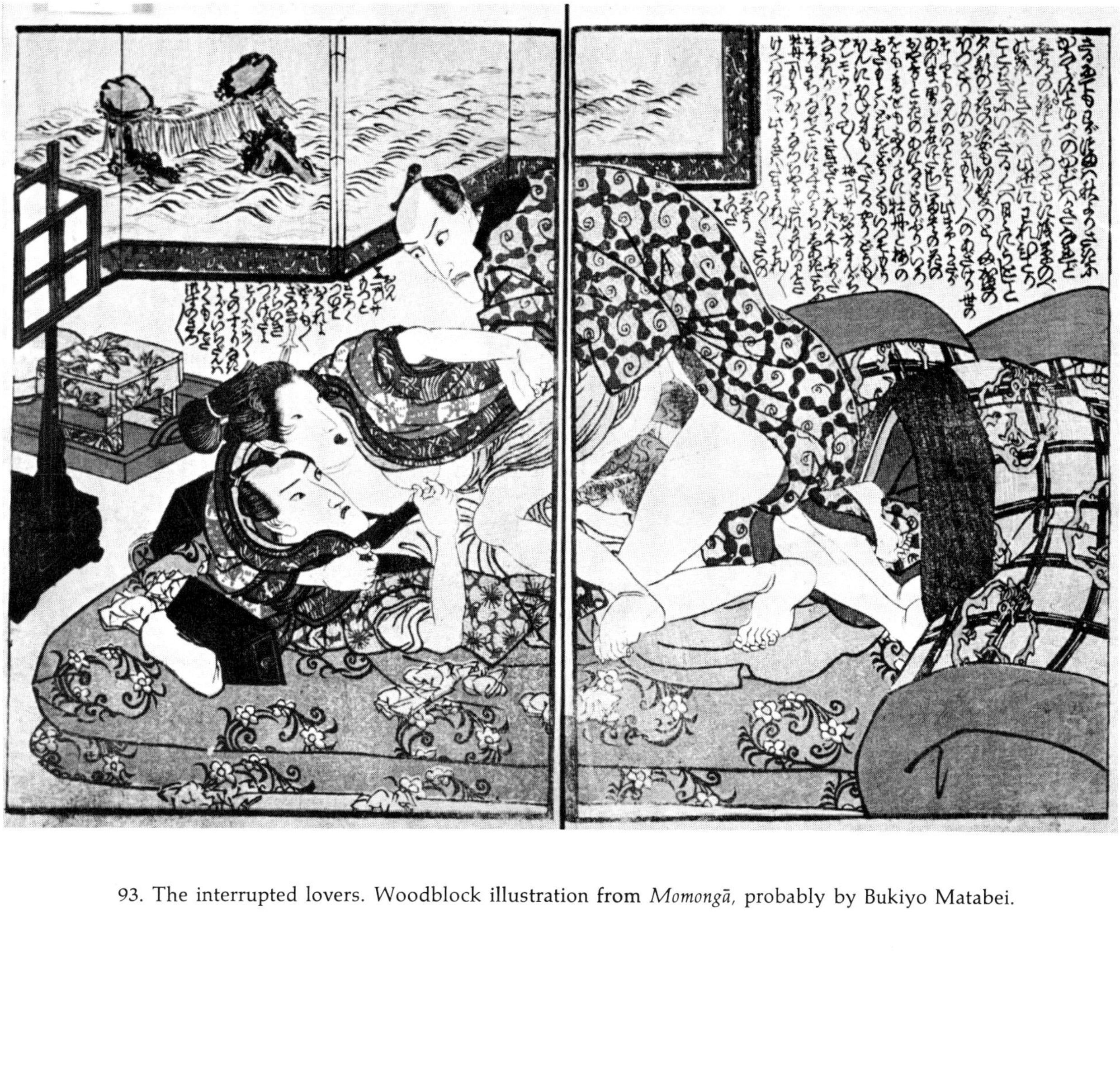

93. The interrupted lovers. Woodblock illustration from *Momongā,* probably by Bukiyo Matabei.

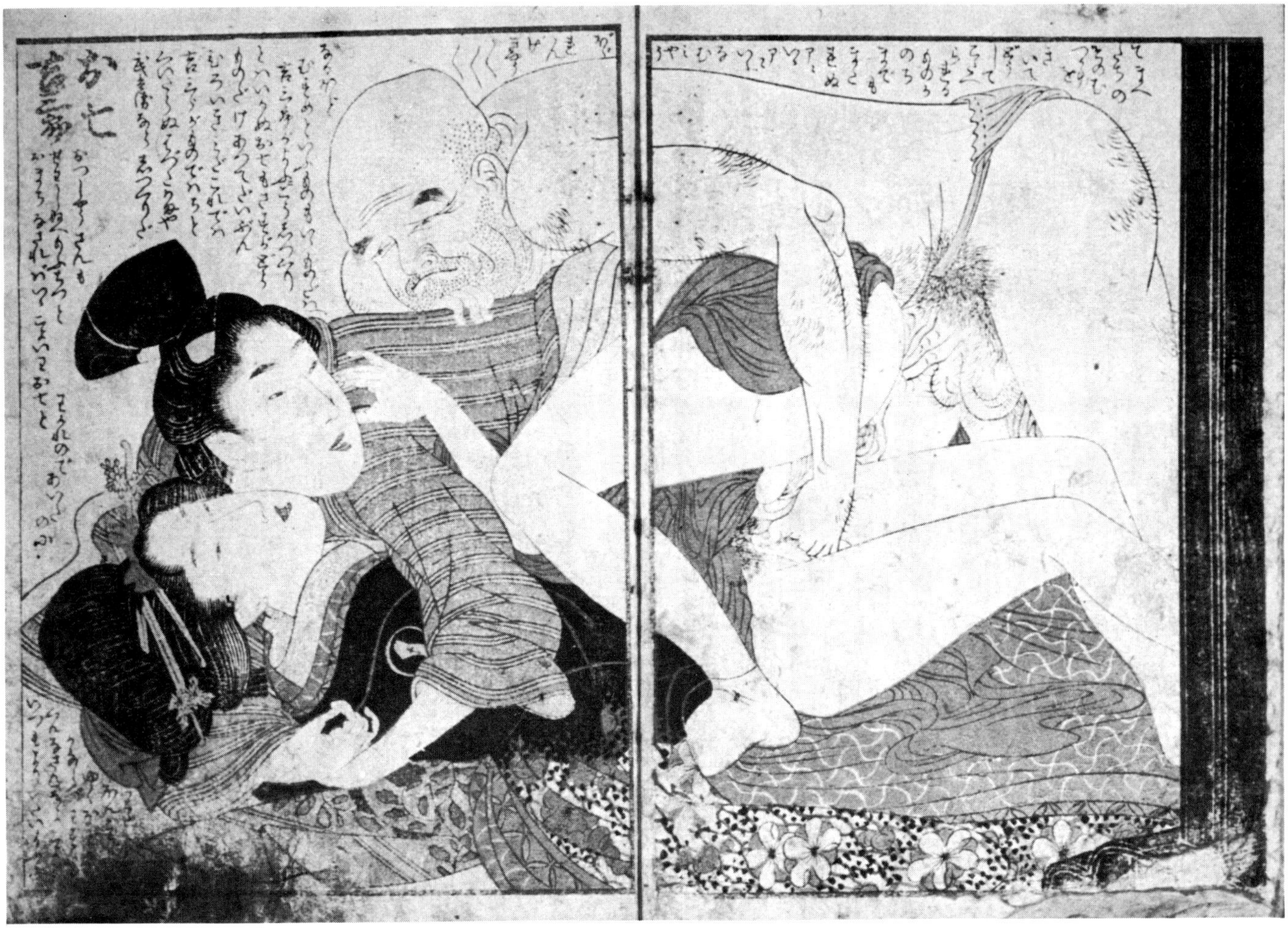

94. Courtesan, youth, and monk. Illustration, by Utamaro, from *Michiyuki Koi no Futusao* (about 1805).

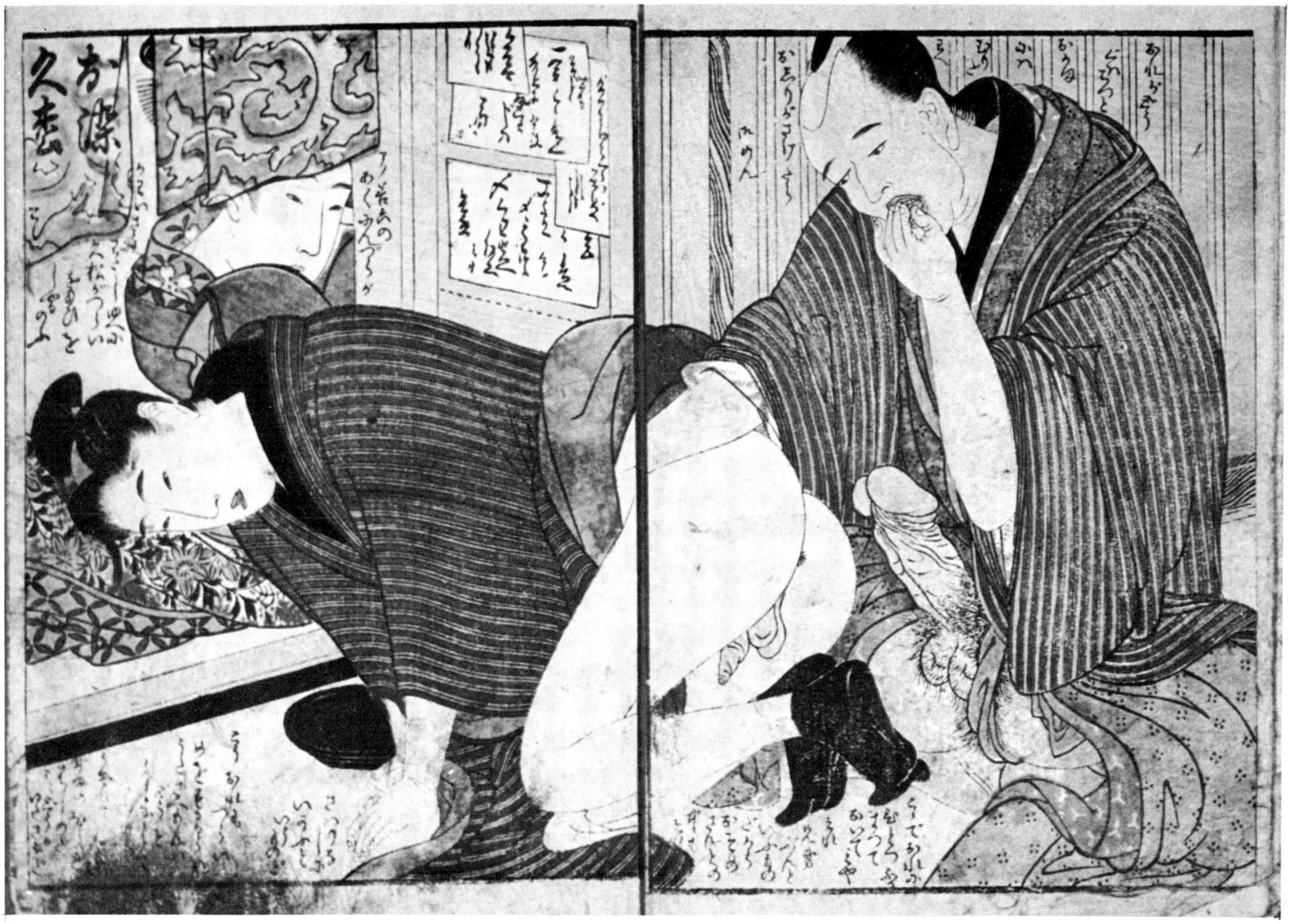

95. Frustration. Illustration by Utamaro, from *Michiyuki Koi no Futusao.*

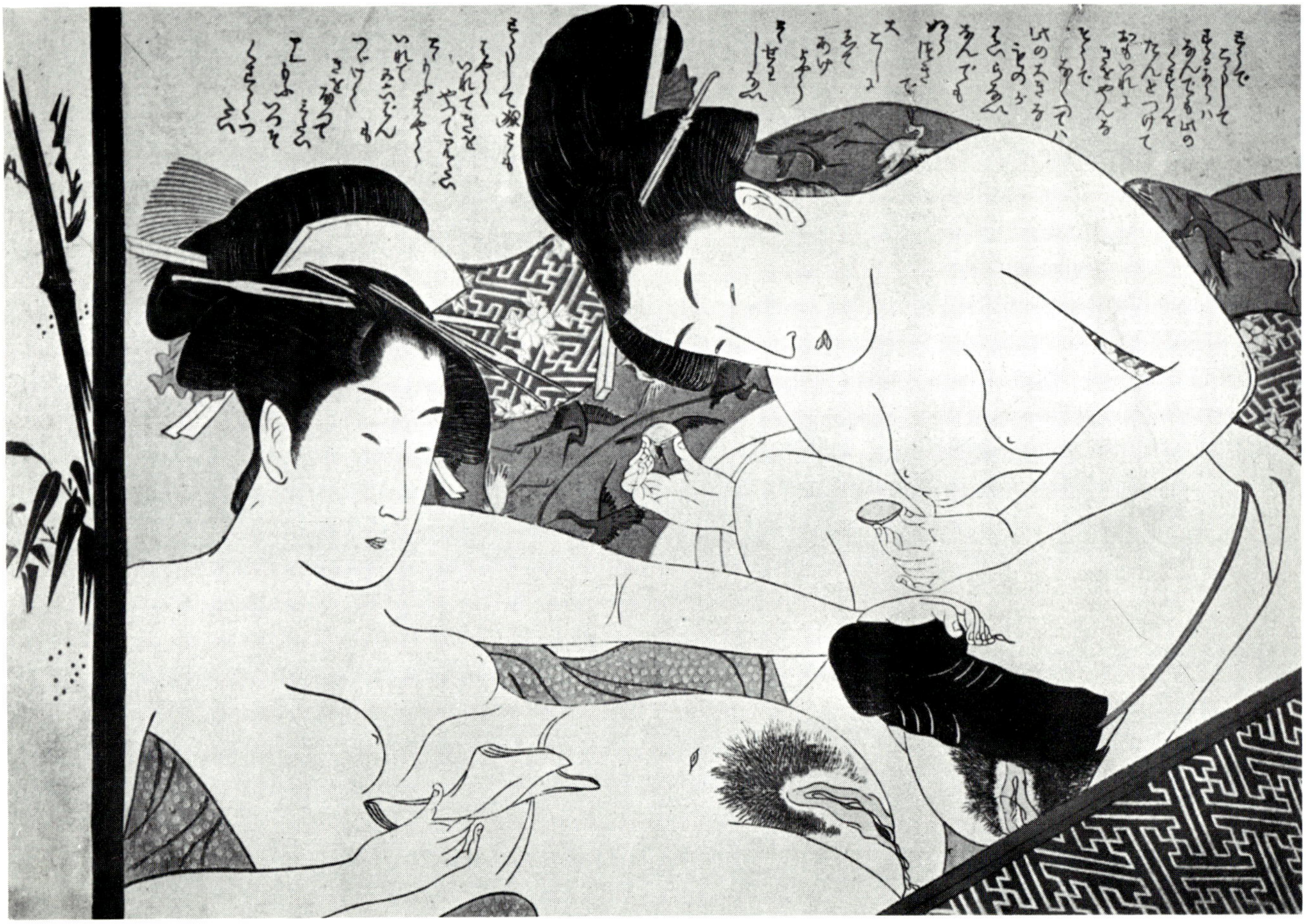

96. Two lesbians. Large color print by Utamaro.

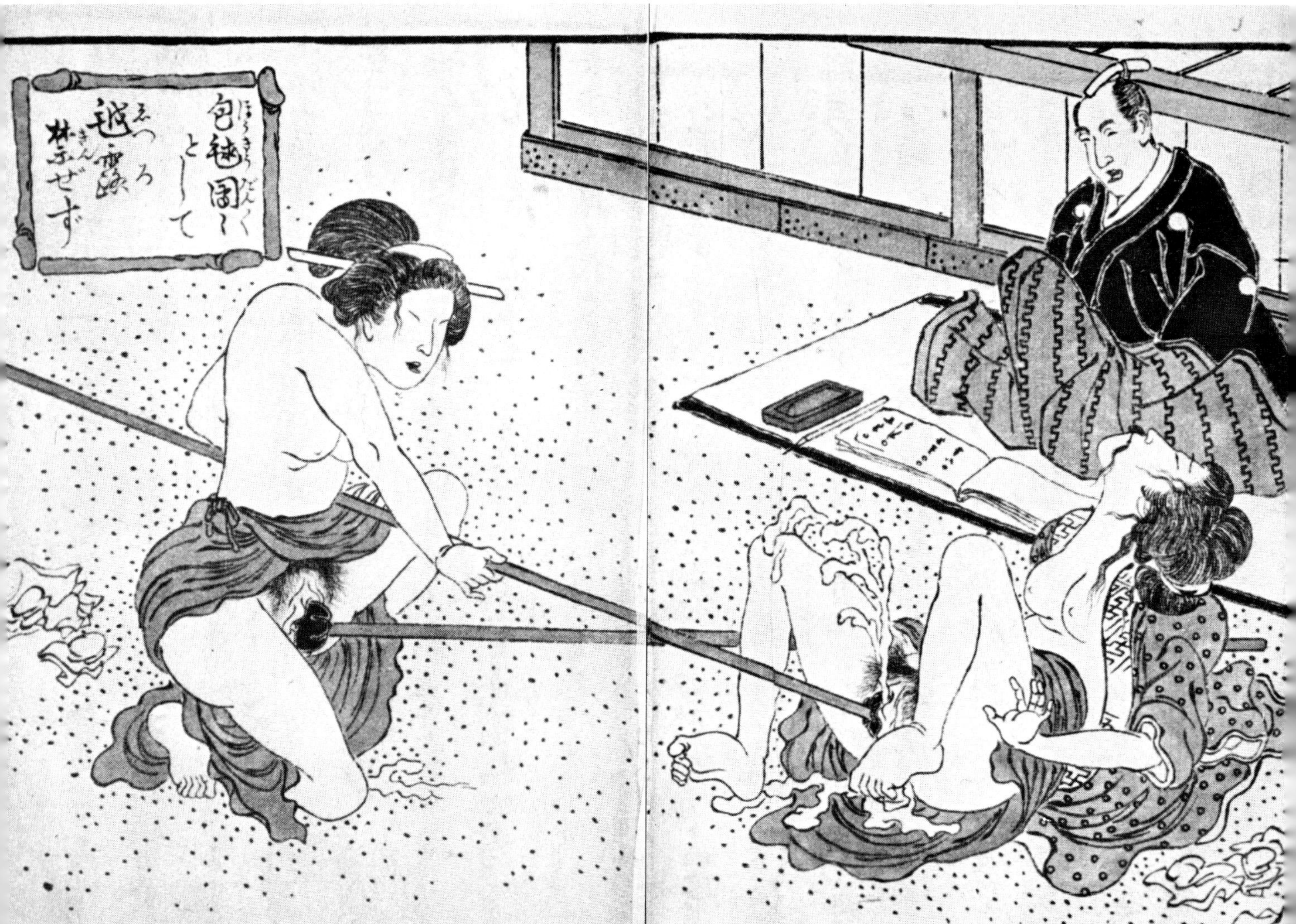

97. Lesbian joust. Woodblock illustration from *Kaisei Suikoden* (*Epic of Sex*), attibuted to Eisen (1790–1848).

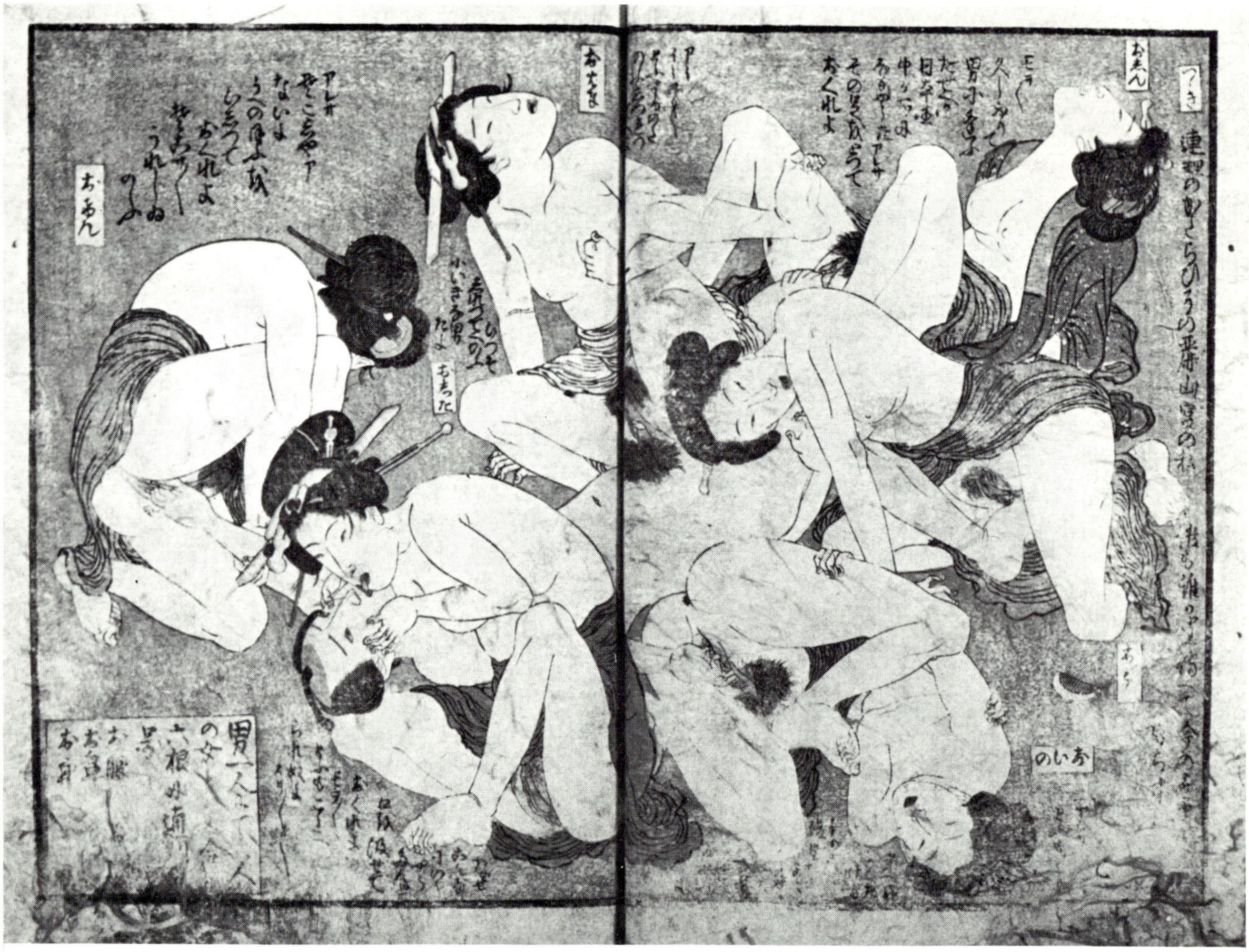

98. Orgy: one man and six women. Woodblock illustration from *Kamigata Koishusyō* (*The Loves of a Kabuki Actor*). Attributed to Kunisada (about 1840).

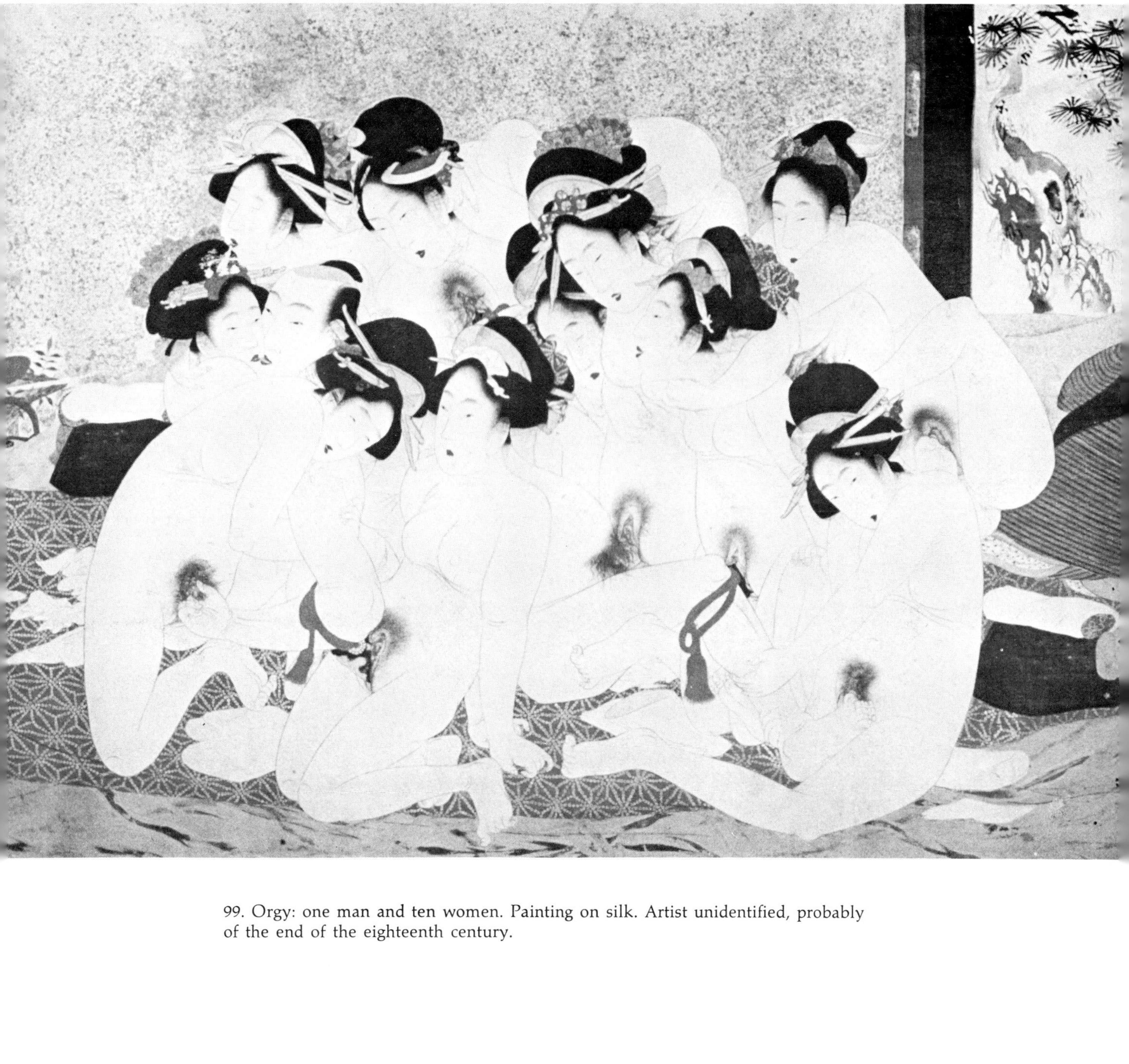

99. Orgy: one man and ten women. Painting on silk. Artist unidentified, probably of the end of the eighteenth century.

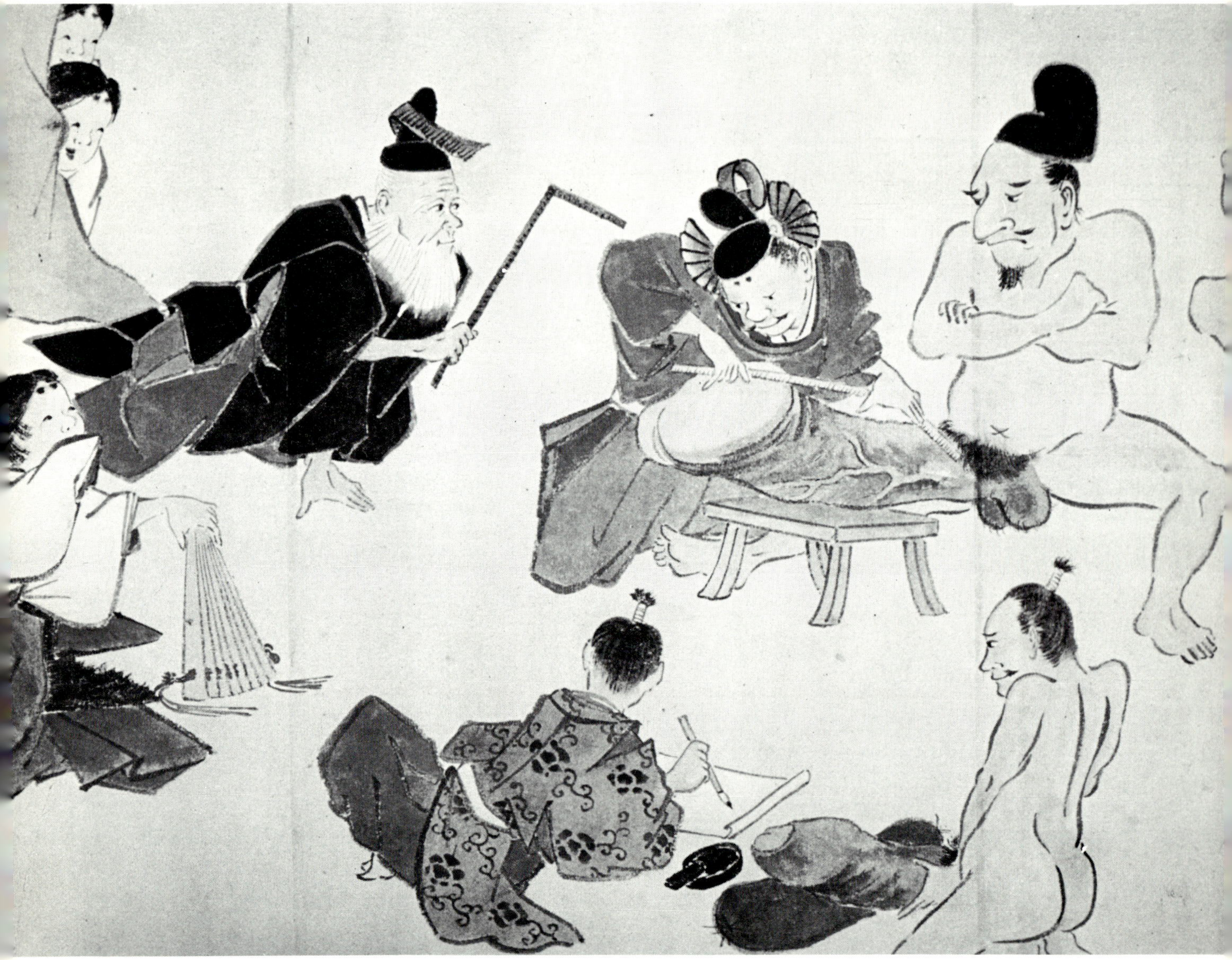

100. Sex contest. Scenes from *Yōbutsu-Kurabe* (*The Phallic Contest*). A nineteenth-century copy of a twelfth- or thirteenth-century original.

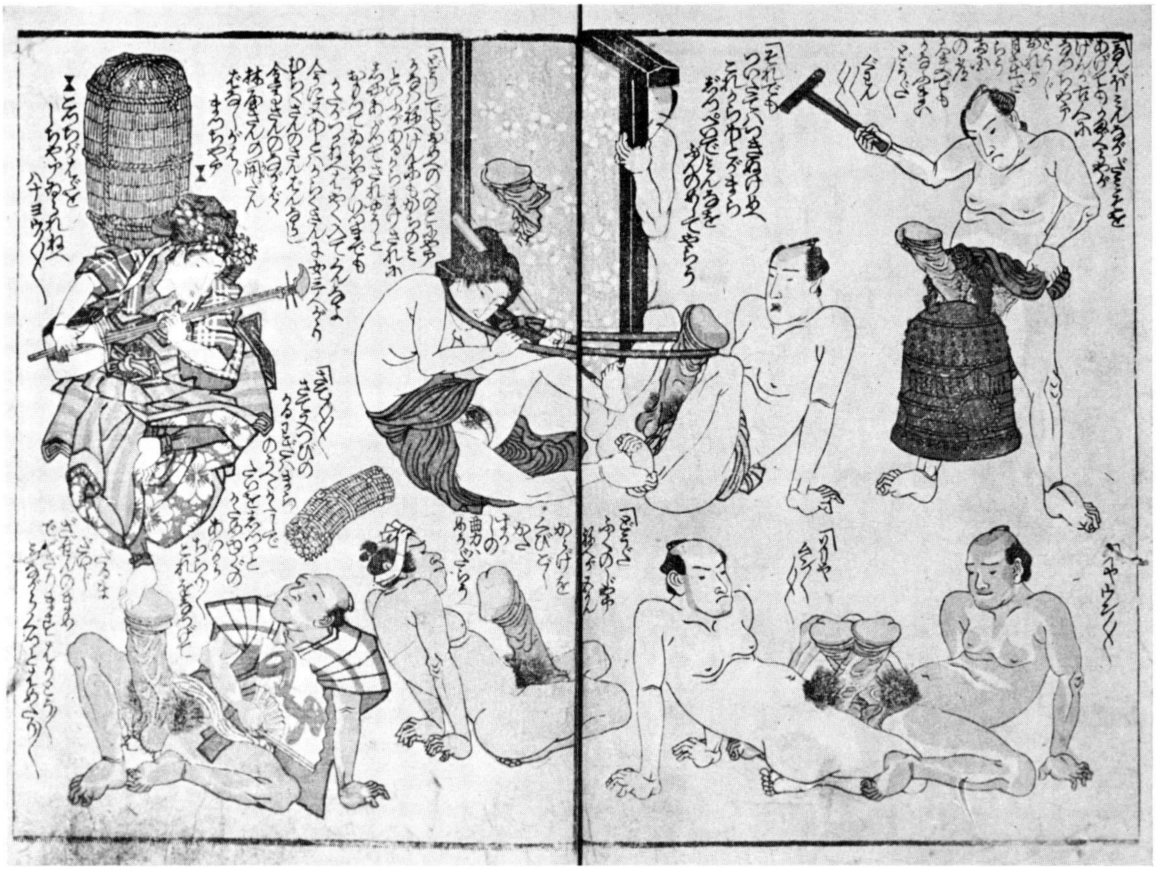

101. The power of the penis. From *Momongā,* illustrated by Bukiyo Matabei.

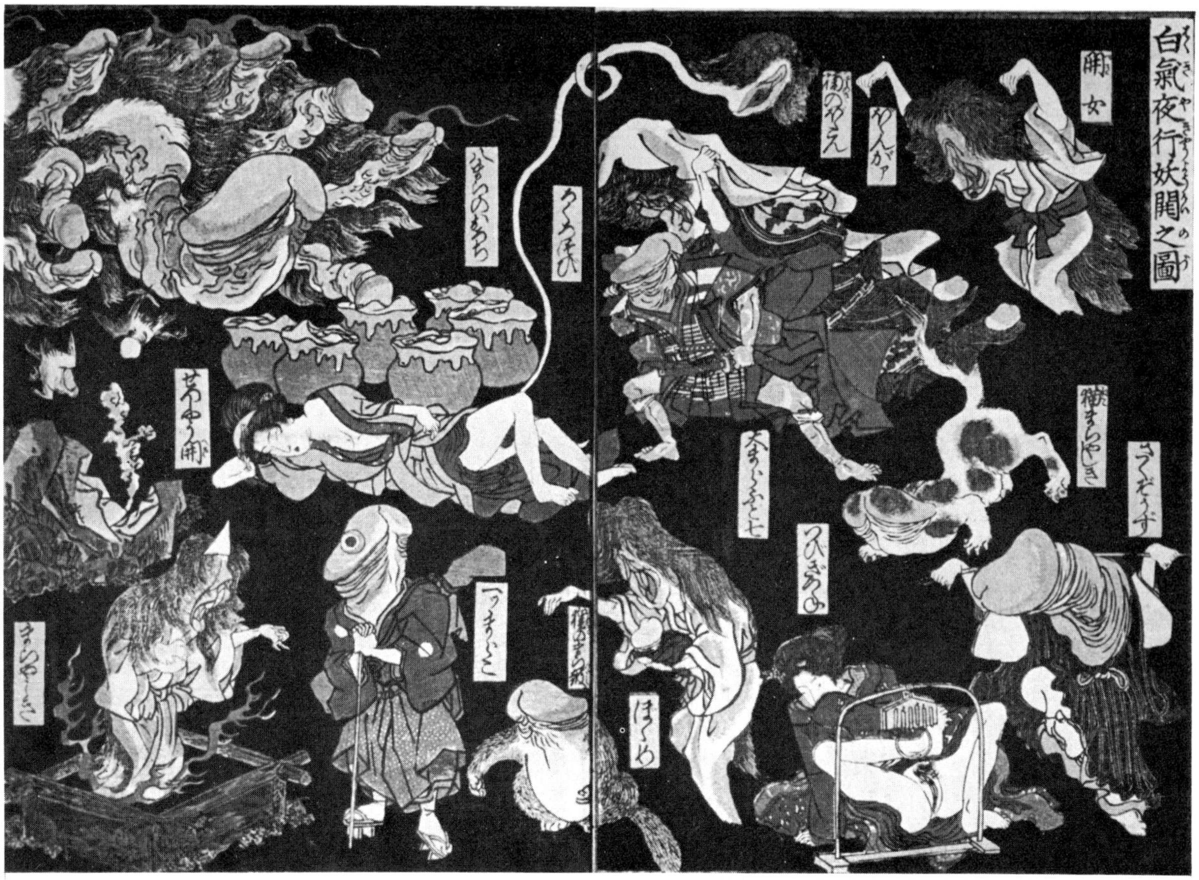

102. Sexual transformationism: humanized penises and vulvas. From *Hyakki-Yakō* (*Veritable Pandemonium*), illustrated by Kunisada.

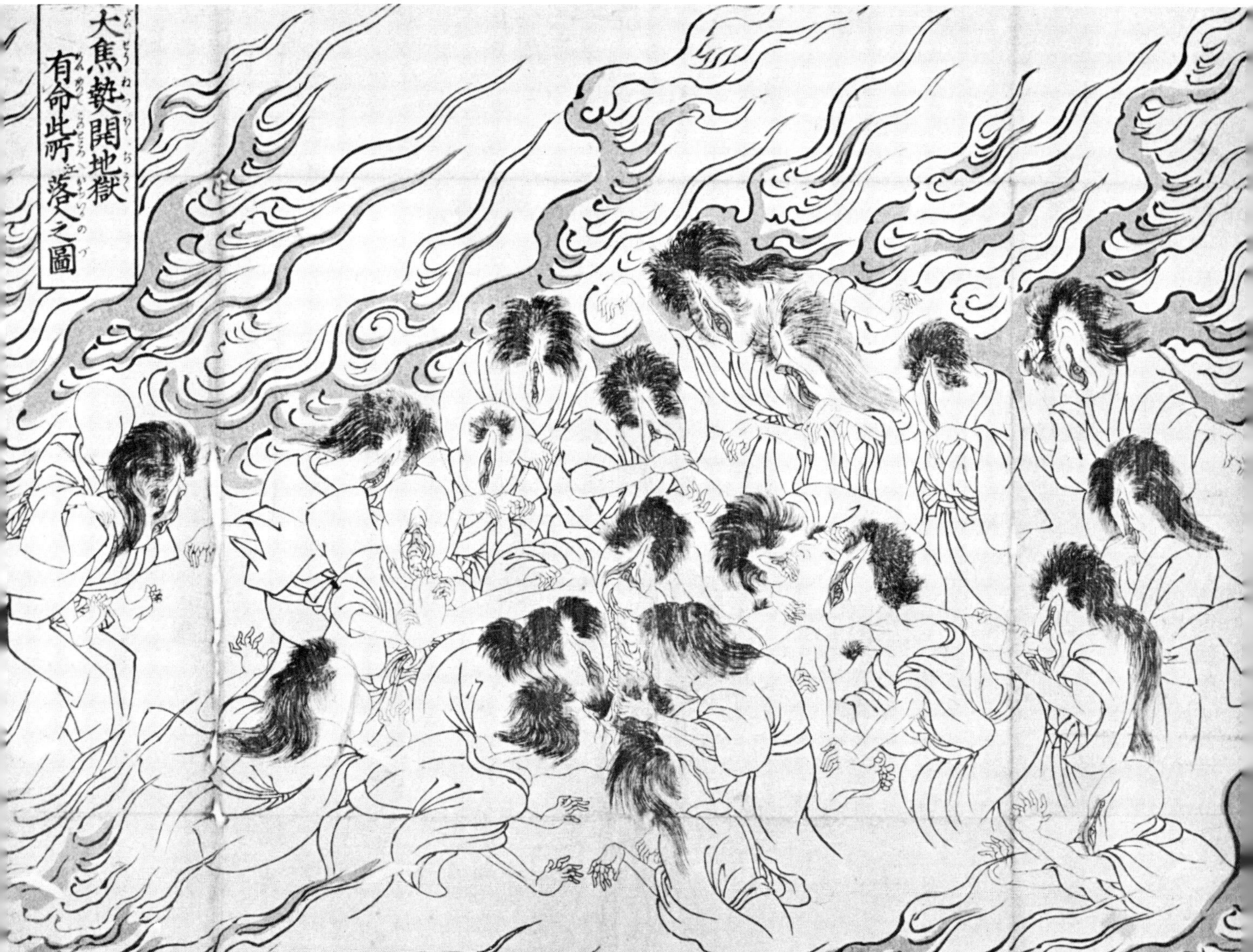

103. The purgatory of fiery vulvas. Large color print by an unidentified artist.

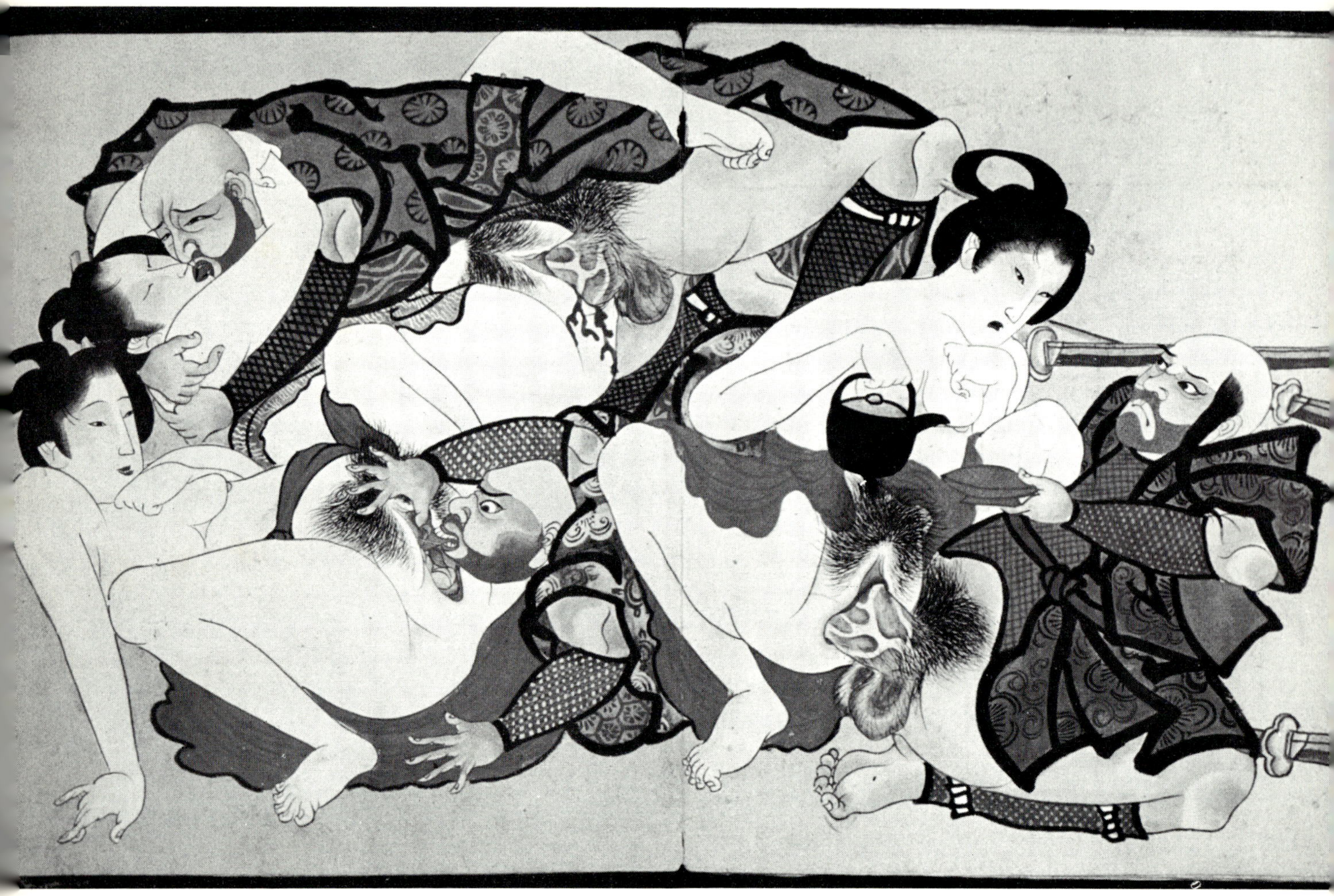

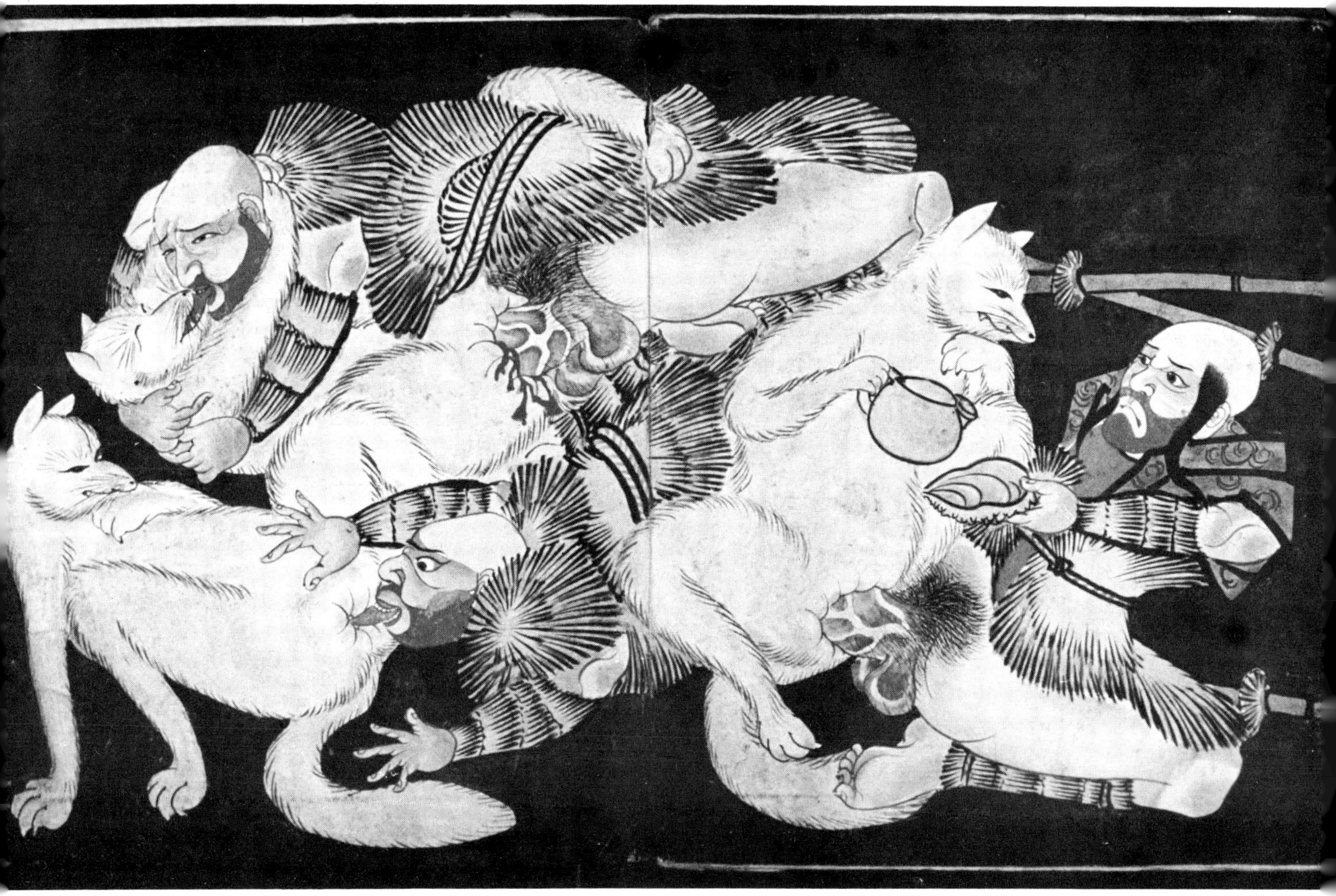

104–105. Sexual witchery: women into foxes. Two scenes from a painted handscroll by an unidentified artist.

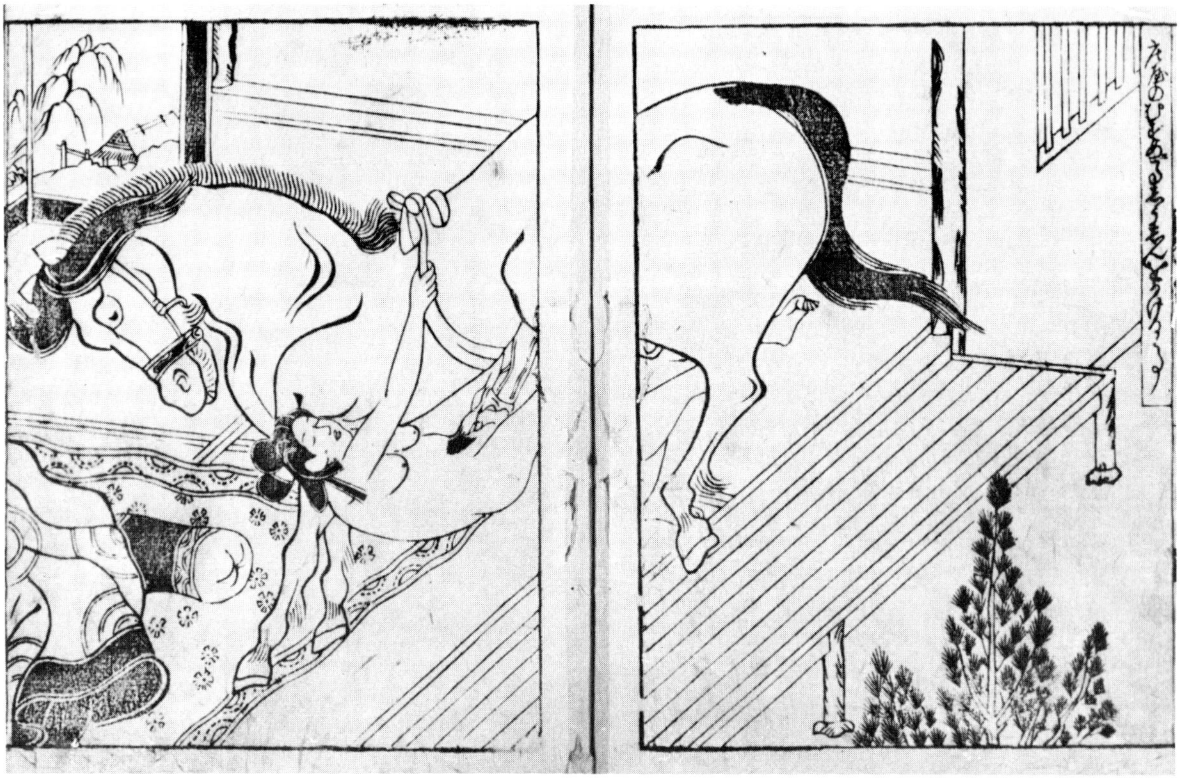

106. Woman and horse copulating. From *Kōshoku Hanasusuki* (*Pampas Grass*) by Yoshida Hambei (about 1705).

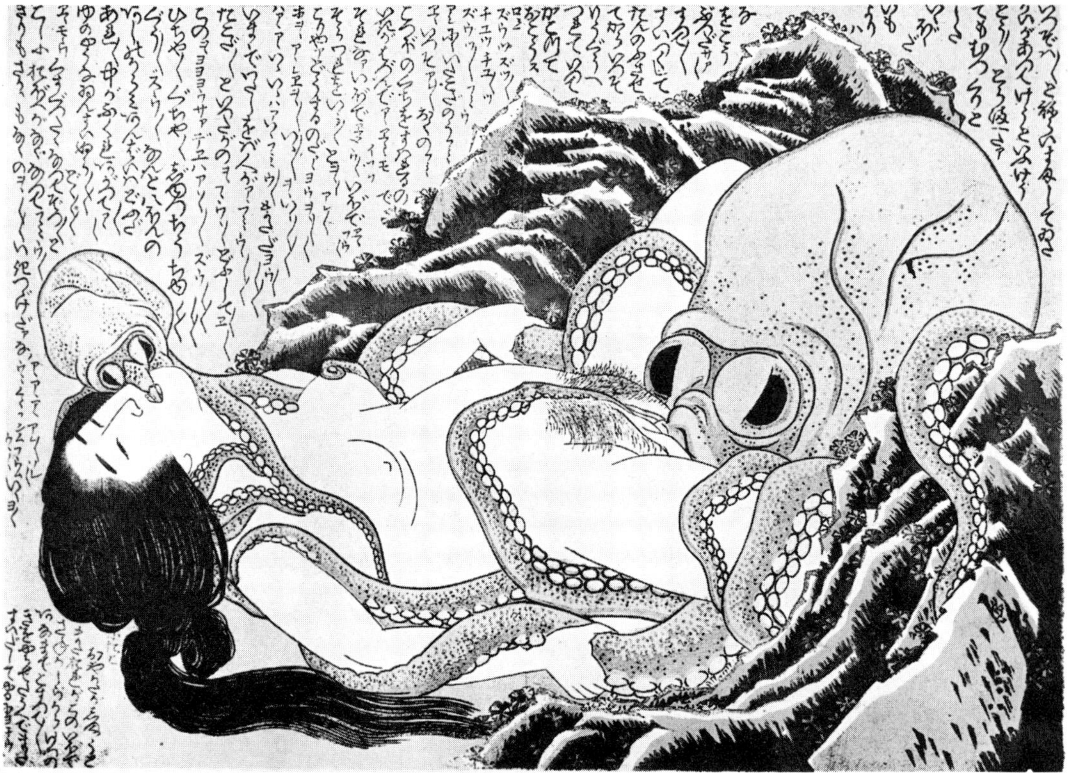

107. The dream of the fisherman's wife. Large print (about 1820) by Hokusai (1760–1849).

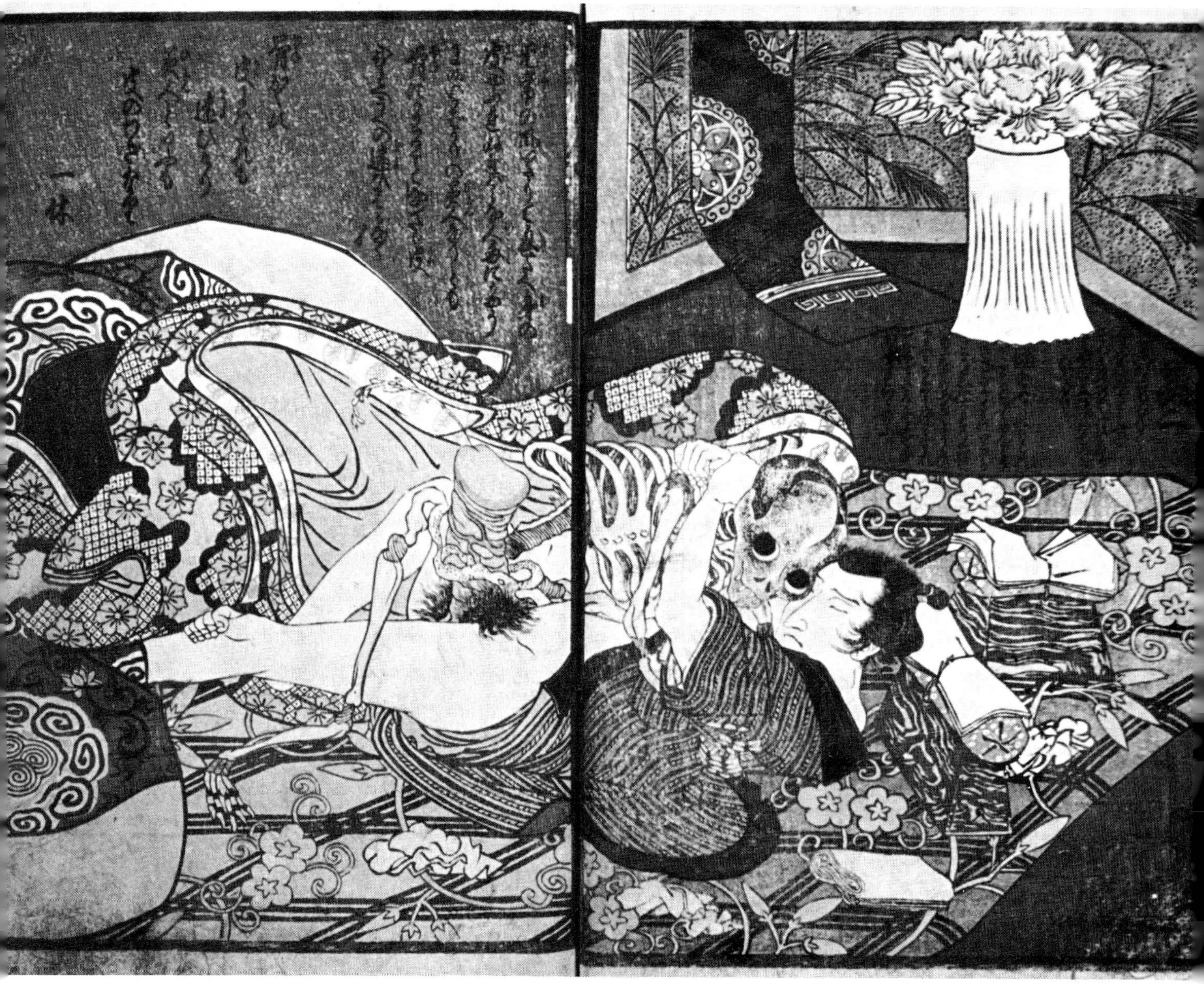

108. The ghostly lover. From *Kaichū Kagami* (*A Pocket Mirror*), illustrated by Kunisada (about 1809).

4

The Metaphors of Love and Birth in Michelangelo's *Pietàs*

LEO STEINBERG

In March 1549, the Florentine church of Santo Spirito installed a life-size marble copy (Fig. 109) of Michelangelo's first masterwork, 109 the long-revered Roman *Pietà* (Fig. 110). The copy had been 110 executed by an artist of modest talent, Nanni di Baccio Bigio, but it was neither the mediocrity of the work nor its inaccuracy that aroused the indignation of a contemporary Florentine. His unsigned letter begins by denouncing certain "dirty and filthy marble figures" (Bandinelli's nude *Adam and Eve*) which had just been placed in the cathedral; it proceeds to our copy of the *Pietà*, unveiled in the same month: "They say that it derives from that inventor of obscenities, Michelangelo Buonarroti, who is concerned only with art, not with piety. All the modern painters and sculptors, pursuing Lutheran whims, now paint and carve nothing for our holy churches but figures that undermine faith and devotion."[1]

One's first impulse is to reject these words as blind bigotry. We know Michelangelo's *Pietà* so well, its religious intention seems so self-evident, and our respect for Michelangelo's canonic art runs so deep, that we can hardly conceive the set of values by which this of all works could become an affront. But a zealot of the Counter Reformation apparently found the impure mind of its inventor confirmed in this work, so that he could bracket it with the offending nudities of Bandinelli. Perhaps he was seeing what no one had been disposed to see before: a smooth marble group which, under cover of a devotional theme, displayed an exceptionally beautiful naked youth in the lap of a girl.

[1] The full text was first published in Giovanni Gaye, *Carteggio inedito d'Artisti* (Firenze, 1840), II, 500. See also Charles de Tolnay, *Michelangelo: The Final Period* (Princeton, 1940), V, 68–69. Henceforth cited as Tolnay, V.

Something of the pious resistance to Michelangelo's group may be learned by comparing the original with its various copies and observing what it is that the copies reject. In the comparison it becomes more than ever apparent that the limbs of Michelangelo's Christ are exquisite not in refinement alone but in their relaxation; and that their suppleness suggests living warmth more than the flaccid or rigid joints of the dead. They recall the divine sleeper in Botticelli's *Venus and Mars,* painted twelve to fifteen years
111 earlier (Fig. 111). In Michelangelo's group, the Christ's groping resistless members yield to their couch as bodies do in deep sleep
112 (Fig. 112).[2]

It is exactly these qualities in the male figure—intimate adaptation and relaxation—that the copies avoid. The first, completed in 1532, is a marble group commissioned from Lorenzetti
113 for Santa Maria dell'Anima (Fig. 113). Here the head of the Christ slumps on the chest and the dropped right hand loses its will. The fainting languor which Michelangelo's figure shared with Botticelli's slumbering Mars gives way to the torpor of death.[3]

[2] For the physiological differences between sleep and death, see John Glaister's standard *Medical Jurisprudence and Toxicology* (Baltimore, 1957), pp. 110 ff., where the changes following death are summarized. Immediately after death, there is general and complete muscular relaxation, called "primary flaccidity" to distinguish it from the secondary flaccidity which follows the departure of *rigor mortis.* The primary condition lasts several hours, often as many as ten or more. It gives way to a progressive rigidity as dehydration brings about a shortening of the muscle fibers, causing the arms and legs to bend and the fingers to curl. Depending on atmospheric conditions, *rigor mortis* may last several days. Many late medieval representations of the dead Christ may be intended to represent this state.

Michelangelo's Christ is obviously not an object for medical *post mortem* examination. It exists in a poetic realm—open to faith and hope as forensic medicine rarely is—where the fraternity of sleep and death is a natural law. But it is certain that the sculptor understood the respective anatomies of sleep and death. He knew that a sleeper's muscles retain some tone, and that his surface veins remain blood-filled—as do the limbs and the veins of this Christ. Thus, whether seen with professional or devotional eyes, Michelangelo's Christ is a body asleep. In the language of metaphor, its "inaccuracies" as a corpse are the pledge of its waking. For Michelangelo, as for St. Paul, the risen Christ is "the firstfruits of them that slept" (I Cor. 15:20).

[3] For the disputed attribution of this work either to Lorenzetti's young pupil Nanni or to the aging master himself, see Rudolf Wittkower. "Nanni di Baccio Bigio and Michelangelo," *Festschrift Ulrich Middeldorf* (Berlin, 1968), pp. 248 ff.

Similar changes mark the free copy of the *Pietà* carved in 1543–1546 by Michelangelo's one-time pupil Montorsoli for a Genoese church (Fig. 114). And even the two reproductive engravings published in 1547 modify the original. In Salamanca's print (Fig. 115)[4] the torso of Christ is propped up, almost upright, iconic, as if to approximate the traditional Man of Sorrows. In Bonasone's more faithful version (Fig. 116) the dogmatic emphasis is achieved by setting the figures against the instruments of the Passion. 114 115 116

Finally, in the marble copy by Nanni di Baccio Bigio (Fig. 109), the departures from the original which Nanni permits himself are hardly explained by lack of talent alone. Some of his brutalizations must be deliberate. He may or may not have responded, as Vasari did, to the *bellezza* of the original, to its "sweet air and concordance," to the common intuition that in Michelangelo's group the very pliancy of Christ's limbs in adapting to Mary's conveys, beyond the apparent death, some profounder satisfaction of harmony. His copy, at any rate, emphasizes a cramped angularity, especially in the legs; and in the Virgin's face he replaces frail, girlish beauty with features afflicted and bloated. These alterations in a copy which purports to reproduce a revered model suggest a rebuke to the original; they correct its erotic appeal.[5] 109

If one considers these late "corrections" and, on the other hand, the agonized tragic *Pietàs* that prevailed in all European art to the end of the fifteenth century, Michelangelo's Roman *Pietà* of

[4] Listed as by Salamanca in Nagler's *Allgemeines Künstler-Lexicon* (Munich, 1845), XIV, 204. Its legend, "*Antonius Salama(n)ca quod potuit imitatus ex(s)culpsit 1547,*" indicates an early essay by the engraver whose activity as a publisher in Rome is documented from the mid-1540's to 1562. He soon became successful enough to employ others to work the plates. But (notwithstanding Tolnay, I, index and Fig. 176) there seem to be no grounds for attributing this print to Bonasone.

[5] Wittkower (*op. cit.*) sees "a criticism of the original" in the changed head position of the 1532 copy, but seems to regard other changes "which Nanni felt free to incorporate" in his imitations as "personal vagaries." It is important to stress that Nanni moves in a stream. Pope-Hennessy suggests as much when he cites Montorsoli's "copy"—with its haggard old Virgin—as evidence that Michelangelo's "break with conventional iconography was not universally acceptable." See his *Italian High Renaissance and Baroque Sculpture* (London, 1963), p. 8.

1498 stands forth as an interlude of disturbing beauty. And the reproof of its loveliness, implicit in the work of his copyists, is as telling as the outspoken bigotry of the anonymous pamphleteer for whom even Nanni's modifications had not gone far enough.

His letter of 1549 does not tell exactly how the *Pietà* had offended. We can guess, nevertheless, because his protest accords in tone and content with a more famous blast against Michelangelo, an open letter of 1545, in which the nudity of the saints in the *Last Judgment* was denounced as fit for a brothel wall. That earlier attack had been launched by Aretino, and it was this same subtle publicist who in a letter of 1537 put into writing what must have been a familiar charge against the *Pietà*—that the Virgin was too young for the Son.[6]

Needless to say, the word "young" is too simple for Michelangelo's image. What the sculptor has done is to place the head of a delicate girl upon the frame of an earth mother, comparable to those looming Etruscan tomb figures, of which one, seated on a sphinx throne, had already served Donatello as the type of the Virgin. The ambivalence of the Madonna's scale helped solve an old problem. In traditional *Pietà* groups it had always been difficult to maintain the full-grown male body on the slighter scaffolding of the woman. Michelangelo, by several imaginative adjustments affecting both figures, discovers them in a single cone. The Christ figure's apparent length is checked by being flexed both at groin and waist, and again by its double curvature, not only dipping between the Virgin's thighs but wound in a crescent about her (Fig.
112 112). And the body is actually reduced in proportion, evoking those *trecento Pietàs* which gave the dead Christ the symbolic size of a child.

[6] See the *Lettere sull'Arte di Pietro Aretino,* ed. Ettore Camesasca, with commentary by Fidenzio Pertile (Milan, 1957–1960), I, No. LXIII, 102. Writing to Fausto Longiano on December 17, 1537, Aretino discusses the prerequisites of good judgment in art, arguing that it takes more than grammar and a knowledge of rules. Michelangelo's *Pietà* is then cited to illustrate want of judgment: "Thus even he who knows whatever is needful about sculpture and painting, nevertheless the marble of Our Lady . . . shows her much younger than her son. . . ." The passage occurs only in the first sixteenth-century edition of the Letters published by Marcolini.

But, for all this, it is still a grown man that lies mysteriously banked on the young woman's lap. To enable this lap to contain his extended length, the sculptor keeps expanding the Virgin's body. The augmentation begins at her head, a small head enveloped in many layers of drapery. And this superfluity of cloth, rather than the head itself, scales the next phase. Turbulent draperies mask a continuous escalation of breast, shoulders, and waist; they are massed about knees and legs that seem measureless.

The result is that very solution to the problem of coordination which had baffled previous attempts. The solution is found in the anatomic anomaly of continually shifting proportions. But this solution—the conjunction of maiden features and pylon limbs fronting a cavernous lap—is only as anomalous as the paradox of Virgin motherhood.[7]

Such observations are necessarily modern. Earlier critics lacked the theoretical presuppositions that would have allowed them to see prestigious works of the Renaissance guilty of deliberate

[7] Almost every formal recourse invented by Michelangelo is interpretable on a symbolic plane. The crescent curve of Christ's body which curtails its apparent length also serves to intensify the physical union of Mother and Son; his supine form, curled about Mary, whose own upright form bends over his, creates a pattern of interlocking and reciprocity. But this sharp bend, which Christ's body owes to the hold of Mary's right hand, also displays and stretches the wound in his side. And it is a traditional requisite of *Pietà* compositions to make the wounds of Christ show. Cf. Curt Gravenkamp, *Marienklage* (Aschaffenburg, 1948), p. 58, quoting a medieval German poem to the Mater Dolorosa:

Ich man dich an das iammer groz,
daz er toter in dein schoz
wart geleit mit fünf wunden . . .

Thus the acute bend of Christ's body in Michelangelo's group implies an *ostantatio vulnerum.*

More suggestive still is the formal analogy of Michelangelo's Virgin Mother with the Etruscan type cited. These large limestone figures, with underscaled detachable heads, are cineraria, hollow inside to hold the ashes of the deceased. Thus the enthroned mother figure in the Archeological Museum in Florence is herself a tomb, though she holds a swaddled child in her lap. The child then, born of its tomb, is born anew. And to the extent that the Etruscan figure, familiar to Donatello (cf. Cornelius Vermeule, *European Art and the Classical Past,* Cambridge, 1964, Figs. 30-31), is allowable as one of Michelangelo's sources, his Christ also (designed for a tomb) becomes "the firstborn from the dead."

inconsistencies, such as unstable scale. They could only point to this or that portion as either too delicate or too gross. The "shoulders of a washerwoman," which the great eighteenth-century critic Milizia descried on Michelangelo's Virgin, seemed to him a mere lapse of judgment, an offense to eighteenth-century standards of breeding and elegance. The sixteenth-century observer, if inclined to be critical, would direct his objections to the impropriety of the Madonna's head: too young for her role in the *Pietà*.[8]

Clearly, whatever suspicions or fantasies Michelangelo's image may have aroused, it was only in this particular that his critics could show actual error: the grieving Madonna, a matron forty-seven years old, had been reduced to a nubile girl lamenting a youth. Hence it was on this sole point that articulate criticism could focus. And the copies that invest the Virgin with a respectable age confirm the currency of the objection.

Our anonymous bigot of 1549 is not altogether alone. And this may explain why both editions of Vasari's Michelangelo *Life* (1550 and 1568) strike back defensively and seek to meet the religious reproach with superior theology: "Though some fools say that he has made the Virgin too young," writes Vasari, "they ought to know that spotless Virgins keep their youth for a long time, while people afflicted like Christ do the reverse."

That this apology was Michelangelo's own, and that the matter disturbed him, emerges from the corresponding passage in Condivi's Michelangelo *Life*, written in 1553 under the master's direction. Citing the Virgin's excessive youth, Condivi lets the master explain it in a prolix and unusually argumentative speech. "Are you not aware," Michelangelo begins, "that chaste women maintain themselves much more fresh than the unchaste? How

[8] The general praise of the Virgin's beauty, "perfect proportions," and immutable youth (to be found, for instance, in Savonarola's Sermon 24 from the *Amos and Zacharia* series, delivered March 11, 1496; Venice, 1544 ed., pp. 238v–239) is not relevant to our theme. For the concept of the Madonna's timeless beauty was almost never appropriated to the tragic *historical* moments of Crucifixion, Descent, Lamentation, Entombment, or to the symbolic moment of the *Pietà*. The Virgin in Renaissance *Pietàs* usually looks her age. Aretino's sneer at the inordinate youth of Michelangelo's figure indicates that he knows of no way to justify it.

much more so a virgin in whom there had never arisen the least lascivious desire that might have affected her body?"

"A consideration worthy of any theologian," says Condivi at last, closing the subject.

It matters little whether Michelangelo invented or adopted the argument. Its moralized physiology served him as a defensive screen, as a rare point of doctrine to justify the Madonna's bridal radiance in mourning her Son. The simple truth is proclaimed in the anonymous poem with which Vasari ends his eulogy of the *Pietà.* Its closing words, addressed to the marble Virgin of Nanni's Florentine copy, invoke ". . . thy spouse, son and father, / Thou his only spouse, daughter and mother."[9]

There is nothing new or heretical in these lines. The Virgin had been extolled as the bride of Christ since the twelfth century. It was then that the "Beloved" of the Biblical Song of Songs, traditionally interpreted as Ecclesia, the Church of Christ, came to be identified with the Virgin. But the medieval Virgin as Bride of Christ was an allegory or mystic approximation, a poetic equation that involved Mary and Church as interchangeable concepts. The Mary who was both Mother and Bride was, so to speak, projected into a pre-existent figure of speech. And in the representational arts, even this figure was visualized only in contexts that were at the furthest remove from the life of the flesh—in scenes of the Virgin's death, or at her coronation in heaven; in allegorical triumphs of the Virgin as Church, or in theological commentaries on Canticles.[10]

[9] *Nostro Signore, e tuo/ Sposo, figliuolo e padre,/ Unica sposa sua figliuola e madre.* See Vasari, *Le Vite . . .* , Milanesi ed. (Florence, 1906), VII, 152. All Vasari quotations in this study refer to the Milanesi edition.

[10] Summaries of orthodox doctrine and poetry describing the Virgin as *Sponsa Dei,* and specifically as Bride of Christ, are contained in Yrjo Hirn, *The Sacred Shrine* (1909; Beacon Press edition, Boston, 1957), especially pp. 291 ff., and the chapters "Annunciation" and "Incarnation." See also Henri de Lubac, *Méditations sur l'Eglise* (Paris, 1953), Ch. 9; in English as *The Splendour of the Church* (Glen Rock, N.J., 1963), pp. 198 ff. The classic formulation occurs in the authoritative Commentary on Canticles written in the twelfth century by Honorius of Autun: "Everything that is said of the Church can also be understood as being said of the Virgin herself, the bride and mother of the Bridegroom." (Quoted in Panofsky, *Early Netherlandish Painting,* Harvard, 1953, I, 145.) In an

But in Michelangelo's imagery, the old symbolic equations
are so concretely embodied that even the tragic presentment of the
117, 118 *Pietà* is sensualized (Figs. 117 and 118). Michelangelo's critics had
every right to protest, for the artist had imported an unfamiliar,
perhaps disturbing component. His *Pietà* not only rendered the
mother youthful enough to be mourning a lover; it compounded
her Christian grief with the pagan passion of an Aphrodite lament-
119 ing the dying Adonis laid on her lap (Fig. 119).[11] Michel-
angelo's treatment of the *Pietà* gave the Christian theme for the
first time a kind of formal and psychic equivalence to the Venus
lament.[12] It established, for the whole sixteenth century, the inter-

---

earlier poetic image Mary's womb was hailed as "the bridal bed of the royal spouse" (St. Gregory, *Hom. XXXVIII in Evangelia,* No. 3, Pl. 76, 1283). Andrew of Crete (ca. 700) invoked the Virgin as "God's living marriage chamber" (*Domini Dei thalamus animatus;* cf. Pat. Gr., Vol. 97, 1315). And with San Bernardino of Siena (canonized in 1450, his collected sermons published in 1495) the metaphor, linked to the Virgin-Church equation, is brought down to Michelangelo's immediate religious environment. The great Franciscan revivalist calls the Virgin *"sponsa Dei, et totius Trinitatis triclinium et specialissimum Filii Dei reclinatorium"* ("Bride of God, and triple couch of the whole Trinity and the special reclining couch of God's son"; see Bernardini Senensis *Opera Omnia,* Quaracchi-Firenze, 1956, IV, Sermo LI, 548). The sermons of Savonarola, too, continually refer to the Virgin as the *"Sponsa Iesu,"* and her joys are described in amorous passages from the Song of Songs. (See Savonarola, *Sermoni e Prediche,* per Ranieri Guasti, Prato, 1846, Sermone 13, p. 134.)

[11] The compositional Venus and Adonis type which so closely anticipates the
119 arrangement of a *Pietà* is remarkably rare. Our Fig. 119 is a line engraving by Giovanni
Paolo Lasinio of a destroyed Pompeian fresco from the atrium of the House of the Surgeon. (See G. B. Finati and others, *Real Museo Borbonico.* Naples, 1827, Vol. IV, Pl. XVII. The only reference to the destruction of the painting occurs in P. Fumagalli, *Pompeia,* Firenze, 1824–1827, p. 40. See also W. Helbig, *Wandgemälde der verschütteten Städte Campaniens,* Leipzig, 1868, No. 336. Drawings of the fresco made after Lasinio's engraving are reproduced in Roux and Barré, *Herculaneum et Pompei,* Paris, 1875, Vol. III, Pl. 105; and in S. Reinach, *Répertoire de Peintures Grecques et Romaines,* Paris, 1922, p. 65, 4.)

The type of the Pompeian fresco must have been known in other examples. It
would otherwise be hard to explain such a work, for instance, as Annibale Carracci's
120 *Pietà* of ca. 1599 in the Naples Museum (Fig. 120). Carracci's composition, clearly
developed from Michelangelo's marble group, also comes strikingly close to the pagan original.

[12] Cf., for example, Rosso's *Death of Adonis* and his *Lamentation,* reproduced in K. Kusenberg, *Le Rosso* (Paris, 1931), Pls. L, LXIV, LXXX, 2.

changeability of the two themes—not by diluting the Christian content of the *Pietà*, but by grasping its mystic sense.[13]

Michelangelo's explanation that it was chastity which preserved the Virgin's bloom is a rationalization, designed to absolve or explain away this specific feature without venting its secret. It is significant that, even as he offers his plea to his literary defenders, a new *Pietà* is taking shape under his hands, but the Madonna's youth is not again featured.

The second marble *Pietà* is the unfinished, overlife-size, four- 121
figure group in the Cathedral of Florence (Fig. 121). It was begun about 1547, when the artist was seventy-two, and was worked on, mostly at night, for eight or nine years. There was no commission for it; it was done, we are told, "as a pastime" and "because carving kept him in good health."[14] We are further told by Vasari that

[13] Rilke's *Pietà*, a poem of 1906, seems clearly inspired by art, probably by the thought of Michelangelo. The erotic tenor of Rilke's vision is so intense that the poem was first published under the bowdlerizing title "The Magdalene."

> Thus do I, Jesus, see your feet again,
> That I was wont to see a timid youth's,
> Feet that my trembling hands undressed and laved;
> Oh how they stood distraught amid my hair
> Like deer entangled white in a thornbush.
>
> I gaze upon your never yet loved limbs
> As if ne'er seen before this night of love.
> We never yet together laid us down,
> And now there's but to wonder and to wake.
>
> But see, Beloved, how your hands are torn—
> Not torn by me, not by my lover's bite.
> Your heart gapes open wide and all may enter
> By that same gate that was to have been mine.
>
> Now are you weary and your weary mouth
> Has no desire unto my bruised lips—
> O Jesus, Jesus, did we miss the hour?
> How wondrously we perish, you and I.

[14] See Vasari, VII, 217, 243 f., and 281 f., for all Vasari references to the Florence *Pietà*.

Michelangelo had destined the work for his own tomb, and that the summit figure of the hooded male penitent was his ideal self-portrait. Finally, Vasari reports that, after almost a decade of labor, Michelangelo destroyed the group and then let a pupil reassemble the pieces. In the reconstructed group as we have it, the Christ figure is deprived of one leg.

The missing limb is rarely missed by observers, so well does the figure in its truncated state seem to work. Some have regarded the lack of the other leg as inevitable; others have welcomed its loss as an artistic gain.[15] It is to those who take this position, or who for any reason whatever deplore the attempt to put back what Michelangelo had removed, that I offer this consideration: Michelangelo did not conceive a Christ with amputations. He planned a whole, and whatever that whole was meant to embody, he lived with and worked on for eight or nine years. Any thought that Michelangelo entertained for nearly a decade is worth thinking again. Hence we may well ask how the missing member completes Michelangelo's group.

There is only one action possible for the missing leg. The left groin still shows a slot or socket for its insertion, presumably for a replacement to be cut from a separate block. And the Virgin's thigh shows a depression where the leg would have rested, like a wake left behind by its passage. It is indeed in this only possible pose that the leg appears in a number of painted and engraved

[15] Thus Henry Thode, *Michelangelo, Kritische Untersuchungen* (Berlin, 1908–1913), II, 278; "*Für das linke Bein Christi ist gar kein Platz vorhanden. . . . Die einzige Möglichkeit es anzubringen wäre die gewesen es vorne über Marias Bein herabhängen zu lassen. . . . Dies aber hätte eine nicht nur unschöne, sondern unmögliche Stellung ergeben.*" Thode is followed by W. R. Valentiner in *The Late Years of Michel Angelo* (New York, 1914), pp. 24–25: "Michelangelo's failure to finish it entirely was probably due to the impossibility of adding the missing left foot of the Christ. . . . One feels astonished that such an omission could have occurred in the master's composition." And finally, Herbert von Einem, *Michelangelo: Die Pietà im Dom zu Florenz* (Stuttgart, 1956), p. 6: "*Rätselhaft ist das Fehlen des linken Beines Christi. Wir wissen dass es vorhanden gewesen ist. . . . Aber es ist keine Frage, dass sein Fehlen ein künstlerischer Vorzug ist. Sollten wir hier den Grund fassen können, warum Michelangelo das Werk aufgegeben hat?*"

reconstructions of the late sixteenth century (Fig. 122).[16] The left leg of Christ is slung over the Virgin's thigh. It forms a connection which in subsequent sixteenth- and seventeenth-century art becomes a common and unmistakable symbol of sexual union. 122

The word "symbol" is crucial. Looking at a seventeenth-century genre scene of lovers linked in this pose, one might mistake it for something "taken from nature" (Figs. 123 and 124). 123, 124
But, in fact, the scheme of two figures of opposite sex seated side by side, with the leg of one bridging the thigh (or both thighs) of the other, is a received convention. It is as a symbolic form that artists such as Govaert Flinck and Jacques de Gheyn naturalize it into their style.

During the seventeenth century this token gesture was finally vulgarized. By the mid-1600's it had come to seem no less appropriate to bourgeois than to divine lovers. Then, not before, does one see it performed by common soldiers or unbuttoned wenches besieging the Prodigal Son (Fig. 125).[17] The transition is best 125
observed in late-sixteenth-century Northern works, where the motif is domesticated by way of allegory and moralization (Fig. 126).[18] 126
But in the decades that more closely concern us, one discovers—tracing the motif backward in time—that the slung leg (its sex interchangeable and in Italy usually assigned to the woman) becomes progressively less profane, almost solemn in context. In the

[16] Engraving attributed to Cherubini Alberti, ca. 1580, after Michelangelo's *Pietà*, Bartsch, VII, 23; Lorenzo Sabbatini, *La Deposizione*, before 1576, altarpiece in the sacristy of St. Peter's, Rome; a free copy of it by Antonio Viviani in S. Maria dei Monti, Rome. Both described in Baglione's *Vite*, pp. 18 and 103. An execrable wax copy which first appeared in a Florentine private collection in the mid-nineteenth century (full bibliography in Vasari, VII, 244 n.) has been repeatedly cited by Goldscheider as the master's "first version."

[17] See Appendix A, pp. 272–275; "The Slung-Leg Motif."

[18] Cf. the drawing by Jacques de Gheyn at Christ Church, Oxford, entitled *Man and Witch Seated on a Monster* (see *Paintings and Drawings from Christ Church, Oxford*, Exhibition Catalogue, The Matthiesen Gallery, London, 1960, No. 24, Pl. LV). Our Fig. 123 is a detail from the same artist's drawing at the Fogg Art Museum, Cambridge, called *A Crossbowman Assisted by a Milkmaid* (published by Jakob Rosenberg in *Art Quarterly*, Summer, 1954, pp. 166 ff.). For the engraving made after De Gheyn's drawing, see Hollstein, VII, 108.

quarter-century that immediately follows Michelangelo's abandonment of the *Pietà*—that is, before 1580—the slung leg occurs only in allegories or in Biblical and mythological scenes. By 1550 the motif is assimilated to scenes of Lot and his daughters—perhaps because the sexual act represented is at the opposite pole from trivial or private lust, being rather a desperate if misguided attempt to save
127 the human race from extinction (Fig. 127). In a few rare instances the slung-leg motif occurs in Lesbian situations: once in a Fontaine-
128 bleau School engraving, *Women Bathing* (Fig. 128; mid-1540's, attributed to Jean Mignon after Luca Penni)—a work unique in exhibiting the motif without mythological pretext; and more significantly in a drawing by Giulio Campi in which Jupiter, in
129 Diana's person, seduces Callisto (Fig. 129). Here, in the Callisto context, the slung leg could be especially useful; in a scene of apparently sterile erotic play between two seeming women, it intervened as the sign of a fecund moment.[19]

The slung leg in sixteenth-century art is invariably a token of marital or sexual union, of sexual aggression or compliance. As a conventional sign it is so unambiguous and legible that when a given story calls for the awkward depiction of a nymph loved by a horse (as happens in the rare myth of Philyra and Saturn in equine disguise), it is the slung leg that conveys the message
130 (Fig. 130).

[19] Cf. the engraving by Daullé after Poussin, *Jupiter as Diana Seducing Callisto* (reproduced in the *Gazette des Beaux-Arts*, July–August 1962, "Catalogue des Graveurs de Poussin," p. 168, A336. For the attribution of the original painting, now in Philadelphia, see A. Blunt, *Poussin, A Critical Catalogue*, New York, 1966, p. 175, R83). The wittiest use of the motif is Carracci's. Cf. the engraving by Bernard Picart, 1707, after Annibale Carracci's painting then in the Collection of the Duc d'Orleans (reproduced in E. Fuchs, *Die Weiberherrschaft in der Geschichte der Menschheit*, Munich, 1913, I, Fig. 176). Here the erotic group works as a "flashback." The nymph at the right points to Callisto and looks out at the spectator as she performs the slung-leg act on her fellow nymph so as to explain Callisto's condition.

The group recurs with similar propaedeutic intent in the *Pan Subdued by Cupid* engraving of Agostino Carracci (B. 116). Agostino's own variant, a doubling of the motif, is assigned to a couple engaged in complex mutual leg slinging to expound the principle of *Reciprocal Love* (B. 119).

Most relevant to this inquiry is the incidence of the motif from its first emergence before 1520 to about 1547, when Michelangelo's *Pietà* was begun. During this quarter-century the motif is extremely rare, confined to a few prints, drawings, and small cabinet pictures; and not only is it reserved for divine and heroic lovers but it tends to remain within a context of marriage.

The currency of the motif is established in the late 1520's and 1530's by engravings after Perino del Vaga and others of Raphael's circle, the subjects being the loves and nuptials of divine couples: Mars and Venus, Bacchus and Ariadne, Neptune (as suitor) and Thetis (Figs. 131 and 132). And finally, as the earliest 131, 132
significant occurrence of the motif *in its canonic form,* it appears in the *Isaac and Rebecca* fresco in Raphael's Vatican Logge (Fig. 133): 133
"Abimelech, King of the Philistines, looked out at a window and behold, Isaac was sporting with Rebecca, his wife" (Gen. 26:8). We need hardly remind ourselves that the Old Testament scenes in "Raphael's Bible" refer by anticipation to Christ. So, too, Isaac's "sport with Rebecca" is a link in the chain of Christ's ancestry—which may explain such of the fresco's features as the fountain, the benediction of the great sun, and the brightness at the young patriarch's loins.

Variant forms of the motif appear shortly before 1520. Not all can be traced to Rome, nor to a single milieu. And this emergence of a purely symbolic gesture over a period of some ten years in various artistic circles suggests that one or several antique models had come to be known—by hearsay perhaps to some, by actual acquaintance to Raphael and his school. The presumed model, however, turns out to be strangely elusive. It is not found in antique *symplegmata,* the ancient name for groups of figures interlocked in combat or love. It does not appear among the countless vase and wall paintings of antiquity that depict sexual relations. They may have ignored it precisely because it was clearly non-functional and associated with hieratic use. And this seems borne out by one splendid antique example that came to light recently when six tombs of the time of Alexander the Great were

uncovered at Dherveni near Salonika in northern Greece.[20] Their most spectacular yield was a splendid gilt bronze krater for cremated ashes, three feet high, displaying continuous relief decoration of satyrs and maenads dancing. The dance centers upon a ritual action—the uncommon scene of the marriage of Bacchus and Ariadne. The scene is so rare, yet in this representation so precise and perfected, it suggests the possibility that we are privy to that mimetic ritual which in antiquity formed part of the secret mysteries of Dionysus.[21] The bride is seated and draped, her veil held out in the traditional bridal gesture. She turns toward her divine spouse, a naked god, his leg flung over her
134 thigh (Fig. 134).

Let me assume that the type of this image had become known in Rome before 1520. This would account for the multiple emergence of a purely symbolic action and for the close resemblance of the slung leg in Renaissance works to that of Dionysus on the Dherveni krater. The model need have been no more than a small gem or cameo seen and understood by a handful of men. Present evidence indicates that a few Roman artists of the second and third decades of the Cinquecento knowingly adopted the slung leg as an antique symbolic form, implying a context of heroic or sacred love, or, more exactly, of divine marriage.

The antique derivation alone may have lent the slung-leg motif a dignity not normally associated with sexual sport. But only

[20] See J. Makaranos in *Archaiologikon Deltion*, Vol. XXVIII (1963) (Athens, 1965). Summaries appeared in *DU*, October 1965, and *Horizon*, Fall 1966. The most recent discussion is in T. B. L. Webster, *The Art of Greece: The Age of Hellenism* (New York, 1965), pp. 20–23.

[21] Cf. Erwin Panofsky, *Tomb Sculpture* (New York, 1964), p. 34: "Ariadne's 'Sacred Marriage' to Dionysus is not entirely absent from Roman monuments but it is rare and told without enthusiasm." Panofsky refers to his single illustration of the subject from Roman art (his Fig. 109, from an urn in the Vatican Museum, Rome). It shows the couple standing side by side and joined by the ritual clasping of hands. "A mimetic marriage was, it is clear, an element in the rites of Dionysus," wrote Jane Harrison (in *Prolegomena to the Study of Greek Religion*, 1903; Meridian Books, New York, 1955, p. 538). Could it be that the symbolic action of the slung leg on the Dherveni krater had its source in this secret mimesis of Dionysian mystery plays?

Michelangelo could reconceive the pose as a consecration. It is as though, for him, the whole meaning of the myth of Dionysus and Ariadne must be expressible in the language of physical action. Ancient poets may have believed that the mortal Ariadne, killed by the love of the god, was by that gift of death rendered immortal. But their artistic idiom never attempted to conflate love and death in one motion. Now, as Michelangelo meditates on the ancient gesture, death and love coalesce in it and the slung leg unites Mary and the crucified Christ in mystic marriage.

At least two sixteenth-century artists followed Michelangelo in making love and death converge in the slung-leg motif. One is the Dutch sculptor Hubert Gerhard, who had studied in Florence in the 1580's. In his bronze group, *Tarquin and Lucrece,* at the
Metropolitan Museum, New York (Fig. 135), the rising leg of the 135
ravisher is both sexual and murderous. The other is Luca Cambiaso in a painting probably of the 1550's (now lost but recorded
in an engraving by G. M. Le Villain; Fig. 136), in which a fond 136
Venus and a dying Adonis form a close-knit, almost sculptural group. Cambiaso's Adonis, at once amorous and amort, engages his paramour with his left leg in direct imitation of Michelangelo's Christ. In Michelangelo's group the themes of love, death, and communion are even more intimately interfused. There can be no question that he conceived the action of the left leg in perfect awareness of what it meant.

The leg does not of course work as a separable appendage; its action is vital within the strangely polymorphous anatomy of the entire Christ figure. For this body from head to toe is not of a uniform age. The full hair and low brow indicate the young man cut off at thirty-three, and the arms are sheer vigor. But the loins are senescent; and both legs—like the right leg even now—must have been gaunt, desiccated, and old. To unsex the erotic gesture it was perhaps necessary to assign it to a limb whose flesh was already spent.

These internal changes are only one manifestation of the Christ's two-natured anatomy. The parts of the body act like parts in a play—in opposition to one another. The body seems both to rise and to fall; it collapses, yet in an expansive embrace; it is literally zoned and quartered, abnegation and eagerness alternating. This is not a *contrapposto* evolved from the studied agility of man's body, but rather the coherence of many thoughts in one personification.[22]

One movement only is unequivocal. Neither muscular nor gravitational, it suggests an ineluctable trend, like the drift of a system in space. The entire group seeks one direction; the Christ presses forward, urged on to where his and the Virgin's body wind about one another. Here, at the focus of interpenetrant union, the sculptor implanted the mounting left leg. Of all possible symbols of marriage, Michelangelo chose that which symbolized its consummation.

Even with the clear sign removed, the message was read by at least one observer who acknowledged the mystic eroticism of the *Pietà.* De Tolnay saw bliss and marriage where the ostensible subject allowed only for grief. "With closed eyes and a face transfigured by supernatural bliss," he wrote, the Virgin "receives him into her arms. . . . St. Joseph of Arimathea unites mother and son in a kind of ultimate *sposalizio* . . . This spiritual marriage is the essence of the *concetto.*"[23]

Three things follow from the interpretation of the missing leg of the Christ: First, a closer pattern of symbolic and formal coherence for the entire group. Second, a new way of thinking about Michelangelo's reasons for destroying the group. Third, the possibility of identifying the slung-leg motif in other classes of monuments. I shall treat each in turn.

1. *Does the marital symbolism of the missing leg enhance the coherence of the whole group?*

The Virgin is not alone in being the Spouse of Christ. In

[22] See Appendix B, pp. 275–277, for a closer analysis of the Christ figure.
[23] Tolnay, V, 87.

Christian tradition, Christ as bridegroom is as multi-present as is His body in the Host of the Altar. The Church is his Bride. The human soul is his bride. The nun who has taken the veil is his bride. So is St. Catherine, whom he espouses with the same words from Canticles—"Come unto me, my fair love and my spouse"—which also welcome the soul of the Virgin. And so, in the medieval tradition exemplified by the *Biblia Pauperum*, is Mary Magdalene: "We read in the Song of Solomon, third chapter, that when the bride had found her beloved she said, 'I have found him whom my soul loveth, and I will again hold him and will not let him go.' This bride is a type of Mary Magdalene, who, seeing her spouse, that is Christ, would fain have held Him . . ."[24]

This introduces the other woman, the Magdalene figure on our left. We do not much like looking at her because, after Michelangelo's destruction of the unfinished group and its subsequent restoration by Tiberio Calcagni, it was this figure that was most overworked, scaled down, pettified. Nevertheless, in the role he has made her play, as Magdalene and as counterpart of the Virgin, she is all Michelangelo's.

She is embraced. That she is truly embraced, not merely caught in the peripheral sweep of a circuiting rhythm, is confirmed by one small nuance. The drapery fold between the Magdalene's breasts that flows down her abdomen is not her own garment but the loose end of Christ's winding sheet. Released from his chest, it presses gently against her body. The delegated caress of the shroud confirms the Magdalene as an object of love.

At this point we touch a vast medieval tradition concerning the erotic association of Christ and Mary Magdalene.[25] Thus Rabanus Maurus in the ninth century: "Mary Magdalene suffered

[24] From the *Biblia Pauperum*, transcribed in A. Didron, *Christian Iconography*, trans. by E. J. Millington (New York, 1965), II, 423. Savonarola, too, in his fervent evocation of the Passion story, exhorts the Magdalene to weep ever more copiously for her "Sweet Spouse" *(Tractato dello Amore di Jesu Christo*, Firenze, 1492, unpaginated).

[25] See Appendix C, pp. 277–280, for the sources cited in this paragraph and for further comments on the role assigned to the Magdalene in the iconography of the Passion.

as lovers are accustomed to suffer, and mourned inestimably concerning the corporeal absence of her beloved lover." Passion plays kept the tradition alive. In the *Noli me tangere* scene of a late-fifteenth-century English play, Mary exclaims: "O mine heart, where hast thou been./ Come home again and live with me!" And in the anonymous fourteenth-century Italian *Life of St. Mary Magdalene,* she cries out: "Oh, most blessed cross. Would that I had been in thy stead, and that my lord had been crucified in my arms, my hands nailed against His . . . so that I had died with him, and thus neither in life nor death ever departed from Him."

An erotic energy derived from these un-Biblical fantasies invests Michelangelo's group. The Magdalene's approach to Christ's body betrays a sexual intimacy either uninterrupted or generated by death.

But the Magdalene is not simply a paramour.[26] She is here what she is to the whole Patristic tradition—the sinner in the flesh, the forgiven harlot, repentant. Her pardon is everyman's hope. "For whereas sin abounded," says the *Golden Legend* speaking of her salvation, "Grace overabounded and was more. . . ."

It is in her dual role as lover and penitent that she too inhabits the *essential conception* of the *Pietà.* She is the counterpart of the Virgin in a single bilateral scheme. "It is she whom he loved more than any other woman in the world, save the Virgin Mary," says the fourteenth-century *Life.* The two Marys are continually paralleled in the sermons. Both stand for the Church—the sinner turned, and the one without sin, personifications of Penitence and Immaculacy. Together, bracing and being embraced, they sustain the dead body like the heraldic supporters of an escutcheon. Both are, or were meant to be, folded within the limbs of Christ's body.

Finally, the secret intimacies that connect the two Marys and Christ help to define the unity of the entire group. Critical accounts of the work, overlooking the sensual bonds, have tended

[26] See below, pp. 277-280.

to reduce one or two of the figures to subsidiary roles. Even Tolnay assigned no essential part to the Magdalene—nor to the cowled figure whom he called a "personification of Providence"—for he saw the "essence of the *concetto*" in the union of only two figures. Yet an indivisible pathos unites the whole group as its secret intimacies begin to tell. Each Mary's figure is passed three times by Christ's body; each is received. But the more closely bound they are to the Saviour, the more does the hooded penitent at their back stand alone. Since Michelangelo had planned to erect this image of Christ at his tomb, it is fitting that he should have projected his likeness upon the Joseph of Arimathea who, after the descent from the Cross, received Christ in his sepulchre.[27] Between this unused tomb of Joseph and Mary's unopened womb elaborate analogies had been drawn since St. Ambrose.[28] And St. Augustine closes his Sermon 248, "De Sepultura Domini," with words that work like a commentary upon Michelangelo's group: "Joseph [of Arimathea] was not less moved than Mary. If indeed she received the Lord deep in her womb, he received him deep in his heart." They are at one, therefore, in the communion of grief. But the contrast is no less poignant, for the women serve—in a given visual corollary—to isolate the hooded mourner who bears Michel-

[27] The identity of the topmost figure is discussed by Wolfgang Stechow in "Joseph of Arimathea or Nicodemus," in *Studien zur Toskanischen Kunst,* Festschrift Heydenreich (Munich, 1964), pp. 289–302. After an impressive accumulation of scholarly argument on both sides, the question remains undecided. But it appears to me, as I think it does to Professor Stechow, that the weight of probability continues in Joseph's favor.

[28] See Hirn, *Sacred Shrine,* Ch. 7, esp. pp. 337 ff. Hirn quotes the Ambrosian Easter Hymn: "Thou who wast before born of a Virgin, art born now of the grave"; and from Ephraim Syrus (ca. 306–378), who compares Christ's emergence from the sealed grave to the fact of Mary's anatomical virginity: "Thus didst thou show, O Lord, by thy resurrection from the grave, the miracle of thy birth, for each was closed and each was sealed, both the grave and the womb. Thou wast pure in the womb and living in the grave, and Mary's womb, like the grave, bore an unbroken seal."

". . . No less honor is due to the tomb which raised the Lord than to the womb of Holy Mary which brought him forth," says St. Augustine in Sermon 248, "De Sepultura Domini," *Patrol. Lat.,* Vol. XXXIX, col. 2204. See also St. Ambrose, *Liber de Virginitate,* I, iii, 14, in *Patrol. Lat.,* Vol. XVI, col. 283.

angelo's face. His only contact with Christ's body is with the arm that embraces the sinner, and his towering solitude contrasts with the communion of lovers under his hands.

2. *Is it likely that the outright carnality of the symbolic slung leg helped to motivate the destruction of the* Pietà?

Let us hear Michelangelo, as Vasari reports him, speak of this work. Since it was uncommissioned, it was, we are told, done for a pastime, for recreation, and "because the use of the mallet kept him [he was then seventy-five!] in good health." As an apology for an intended tomb monument, such remarks seem evasive almost to the point of flippancy. We then learn that the work was destroyed. And Vasari, because he cannot imagine why, offers three reasons: the marble, he says, was marred by many flaws. (But Michelangelo himself speaks of only one troublesome vein in the stone, and furthermore this is not convincing ground for destroying a work nearly completed.) Second, says Vasari, the marble was hard, making the sparks fly from the chisel. (But though this might be reason for abandoning the work, it hardly explains the added labor of breaking it up; and furthermore, what remains of the stone shows Michelangelo equal to it.) Third and last, says Vasari, "the artist's standards were so high that he could never be content with what he had done." (But how should such general discontent explain a unique instance of mutilation? Though the Florentine *Pietà* is not the poorest of Michelangelo's works, it is the only one he took the trouble to smash.)

Elsewhere in Vasari's account, the sculptor himself being pressed to explain "why he had ruined such a marvelous work," he responds with a tangle of incongruous motives: "It was because of the importunity of his servant Urbino, who nagged at him daily that he should finish it; and that among other things a piece of the Virgin's elbow had broken off, and that even before that he had come to hate it, and he had had many mishaps because of a vein in the stone; so that losing patience he broke it, and would have smashed it completely had not his servant Antonio asked that he give it to him just as it was."

The story ends with Michelangelo consenting to let a young

pupil, Tiberio Calcagni, reassemble the group on behalf of a wealthy admirer who promises to pay 200 ducats in gold to the servant Antonio, who now owns the pieces.

Here again are some patent evasions. Michelangelo says he has come to hate the work to the point of wanting it utterly smashed; but he attacked only that corner of the block which involved Christ's left leg and arm. He then allows the group, including the arm, to be restored—but not the leg. And there is indication that he had broken this leg into fragments. For the inventory of his house taken in 1566 (after the death of Daniele da Volterra, who had taken it over) includes "a marble knee from the *Pietà* of Michelangelo"—presumably from this work. A knee only was allowed to survive.[29]

One other incident points to the leg as the focus of special concern. It is a short anecdote which Vasari tells, at the end of his Michelangelo *Vita,* to illustrate an interesting character trait:

> One night Vasari was sent by Pope Julius III to Michelangelo's house for a drawing. He found the master working on the marble *Pietà* which he broke. Recognizing the knock, Michelangelo rose and took a lantern. When Vasari had explained his errand, he sent Urbino [his servant] for the design and began to speak of other things. Vasari meanwhile cast his eyes upon a leg of the Christ which Michelangelo was working on and was trying to alter, and in order that Vasari might not see it, he let the lantern fall, and being now in the dark, called Urbino to bring a light; in the meantime, stepping out of the room where he had been, he said, "I am so old that death frequently drags at my cloak to take me, and one day I myself will fall like this lantern and so the light of my life will go out."

A dark story, not the kind that yields solid evidence. It contributes nothing to our purpose if we assume that Michelangelo kept open house in his studio, and that the *Pietà* was normally left

[29] *"Un ginocchio di marmo della Pietà di Michelangelo."* See E. Steinmann and R. Wittkower, *Michelangelo Bibliographie* (Leipzig, 1927), No. 778: *Il Buonarroti,* ed. Benvenuto Gasparoni (Rome, 1866), I, 178.

exposed, so that Vasari would have known the *concetto* from previous visits. On the other hand, if Michelangelo was normally secretive about all or any of his unfinished works, and if, carving the *Pietà* by night, he normally kept it covered by day, then Vasari's story gains interest. The question cannot be wholly resolved. But it is worth recalling that Michelangelo's secretiveness was proverbial. Forty years after his death, Van Mander writes in his *Schilderboek* that Hendrik Goltzius never allowed unfinished works to be seen and that, "in this as in many other things, he resembled the great Michelangelo." In the first (open house) alternative, assuming Michelangelo's friends to be familiar with the work in hand, the sculptor's embarrassment on the occasion of Vasari's nocturnal call would be due to some fresh mishap in the carving, caused perhaps by the emery vein. Such a hypothesis makes it fortuitous that the location of the vein coincides with that of the slung leg (whose eroticism, being merely symbolic, would hardly have caused the sculptor anxiety). A flaw in the marble becomes the sufficient reason for the destruction of the *Pietà*. Michelangelo would have been moved to destroy his work by a succession of accidents to the stone and the vexation that followed. The destructive act tells us nothing that is not technical about the work, nor about the artist beyond proving his irascible temper.

There is now a new way of posing the problem. The Florentine *Pietà* employs a direct sexual metaphor on a scale unprecedented in Christian devotional art. Michelangelo's figurative use of the human figure recalls the poetic idiom of those earlier mystics and preachers who described the ultimate religious experience in figures of physical love. St. Bernardino of Siena, for instance, says sexual ecstasy when he means mystic transport, and there is nothing uncommon in this kind of *wording.*[30] But poets and mystics

[30] "Sometimes the soul, through the penetrating alterations of love, enters the marriage bed of heavenly mysteries . . . and not lacking are visions most lofty in which the soul tastes what it is to be almost translated into the profound and infinite abyss of God. It happens also that, in some unthinkable and most fervent act of love [*ferventissimo actu amoris*] in one glorious moment, a spiritual marriage with Christ

had the freedom of figurative speech as an ancient charter. It was another matter to claim such poetic license in the concretions of palpable sculpture. Now, with the reformist atmosphere settling on Rome, Michelangelo may have feared that his intentions would be misread by censorious and prurient men who, like the Florentine anonymous of 1549, expected to find his inventions obscene. He may have felt certain more inward resources of confidence failing—confidence in the transcendent eloquence of the body—in the possibility of infinitely spiritualizing its anatomic machinery while still respecting its norms. Perhaps it was simply the coarsening of his metaphorical idiom in the work of others that crowded and threatened his confidence. Or, more specifically, that the vulgarization of the slung-leg motif during the very years of his work on the *Pietà* rendered the pose increasingly unacceptable. Such conjectures suggest alternative or additional motives for Michelangelo's destructive act. They keep open the possibility that he shattered his work, not because he was vexed by a servant's nagging, and not because part of the Virgin's elbow had splintered off, but that he destroyed it in despair: that he saw himself pushing the rhetoric of carnal gesture to a point where its metaphorical status passed out of control; that he felt himself crossing the limit of what seemed expressible in his art. His demolition then would be a renunciation, comparable to that which sounds again in the final lines of his sonnet:

> To paint or carve no longer calms
> the Soul turned to that Love divine
> Who to embrace us on the Cross opens his arms.[31]

---

is consummated." St. Bernardini Senensis, *Opera Omnia* (Firenze, 1956), Tomus IV, Sermo LI. "De admirandis gratiis beatae Virginis," p. 549.

An Early Christian example of sexual metaphor relevant to the *Pietà* theme occurs in the *Symposium* of Methodius of Olympus (summarized in Herbert A. Musurillo, *The Fathers of the Primitive Church,* New York, 1966, p. 213): "Christ's final act was to sleep in the ecstasy of his Passion, during which he procreated through the virgin Mother Church all those who would be baptized in his blood."

[33] Sonnet CXLVII, "Giunto è già 'l corso della vita mia," sent to Vasari on September 19, 1554.

The date of the sonnet falls within the year of the destruction of the *Pietà*.

3. *Does the interpretation of the slung-leg motif carry over to other classes of monuments?*

There can be no doubt that the motif is sexual when it couples adults. The question arises whether we are to recognize the same symbolic charge in images of the Virgin and Child. In the early sixteenth century (in pictures by Raphael, Puligo, Andrea del Sarto, some half dozen Michelangelo drawings, etc.) the motif of the infant's leg arched over the mother's thigh is so common as to suggest either that it is wholly innocent or that, being thoroughly understood, it was felt to be more safely assigned to the lively Child than to the man. This latter assumption would add another to the many proleptic themes of Renaissance art which show the Child anticipating whatever the Christ is destined to do—embracing some token of his Passion, raising his hand in preachment, benediction, or judgment, prefiguring the sleep of his death, espousing St. Catherine, and so on. In Michelangelo's early marble *tondo*, the *Madonna Taddei*, as in Andrea del Sarto's Madonnas of the 1520's, the Child's leg scaling the Virgin's thigh is presumably innocent; doubt on this score may even meet with resentment. On the other hand, the infant's pose may have been at first playful, athletic, striding forth, to become erotic only by gradual adapta-
137, 138, 139, 140 tion to the slung-leg motif (Figs. 137–140). One's assurance in the abiding innocence of the motif is shaken on comparing certain works of slightly later date in which the Child seems cast in a similar role. Thus, remarkably similar poses are struck by the Christ Child in Cambiaso's *Mystic Marriage of St. Catherine* (Fig.
141 141), and again in a Parmigianino design preserved in a
142 seventeenth-century engraving by Schelte à Bolswert (Fig. 142). Here the "innocence" of the pose can no longer be argued, particularly when it is found, by comparing Giulio Romano's
143 *Cupid and Psyche* (Fig. 143),[32] that, regardless of the boy's age, this

[32] See Frederick Hartt, *Giulio Romano* (New Haven, 1958), Vol. I, Catalogue of Drawings, No. 139, and pp. 88–89; and Vol. II, Fig. 149. Hartt dates the drawing

bestriding a woman's thigh is an unmistakable gesture of male appropriation. In Parmigianino's design the erotic tenor is further emphasized by the riper age of the Child: not a babe, but the young Saviour embracing with one hand the urn of his Passion while his other hand grasps Mary's shoulder. This seizing a shoulder is another ceremonial gesture of possession taking. It demonstrates *manus,* the dominion over a person—specifically, in Roman Law, the husband's power over his wife. It places the woman *in manu.*[33]

There is a wide frame of reference for these sixteenth-century images in which the nuptials of the heavenly spouse are prefigured in the approach of the Child. The emotions projected into such pictures may not always have been formal doctrine, but their part in the religious imagination of Mediterranean Europe was vital. A millennial procession of symbolic equations had left thought and feeling caught up in constellations of metaphors—metaphors in which subtle theological formulas and secret fantasies consorted together. The Old Testament's Song of Songs, which in the Rabbinical exegesis declared God's love for Israel, became, in the Christian translation, Christ's love for his Church. "It can be

(Louvre 3497), which he connects with Giulio's first Mantuan period, in 1526.

The proliferation of infant slung legs during the 1520's suggests the effect of a single powerful stimulus; that this may have been Michelangelo's *Madonna Medici* becomes the more likely in view of Pope-Hennessy's recent insight that the work had been made in the preceding decade to form part of the Julius Tomb.

[33] With hand laid on shoulder, Eros takes hold of Paris (Hellenistic relief, Naples); Hercules reclaims Alceste from Hades (Pompeian fresco); Death takes a youth (etching by the Housebook Master, Lehrs 53); Eve appropriates Adam (Ludwig Krug relief, 1514, Berlin-Dahlem); Mars seizes Venus (Marcantonio Raimondi engraving, B. 325); and the newborn Christ Child claims the Madonna (Filippo Lippi's *Madonna Adoring the Child with Two Angels,* 1457, Uffizi, our Fig. 144). In Roman law the *manus* 144
injectio demonstrated the ceremonial seizure of a slave or a debtor (see R. Brilliant, *Gesture and Rank in Roman Art,* Conn. Acad. of Sciences, XIV, 1963, 215, for full bibliography). As a token of marital status, from Roman and early Christian times onward, the gesture is as common as it is self-explanatory.

In a drawing of the *Lamentation* at the British Museum (Fig. 145), catalogued as 145
by Michelangelo and datable in the late 1530's, the dead Christ, cradled in Mary's lap, lays his left hand on her shoulder. (J. Wilde, *Italian Drawings in the British Museum: Michelangelo,* London, 1953, No. 64r.)

said frankly and safely," writes St. Gregory the Great, "that when in the mystery of the Incarnation the Father celebrated the wedding of his royal son, he gave him the Holy Church as his companion. The womb of the Virgin Mother was the nuptial couch of this bridegroom."[34]

But from the second century onward, Mary herself becomes a type of the Church. Before long the Church is figured in Mary as Mary is in the Church. Christ is the bridegroom of the one as of the other. By the twelfth century, Ecclesia, herself Virgin and Mother and Beloved of Christ, has become in every respect interchangeable with the Virgin. As in the doctrine of Perichoresis, which describes the two natures of Christ, Mary and Church wholly inhere in each other. "Everything that is said of the Church can also be understood as being said of the Virgin herself, the bride and mother of the bridegroom."[35]

In the reading of Canticles, and in its pictorial complement, the Beloved embraced by Christ became and remained an ambivalent symbol. In illuminated twelfth-century Bibles, or in manuscript commentaries on Canticles, the initial "O" of the opening "*Osculetur me oscula oris sui*" may enclose lovers who share even their single halo; but the lady's identity, whether Virgin or
146 Church, is undefined (Fig. 146).[36]

But another type exists which seems to demand a simple Marian interpretation: the bridegroom of Canticles takes form as
147 the newborn Christ—as in the Lyons Bible (Fig. 147).[37] Here the historiated initial which opens the "Let him kiss me with the kisses of his mouth" contains a Madonna and Child, the Child coming as bridegroom, as lover, as man, striding toward her, embracing,

[34] Quoted in de Lubac, *Splendour . . .* , p. 209, from S. Gregory, *Hom. XXXVIII in Evangelia*, No. 3, *Patrol. Lat.*, Vol. LXXVI, col. 1283.

[35] Honorius of Autun, *Commentary on Canticles, Patrol. Lat.*, Vol. CLXXII, col. 494.

[36] Twelfth-century manuscript of St. Jerome's *Expositio in Canticum Canticorum*, Abbaye de Saint-Amand, Lat. 1808, fol. iv.

[37] Lyons, ms. 410, fol. 207v, second half of the twelfth century: *Bibliothèque Nationale, Les Manuscrits à Peintures en France du VIIe au XIIe Siècle* (Paris, 1954), No. 330.

their cheeks sharing one contour, so that their eyes touch and their coupled lips align as in a kiss folded out.

There is a tradition here which reaches both forward and backward. An engraving by Abraham van Merlen, a Jesuit illustrator of about 1600, shows the Madonna and Child over the legend—"My beloved is mine, and I am his. . . . He shall lie all night betwixt my breasts" (Cant. 2: 16 and 1: 12; Fig. 148. Cf. the 148
inscribed arch in Fig. 140). On the other hand, the Lyons Bible 140
initial, painted by an unknown Byzantinizing illuminator, points back to the Byzantine Madonna of "sweet love," the Glykophilousa. It is here and in its derivatives that one finds, in the tender contact between the Mother and Child, the first veiled erotic allusions to their mystic marriage.[38] The intent of countless later Madonna and Child confrontations in art is to reveal the Child Jesus as fully the Christ and fully man who, having chosen his mother, now chooses her for his Virgin bride.

Nowhere were such thoughts more compellingly realized than in the preaching of Savonarola, which Michelangelo heard in his youth. In Savonarola's remarkable expostulation for the pregnant Virgin, his *"Sponsa Iesu,"* Mary yields dramatically as mother and bride to the awaited Bridegroom. Addressing herself to the Father, she pleads that he vouchsafe her a delivery as hurtless as her conception had been: "Even as I conceived him without shame and without violence to my virginity, so, by Thy grace, let me now bring him forth without pain, abiding ever virgin and chaste."[39]

So far we are on traditional ground. Savonarola merely presents as dramatic monologue what earlier fathers, such as Andrew of Crete (ca. 700 A.D.) expressed by apostrophe: "Your chastity, O Virgin, has remained as it was in the beginning, inviolate. For

[38] See Appendix D, pp. 280–283, on the wooing motif of the touched chin.

[39] *". . . così come io lo ho conceputo senza pudore e senza violamento della mia verginità, così ora per tua grazia, lo partorisca senza dolore perseverando vergine e illibata."* (*Sermoni e Prediche di F. Girolamo Savonarola,* Prato, 1846, Vol. I, Sermo XIX, "Della Natività di Cristo," 485).

Christ the sun, like a bridegroom from the bridal chamber, has come forth from you."[40] But the traditional evocations of sun and bridegroom, derived from the Psalms, grow strangely sensual in Savonarola's lines for the Virgin as they turn into direct address: "Come forth then, my Son, even as the bridegroom from his bridal chamber. Issue forth from my womb . . . Gladden your handmaid's soul, fulfill at last your mother's desire, my soul has desired you and desires you continually, Jesus mine, I can wait no more, I am consumed, I melt, I languish in love."[41]

For Savonarola the delivery of the Christ Child was not only, as it had seemed to earlier visionaries, quick, painless, and without lesion; it was pleasurable, and the pleasure ecstatic. And the Infant Bridegroom who came forth in such sheer virility must be tremendous and ardent.

In sheer virility he appears in Michelangelo's *Madonna*
149 *Medici* (Fig. 149). The Christ Child is an infant Hercules, sitting forward, straddling his Mother's thigh. His upper body swerves through an astonishing 180 degrees, and he appears to be nursing. But his left hand, grasping the Virgin's shoulder, leaves infancy as far behind as does the precocious athleticism of his physique.

This Child is many things. As Infant Hercules, he absorbs the titles of championship and apotheosis implicit in the old hero cult.[42] And the linen bands that cross and recross his body suggest

[40] Andreas Cretensis, *Canon in Beatae Mariae Natalem*, Migne, *PG*, 97, 1323.

[41] "*Egredere igitur, fili mi, tanquam sponsus de thalamo suo. Esci del ventre mio . . . Letifica l'anima dell'ancilla tua, adempe oromai il desiderio della madre tua, l'anima mia t'ha desiderato e desidera continuamente, Gesù mio, io non posso più aspettare, io mi consumo, io mi sento tutta liquefare, io languisco d'amore.*" For speculations concerning this startling confession, see Appendix E, pp. 283–285.

[42] Hercules as a prefiguration of Christ is discussed in Marcel Simon, *Hercule et le Christianisme* (Paris, 1955). We may add that in the history of representational imagery, the Infant Hercules also prefigures the prolepses of the Christ Child, as when he appears with the Apples of the Hesperides in his little hands (statuette at the Conservatori Museum, Rome). "Herakles' long journey to the Far West has in this case been assigned to his babyhood," commented Dorothy Kent Hill (in "Ancient Representations of Herakles as a Baby," *Gazette des Beaux-Arts*, Series VI, XXXVI, April 1948, 199). The concept is better explained as a future tense in the grammar of representation.

a stripping away either of swaddling or winding sheet, or of both at once, one in the character of the other, defining the divine man in his twofold emergence.

Why the crossed legs of the Virgin? Tolnay suggested that the Madonna's legs were crossed so as to elevate the Child "to bring it closer to the bosom." But in three surviving Michelangelo drawings that anticipate the *Madonna Medici* (Figs. 150–152)[43] the Child is already fast at the breast though the Mother's legs are uncrossed; it is rather her lofty shoulder that is out of reach. What the crossing of the Madonna's legs accomplishes is to lift the Child far above her breast level; evidently the literal contact here was dispensable since the mere direction of the Child's turn would suffice to suggest suckling. But with the Madonna's legs crossed, the Child rides the high crest of her thigh. Now all his body, his straddling seat and his grip on her shoulder, reveal in the Child the divine lover electing his spouse. 150, 151, 152

Much of Michelangelo's idiom is unintelligible so long as its indwelling sexuality remains unexplored. His bodies, in action or immobilized, are possessed by their sex. But sex here means

[43] All three drawings (Figs. 150–152) show the Virgin with the nursing Child, who sits astraddle on one of her thighs spiraling inward. While his right hand reaches her breast, his left hand remains comparatively unemployed—and is omitted in the earliest of the three drawings (the Louvre version; proposed datings run 1503 to 1524). Even here, however, Mary's gesture shows that the Child, following Byzantine precedent, would have allowed his left hand to be held by the Mother—as he does in the Vienna version (proposed datings 1506 to 1524). This traditional solution leaves one hand of the Christ idling in a manner which no matured Michelangelo work will permit. Accordingly, in the London drawing, demonstrably later than the other two, the Child's left hand is almost released for action—but only to become redundant, for now both hands attach the same feeding breast. 150, 151, 152

Michelangelo evidently felt this to be a problem unsolved; but the drawings do not as yet offer the structural base for the solution—that of extricating the Child's hand to seize Mary's shoulder. So long as the Child sits on thighs that remain uncrossed, the Mother's shoulder remains inaccessible to his arm. If the Madonna was not to forfeit her regal height, the Infant could reach her remote shoulder only by being raised on her arm or by standing up on her lap, as he does in Gothic Madonnas; but these adjustments would have surrendered the straddling motif.

the full sexual cycle—courtship and brooding fertility, coupling and birth, and, beyond birth, a sexual symbolization of parenthood.

The thighs, knees, and feet of the mother are, or become, outward tokens of the maternal womb; the child's place with respect to these members indicates filiation. If this sounds self-evident, it is not self-evident visually, for a visual image of birth or of actual procession attends neither the word nor the mental picture of "child." The English word "issue," medieval in origin and more vivid in describing physical derivation than the Italian *progenie* or *stirpe* (offspring), has no precise parallel in Italian. Its equivalent appears in Italian Renaissance art.

Again, the theme of a child held between his parent's knees may seem commonplace. Yet it does not enter art as an observed phenomenon, but evolves from the most schematic representations of sonship—from the Trinity type known as the *Gnadenstuhl,* or Throne of Mercy, and from the family groups of the Virgin and Child with St. Anne.

In the Trinities that developed in the Romanesque art of the North, God the Father is seated, accepting the Crucifix. Devotional images of this type came to enjoy wide popularity in Italy after the mid-fourteenth century, and it is in these pictures of Father and Son that the crucified Christ, often diminutive as a toy, first appears between the progenitor's knees. But the word "between" claims too much. In the comparatively flat Trecento style a Corpus Christi hung at the Father's knees conveys little sense of palpable interposition. One is not certain that the Trecento artist ever intended the visual effect of a child sprung from paternal loins.

It is hard to say just when the anatomical symbolization of parenthood becomes intentional. It is clearly intentional after the mid-fifteenth century, when the modified form of the Trinity group becomes an emblem of manifest filiation. As the size of the cross expands to make the scale of Son and Father agree, the Corpus descends below the feet of the Father; and as plastic-spatial relationships are intensified, the parental thighs clasp the Son's body (Figs. 153–156).[44] 153, 154, 155, 156

Christ's human descent through St. Anne, the Virgin's mother, inspired another devotional image of the Trecento.[45] The succession of generations was at first rendered schematically by means of relative size and precession: the Christ Child precedes the Virgin, who sits in front of St. Anne; the grandmother, grandiose and overscaled, looms behind the Mother and Child and outmeasures her adult daughter by as much as the Virgin exceeds the size of the Child. The scheme is concentric; the diminishing scale shows

[44] The Trinities illustrated are: Orcagna School, 1370, London; Masolino, ca. 1425, Detroit; Pesellino, *Trinity with Saints,* 1455, London; and Granacci's *tondo,* 1512, Berlin. All four are Florentine and formed part of Michelangelo's artistic environment. Several others could be cited as likely influences upon his youth, notably Baldovinetti's Trinity Altarpiece of 1473. (Those of Masaccio and Castagno in which God does not appear seated represent a different type.) Francesco Granacci, the author of our Fig. 156, was Michelangelo's childhood friend and fellow apprentice. 156

For discussions of the *Gnadenstuhl* Trinity, see Millard Meiss, *Painting in Florence and Siena after the Black Death* (Princeton, 1951; Harper Torchbooks, 1964), p. 34; and most recently Otto von Simson's important essay "Über die Bedeutung von Masaccios Trinitäts Fresco in Sta. Maria Novella," *Jahrbuch der Berliner Museen,* VIII (1966), 119–159.

[45] The St. Anne family group was developed in the fourteenth century to express the Franciscan tenet of the Virgin's Immaculate Conception. As the receptacle of the *conceptio immaculata,* the Virgin's mother gained ever greater importance within the divine plan. Images of the three-generation group proliferated, known in Italy as *Sant'Anna Metterza,* in Germany as *Die heilige Anna Selbdritt.* Northern representations usually show the two mothers standing or seated side by side; St. Anne, who is nearly always larger in scale, sometimes embraces her daughter, sometimes carries her miniature adult form like an attribute on one arm, while the Christ Child rests on the other. There is no attempt in the Italian mode to symbolize physical generation.

For an entertaining survey of the St. Anne cult in Europe after 1480, see A. Chastel, *The Age of Humanism* (New York, 1963), pp. 105 ff. The especial veneration of the Florentines for St. Anne as patroness of their city dates from the liberation of Florence from the tyranny of Brienne, Duke of Athens, on St. Anne's Day, July 26, 1343. See Giovanni Villani's *Cronica,* written from 1300 to 1348; ed. Florence, 1823, VII, 54. The fullest account of the subject from the points of view of religion and (more naïvely) art history, is Beda Kleinschmidt, *Die heilige Anna,* Düsseldorf, 1930. I have not followed his system of classification in the distinction of types, nor the more sophisticated system proposed in H. Aurenhammer's *Lexikon der Christlichen Ikonographie,* (Vienna, 1960), s.v. "Anna Selbdritt."

each progeny enfolded or circumscribed in its matrix (Figs.
157, 158 157 and 158).[46]

This venerable Trecento schema remained authoritative for well over a century. One finds it preserved, despite the updated style in the figures, in pictures as late as the Signorelli school or even Correggio.[47] Nevertheless, new solutions emerge throughout the 1400's, their fullest realization coming in works of the High Renaissance—in Fra Bartolommeo, Leonardo, and Michelangelo. Fra Bartolommeo's system departs from the concentric Trecento scheme by substituting an echelon structure. His *Pala di Sant'Anna*
159 of 1512 (Fig. 159) indicates precession by the setting of podium and throne; the Virgin is seated below her mother in a literal show of descent. Another scheme, dispensing with props, enthrones the full-grown Virgin on her mother's lap—either facing forward
158, 160 (Figs. 158 and 160), or side-saddle in the solution made famous
161, 168 by Leonardo (Figs. 161 and 168).[48] Lastly—and this becomes

[46] The examples reproduced are Traini's picture at Princeton and the fourteenth-century carved-wood group from Or San Michele, now at the Bargello, Florence. The association of the Florentine St. Anne cult with victory explains the strangely
158 archaic character of the Bargello group (Fig. 158), originally placed over her principal altar in Or San Michele. The group is clearly patterned on the Byzantine Madonna type known as the Nikopoia, the bringer of victory. Because of its rigid, hieratic frontality, the type had long passed out of favor in Italy. Its pattern was adapted and doubled at Or San Michele not as a stylistic regression, but as visual evidence that the Virgin's power of bestowing victory derived from St. Anne. The effect of this work, or rather of its authoritative sacred location, was to leave Renaissance realism with another magnificent paradox on its hands—how to reconcile ideality with absurdity, or one adult woman perched, in beauty and dignity, on the lap of another.

[47] See the *Sant'Anna Metterza* by Bicci di Lorenzo (1373–1452) in The Bob Jones University Gallery, Greenville, S.C.; the similar panel by the "Stratonice Master" (active 1475–1490) in the Lord Lee of Fareham Collection, London; the Signorelli school piece at Castiglione Fiorentino, attributed to Papacello (d. 1559; see *Signorelli, Klassiker der Kunst*, Berlin, 1927, p. 191); the little Correggio panel of ca. 1515 in the Kress Collection, Washington National Gallery.

[48] The Virgin sits on St. Anne's lap in the canonic fourteenth-century image from
158 Or San Michele (Fig. 158). She does so in Gozzoli's picture in the Pisa museum (Fig.
160 160) and, almost a century later, in Girolamo dai Libri's picture in London (National Gallery No. 748, dated 1518). Leonardo's side-saddle scheme is anticipated in Luca di Tommè's polyptych, dated 1367, in the Siena Pinacoteca, and in an engraving
161 (before 1470) by the Master E. S. (copy by Meckenem, Geisberg 332; Fig. 161). The engraving also anticipates Leonardo in that the Child is placed on the ground.

Michelangelo's way—the forms of mother and daughter are nested so that all primary motion is a visible coming forth, like a birth (Fig. 162).[49] But this fertile posture, the legs parted wide enough 162
to encompass a seated adult, is originally a borrowing from the severe Trinity scheme discussed above. To convey kinship by generation, the Father's spread thighs are adapted to the pose of St. Anne.

As the crucified Son fills the open lap of the Father, and as Mary fills that of St. Anne, so the manifest filiation principle is applied *a fortiori* to the placing of the Christ Child. Whether one looks at the Mantegnesque *Holy Kinship* in the Gardner Museum, Boston (Fig. 164), or at Michelangelo's *Bruges Madonna* (Fig. 165), 164, 165
the stationing of the Child between the Mother's legs as her body's issue is clearly adapted from the older symbolic visualizations of progeniture.

But this final type presupposes another significant fifteenth-century development: Mary's lap relaxes to become an ever more flexible and articulate structure. The Trecento lap as pedestal or as solid throne is resolved into twin thighs. The Virgin's legs assume the freedom of separate gesture, and the interval they contain becomes a stage for the Child. The Christ Child cradled in a deep lap, or standing between Mary's shins as between pillars—these are among the new themes of the late Quattrocento. And each of these themes may be activated to suggest the Child coming forth.[50]

[49] The outstanding examples of "nesting" to indicate offspring are Michelangelo's two surviving drawings on the theme of St. Anne: that of ca. 1502 at Oxford (Fig. 162) 162
and the somewhat later study at the Louvre. The principle was adopted by Francesco da Sangallo, ca. 1522, in the monumental marble group which, on the St. Anne altar at Or San Michele (Fig. 163), replaced the old wooden effigy now at the Bargello 163
(Fig. 158). Sangallo's symbolism is biological instead of hierarchic, substituting the 158
authority of an unexecuted Michelangelo project for the authority of tradition. But his product, with its mechanical encapsulation of Mothers, is one of the vulgarest sculptures in Florence; it demonstrates the implausibility of the nested family group when unredeemed by tenderness and imagination.

[50] The Child climbs up from between the Madonna's parted thighs in the Prato Master's *Trivulzio Madonna* (late 1440's; Milan, Castello Sforzesco; reprod. in C. Shell, "The Prato Master," *Art Bulletin*, September 1961, Fig. 6). In Benozzo Gozzoli's *Madonna and Child Enthroned with Saints* (1461; London, National Gallery, No. 283; Fig.

A central figure in these preoccupations is Leonardo da Vinci. Most of the fifteenth-century precedents he inherited were rational and naturalistic; the contact between the Child and the Mother was rarely implausible. It is Leonardo who uses his greater naturalistic resources for the further metaphorization of the Son-Mother relationship. In his London cartoon of the St. Anne group with St.
168 John (Fig. 168), the Christ Child is floated into space as if by an energy located in Mary's abdomen. If the Child is on the ground,
169 as in the Louvre *St. Anne* (Fig. 169), then he seems to have sprung from between Mary's feet. Leonardo's drapery studies for the
170, 171 Virgin's lower body in this same painting (Figs. 170 and 171) are strangely emphatic in separating the legs, outlining even the *mons Veneris,* as if in relentless meditation on the organs of parthenogenesis.

The devices evolved during the opening years of the sixteenth century, chiefly by Leonardo and Michelangelo, retained their force at least to the mid-Cinquecento. In countless images of the Madonna, from the most hieratic to almost genre-like presentations, the child issuant is the charge.[51]

---

166 166), the Christ Child, striding forward on his Mother's lap, appears literally to emerge from behind her rose-colored tunic. The expressive and formal problems thus broached by the mid-fifteenth century seem to have become matter of special interest in the Northern Italian centers of Ferrara and Padua. See, for instance, Cosimo Tura's *Madonna and Child* in the Washington National Gallery; or Francesco Cossa's great
167 *Pala dei Mercanti* of 1472 in the Bologna Pinacoteca (Fig. 167). Finally, a wealth of symbolic action appeared in Northern engravings toward the end of the fifteenth century. Thus the Master I.A.M. of Zwolle (whose *St. Anne* engraving, Lehrs 13, uses the modern step-down design to express "descent") also engraved a mystic *Madonna and Child,* Lehrs 10, wherein the Child, obviously "issuant," floats out into space to embrace a large Cross. It comes astonishingly close to Leonardo's inventions of the Child issuing from Mary either to caress St. John or to mount his Passion in the form of a lamb. Evidently the generation of the Italian High Renaissance availed itself of these Northern prints to help resolve the apparent conflict between dogmatic symbolism and naturalism.

[51] After 1500 the motif of the issuant child is recognizable in works of Piero di Cosimo, Andrea del Sarto, Sodoma, Franciabigio, Puligo, Sebastiano del Piombo, Giulio Romano, Garofalo, and others. It is most powerfully used by Parmigianino. A *Holy Family* engraved after Parmigianino by the Master L.D. of the School of Fontaine-
172 bleau shows the Child literally stepping out of the Virgin's body (Fig. 172). In a pen-

Nowhere is this code of expressive signs a profounder necessity than in Michelangelo's work. The Christ Child in Michelangelo's imagination exists throughout in an emergent relationship to Mary's body. Just as in his drawings of the Resurrection one foot of Christ, no matter how impetuous the ascent, trails at the tomb, so his Christ Child, even when striding out, leaves one lingering foot pointing his origin. The Child displays "whenceness" like a physical attribute.[52]

Michelangelo's insistence on these symbolic connections is almost obsessive and spans all his working life, from the *Bruges Madonna,* whose Child steps forth from her body (Fig. 165), to 165
the late *Epiphany* cartoon in the British Museum (Fig. 174). Here 174
the young St. John in the lower right is discovering God newly incarnate as the fruit of a woman's womb, the physical facts being stated with astounding simplicity.

Michelangelo's determination to see Christ as the Virgin's issue helps to understand yet another *Pietà,* a design of the 1530's known as the *Pietà for Vittoria Colonna.*[53] The Marchesa Vittoria Colonna, to whom the artist dedicated the work, was a poetess and Catholic reformer in whose circle Michelangelo had undergone a religious conversion. The drawing he made for her may be the

---

and-wash study for an enthroned *Virgin and Child* (Fig. 173) the Christ Child—a boy of 173
more than infant years—again surges upward from the inmost lap of the seated Madonna, but in a soaring pose which deliberately anticipates the Ascension.

[52] "Whenceness" is shown as well by Michelangelo's Isaac writhing between Abraham's knees in the Sacrifice scene. Cf. the drawing of ca. 1535 in the Casa Buonarroti, Florence (Berenson, *The Drawings of the Florentine Painters,* Chicago, 1936, No. 1417, Fig. 721). There are precedents in Mantegna and Baldovinetti, sequels in Pontormo and Rembrandt, indicating how widely the metaphor of manifest filiation was understood. Shakespeare too (in the Prologue to *Romeo and Juliet*) sees his star-crossed lovers take their life "from forth the fatal loins of these two foes."

For Michelangelo's studies of the *Resurrection of Christ,* see Berenson, *op. cit.,* Figs. 696–699. For striking examples of the issuant child among Michelangelo drawings, see Berenson, Figs. 596, 626, 627, 628, 656, 759, 762.

[53] See Tolnay, V, 60–64, for full documentation of the *Pietà for Vittoria Colonna,* and his Pl. 159 and Figs. 340–358.

disputed sheet preserved at the Gardner Museum in Boston (Fig.
175 175). The *concetto,* at any rate, lives in a score of engravings and painted copies. Translated into relief, it survives in two monumental examples as well as on countless paxes, doors of small tabernacles, and liturgical ornaments. Variants and adaptations of the design in sixteenth- and seventeenth-century art are innumerable. Judged by its influence, its appeal and proliferation, the *Colonna Pietà* is Michelangelo's most successful invention.

The design is syncretic. With the theme of the *Pietà,* and with the setting of Golgotha, it compounds three further iconographic types, yet without blurring their distinct traits. The traditional tragic *Pietà* is re-formed in the image of the Virgin with
164 the Infant between her knees (Fig. 164), so that protected Child and crucified God appear in one person. And the grouping of Christ with angelic supporters imports a mystical connotation by absorbing yet another devotional image: the dead Saviour, Man
176 of Sorrows, upheld at his tomb by attendant angels (Fig. 176).[54]

The resultant fusion seems strangely schematic, and Tolnay is probably right to describe the *Colonna Pietà* as somewhat stiff and abstract—"the diagram of a doctrine." But these terms, doctrine and diagram, are so interfused that to expound the doctrinal content is simply to see the picture itself.

Consider the ground level first. It does not reach to the base of the picture, but stops in an upper stratum at the feet of the Virgin and the two angels. These feet rest on firm earthen ground, and it follows that the zone below is not "a kind of pedestal," but a sheer drop. It represents the inside wall of the grave—a feature best understood in those versions of the design which, like the great marble relief in the Vatican Library (Fig.

[54] The connection with the image of the Man of Sorrows, as developed by Donatello, was first pointed out by Thode (*Kritische Untersuchungen,* II, 492). As a woodcut illustration to Saronarola's *Dell' Umiltà,* 1492, it became familiar to every Florentine. The most impressive examples of the type are Northern Italian: Giovanni Bellini
176 (Museo Correr, Venice), Cosimo Tura (Vienna; here Fig. 176), and Marco Zoppo (Monograph by E. Ruhmer, Vicenza, 1966, Pls. 3 and 7).

177), are demonstrably closest in origin to Michelangelo's shop. 177
The significance of the idea was of course quickly grasped. Several *Pietàs* of the 1540's, dependent on Michelangelo's model, show a freshly dug grave at the foot of the cross ready to receive the deposed body (Figs. 178 and 179). But more than all imitators, 178, 179
Michelangelo so orders his space that the worshipper confronting the image must visualize himself inside the grave. It is as though the spatial conditions of the picture realized the words of Notker Balbulus' antiphon—*media in vita in morte sumus*—"in the midst of life we are in death."[55]

The fall under the Virgin's feet is a detail. More emphatic in conveying the imminence of the descent is the pattern of the whole image, its kinship with the scheme of the Trinity discussed above. These "Thrones of Mercy" are the unmistakable analogues for the motif of the seated parent holding the crucified Christ between parted legs. And it was in these images, as Quattrocento painters developed them, that the change of level from the feet of the Father to those of the incarnate Son came to symbolize distinct phases of the redemption—from the Trinity in its heaven to Christ sacrificed in the world. In Pesellino's Trinity Altarpiece (Fig. 155), the stratification is confirmed by the scene shift from a 155
schematic heaven to a landscape on earth. Michelangelo's *Colonna Pietà* shifts from earthly life to the state of death, but the going down is implicit in the analogous pattern. And every action of Michelangelo's Christ—the cast of his head, the pointing fingers, the centered feet—all converge on one purpose. It is a dead body willfully seeking its destination—perhaps in Adam's tomb, which tradition sites under the Calvary Cross, or in its own, the actual

[55] Remarkable anticipations of Michelangelo's thought occur in a poignant drawing by Marco Zoppo for an Entombment (Frankfurt, Staedel Institut, No. 3476; Ruhmer, *op. cit.*, Pl. 54) and in Dürer's drawing in Bremen, dated 1513 (Winkler, IV, 578). In both works the spectator's vantage point is within or on this side of the tomb. The same *concetto* may explain the difference between Caravaggio's "Entombment" in the Vatican, where the body is being laid on the stone of unction, and Rubens' copy of it at Ottawa, transformed into an authentic Entombment. (See Mary Ann Graeve, "The Stone of Unction . . . ," *Art Bulletin*, XL, 3, Figs. 1 and 3.)

mileage from Calvary to Christ's burial cave being erased. It would not be against the nature of Michelangelo's "diagram" to compress spatial relations and, at the same time, to collapse in the single notation of death the historic distance between the tombs of the First and the New Adam.

The next phase of the diagram is made legible in the symbolic parturience of the Madonna's spread thighs. We are made to see both birth and burial, a visible approximation that gives body to an ancient verbal tradition. The Church Fathers had dwelled continually on the similitude of Christ's unused grave and the uneared womb of his Mother, two earthly tabernacles chosen to house the divine.[56] Once the godhead dwelled in a Virgin's womb to emerge from it bodily for the Incarnation, and it deigned to enter a sepulchre to emerge from it bodily for the Resurrection, each emergence being miraculous, without breaking the seal. Womb and tomb were twinned analogically.

But an analogy understood as a correspondence of stable terms would be too static to describe Michelangelo's aim. His image is energized by motion and sequence. There is work being done by the angels. He has made it their task to be visibly withdrawing the body of Christ, lifting it, as midwives might, out of the Virgin's lap, thence to lower it into the tomb.[57] All duration collapses; the span of life from birth to entombment shrinks into a sign.

The direct birth-to-burial passage in turn illuminates the Virgin's action. She is in the attitude of an *orant,* performing the ancient gesture of prayer. But in the present context her pose takes

[56] See above, note 28.

[57] I believe that Michelangelo fully intended to evoke the act of childbearing. Whoever examines sixteenth-century illustrated books on obstetrics and modern histories of the subject will find that it is only in antique (or in classicizing) delivery scenes that women in childbirth recline. In representations from the thirteenth century onward, the expectant mother is shown sitting up, often in a posture that comes astonishingly close to that of the Virgin in the *Colonna Pietà.* (See E. Roesslin, *De Partu Hominis . . . ,* 1532, and its German versions of 1513; Jacobus Rueff, *De Conceptu et Generatione Hominis,* Zurich, 1554; and Samuel Janson, *Korte en bondige Verhandeling . . . ,* Amsterdam, 1685, especially Book VI, Fig. 21.)

on additional meaning. In other *Pietàs,* the Virgin naturally supports the dead body and touches it with one or both hands. In Michelangelo's image, the suspension of this common necessity becomes an act of willed resignation. The Virgin's desistence, raising her hands at this moment, disengaging them even as the body is being taken, suggests that she is letting it go, so that the death of Christ becomes—not as a dogma, but as an immediate visual intuition—her sacrifice also.

This at least is what her gesture might signify in dramatic-psychological terms. Mary's hands, inasmuch as they refer to the lower half of the design, acquiesce in the process which draws the life she bears to its grave. But the conventional meaning of Mary's gesture is equally operative. Together with her uplifted glance it defines the third theological dimension, the hope and promise of resurrection. She initiates all that energy which in the upper portion of the design appears to ascend. And it is her action which is taken up and transmitted by the arms of the Cross (Fig. 180).[58]

It may well be as a comment on her personal sacrifice that we 180
are to read Dante's line inscribed behind her on the shaft of the Cross: *"Non vi si pensa quanto sangue costa"*—"they care not there (on earth) how much blood it cost"—"an inscription obviously to be attributed to the Virgin," as Tolnay says. But Dante's words, spoken by Beatrice (*Paradiso,* Canto XXIX, 91), refer to the arbitrary interpretations of Scripture preached by men who forget "what it cost in blood to disseminate it in the world." Thus, although the application of these words to the personal sacrifice of the bereaved mother is not ruled out, neither is their original

[58] Of the many engravings of the *Colonna Pietà,* only the two earliest, Bonasone's of 1546 (B. XV, 64) and Beatrizet's of 1547 (B. XV, 25), correctly transmit Michelangelo's unique design for the Cross. Their versions agree with each other and with Vasari's description. But Bonasone, unlike Beatrizet (cf. Tolnay, V, Fig. 341), has misunderstood the lowermost zone of the composition by rendering it almost a horizontal ground. For the type of the Cross and its implicit allusion to the Tree of Life, see G. Francovitch, "L'Origine e la diffusione del Crocefisso gotico dolorosa," *Kunstg. Jb. der Bibl. Hertziana,* II, 1938, pp. 150 ff.

reference to the promulgation of orthodoxy. And this suggests that the speaker is not Mary alone, but Mary-Ecclesia, the Virgin as Church. Her gesture certainly is adaptable to her dual role; for the *Orans,* the familiar figure who stands with palms outspread in the frescoes of Rome's Christian catacombs, was a figure often interpreted as the Church.

A reading of Michelangelo's Virgin as both woman and personification reconciles us to her monumentality, to the reach of her arms, the pillar strength of her legs, her place at the grave, and her all-apparent mediation between mortal birth and heaven. It may even justify the contrived, abstract, almost perfect hexagonal geometry of the design. The *Pietà for Vittoria Colonna* is the diagram of a catechism. There has perhaps never been an image which precipitates so much creed and thought in one compact appearance. Vittoria Colonna herself wrote to the artist in a letter that seems to refer to this work: "I had the greatest faith in God that he would give you a supernatural grace to make this Christ: then I saw it so marvelous that it surpassed in all ways all my expectations. . . . One could not wish more, nor come to wish so much"[59] It is significant for Michelangelo that the fixed pivot of this elaborate summa of doctrine and faith is the birth mystery.

181 To this work, the *Colonna Pietà,* Michelangelo returned more than thirty years later to conceive from it the *Pietà Rondanini,* his ultimate sculpture (Fig. 181). The block from which it is carved had passed through two previous phases before reaching its present condition. In 1552–1553, Michelangelo had roughed it out for a *Pietà* composition of which no certain record survives. Then, in the mid-1550's, after abandoning the Florentine *Pietà,* this smaller stone was taken in hand and radically reworked. Either its original 1552 phase or this revision of 1555 is reflected in the first two of five drawings on a single sheet at the Ashmolean Museum, Oxford

[59] Tolnay, V, 61.

(Fig. 182).[60] These faint sketches are studies for a compact three-figure group: the dead Christ flanked by two supporting male figures. They form an Entombment, but in a grouping clearly dependent on the *Colonna Pietà,* especially in the square yoke formed by the arms of Christ. The three remaining drawings on the Oxford sheet, showing the Virgin and Christ alone, seem at first glance to be unrelated; and yet, it is another feature of the *Colonna Pietà* that they take up, for they express the Entombment idea exactly as the *Colonna Pietà* had developed it—by change of level. These three sketches determined the design of the *Rondanini Pietà* from 1555 until just before its last transformation in 1564, the year of the artist's death at eighty-nine. 182

As the work has come down to us, the Virgin alone supports the dead Son, his pendent body already far sunk beneath her own solid footing, yet their two forms so consubstantial that we seem to be witnessing some aboriginal separation (Figs. 183 and 184). 183, 184
This effect of absolute fusion came at the end. It came with the last mutilating revisions Michelangelo made. Cutting away the whole upper portion of the completed Christ figure, he tried to make the loved form issue again from the diminishing core of the stone. At the cost of the work itself, he tried once more to enact the Incarnation from Mary's body. And in this final happening, which still absorbed him in the week of his death, he brought about those destructive changes which reduced the near-finished group to its present abbreviation, and which Tolnay's technical section inventories as follows: "He reduced the size of the group and made vertical the position of the body of Christ to join it more closely to that of the Virgin. . . . He achieved this effect by hewing the new body of Christ directly from the part of the block belonging to the Virgin: the new head of Christ is carved from the right shoulder of the Virgin, the new arms of Christ from the sides and thighs of the Virgin's body."

[60] See Tolnay, V, 220, for an analysis of the chronological sequence of the studies on the Oxford sheet; and pp. 89–91 and 154–155 for a lucid account of the complex genesis of the *Rondanini Pietà.*

APPENDICES

A. THE SLUNG-LEG MOTIF

The attempt to construct a history of the slung-leg motif is somewhat foolhardy, since any new find may modify the structure and examples are bound to keep turning up. But to forestall an undue expansion of the inventory, let me define what I consider the chief limiting feature of the motif. Pairs of lovers of whom one sits on the lap of the other, or on one thigh within his lap, are ruled out. The "canonic form" requires that each partner maintain his own seat, so that the leg that is thrown across becomes a gesture toward the other, a wooing or claiming, an action that visibly changes a relationship or establishes a condition. Whereas the settled intimacy of the lap-sitting pose, even though it include a slung leg, suggests the condition itself. (E.g., the Michelangelesque *Adam and Eve* drawing at the Musée Bonnat, Bayonne; see Jacob Bean, *Les Dessins Italiens de la Collection Bonnat,* Paris, 1960, No. 66.)

Also ruled out are certain late-fifteenth-century Italian *Pietàs* (e.g., a Ferrarese bronze relief in the Victoria and Albert Museum, London; Pope-Hennessy Catalogue, Pl. 337), in which the Christ figure, extended across the Virgin's lap, allows its right leg to slip to the ground. The left leg remains arched over the Virgin's thigh without, however, constituting the appropriative action.

Ruled out on yet another count are seated couples with elaborately intertwined legs, as in Robetta's *Allegory of Envy* engraving of ca. 1520 (B. XIII, 24; A. M. Hind, *Early Italian Engraving,* London, 1938–1948, D. II, 31, and Pl. 294); or as in Mabuse's picture of *Hercules and Dejanira* of 1517 in the Barber Institute, Birmingham. (See H. Pauwels, *Jan Gossaert, genaamd Mabuse,* Rotterdam Exhibition Catalogue, 1965, Pl. IV.) I would call these the "hearsay type," since they suggest a knowledge of the symbol but not of its visual form. In the work of Mabuse, who sojourned in Rome during 1508–1509, the motif appears twice more in similarly unorthodox fashion: in a drawing of *Adam and Eve* at the Albertina, dated 1525 (Rotterdam Catalogue, 61), and most significantly in his early woodcut of ca. 1515, *Hercules and Dejanira.* In both of these it is the husband's leg that crosses the wife's. The woodcut has further importance as a likely source for Rubens' *Shepherd and Shepherdess* in Munich.

The earliest instances of the motif in "correct" visual form occur in Italy soon after 1500. They show the woman's leg raised, so that the male knee assumes a quasi-penetrant function—a variant which may have been served by a separate prototype. I cite Riccio's small bronze *Satyr and Satyress* in the Victoria and Albert Museum, London, and two rare engravings with obscure subjects. First, *The Faun Family* by the Bolognese Master I. B. with the Bird: a Leonardesque nymph loops the knee of a laurel-crowned wild-man (B. XIII, 248, 7; Hind, V, 256, 6 and Pl. 837). Second, an Agostino Veneziano engraving of 1516 (B. XIV, 241)—after a Bandinelli design, according to Bartsch. Bartsch's title, "The News Brought to Olympus" (retained in Passavant, *Peintre-Graveur,* VI, 57, 60) is a confession that the subject is unidentified. The pattern of the amorous group in the sky seems to anticipate both Raphael's Isaac fresco and some of the action of Michelangelo's Christ.

Raphael's fresco of 1520, which was probably executed by Perino del Vaga, is followed in 1527 by the Caraglio engravings after Perino's designs (B. XV, 11 and 14), and by one undescribed and undated engraving of *Venus and Mars,* attributed to Giorgio Ghisi after Giulio Romano (illustrated Bartsch, Vol. 15a, unpublished; Institute of Fine Arts Library, N.Y.U.). That these prints were chiefly responsible for the diffusion of the motif is confirmed by a majolica dish at the Metropolitan Museum, New York, dated Urbino 1542, and attributed to the shop of Orazio Fontana. Here the Caraglio-Perino *Neptune and Thetis* (B. 11) is adapted to a *Story of Venus and Mars.* The dispersion of prints may also account for the occurrence of the motif in two Venetian pictures of the 1530's:

Bonifazio's *Lot and His Daughters* in the Walter P. Chrysler Collection, New York; and the *Mythological Scene* in the London National Gallery (No. 1123), formerly given to Bonifazio, now catalogued as "Venetian School." The set of engravings of the *Loves of the Gods* by Bonasone (esp. B. 151 and 155) again displays our motif but cannot be dated with certainty before the mid-century.

Indicative of the eloquence of the leg as a conjugal symbol is this remarkable record of the proxy marriage of an English Princess, Sister of Henry VIII, to a decrepit French King:

> Consummation of the marriage by proxy between the Princess Mary and Lewis XII.
>
> Last Sunday the marriage was concluded *per verba de praesenti.* The bride undressed and went to bed in the presence of many witnesses. The Marquis of Rothelin, in his doublet, with a pair of red hose, but with one leg naked, went into bed, and touched the Princess with his naked leg. The marriage was then declared consummated. The King of England made great rejoicing, and we at Abbeville did the same. 18 Aug. 1514.
>
> (From Great Britain, Public Record Office, *Letters and Papers . . . of the Reign of Henry VIII . . . ,* I, Part 2, 1509–1514. London, 1862, p. 861.)

The impetus for the "deconsecration" of the motif derives from its early association with the theme of Lot and his daughters. (The early instances have been cited; seventeenth-century examples, as in works by Elsheimer, Stanzione, Vouet, and others, are common.) The same Biblical subject further popularized the assumption of the slung-leg pose by the woman. The motif remains with the woman in most Italian sixteenth-century examples. Rodin understood the full implications of the motif when he revived it, as part of the woman's enterprise, in *Le Baiser.* In the seventeenth century the hoisted leg is usually male again—or else improper (e.g., Thamar playing the harlot with Judah in the picture by Pieter Lastman in the Dr. David Arnon Collection, New York City, engraved by both Pieter Nolpe and Jan van Noort). The woman who so engages her lover in the Jan Steen picture at Vienna serves, along with other engaging perversions, to define *The World Upside Down.* Ultimately, by way perhaps of the Italian comedy and the circus, the slung leg passes into broad comedy and ends up as a Marx Brothers routine.

B. THE FIGURE OF CHRIST

The attitude of the Christ (Fig. 121) is, as Vasari observed, utterly 121
unprecedented. It is incomprehensible. From the point of view of its antecedents, it seems compounded from incompatible sources. The upper body, with falling head and outspread arms obliquely supported, is familiar both as a dying Niobid on Roman sarcophagi and as a Christ figure in a descent from the Cross (e.g., Roger van der Weyden's picture in the Escorial, engraved 1565 by Cornelis Cort). But in these partial precedents the lower limbs invariably trail away, whereas in Michelangelo's Christ, the forward thrust of the knees resumes the directional lead of the head. Such leg work indicates action and vital desire directed, as a lover's would be, toward an object of passion. But then, unlike Michelangelo's Christ, figures whose lower body is so disposed always advance chest and shoulders to bring the arms into play.

The discrepancy of upper and lower zones encourages a psychological viewpoint—that is, to regard every attitude as expressive gesture and the entire body as a scene of conflicts. Thus the erotic energy of the leg mounting the bride is belied by the elbows-out arm and the shoulder twisted away, as if to renounce a love, the same love, which the head seeks again. Similarly, the lingering tenderness of the right arm embracing the Magdalene is belied by the averted loins. Every part of this breaking body responds to a twice-turning will.

But such psychological readings become suspect as soon as we realize that there exists another determinant for the pose, one which the loss of the left leg makes strikingly clear. Seen as a formal pattern, the Christ's attitude—that same action of arms in a single arc intersecting the S-curve of the body—displays an unmistakable kinship with the ancient *Discobolos.* John Shearman has pointed out "how popular the *Discobolos* pose became in the sixteenth century," citing Pontormo's use of it for an angel of the Annunciation, Bandinelli using it for his self-portrait in Boston, and Titian, in 1545, for the suppliant nephew in the *Portrait of Pope Paul III* at Naples. (Shearman, *Mannerism,* Penguin Books, 1967, p. 85.) One reason for this remarkable adaptability was the fact that copies of the *Discobolos* known in the sixteenth century were too fragmentary to associate with a specific content; they were not even recognizable as representing an athlete. They were simply the model of an energetic male form defined in a circular orbit and so turned that its every part appeared unforeshortened.

This immediately suggests a new set of governing considerations for Michelangelo's Christ. The parts of his body seek an ideal plane, every limb revealed in its longest extension, legs and head in side view, shoulders full front, extended arms tracing a circle. Thus, from a formalist point of view, the pose of the Christ seems conditioned not so much by the joining of disparate models, and less by any expressionism of conflict, than by an esthetic principle of maximum visibility.

And yet again, this formal solution, almost archaic in its insistent clarity, is so strangely appropriate to a theological program that, suspecting a symbolic intention, one looks again and from a new point of view. Of the three living figures who support the Christ, each is foreshortened and in part obscured. And it is immediately apparent that any similar effect in the Christ figure, allowing concealment and foreshortening of the divine limbs, would be an imperfect theophany. The adaptation to the *Discobolos* pose lays out the body of Christ in the space of a giant disc; to the concrete three-dimensional life of the supporting figures, it opposes the radiant clarity of abstraction.

In the traditional scheme of the *Pietà,* Christ's body appeared in profile so that some of its substance, especially the distant arm, was unseen, and the showing of the wounds was made difficult. In his

Roman *Pietà* (Fig. 110), Michelangelo had been content to adopt 110
an old compromise remedy—a slight tipping of the body's sup-
porting plane. In all his subsequent attacks on the subject, in
drawings as well as in the late marble groups, the Christ figure is
wholly displayed. This resolution was unexpected. Writing about
the Christ in Michelangelo's *Pietà for Vittoria Colonna* (Fig. 175), 175
the Bishop of Fano remarks: "Though he is in the form of a
Pietà, nevertheless his whole body is seen." (Letter of May 12,
1546, to Cardinal Ercole Gonzaga. See Thode, *Kritische Untersuch-
ungen*, II, 494). It is Michelangelo's invention to have reconciled the
formal principle of full visibility with the *Pietà* theme and its
required show of the wounds.

C. MARY MAGDALENE'S LOVE

The medieval sources bearing on the Magdalene's erotic attachment to Christ are brought together in Helen M. Garth's exemplary study, *St. Mary Magalene in Medieval Literature* (Baltimore, 1950). I have drawn heavily on Miss Garth's Chapter 4, "The Personality of Mary Magdalene," which supplied my references to Rabanus Maurus (p. 70) and the later Passion Plays. It is in these plays that the Magdalene's melancholy becomes pure erotomania. Thus in the Digby Mystery Play called *Christ's Burial and Resurrection* (Garth, p. 69): "Schew my best love that I was here!/ Tell hym, as he may prove,/ That I am dedly seke/ And all is for his love." Or again in *The Lamentatyon of Mary Magdaleyne*, a poetic English portrayal of her grief formerly attributed to Chaucer;

> A due, my lorde, my love so faire of face,
> A due, my turtel dove so fresshe of hue,
> A due, my myrtle, a due, al my solace,
> A due, alas, my savyour lorde Jesu.

In the anonymous Italian fourteenth-century *Life of St. Mary Magdalene* (Valentina Hawtrey trans., London, 1904, pp. 236–237),

the Magdalene's address to the Cross is erotic in form no less than in content. The lover envying whatever object has contact with the beloved is a commonplace of love poetry. "Would that I could become a pipe, so that he might breathe upon me!" says Chloë as she watches Daphnis in Longus' famous romance (third century A.D., trans. Moses Hadas, New York, 1953, p. 25. Cf. Romeo's sigh in the Balcony Scene, Act II, sc. ii: "Oh, that I were a glove upon that hand, that I might touch that cheek!"). This is the pattern of the Magdalene's cry, "Oh, most blessed Cross! Would that I had been in Thy stead, and that my Lord had been crucified in mine arms . . ." A Rodin sculpture, called *La*
185 *Madeleine* (Fig. 185), in which the despairing woman, alone with Christ, presses herself naked against his crucified body, comes so close to this spirit of star-crossed love that one would take it for a rehearsal of the Gothic text. But what at first sight appears as *fin de siècle* romanticism turns out to be deep-rooted Catholic. The subtlest artists of the sixteenth and seventeenth centuries understood well enough that the crucifix in Mary Magdalene's hands
186, 187 could be an object of erotic fantasy (Figs. 186 and 187). Some, especially certain Northerners such as Isenbrandt and Engelbrechts, allowed the Magdalene on Calvary to kneel in such manner as to
188 take the upright Cross between her thighs (Fig. 188). The motif appears with more propriety in certain sixteenth-century Italian Crucifixions, such as that engraved by Phillip Soye after a design by an unidentified Michelangelizer (reproduced in *Fortuna di Michelangelo nell'Incisione,* exhibition catalogue by M. Rotili, Benevento-Rome, 1964, No. 122, Fig. 47).

In pictures of the Deposition, the Magdalene sometimes appears anointing one of Christ's hands; but the more common rendering shows her embracing, kissing, or embalming the feet—as she had done at the Feast in the House of Levi. And several Italian High Renaissance painters find ways of relating the wounded crossed feet of Christ directly to the Magdalene's open body. I refer to such works as Caroto's *Lamentation* of 1515 (Berenson, *Central and North Italian Schools,* London, 1968, Vol. III,

1880); Moretto da Brescia's *Pietà* in the National Gallery, Washington, datable in the 1520's; Correggio's *Deposition* of 1522 in the Parma Gallery; Lanino's *Deposition* of 1558 at Turin (Berenson, *op. cit.*, 1278); and others.

Michelangelo's own meditations on the subject of the Deposition rarely fail to define the Magdalene's erotic character. See especially the reworked Michelangelo drawing for a Descent from the Cross, ca. 1545–1555, at the Ashmolean Museum, Oxford (Fig. 189). Michelangelo here participates in one of the great minor themes of sixteenth-century art: the insinuation of disturbed physical love in scenes of *Pietà* and Entombment. Few subjects offered such challenge and so many pitfalls to an artist's ardor and indiscretion. 189

But it would be a preposterous impoverishment of the tradition to regard Mary Magdalene as only, or as primarily, a medieval sex symbol. Her symbolic roles are almost as rich and multiple as those of the Madonna. She could be Eve again, or a type of the Virgin, or even the Holy Church. As an example of the Magdalene's identification with the Virgin, Miss Garth cites the *Discourse on Mary Theotokos* by Cyril, Archbishop of Jerusalem (from E. A. Wallis Budge, ed., *Miscellaneous Coptic Texts*, London, 1915, pp. 629–630). The Virgin is speaking: "My father was Joakim . . . My mother was Anna . . . I am Mary Magdalene because the name of the village wherein I was born was Magdalia." Later in the same *Discourse* (Budge ed., p. 646) the Virgin on her deathbed appoints Mary Magdalene to her own place on earth, saying to the Disciples: "Behold your mother from this time onwards" (Garth, pp. 22–23).

The Magdalene as the type of Eve occurs in the Homilies of Gregory the Great ("Lo, the guilt of the human race is cut off whence it proceeded . . . for a woman tells the words of the Life-Giver as [Eve] told the words of the death-bearing serpent"—Garth, p. 79); and in the Sermons of St. Peter Chrysologus: "In this latter day a woman runs to grace, who earlier ran to guilt. In the evening she seeks Christ who in the morning knew that she had lost Adam. She who had taken perfidy from Paradise hastens to take faith from the sepulchre; she hastens to snatch life from death, who had snatched death from life" (Sermons LXXIV and LXXVII, Migne, *Patrol. Lat.*, v. 52, col. 409; quoted in Garth, p. 79).

In his commentary on Matthew 28:1 ("As it began to dawn . . . came Mary Magdalene and the other Mary to see the sepulchre"), St. Peter Chrysologus points out that the singular *venit* (came) is used rather than *venerunt*. In this, he says, the unity forms one person in two names, rather than two persons of one name, and indicates a changed woman who is mystically both Eve and Mary Magdalene. "She who led Adam to the death came; she who received Christ from the dead came" (Garth, p. 79).

The Magdalene as Ecclesia is, says Miss Garth, "the most usual analogy made by medieval writers." St. Odo of Cluny (Sermo II, *Patrol. Lat.*, v. 133, col. 716) explained that since *Magdalus*, from the Hebrew *migdal*, or *tower*, refers to the Church, "mystically this blessed woman herself signifies the Holy Church" (Garth, pp. 78 and 83). Ronald Steinberg kindly reminds me that the Magdalene-Church equation was especially dear to Savonarola.

D. THE CHIN-CHUCK MOTIF

The motif of the Child touching the Virgin's chin occurs in the Byzantine Madonna type known as the "Virgin of Sweet Love," or Glykophilousa. As a love gesture expressing a tenderness at once childlike and faintly precocious, it passes into the art of the West. There, from the twelfth to the seventeenth century, and irrespective of its use or disuse in life situations, the "chin-chuck" remains a conventional iconographic sign for sexual love—in iconic devotional imagery as well as in secular erotic art.

Historically speaking, the chin-chuck is even more venerable than the slung-leg motif. Its origins—whether in passion, ritual, custom, or art—seem indeterminable. Homer (*Iliad*, I, 501–502, and X, 454–455) uses the chin-touching gesture as one of supplication, and it so functions in Archaic Greek art: a victim will touch his antagonist's chin to plead for his life (e.g., Corfu Pediment, Priam seated at left; Nessos Amphora, Athens, National Museum, both ca. 600 B.C.). From the early seventh century onward, the Homeric gesture, presumably still the familiar suppliant's touch, adapts itself to purely erotic play. Theseus, chucking her chin, woos Ariadne on a Tarentine clay relief and again on a Cretan vase (Schefold, *Frühgriechische Sagenbilder,* Munich, 1964, Pl. 27 a and b). Several Attic vase paintings of ca. 540–530 B.C., depicting scenes of "Man Wooing Boy," show the bearded suitor caressing the chin of the *eromenos,* the beloved.

An Egyptian relief from Medinet Habu shows Ramses III (twelfth century B.C.) welcoming his concubine with a chin-chuck; but whether an Egyptian custom furnished the impetus for the erotic reinterpretation of the Homeric gesture is not yet clear. Nor can we demonstrate an unbroken continuity from ancient monuments to those Byzantine icons where the chin-chuck occurs. Eros caresses the embraced Psyche's chin (e.g., third-century sarcophagus from Tarsus, Metropolitan Museum, New York), and this late Antique adaptation of the motif to the redemptive allegory of divine love may have prepared it for its Christian translation. At the same time, the gesture may actually have survived in flirtatious lovemaking. One thing seems unlikely: that a gesture of ancient sex connotation in the art and love practice of the Eastern Mediterranean should appear entirely stripped of these connotations in Constantinople.

In Byzantine iconic art the Child caressing the Virgin's chin seems to be a thirteenth-century development, and I suspect that its reference is to a refrain in the Song of Songs (2,6 and 8,3): "O that his left hand were under my head, and that his right hand embraced me!" That these words had acquired a specifically sexual connotation emerges from a remarkable exegesis in the 22nd Epistle of St. Jerome (*Select Letters of St. Jerome,* trans. F. A. Wright, London, 1933, pp. 93–95). Applying a verse from Daniel (2,45) to the virginal birth of Christ, Jerome interprets as follows: "He is foretold to be 'a stone cut out of the mountain without hands,' the prophet signifying thereby that He will be born a virgin of a virgin. The word 'hands' is to be taken as meaning the marital act, as in the passage: 'His left hand is under my head and his right hand doth embrace me.' "

Now it is these very lines which appear as superscriptions in late Gothic Canticles illustrations that depict Christ and his spouse in the commonest lovers' pose—the lady resting against the knees of her lover who places his caressing hand at her chin (see the fifteenth-century Dutch blockbook edition, Schreiber 14, Pl. 7; reproduced in A. M. Hind, *History of Woodcut* I, Fig. 101). It seems probable that the artist of the Byzantine Glykophilousa similarly assimilated the vague Biblical "under my head" to the more precise and familiar visual formula of the touched chin.

A Romanesque figured capital of the early twelfth century (Toulouse, Musée des Augustins; reprod. in W. Oakeshott, *Classical Inspiration in Medieval Art,* London, 1959, Pl. 24a) displays, in its action, a surprising likeness to the Egyptian Ramses relief. It shows the enthroned King Herod touching Salome's chin exactly as King Ramses had touched that of his concubine.

In the later thirteenth century the chin-chuck becomes commonplace in Western art, especially in Gothic France. For the first time within the same cultural ambience it occurs simultaneously in cult figures and representations of lovers' trysts. Ivory statuettes of the Madonna and Child (the Virgin usually crowned as Queen of Heaven) display the motif as often as do ivory caskets or combs depicting the meeting of lovers. In the Trecento, the motif of the Child touching his Mother's chin is widely adopted by major masters of Florence, Siena, Bohemia, and elsewhere. It remains common in Madonna images both north and south of the Alps throughout the fifteenth century and receives universal currency through the dis-
190 semination of prints and plaquettes (Fig. 190).

At the same time the motif retains its full usefulness as a formula for erotic love—e.g., among beneficiaries of the Fountain of Youth and even in allegories of Lust. It is notable that, like the slung leg, the chin-chuck from the late fifteenth century onward can be administered by the female partner. In the century following it becomes
126 reciprocal (Fig. 126, group at left). And it becomes generally more adaptable. Giulio Romano uses it in a context of near-pornography. In his *Jupiter Visiting Olympia* fresco at the Palazzo del Te, the god approaches his bedfellow with tumid member and chin-seeking hand

(see Hartt, *Giulio Romano,* New Haven, 1958, Pl. 263 as well as Pl. 178). The gesture is used by Primaticcio for a *Ulysses and Penelope* (Toledo Museum), by Garofalo for a *Diana and Endymion* (Dresden), by Frans Floris for *Lot and His Daughters* (engraved by C. Cort, B. de Haan Cat. 10, Pl. 4), by Cambiaso for a *Venus and Adonis* (Rome, Borghese, Fig. 191), and in a German woodcut of 1537 for a moral- 191
izing representation of a procuress at work ("Die Kupplerin" by Heinrich Vogtherr the Younger, Geisberg, *Einblattdrucke . . . ,* No. 1469). But Veit Stosz, in one of the most fiercely tragic and moving *Pietàs* ever engraved (Lehrs, VIII, 260, 3; here Fig. 192), assigns the 192
gesture to the disconsolate Virgin.

In sixteenth-century art, a Madonna whose chin is held or chucked by the Child is unmistakably an object of adult devotion (e.g., Burgkmair's woodcut of 1518, B. VII, 8; Cornelius van Cleve's Detroit *Madonna;* Luca Cambiaso's *Virgin and Child* at the Hague; Agostino Carracci's engraving, B. XVIII, 31; and others). But the motif is also adapted to the expression of the Christ Child's love for St. John (Leonardo, Raphael, Fra Bartolommeo, Parmigianino, and others). Parmigianino makes St. Catherine at her mystic wedding chin-chuck the Child (Bologna), while Cambiaso makes the Child chuck the chin of the Magdalene (Genoa, Palazzo Bianco;
Fig. 193). 193

Artists of the seventeenth century still understood the convention and used it accordingly—as when Caroselli, in an *Allegory* formerly in Berlin, makes the Spirit of Painting chuck the chin of Natura; and better still, when the French sculptor Puget, carving an ambitious variant on Michelangelo's Medici Madonna, substitutes—as an equivalent marital symbol—the chin-chucking for the shoulder-grasping motif (Fig. 194). 194

E. SAVONAROLA'S RHETORICAL FANTASY (see p. 258)

What causes a man to project such orgastic sensations upon the pregnant Madonna, or to seek identification with her as birth giver? Having no access to Savonarola's individual psychology, we can only set forth certain theoretical possibilities. These may be designated dramatic, erotic, and sacramental—or, respectively, female, male, neuter.

First: contemporary woodcut representations of Savonarola preaching show him addressing an audience which, conforming to the then common practice, was segregated by sex. Any turn of his head would thus make him aware of the sex of his audience and their peculiar response. Judging from Savonarola's concern for the elegant printing of his published sermons, and from his florid style, we may suspect that he had a normal modicum of vanity about his rhetorical prowess. A histrionic ambition could have projected him into an intense state of identification with the woman whose emotions he was describing to a rapt female audience.

A second theoretical possibility is identification by way of a peculiar perversion of male eroticism. The history of sexual fantasy records one in which the male lover conceives himself penetrating the woman from within her womb, so that the process of birth becomes a sexual possession. Its most explicit statement occurs in a sestet entitled "The Wish," by the notorious Restoration rake, the Earl of Rochester:

> O that I now cou'd, by some Chymic Art,
> To sperm convert my Vitals and my Heart,
> That at one Thrust I might my Soul translate,
> And in the Womb myself regenerate:
> There steep'd in Lust, nine Months I wou'd remain:
> Then boldly . . . my passage out again.
>
> (*Collected works of John Wilmot, Earl of Rochester,*
> edited by John Hayward,
> London, 1926, p. 220.)

It may be that Rochester's egressive coitus is no unique private fantasy. It reeks of theology, but in the negative sense, like the Black Mass—that is, the devil's side of the coin, the nightmare twist given to the quintessential Christological myth. (Cf. Claes Oldenburg, "America: War & Sex, Etc.," *Arts Magazine,* Summer 1967, p. 32;

detail, lower left, of a drawing entitled "Clinical Study . . .") The second possibility then is that Savonarola drew from a well of repressed male sexuality what he sublimated in his remarkable Virgin's expostulation.

The third possible ground for identification is asexual, or priestly. I quote from Henri de Lubac, *The Splendour of the Church* (Deus Books, Paulist Press ed., 1963, pp. 206 and n. 87; first published as *Méditations sur l'Eglise,* Paris, 1953): "The spiritual maternity of the Church . . . includes that power over the Eucharist by the exercise of which the Church, we may say, carries out a sort of maternal function with regard to Christ himself. Hence those comparisons, sometimes rather daring, between Our Lady and the priest and those speculations on Our Lady's priesthood . . . It was natural enough to consider, after the gift of life in Baptism, and that of the Word in the preaching which gives birth to faith, the sacramental sentence which makes present the body of Christ, as did Mary's Fiat at Nazareth. From the twelfth century onward we repeatedly come across the exclamation: 'O truly to be venerated is the dignity of priests, for in their hands, as in the womb of the Virgin, Christ is incarnated anew.' "

A priest for whom the transubstantiation of the Host was absolute reality might indeed have experienced a sense of identification with the Virgin birthgiver, since (in the words of the German Catholic theologian Scheeben, quoted in de Lubac, n. 87) he too "engenders the God-Man in his sacramental existence."

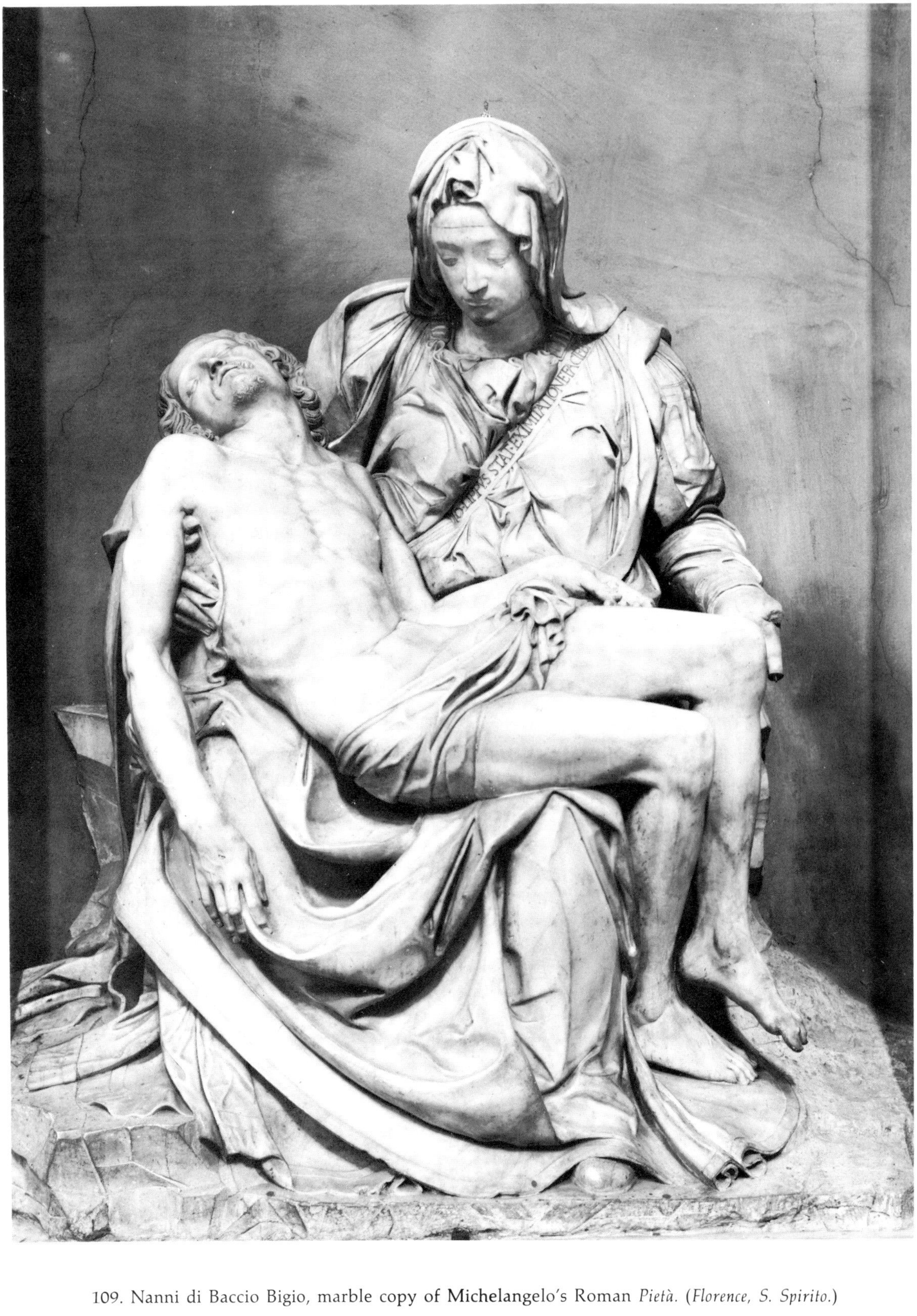

109. Nanni di Baccio Bigio, marble copy of Michelangelo's Roman *Pietà*. (*Florence, S. Spirito.*)

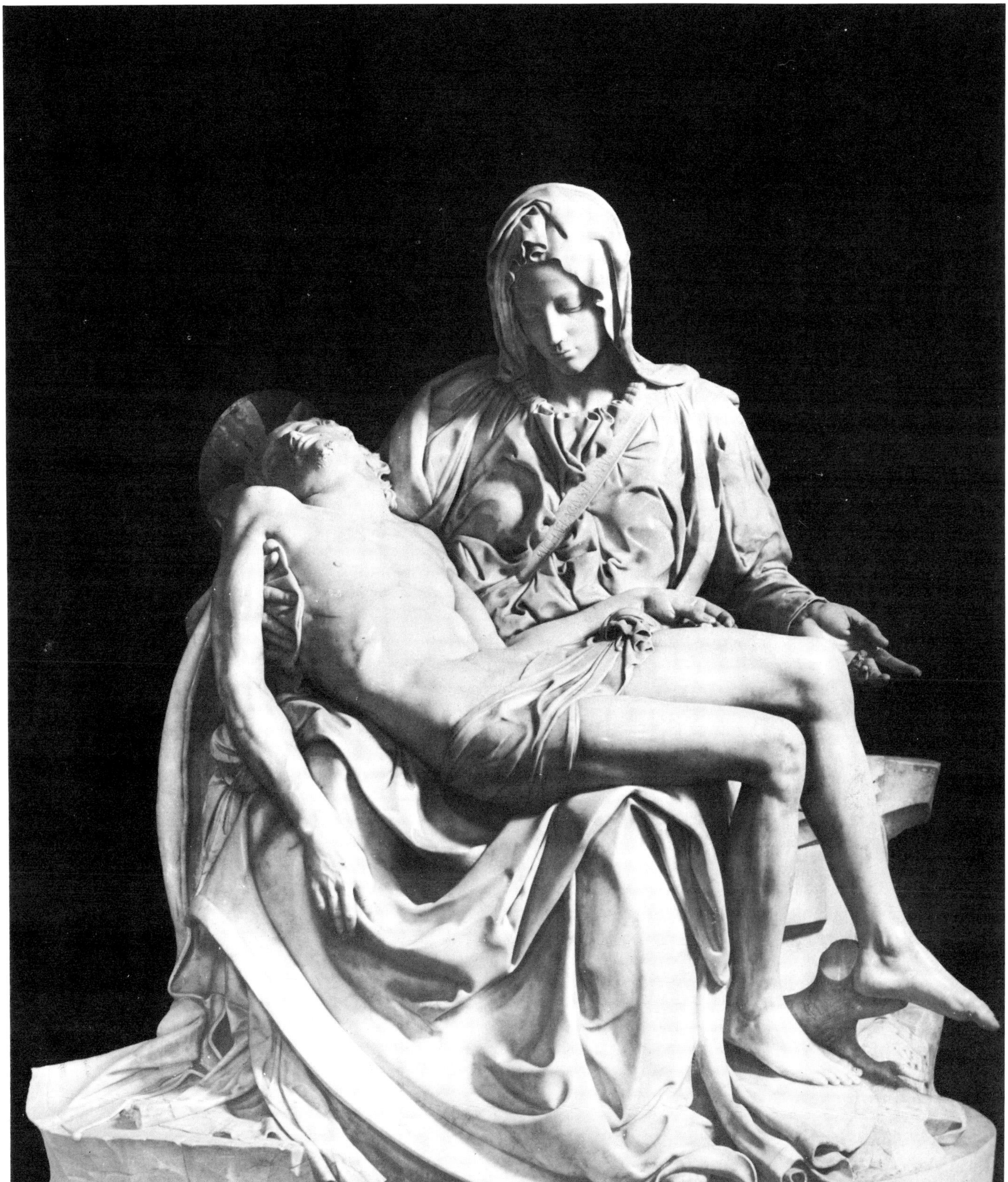

110. Michelangelo, *Pietà.* (*Rome, St. Peter's.*)

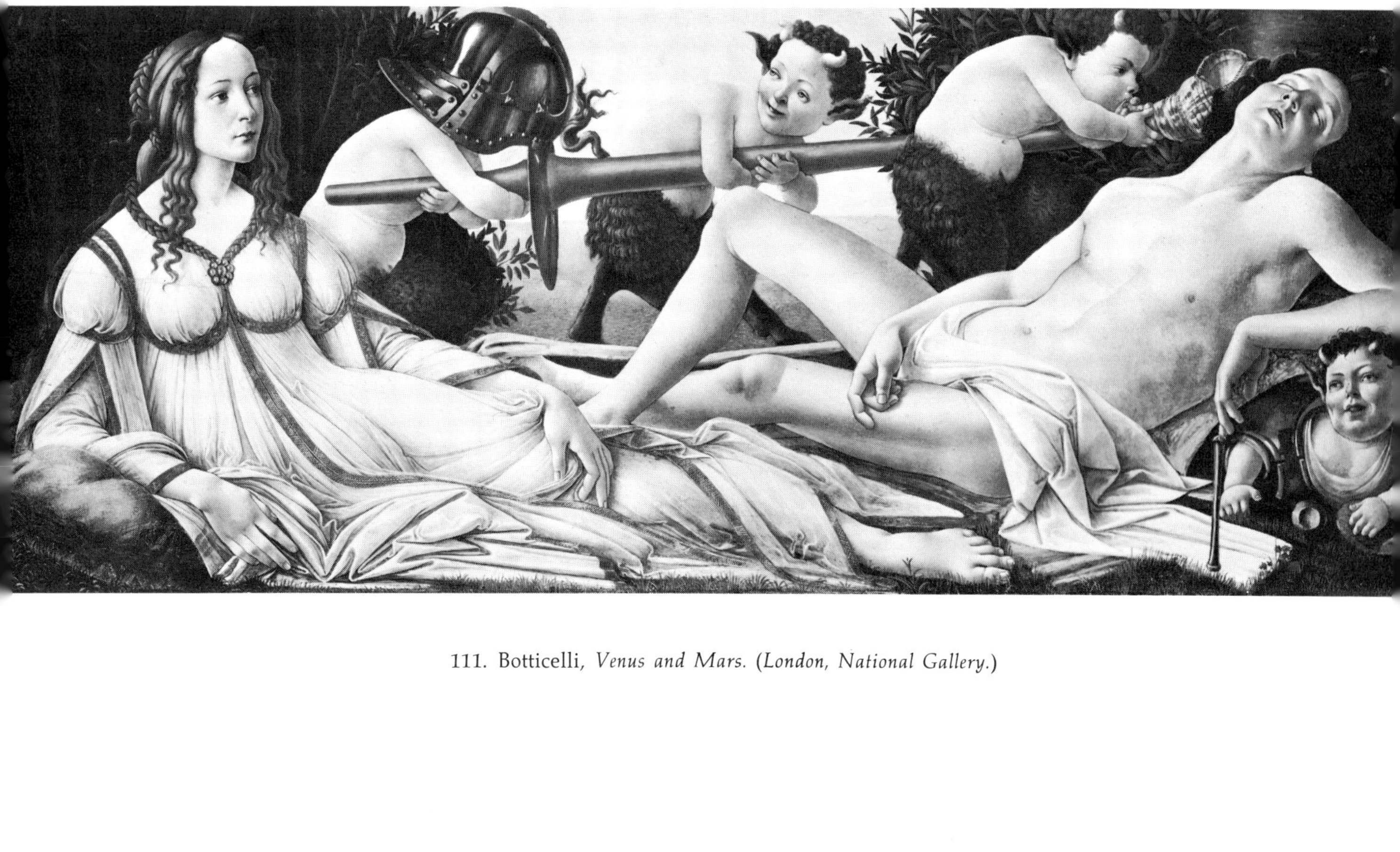

111. Botticelli, *Venus and Mars.* (London, National Gallery.)

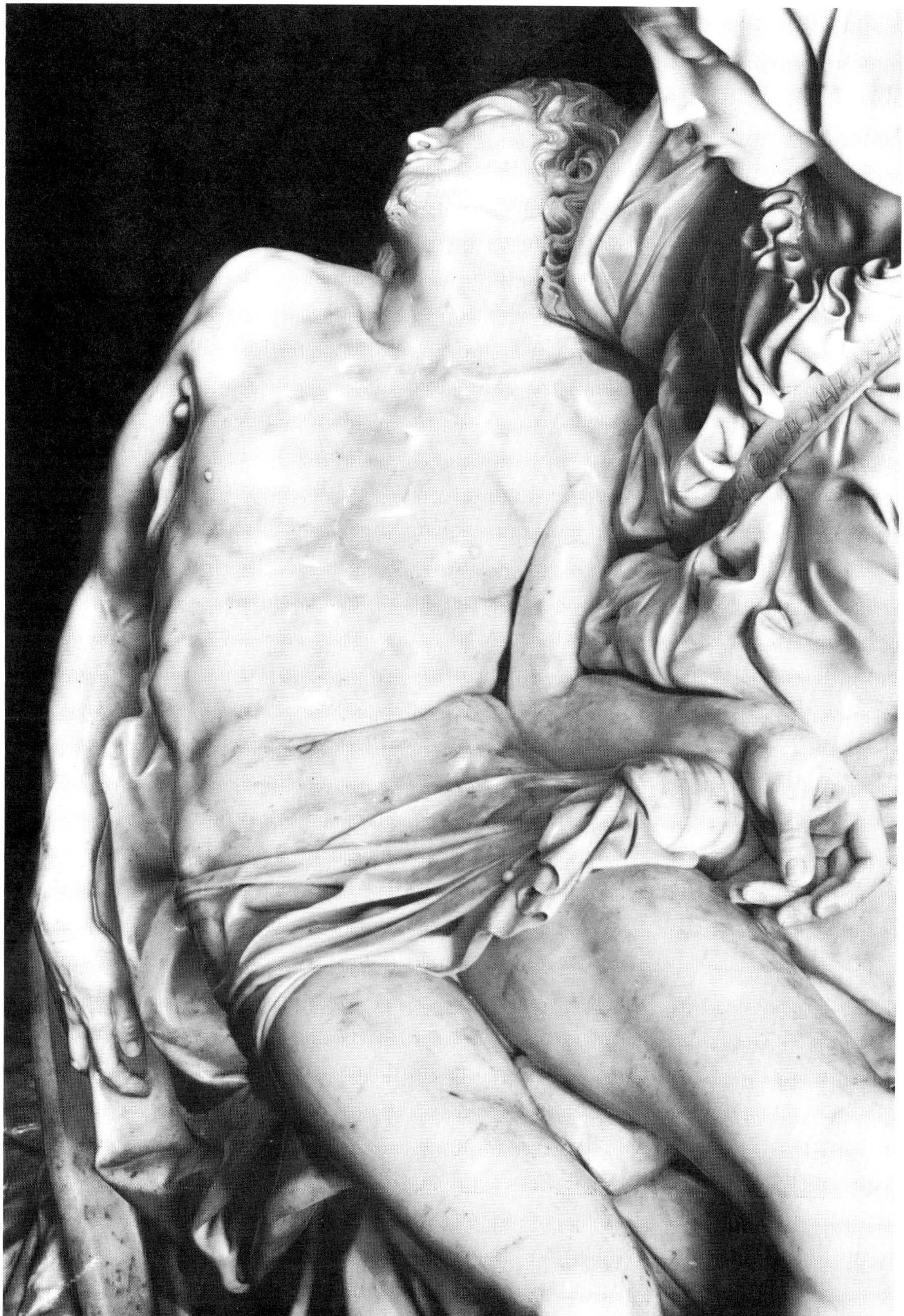

112. Michelangelo, *Pietà* (detail). (*Rome, St. Peter's.*) (Photo: Arnold Newman, in Robert Coughlan, *The World of Michaelangelo,* Time-Life Books, © 1966 by Time, Inc.)

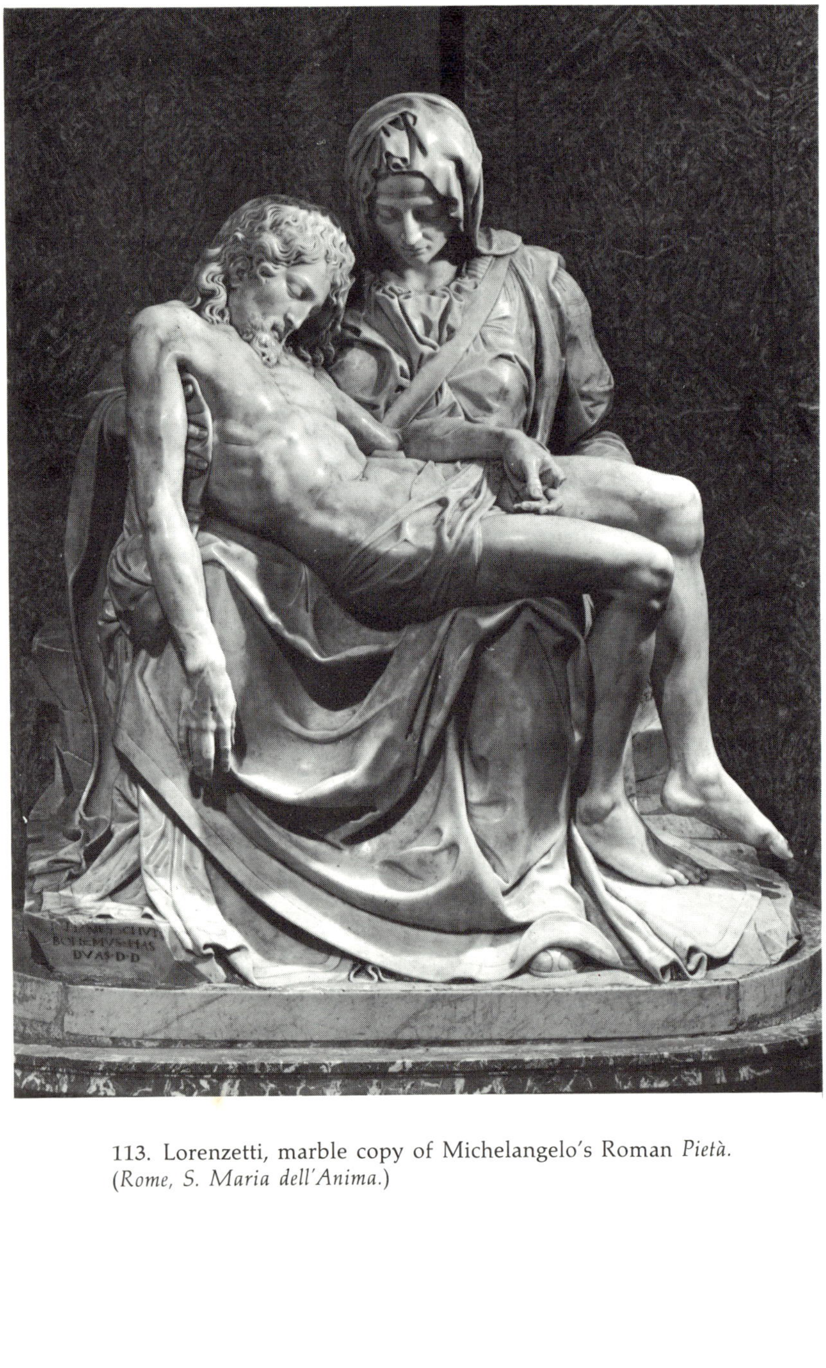

113. Lorenzetti, marble copy of Michelangelo's Roman *Pietà*. (*Rome, S. Maria dell'Anima.*)

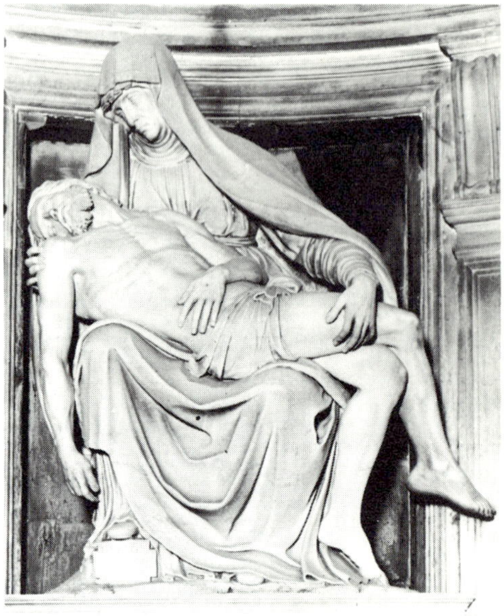

114. Montorsoli, *Pietà*. (*Genoa, S. Matteo.*)

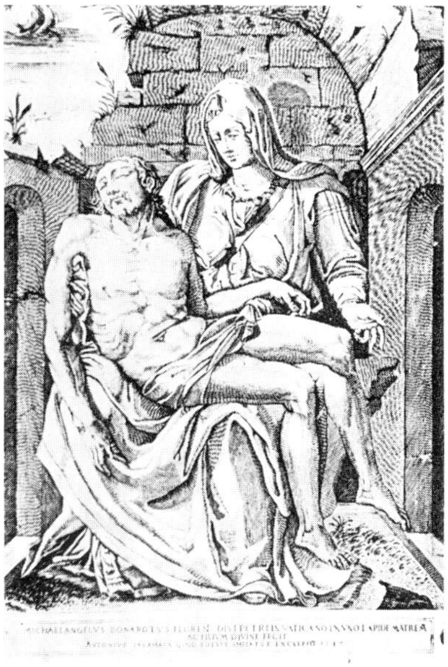

115. Salamanca, engraving after Michelangelo's Roman *Pietà*.

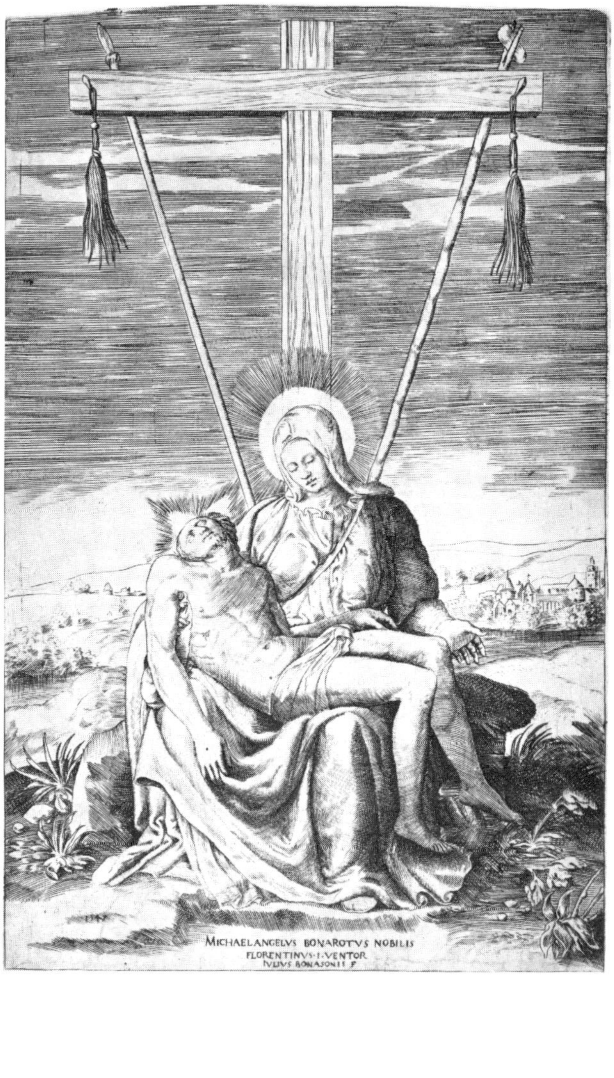

116. Giulio Bonasone, engraving after Michelangelo's Roman *Pietà*. (*New York, The Metropolitan Museum.*)

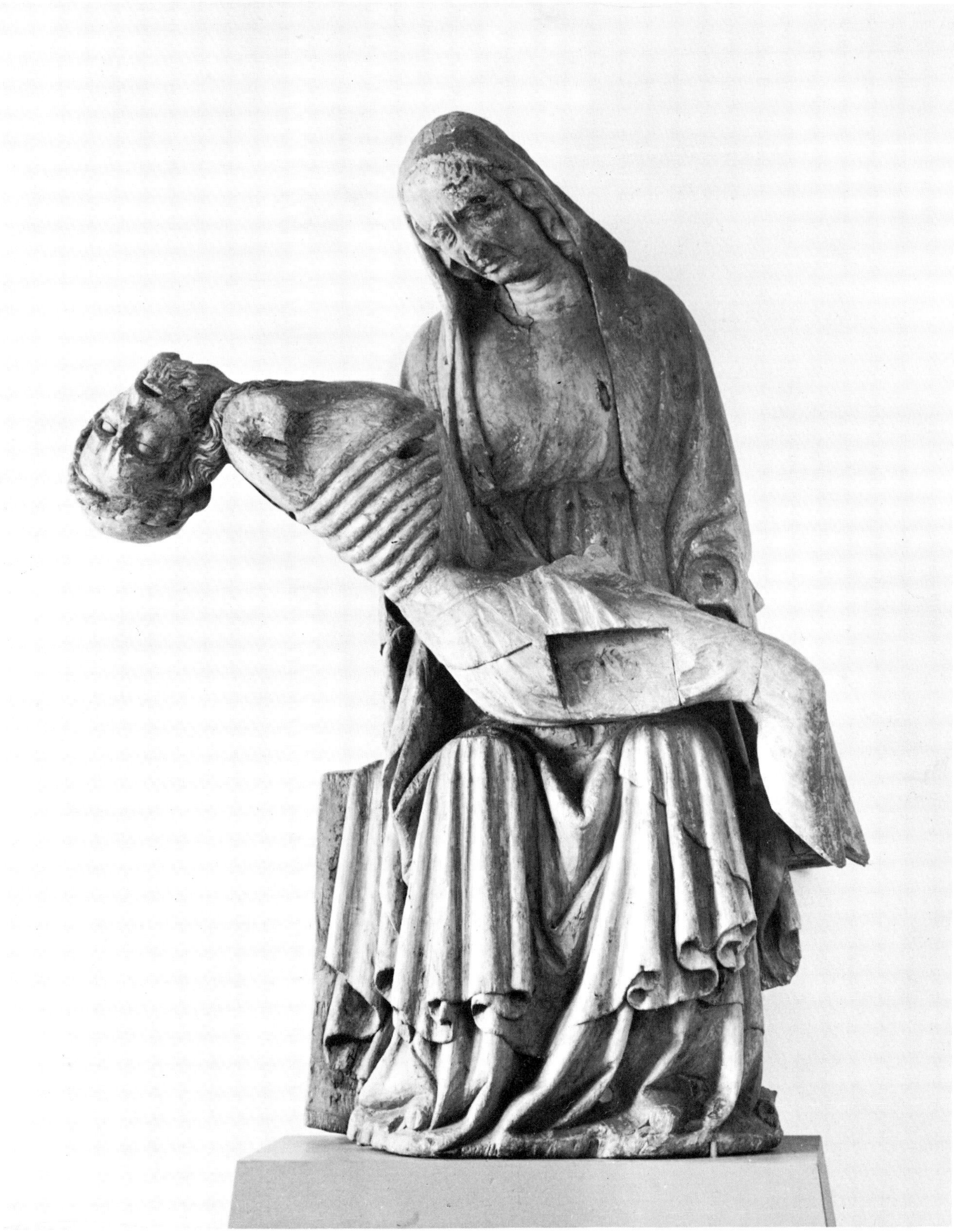

117. German anonymous, early fourteenth century, *Pietà*. (*Coburg, Kunstsammlung der Veste Coburg.*)

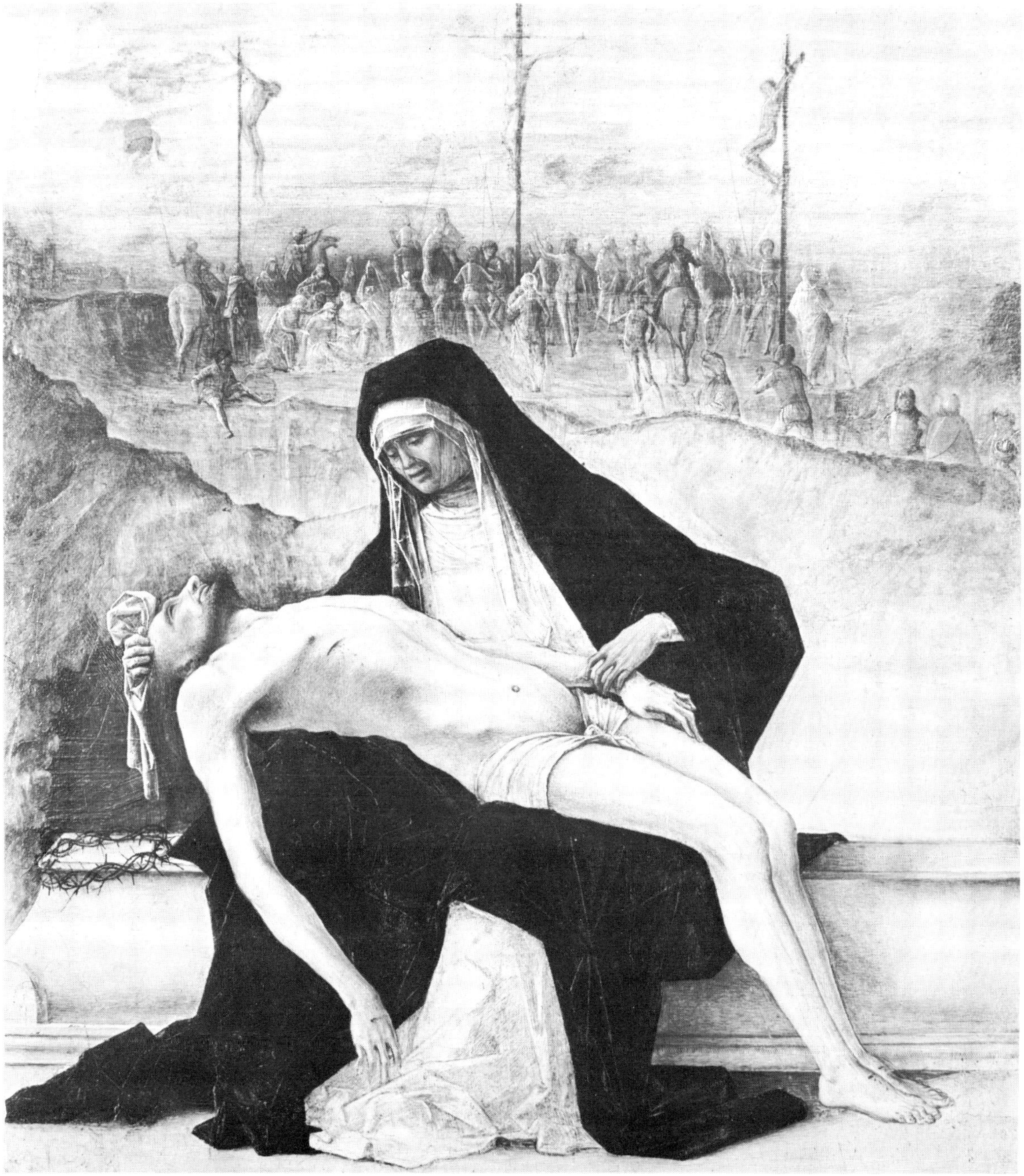

118. Ercole Roberti, *Pietà.* (*Liverpool, Walker Art Gallery.*)

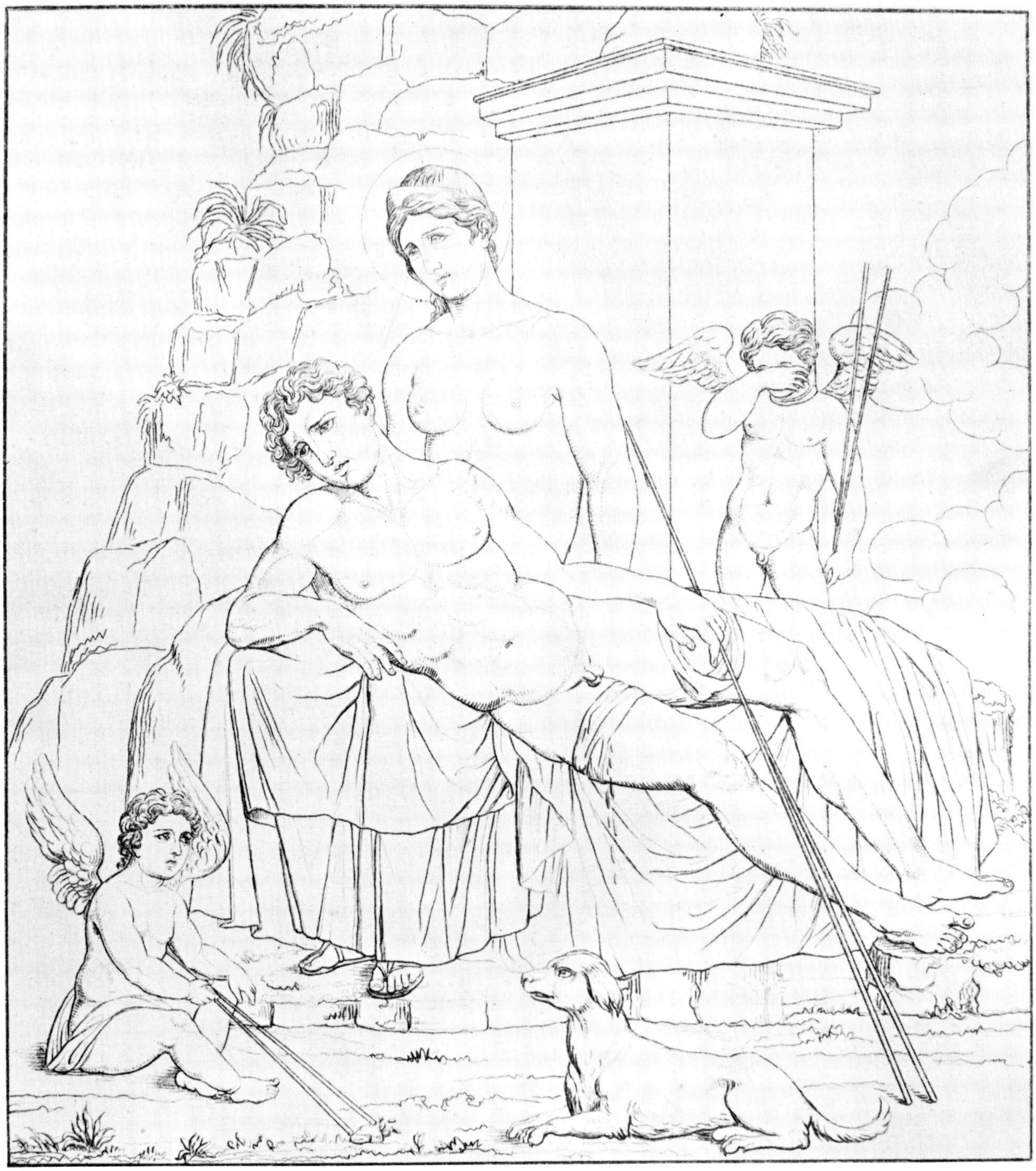

119. Pompeian painting engraved by Giovanni Paolo Lasinio, *Venus and Adonis.* (From *Real Museo Borbonico,* 1827, Vol. IV, Pl. XVII.)

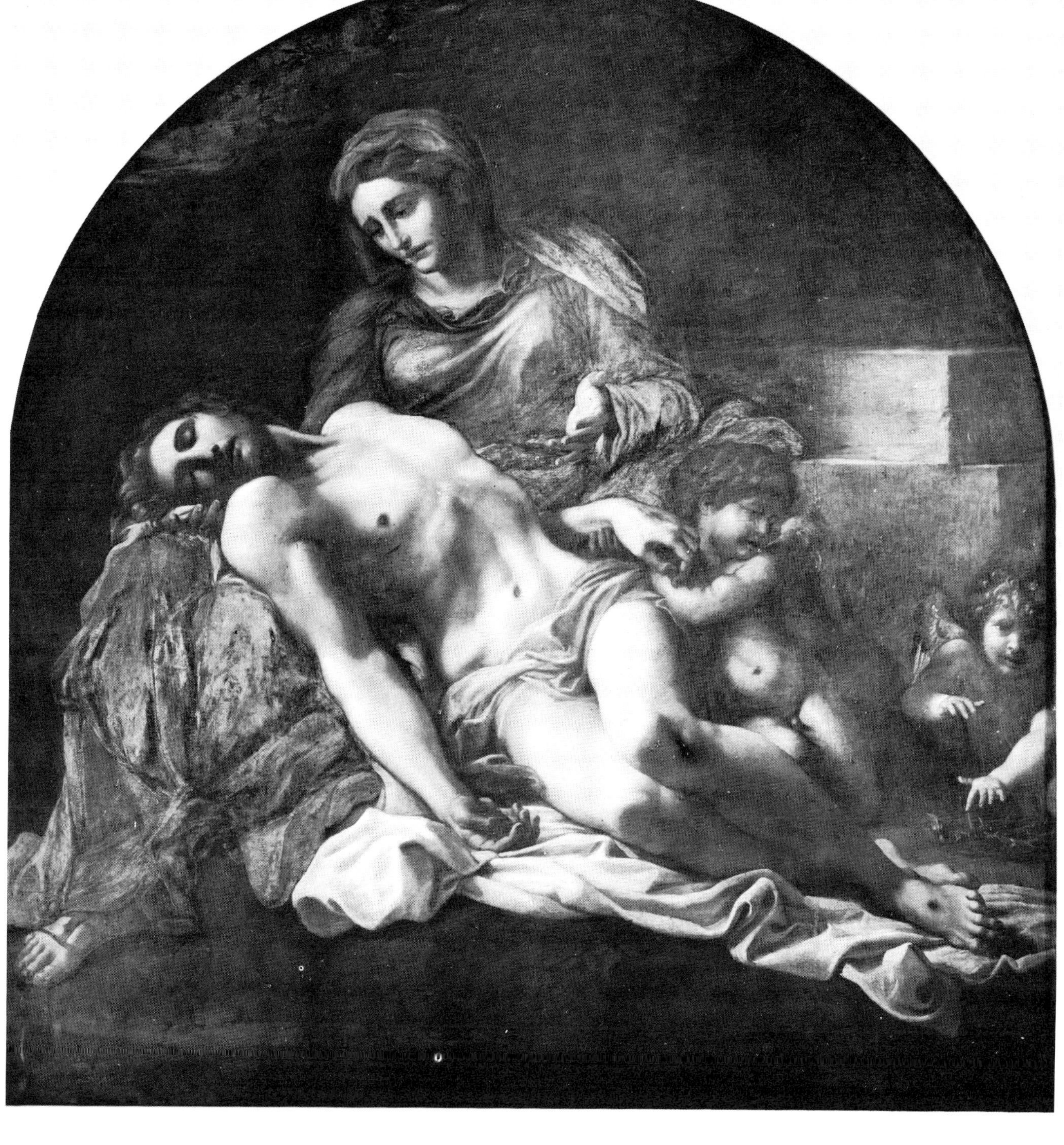

120. Annibale Carracci, *Pietà*. (*Naples, Capodimonte.*)

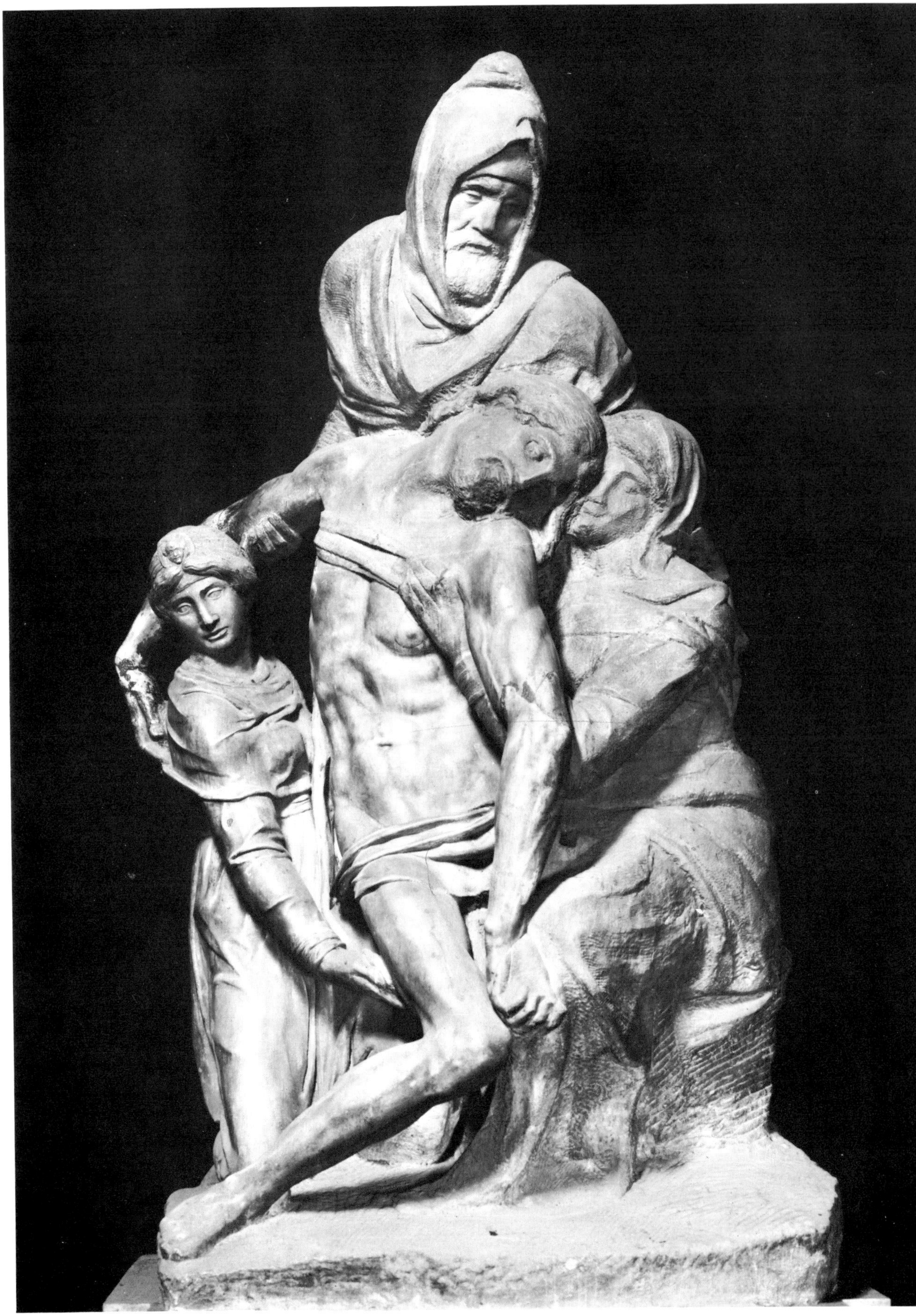

121. Michelangelo, *Pietà.* (*Florence Cathedral.*)

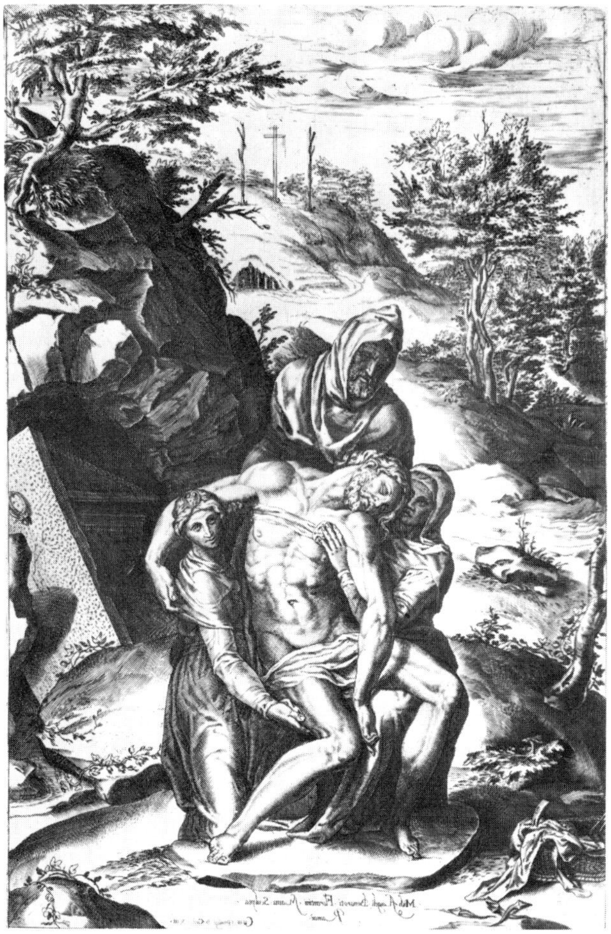

122. Cherubino Alberti, engraving (reversed) after Michelangelo's Florentine *Pietà* (*London, British Museum.*)

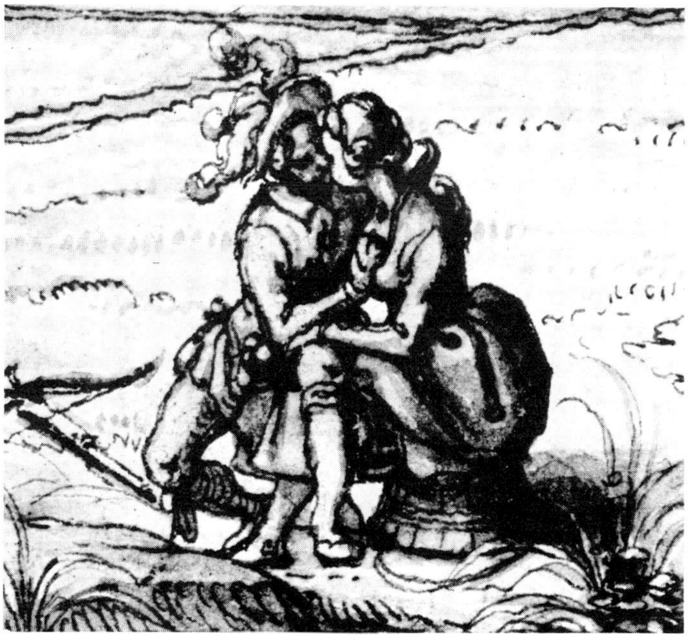

123. Jacques de Gheyn, *Crossbowman and Milkmaid* (detail, reversed). (*Cambridge, Fogg Art Museum, Harvard University, gift of Meta and Paul J. Sachs.*)

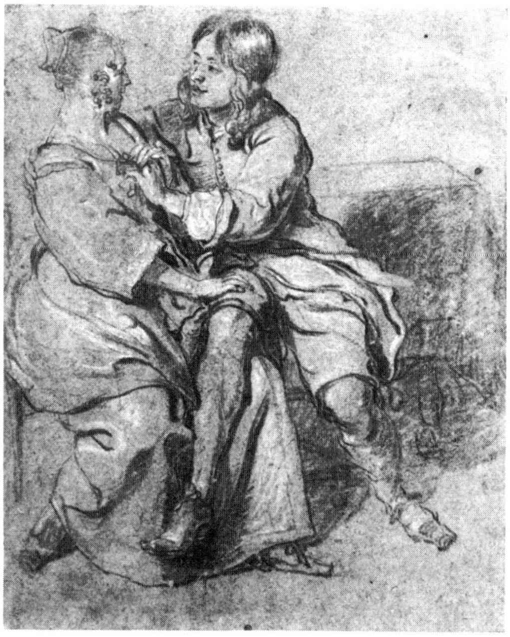

124. Govaert Flinck, *Lovers.* (*Paris, Cabinet des Dessin, Louvre.*)

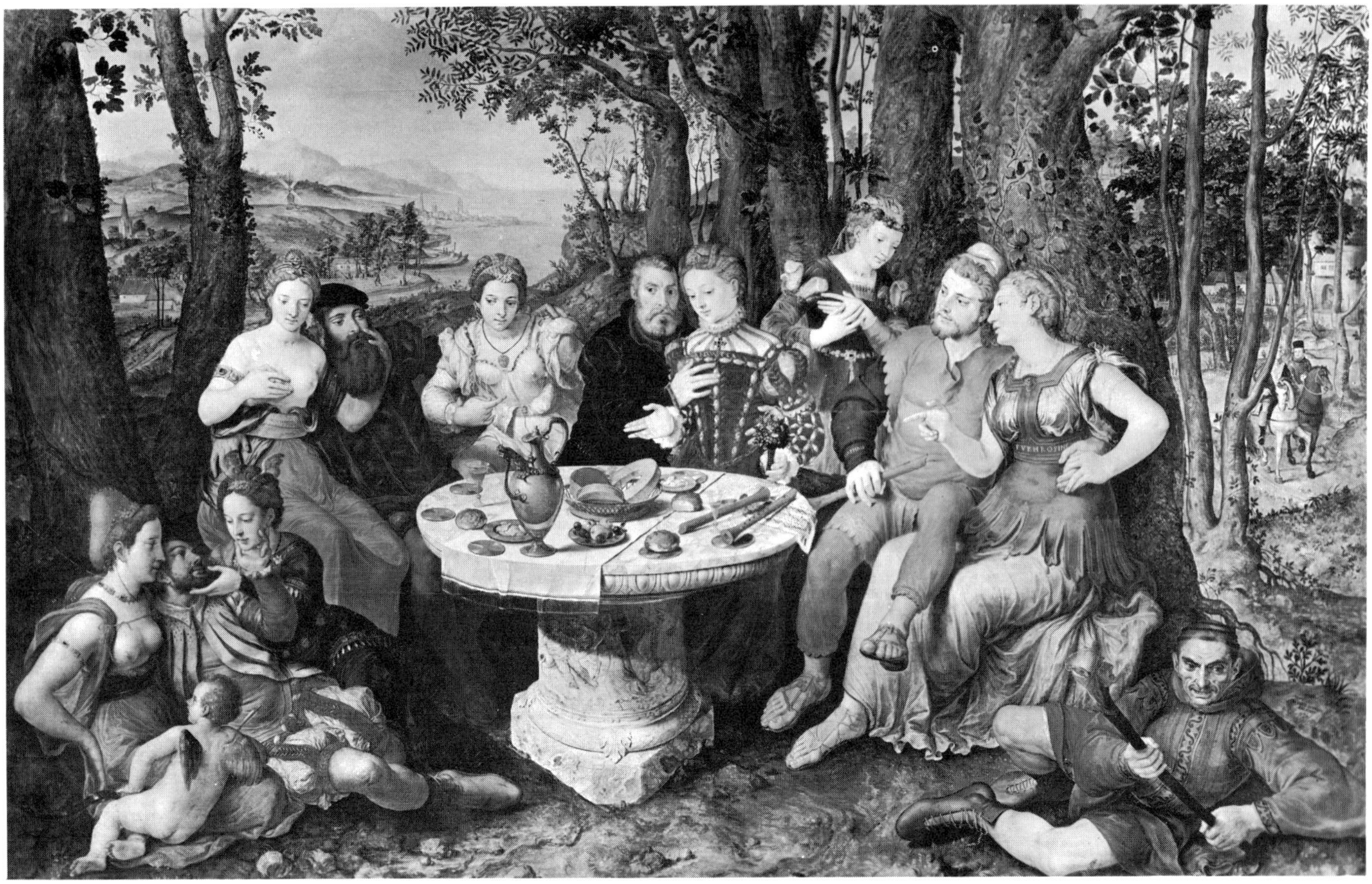

126. Peter Pourbus, *Allegorical Love Feast.* (*London, Wallace Collection.*)

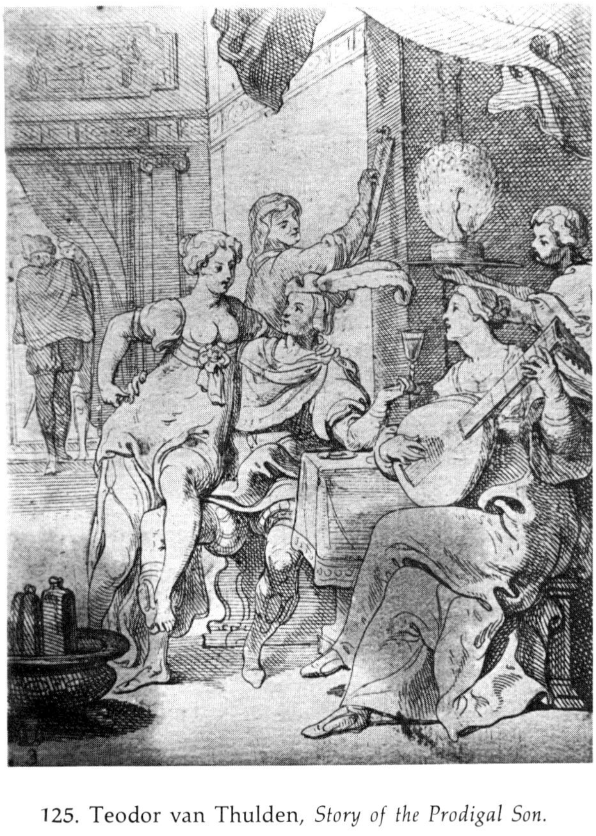

125. Teodor van Thulden, *Story of the Prodigal Son.*

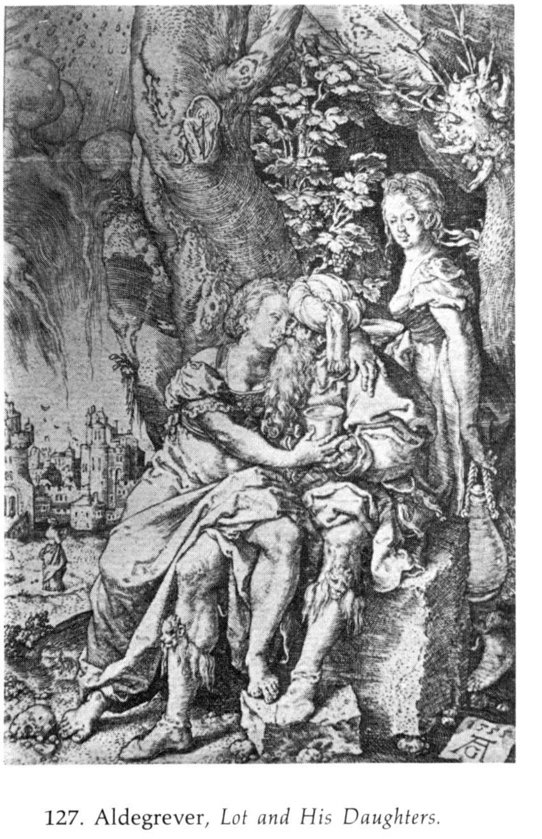

127. Aldegrever, *Lot and His Daughters.*

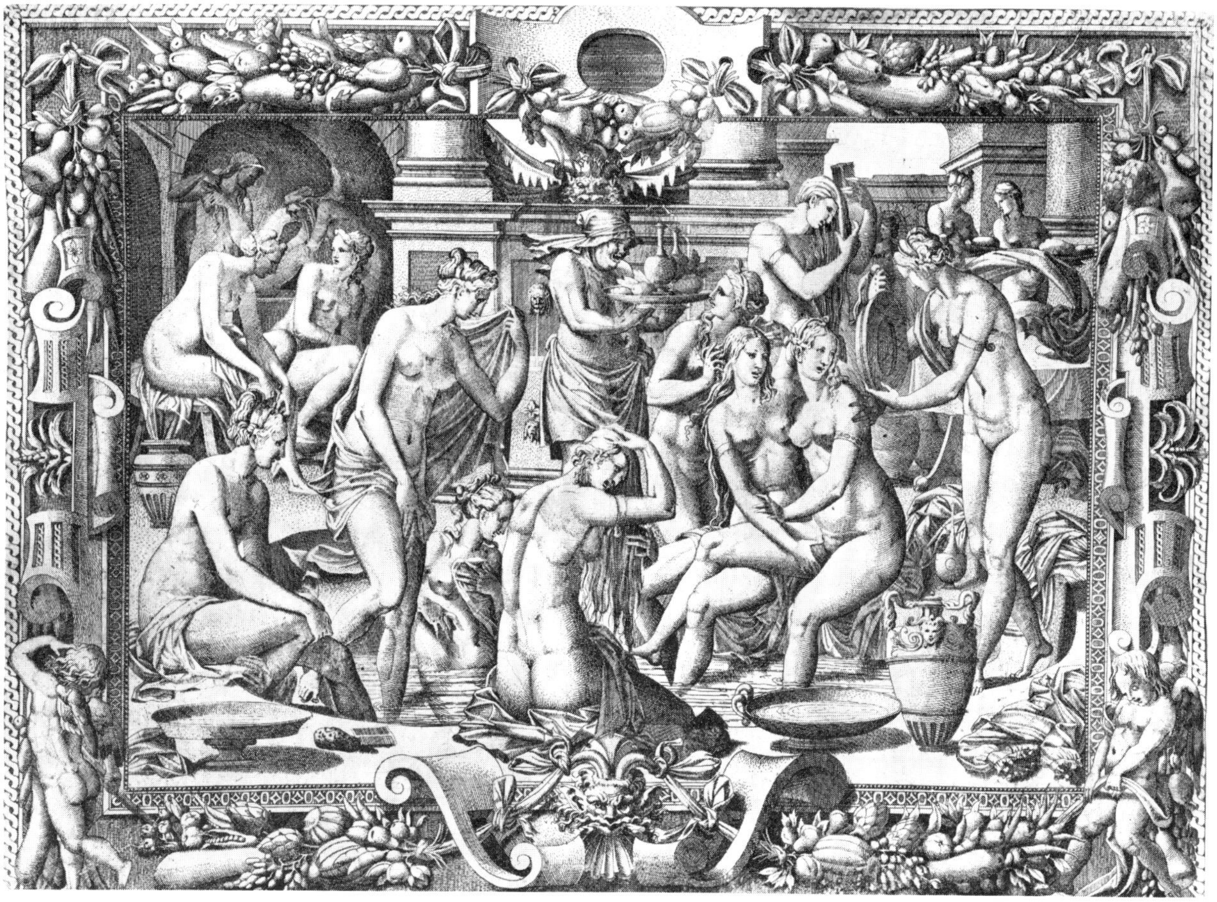

128. Jean Mignon, *Women Bathing.* (*Vienna, Albertina.*)

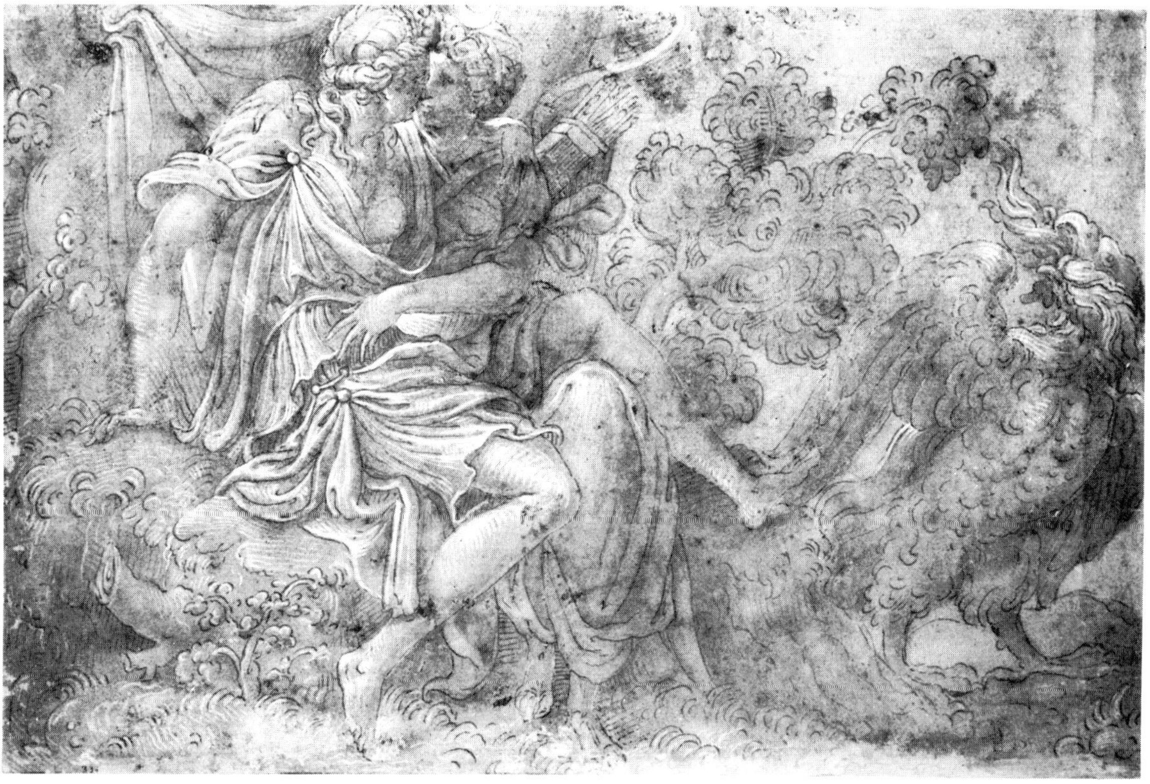

129. Giulio Campi, *Jupiter and Callisto.* (*New York, H. Shickman Gallery.*)

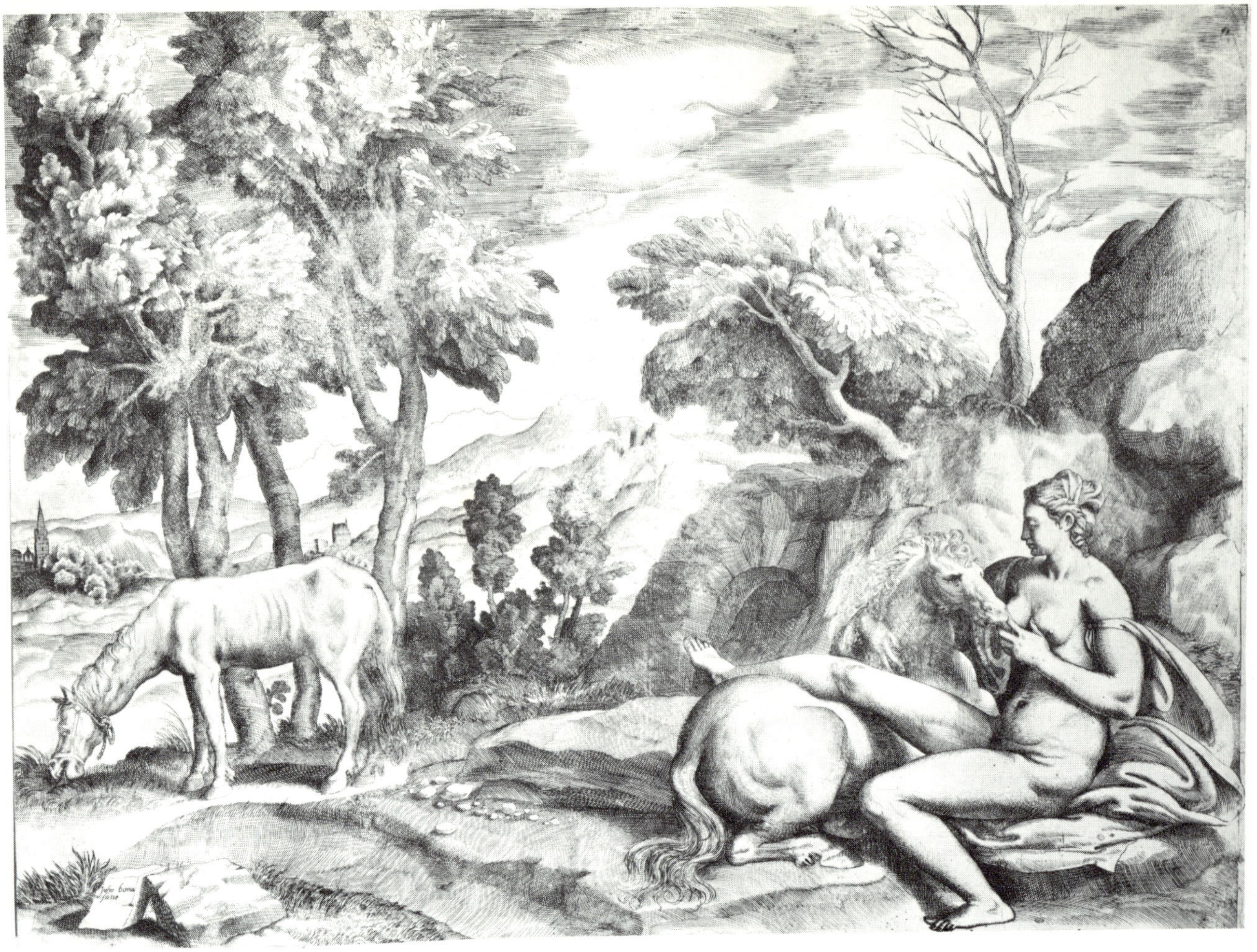

130. Giulio Bonasone, after Giulio Romano, *Saturn and Philyra.* (*New York, **Metropolitan Museum**, Whittelsey Fund, 1959.*)

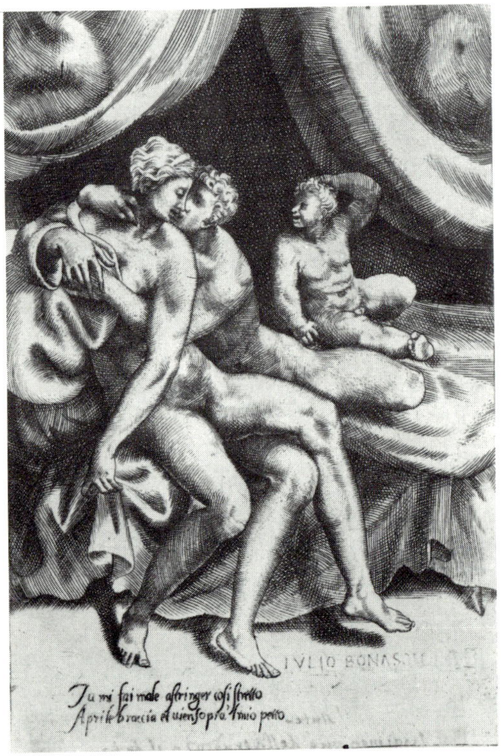

131. Giulio Bonasone, scene from *The Loves of the Gods.* (*London, British Museum.*)

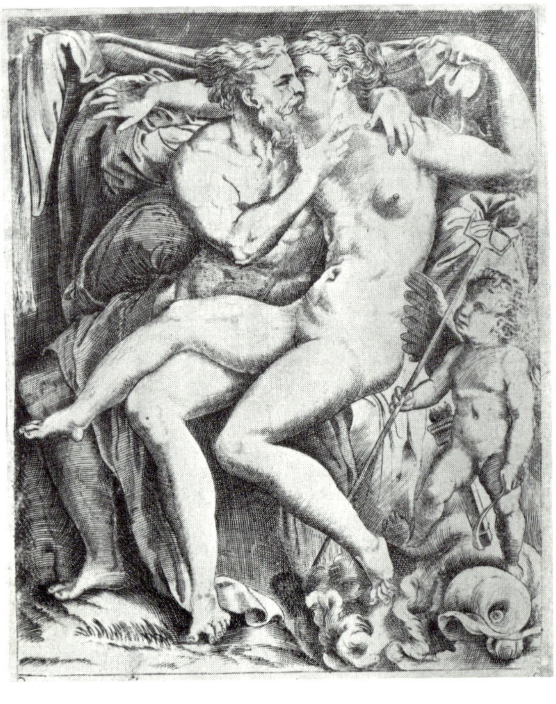

132. Caraglio, after Perino del Vaga, *Neptune and Thetis.* (*London, British Museum.*)

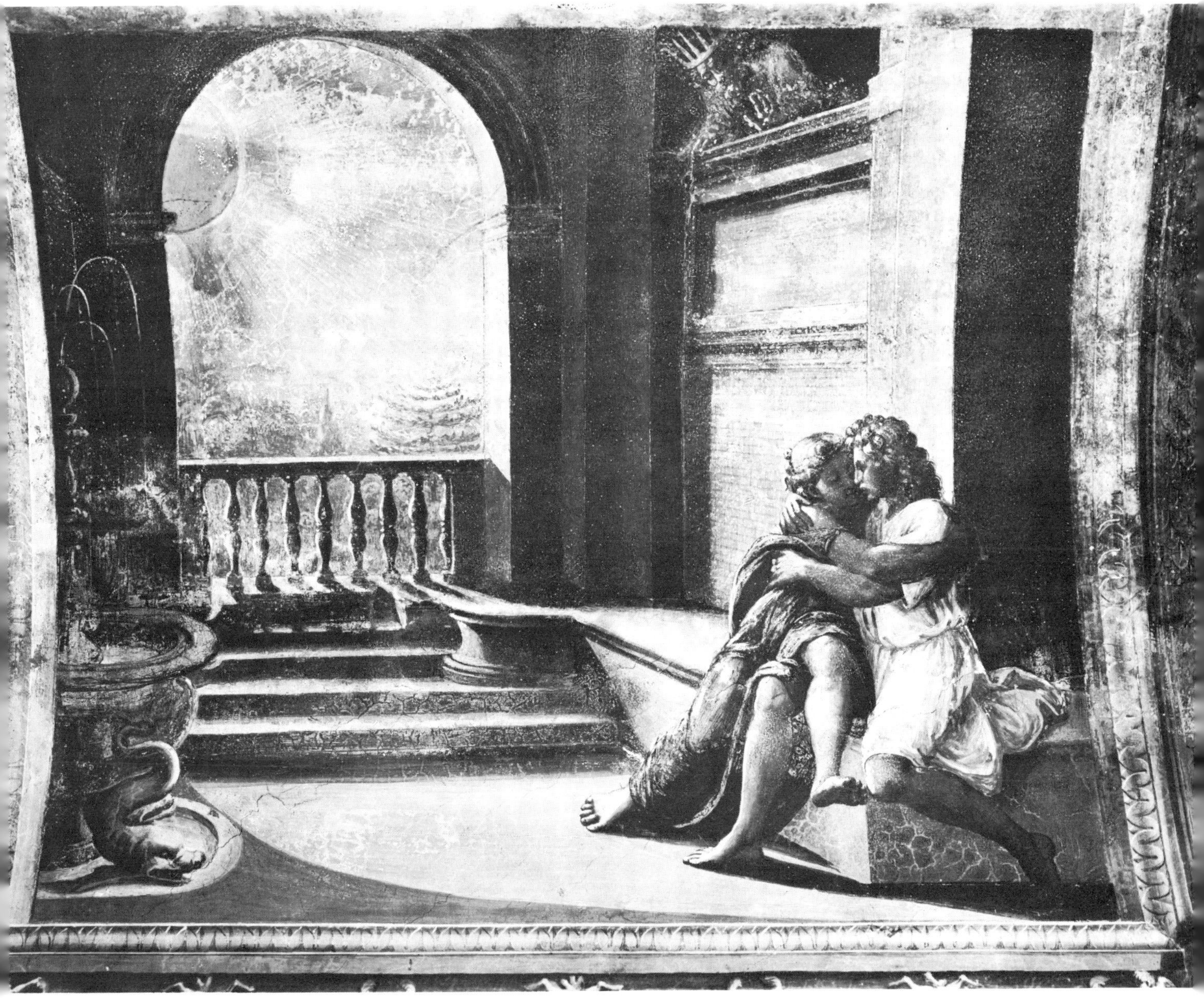

133. Raphael School, *Isaac and Rebecca Spied on by Abimelech.* (*Vatican Logge.*)

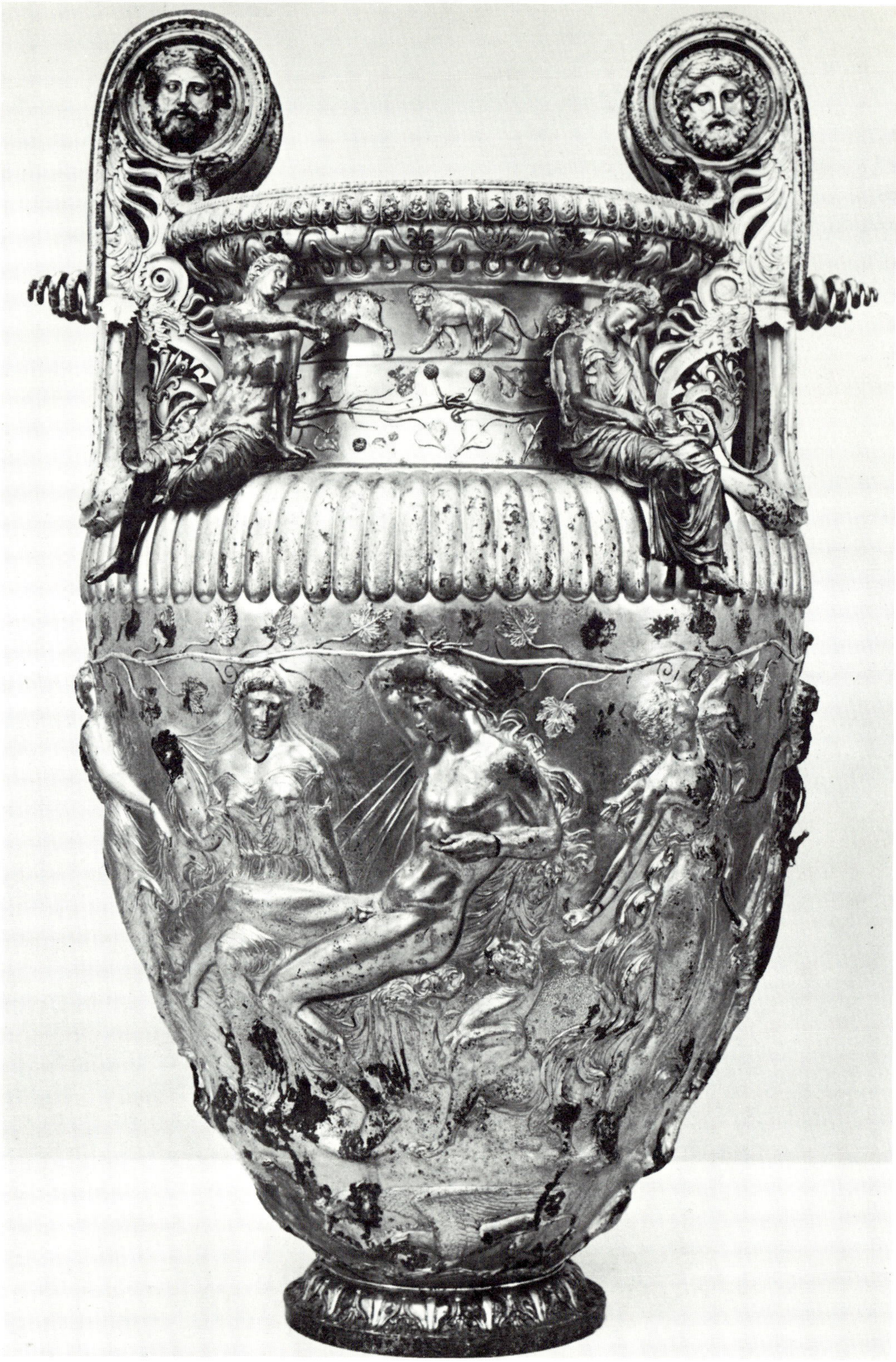

134. Bronze krater from Dherveni, ca. 320 B.C. (*Salonika, Archaeological Museum.*)

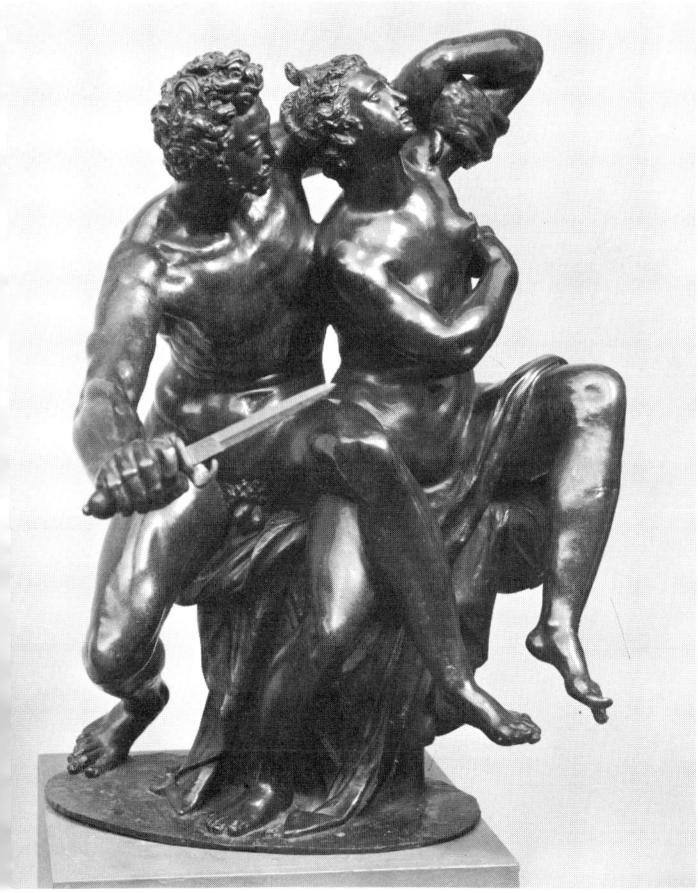

135. Hubert Gerhard, *Tarquin and Lucrece.* (*New York, The Metropolitan Museum, Edith Perry Chapman Fund, 1950.*)

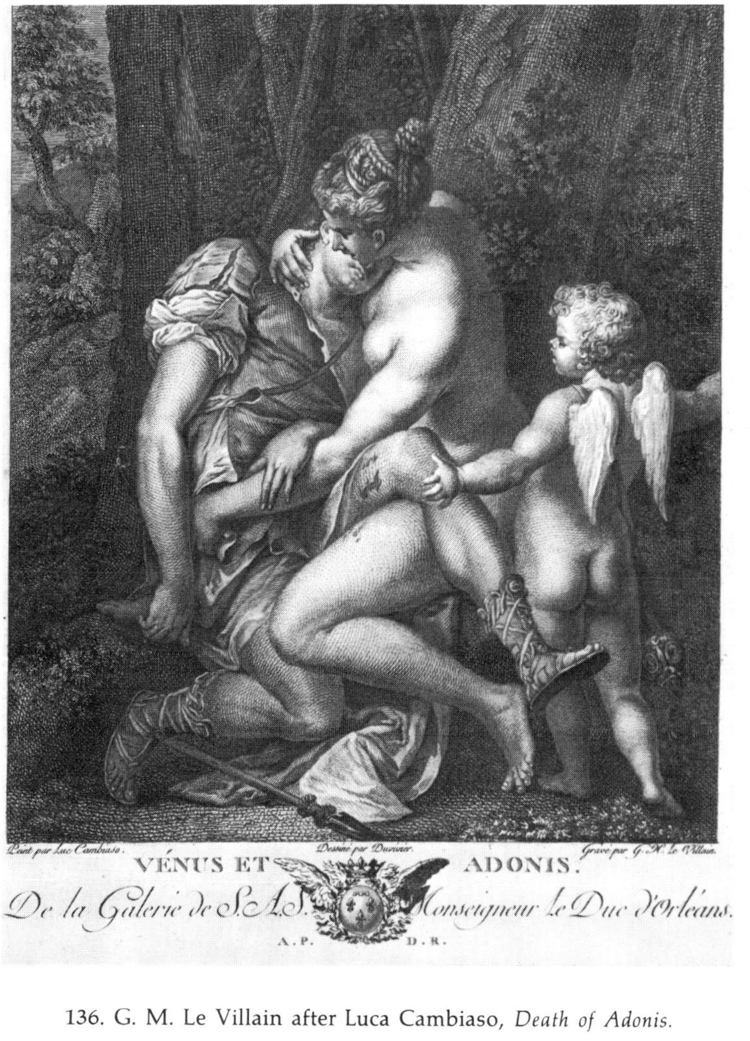

136. G. M. Le Villain after Luca Cambiaso, *Death of Adonis.*

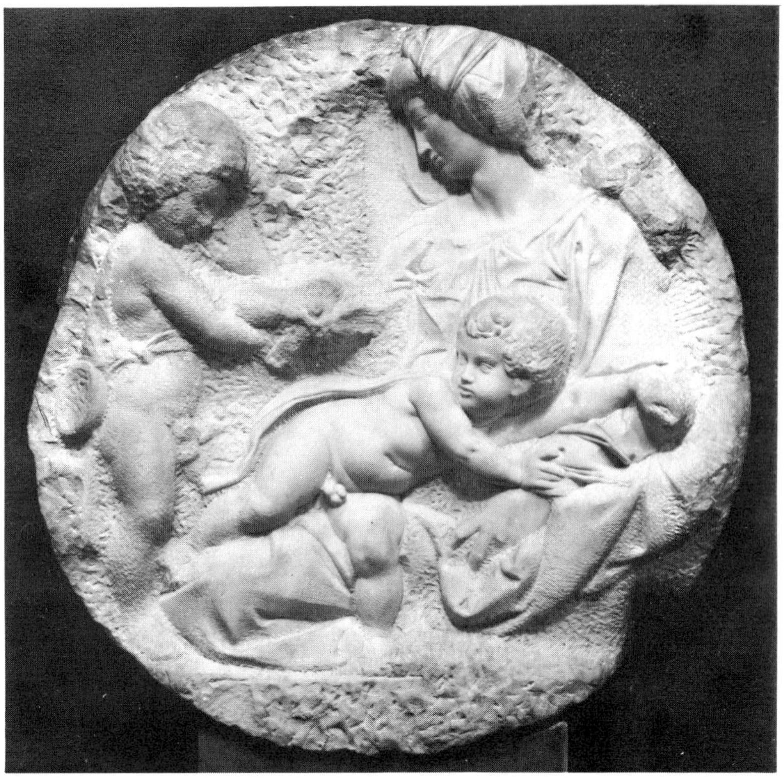

137. Michelangelo, *Madonna Taddei.* (*London, Royal Academy of Arts.*)

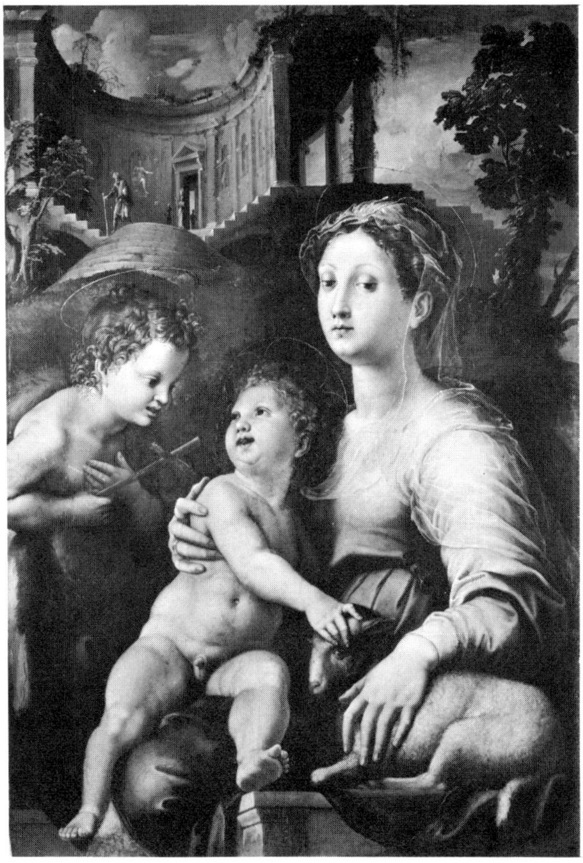

139. Raffaello dal Colle, *Madonna and Child with the Young St. John.* (*Baltimore.* **Walters** *Art Gallery.*)

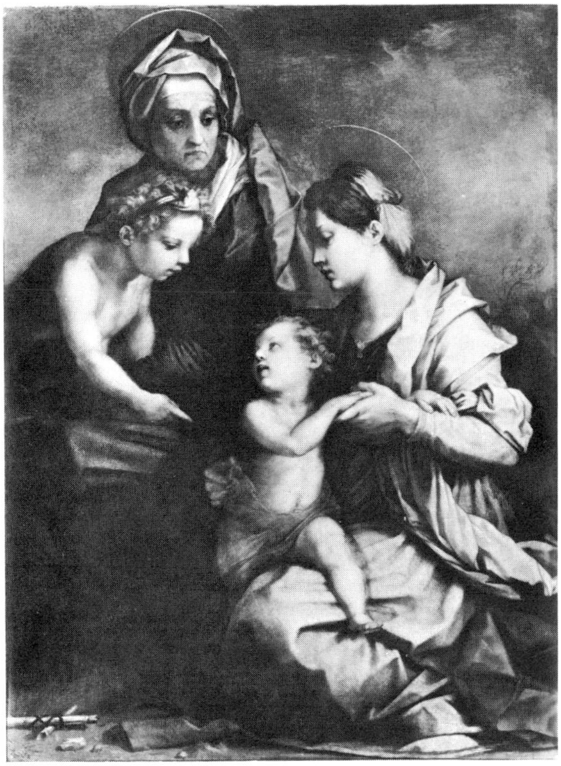

138. Andrea del Sarto, *Holy Family.* (*Florence, Pitti Palace.*)

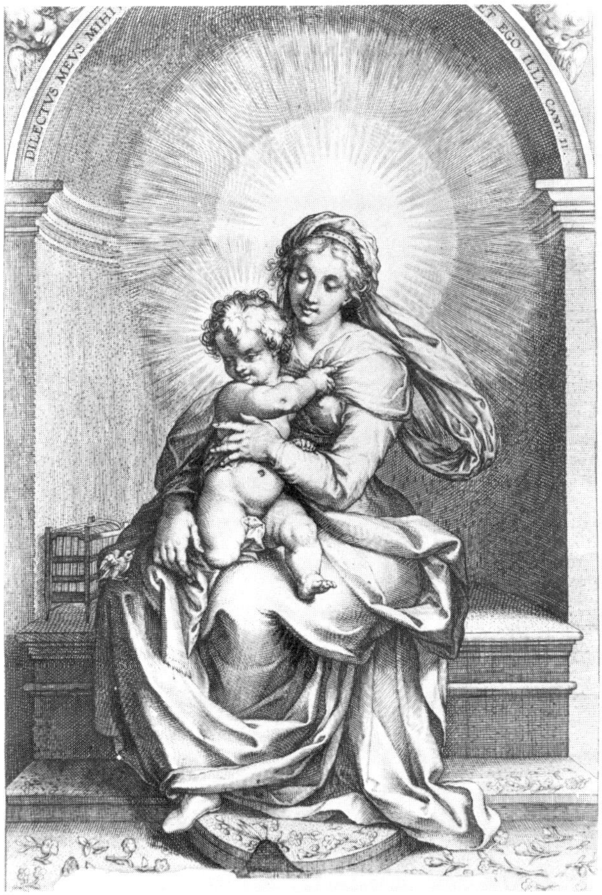

140. J. B. Barbé after Fr. Francken the Younger, *Virgin and Child.* (*Hollstein, I, p. 99, 1A.*)

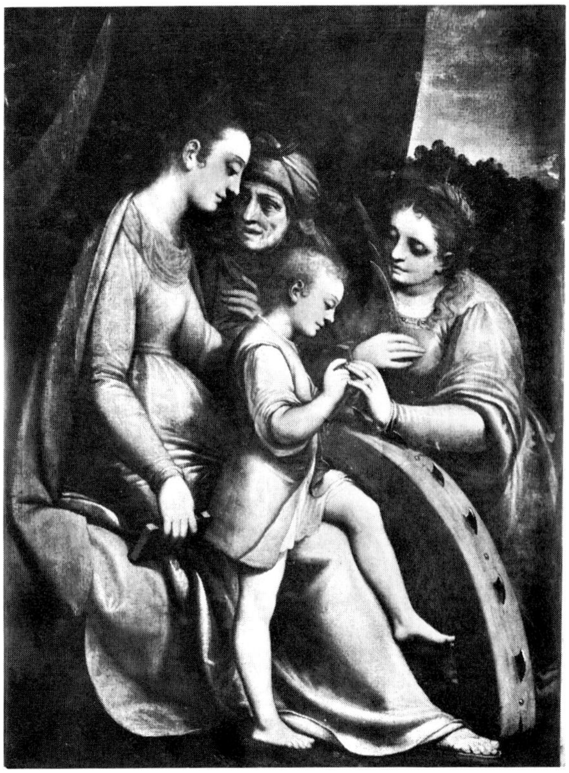

141. Luca Cambiaso, *The Mystic Marriage of St. Catherine.* (*Naples, Leonetti Collection.*)

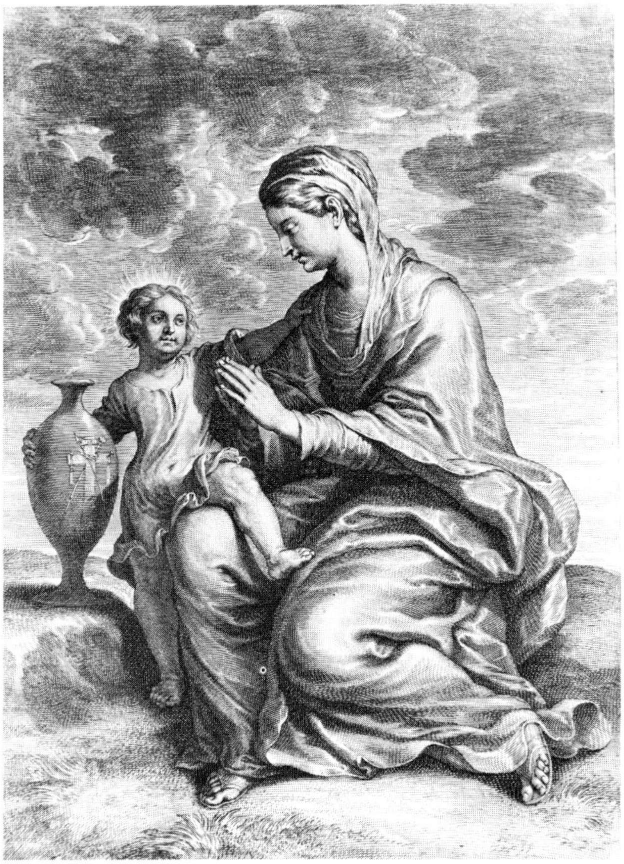

142. Schelte à Bolswert after Parmigianino, *Madonna and Child.*

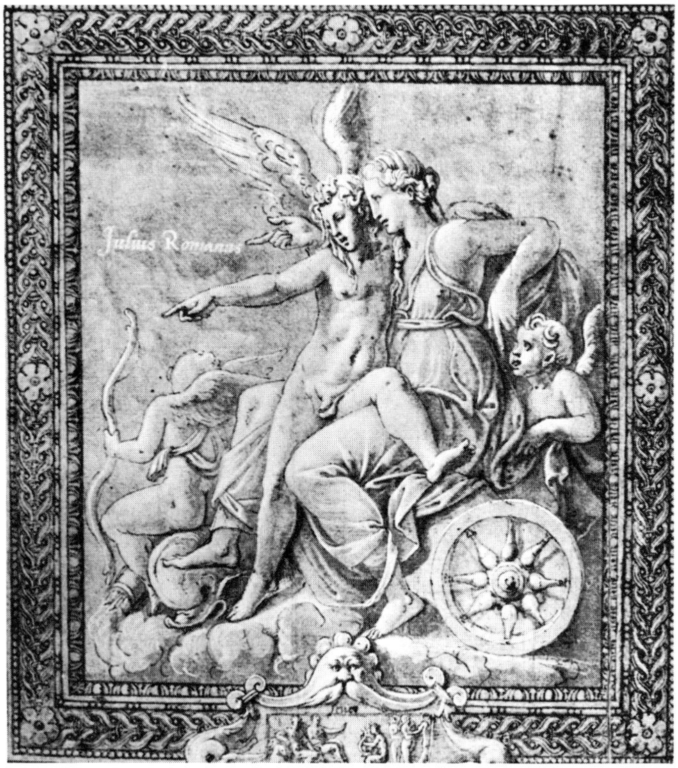

143. Giulio Romano, *Cupid and Psyche,* drawing for the Stalle del Te, Mantua, (*Paris, Cabinet des Dessins, Louvre.*)

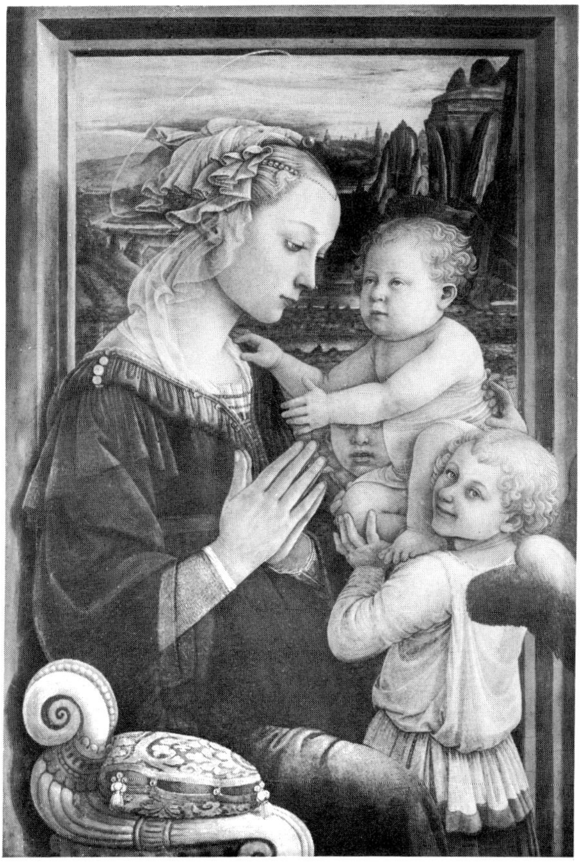

144. Filippo Lippi, *Madonna Adoring the Child with Two Angels.* (*Florence, Uffizi.*)

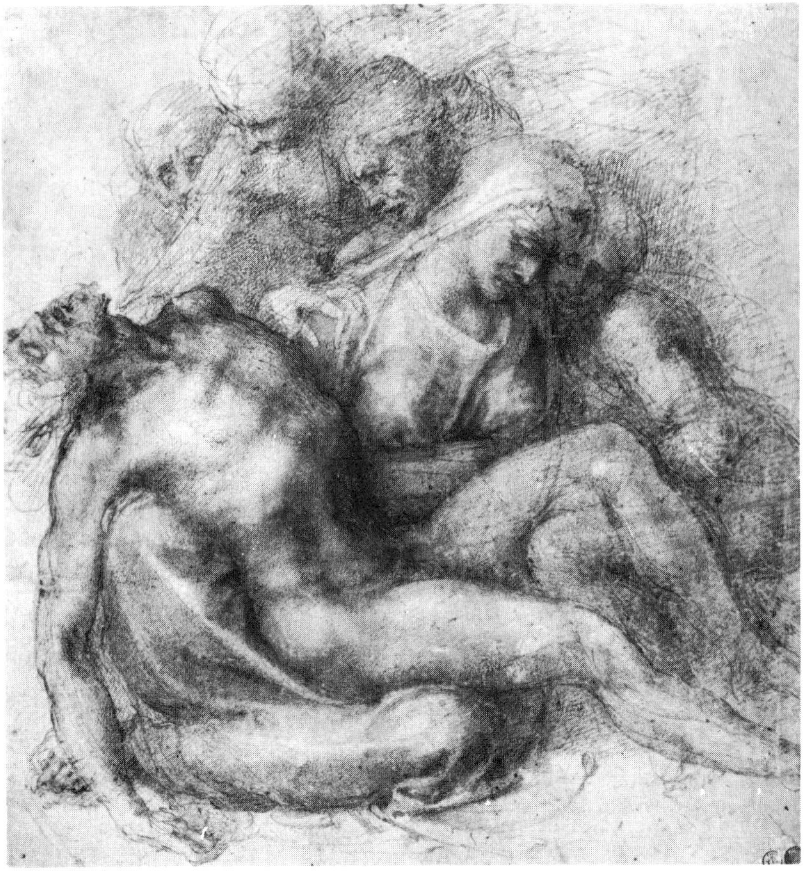

145. Michelangelo (?), *Lamentation.* (*London, British Museum.*)

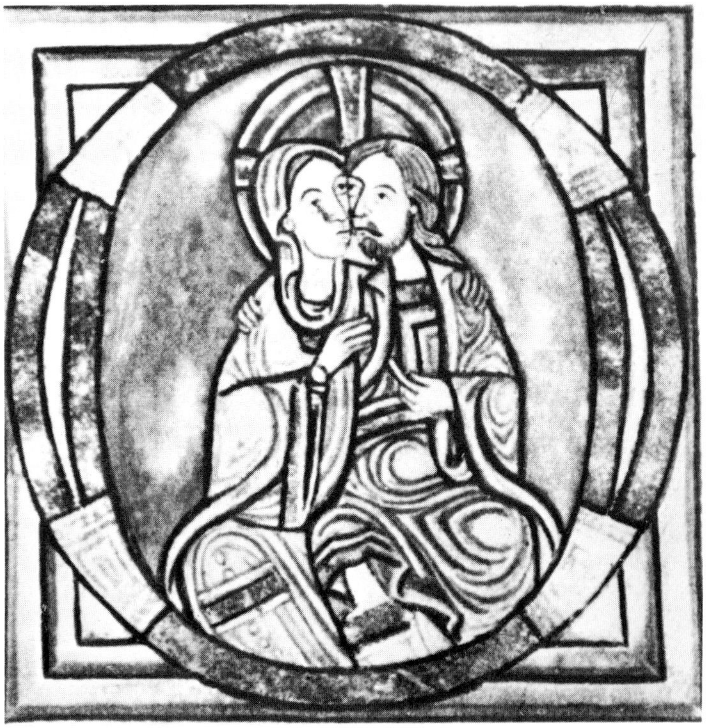

146. Bride and Groom from St. Jerome, *Commentary on the Song of Songs,* twelfth-century manuscript at Saint-Amand.

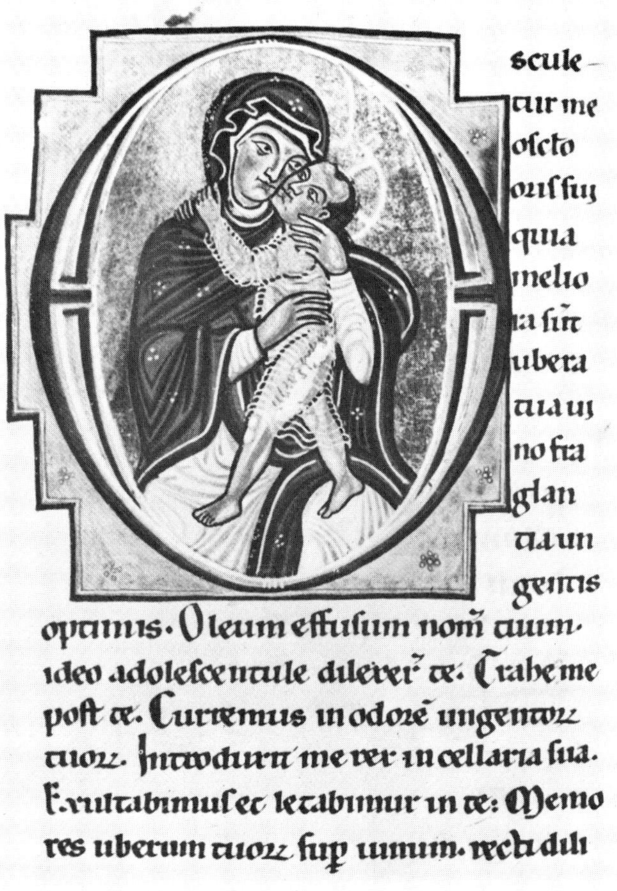

147. Lyons Bible, *Virgin and Child,* twelfth century.

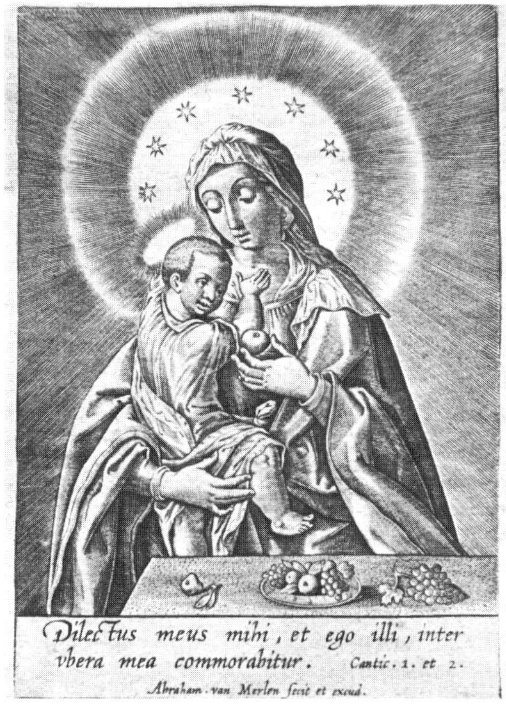

148. Abraham van Merlen, *Virgin and Child.*

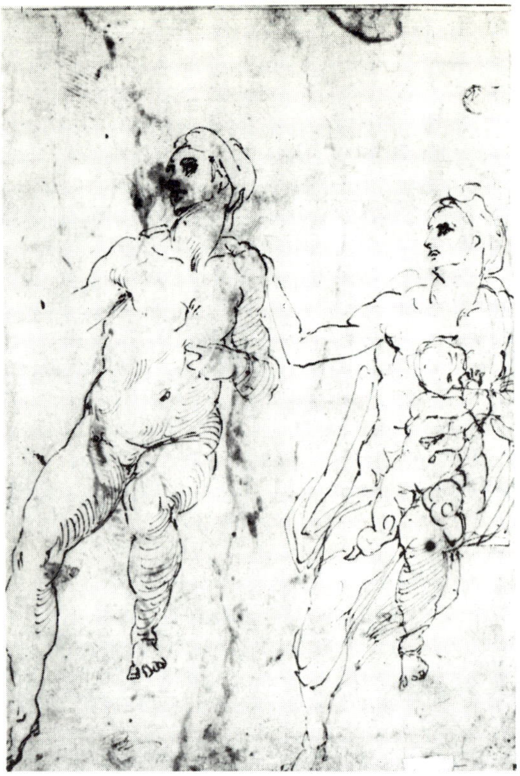

150. Michelangelo, *Madonna and Child.* (*Paris, Cabinet des Dessins, Louvre.*)

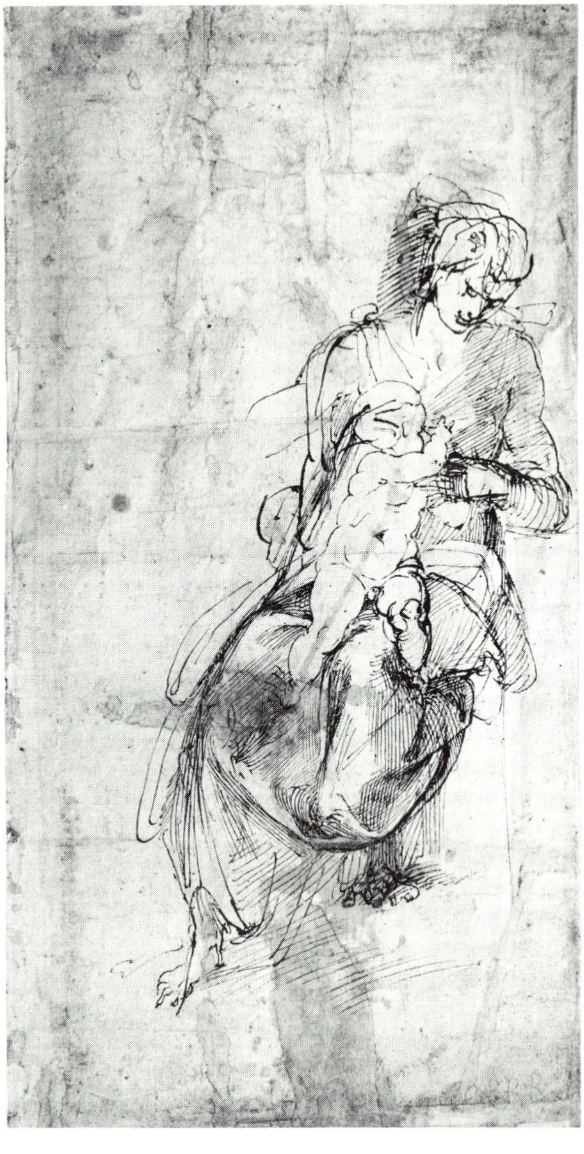

151. Michelangelo, *Madonna and Child.* (*Vienna, Albertina.*)

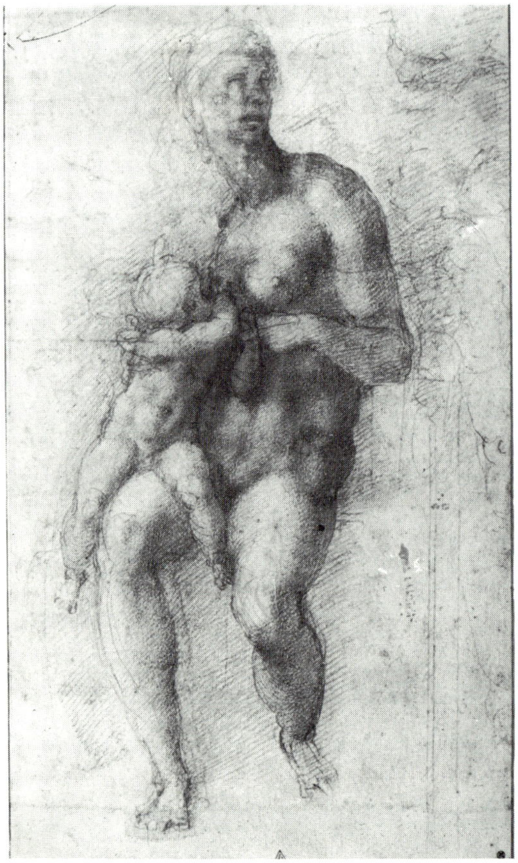

152. Michelangelo, *Madonna and Child.* (*London, British Museum.*)

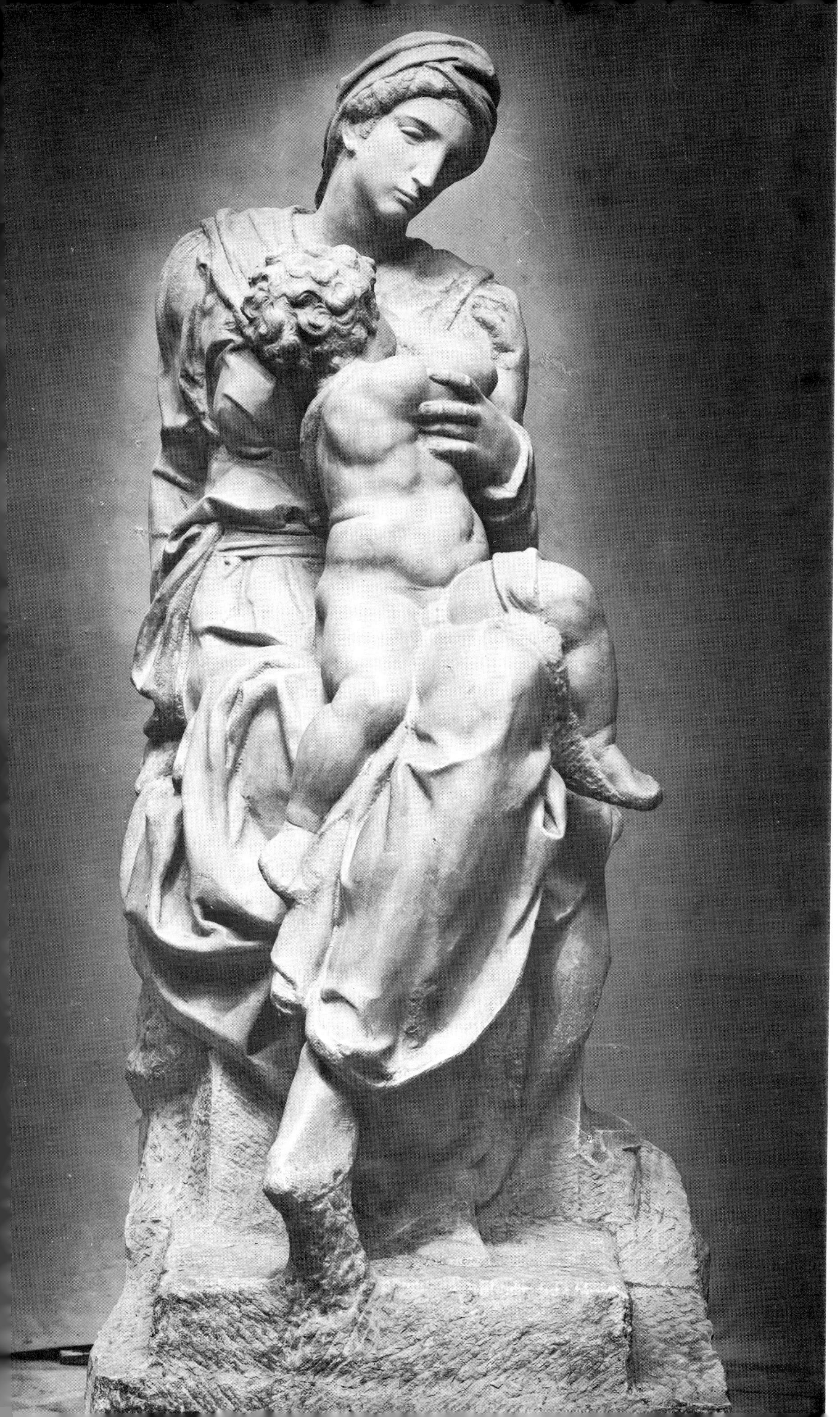

149. Michelangelo, *Madonna Medici.* (Florence, S. Lorenzo.)

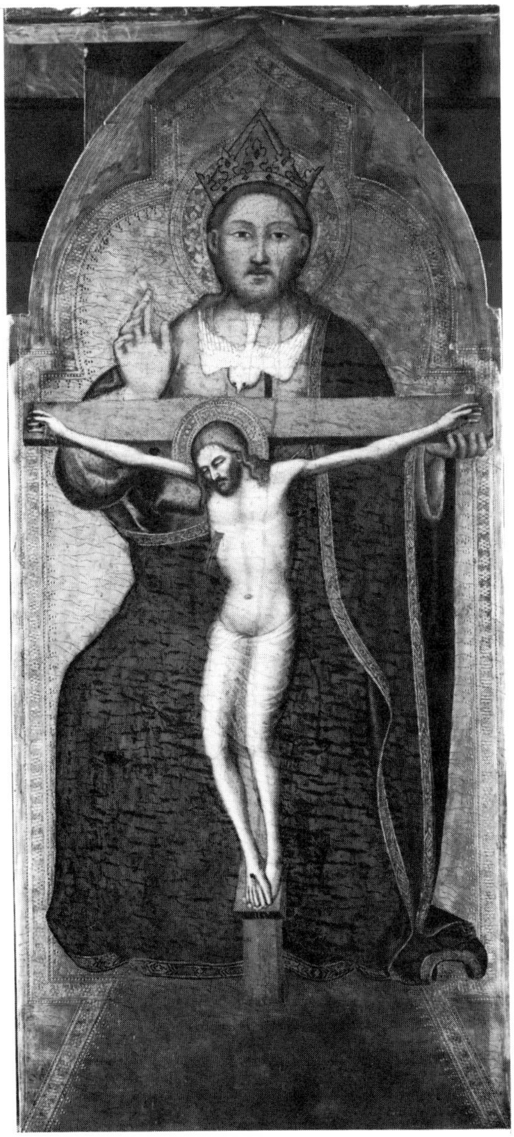

153. Orcagna School, *Trinity.* (*London, National Gallery.*)

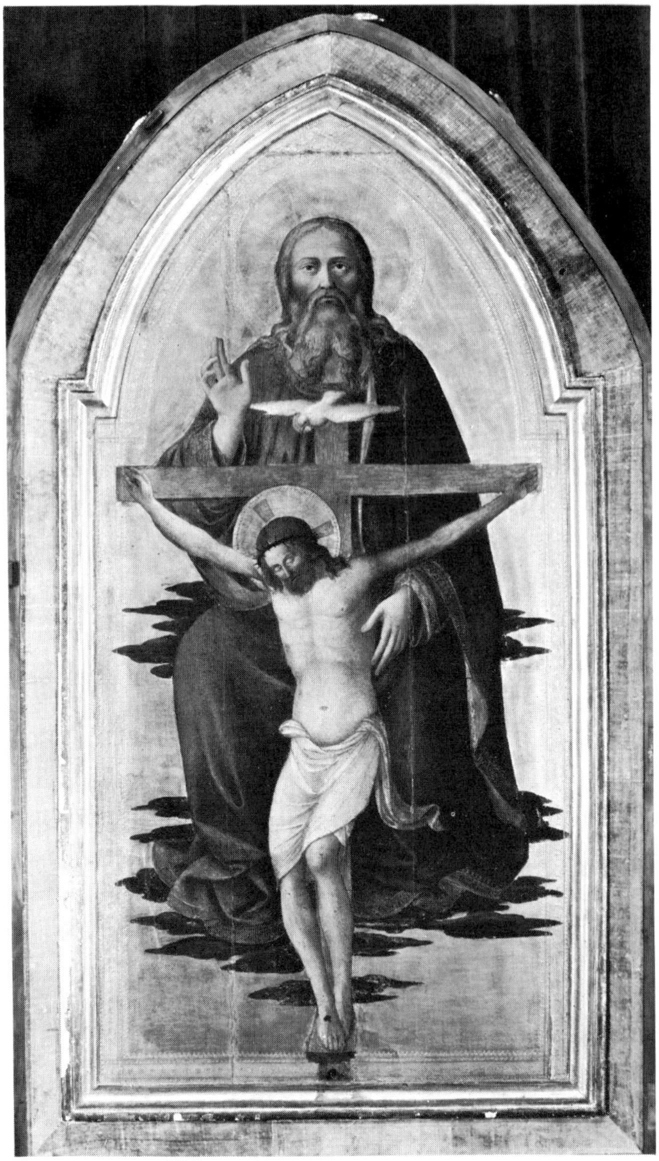

154. Masolino, *Trinity.* (*Detroit, Institute of Arts.*)

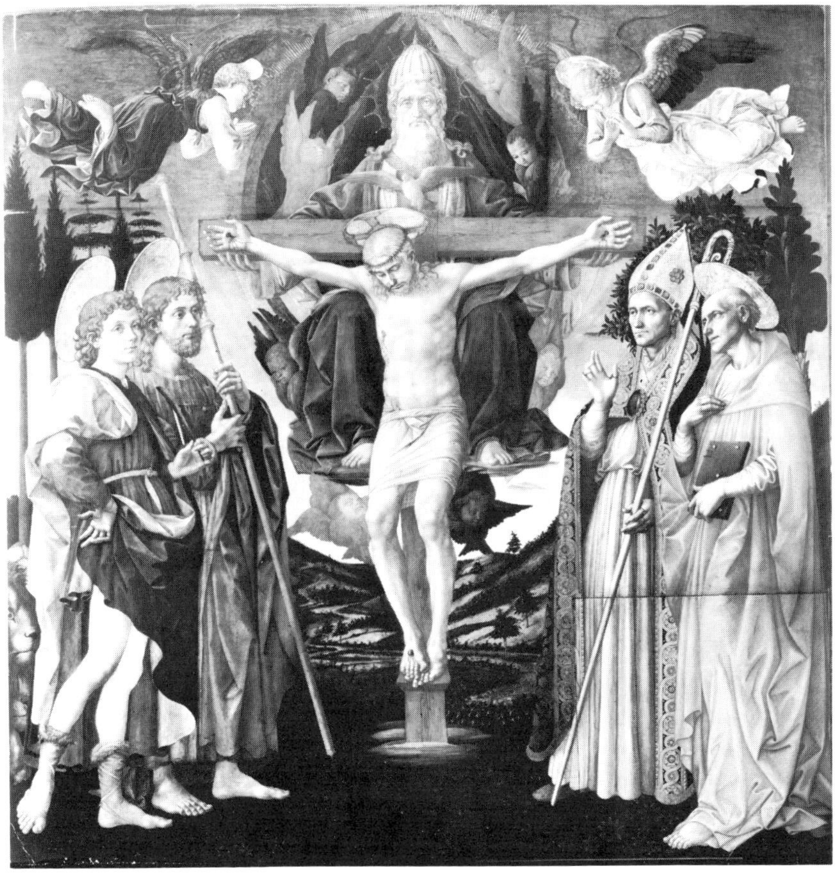

155. Pesellino, *The Trinity with Saints.* (*London, National Gallery.*)

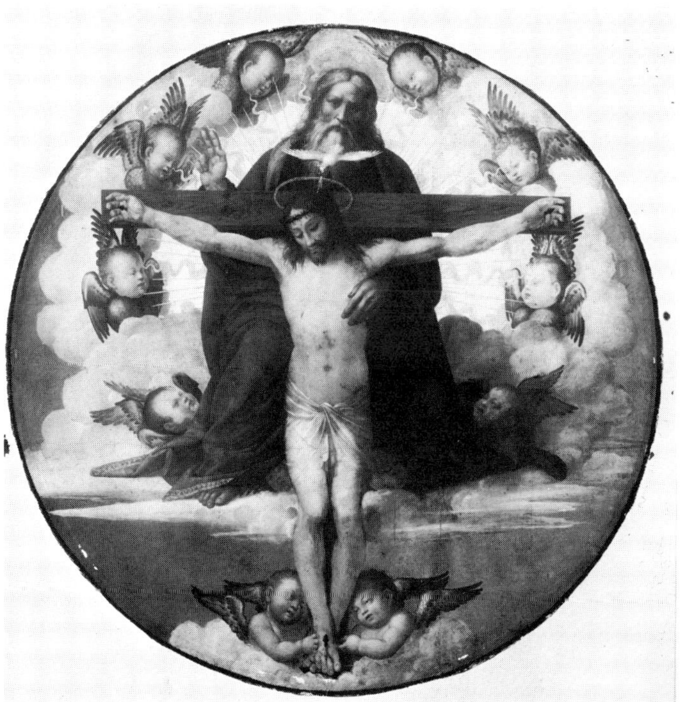

156. Granacci, *Trinity.* (*Berlin, Gemäldegalerie, Staatliche Museen.*)

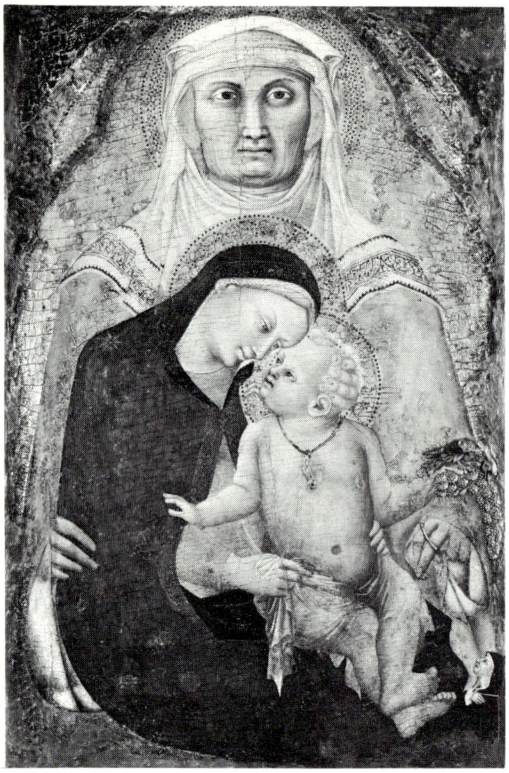

157. Traini, *Virgin and Child with St. Anne.* (*Princeton University, Art Museum.*)

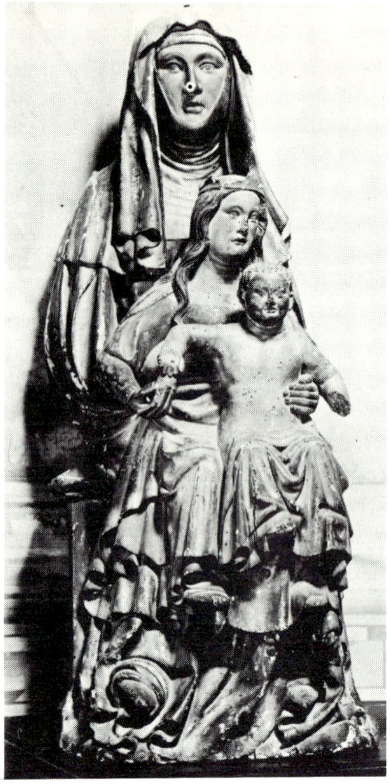

158. Anonymous fourteenth century, *Virgin and Child and St. Anne.* (*Florence, Museo Nazionale.*)

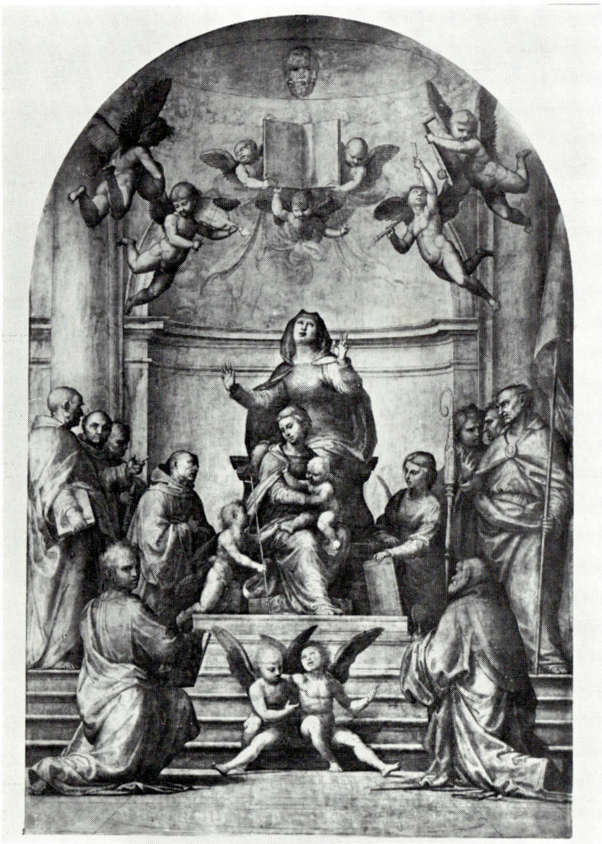

159. Fra Bartolommeo, *Madonna Enthroned with Saints.* (*Florence, San Marco.*)

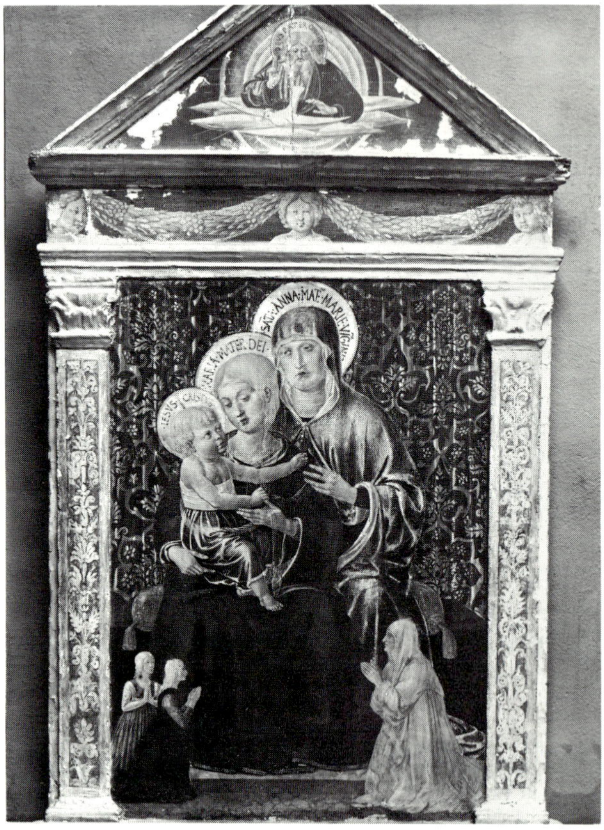

160. Benozzo Gozzoli, *Virgin and Child with St. Anne.* (*Pisa, Museo Civico.*)

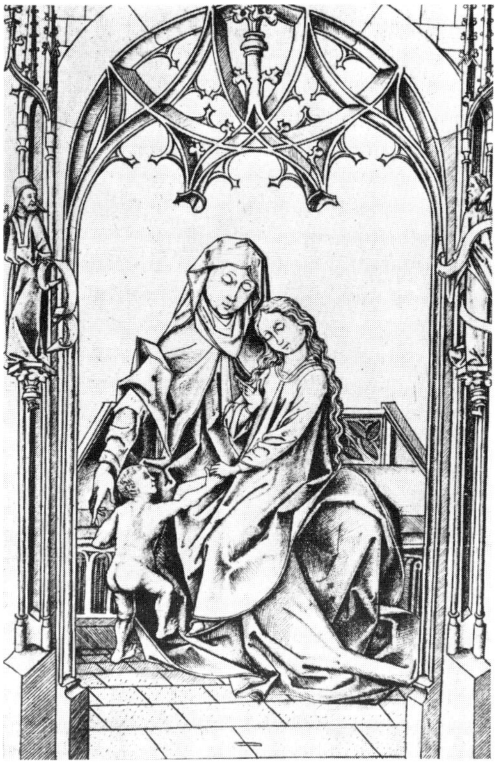

161. I. van Meckenem after Master E. S., *Virgin and Child with St. Anne.*

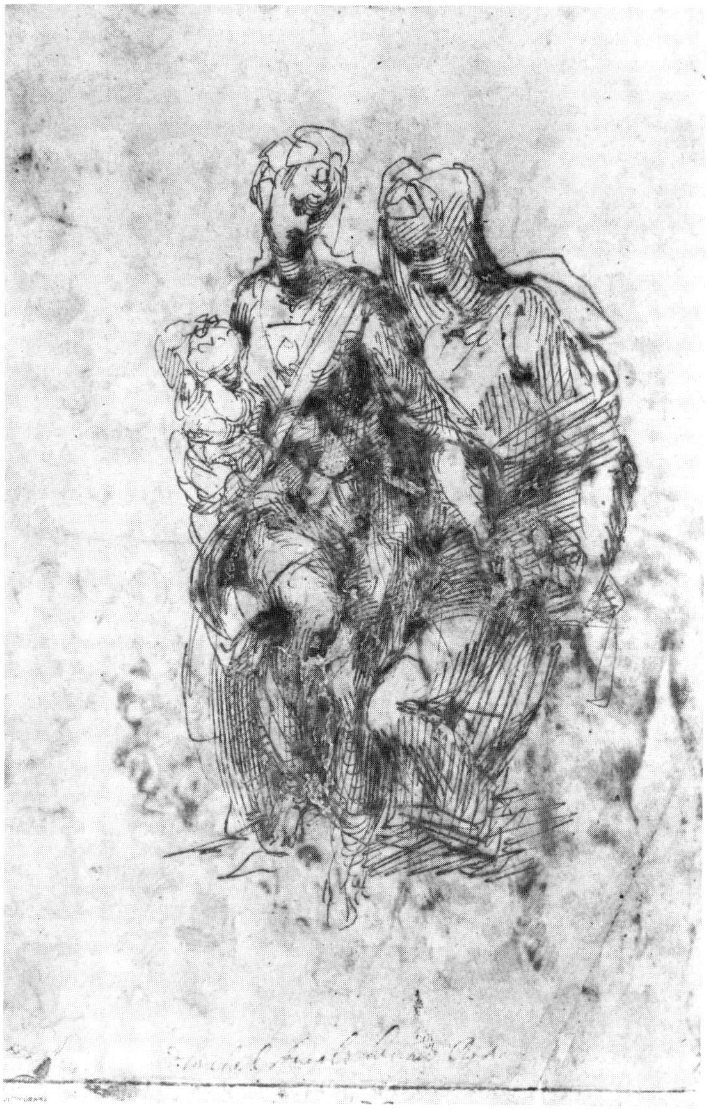

162. Michelangelo, *Virgin and Child with St. Anne.* (*Oxford, Ashmolean Museum.*)

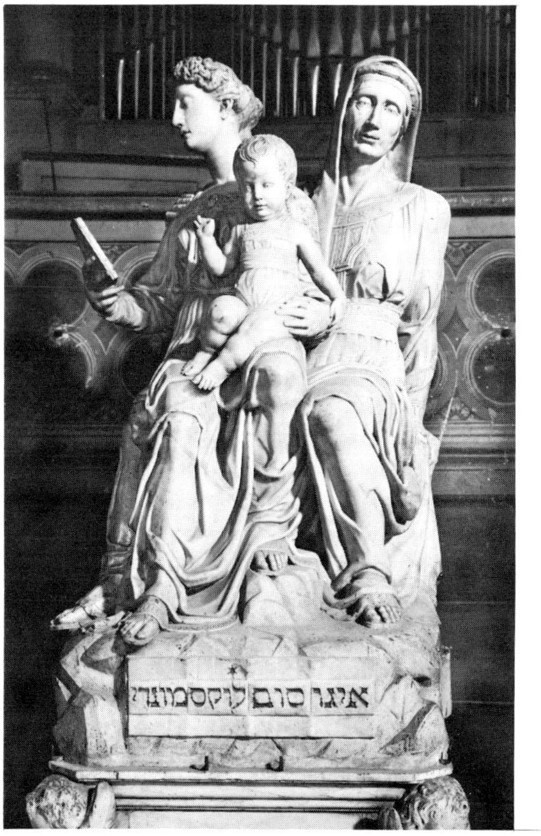

163. Francesco da Sangallo, *Virgin and Child with St. Anne.* (*Florence, Or San Michele.*)

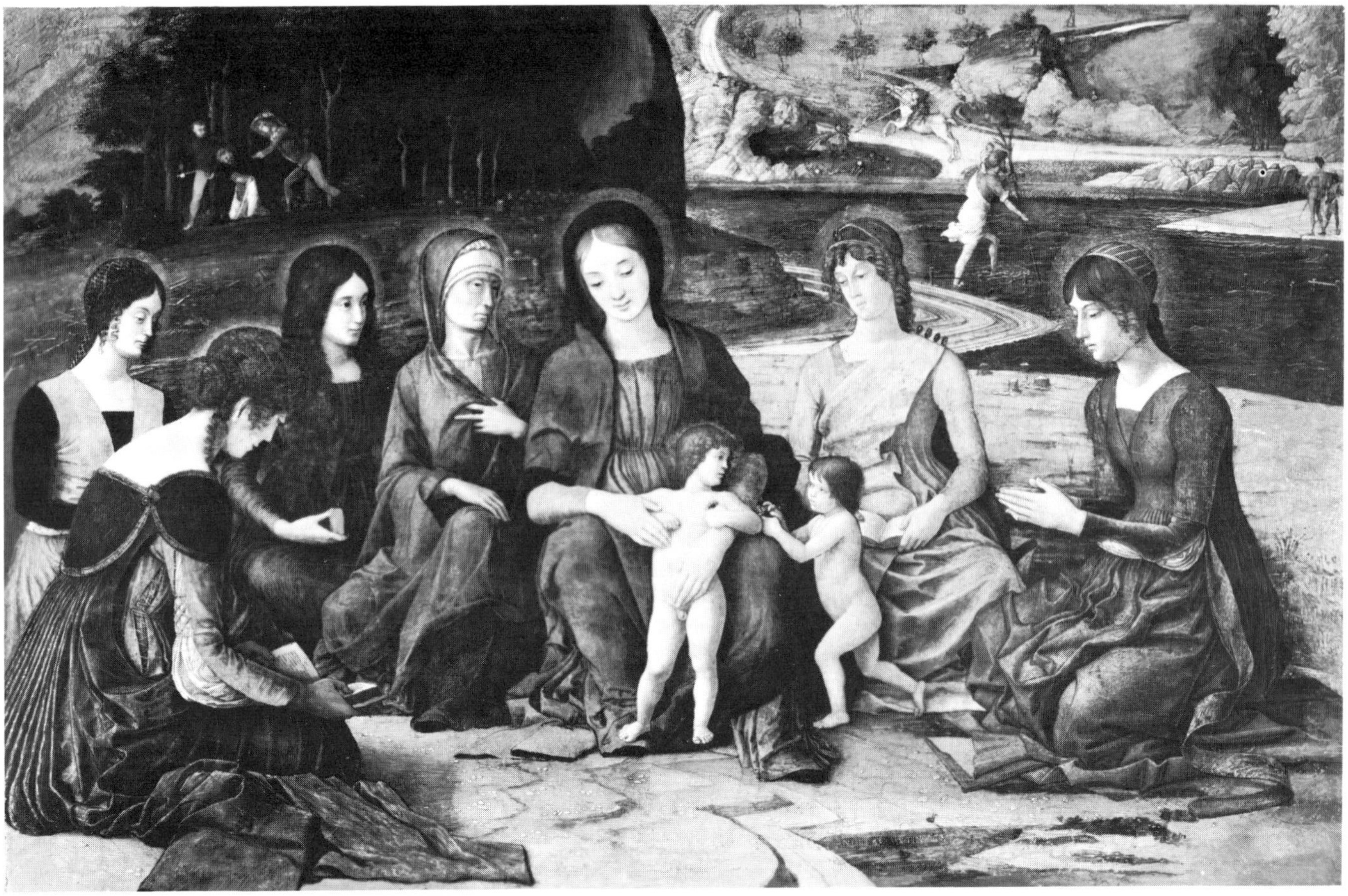

164. Mantegna School, *Holy Kinship.* (*Boston, Isabella Stewart Gardner Museum.*)

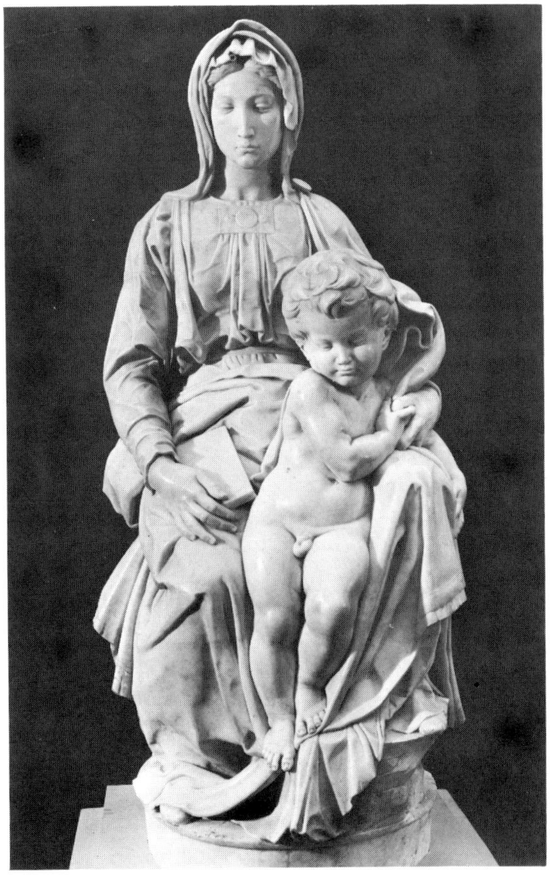

165. Michelangelo, *Bruges Madonna.* (*Bruges, Notre Dame.*)

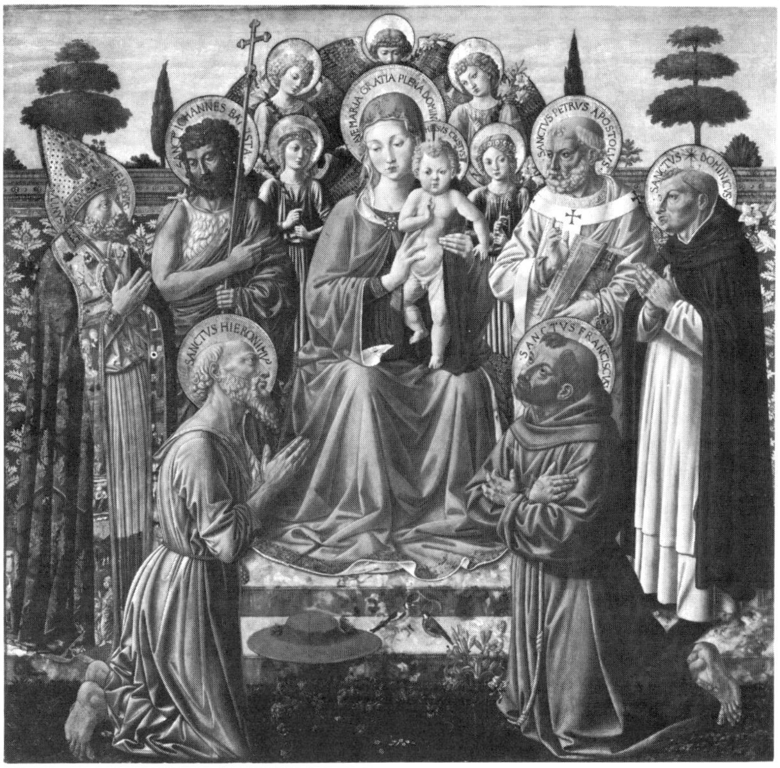

166. Benozzo Gozzoli, *Madonna and Child Enthroned with Saints.* (*London, National Gallery.*)

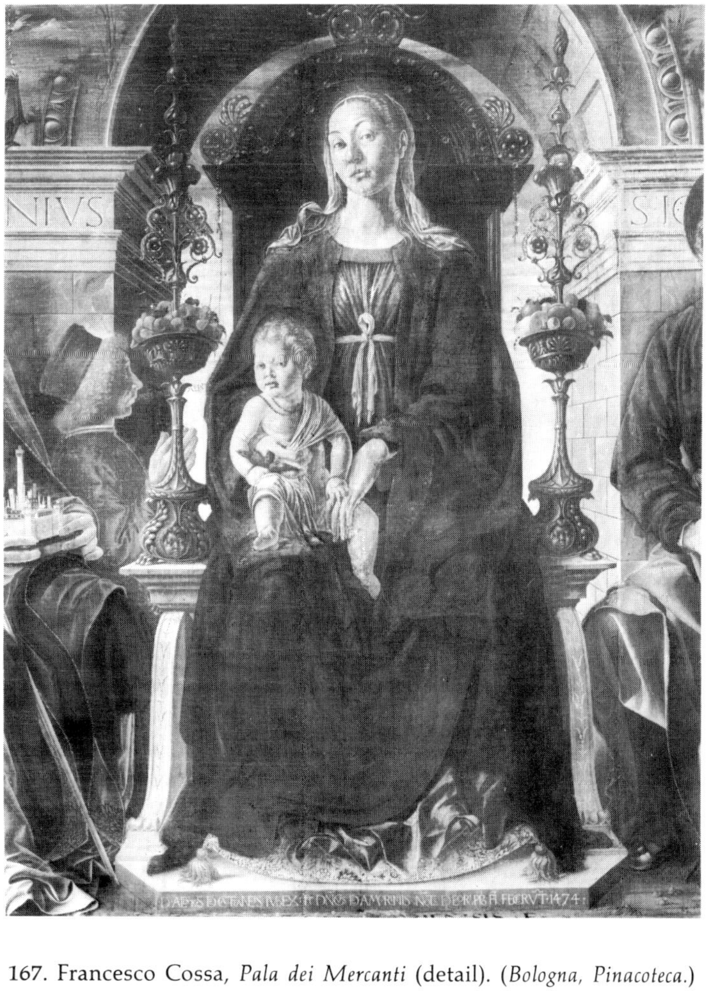

167. Francesco Cossa, *Pala dei Mercanti* (detail). (*Bologna, Pinacoteca.*)

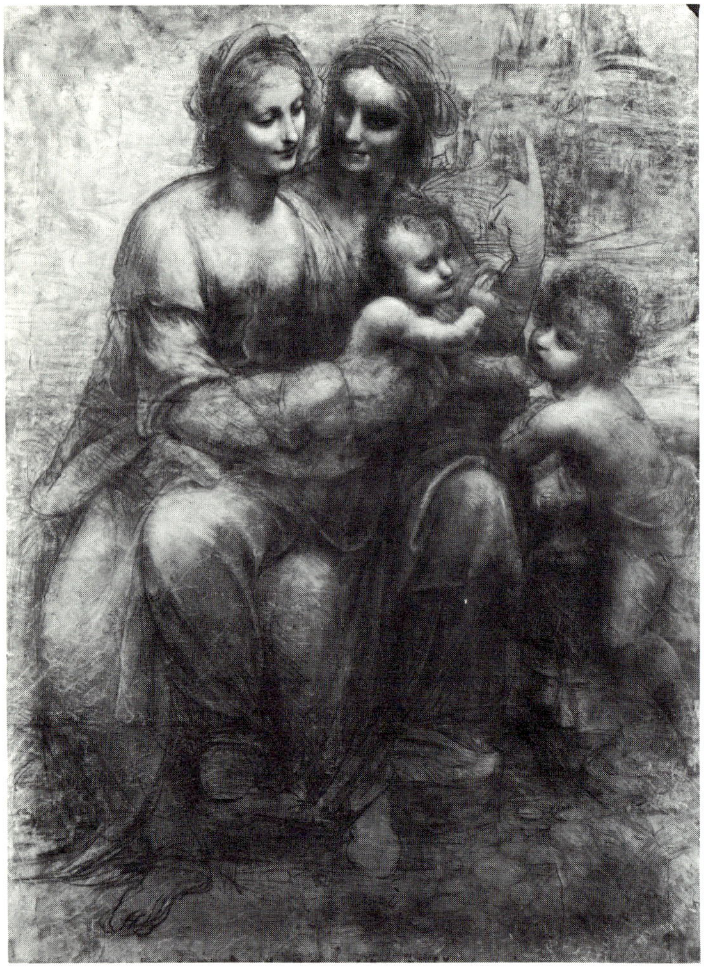

168. Leonardo da Vinci, *Virgin and Child with St. Anne.* (*London, National Gallery.*)

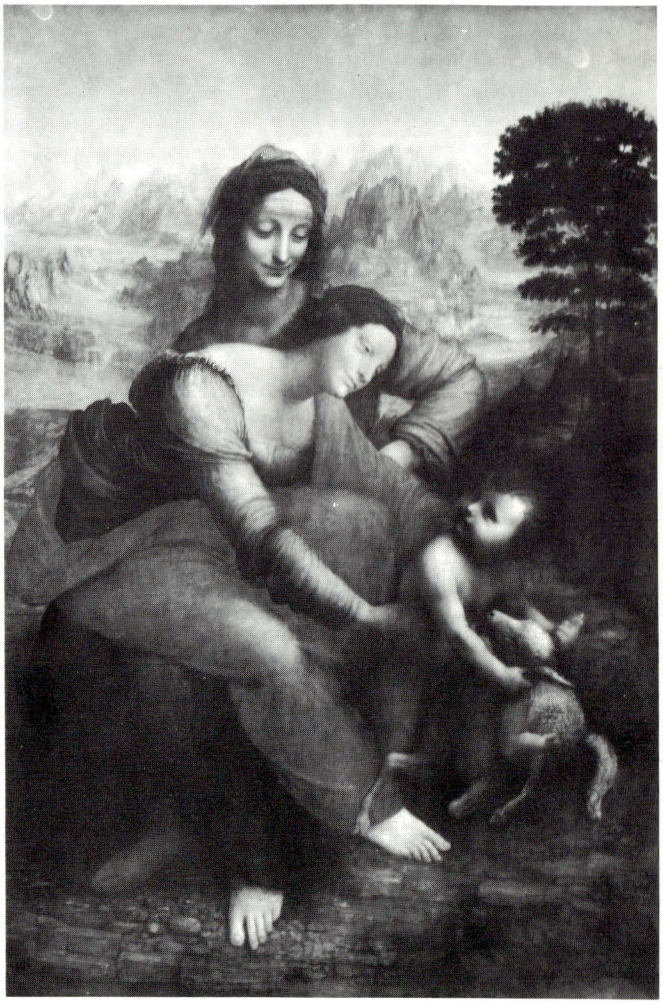

169. Leonardo da Vinci, *Virgin and Child with St. Anne.* (*Paris, Louvre.*)

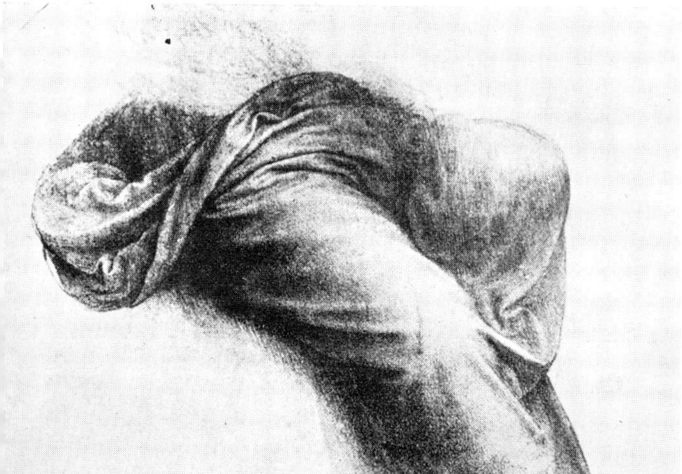

170. Leonardo da Vinci, *Study for a Seated Virgin.* (*Paris, Cabinet des Dessins, Louvre.*)

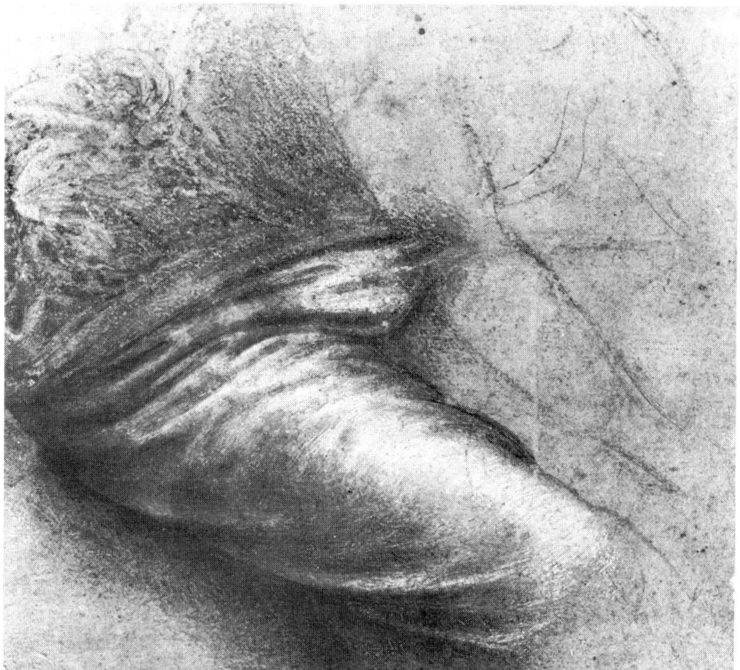

171. Leonardo da Vinci, *Study for a Seated Virgin.* (*Windsor Castle, Royal Collection.*)

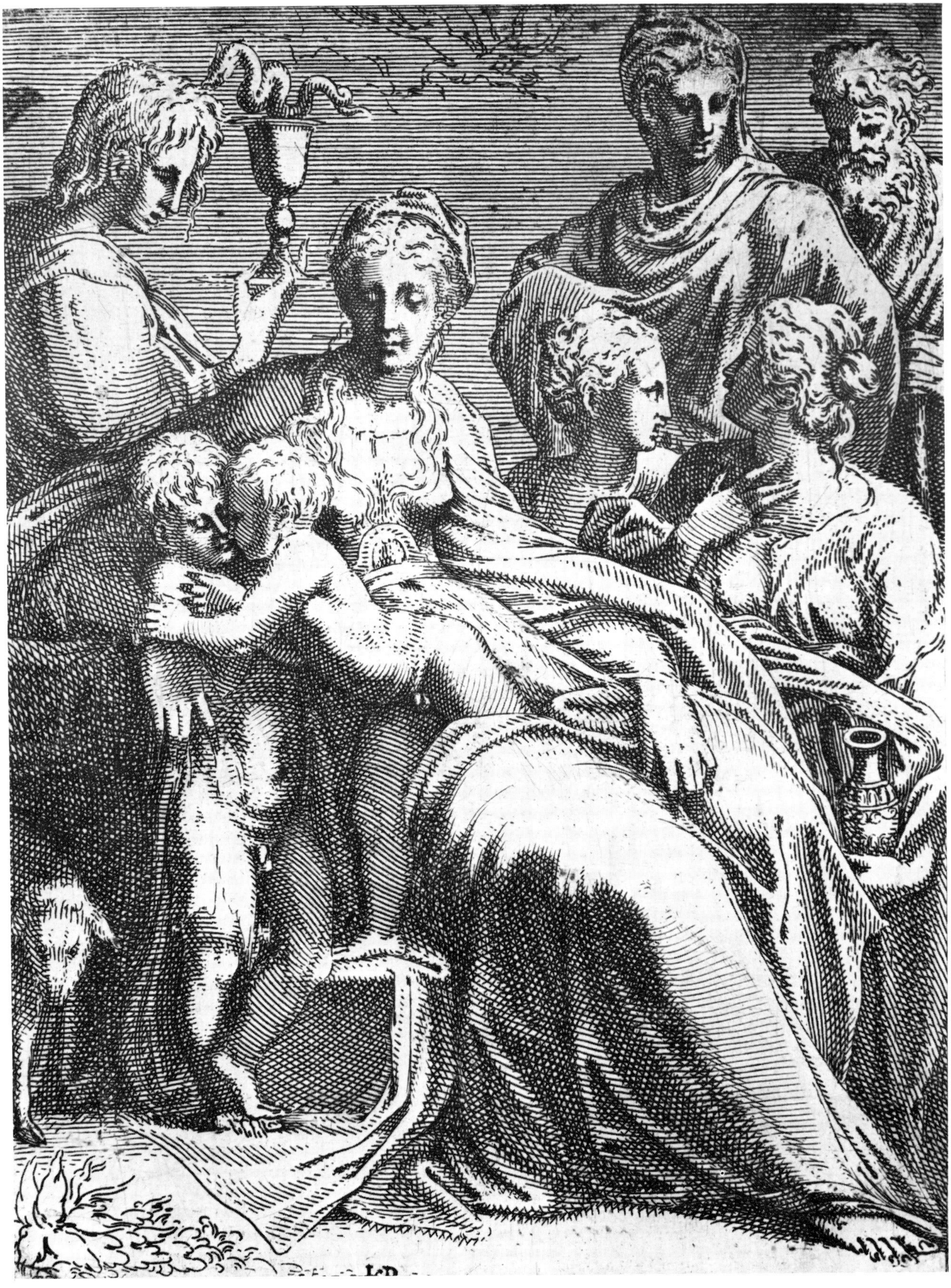

172. Master L. D. after Parmigianino, *Holy Family.*
(London, British Museum.)

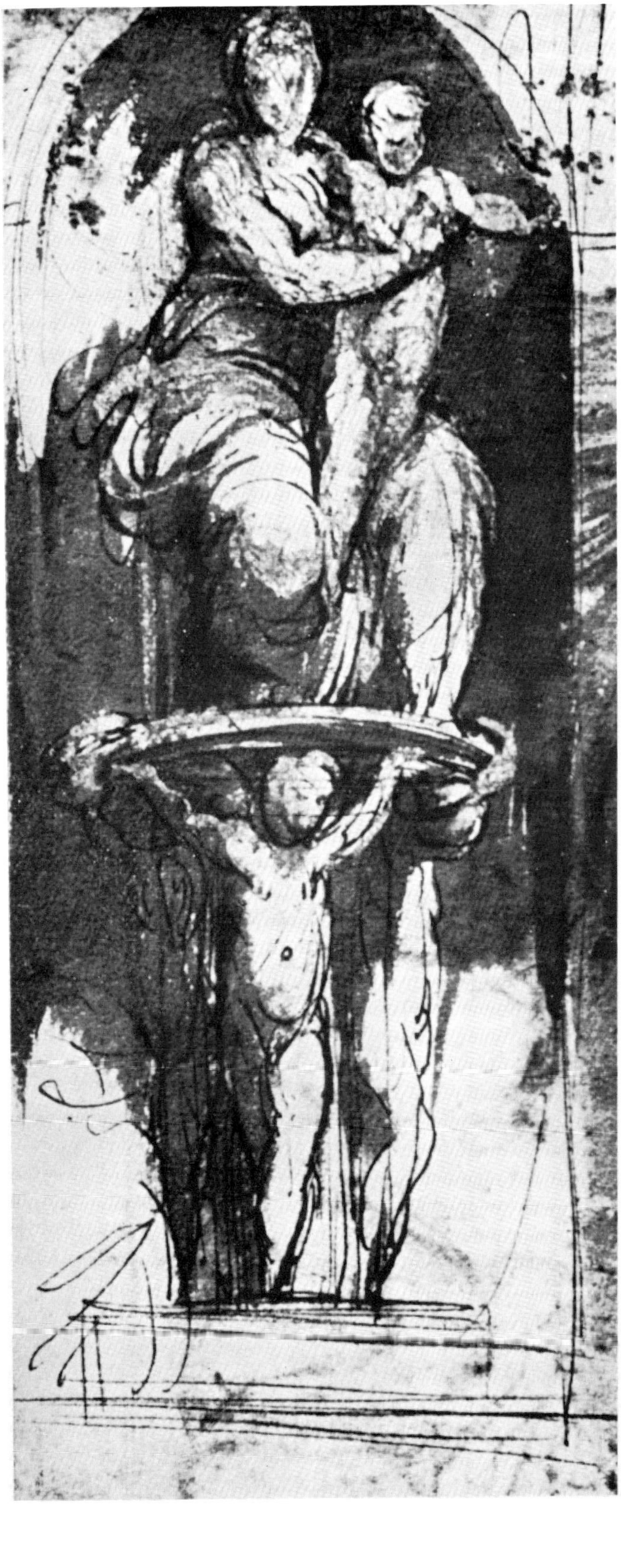

173. Parmigianino, *Study for the Virgin and Child.* (Chantilly, Musée Condé.)

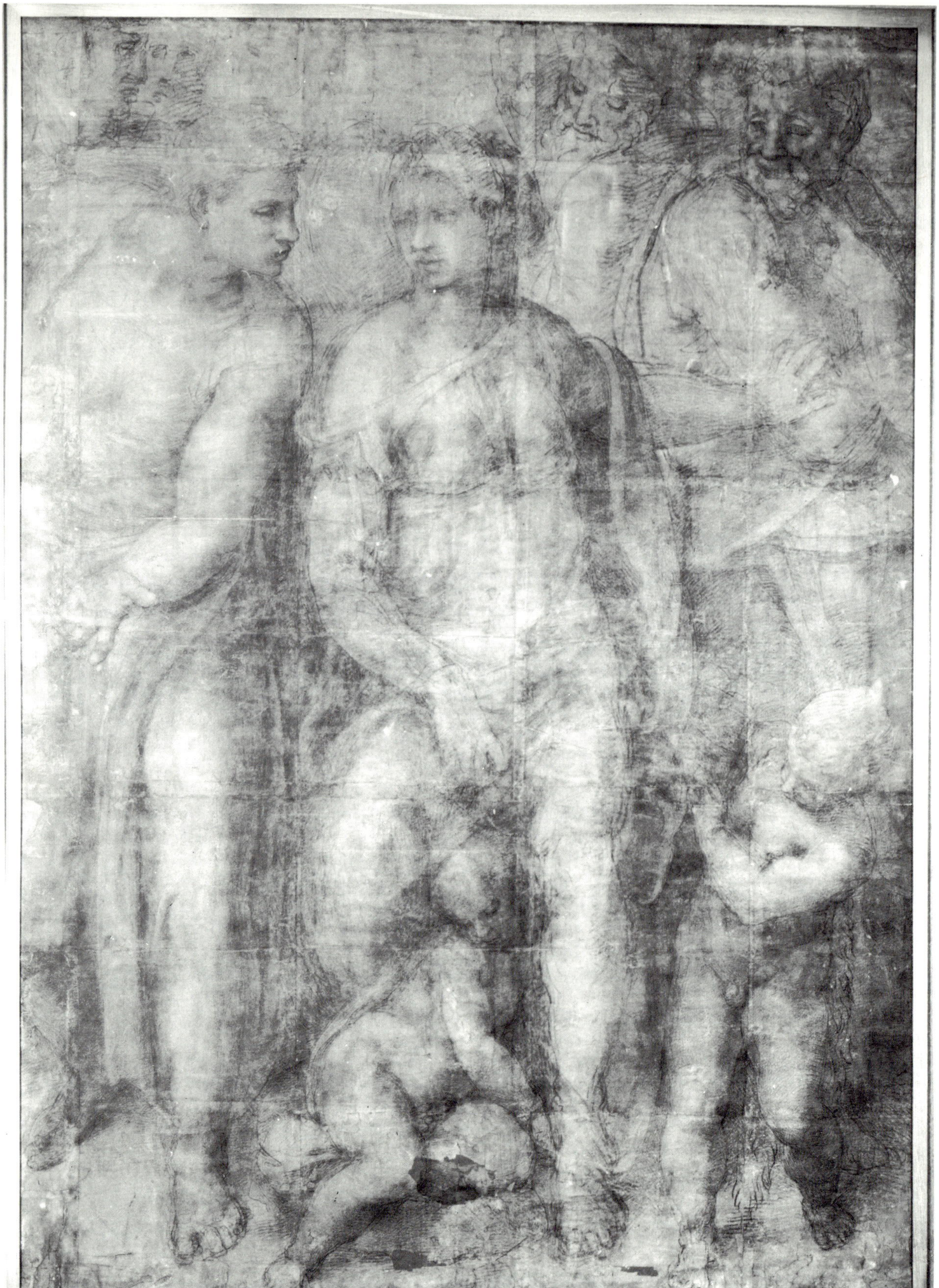

174. Michelangelo, *Epifania.* (*London, British Museum.*)

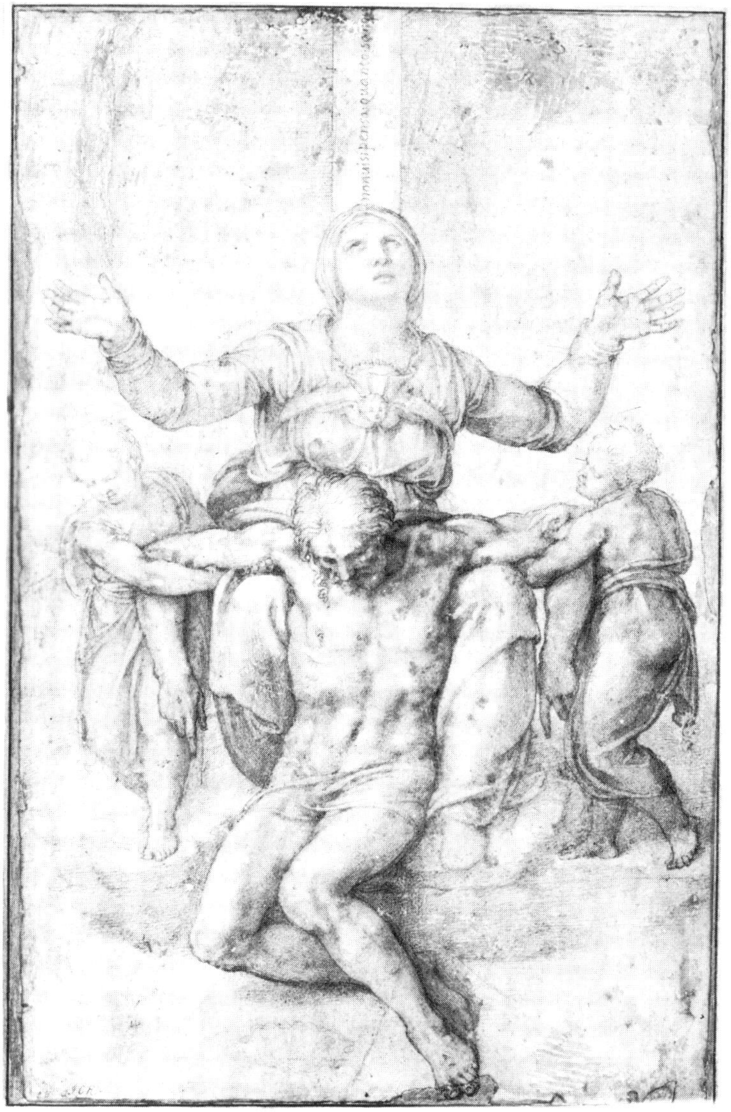

175. Michelangelo (?), *Pietà for Vittoria Colonna.* (*Boston, Isabella Stewart Gardner Museum.*)

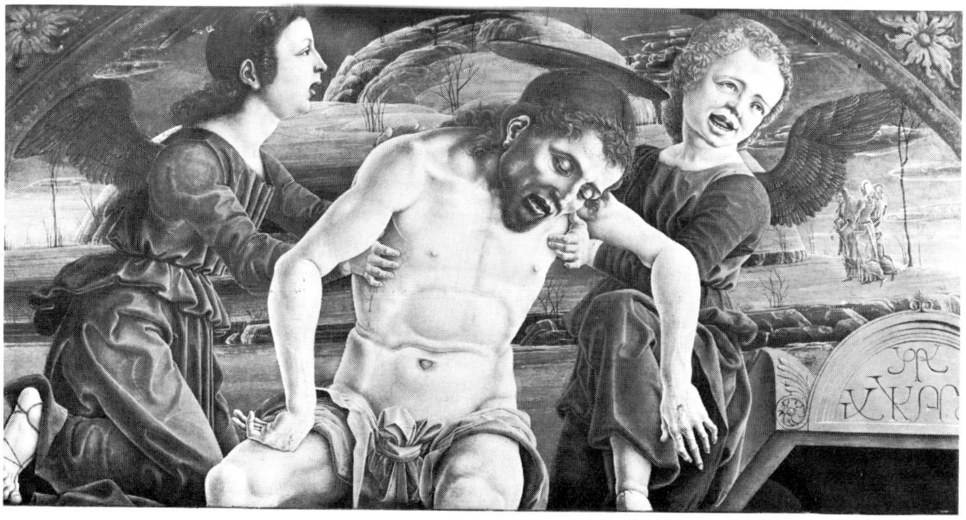

176. Cosimo Tura, *Dead Christ Supported by Angels.* (*Vienna, Kunsthistorisches Museum.*)

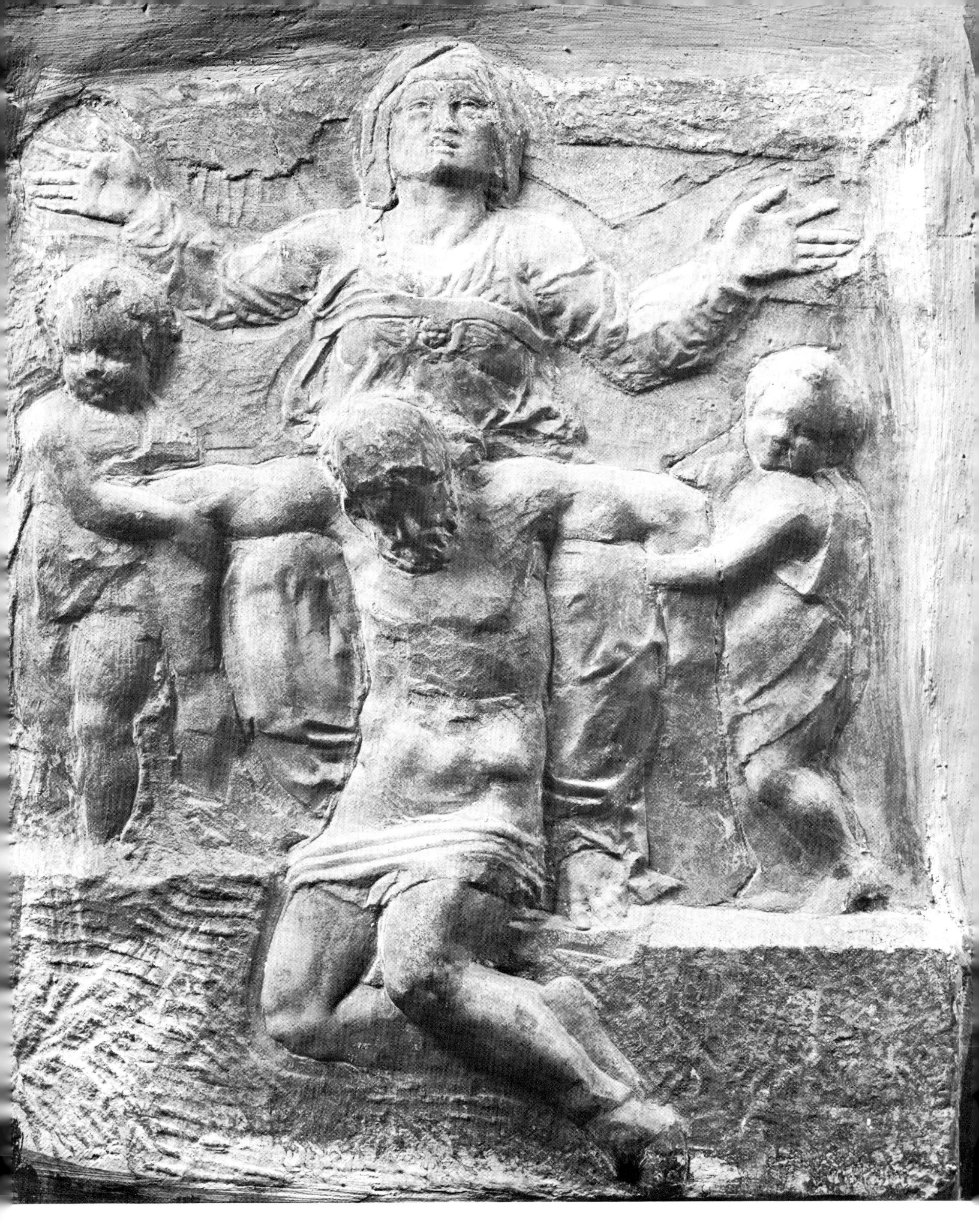

177. Michelangelo School, *Pietà for Vittoria Colonna.* (*Vatican, Museo Cristiano.*)

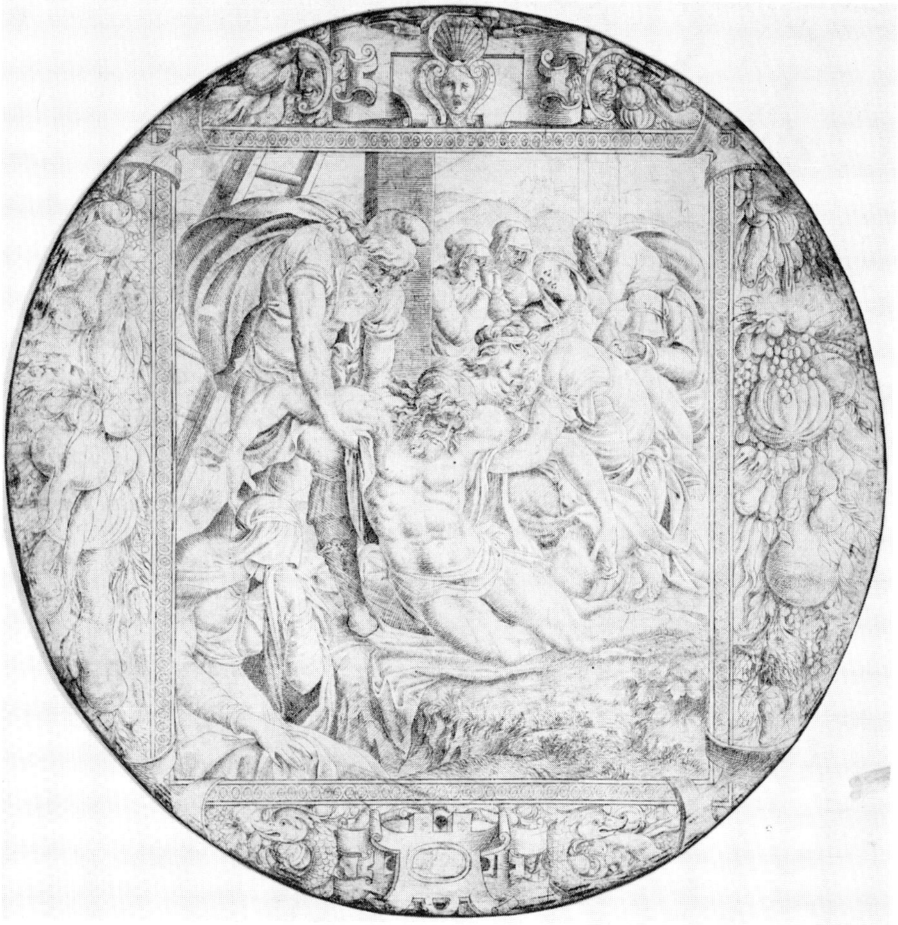

178. School of Fontainebleau. *Descent from the Cross.* (B., XVI, 25.)

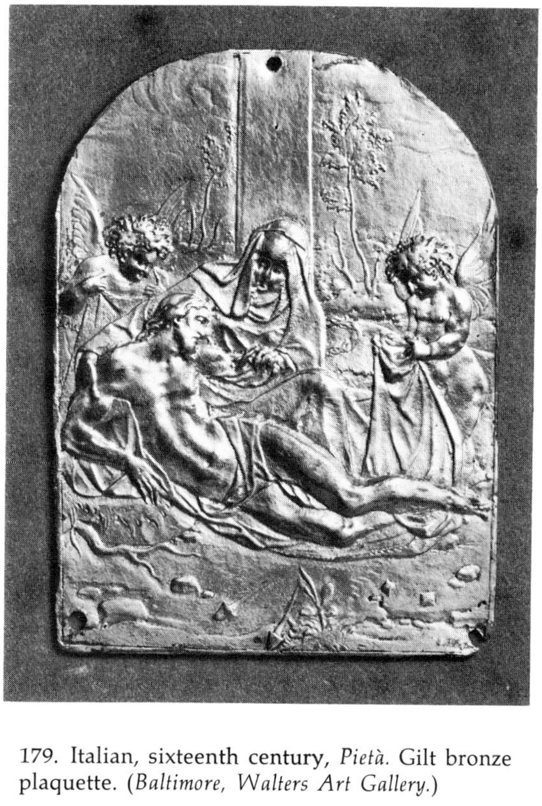

179. Italian, sixteenth century, *Pietà*. Gilt bronze plaquette. (*Baltimore, Walters Art Gallery.*)

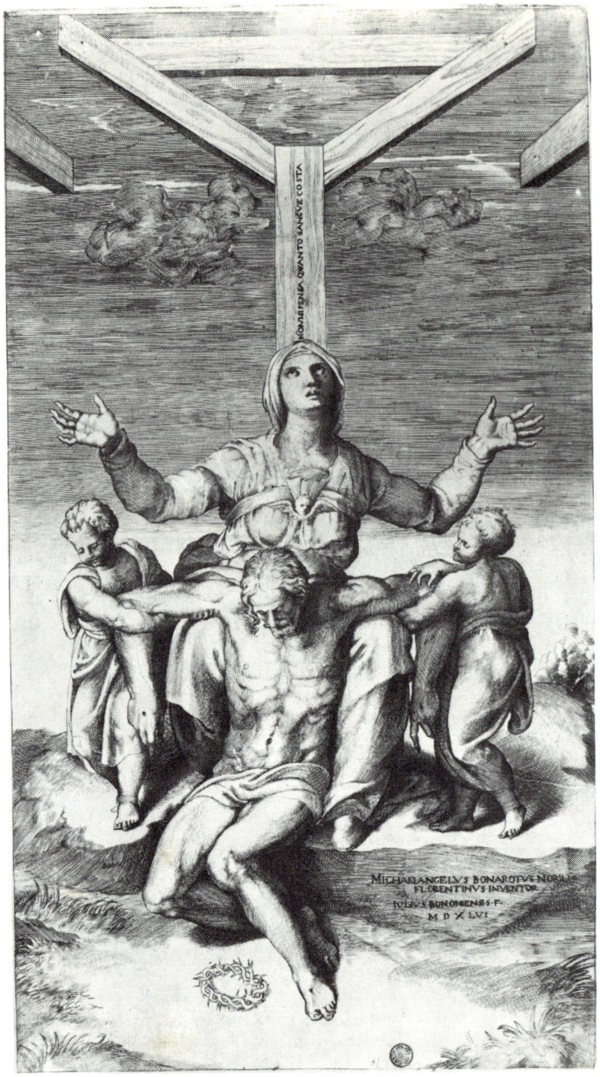

180. Giulio Bonasone, engraving after Michelangelo's *Pietà for Vittoria Colonna.* (*London, British Museum.*)

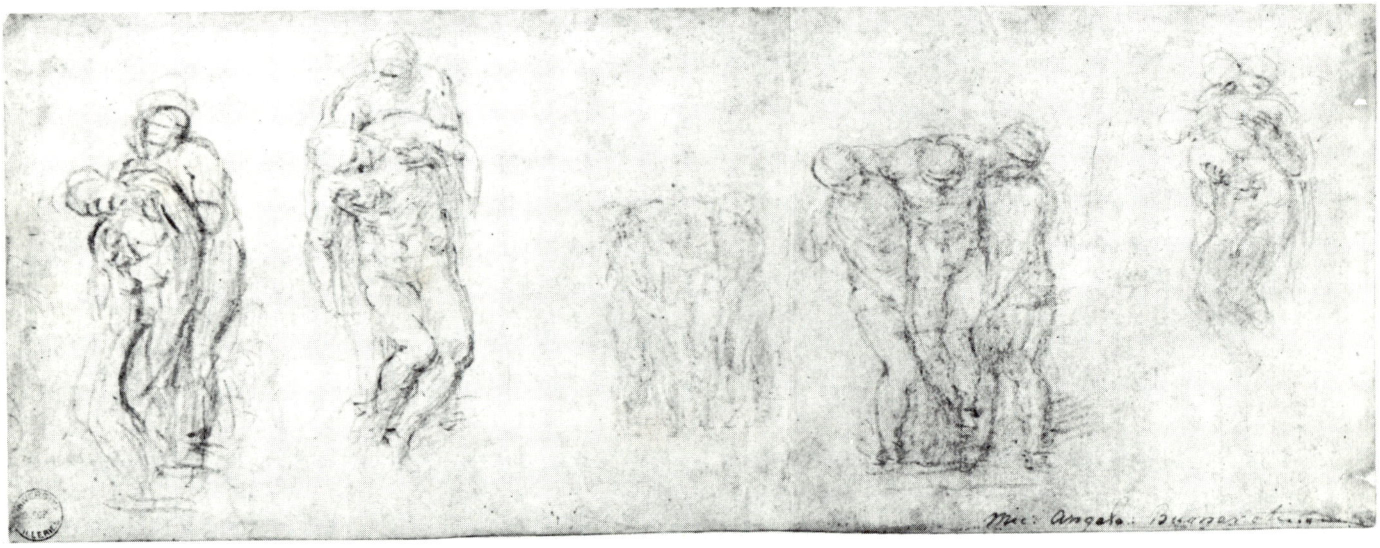

182. Michelangelo, *Studies for the Rondanini Pietà.* (*Oxford, Ashmolean Museum.*)

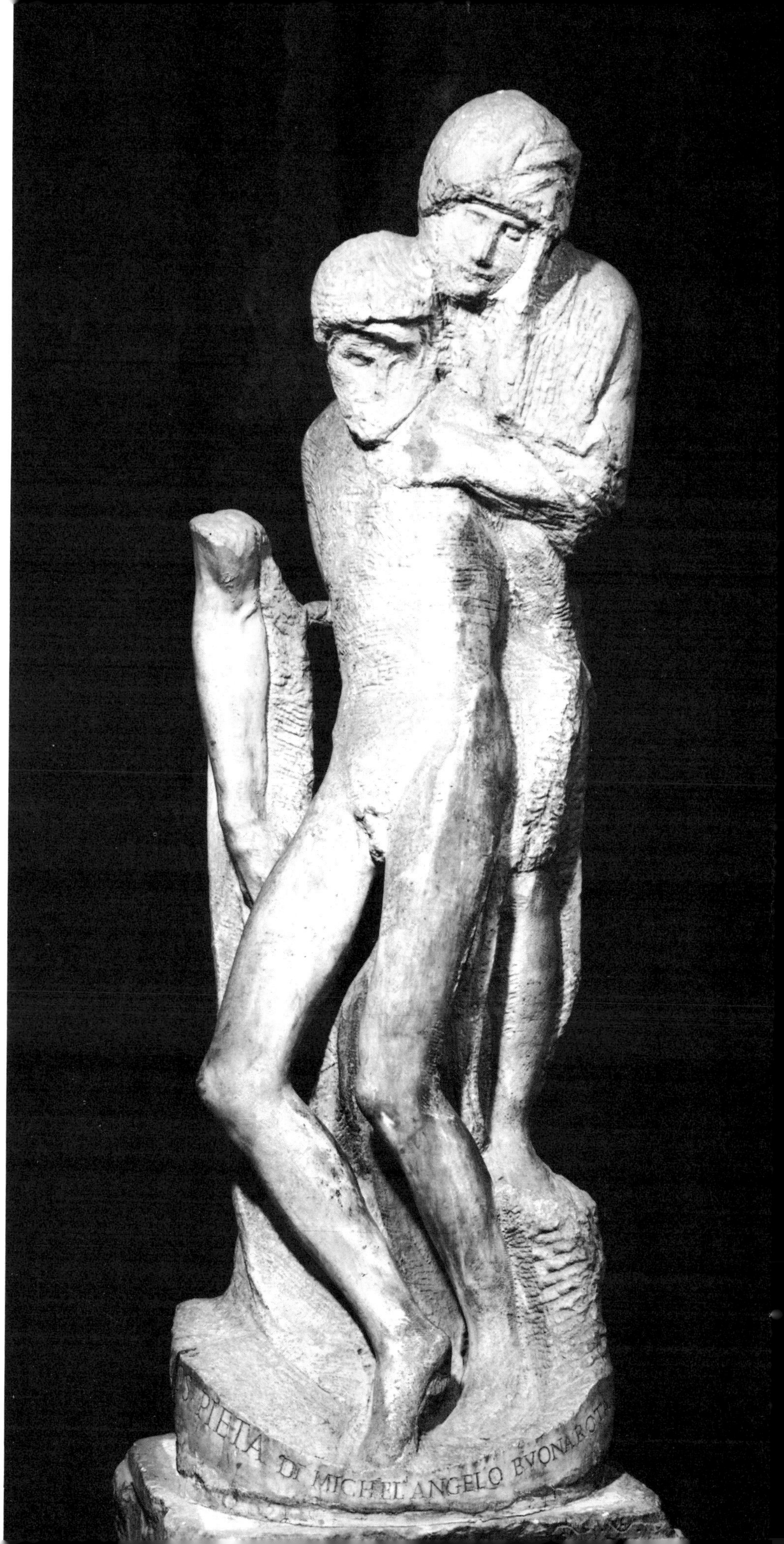

181. Michelangelo, *Pietà Rondanini.* (Milan, Castello Sforzesco.)

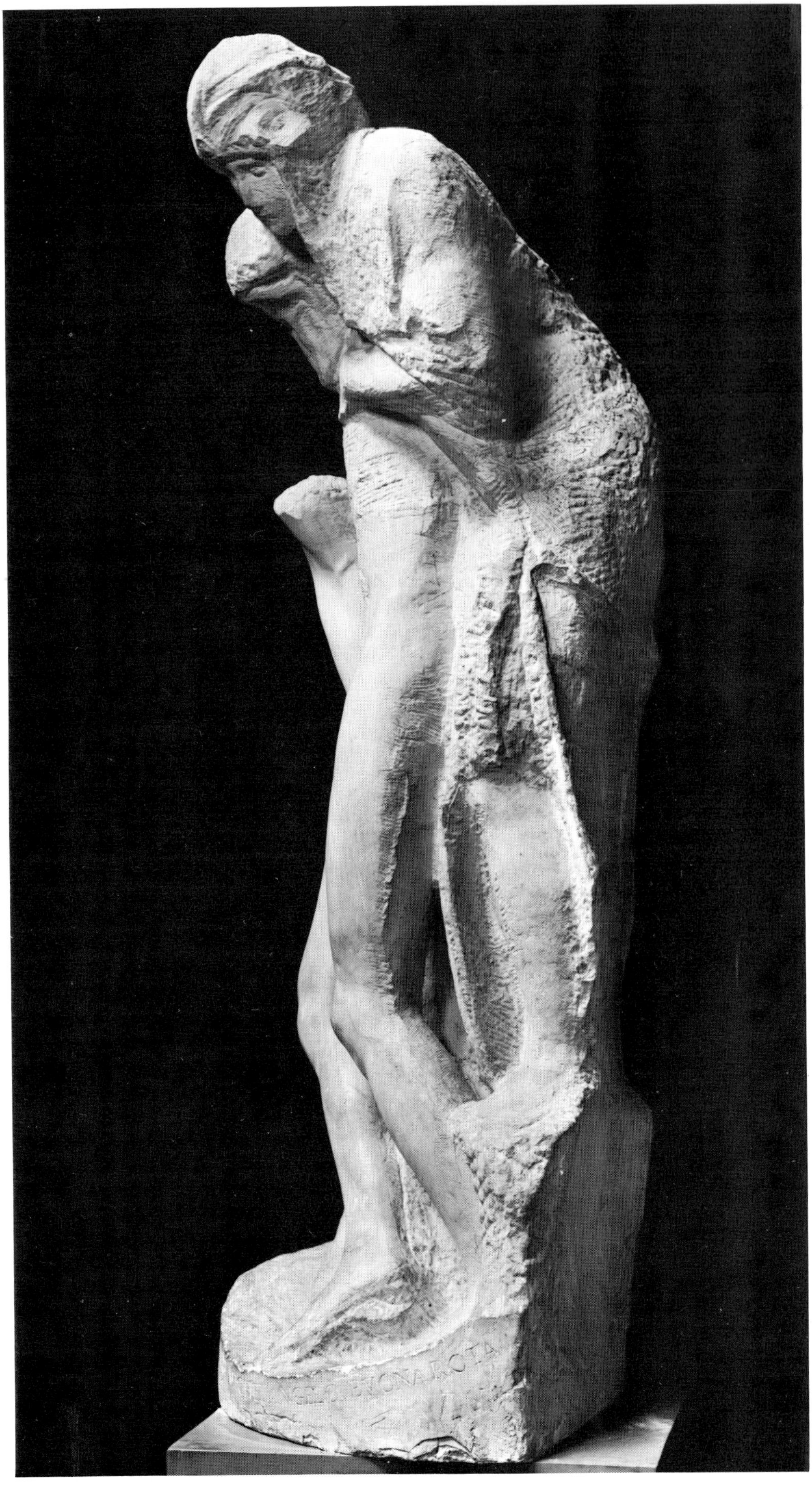

183. Michelangelo, *Pietà Rondanini.* (*Milan, Castello Sforzesco.*)

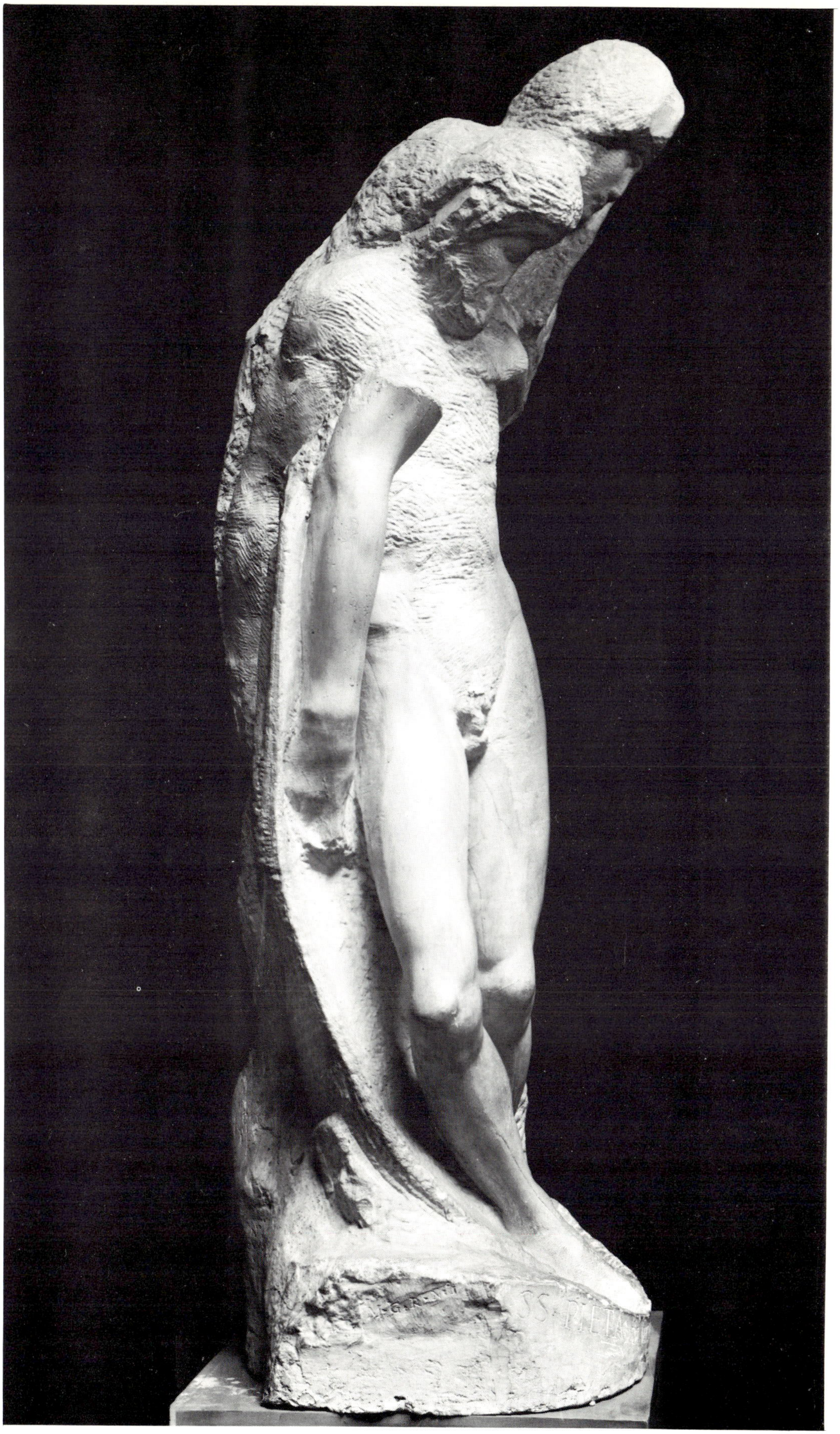

184. Michelangelo, *Pietà Rondanini.* (*Milan, Castello Sforzesco.*)

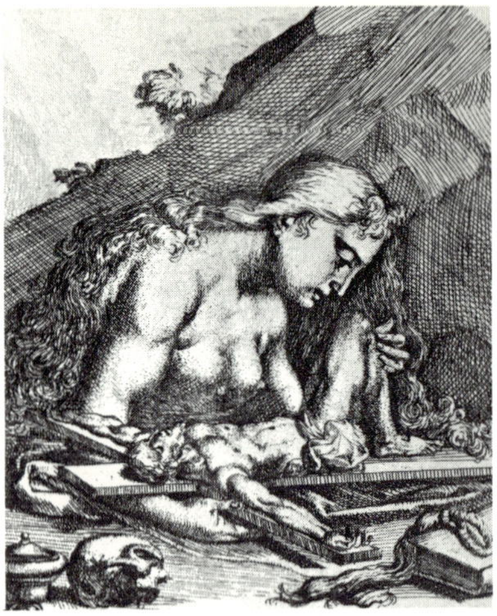

186. Marcantonio Bellavia after Annibale Carracci. (*Pensiere diversi . . .* , Pl. 10.)

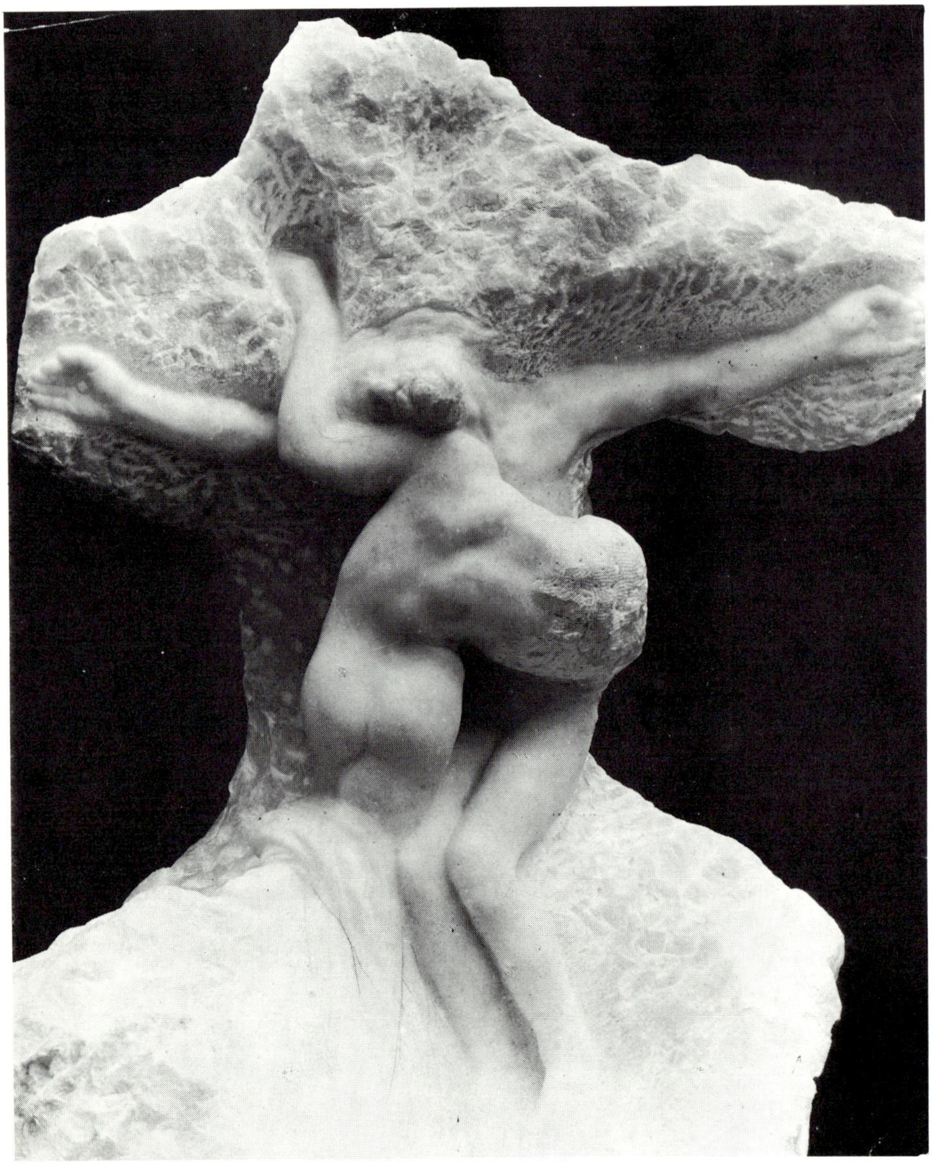

185. Rodin, *La Madeleine.*

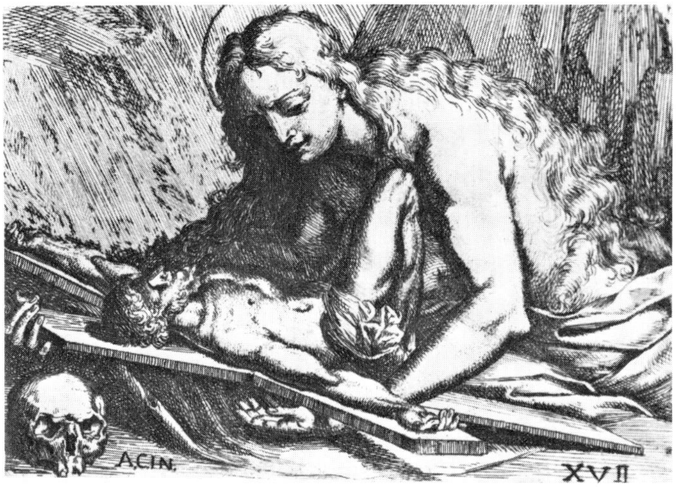

187. Marcantonio Bellavia after Annibale Carracci. (*Pensiere diversi . . . ,* Pl. 17.)

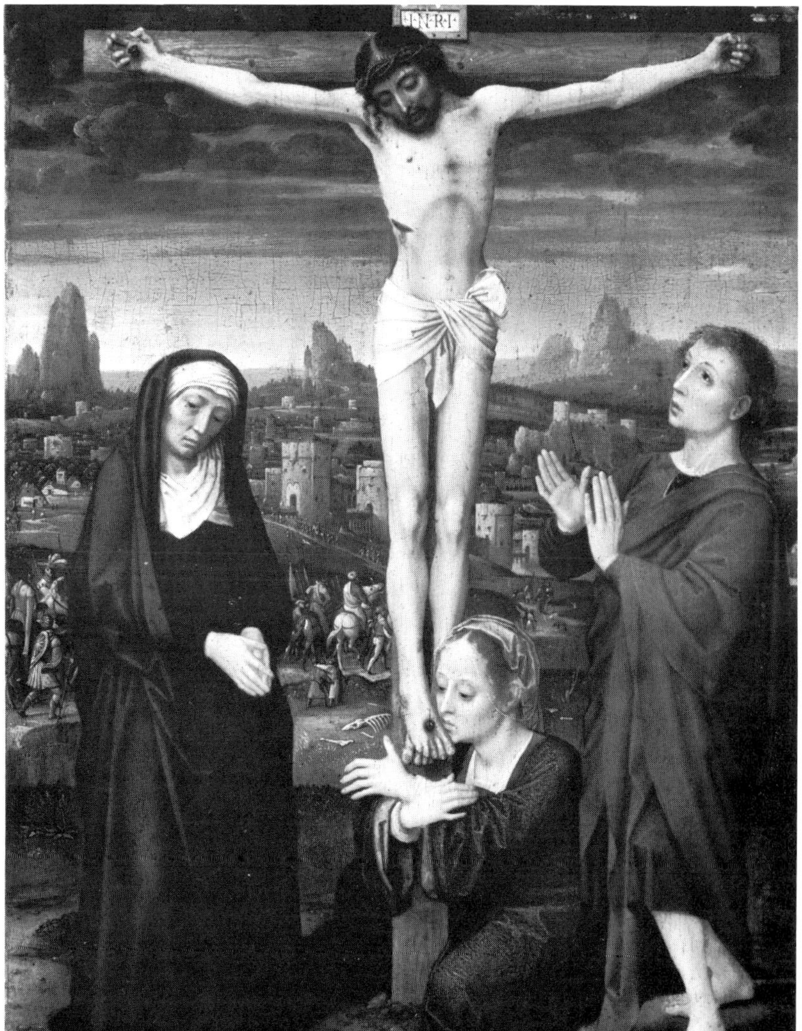

188. Isenbrandt, *The Crucifixion.* (*Los Angeles County Museum of Art.*)

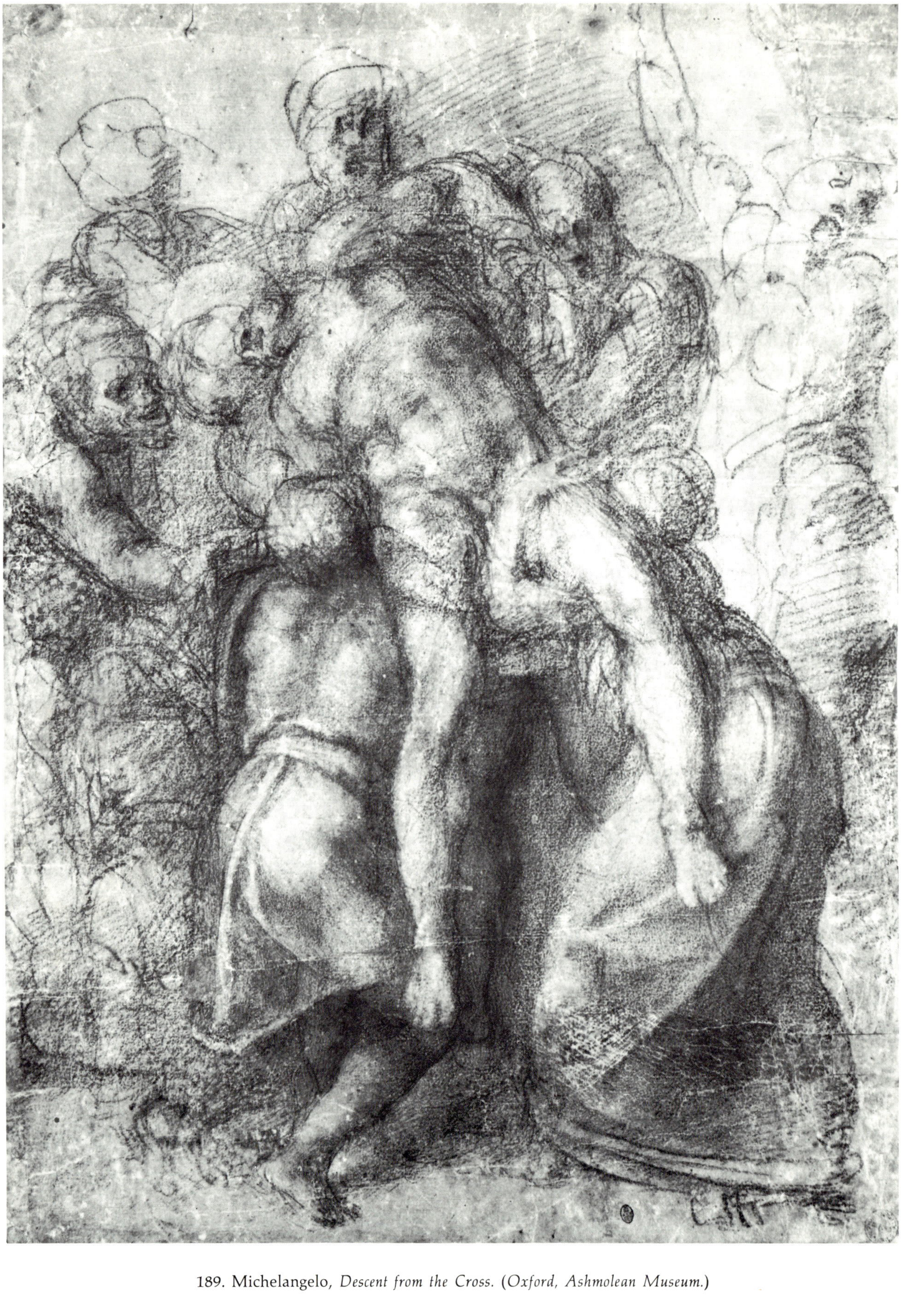

189. Michelangelo, *Descent from the Cross.* (*Oxford, Ashmolean Museum.*)

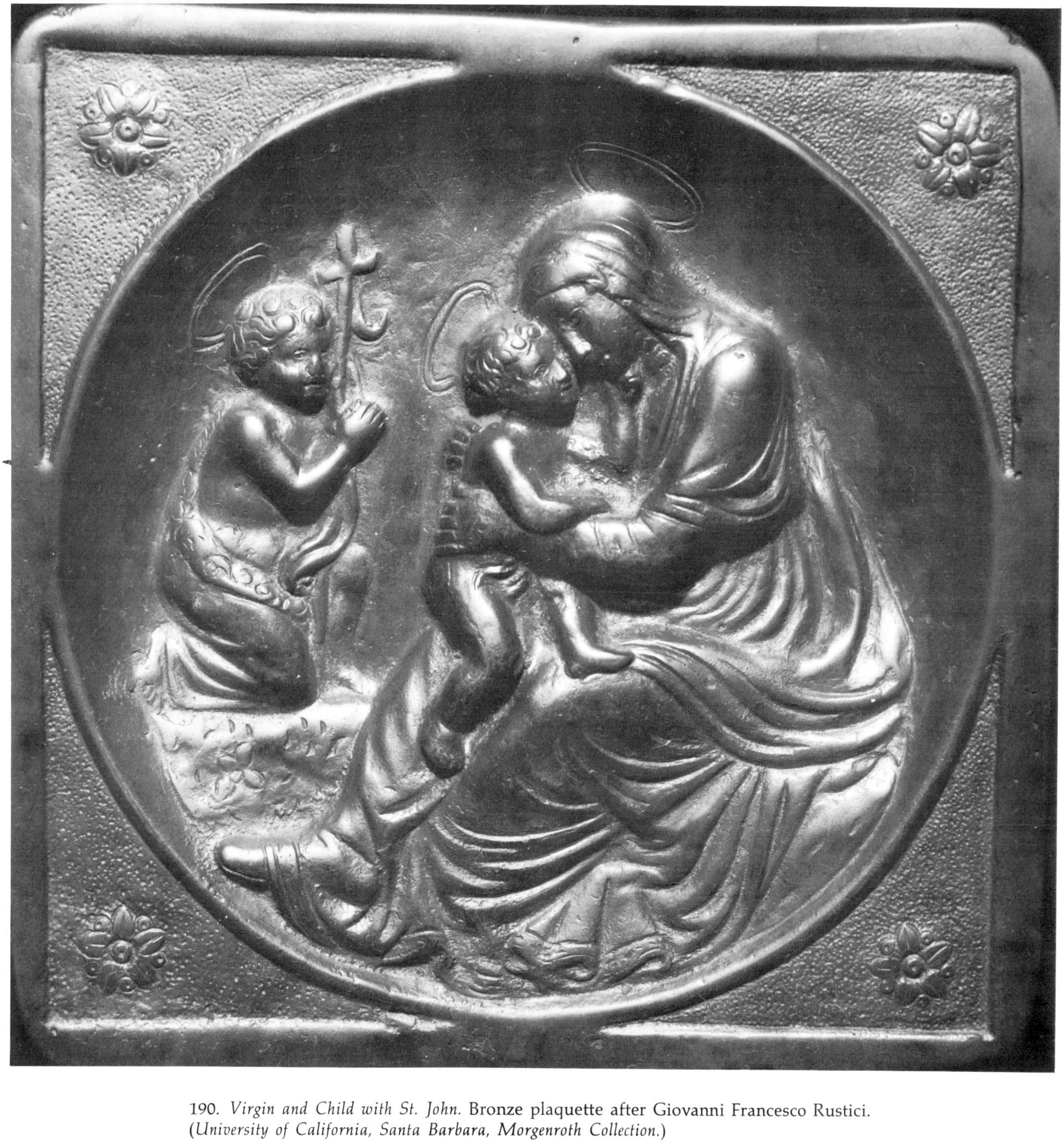

190. *Virgin and Child with St. John.* Bronze plaquette after Giovanni Francesco Rustici. (*University of California, Santa Barbara, Morgenroth Collection.*)

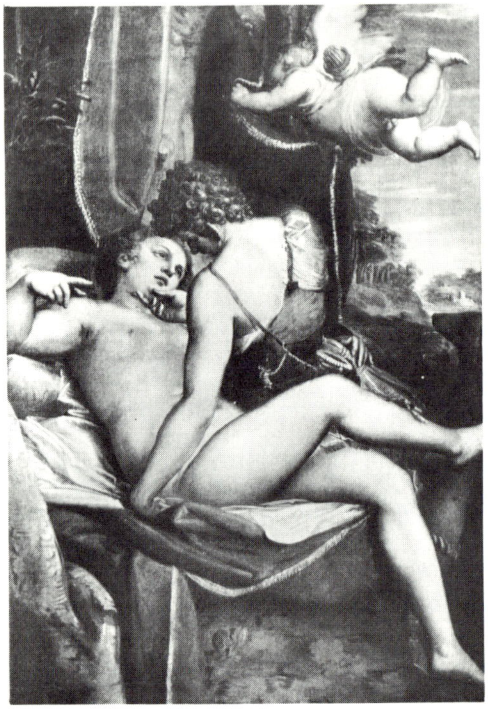

191. Luca Cambiaso, *Venus and Adonis.* (Rome, Galleria Borghese.)

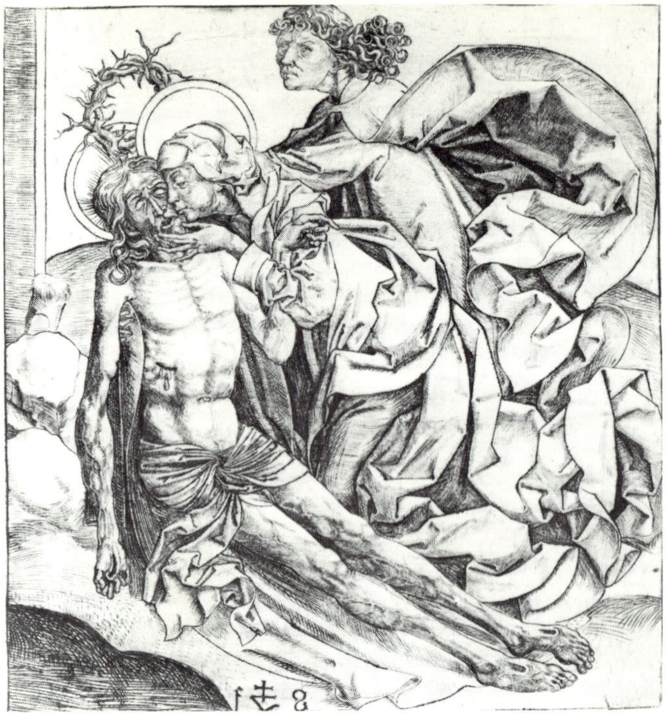

192. Veit Stosz, *Pietà.* (London, British Museum.)

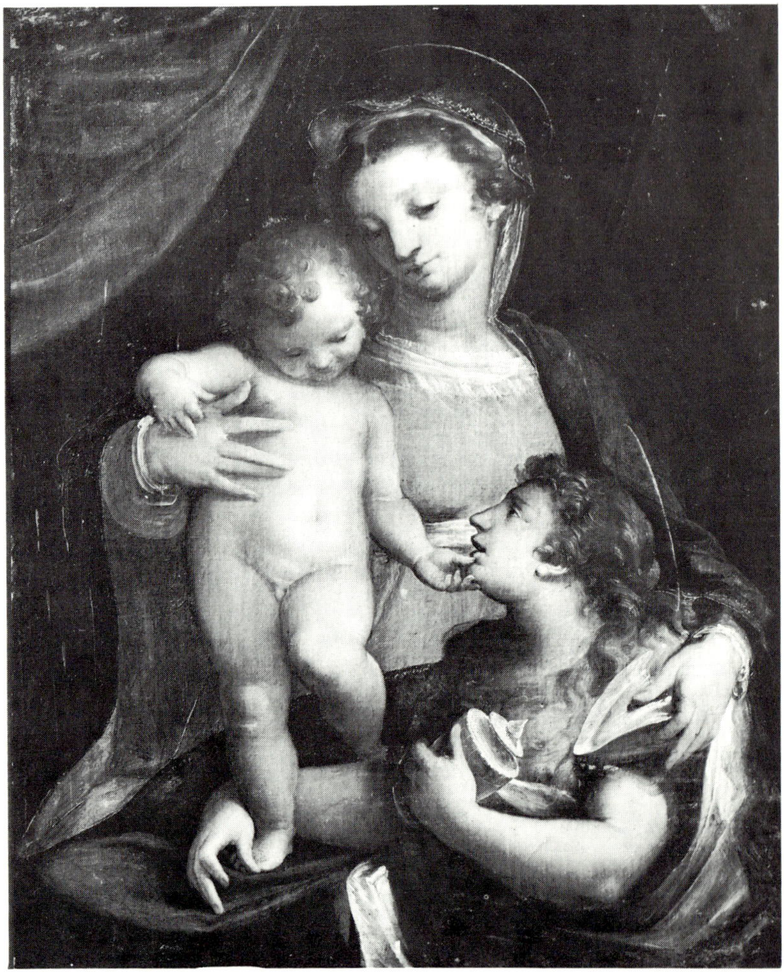

193. Luca Cambiaso, *Madonna and Child with the Magdalene.* (Genoa, Palazzo Bianc

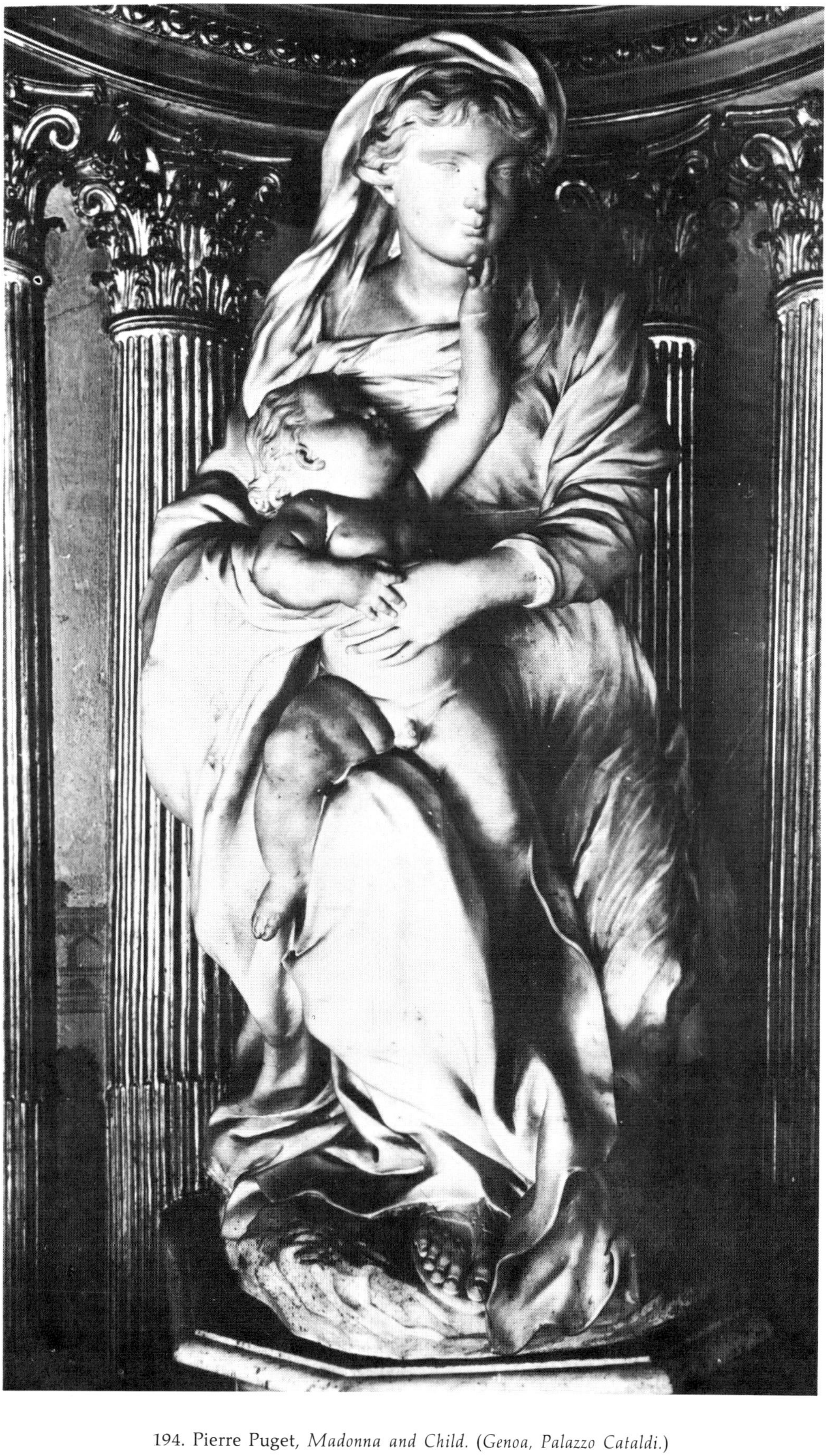

194. Pierre Puget, *Madonna and Child.* (*Genoa, Palazzo Cataldi.*)

5

Picasso and the Anatomy of Eroticism

ROBERT ROSENBLUM

No other great artist of our century has explored so wide a variety of human experience as Pablo Picasso; nor has any other modern artist considered the diversity of human behavior from so many different and even contradictory viewpoints. Within Picasso's vast scope, sexual themes are recurrent, and are subjected, in general, to interpretations consonant with the artist's preoccupations of the moment. Thus, in the early, pre-Cubist years, Picasso's occasional excursions into erotic art reflect, on the one hand, the libertine ambiance of an artist's Bohemia[1] or, on the other, the passive desperation of the ascetic figures who populate the works of the "Blue Period."[2] In the Cubist years, the rare references to sexual themes are, expectedly, intellectualized in the form of witty and risqué verbal puns concealed within a complex formal structure;[3] and in the Neoclassic years of the late teens and early 1920's, sexual motifs are generally interpreted in the guise of classical erotic mythologies.[4]

[1] As in the bedroom scene of the artist himself and a nude woman in the act of fellation; illustrated in Ove Brusendorff and Poul Henningsen, *Love's Picture Book* (Copenhagen, 1960), II, 112.

[2] For example, the 1904 drawing of a lean and bony couple who copulate in a joyless grip; illustrated in David Douglas Duncan, *Picasso's Picassos* (New York, 1956), p. 204.

[3] As in the clipping that spells out TROU ICI and is pasted under a lingerie advertisement in a Cubist collage of 1912; illustrated in Christian Zervos, *Picasso: oeuvre catalogue* (Paris, 1932 ff.), II (2), 378 (hereafter abbreviated as *Zervos*).

[4] For example, in a series of drawings of a centaur abducting a woman (1920), probably to be identified as the myth of Nessus and Dejanira. For illustrations, see the exhibition catalogues *Hommage à Picasso* (Paris, Petit Palais, 1966–1967) (dessins, No. 66) and *Picasso: 75th Anniversary Exhibition* (New York, Museum of Modern Art, 1957), p. 51, where three of these drawings are reproduced.

Such motifs, however, are relatively peripheral to Picasso's art until the mid-1920's. Then, for nearly a decade, the multiple aspects of sexual experience become a major obsession in his imagery, a phenomenon that may be explained, in part, by both public and private reasons. In public terms, this surge of interest in sexuality is a direct parallel to the official launching of the Surrealist movement in 1924, with its willful efforts to create an art and a literature that could release those suppressed wellsprings of erotic impulse which Freud had found basic to an explanation of human behavior.[5] And in private terms, this new fascination with the erotic may also reflect the particular tensions of Picasso's own life during these years, a period in which a growing hostility toward his wife, Olga Koklova, in the late 1920's was followed, in the early 1930's, by a period of erotic harmony in the person of a new mistress, Marie-Thérèse Walter.[6] Whatever the value of such speculations (and it should be cautioned that an art as complex as Picasso's can seldom be explained satisfactorily by a single, one-to-one correlation with the events of his personal life), there is no doubt that during the years that concern us here, from about 1927 to 1933, Picasso devoted much of his energy to the creation of images corresponding to the psychological and physiological realities of sexual experience.

These realities, as interpreted by Picasso, cover an enormous range. At times, sexual impulses, particularly those of women, are seen as menacing, brutal, and destructive; in other cases, these forces are viewed as almost Rabelaisian jokes that turn man into a clumsy, comical creature; and elsewhere, eroticism is celebrated as a lyrical, tender experience saturated with the magic of love and the miracle of procreation. Needless to say, these interpretative

[5] I have elaborated the problematic relationship of Picasso to Surrealism in a short essay, "Picasso as a Surrealist," in the exhibition catalogue *Picasso and Man* (The Art Gallery of Toronto, 1964), pp. 15–17; reprinted in *Artforum*, V (September, 1966), 21–25.

[6] The importance of Picasso's amorous life to the sexual character of his work of these years is stressed in the important study by Jan Runnqvist, *Minotaurus: en studie i förhallandet mellan ikonografi och form; Picassos konst 1900–1937* (Stockholm, 1959); and in John Berger, *The Success and Failure of Picasso* (Harmondsworth, 1965).

possibilities are by no means mutually exclusive, but form, rather, only some of the major leitmotifs which Picasso explores and combines in the rich, multi-leveled visual metaphors of these years.

The image of female sexuality as a monstrous threat dominates the work of the late 1920's, especially in paintings that juxtapose a male profile of classical beauty with a female head of grotesque ugliness. Characteristically, these works may be read on many levels, both public and private, aesthetic and psychoanalytic. Thus, if they may be seen as demonstrations of Picasso's capacity, after the critical years of Cubism, to work simultaneously within different and contradictory styles (a point made explicit in the artist-and-model series executed in 1927–1928[7]), they also suggest an image of hostile sexual confrontation between male and female, which may in turn originate in the growing personal frictions between the artist and his wife Olga.[8] In all of these works, the rationally ordered artist's world of rectilinear framing elements and of timeless serenity is shrilly assaulted by female heads of night-
mare horror and violence. In one (Fig. 195), the female head 195
almost seems to be an internal, psychological menace, a gaping maw with savage teeth and red barbed tongue that assails the profile from behind and from within its contours. In another
(Fig. 196), this succubus is momentarily caged, squirming, within 196
a frame, although a spearlike tongue form protrudes to assault the
male profile's open mouth. And in another (Fig. 197), an amoeboid 197
head, with a stitched mouth, swells toward the artist and threatens the space between him and the T-shaped form suggestive of picture frames, stretchers, and easels.

In such female heads, humanity is reduced to a subrational, bestial level, almost a pictorial equivalent of Freud's concept of the id. Indeed, in their descent down the ladder of evolution to primitive biological forms and functions, these heads can often

[7] Especially in the version that represents a grotesquely disfigured model who is translated by the artist into the traditional beauty of a classical profile (*Zervos,* VII, 243).

[8] Indeed, the profile is frequently identified as a self-portrait. See, for example, Roland Penrose, *Picasso: His Life and Work* (2nd ed.; New York, 1962), p. 235.

take on strong sexual connotations, even to the point where human physiognomy is related, in visual puns, to sexual organs. That such associations were fully as much in the mind of Picasso as in that of the viewer attuned to psychoanalytic speculations may be demonstrated by several drawings of 1929, preparatory to a painting of 1930, the *Crucifixion.*[9] Here, in studies of female figures wracked
198, 199 with grief (Figs. 198 and 199), the head is thrown back, upside-down, in a manner that confounds it with a view of the female pubic region. In the variations upon this theme, the metaphor is expanded in fantastic reshufflings of anatomy that produce startling biological configurations that may be read simultaneously as mouth and vulva, breasts and testicles, nose and penis, head hair and pubic hair.

Such preoccupations with Freudian sexual metaphors were not unique to Picasso, but were shared by much Surrealist imagery of the 1920's and 1930's, not only in the work of Miró but in that of the more photographic double and triple images invented by masters such as Dali and Magritte. A case in point is Magritte's
200 *Rape* of 1934 (Fig. 200), in which a female head and torso are combined in a visual pun that recalls as well the erotic double images of popular postcards published in the Surrealist magazine
201 *Minotaure* (Fig. 201).[10] Yet Picasso's art, freed from the realist premises of Dali's or Magritte's Surrealism (which permit only a finite number of readings of a multiple image), could create infinitely more evocative puns and metaphors. Thus, in his treatment of the human head alone, the sexual analogies invented are
202 prodigious. In one case, that of a harlequin head (Fig. 202), the mouth is aligned vertically to produce a vulva shape; in another, a
203 fantastically scaled dream monument (Fig. 203), the vertical slit of the mouth is armed with tiny sharp teeth which evoke that Freudian metaphor of psychosexual castration fear, the *vagina*

[9] *Zervos,* VII, 287. The *Crucifixion* and the related drawings are briefly discussed by Penrose, *op. cit.,* p. 235.

[10] No. 3–4 (1933), p. 89. Magritte's *Rape* was also used to illustrate the cover of André Breton, *Qu'est-ce que le Surréalisme?* (Brussels, 1934). For a reproduction of this cover, see Patrick Waldberg, *René Magritte* (New York, 1965), p. 158.

dentata. At times, the metamorphosis of a head into sexual organs is associated with a sleeping female figure, as if the relaxation of consciousness exposed the sleeper's repressed sexuality. Thus, in two paintings of 1927 (Figs. 204 and 205), a nap in an armchair 204, 205
permits the female sitter's mouth to open in sphincteral forms, round and oval, whose inherent savagery is emphasized by the continuous rings of teeth and, in one case, by the upward projection of a pointed red tongue. Or in other paintings of wakeful sitters (Figs. 206 and 207), the soft, padded comfort of an armchair 206, 207
is confounded with limp limbs which take on a potentially erectile quality that underscores the gross sexuality of the mouth's gaping, voracious slit. Such metaphors are paralleled closely in the work of Picasso's compatriot Miró, whose *Woman* of 1934, for example, offers analogies to these translations of the female head and body into primitive organs of almost exclusively sexual function (Fig. 208). Similarly, in Picasso's sculpture of the early 208
1930's, the bronze female heads often appear to be composed of pendulous, phallic forms that become synonymous with hair and nose (Fig. 209).[11] 209

The sexual creatures Picasso invented range from sadistic monsters, armed with fanged teeth, barbed tongues, and cutting carapaces, to unicellular blobs, whose tumescence transforms them into ludicrously clumsy shapes barely capable of performing their urgent functions. Such is the case in a drawing of 1927 (Fig. 210), 210
in which the setting is a seaside resort, a locale that often creates in Picasso's work of these years an ambiance where the human species can cavort, far from civilization, in a maximum of animal abandon. Here, a grotesquely swollen female nude, composed entirely of the same erectile tissue, attempts, with a fingerless hand, to manipulate a key in the lock of a beach cabana.[12] This action, recurrent in Picasso's seaside paintings and drawings of the late

[11] The sexual metaphors of these sculptures are underlined in Berger, *op. cit.*, pp. 159–160.

[12] Picasso himself has referred to his fascination for keys and to their appearance in these scenes of bathers. See Antonina Vallentin, *Picasso* (Paris, 1957), p. 90.

1920's, introduces yet another metaphor whose sexuality would be apparent even without knowledge of Freud.[13]

Even more androgynous and tumescent is the sexual monster
211 in another drawing of 1927 (Fig. 211), whose pneumatic plasm has expanded to a gravity-defiant stiffness that stands with momentary monumental grandeur in a hideous yet comical parody of the distorting protuberances produced by sexual excitement. These bizarre beings continue into the early 1930's, as in the *Bather with*
212 *a Ball* of 1932 (Fig. 212), in which another humanoid creature is seen in pursuit of her prey, a beach ball.[14] Appropriate to the imagery of the seaside game she plays, the flesh of the woman first evokes the rubbery gray matter of a beach ball itself, and then, in an inspired pun, goes on still further to confound human anatomy with the gummy substance of another object familiar to the seashore, a squid. As the human head is transformed into an inflatable bulb and the wind-blown hair turns into jet-propelled tentacles, the vertical mouth becomes simultaneously a squid's air vent and a vulva, so that, finally, the whole figure is metamorphosed before our eyes into a submarine creature obeying a primal urge.[15]

The protean fertility of Picasso's genius for inventing such complex biological fantasies is nowhere illustrated more succinctly than in the series of erotic anatomical drawings, dated February 22, 1933, which were published in *Minotaure* under the title *Une*
213 *Anatomie* (Fig. 213).[16] Here, not only are male and female organs juggled into totally ambiguous hermaphrodites, but sexual functions are even conflated with man-made mechanical and

[13] It may be noted that the sexual connotation of inserting a key in a lock is so basic that the Italian slang word for copulate is *chiavare.*

[14] I have also discussed this picture briefly from a somewhat different viewpoint in "The Unity of Picasso," *Partisan Review*, XXIV (Fall, 1957), 593.

[15] The confounding of a cephalopod with a human being is prefigured, incidentally, in Hokusai's print of an octopus in amorous play with a woman (illustrated in Chapter 3 of this volume, Fig. 107). Other sexual associations between human and marine creatures are found often in Surrealist imagery, as in Magritte's *Collective Invention* of 1934, which parodies the newborn Venus on the seashore as half-fish, half-human; illustrated in James Thrall Soby, *René Magritte* (New York, 1965), p. 28.

[16] No. 1 (1933), pp. 33–37.

carpentered parts. Funnels, chairs, cups, paired balls suspended by wires, are all absorbed by these erotic creatures, whose very torsos and heads can become ithyphallic and whose precarious equilibrium between the mechanical and the organic evokes a bawdy circus of sexual acrobatics.[17]

In most works of these years, diverse sexual behavior is conveyed through single figures, almost always female or androgynous, rather than through sexually active couples. Nevertheless, some works of this period do represent sexual couplings, interpreted with a comparably amazing variety that can swiftly change from the tragic to the comic, the sadistic to the gentle, the grotesque to the beautiful. In a pair of kissing heads of 1931
(Fig. 214), one finds a whimsical statement of the discrepancy 214
between sexual passion and modern manners. Man and woman assault each other with a familiar animal savagery of bristling hair, gnashing teeth, and barbed tongue, yet the lady closes her eyes demurely and the pair modestly conceal their bodies under what would appear to be a sheet. The juxtaposition of brute sexual instinct with the constraints of modern civilization recalls the irony of many of Picasso's other works in which the orderly trappings of modern man—beach cabanas, armchairs, middle-class interiors—are startingly contrasted with the revelation of a monstrously primal sexual force.

In an earlier related work of a kissing couple (Fig. 215), the 215
situation is far less specific in time and place, so that the couple now seem more unequivocally primitive in their clashing encounter. Sexually differentiated only by the pattern of their hair, this man and woman are about to devour each other with spearlike

[17] These comical forms, both hermaphroditic and mechanistic, are verbally paralleled by the well-known limerick:

> There once was a man from Racine
> Who invented a fucking machine.
> Concave and convex,
> It would fit either sex,
> With a bucket beneath for the cream.

tongues and locking noses, a grotesque reminder of the physical awkwardness and sadism implicit in an erotic kiss. Members of the same species are seen copulating in other works of these years, such as a painting of 1931 that again uses the seashore as an
216 environment conducive to bestial liberty (Fig. 216). Once more, the cabana introduces the irony of a modern setting, almost a symbolic shell of decorum into which the figures can retreat after they have disrobed and abandoned themselves to natural biological forces. Balanced in a difficult interlocking of heads, limbs, and torsos, they look at once animal and human, their brute energies countered by the almost tender caress of the male's caliper-like left arm, their tough hides softened by the suggestion of pink, sunburnt flesh.

Although the representation of a copulating couple is relatively rare in Picasso's work, in one year, 1933, he did execute a number of astonishingly imaginative variations upon this theme. At times, the motif was seen in classical guise, with one of Picasso's recurrent mythological symbols, the minotaur, as a male assailant
217 who rapes his partner (Fig. 217).[18] Half-bull and half-man, the minotaur is particularly appropriate to Picasso's frequent association of sexual desire with the eruption of bestial forces, though it should also be noted that this theme of pagan eroticism was paralleled at the same time by Matisse, whose illustrations for Mallarmé's *L'Après-midi d'un faune,* reproduced in the same number of *Minotaure*[19] as Picasso's *Une Anatomie,* similarly represented a subhuman mythological creature, a satyr, pursuing a nymph
218 (Fig. 218). But, characteristically, Picasso explored this theme down to its biological roots in a series of brilliant metamorphoses.[20]
219 In one drawing (Fig. 219), the locked limbs and torsos still seem as

[18] For another version of this minotaur rape, see *Zervos,* VIII, 12.

[19] No. 1 (1933), p. 72. These drawings were preparatory studies for the de luxe Skira edition, *Poésies de Stéphane Mallarmé* (Lausanne, 1932).

[20] These metamorphic copulation drawings, oddly enough, seem to be ignored in the Picasso literature, with the exception of Runnqvist, who briefly mentions them and illustrates one of them (*op. cit.,* p. 122).

human as in the minotaur drawing, but the heads of the sexual partners are transformed into images of more basic sexual instinct—that of the male becomes phallic, that of the supine female becomes a multiple organic form that suggests buttocks, vulva, and leaf. The equation of sexual passion with the unleashing of primal animal urges is seen even more fantastically in a drawing
of a couple copulating on a beach near a cabana (Fig. 220). Here, 220
the intricate maneuvering of limbs and torsos is geared solely to the brutal plunge of a gigantic penis into the female, an act whose inexorable force reduces the partners to a pair of brontosaurus-like monsters, whose tiny, reptilian heads look pitifully helpless and exhausted. Even lower on the biological ladder than these love-making fossils is another copulating couple who now pertain far more to a submarine species of crustaceans or mollusks than to
the human race (Fig. 221). Their male and female hair flowing like 221
antennae in aquatic currents, they lock shells in an armored sexual embrace. Other copulation drawings of 1933 introduce more comical elements. In one, the sexual encounter takes place on what appears to be a bed, a civilized intrusion that makes the couple's
animal metamorphoses all the more bizarre (Fig. 222). Both male 222
and female fingers turn into clumsily outstretched, doglike claws, whereas the heads descend to even lower biological realms. Once again, the female head turns into buttocks, vulva, and leaf, whereas the phallic shaft of the male neck blossoms into a kind of sea anemone, its antennae alertly extended. In another pure line drawing of a copulating couple, sexual activity is confounded not
only with organic but with mechanical metaphors (Fig. 223). Here, 223
above the serene horizon of the sea, the male, from the waist up, is miraculously airborne, a fantastic Freudian flying machine. His head becomes a steering wheel that permits him to locate and to drop his mechanistic genitals just above their female goal, the rotund womb of a fertility goddess, whose round head and buttocks are merged in generative harmony with the circular plant growth of the earth below. In yet another copulation drawing from this series, Picasso distills an image of such purity and economy

that we might not recognize its sexual theme without knowledge of
224 the related drawings of 1933 (Fig. 224). Here, only a minimum of organic shapes creates the quintessential statement of copulation—above and airborne, the tense thrust of the male genitals and blocky torso; below and earthbound, the swollen belly and buttocks and the extended head of an archetypal supine female form. And the whole is seen in the context of a natural setting that offers an encompassing trinity of earth, water, and sky. Again, it may be worth mentioning that, although the genius of these drawings is uniquely Picasso's, their conception and form are paralleled in the work of other artists, in particular Miró, whose art so often bears
225 analogies to Picasso's. Thus, Miró's *Lovers* of 1934 (Fig. 225) similarly turns a human couple into a grotesquely encumbered pair of subhuman creatures who desperately manipulate their amoeboid bodies and tiny heads to accommodate the urgent thrust of an enormous red penis.

Indeed, in his exploration of sexual imagery, Miró at times may even have preceded Picasso, especially in his conception of the female figure as a wellspring of procreative forces, a conception which Picasso investigated intensively only in the early 1930's.
226 As early as 1924, Miró's *Maternity* (Fig. 226) announced this theme: a creature both mammalian (to judge from the breasts viewed frontally and in profile and the young that suckle at them) and submammalian (to judge from the featureless head and antennae) becomes a metaphor for biological fertility, a theme further underlined by the wriggling spermatic form that flows toward the egglike
227 breast.[21] Or in the *Nude* of 1926 (Fig. 227), Miró metamorphoses a female form into a burgeoning tree, a Freudian Daphne from whose maternal trunk leaves and fruit blossom forth. Such veneration of female sexuality as a positive, life-giving force contradicted the pessimistic mood of Picasso's female monsters of the late

[21] The same theme is made as explicit in another Miró of 1924, *The Family,* in which the central female figure is dominated by a large vagina that forms the burgeoning, life-giving core of the entire family; illustrated in James Thrall Soby, *Joan Miró* (New York, 1959), p. 38.

1920's, whose sexual attributes and functions are usually destructive, like those of a female praying mantis.[22] But soon after, in the early 1930's,[23] Picasso adapted this alternate interpretation at a time when his wife Olga was replaced by a new mistress, Marie-Thérèse Walter, who seems to have inspired a series of works that view the female form as a passive, fecund vessel of biological mystery rather than as an aggressive, menacing trap.[24]

In *Woman with a Flower* of 1932 (Fig. 228), the Miró-like head 228
and hair become a pun on a sprouting seed, a germinal image which is further elaborated in the vigorous, tendril-like arms that pinwheel outward from the fruitlike breasts, and the curling stem and flower that likewise seem to grow from the fingers themselves. Generative metaphors are even richer in a series of reclining or sleeping nudes of 1931–1932 that may reflect the penchant of the blond, voluptuous, and placid Marie-Thérèse for napping and slumbering. In one of these works of 1931 (Fig. 229), the relaxation 229
of consciousness induced by sleep turns the figure into a human still life. A green leaf sprouts from the extended fingers; two pears in the right foreground are echoed by the two ripening breasts; the lunar and seedlike head, enclosed in a dark, uterine cushion, matures with the solar heat of dawn, whose warm rays are echoed in the fiery, radiant patterns of the wallpaper. Similarly, in another sleeping nude of 1932 (Fig. 230), human and vegetal images are 230
again confounded. Here, a philodendron plant, nurtured by the orange-red heat of the rising sun, virtually grows from the loins of

[22] The simile of a praying mantis is borne out, in particular, in such insectile heads, complete with vertical mandibles, as found in the *Seated Bather* of 1930 (*Zervos*, VII, 306).

[23] The date of the beginning of Picasso's relationship with Marie-Thérèse is frequently given as 1932, but Berger (*op. cit.*, p. 154) gives it as 1931. That Picasso did, in fact, know her in 1931 is suggested by the appearance in paintings of that year of the blond, lunar head associated with Marie-Thérèse. See, for example, the 1931 Cecil Beaton photograph of Picasso before such a painting; illustrated in Ronald Penrose, *Portrait of Picasso* (New York, 1957), p. 56.

[24] The profound impact of Marie-Thérèse on Picasso's art is particularly emphasized in Runnqvist, *op. cit.*, pp. 108–117, and in Berger, *op. cit.*, pp. 154 ff.

the nude sleeper, just as a white flower blossoms from her fingers, and her blond hair becomes a pun upon a seed that appears to be fertilizing an ovarian breast. It is worth noting that even in still
231 lifes of these years, like one of 1931 (Fig. 231), both the fruit and the inanimate forms of the table legs, pitcher, and bowl are charged with an intense, organic vitality, a tangle of churning, burgeoning shapes whose black spots within swelling spheres evoke the germinal force of fertilized seeds.

These metaphors of procreative magic and energy attain their richest form in two paintings of 1932 that introduce a mirror as yet another motif that may generate sexual imagery. In the earlier of the two, *The Mirror,* a sleeping blonde is seen before a mirror whose circular shape is warped into a more spiraling organic form
232 of uterine connotations (Fig. 232). Indeed, the image reflected in the mirror is not that of the sleeper's head, but that of her buttocks and groin, from which curls forth, along the reflection of the yellow seedlike hair, a green stem, as if from a fertilized seed. Such a conception of woman as a virtually headless bearer of pulsating, biological forces was familiar to these years, witness Arp's so-called Human Concretions[25] of the 1930's or even the photographs by Picasso's friend Brassai, whose studies of female nude torsos, their heads excluded from the camera's range of vision, were reproduced in the first issue of *Minotaure*[26] and offered a photographic equivalent to this equation of the female nude
233 with a primal goddess of fertility (Fig. 233).

In Picasso's art, these meditations reached their summit in the
234 great painting of 1932, the *Girl before a Mirror* (Fig. 234), whose imagery, like that of another masterpiece completed in the 1930's, James Joyce's *Finnegans Wake,* is so dense and metamorphic in its constantly fluid evocations of human and biological archetypes that

[25] Arp applied this generic title to many of his sculptures of this decade which reduce the human organism to a sub-intellectual, biological state of germinating plasm. The best-known example is that of 1935 in the Museum of Modern Art, New York, illustrated in James Thrall Soby, *Arp* (New York, 1958), p. 65.

[26] No. 1 (1933), p. 43.

only a few of its multi-leveled metaphors may be suggested here.[27] However, it can at least be said that this work synthesizes many of the sexual themes that preoccupied Picasso at this time. For one, female sexual impulses are conveyed in a series of transformations that evoke these welling biological forces and that contrast virginity and consummation. Thus, the lavender profile view of the girl, enclosed by a white veil-halo, suggests an overt innocence that opposes the more covert frontal view of a rouged cheek and lipsticked mouth upon a glowing, golden face; moreover, the ripening forms of breasts, womb, and buttocks are temporarily constrained by the rectilinear armature of the corseted, skeletal form which holds the figure taut from behind and by the angular frontal silhouette which suppresses the organs of generation that swell toward fulfillment. Furthermore, this tense ambiance of the awakening of sexual desire is underlined by the androgynous puns so common to Picasso's work of these years and soon to receive their most explicit statement in *Une Anatomie* of 1933 (Fig. 213). 213
Thus, the anatomies of both the girl and the mirror image that she embraces and contemplates evoke their male counterparts. In particular, the upraised left arm of the girl becomes, especially in conjunction with the testicular pair of breasts directly below it, an ithyphallic form whose sprouting fingers, in turn, metamorphose it into an image of generation, a kind of Aaron's rod. Later, in *Guernica,* when concerned in a different way with the female as the perpetuator of the human species, Picasso would again seize the visual and poetic analogy of male and female reproductive forms, this time by the close pairing of the testicles of the victorious bull with the breasts of the woman grieving over her dead infant.[28]

[27] The only close study of this painting is that by Carla Gottlieb, "Picasso's *Girl before a Mirror,*" *Journal of Aesthetics and Art Criticism,* XXIV (Summer, 1966), 509–518. Some highly suggestive comments about its multiple symbolism are found in Wylie Sypher, *Rococo to Cubism in Art and Literature* (New York, 1960), p. 280.

[28] The possibility of a sexual interpretation of *Guernica* has been suggested briefly by James. R. Mellow in "Picasso and the Shy Psychologist," *Lugano Review,* I (Summer, 1966), 99.

Once more, as in the sleeping nudes of 1931–1932, the *Girl before a Mirror* conveys the procreative attributes of sexual desire by a kind of vegetal imagery. The hair that adorns the girl's virginal profile is again seedlike; its mirror reflection is of a green tendril. Indeed, the anatomical zones of sexual function are generally verdant; and the breasts are like ripening fruits that exert organic, burgeoning pressures upon the concentric arcs and circles that surround them. Perhaps most telling is the black, nipple-like spot on the breast reflected at the right of the mirror. As if newly fertilized, this egg shape blossoms forth with a green sprout that in turn is continued above in the green protective layer which surrounds a half-formed head of strange, primitive mystery, both embryo and death mask. Uterus and shroud, the oval enclosure of the mirror image carries within it the wonder and terror of the ultimates of human experience. For Picasso in the *Girl before a Mirror,* these ultimates meant primarily the biological cycle of life, death, and rebirth, a cycle perpetuated by those sexual tensions which, from 1927 to 1933, also created a reigning muse, alternately monstrous and lyrical, for his art.

FIGURES

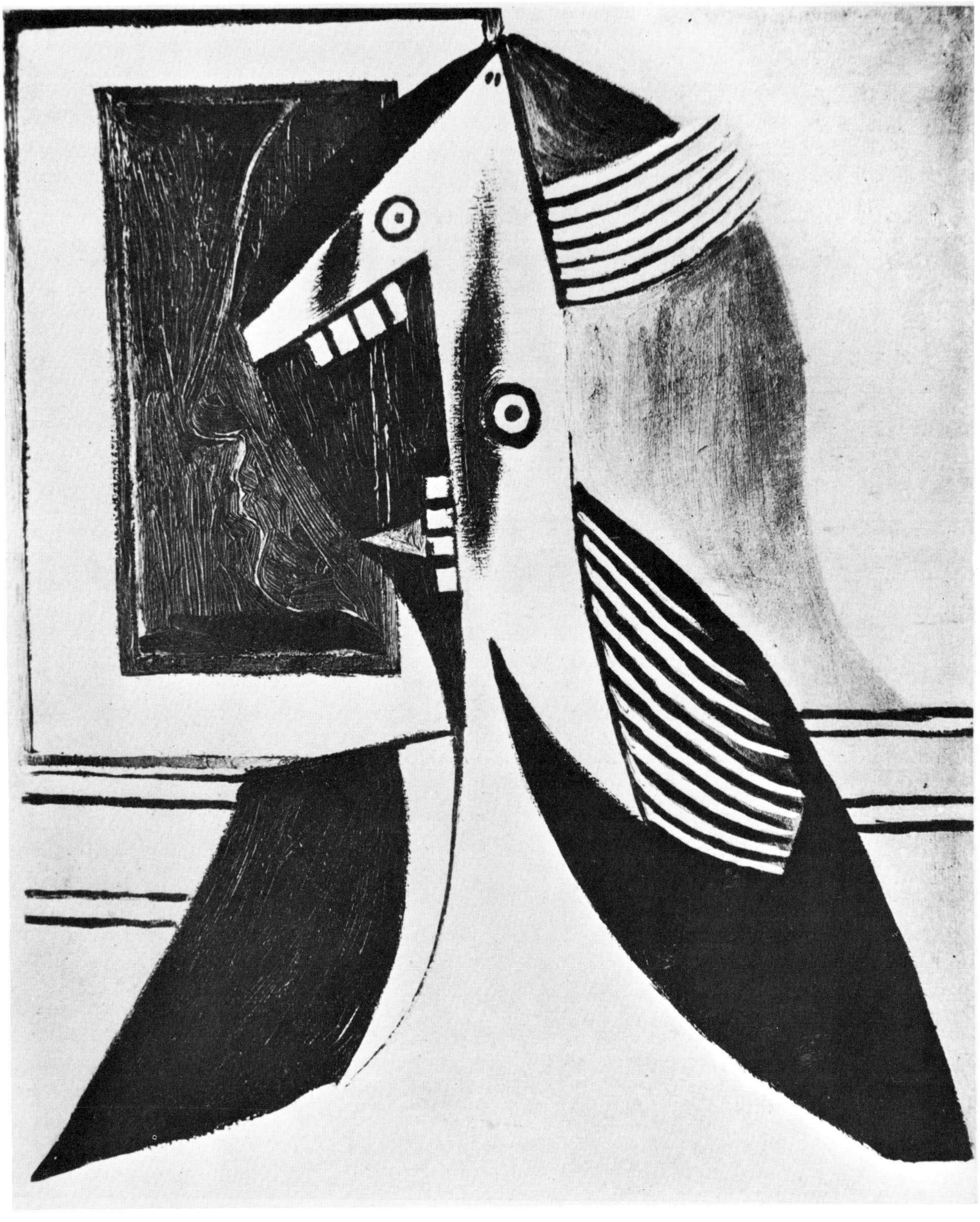

195. Picasso, *Woman's Head and Profile*, 1929. (**Philadelphia**, Collection of Mrs. J. Wintersteen.)

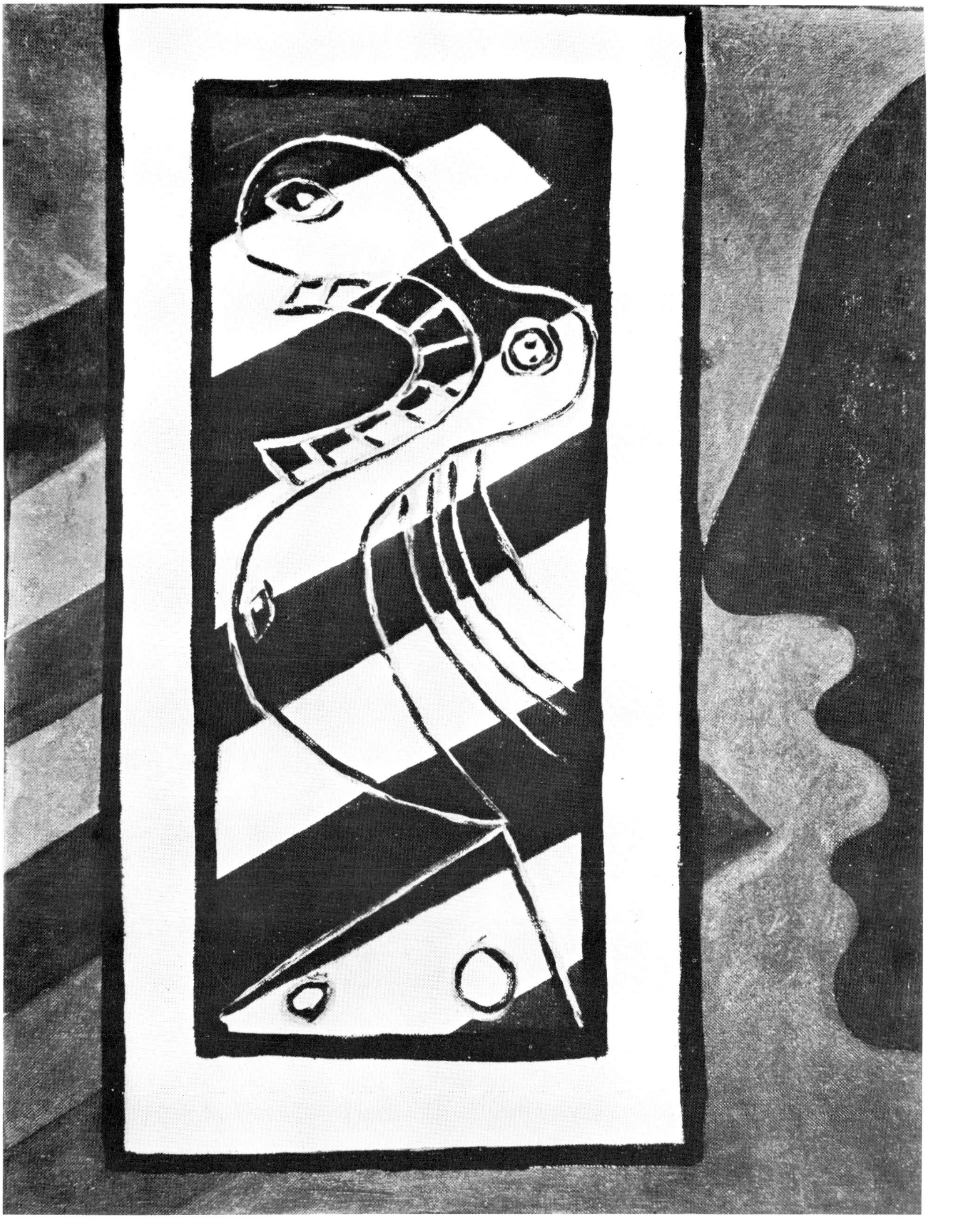

196. Picasso, *Woman's Head and Profile,* 1927–1928.

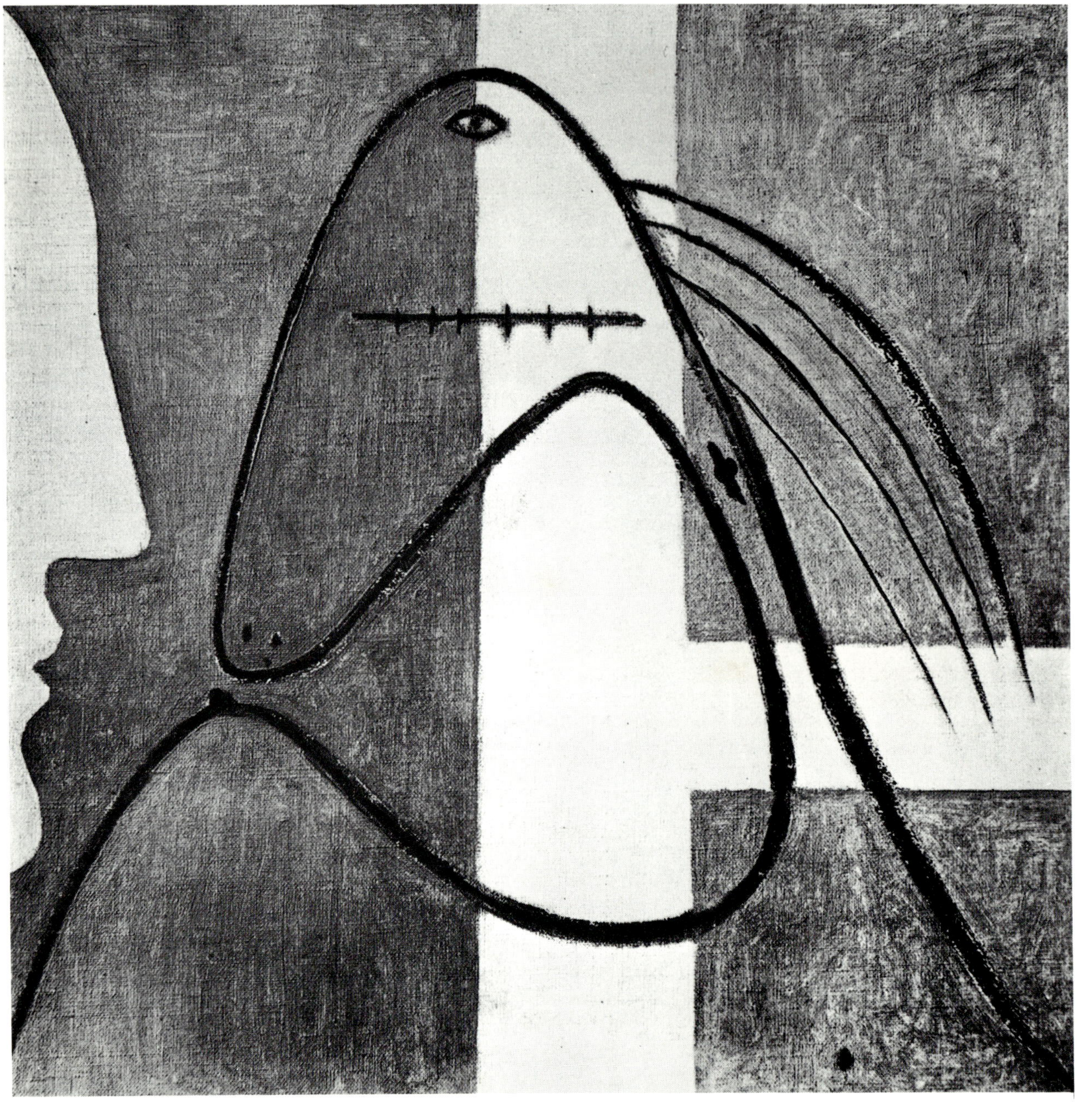

197. Picasso, *Woman's Head and Profile*, 1928.

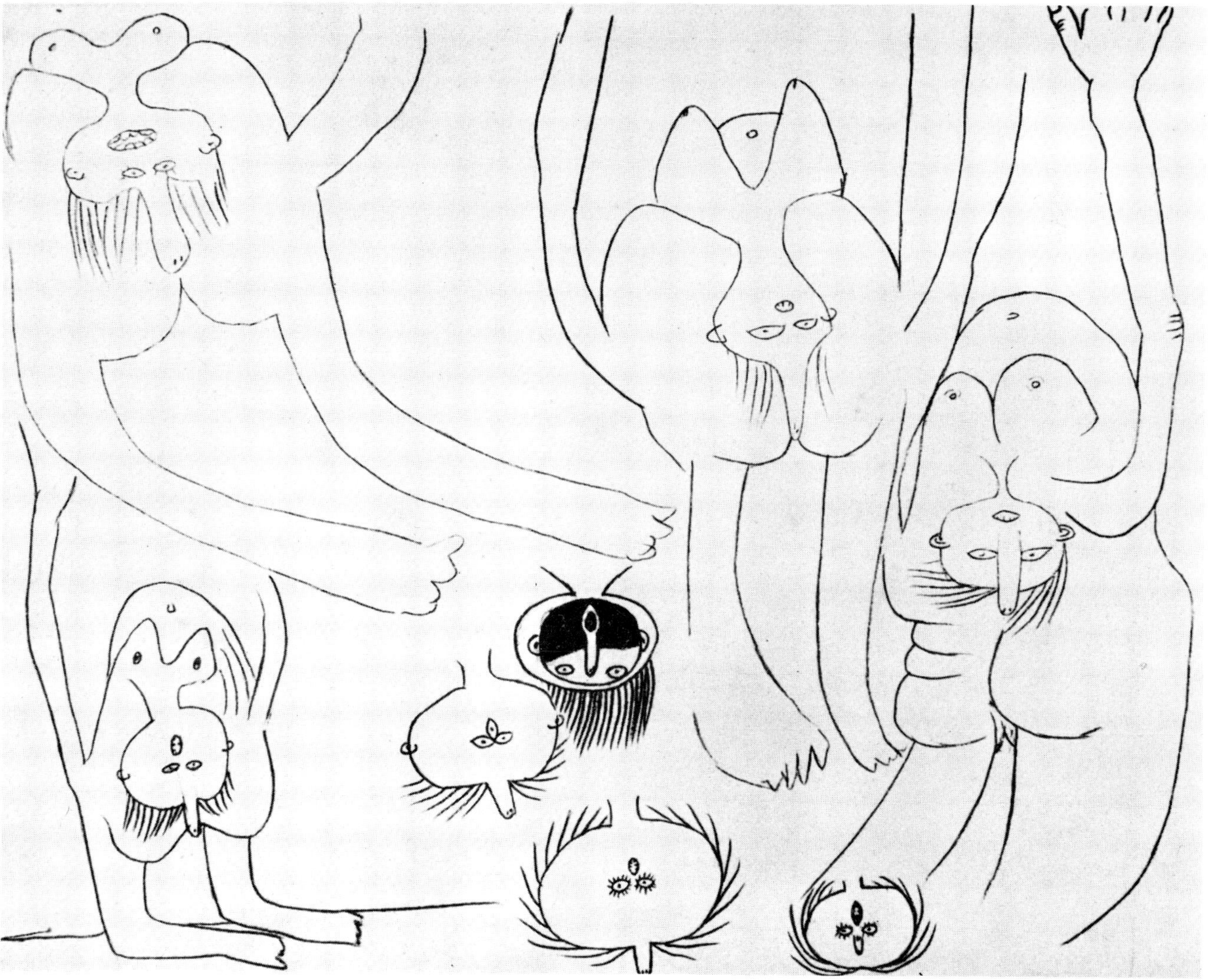

198. Picasso, *Drawing for Crucifixion*, 1929.

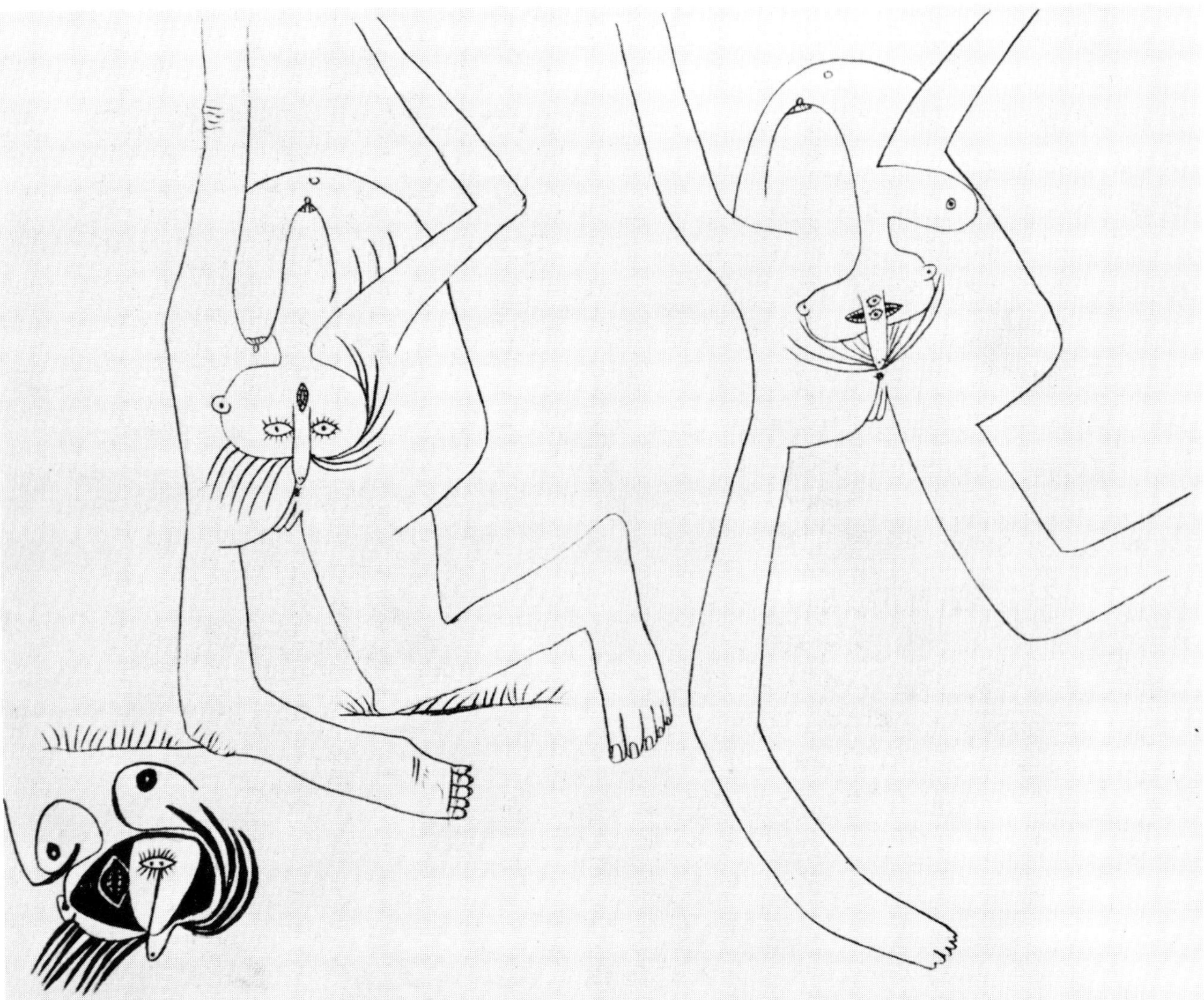

199. Picasso, *Drawing for Crucifixion,* 1929.

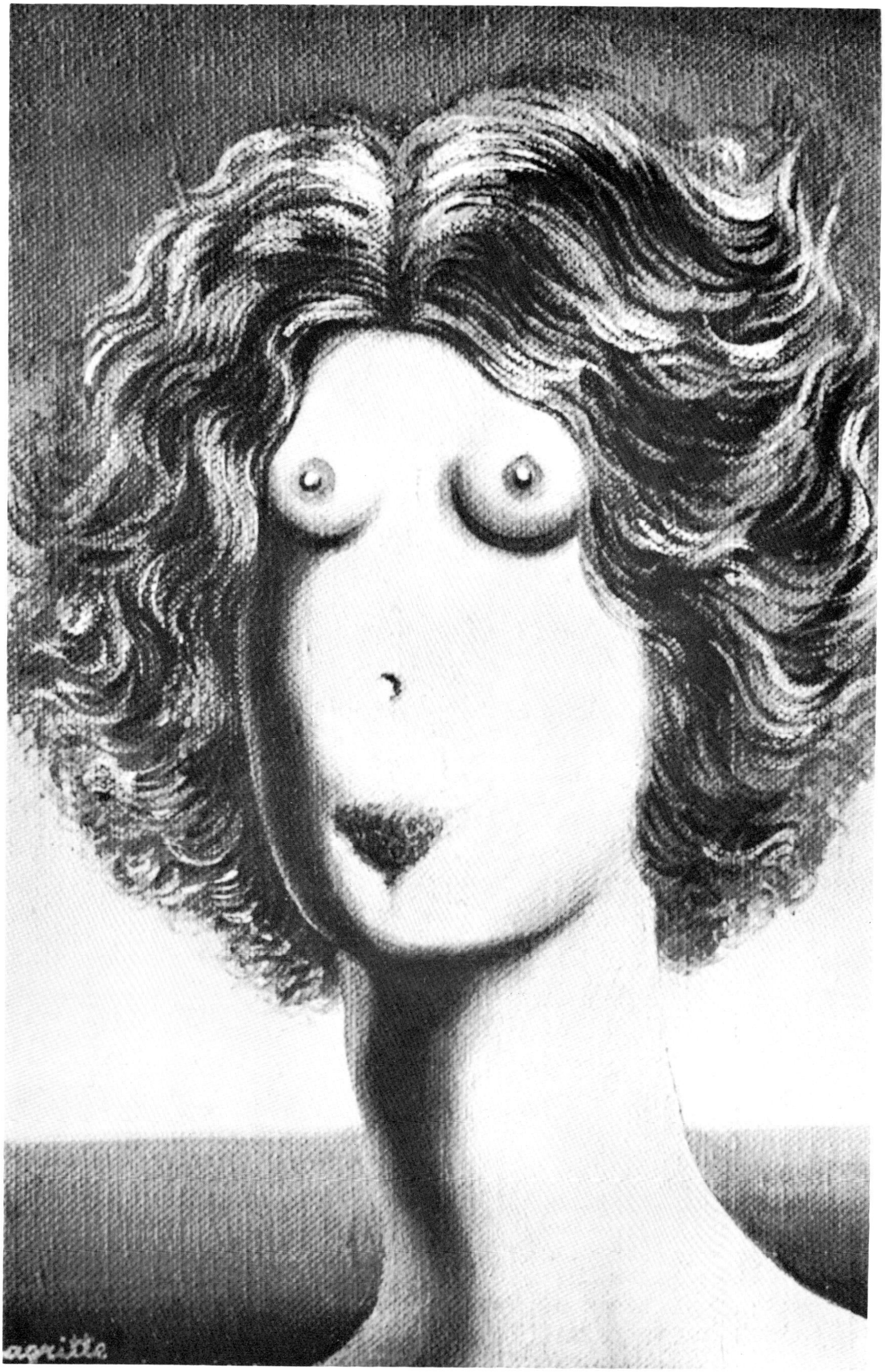

200. René Magritte, *Rape,* 1934. (*Brussels, Collection of Mrs. Jean Krebs.*)

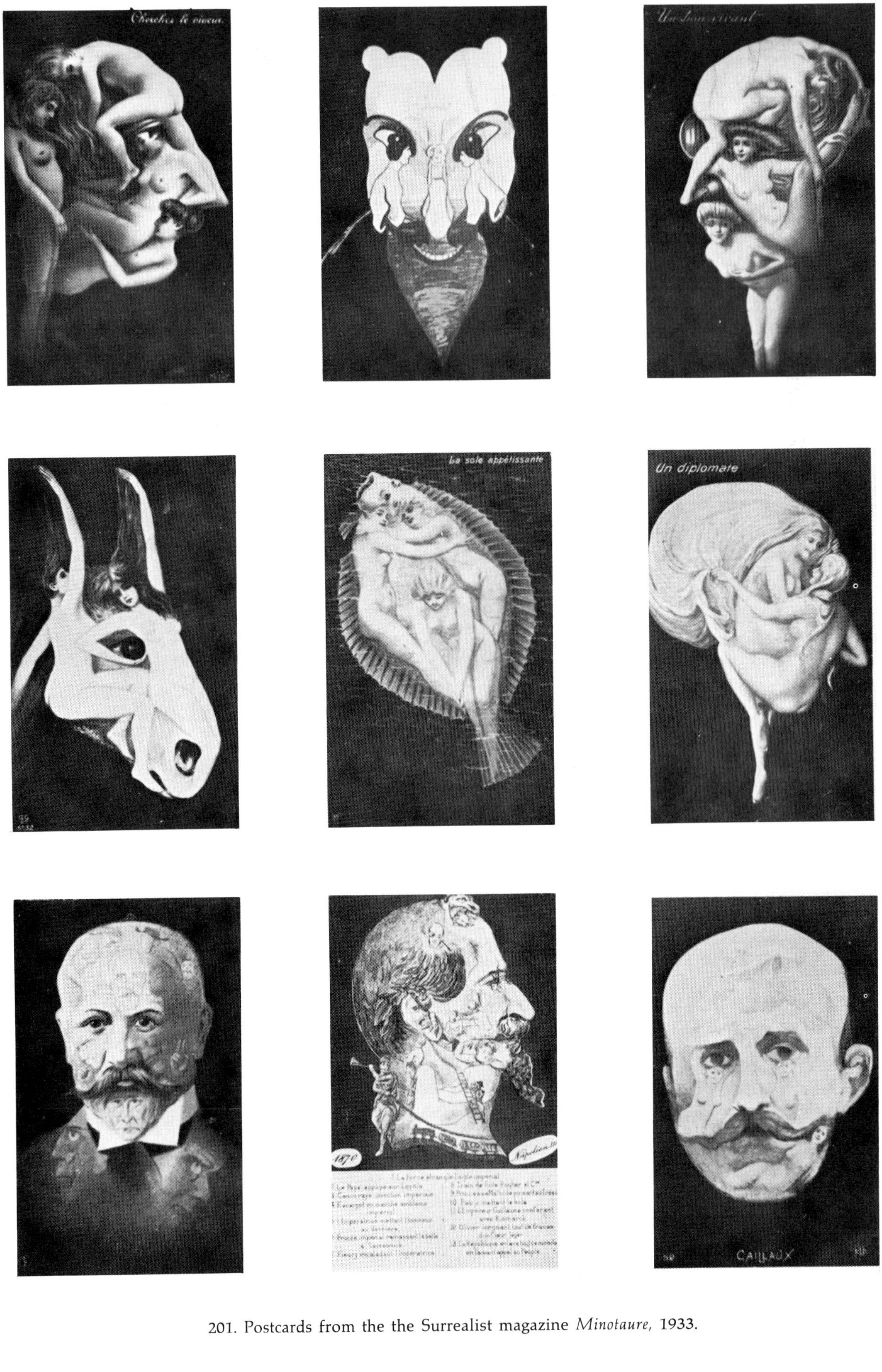

201. Postcards from the the Surrealist magazine *Minotaure,* 1933.

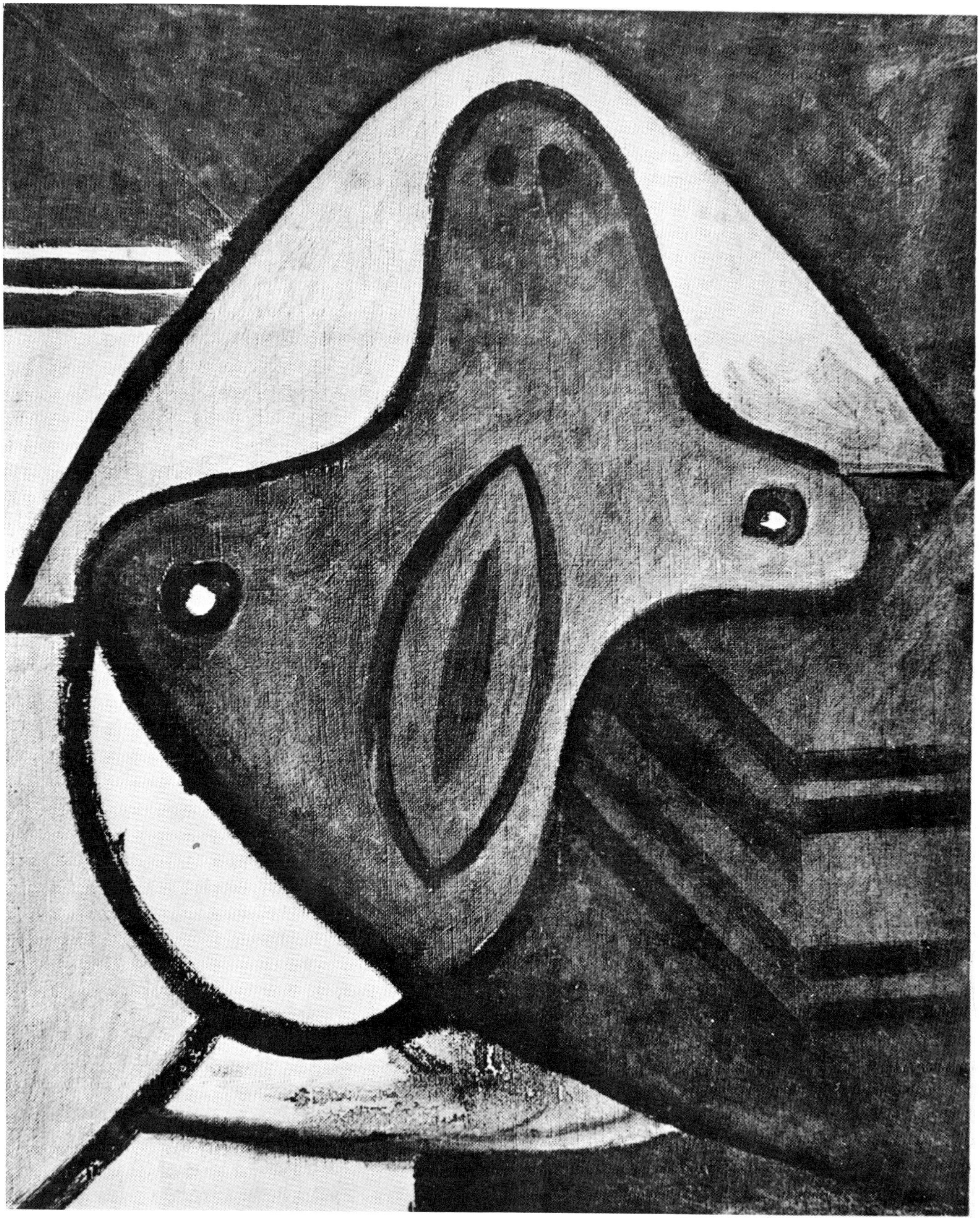

202. Picasso, *Harlequin*, 1927.

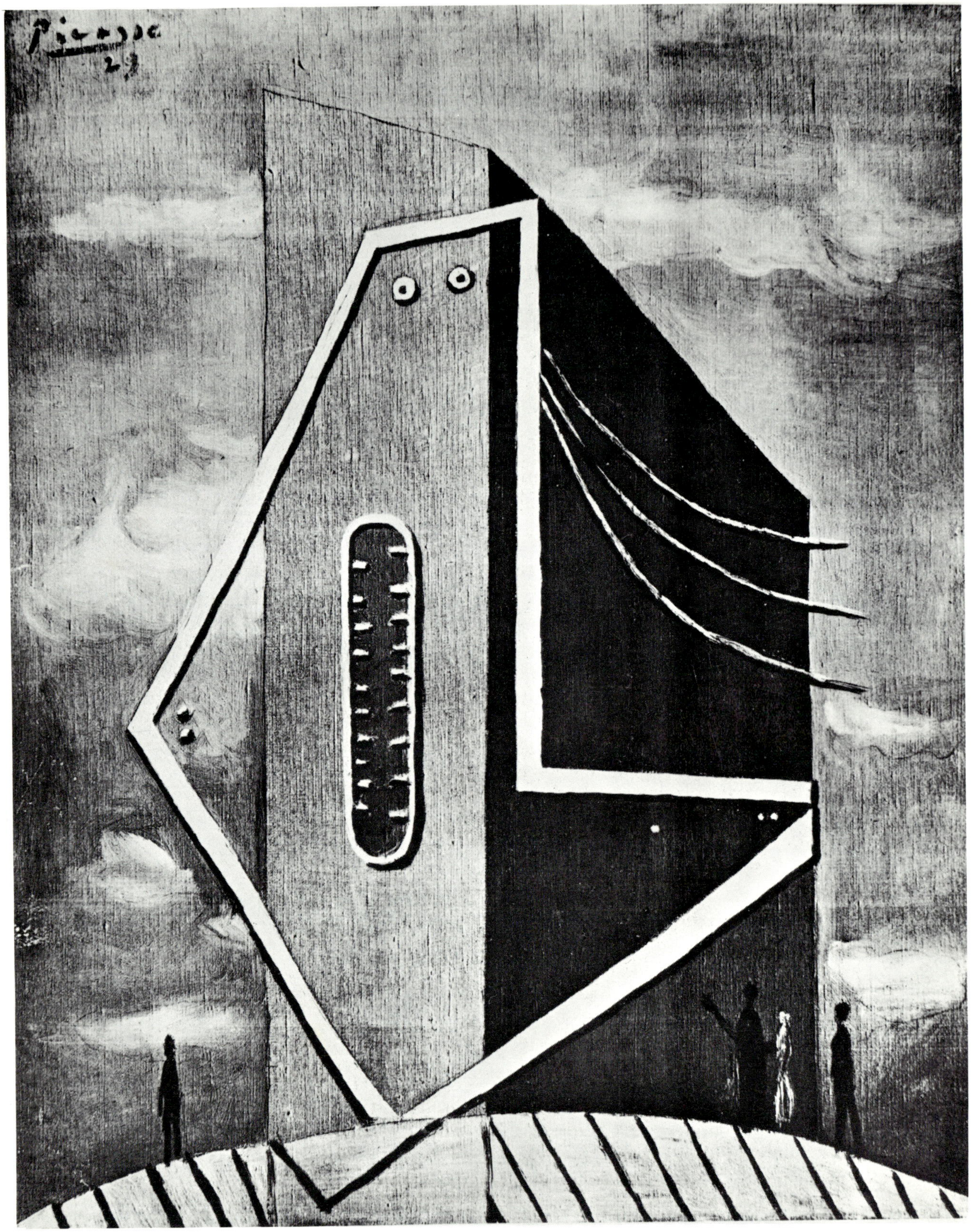

203. Picasso, *Monument: Woman's Head,* 1929.

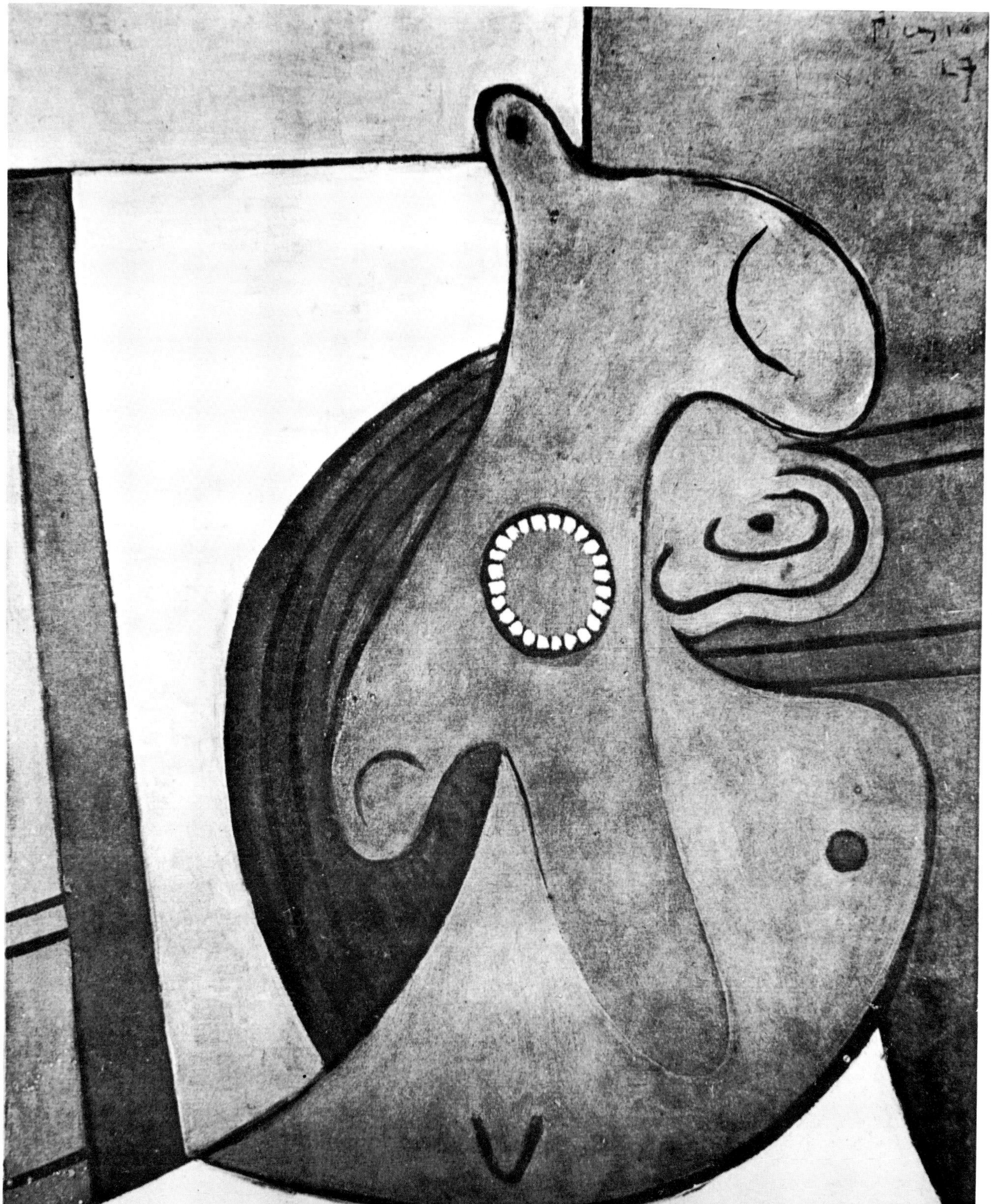

204. Picasso, *Sleeping Woman in Armchair,* 1927. (*New York, Collection of Samuel A. Berger.*)

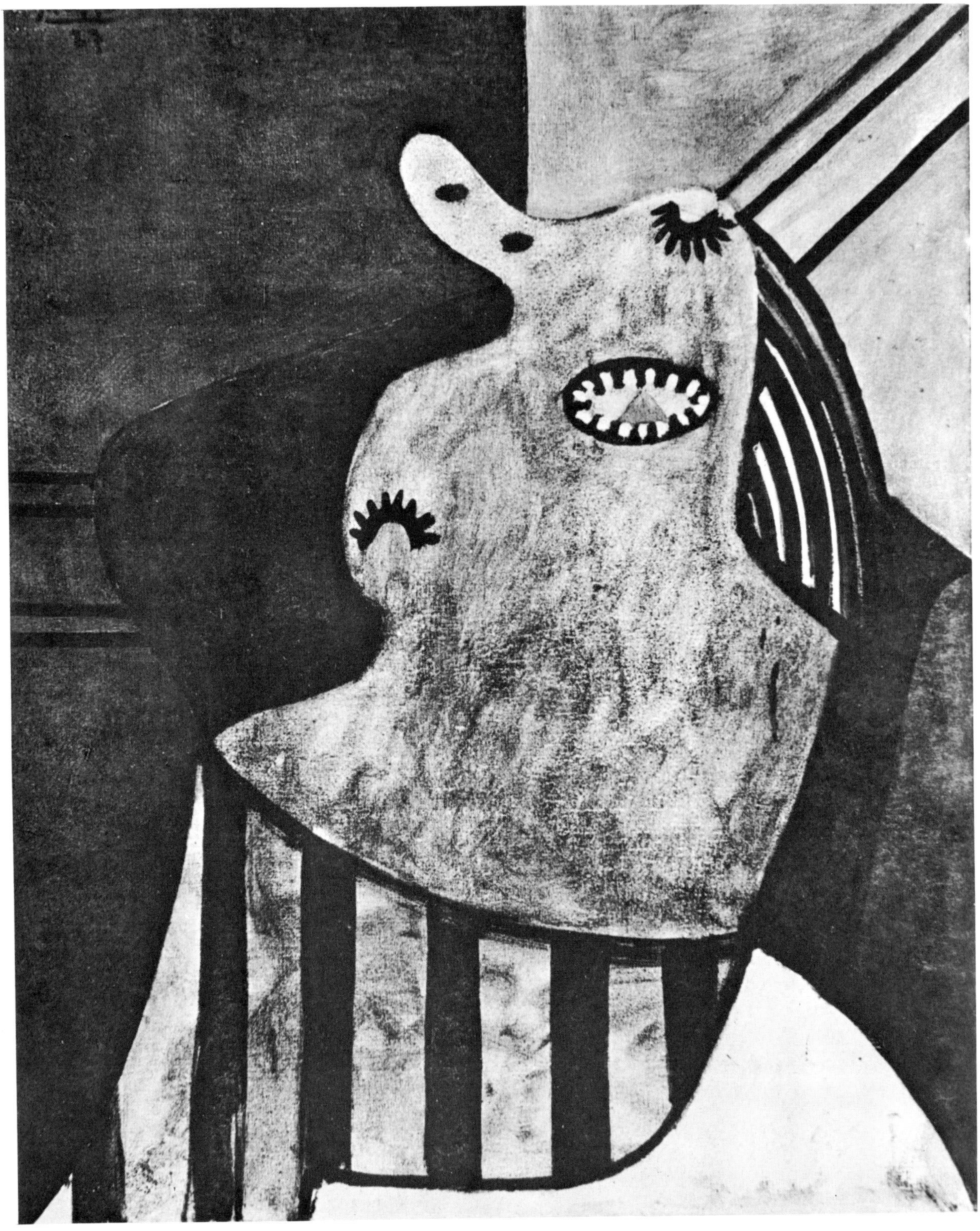

205. Picasso, *Sleeping Woman in Armchair*, 1927. (*Brussels, Collection of Betty Barman.*)

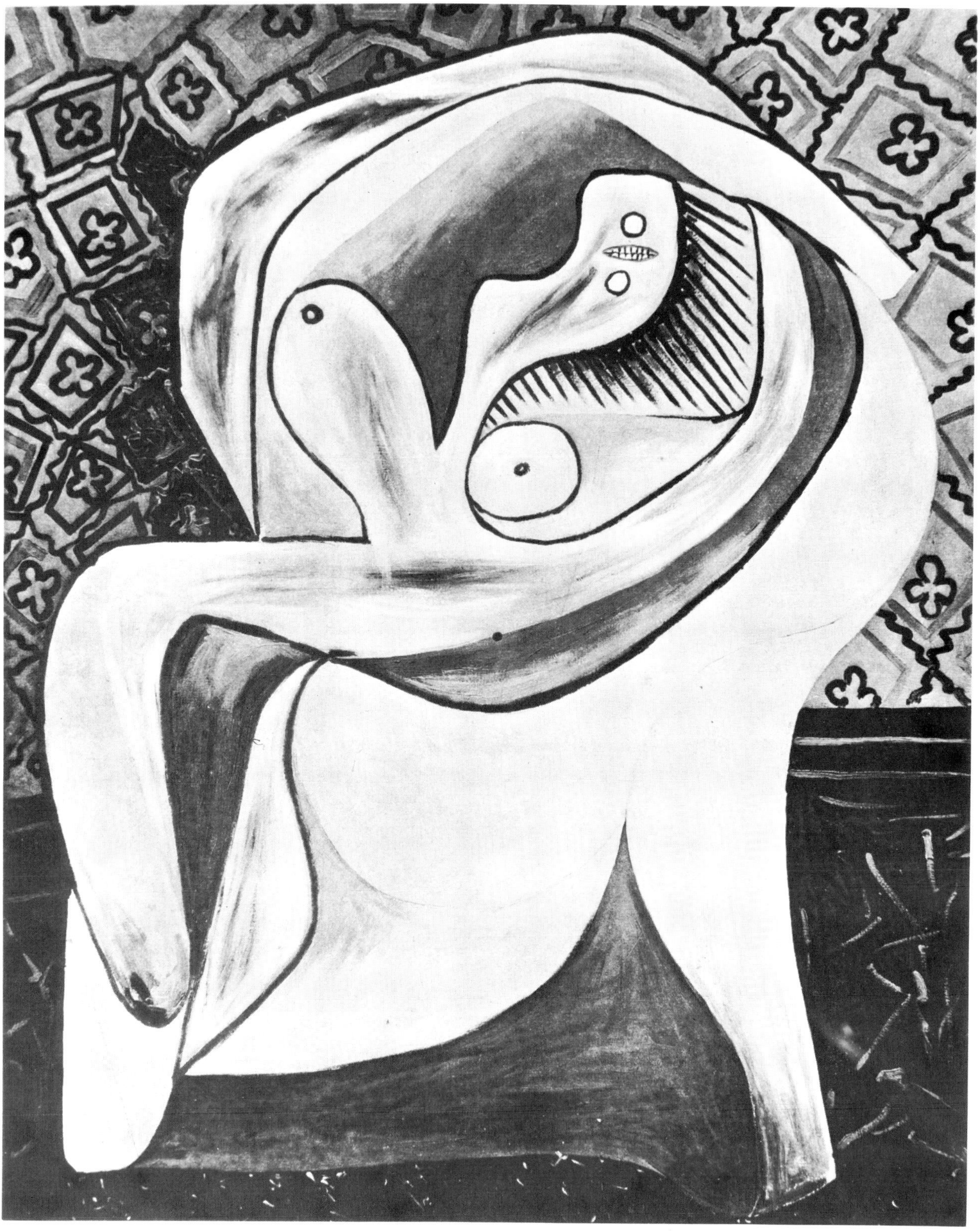

206. Picasso, *Woman in Armchair,* January 22, 1932.

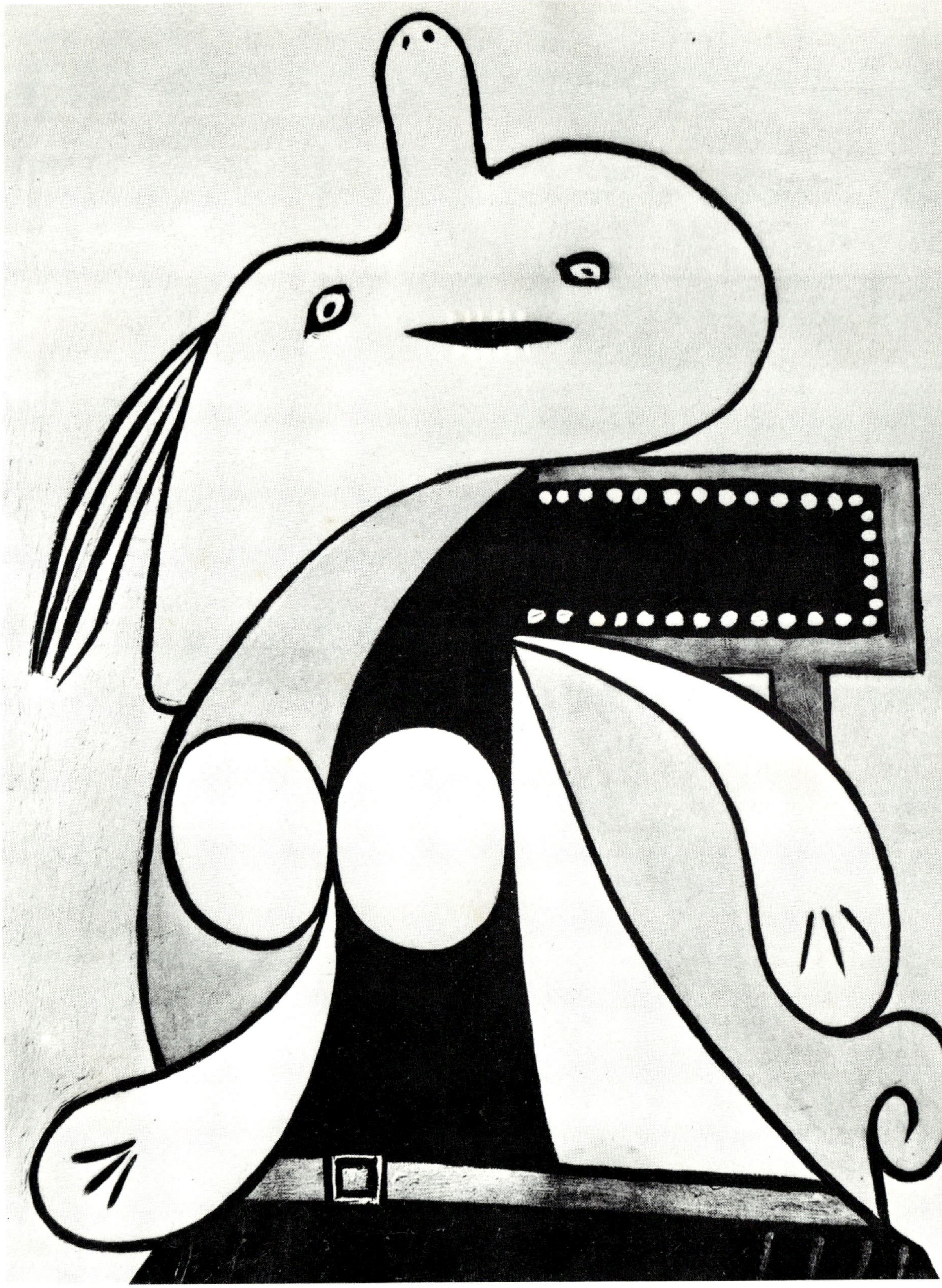

207. Picasso, *Woman with Yellow Belt*, January, 1932.

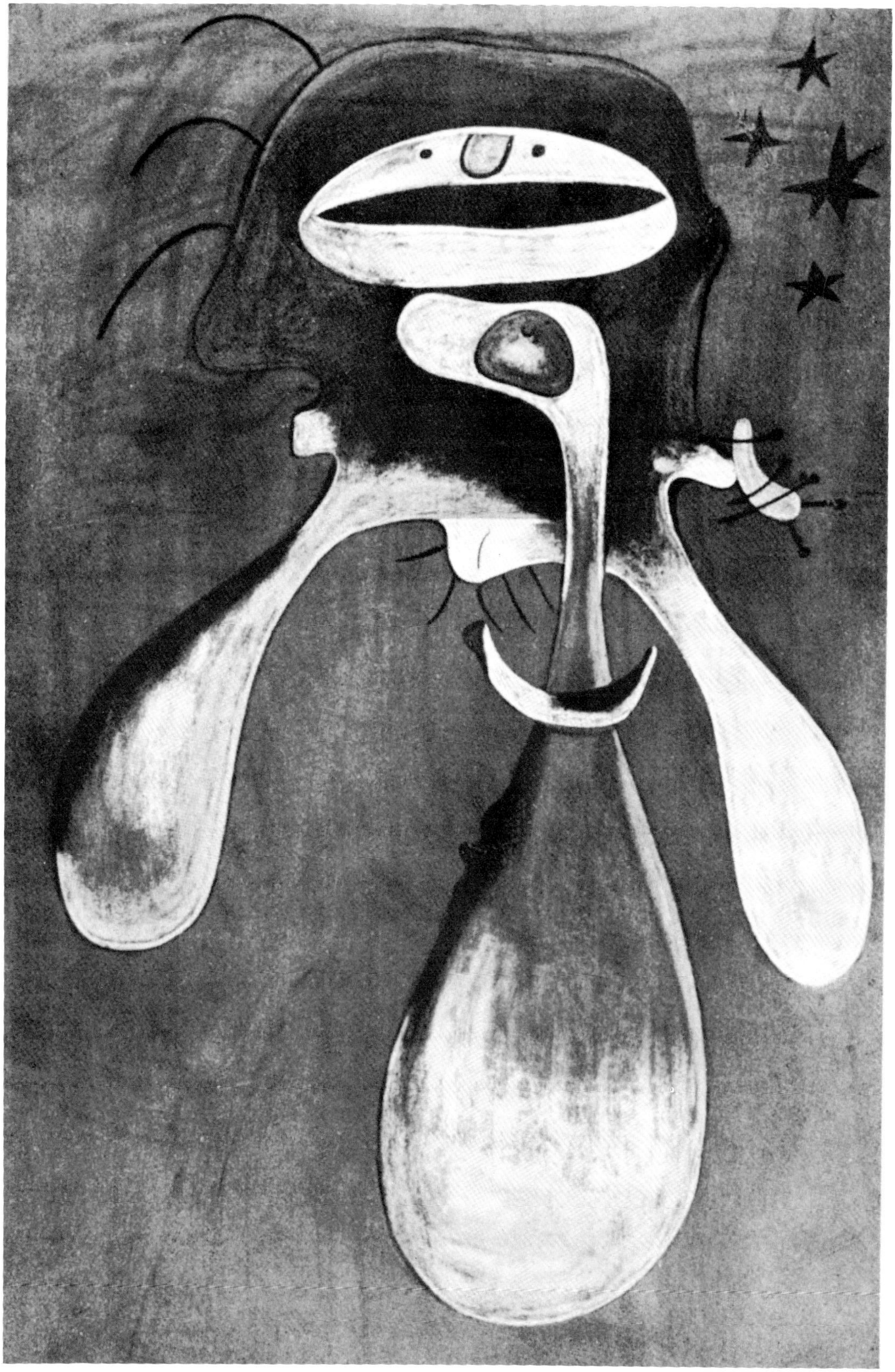

208. Joan Miró, *Woman*, 1934. (*Paris, Galerie Maeght.*)

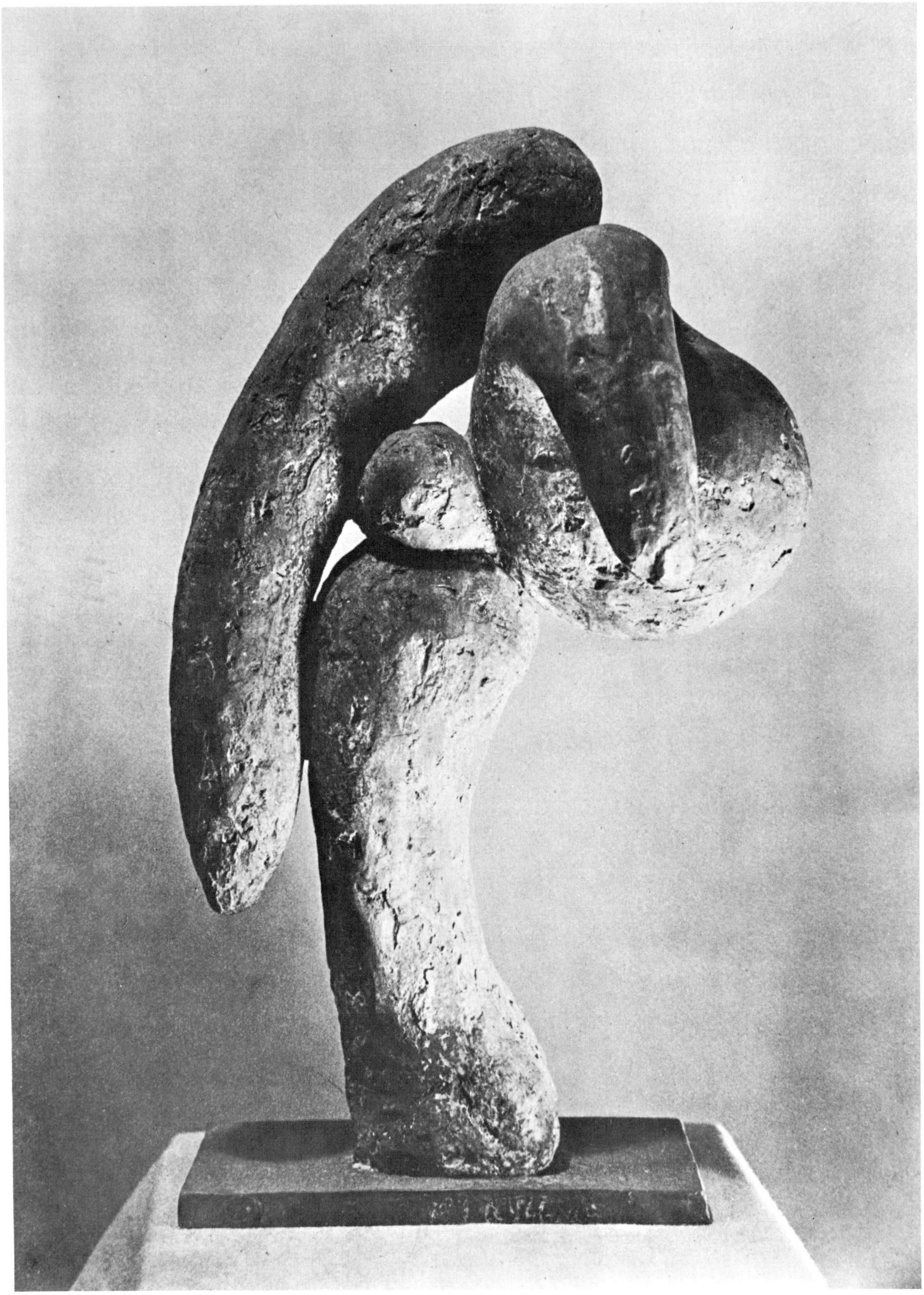

209. Picasso, *Woman's Head* (bronze), 1932. (*Collection of the artist.*)

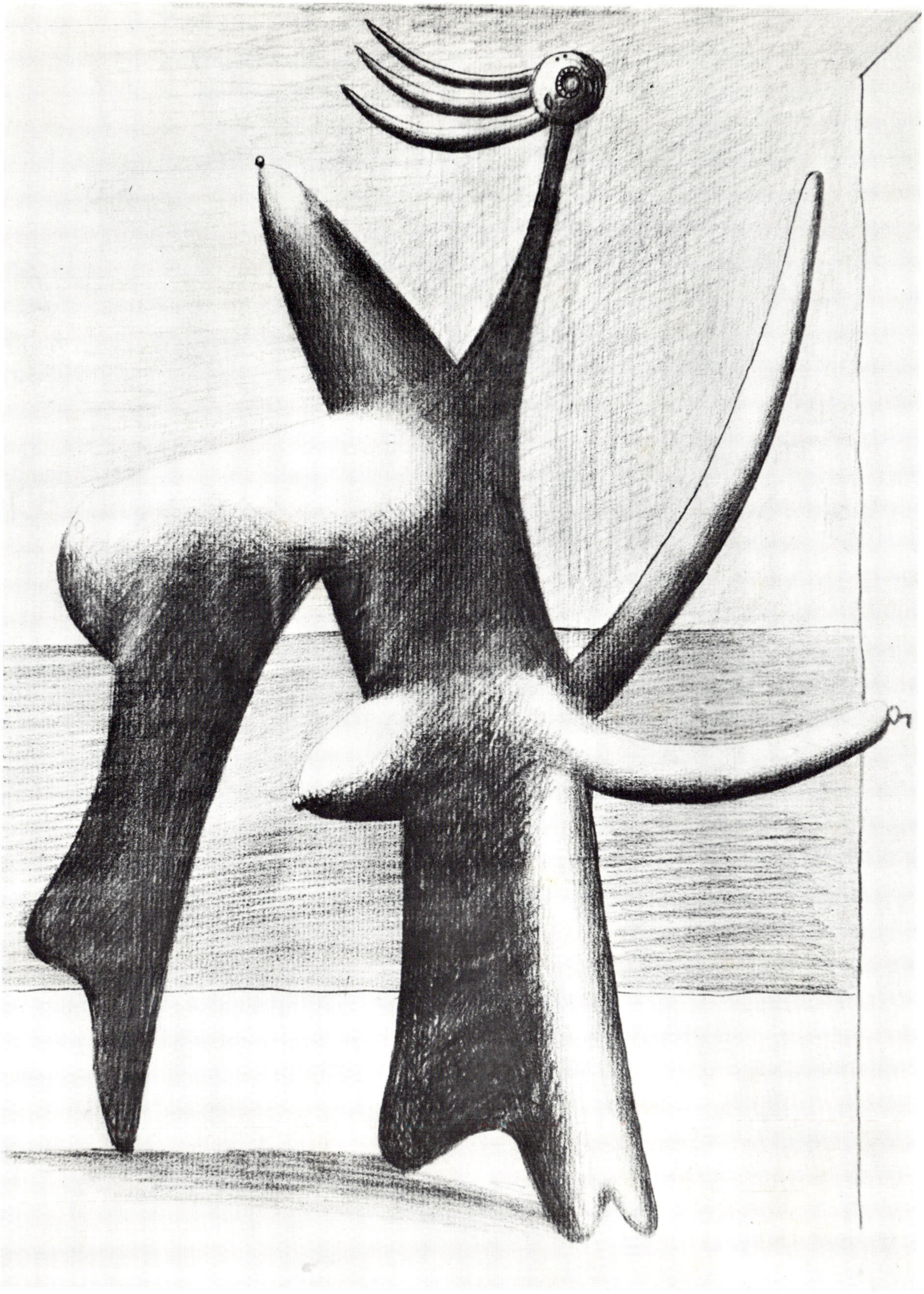

210. Picasso, *Drawing,* Summer, 1927.

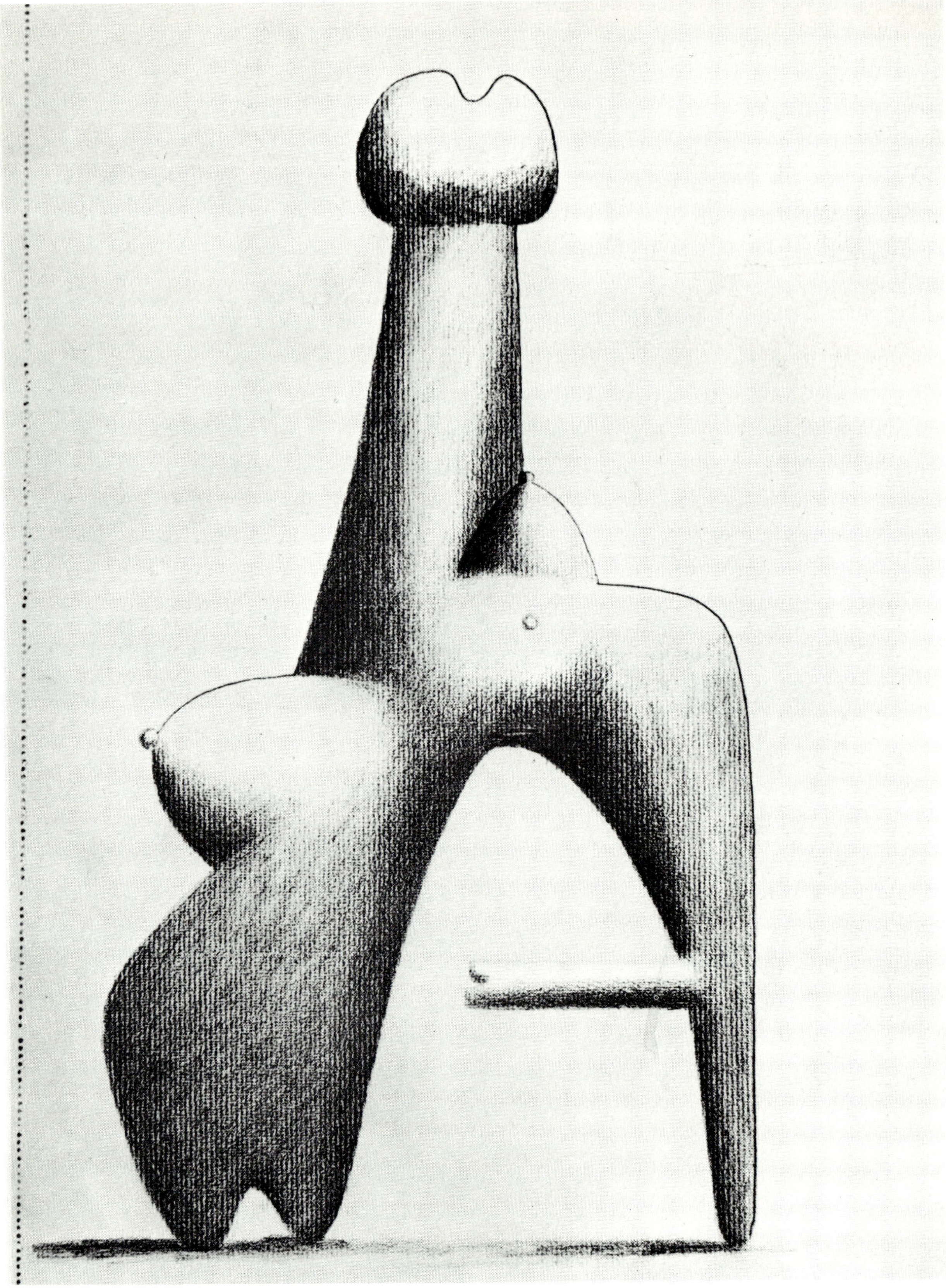

211. Picasso, *Drawing,* Summer, 1927.

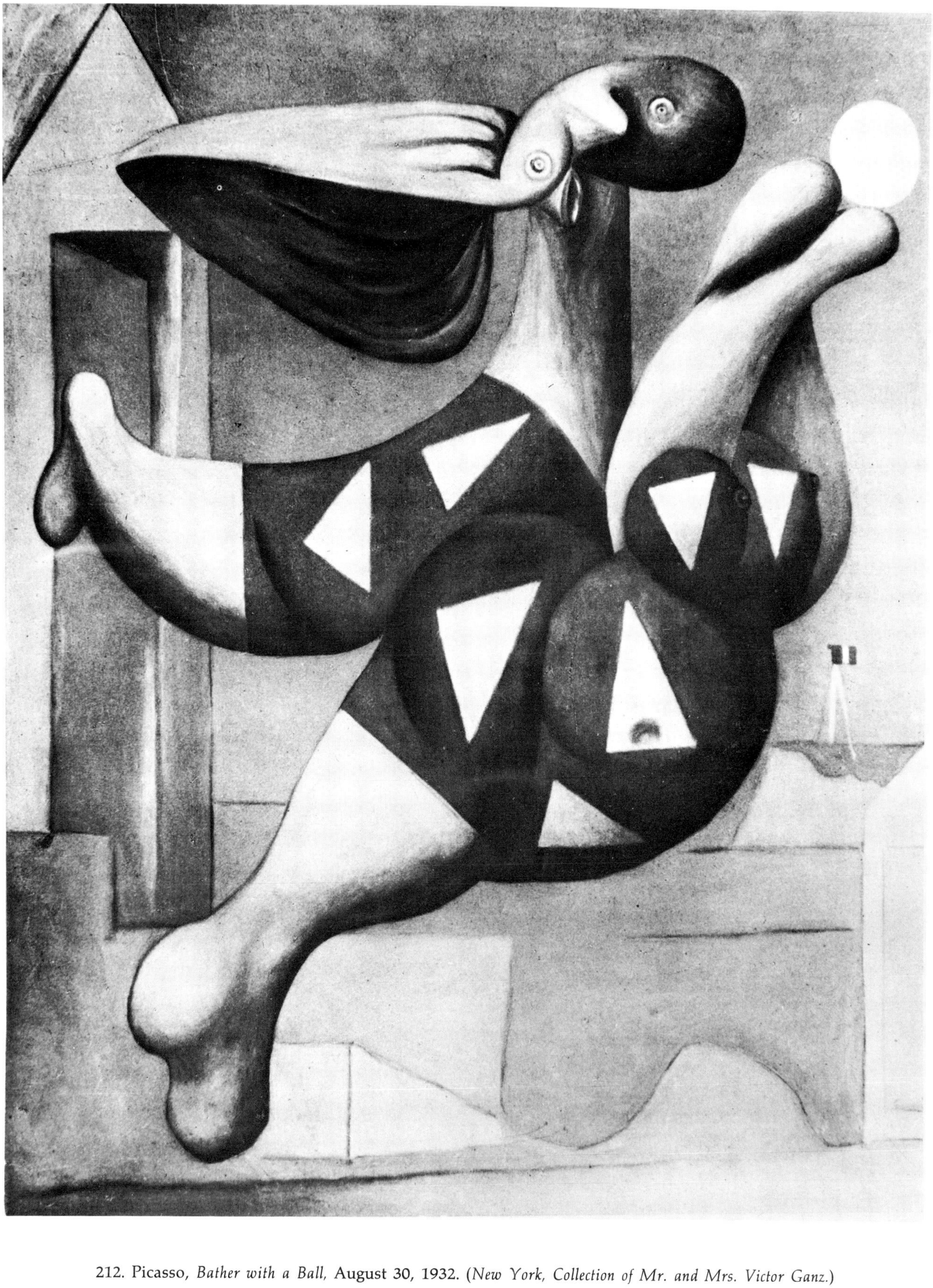

212. Picasso, *Bather with a Ball*, August 30, 1932. (*New York, Collection of Mr. and Mrs. Victor Ganz.*)

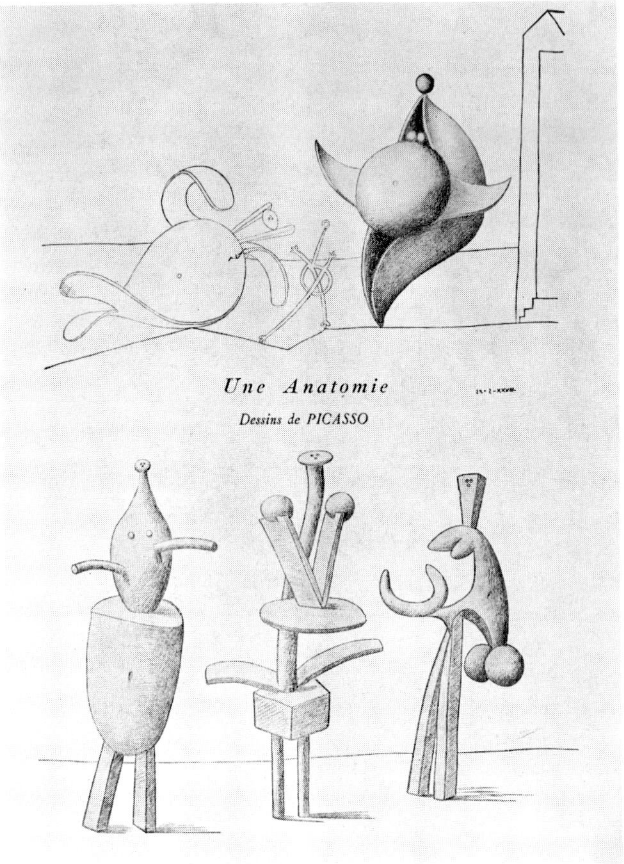

213. Picasso, *An Anatomy*, February 22, 1933.

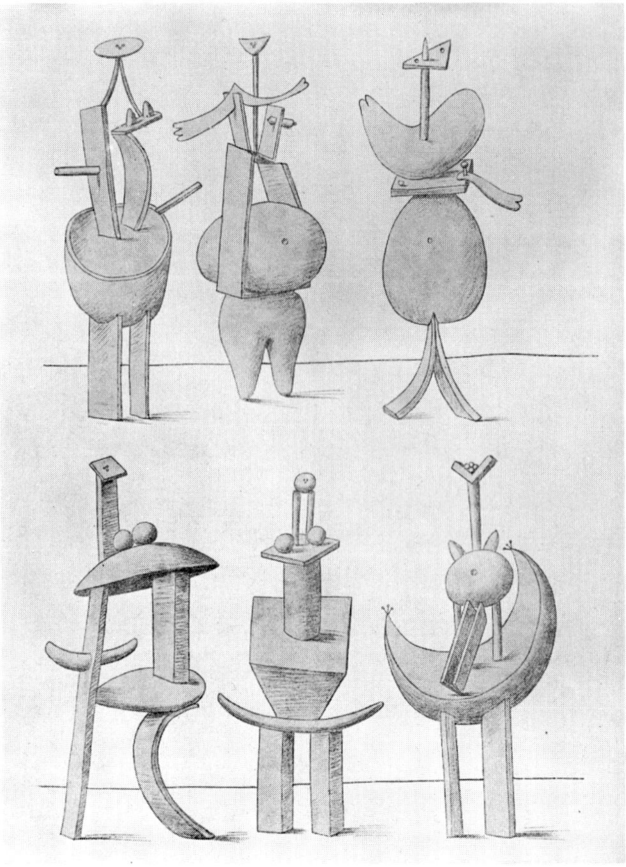

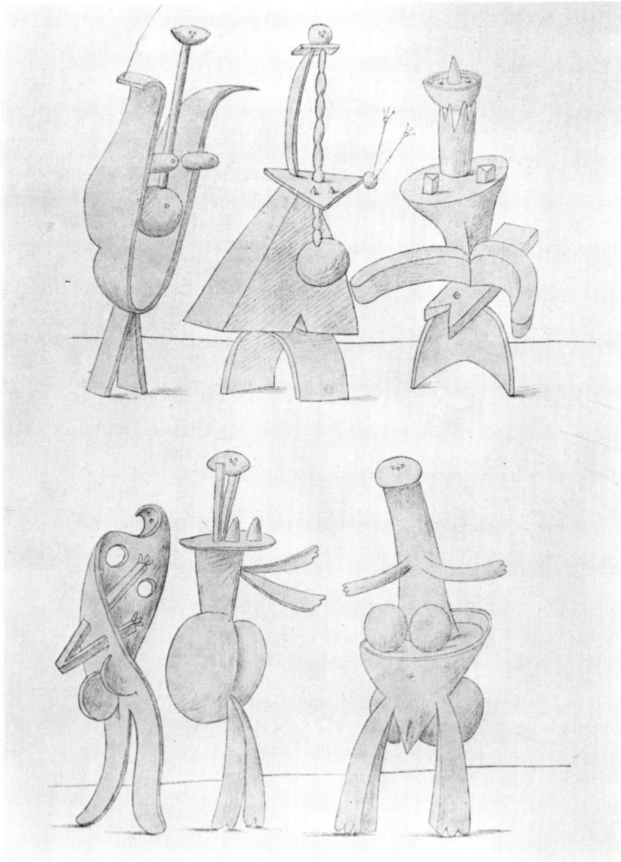

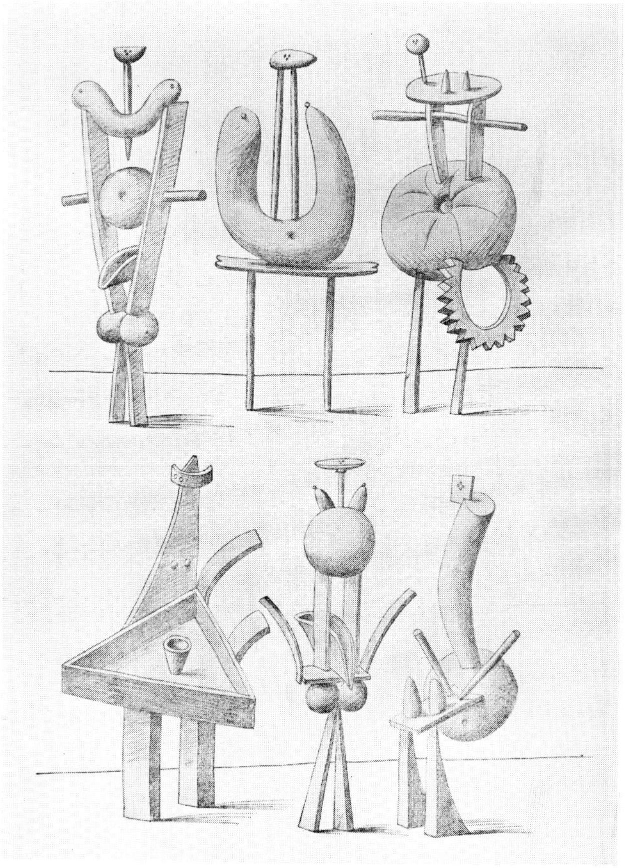

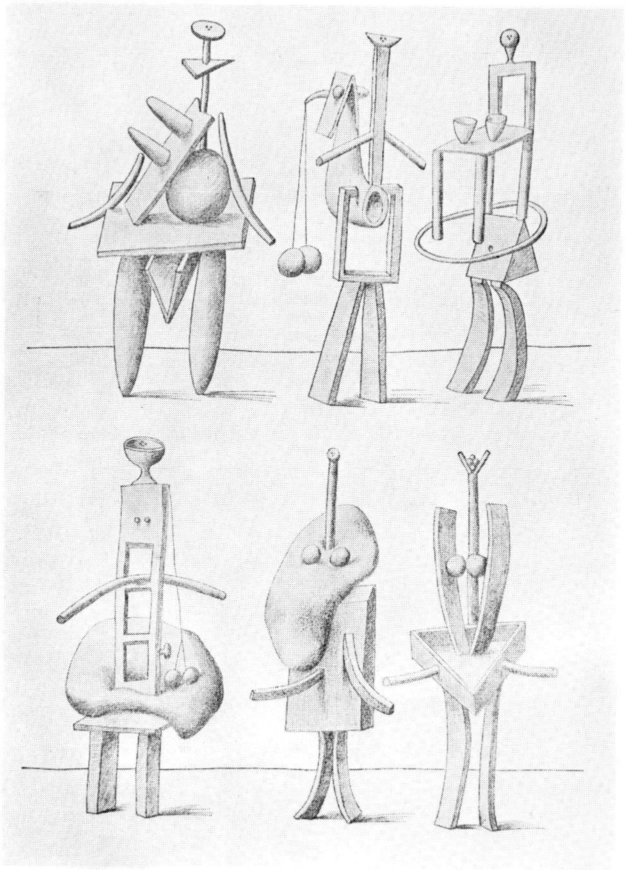

213. (*Continued.*)

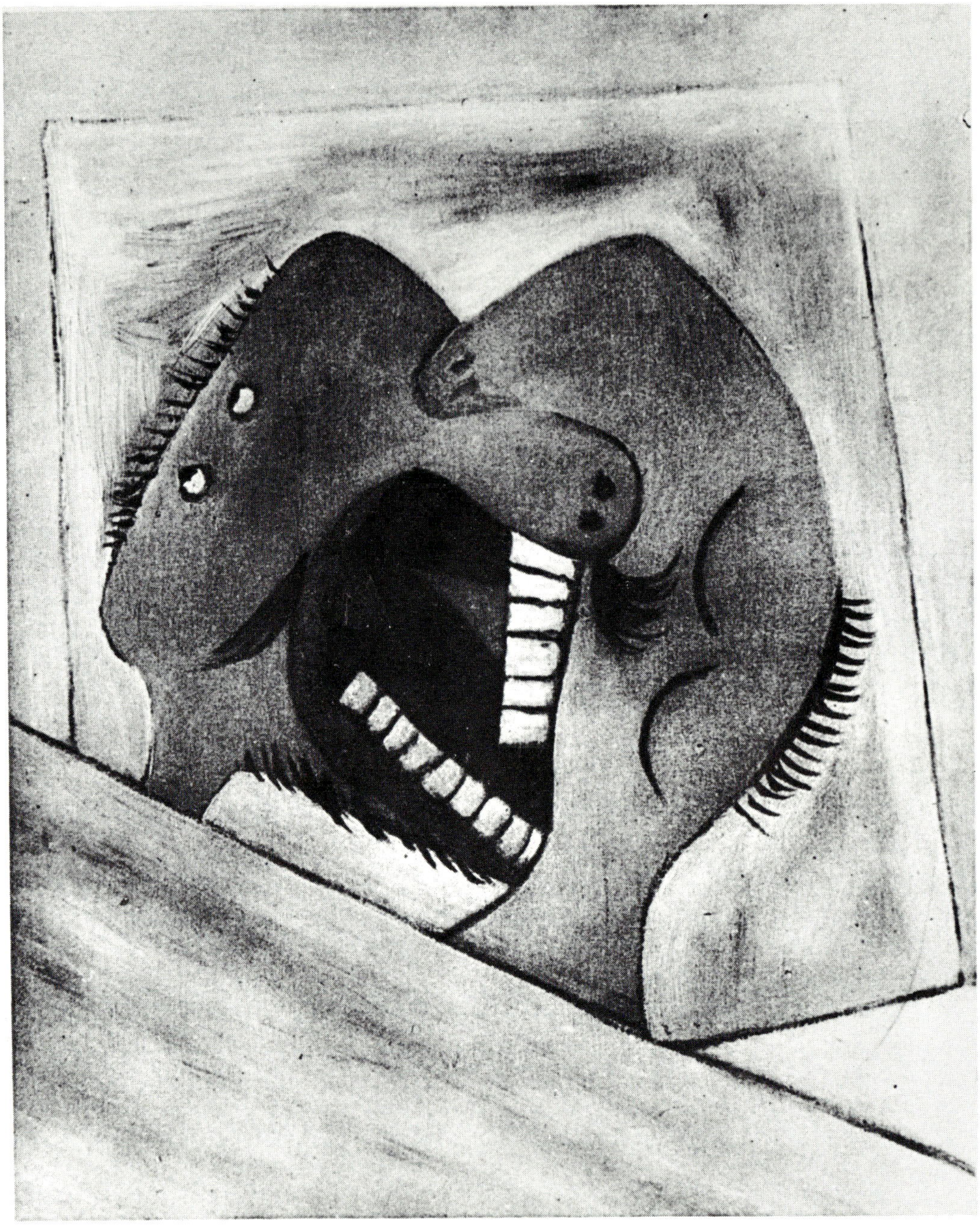

214. Picasso, *Two Heads,* 1931.

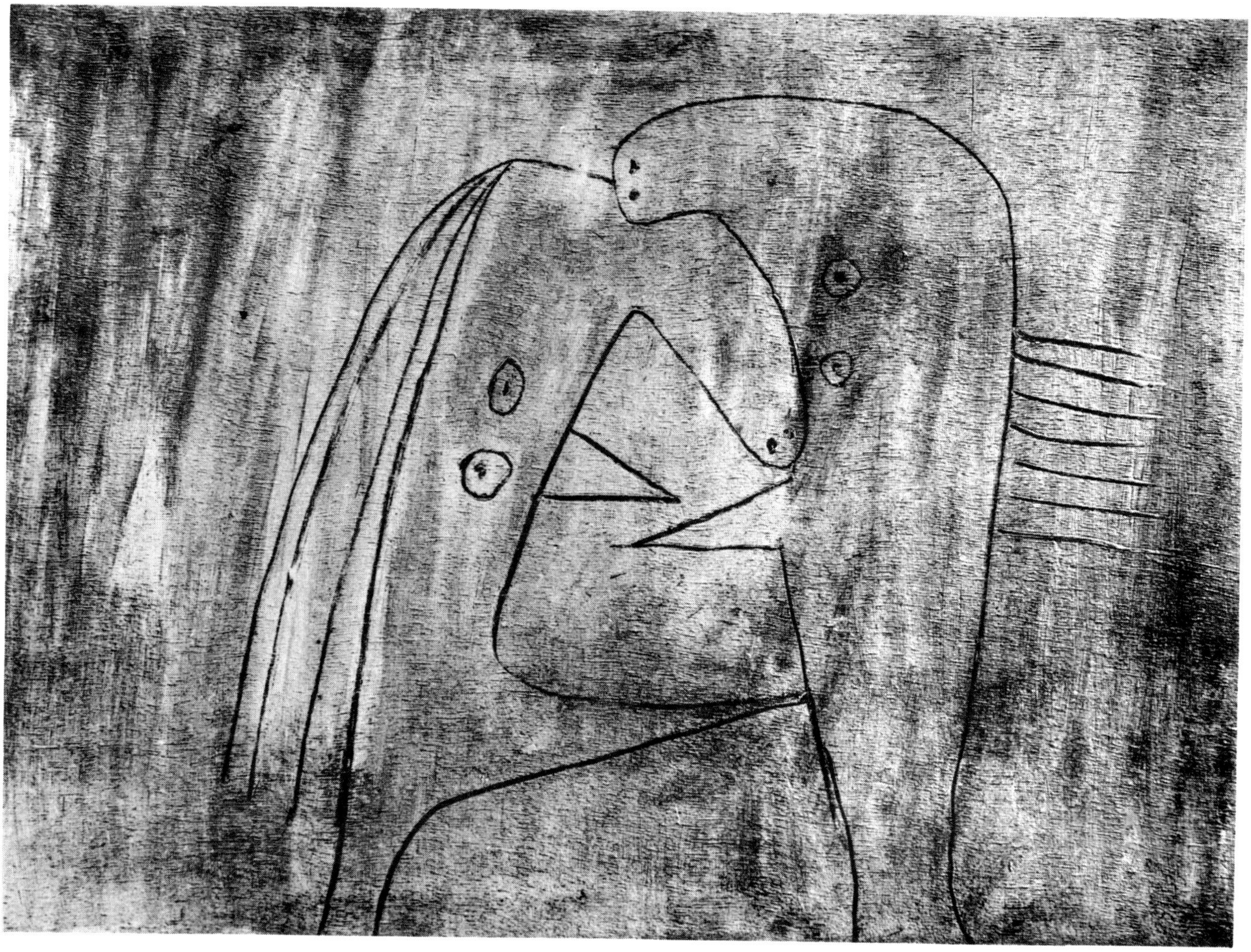

215. Picasso, *Two Heads*, 1930.

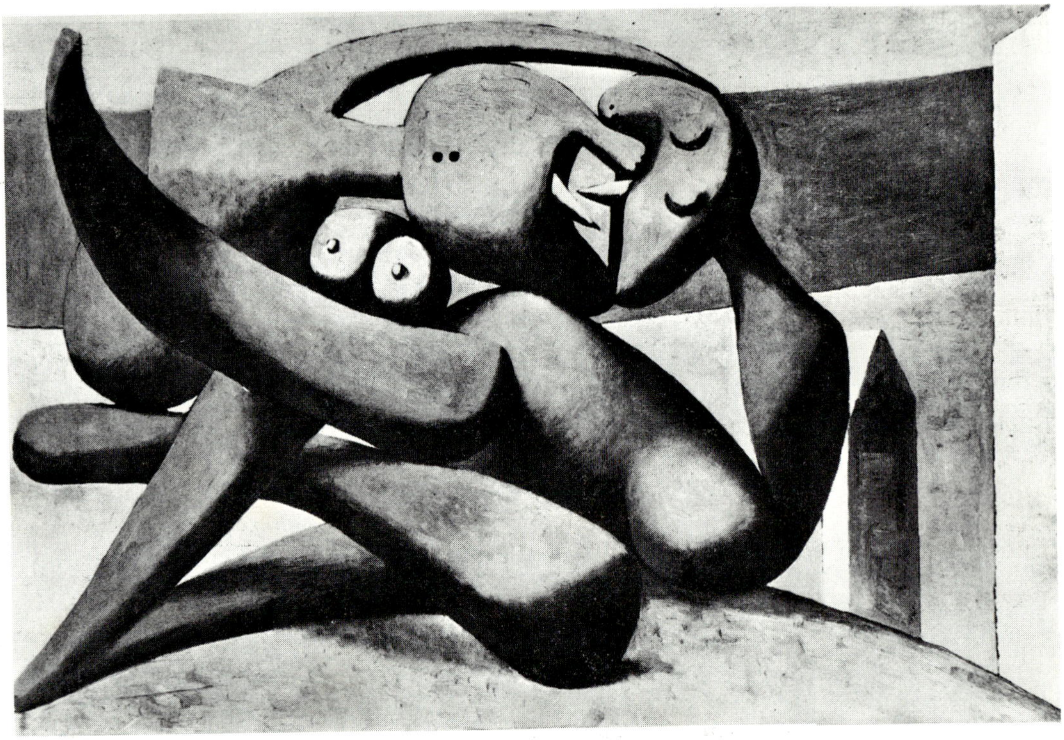

216. Picasso, *Figures by the Sea,* 1931.

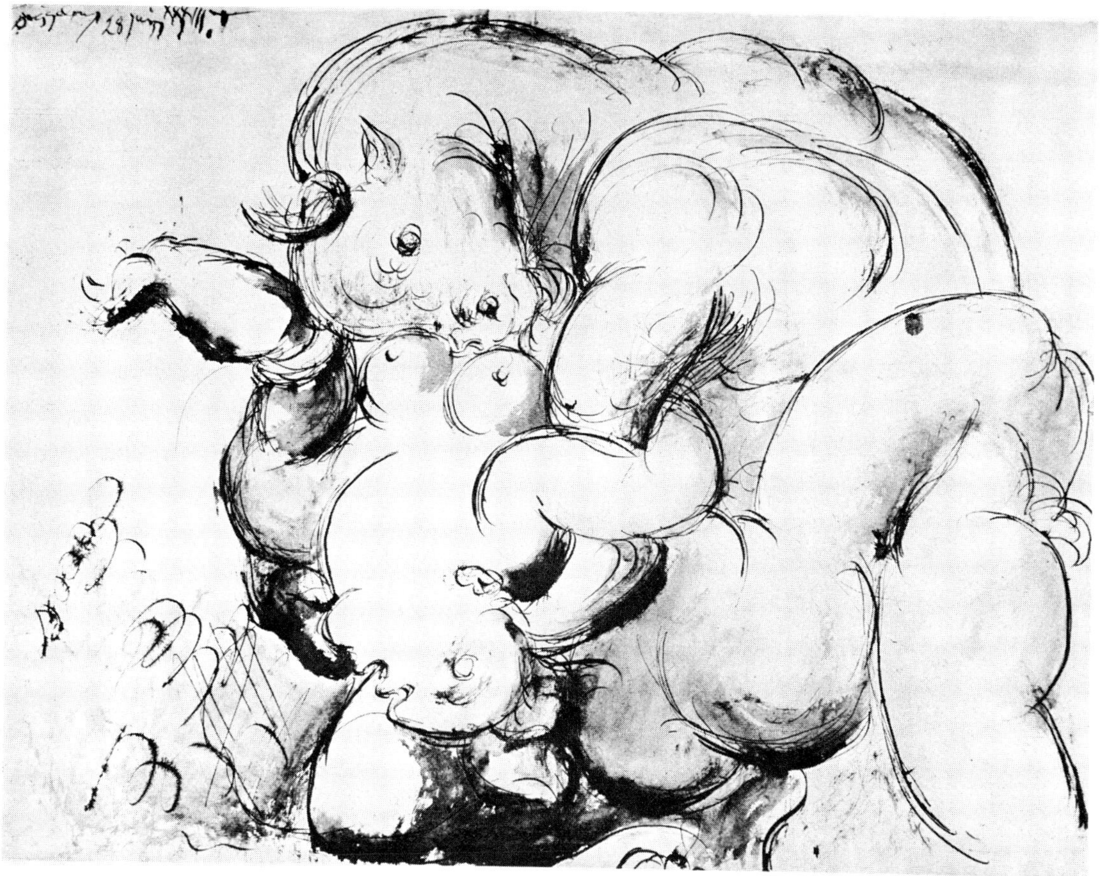

217. Picasso, *Minotaur* (drawing), June 28, 1933.

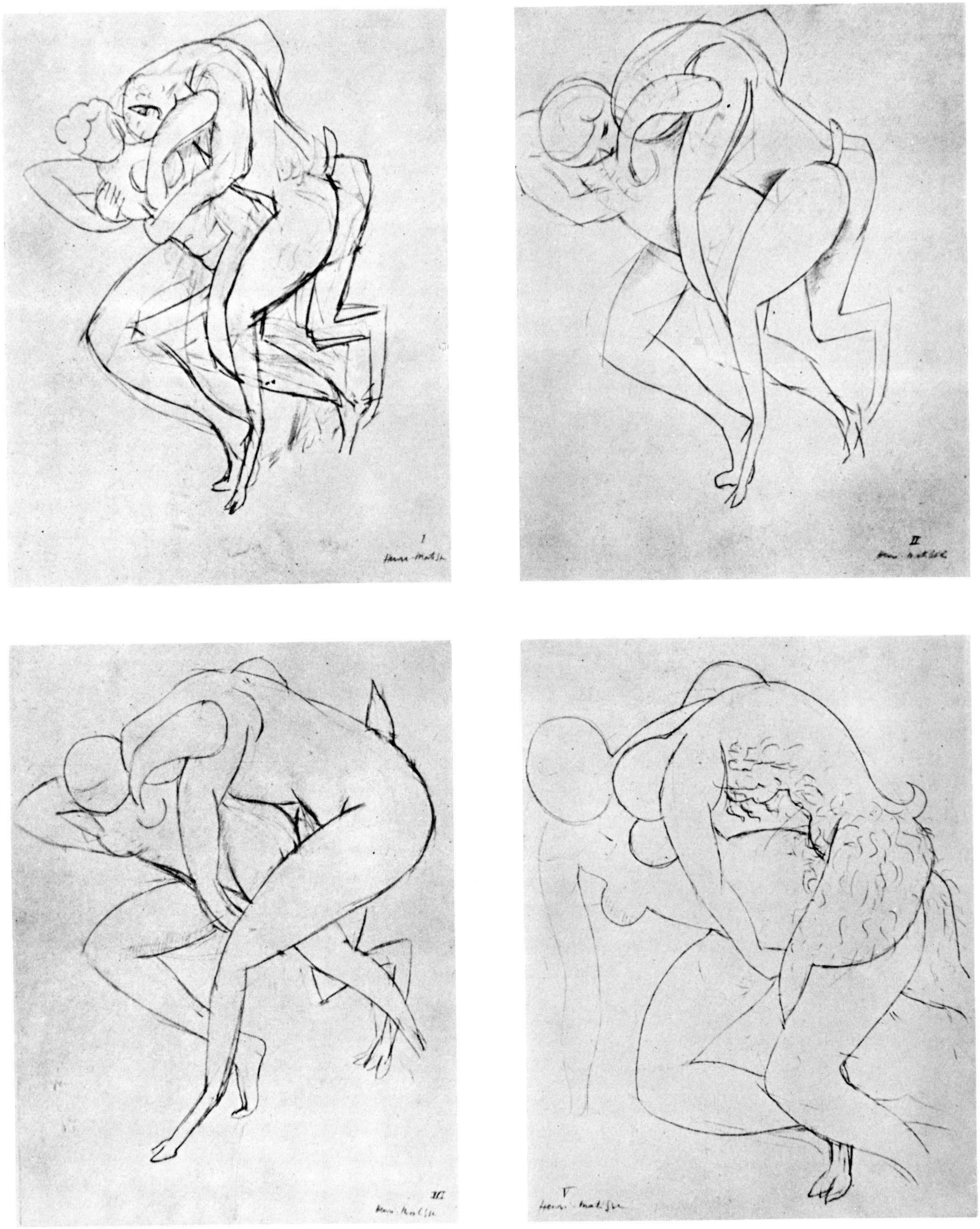

218. Matisse, illustrations for Mallarmé's *L'Après-midi d'un faune,* 1933.

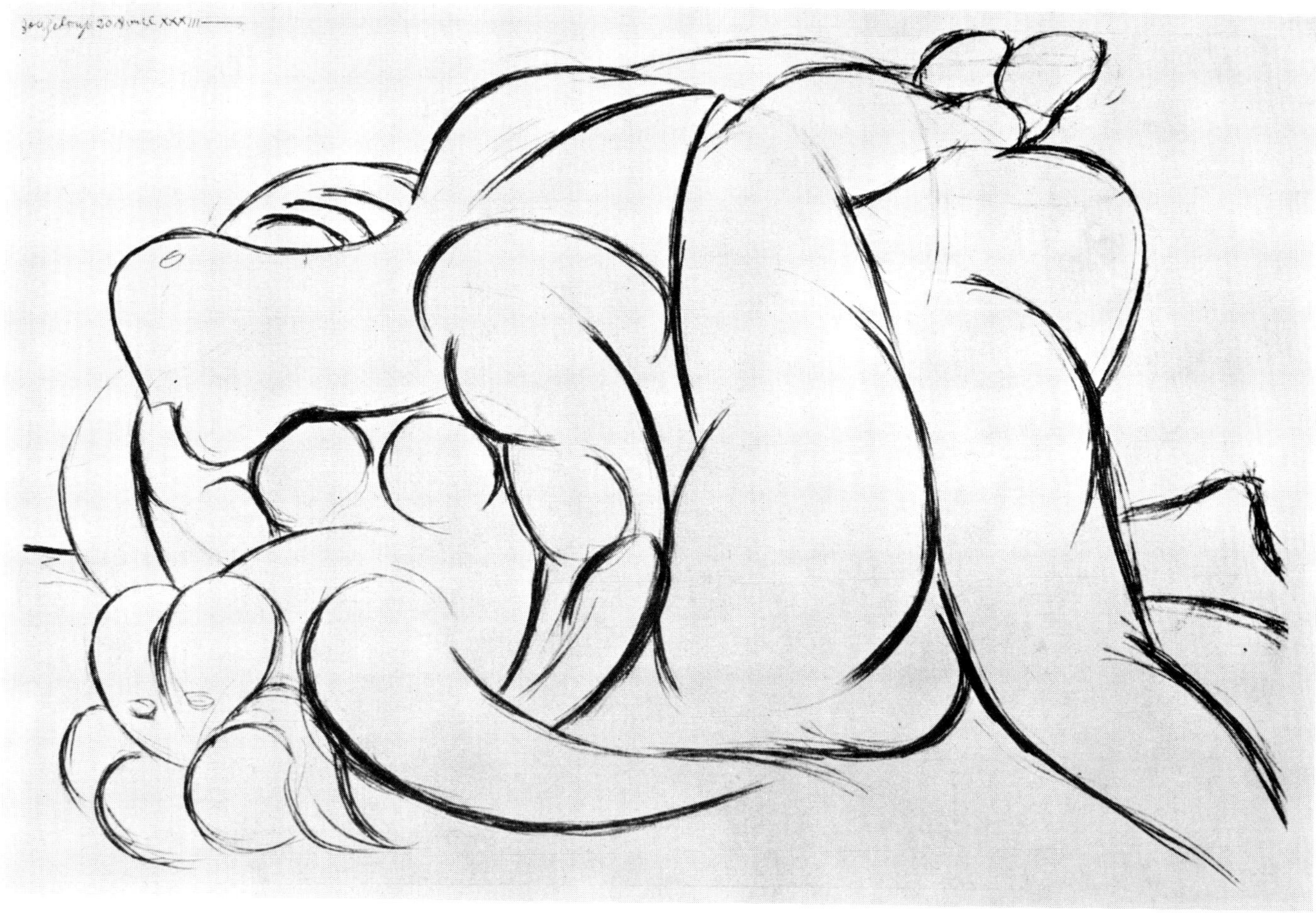

219. Picasso, *Two Figures* (drawing), April 20, 1933.

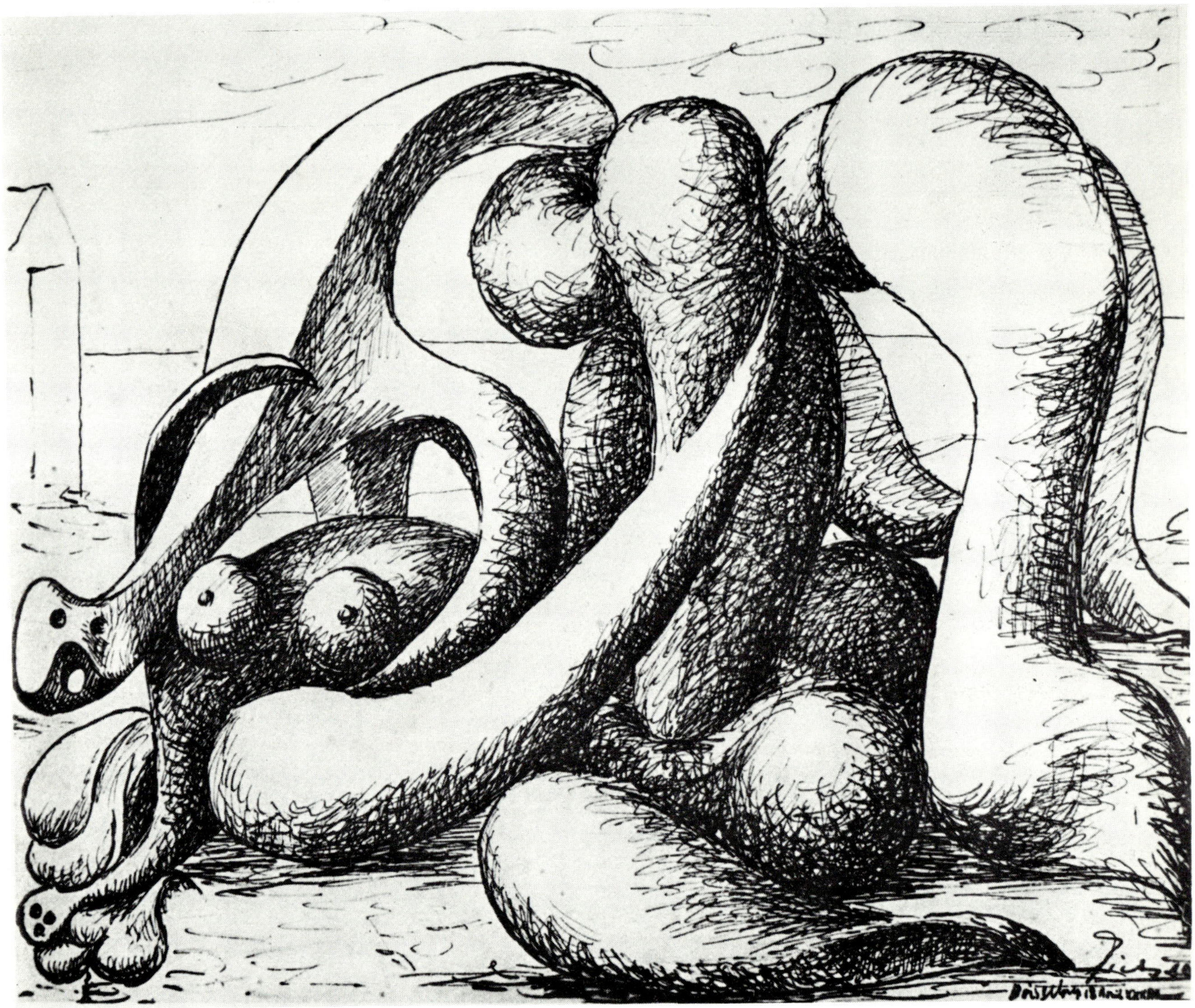

220. Picasso, *Two Figures* (drawing), April 18, 1933.

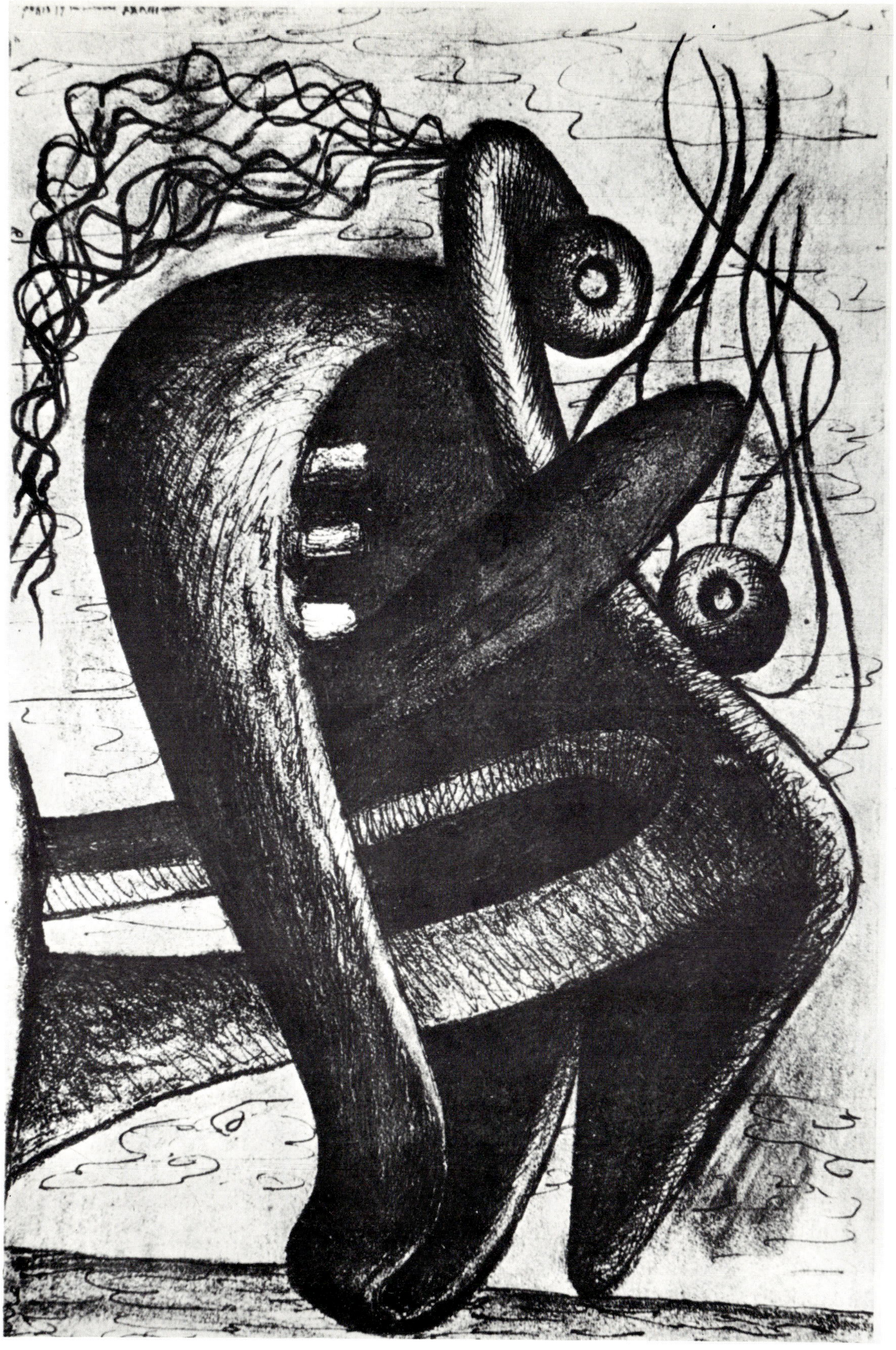

221. Picasso, *Two Figures* (drawing), November 19, 1933.

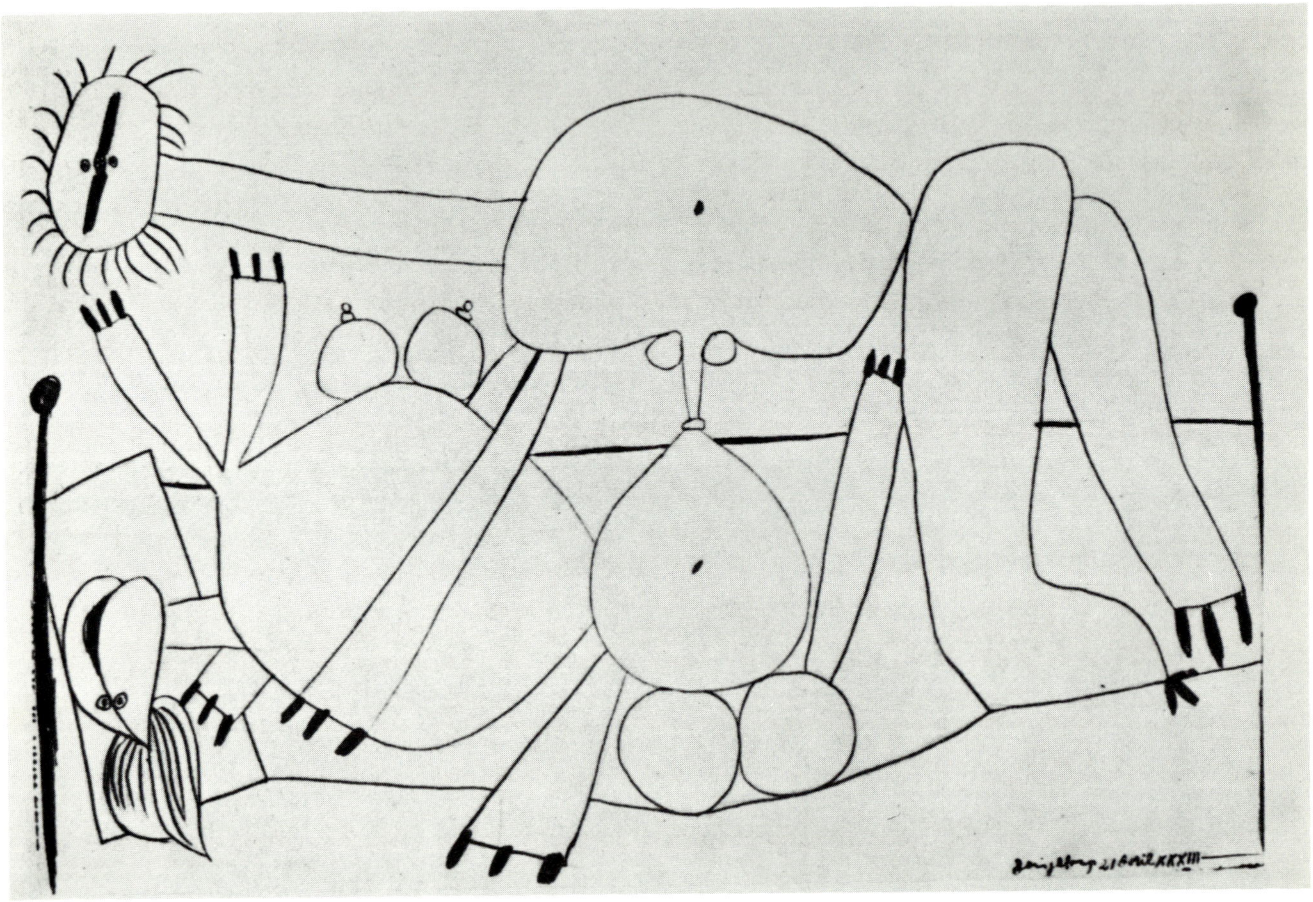

222. Picasso, *Two Figures* (drawing), April 21, 1933.

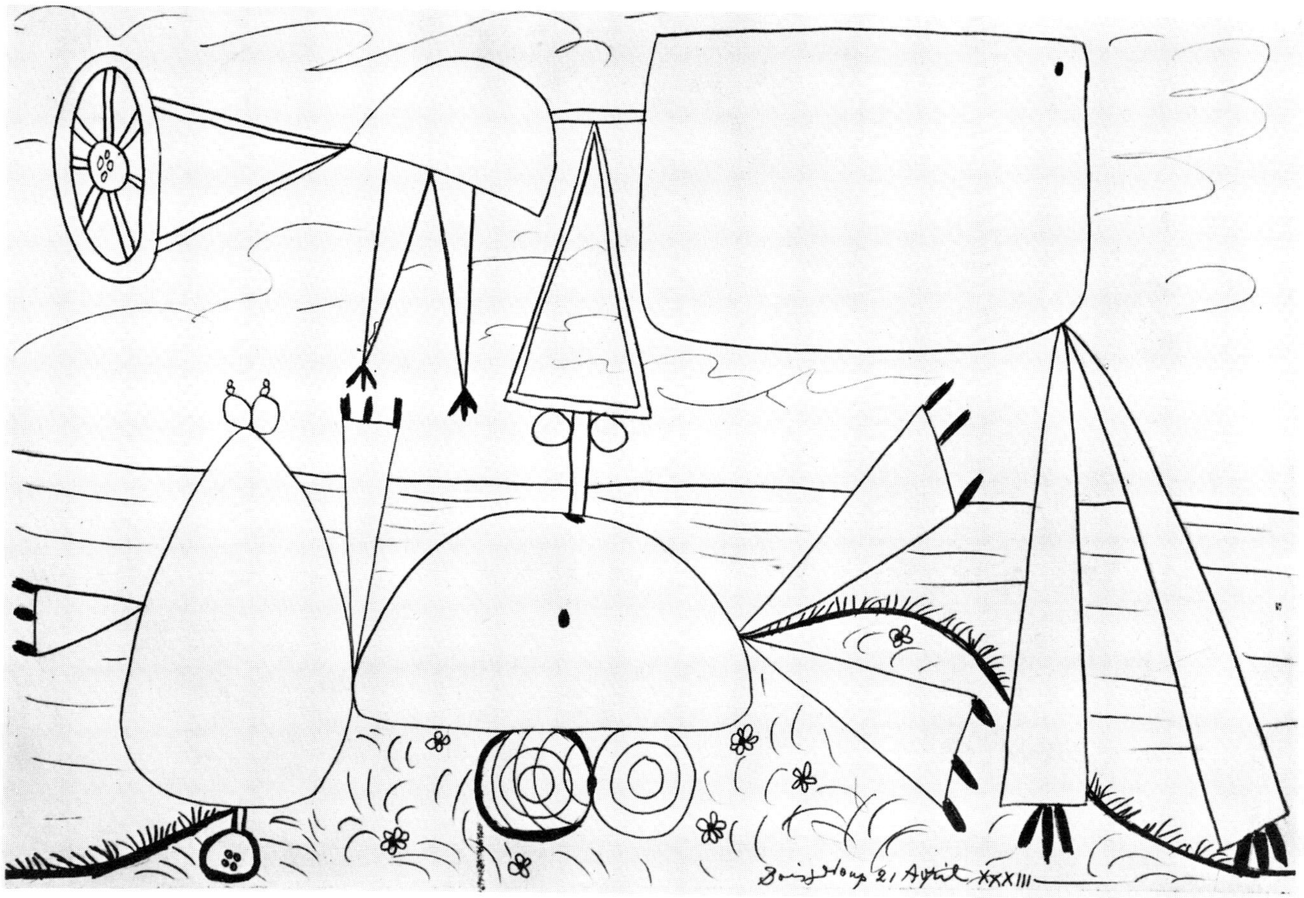

223. Picasso, *Two Figures* **(drawing),** April 21, 1933.

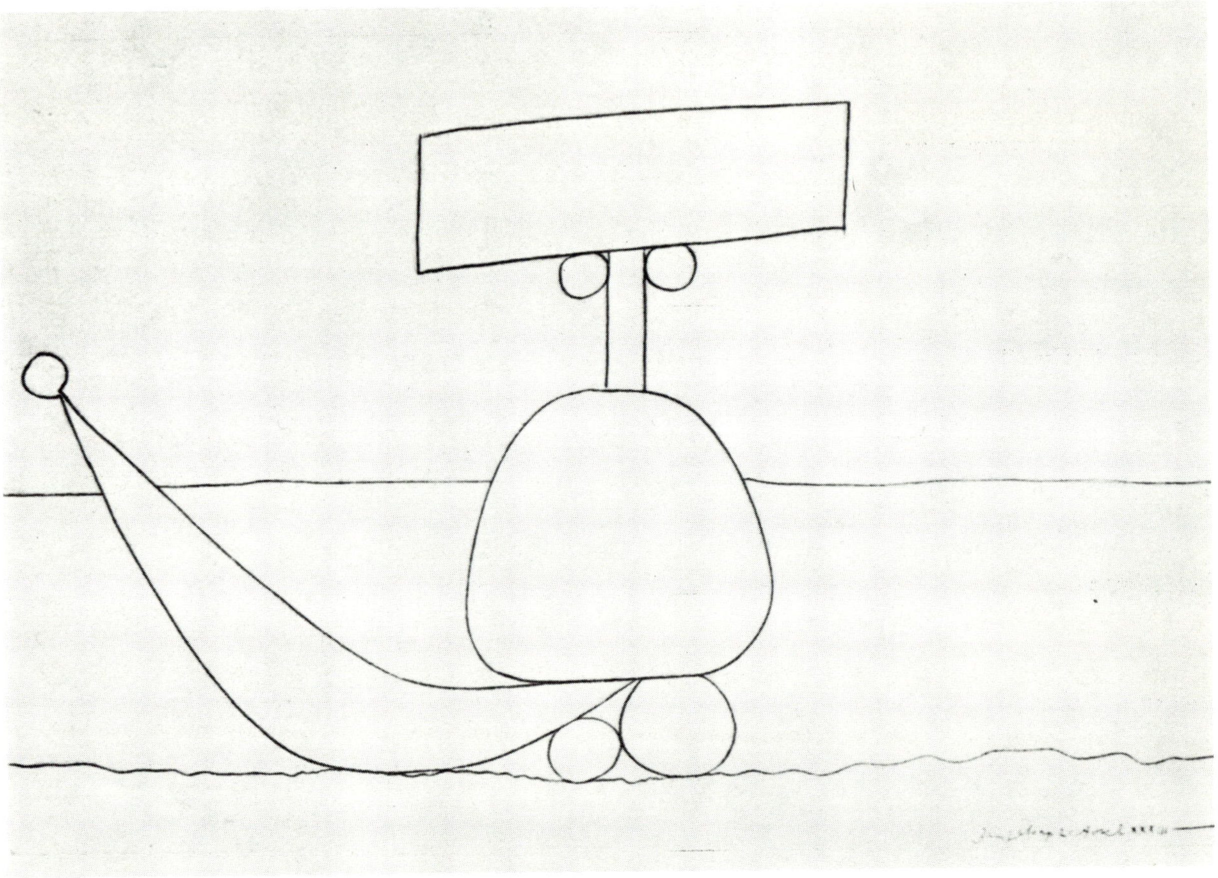

224. Picasso, *Two Figures* (drawing), April 21, 1933.

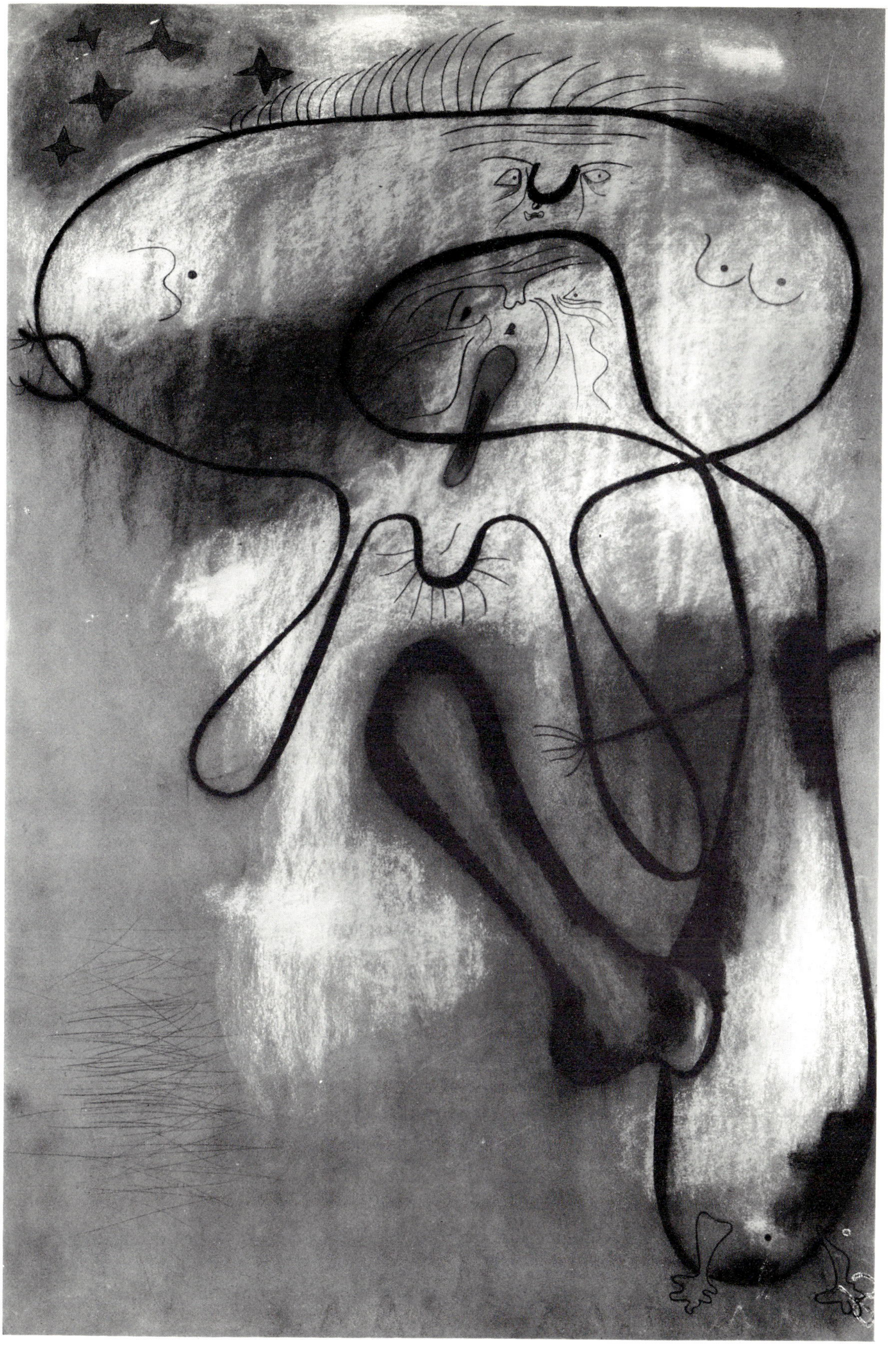

225. Miró, *The Lovers*, 1934. (***Philadelphia Museum of Art***, *Collection of Louise and Walter Arensberg.*)

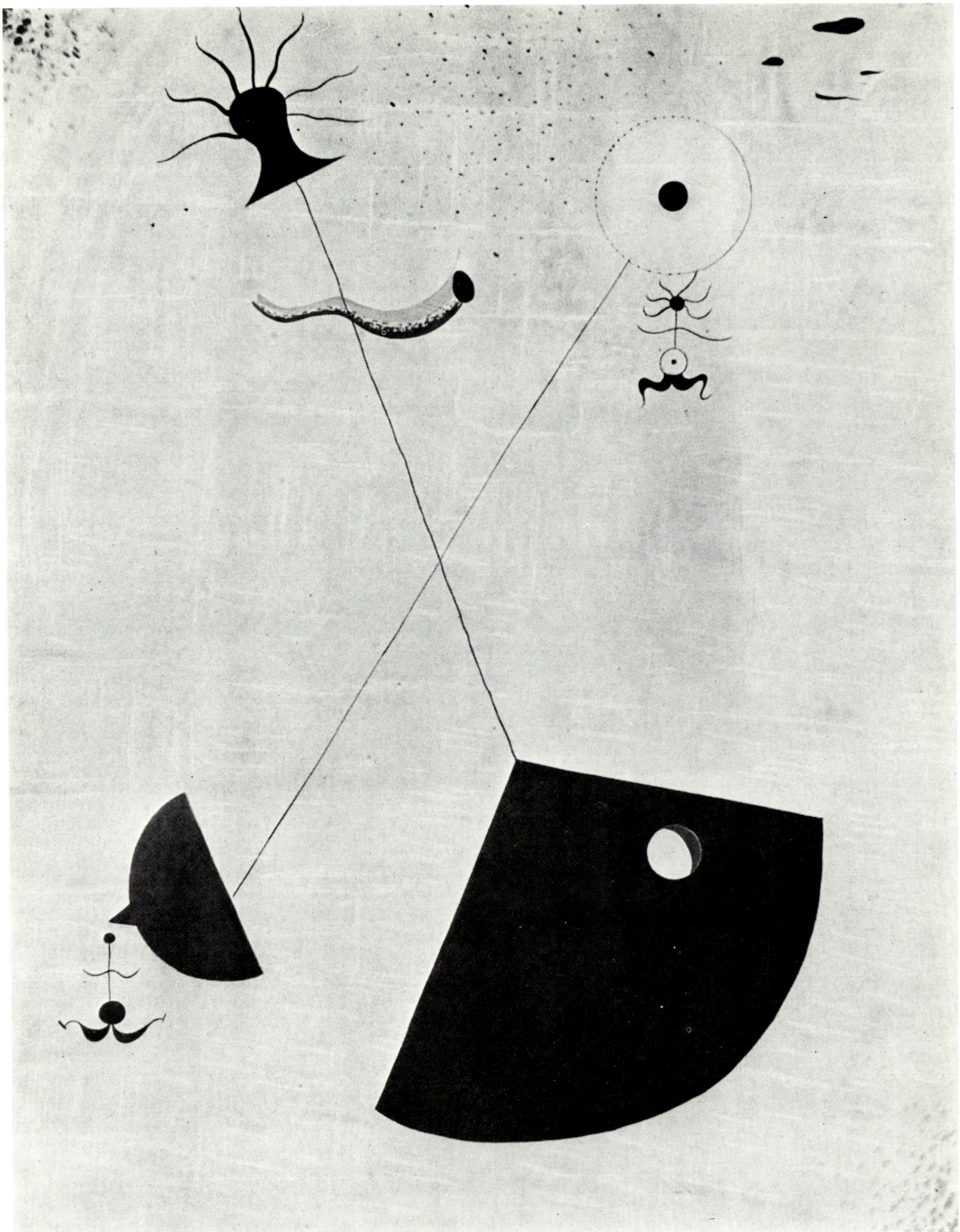

226. Miró, *Maternity*, **1924. (***London, Collection of Roland Penrose.***)**

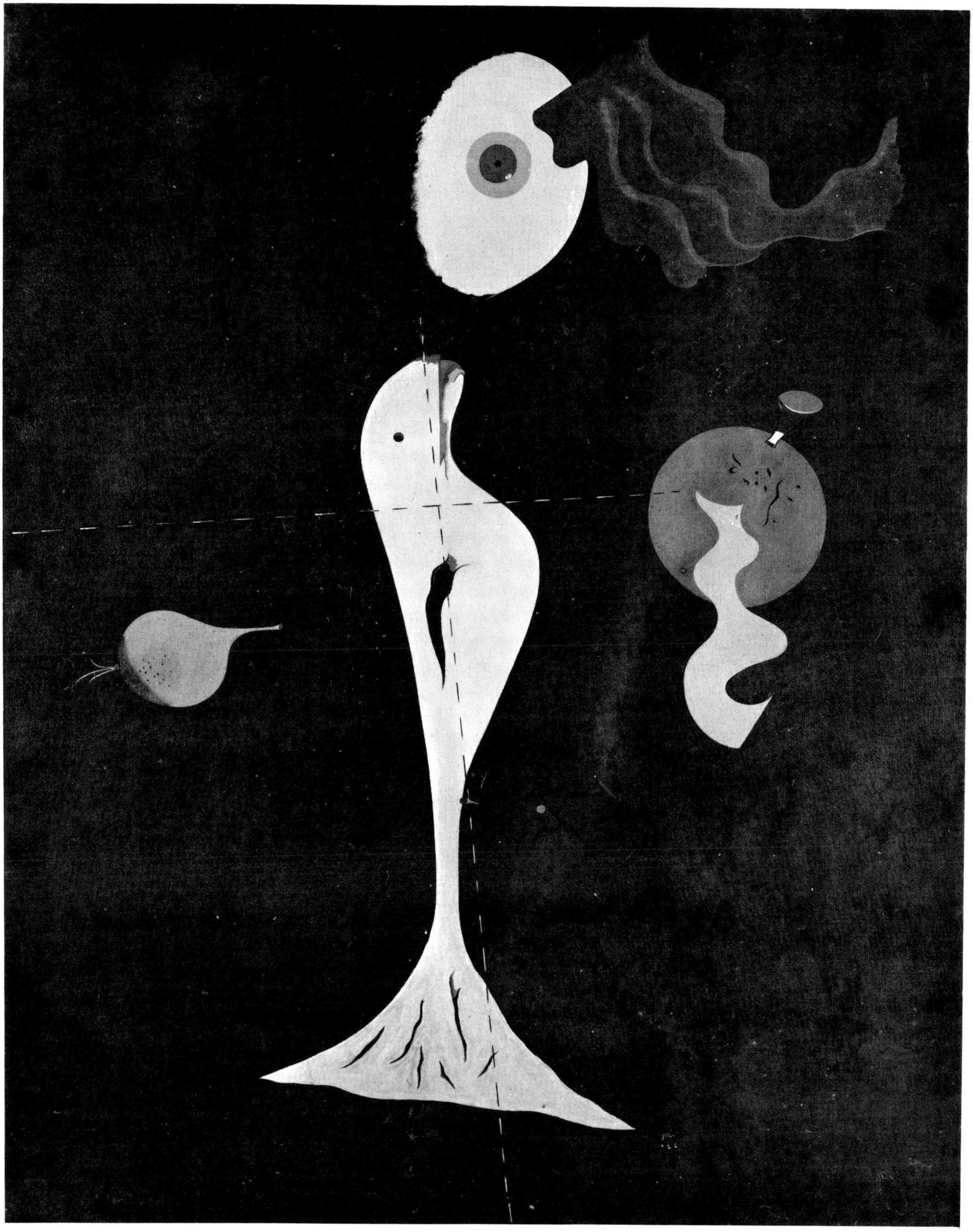

227. Miró, *Nude*, 1926. (*Philadelphia Museum of Art, Collection of Louise and Walter Arensberg.*)

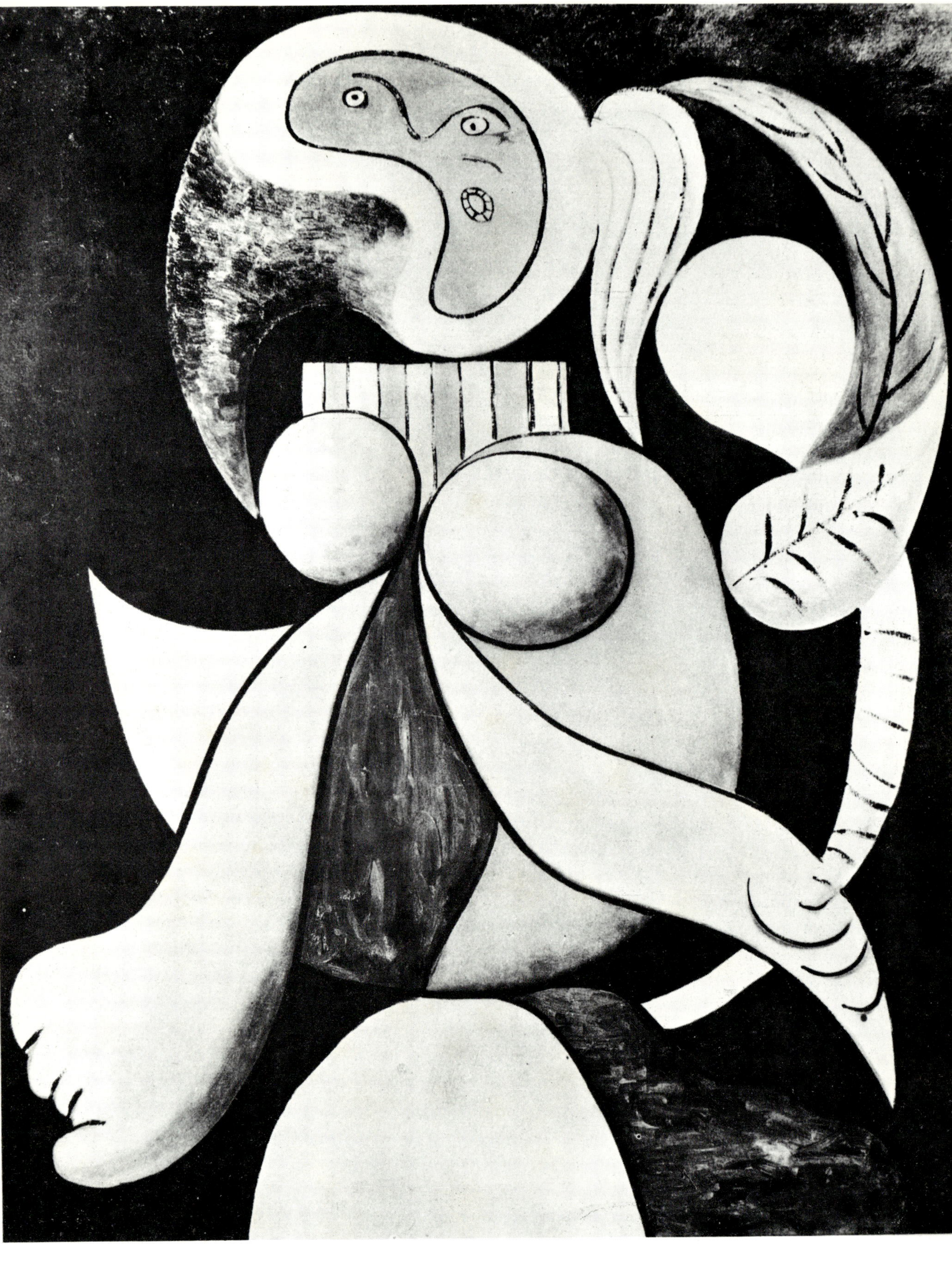

228. Picasso, ***Woman** with a Flower,* April 10, 1932.

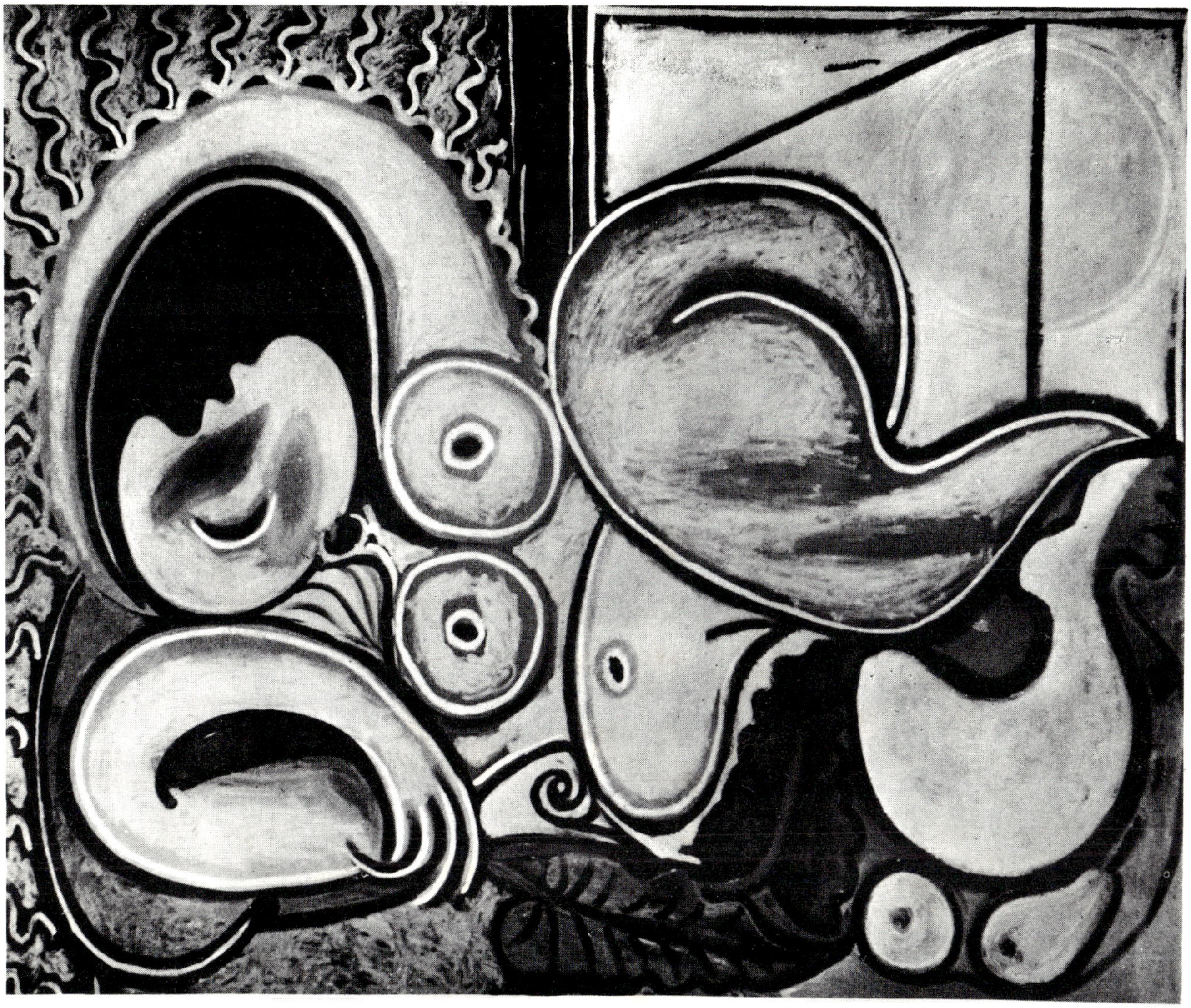

229. Picasso, *Sleeping Nude,* 1931.

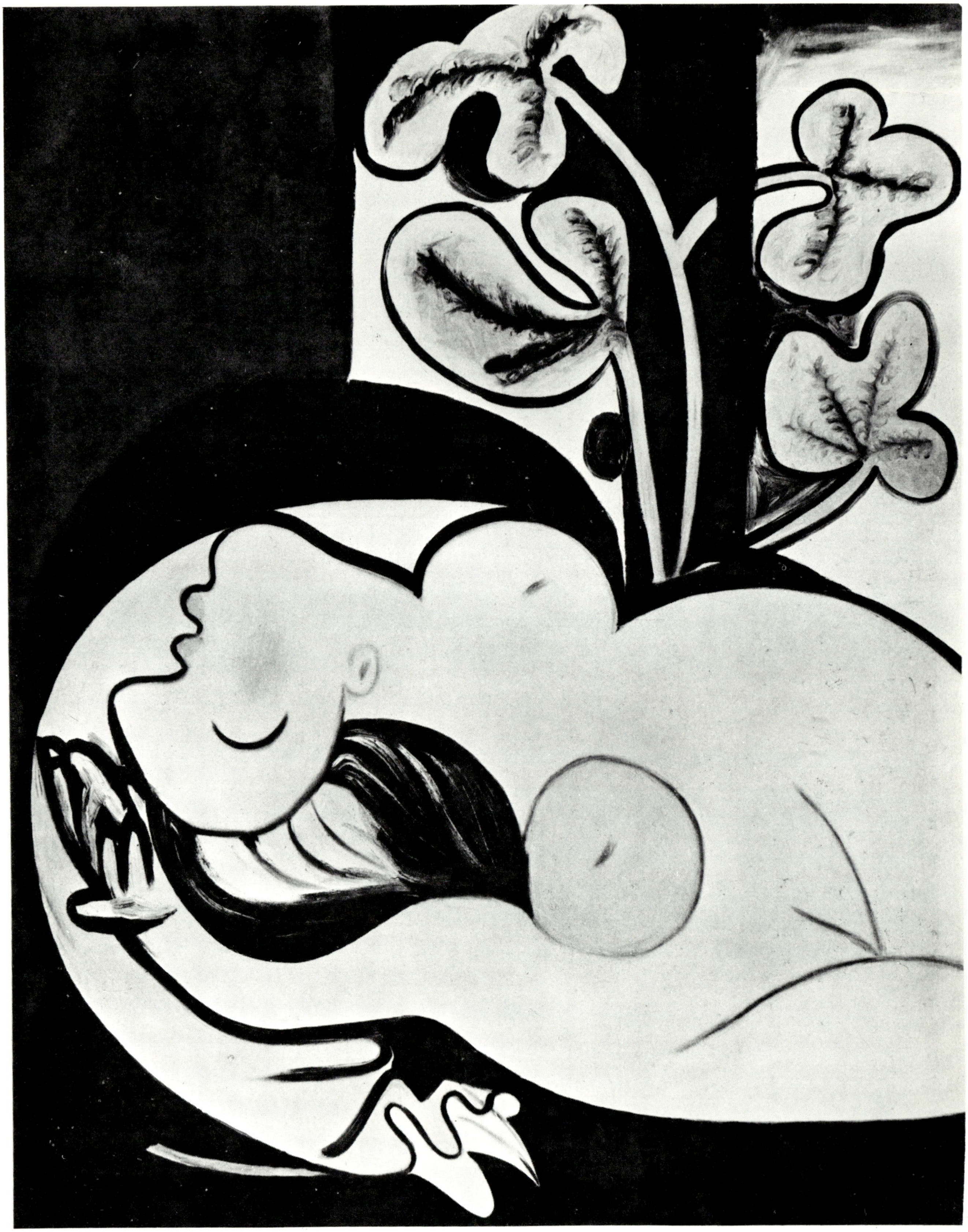

230. Picasso, *Sleeping Nude,* March 9, 1932.

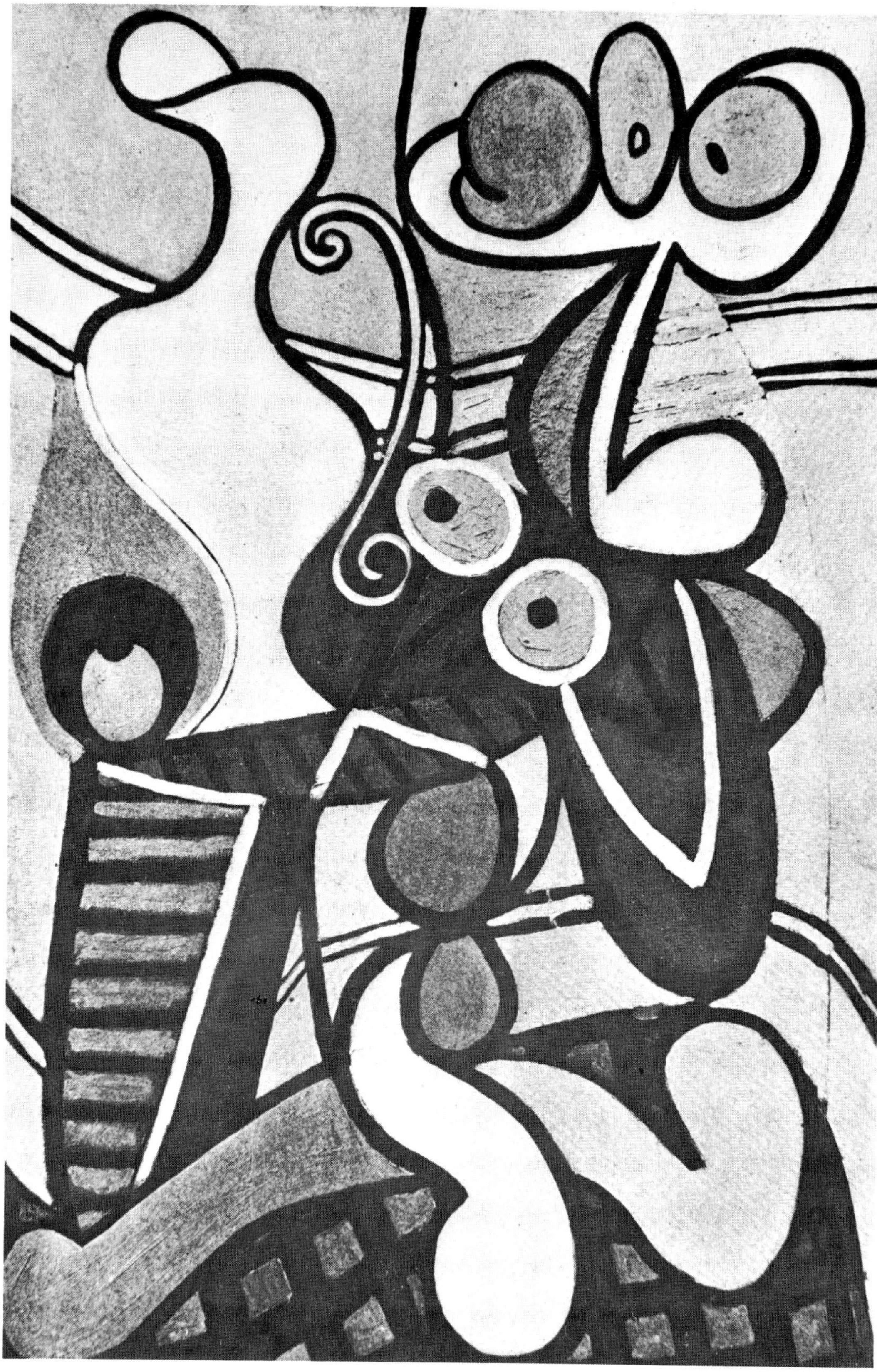

231. Picasso, *Still Life on a Table,* March 11, 1931.

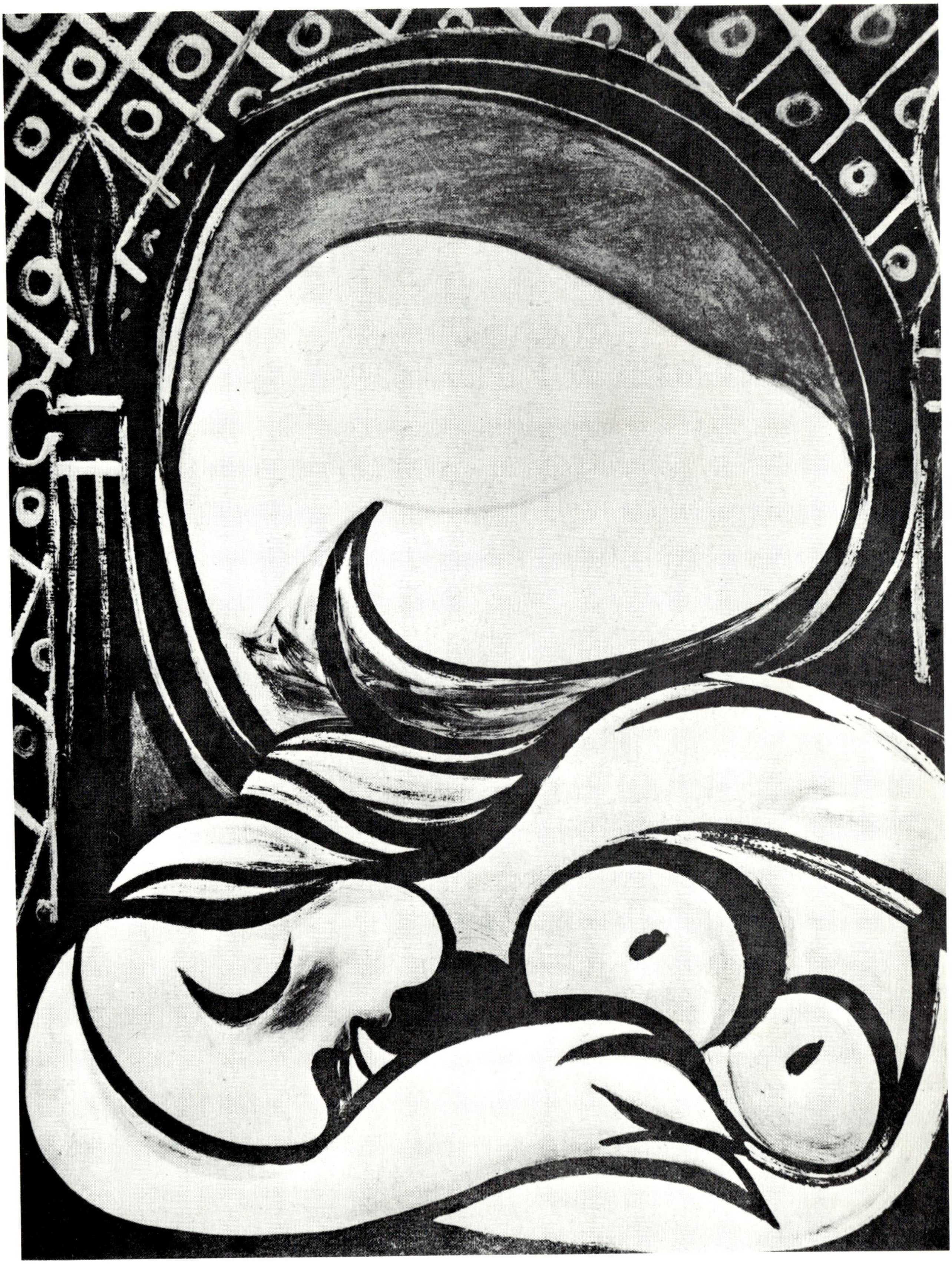

232. Picasso, *The Mirror*, **March 14, 1932.** (*Gustav Stern Foundation.*)

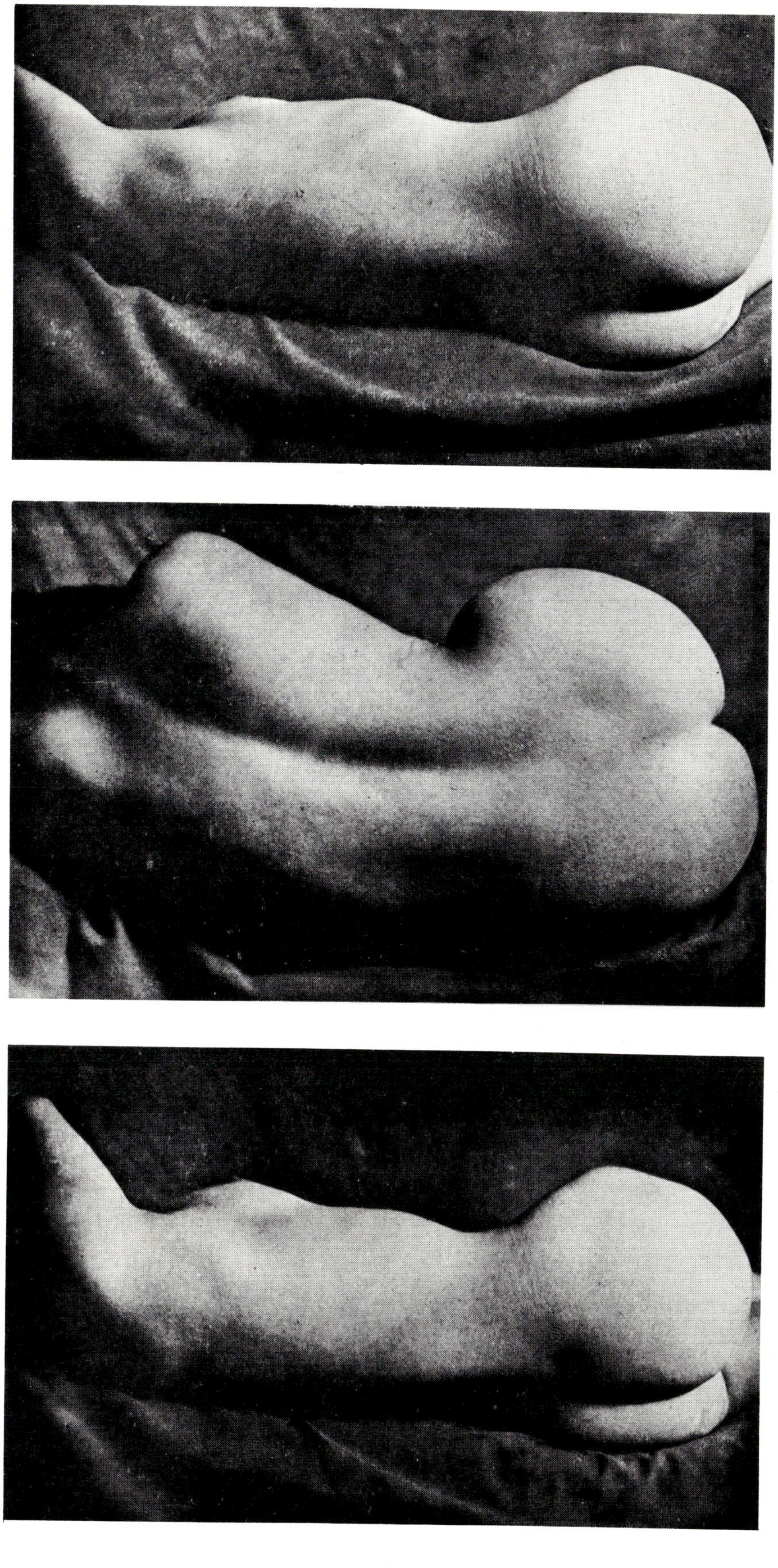

233. Brassai, *Nudes,* 1933.

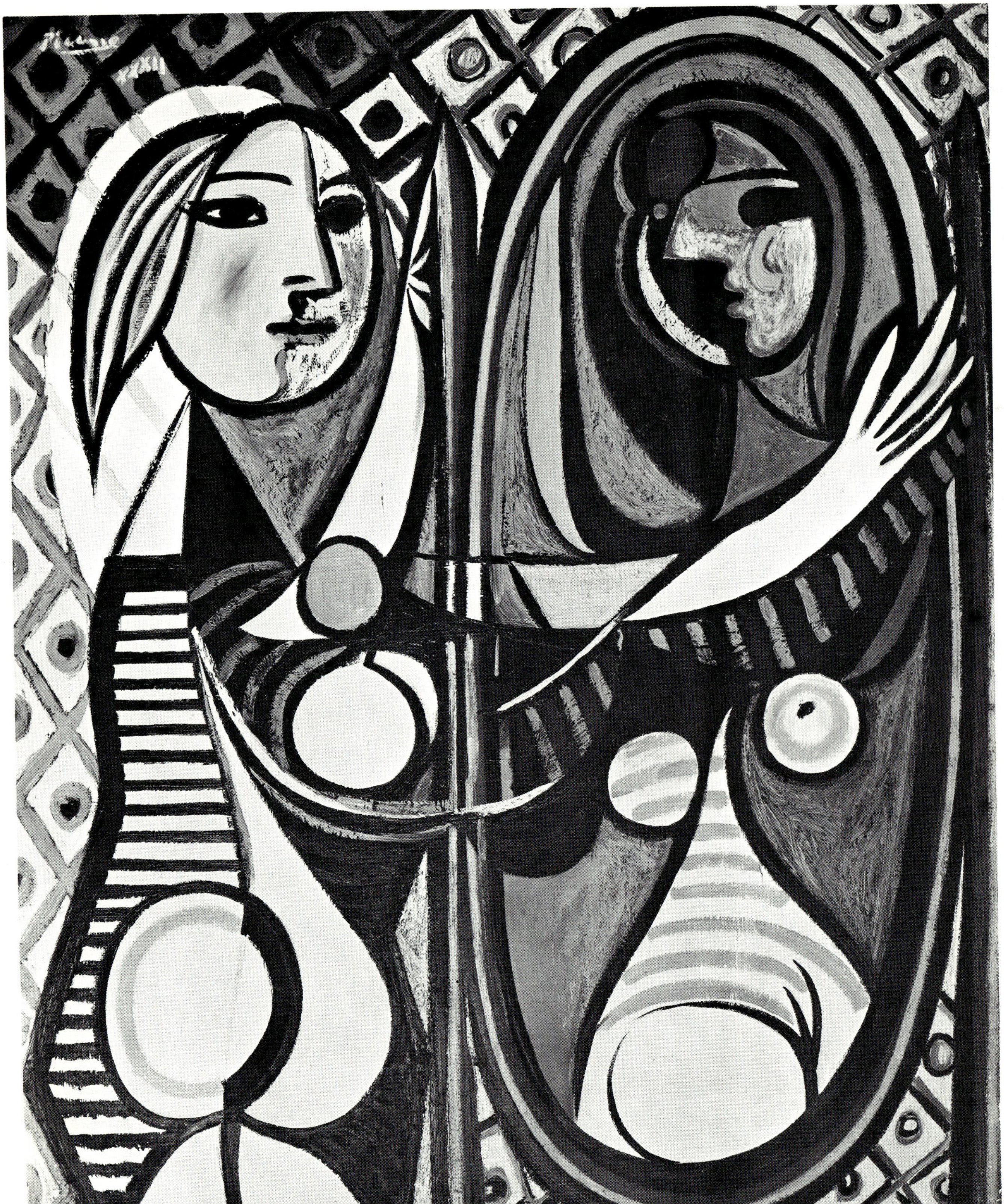

234. Picasso, *Girl before a Mirror*, March 14, 1932. (*New York, Collection of the Museum of Modern Art, gift of Mrs. Simon Guggenheim.*)

Acknowledgments

The authors and publishers wish to make grateful acknowledgment to the following for providing photographs and granting permission to reproduce the art works in their collections:

CHAPTER 1

Alinari photographs, *2, 5, 8.*
American School of Classical Studies, Agora Excavations, Athens, *47.*
Antiken-museum und Skulpturhalle, Basel, *19.*
Athens National Museum, *3.*
Bettmann Archive, Inc., New York, *28.*
British Museum, London, Courtesy of the Trustees, *12, 18, 22.*
Capitoline Museum, Rome, *2.*
French School of Archeology, Athens, *29.*
Louvre Museum, Paris, *17, 21* (photo: Chuzeville).
Martin v. Wagner-Museum, der Universität Würzburg, *10, 11.*
The Metropolitan Museum of Art, New York, *9, 39.*
Museum of Fine Arts, Boston, *4, 27.*
National Museum, Rome, *32.*
Staatliche Museen, Berlin, *13, 14, 15, 16, 20, 25, 26.*
Staatliche Museen, Antikenabteilung, Berlin, *34, 35, 36, 37, 38, 40, 41.*
Verlag für Kulturforschung, Hamburg, *44.*

Acknowledgment is also made to these publications:

Giulio Farina, *La Pittura Egiziana* (Fratelli Treves, Milan, 1939) (by permission of Aldo Garzanti Editore, Milan), *48.*
A. Furtwängler and K. Reichhold, *Griechische Vasenmalerei* (Bruckmann, Munich, 1904), Series 3, Text 2, *7, 23, 24.*
P. Herrmann, *Denkmäler der Malerei des Altertums* (Bruckmann, Munich, 1904–1931), 33.
Hans Licht, *Sittengeschichte Griechenlands*, Ergänzungsband, "Die Erotik in der Griechischen Kunst" (Paul Arentz, Zürich, 1928), *31, 43, 46.*
Gaston Vorberg, *Ars Erotica Veterum* (Julius Püttmann, Stuttgart, 1926), *42, 45.*

CHAPTER 2

Photographs by William Dellenback, Institute for Sex Research, Bloomington, Indiana.

CHAPTER 3

The author is greatly indebted to his colleagues Professors T. Uehara and K. Yasuda of the Department of East Asian Languages and Literature, Indiana University, for their help in the interpretation of the many texts found in the illustrations.

The following illustrations are reproduced from works in the collections of the Museum of Fine Arts of Boston, which has graciously accorded permission to use them:

73, 74, 75, 76, 77, 80, 82, 83, 84, 85, 86, 87, 88, 89, 90, 91, 92, 93, 94, 95, 97, 98, 99, 100, 101, 102, 104, 105, 106.

From other sources:

François Poncetton, *Les Érotiques Japonais* (Éditions du Siècle, Paris, 1925), *72, 96, 107.*
Marianne Densmore, *Les Estampes Érotiques Japonaises* (Cercle du Livre Précieux, Paris, 1961), *79, 81.*
Institute for Sex Research Collections, *78, 103, 108.*

CHAPTER 4

Albertina, Vienna, *128, 151* (photo: Alpenland).
Alinari photographs, *109, 110, 120, 121, 133, 138, 144, 149, 158, 159, 160, 163, 165, 167, 177, 181, 183, 184.*
Ashmolean Museum, Oxford, *162, 182, 189.*
Bibliothèque Municipale, Lyons, *147.*
Bibliothèque Nationale, Paris, *115.*
British Museum, London, Courtesy of the Trustees, *122, 131, 132, 145, 152, 172, 174, 178, 180, 192.*
County Museum of Art, Los Angeles, *188.*
The Detroit Institute of Arts, Detroit, *154.*
Fogg Art Museum, Harvard University, Cambridge, *123.*
Gabinetto Fotographico Nazionale, Rome, *113.*
Galleria Borghese, Rome, *191.*
Isabella Stewart Gardner Museum, Boston, *164, 175.*
Kunsthistorisches Museum, Vienna, *176.*
Kunstsammlungen der Veste Coberg, Coberg, *117.*
Cabinet des Dessins, Louvre Museum, Paris, *124, 143, 150, 170.*
Louvre Museum, Paris, *169.*
The Metropolitan Museum of Art, New York, *116, 130, 135.*
Musée Condé, Chantilly, *173.*

Musei Bibliotechi e Scuoli d'Arte, Genoa, *114.*
The National Gallery, London, Courtesy of the Trustees, *111, 153, 155, 166, 168.*
Palazzo Bianco, Genoa, *193* (photo: Gasparini).
Palazzo Cataldi, Genoa, *194.*
Princeton University, The Art Museum, *157.*
Royal Academy of Arts, London, *137.*
Saint Amand Abbey, *146.*
Salonika, Archeological Museum, *134* (photo: Perissinotto, Padua).
Santa Barbara, University of California, Museum of Art, *190.*
H. Shickman Gallery, New York, *129* (photo: Feist).
Staatliche Museen, Gemäldegalerie, Berlin, *156.*
Walker Art Gallery, Liverpool, *118*
The Wallace Collection, London, Courtesy of the Trustees, *126.*
Walters Art Gallery, Baltimore, *139, 179.*
Windsor Castle, Royal Collection, *171.*

From other sources:

Arnold Newman, in Robert Coughlan, *The World of Michaelangelo* (Time-Life Books, New York, 1966), *112.*

CHAPTER 5

Museum of Modern Art, New York, *234.*
Philadelphia Museum of Art, *225, 227.*
Permission SPADEM 1969 by French Reproduction Rights, Inc., for all 32 Picasso works.
Permission ADAGP 1969 by French Reproduction Rights, Inc., for Figs. *208, 225, 226, 227.*

From other sources:

Minotaure (Éditions Albert Skira, Paris, 1933), No. 1, *213, 218, 233,* No. 3–4, *201.*
Christian Zervos, *Dessins de Picasso, 1892–1948* (Éditions Cahiers d'Art, Paris, 1949), *217.*
Christian Zervos, *Picasso, Oeuvre Catalogue* (Éditions Cahiers d'Art, Paris, 1955, 1957), Vol. VII, *195–199, 202–207, 210, 211, 214–216, 228–232,* Vol. VIII, *212, 219–224.*